SALESMANSHIP

HELPING PROSPECTS BUY

THIRD EDITION

by **CHARLES ATKINSON KIRKPATRICK,** D.C.S.

PROFESSOR OF MARKETING
SCHOOL OF BUSINESS ADMINISTRATION
UNIVERSITY OF NORTH CAROLINA

Published by

SOUTH-WESTERN PUBLISHING COMPANY

CINCINNATI 27   CHICAGO 44   DALLAS 2

BURLINGAME, CALIF.   NEW ROCHELLE, N. Y

S52

PREFACE

This is the third edition of a book written for individuals who must influence or persuade, actuate or lead other individuals, now or in the future. It is primarily a text for college students who look forward to selling careers with established firms or on their own. The many students who enter selling and remain in it (rather than moving into management) need a broad college preparation in the principles and practices of professional selling. As do the first two editions, this one serves practicing salesmen for reminder and refresher purposes; it is also suitable for use by those who train salesmen. For students whose main interest is marketing, the book is an introduction to the most significant promotional force of all — personal selling. And one must recognize that the great numbers of new products and services which are marketed each month join the cost-margin-profit squeeze to make selling more challenging year after year.

Because this book is a combination of principles and techniques, it recognizes *why* as well as *what, how,* and *when.* The principles which receive emphasis are basic and lasting; they are the principles which students will apply in business. Techniques include practices to adopt and practices to avoid. Throughout is the assumption that there is no recipe, formula, or set of directions which can be followed by salesmen as a builder follows blueprints and instructions in building a house. Even so, this is a practical book, comprehensive yet thorough, based on what the better salesmen do.

The first part of this edition is a two-chapter section providing important concepts about selling. Next comes a seven-chapter section dealing with the background information a salesman needs. The third part is an eight-chapter section devoted to analysis of the selling process. A final section examines industrial selling and retail selling.

The fundamental conviction of the earlier editions has been kept, namely, that the proper role of a salesman is that of adviser to buyers. The salesman in mind is not interested in making one-time sales; neither is he a mere order-taker, unimaginative and devoid of resourcefulness.

v

This edition continues to emphasize creative selling which leads to continuing, mutually profitable relations between a salesman and his customers. The author and the users of the earlier editions sense no need for radical change.

In an effort to produce a more effective teaching and learning tool, there has been substantial rewriting of certain sections and the inclusion of new sections. Some treatments of topics have been lengthened; some have been shortened. Chapter 3, *The Man for the Job*, and Chapter 8, *Consumer Motivation*, have been redone. A new chapter on industrial selling should be of interest to the rather considerable number of students planning careers in this area of selling. There are new examples, new study assignments, and new case studies.

The author owes much to many. In particular, his thanks and appreciation go to companies which contributed, to instructors who have used the book, to students who have studied it, to salesmen, and to the author's colleagues.

C. A. KIRKPATRICK

CONTENTS

Part A.
The Field of Selling

Part B.   Background for Selling

Part C.   The Selling Process

Part D.   Industrial and Retail Selling

The Field of Selling

Part

A

CHAPTER 1

PERSONAL AND ECONOMIC ASPECTS
OF SELLING

CHAPTER 2

TYPES OF SELLING

CHAPTER 1

PERSONAL AND ECONOMIC ASPECTS OF SELLING

The need for salesmen today is urgent. That need is growing — for more salesmen and for better salesmen. If the 1960–70 decade is truly to be the "Soaring, Sizzling Sixties," then markets must expand to absorb the output of our ever-growing production capacity. The appearance of new and improved products and of new companies is both exciting and challenging in the light of our increasing population. Consumption, much of which is stimulated by selling, must keep pace.

Despite the potential of the present decade, personal selling does not enjoy great appeal as a career. Why? To some, selling means ignorant retail clerks or high-pressure artists who are adept at keeping doors ajar with a foot. Other persons do not realize that principles of selling must be used by *everyone* in business if he or she is to influence individuals — a prerequisite to leadership. These principles, indeed, *can* be used by every person, in business or not, who must have dealings with and get along with people. Indeed, students who have learned something about these principles generally secure more desirable jobs than do their friends who are unaware of them. Some persons have not recognized or admitted to the arrival of the era of the Marketing Man — one who can sell goods at a profit. Some fail to appreciate the value added to products and services by the selling process.

Students wonder whether salesmen can be ethical in their relationships with buyers. Students wonder if a salesman is slowly being worn down between buyers who demand too much and sales managers who expect too much. Students see the job of the salesman as lacking both in security and in social status. So, let's start by taking a hard, objective look at the features of selling as a career.

PERSONAL ASPECTS

Opportunity for Advancement

Few, if any, types of activity offer the bright future for an individual and his family that personal selling offers. Broad trends are partially

3

Advantages of selling as a career

1 — Higher income. In general, the salesman will receive more remuneration than office workers and production personnel.

2 — Opportunity for advancement. The salesman's position is tied more closely to his individual performance than is that of most other workers.

3 — Travel. The salesman has more opportunity to see new places and new things and thus broaden his outlook.

4 — Sense of pride. The salesman knows he represents his company to the trade and to the public in his territory.

5 — Development of personality. The salesman's challenge is a personal one. He learns to deal with people, ideas, and changing conditions.

6 — Freedom. The salesman works mostly on his own initiative with far less supervision than office or factory workers.

7 — Development of responsibility. Because the salesman is "on his own," he trains himself to accept responsibility.

Disadvantages

1 — Lack of normal home life. Travel requirements may prevent a salesman from spending as much time as he would like at home with his family and friends.

2 — Lack of authority. Decisions outside the prescribed rules of the company cannot ordinarily be made by a salesman on the spot. Approvals for necessary commitments are sometimes delayed until the time for action has passed.

3 — Monotony. The salesman often spends more time waiting in line for an audience with the buyer than he does on actual sales presentations.

You can see from the foregoing that we think the advantages of a career in selling outweigh the disadvantages by a fairly wide margin.

Excerpt from a letter written by a president of the Emerson Drug Company.

responsible for this. Our population has been growing and continues to grow. The increase in our capacity of manufacture also continues; the volume of goods and services that our productive plant is able to pour out on our markets is staggering. More and more new products appear, needing salesmen, and the United States consumer continues to want more and better products. The increase in the amount of leisure time each consumer enjoys is opening up new markets. And, most important of all, the rise in national income has placed in consumers' hands buying power with which to pay for more and better goods.

In a narrower, more specific way, each individual salesman who deserves promotion is far more apt to get promoted than are most men in other phases of business. From the moment he begins to succeed and to achieve, regardless of his youth, he must be considered for advancement. Hard work and resourcefulness will move him up faster and farther than they will persons in other types of work. In few other activities can one become a senior or even a junior executive at such an early age. This is because the good salesman does not have to wait long for management to recognize his worth. He can stand for promotion on his record of successful *performance*, not on successful *politicking;* he can substitute a base that cannot be challenged — *sales* — for unsound bases, such as *seniority*. The salesman makes his breaks, and he cashes in proportionately.

This matter of promotion is commented on by an executive of Eli Lilly & Company:

> An important advantage for selling as a career . . . concerns the problem in large companies of "getting lost in the crowd."
> The question has been asked within many companies, "Why do people from sales get all the breaks in managerial selections?" I believe that one important reason is that selling delineates the degree of performance more definitely than any other area of business. Selling can be referred to as the stage, and the top performers get top billing. Average, mediocre, and tolerable performances are also recognized for what they are; and these salesmen become the supporting cast. In other words, to p management has more criteria for knowing who's who in sales than in any other phase of the business.
> Moreover, selling provides more opportunities and demands for further development and self-improvement than other phases of our complex and interdependent business life today.
> Continued growth is a prerequisite for the creative salesmanship required by our modern business society, and thereby prepares people for larger responsibilities. The spotlight is always on; and that in itself discourages introversion, self-satisfaction, and complacency.
> Selling will always provide opportunity for ambitious people with the proper traits, enthusiastic interest, and an eagerness to apply themselves and . . . will continue to be one of the most dependable reservoirs for management personnel.

Where does promotion lead? The successful individual can chart a course for the top in *selling*, or he can move toward a position in *management*. These two are available, of course, within his own company or in other organizations. Advancement in selling is largely a matter of territory or accounts. Advancement in management might be through such jobs as sales supervisor, branch manager, district or zone manager, regional manager, divisional manager, assistant sales manager, sales manager, vice-president of sales, and even president. Advancement in retailing might be to head of stock, assistant buyer, buyer, or selling supervisor. Then there are certain allied activities in marketing into which one might move — advertising, sales promotion, and market research. The salesman may move to a competing company; or, he may go to a related company, leaving a manufacturer to join an advertising agency or an advertising medium, or leaving a retail store to join a wholesaler or a manufacturer. If the individual plans to enter business for himself, his future is brighter if he has learned to sell.

Business used to get its senior management from the fields of production, law, and finance. Now, however, many top managers are coming from the field of selling. Many presidents of today's companies started as salesmen. Management and leadership everywhere depend on the ability to get along with others and to influence them. Salesmen come in contact with all types of people. They learn to sell not only products but also their company and themselves.

Earnings

Good salesmen are paid well. Studies of college and university classes usually show that four or five years after graduation the salesmen have risen more in earnings than any other group. As a general rule, the highest income figures in business are found in selling. In addition, selling ranks highest among almost all fields in *average* earnings. Income for salesmen's families usually ranges from $1,000 to $2,000 more than the national average family income.

Practically all salesmen are paid a salary or commission, or some combination of the two. Many college seniors flatly refuse to enter selling on a commission basis, demanding the salary type of compensation. These seniors group together such factors as steady salary, fringe benefits, large size of company, and prestige of large companies; they consider these more desirable than incentive, opportunity to rise quickly, or even amount of pay. A recent nationwide study indicated that fewer than one-fourth of U. S. salesmen are on commission. It also revealed the interesting fact that salesmen on commission for small companies earn one and one-half times the take-home pay of salesmen on salary for large

Average Monthly Earnings of College Graduates				
	5 Years After Graduation		10 Years After Graduation	
	1957 Report	1959 Report	1957 Report	1959 Report
Accounting...............	$549	577	778	783
Engineering...............	$592	641	740	778
General Business...........	$556	583	768	788
Sales....................	$599	637	826	866

These figures were supplied by Mr. Frank S. Endicott, Director of Placement, Northwestern University. The 1957 report covered the classes graduating in 1951 and 1946; the 1959 report covered the 1953 and 1948 classes.

companies. One thing to remember is that a salesman's profit showing can be determined, and if it is unsatisfactory, the fact that he is on salary need not postpone his dismissal by a single day.

The significant angle is that a salesman sets his own compensation whether he be on salary or on commission. His pay is determined by how much, how hard, and how well he works. His income is in direct proportion to the time, energy, and thought he chooses to spend. His earnings are *not* set by his name, his acquaintances, or the schools he attended. Proof of his control over his pay is the fact that to earn more, all he needs to do is to sell more. There is no ceiling on the size of his income. And, if his own company will not pay him what he is worth, the salesman can show his record to some other company that will.

In being paid on the basis of his own individual production, the salesman differs from others in business. No company can measure precisely what any one of its accountants contributes to the profitable operation of the business. The field of personnel is another in which the determination of personal output or worth of an individual can be done in only the roughest, crudest of manners. The same holds for production, purchasing, finance, and general office work. Not so for a salesman. He can reap what he sows because his sales volume, the gross margin thereon, and his cost to the company can be measured in dollars. Incidentally, it is not uncommon to hear of prizes and bonuses that can be won by a company's salesmen; but you rarely hear of such being offered to production or office workers.

Personal Satisfaction

Despite what some scoffers and cynics may think, dollar income is not the only kind of income a person must have if he is to be and feel successful. Everyone needs psychic income, too. Unless a person's earning activities provide him with what, for him, are the necessary amounts and types of incomes, then that person will be dissatisfied. The last section dealt with dollar income; this section deals with psychic income.

Selling offers the satisfaction of personal growth and development. Because the salesman must think of the needs, the problems, the hopes, and the welfare of others, he cannot afford to be narrow or self-centered. He must learn to get along satisfactorily with all types of persons and to deal with them pleasantly. He must work toward permanent, mutually profitable relationships with his buyers. He will find the development of close, delightful friendships inevitable.

Selling lets the salesman feel necessary and needed, and that feeling gives him satisfaction. As a matter of fact, if and when an individual feels that others no longer need him, his existence can be nothing but barren and his activities little more than futile. To know that a buyer needs help in finding better solutions to his problems, to know that he counts on you to help him find those better solutions, and then to join him in a successful search for them — that is a most rewarding experience and gives the salesman a feeling of personal worth.

Selling gives the salesman the thrill of accomplishment, a major form of satisfaction. A salesman starts by hunting buyers who will benefit from buying his products. He analyzes the problems of those buyers in order to be able to make specific proposals. Then the salesman persuades the buyers to become customers and to begin enjoying the advantages of using his items. Making each sale provides the salesman with one feeling of accomplishment, because he himself, his company, and his new customer all know of his performance. A second gratification is experienced by the salesman as he sees clearly and often how he has benefited buyers.

Finally, selling gives the salesman the personal satisfaction of knowing that he has been of service to his fellow men. Salesmen can feel that they have contributed to society. Salesmen-to-consumers make life more pleasant, safer, more convenient, or easier for their customers. They reduce physical stress and improve health; they reduce mental strain and increase peace of mind. They sell leisure and comfort for housewives, better illumination for pupils in school, and income for widows. Salesmen-to-business help businessmen increase sales volume and reduce costs. Salesmen know happiness because they make buyers happy; they sell satisfaction and, in return, find their own satisfaction.

Security

College students join almost everyone else in wanting a good measure of security. That desire is both understandable and commendable. It is perhaps unfortunate that so many college students believe that the days of growth and opportunity are gone forever. Some students consider selling as a career to be too risky and uncertain. Some contend that they can take a long-shot chance and enter selling — or they can choose security. Even within the area of selling, some graduates insist that the only items to select to sell are large, complex physical products; they want little to do with low-priced, small items, and absolutely nothing to do with intangibles. As suggested earlier, large companies and "safe" departments (accounting, personnel, production) are extremely popular.

One does not need extensive or exhaustive research to discover that companies can continue operating only if their salesmen make sales. When a recession develops, does a company fire its salesmen? As times get tougher, does the need for productive salesmen decline? Of course not. Sales executives say that for a salesman who likes to sell and can sell, there is no job more secure. They say that there have never been enough good salesmen and that, consequently, the ability to sell at a profit is the most effective type of security. Indeed, it is during depressions that demand for competent salesmen is greatest. When times are bad, inefficient salesmen may be fired along with production and office personnel, but the sound salesman most likely suffers no more than a drop in earnings.

Selling is security in other ways. The ability to influence human behavior, to persuade, is essential everywhere and at all times. Employers will pay for that ability. When the management of a company changes, many replacements may be made, but few will be replacements of salesmen, for salesmen are responsible for sales volume and for the sales income budget — the most basic of all budgets. When an individual begins to get along in years, his hold on his job often becomes uncertain because his abilities and faculties may have become somewhat impaired. A person can be, indeed he can *become*, a good salesman at age 40, or 50, or 60. Finally, no machine is going to replace or make obsolete the salesman whose judgment is sound, whose tact and discretion are outstanding, whose thinking is keen.

Respect

Unless a person's economic activities are respectable, his chances of being happy are slim. There are two phases to this matter of respect — self-respect and community respect.

To some students, self-respect and personal selling seem mutually exclusive and mortal enemies. These students look down on selling, considering it a job to take only if nothing better can be obtained. They think of it as dirty and tricky. You will recall, however, that another point of view was presented earlier in the discussion of personal satisfaction. There it was argued that a salesman can adopt for himself a high purpose in life because he knows that his job is as worthwhile as it is essential. He can be a man of integrity. His calling can be one of pride and dignity.

The "community" in community respect consists largely of family and friends. Some students shy away from selling lest they be regarded as objectionable individuals instead of being held in esteem by persons close to them. The prestige of the professions is a dominant element in this desire for community respect. For example, a man known to the writer has earned a Bachelor of Laws degree *and* the Chartered Life Underwriter designation in selling life insurance. The man is a competent lawyer but left the practice of law to sell life insurance, one of the reasons being that he makes more money in selling. But his wife wants him to practice law. As a matter of fact, she is strongly opposed to his being "just a salesman," as she expresses it. Her preference is to be the wife of a professional man. She wants to be known as a lawyer's wife rather than as a salesman's wife, even though a reduction in income is involved.

How different and refreshing are these reassurances from The Firestone Tire & Rubber Company:

> As far as the social standing of salesmen is concerned, if there ever was a time when salesmen were not highly regarded in this country, that time has long been past. Furthermore, in recent years there has been a tendency to improve the caliber of salesmen by more careful selection. Educational requirements are generally higher than they have been in the past, and selling is no longer treated as just a job but as a profession and as a career for which careful training and real ability are required. To be sure, the individual salesman's social standing is determined by his personality, activities, and accomplishments, but certainly no salesman need feel that he is suffering under a handicap socially because he is a salesman.

Is the salesman's social standing in his community low? Let's put it this way. In this country, one of the determinants of social standing is *money* — not so much because of the money itself, but because of the opportunities that money affords. If number of dollars is to continue to be a measure of social status, then selling is perhaps the quickest route to community respect.

Social status, however, is determined not only by number of dollars but also by one's personality, character, conduct of personal affairs, personal and civic accomplishments, and contributions to the community. And certainly members of no one occupation or profession have a corner on any of these elements of success. If a salesman accepts as his sales philosophy the one of "helping prospects buy," he will include in his personal and social philosophy the concept of helpfulness and service. His money income can then help provide for him the opportunity of participation in the life of the community in such a way as to help him attain social position for himself and for his family equal to that enjoyed by members of other professions — doctors, lawyers, ministers, and teachers — in *your* community.

Independence with Guidance

Selling is an independent way of life. The salesman has much control over his time and his activities. He has so much freedom of choice that often he is virtually in business for himself. He works in *his* territory, handling *his* products and *his* prospects and customers as *he* thinks best. There is some supervision, of course, but the salesman in a sense is pretty much his own boss. Typically he drafts his own program or schedule of work and plans his own routing in the light of whom he wants to see when.

This degree of self-management is not attractive to students who do not want to be on their own or to try to map out their own business lives. Some students prefer a job that the company will spell out completely for them. They want detailed instructions on what to do.

More and more companies realize how highly dependent they are on their salesmen. They have developed sound procedures for selecting, training, supervising, and helping young salesmen. Instruction for selling is extensive and intensive. Whatever guidance is either necessary or desired is available on a continuing basis. In selecting his selling job, an individual can get just about the mixture of independence and guidance he prefers.

Travel

Some jobs in selling demand travel, others do not. There is the day-to-day type of travel, and then there is the infrequent move or transfer which perhaps can be classified as another type of travel. Normally, the amount and type of traveling the salesman must do depend on the size of his territory.

There are two or three plus points about salesmen's travel. One is seeing new places; a second is seeing different persons; a possible third is the additional compensation received in some jobs because of the travel required.

On the other side of the ledger, one finds the salesman separated from family and home, from neighborhood and friends. His evenings away from home can be empty, or even filled with activities that do him no good. Sleeping and eating schedules must be adjusted to fit circumstances of the moment. After several swings through his territory, the new places become old, and the different persons talk, look, and act alike. Traveling itself can become boring, exhausting, and dangerous.

Variety

The very nature of selling insures considerable variety for the salesman. Travel, as just indicated, provides variety. Because of loss of customers to death and to competitors, each salesman must ever be on the trail of new prospects, some of whom must be converted into new customers. This means an endless stream of new contacts and new acquaintances. This ever-changing pattern holds true for circumstances, too. Each day is different from other days, each city or market differs from others, and, in a literal sense, no two interviews are identical. Always the circumstances vary. Because no two buyers are alike and no two calls the same, a salesman finds each buyer a new challenge, each call a new test.

Stimulating variety can be found in broader areas. Prices, for example, vary from market to market, from time to time, and even from buyer to buyer. Products dare not remain unchanged too long, or they become obsolete or dated. Competitors stay up late thinking up new ways to woo and win new customers — from other salesmen. Promotional strategy and tactics are always being revised and improved so that their effectiveness is increased. New types of middlemen appear and may be added to a manufacturer's distribution channels. Sales expectations and the potentials of individual markets can change overnight. One can certainly say that selling is not monotonous.

Hard, Interesting Work

The fact that selling is hard work has been hinted at already. We have seen that the selling pattern can be one of irregularity in respect to hours, sleep, meals, and travel. We have seen that the salesman must see buyers where and when they can be seen. Those who sell automobiles, insurance, or farm equipment can testify to sales made in strange settings and at odd hours.

One difficult phase of the salesman's job which has not yet been discussed concerns the buyer's hostility. Many buyers raise buying obstacles and buying defenses the moment a salesman appears. The buyer tells himself that he is being imposed on, and he worries lest the salesman take advantage of him. Many buyers have no confidence in their own ability to analyze products, prices, and proposals. They fear that their decisions may not be sound, and that their selections may be unhappy ones. They convert fear of the soundness of their judgment into fear of the salesman himself. Selling to a buyer who fears both himself and the salesman is not easy work.

The very nature of the salesman's goal makes his undertaking a difficult one because it arouses the buyer's hostility. The salesman must question the buyer's decisions. He must replace or at least rebuild the ruts the buyer knows and loves so well. He must disturb the buyer's precious habits. He must cajole or frighten the buyer out of his state of inertia. He must insist that the buyer think, decide, and act. All of these are painful to buyers. All of them demand of the salesman courage, energy, initiative, and staying power.

A second difficult phase of the salesman's job is the competitive nature of selling. Salesmen must be successful competitors. The salesman, in one sense, competes with the buyer as to which will influence the other. Veteran salesmen have been quoted as telling certain junior salesmen something like this, "Son, you are being too nice. You act as though buyers will buy just because they should buy. You are selling too softly. You'll never succeed until you realize just who the buyer is. He is *The Enemy!*"

Competition is the essence of another relationship, that between a salesman and the salesmen of competing companies. Each salesman tries to hold on to his customers, to keep them from going to competitors. At the same time, each salesman is trying to talk customers away from those same competitors.

Finally, a salesman must compete with himself, against his past performances. He wants each year to be better than the last, and every order from each customer to be larger than previous orders. His own best records can be a salesman's fiercest competition.

Mr. John M. Wilson, National Cash Register Company, makes these observations about selling as hard, competitive work:

Selling is highly competitive. It is the backbone of our competitive way of life. You either compete or you drop out. Look at what has happened to the records in all fields of sport. They are being broken constantly, not by those who set them originally, but by others who have set new standards of performance.

The athlete who only equals the old record isn't given a second thought. It is the fellow who sets a new standard who makes the headlines.

This is to imply not that a salesman must set new records every time he "goes to the post" but that the standards of measurement have changed; he is judged by today's standards and methods. The glib-tongued, back-slapping fellow of a few years ago does not meet these new standards of sales performance.

Salesmen who are growing and developing are high-grade business-men. They are recognized as business counselors or distribution experts who are welcome wherever they go because they sell not only TO a customer but FOR a customer.

Today's salesman is a painstaking, well-trained individual who considers himself in a profession just as much as a doctor, lawyer, or engineer. He reaches this goal by a carefully planned series of professional procedures involving extensive planning, promotion, and presentation.

While it is true that selling is hard, competitive work, it is the most interesting work in the world for those who like it. The salesman is dealing with human beings and their motivation. He works with personal values and personal satisfaction. He experiments with various stimuli and analyzes buyers' reactions to each. The desires and aspirations of individuals are the strings on which he plays. Human nature is his field of study. For the individual who delights in coming to grips with stubborn, contentious buyers and selling them, the basic enjoyment, excitement, and satisfaction he finds in selling can be matched nowhere else.

SOCIAL AND ECONOMIC ASPECTS

Concepts About Selling

Many persons, including many students, are inclined to underrate the role of selling in our society and in our economy. This incorrect attitude is usually the result of inadequate knowledge. When selling is understood fully, false ideas disappear, and in their place appears an appreciation of what selling means to us.

Selling is *not* made up of jokes and drinks, backslapping and smiles, high pressure and high living, gifts, shady deals, and expense accounts. Salesmen are *not* away from home all the time. Their families need *not* suffer any more than other families. Salesmen do *not* have to resign themselves to a life less full, less satisfying, or less happy than other individuals enjoy.

Selling Is Essential. It is a serious mistake to consider personal selling an optional activity insofar as our economy is concerned. The products of our manufacturing and of our agriculture will not sell themselves, no matter how good or how big they are. The same holds true for intangibles. The advice that all one needs to do to succeed is to begin building the mousetrap better is as treacherous as it is untrue. Selling — aggressive, face-to-face selling — is necessary to move the volume of goods that comes from our factories and farms. As for intangibles, how many persons do you suppose buy insurance without any nudging from a salesman?

Selling is essential for high employment. A recent study showed that the typical salesman of a manufacturer is responsible for the steady employment of 31 factory workers. Their dependents, plus his, add up to 109 consumers. Then, moving out of his own organization, the salesman contributes to the continued operation of other enterprises. Railroads get business because manufacturers' salesmen, as well as their own, sell; wholesalers, retailers, storage companies, advertising agencies, advertising media — they, too, stay in business because salesmen are out making sales.

A point sometimes overlooked is that new products are not alone in requiring personal selling. Established products, too, must be sold, year after year. The many changes forever going on in many areas will not allow otherwise. As examples, a manufacturer decides to enter a new market, or he sees some new competitors appear, or established competitors take some dealers away from him, or — and this applies to all sellers — he sees the buyer group changing every day, some disappearing and needing to be replaced. Since advertising alone will almost never keep a product on the market, the manufacturer must make use of salesmen and salesmanship — indefinitely. What would happen if he abandoned personal selling? His sales would drop, his production would have to be cut back, his workers would be laid off, his inventories would rise, and, eventually, he would face bankruptcy.

Selling Is a Productive Activity. It is a misconception that selling adds no value to the goods and services it markets or that it is a parasitic form of promotion. The other side of this spurious coin is that individuals engaged in production and agriculture *are* productive — that they *do* create utility.

The answer to this is that economic exchange is the heart or core of our economy. There cannot be vast consumption without heavy buying, and heavy buying will not be done without extensive selling. Time-, place-, possession-, and information-utility can result directly from the activities of salesmen.

Selling is productive in that, to be successful, it must benefit the buyer as well as the seller. Practically all vendors must receive repeat orders and purchases from their customers if the vendors are to survive profitably. Most vendors must hold a customer's patronage through many successive purchases and over many years. Clearly, no sensible buyer makes repeated purchases from a seller if those purchases fail to benefit him.

Selling Is a Proud Activity. Every sincere, competent salesman is entitled to a feeling of pride from his career in selling. As has been indicated, his activities assure jobs for many other individuals. He guides buyers to better, more profitable products and services, and this is certainly a satisfying experience because he is guiding them to greater satisfaction.

All buyers, be they consumers, middlemen, members of a profession, or purchasing agents, benefit from good selling and are indebted to good salesmen.

A salesman can, does, and must do more than just make money. (It is not clear just why some of the critics of selling belittle the making of money. The position taken in this text is that, all other things being equal, the making of money is desirable, and the making of *more* money is even *more* desirable.) The salesman is the key man in the economic growth of our country. He, in part, makes possible the massive production plant which greatly contributes to our national security. Machines, men, and materials devoted to the manufacture of consumer goods can be converted swiftly to the production of war goods, if necessary.

Finally, because a career in selling pays well, a salesman can treat himself and his family to products and experiences that would otherwise be beyond his reach. He can take great pride in the standard of living he is able to enjoy.

Product Invention and Improvement

The competition among sellers in their selling activities exerts strong, even irresistible pressure on those sellers to compete on another basis — that of product. Manufacturers must constantly ask if they should bring out any new products, if there are product improvements that can and should be made, or if there are any new uses for their present products. In every proposal for product change, there is one basic and all-important question: can the new product, or the improved product, or the new use of product be sold profitably? Unless the answer is affirmative, the proposal has no practical value.

No new product or service can be placed on the market and kept there unless it can be sold successfully. Inventions and improvements mean nothing to the inventor, the worker, the businessman, the consumer, or to our national wealth until they are accepted, and that means *bought* by the public. In the case of new products, both the product and its market must be created from scratch. New and better products do not of themselves create buyer-desire or buyer-demand. The histories of electric lights, typewriters, cash registers, sewing machines, railroad transportation, and insurance prove this point.

The salesman encourages and often demands the improvement of current products and the invention of new ones. His plea is for products which will give him an advantage over the salesmen and products against which he competes. In effect, he tells the inventor to create and improve products; he tells the engineers and production managers to manufacture the items; he signals the advertising manager to go into action. These actions of his can be approved because the salesman himself is going to take the actual products and show them and sell them to buyers. The number of products on the market is increasing. These products must be sold. Many new products are being designed and tested. They will appear on the market just as soon as it is thought that they can be sold in a volume that promises profits. There is a natural tendency on the part of buyers to be cautious about purchasing new types of merchandise. Consumers get new and better products only because and if salesmen can sell them.

Freedom of Enterprise

Personal selling is absolutely essential to the freedom of enterprise we have. Twin pillars support our competitive system. First, the buyer can choose freely from among the products of many sellers. Second, the seller has the opportunity of entering the business of his choice and the privilege of hunting for customers. It appears that a vendor can build up his sales volume in three different ways. One, he can convert nonusers of his type of product into users — of his brand. Two, he can get his present customers to buy greater amounts of his brand than they have been buying. Three, he can persuade buyers who now buy competing brands to begin buying *his* brand. All three of these techniques make extensive use of personal selling.

Competition diminishes with any decline in aggressive efforts by sellers to increase sales. The "American way," as we know it, recognizes that producers must forever be locating new prospective buyers and must sell their wares to some of them. This is best done in a person-to-person, face-to-face manner. Unless sellers compete with other sellers, unless they fight for the buyer's dollars, one of two developments is inevitable. Either there would be dictation by the government, or there would be agreements among sellers, agreements that would set prices, divide markets, control output, and literally abolish competition as we know it today.

High Standard of Living

The activities of salesmen have only one effect on our standard of living, and that is raising it. Salesmen influence our way of life by changing our consumption patterns. They start by making a consumer dissatisfied with his present wants, habits, decisions, and products. Salesmen then tell about their new products, preaching progress and improvement. In this particular undertaking, the salesman functions as both an informer and a reformer. He must educate the buyer about his true circumstances and conditions before that buyer will pay much attention to the salesman's advice and counsel. He must teach the buyer about his problems before he can help him make purchases that will provide a higher standard of living.

The United States consumer is the best-fed, best-housed, best-clothed, best-transported, and best-entertained consumer in the world. There are more comforts of life available to more persons in our economy than anywhere else. The luxuries of today, now enjoyed by only the top-income families, will be taken for granted tomorrow by middle-income families. Two facts help explain this. First, competition among vendors is sharpened by the nature of the selling process with a resultant "break" for the consumer. Second, low prices are possible because of mass production, and mass production depends on the marketing of large quantities. Salesmen play the dominant role in the marketing of such quantities.

A country's standard of living is high or low as a direct result of how many or how few nonessential purchases its inhabitants make. Non-essential products and services raise our standard of living; they are the products and services that are not *bought* — they must be *sold*. Our consumers have *more* wants, and also *more varied* wants than other consumers have. They want their lives to be safer, more comfortable, easier, longer. They live better only as our salesmen sell better.

And our high standard of living *does* rest on and demand selling. No product or service can affect a consumer's living level and increase that consumer's satisfaction until the consumer buys and tries that product or service. This usually requires salesmanship. The public's reception of new products is characterized more by caution, hesitation, skepticism, and postponement than by an impatience to own the new item today. The public is reluctant to accept change, preferring the old, the familiar. Consumers resist new ideas and new products because such will disrupt their beloved routines. Consumers know the old; they are not quite sure of the new; they delay making a change. That delay is ended usually by some salesman who convinces buyers that they should spend some of their money for new and better ways of living. Price cuts, merchandising, advertising, and other promotion will not prove to Mrs. Housewife that she needs a clothers drier, or a waste disposer. Telephones, automobiles, vacuum cleaners, TV sets, air conditioning — all had to be *sold*.

Mr. Walker A. Williams, of the Ford Motor Company, says this:

> Eighty years ago, three-quarters of our working population made things. Those men worked on farms, in mines, and in factories. Today less than half of our labor force is devoted to production. Yet the total of our output has been climbing steadily.
>
> I don't think there can be any doubt but what America's great sales force has been one of the major factors in this trend. Largely because salesmen stimulate the demand for goods, industry found ways to produce more and more things at lower and lower prices for more and more people. As a result, America today enjoys the highest standard of living in the world.

Business Activity

Our economic well-being at any given moment is greatly influenced if not completely determined by three factors: *consumption*, *employment*, and *production*. It is obvious that these three are related; not one of the three can be at a high and healthy level unless the other two are healthy. When all three are at high levels, then we approach a balanced economy because production is matched by consumption, and unemployment is no problem because it is practically nonexistent. Full consumption and full production insure full employment.

If maximum production is to be had, large quantities of products and services must be sold. This justifies the contention that the salesman dictates how much merchandise his company will make, that he is the key to our production. Our mass production, the envy of the world, demands mass marketing, and this demands intensive and extensive selling. Production looks to salesmen to locate prospects for what production manufactures and then to convert those prospects into buyers. It must be remembered that unless a product can be sold profitably its manufacture must stop.

If maximum employment is to be had, then, as in the case of maximum production, large quantities of products and services must be sold. Selling increases consumer spending and thereby acts as a pressure to increase the efforts and activities of consumers to earn. Because of selling, we can have highly specialized labor with its efficient machines and its assembly lines. As a matter of fact, the highly specialized worker is at the mercy of selling. His high degree of specialization demands a large volume of production, and this demands large markets. Selling contributes in a substantial measure to employment throughout all industry and commerce, as these expand in direct proportion to the volume of goods and services sold. In summary, selling causes employment, and employment causes consumption.

Economic Growth

Let us hope that the second half of this century, 1950–2000, will deserve the label "Age of Marketing" as rightly as the 1900–1950 decades are entitled to be known as the "Age of Production." Distribution is the major element in our economy today. Our production has outrun our marketing; our ability to supply exceeds our demand; our big job is to sell the output of our huge productive facilities. We must look to selling to close the gap between our growing capacity to produce and our demand. Our basic problem for the years immediately ahead is that of marketing what we can make. The number, the variety, and the volume of products now on the market bear eloquent witness to the fact that our production problem has largely been solved. Consumption is our problem now, and it is the salesman who is needed to find buyers for our expanded volume of production.

Economic growth assumes continued investment because investment causes the production of additional products. This means more jobs, and jobs mean greater consumer buying power. Growth feeds on buying power. The cycle is something like this: sales cause capital investment — capital investment causes jobs — jobs cause income — and income causes purchases and sales. Investors invest because salesmen assure a market for the product in question, thus reducing the investor's risk to a tolerable point. New companies and new products would never be financed unless salesmen could find or create markets for the products.

Personal selling and advertising are our two basic marketing forces. Advertising is both desirable and necessary, and only the unenlightened salesman is hostile to it. But, advertising cannot do the entire marketing job for the products of our manufacturing and our agriculture. Indeed, the greater portion of this job must be assigned to personal selling. It is the salesman who must shoulder the greater share of the responsibility for the satisfactory operation of our distribution facilities. If our economic future is to be one of growth, then salesmen, aided, to be sure, by advertising, must go to buyers and stimulate demands for more and better products and services. Our growth is and will be limited only by our ability to market. The resignation "Well, our economy is now mature" will be premature so long as we can make and sell in greater amounts.

STUDY ASSIGNMENTS

1. Why do many people rate personal selling low as a choice of career?
2. Should salesmen organize and demand an 8-hour day and a 40-hour week? What are the reasons for your answer?
3. "Every individual operates in the field of selling because each must sell himself, his ideas, and his recommendations." *Is* everyone a salesman?
4. Why do some students believe that other departments in a manufacturer's organization provide more security than does the sales department?
5. What do you consider to be the salesman's most important contribution to society?
6. What yardsticks would you recommend for use in measuring a salesman's success?
7. The terms "hard sell" and "soft sell" have never achieved official definitions. What do *you* think each might involve?
8. Why must a salesman be a keen competitor?
9. "Nothing really happens 'til somebody sells something." Comment.
10. One hears the claim that economic activity breaks down into two undertakings — the making of goods and the marketing of those goods. Products must be produced and then sold. In what ways is a salesman a producer?

CHAPTER 2

TYPES OF SELLING

Classifying selling activities is not an easy undertaking, largely because there are so many variables on which classifications could be based. *Purpose of buyer* is one; some buyers, for example, buy to use or consume, whereas others buy to resell. *Characteristics of salesman* is another; there are inside salesmen and outside salesmen, part-time salesmen and full-time salesmen. *Purchase-sale features* is still another; some are negotiated, others are bid competitively; some involve creative selling, others reflect service selling. Selling can be classified on the basis of *type of item;* some salesmen sell physical products, others sell intangibles; some products are staples while other products are specialties. The *salesman's employer* differs; some salesmen work for manufacturers, some for wholesalers, some for retailers — and some work for themselves. *Skill and training* vary among salesmen; missionary salesmen and sales engineers typically need more than do service salesmen and retail salespersons. Identity of *contact initiator* permits an alternative; sometimes buyers get in touch with salesmen, and sometimes vice versa. *Compensation* is a basis of classification; some salesmen are on straight salary, some on straight commission, some on a type of combination. Finally, this chapter recognizes the *type of buyer:* selling to wholesalers and retailers for resale, selling to purchasing agents, selling to professional men, and selling to consumers.

SELLING TO WHOLESALERS AND RETAILERS

In the area of selling merchandise to middlemen for resale, three relationships are found. A manufacturer's salesman can sell to wholesalers; a manufacturer's salesman can sell to retailers; and, a wholesaler's salesman can sell to retailers. Often the same individual will sell to more than one type of buyer. Here one sees a manufacturer's salesman selling to both wholesalers and retailers, or to wholesalers and institutions, or to wholesalers and chain store warehouses. The same salesman for a wholesaler is seen selling to retailers, to business and industrial buyers, and even to other wholesalers.

21

Buyers in this area display a wide range of buying skill, but in one respect they are unanimous — they buy in response to rational, not emotional, motivation. Their main if not sole concern is for profits, and they know that the only ways to increase profits are to increase sales volume and to reduce costs. More specifically, wholesalers and retailers think in terms of inventory requirements, turnover, unit and dollar sales volume, markdowns, and margins. The manufacturer, the wholesaler, and the retailer — all three know that merchandise is completely and satisfactorily sold only when the customer buys, consumes, and returns to buy more. Thus, middlemen serve consumers as well as themselves when they buy with rational motives.

Selling to dealers for resale consists more of *service* selling than of *creative* selling. *Service* selling is little more than order taking. It is transacting a sale with a buyer who wants to buy and knows what he wants. The salesman fills the buyer's requests and the transaction is over. Service selling is common, for example, in retail stores; a customer comes in, selects two ties, tells a clerk he wants them, pays for them, gets the wrapped ties and a "thank you" from the clerk, and the purchase is completed. What the clerk does is service selling. In *creative* selling, the salesman discovers a buyer-need of which the buyer is unaware and sells his product as the answer. Or, the salesman gets the buyer to act to fill a need he knew about but, up to then, had done nothing about. Or, the salesman entices a buyer away from another, competitive seller. If the retail clerk had sold a better quality tie to the customer just mentioned, or if he had sold three ties instead of two, or if he had sold three shirts to the customer in addition to the ties, then he would have been a creative salesman instead of a clerk.

Regular Dealer-Selling Salesmen

Features of the Job. The individual referred to as a regular dealer-selling salesman may work for a manufacturer, calling on wholesalers and retailers, or he may work for a wholesaler, calling on retailers. The products he sells to these two types of middlemen are items for resale, not for use by the wholesaler or retailer in the operation of his business. For example, this type of salesman sells toothpaste to a drug store, not a cash register for keeping a record of cash; or, he sells canned food to a grocery store, not tires for the grocer's delivery trucks.

The salesman travels over a planned route in a repeated sequence. There is a regularity in the pattern of his call interval which permits each buyer to know when next to expect the salesman. If the salesman calls on a type of retail store that is numerous, then he usually makes numerous calls each day. Much of the salesman's income, sometimes all of it, is in the form of a regular salary. The job provides the individual with a considerable amount of security and with a regular pattern of life.

The job of the regular salesman who sells to dealers demands only a modest amount of creative selling. He must do a certain amount of prospecting, and detection and identification of buyers who could buy from him, and their conversion into customers must be considered to be creative activities. Then, in handling his regular customers, the salesman will, on occasion, discover a buyer-need that was not recognized before and sell the product that will best fill that need. That, too, is creative selling. Finally, any success the salesman has in getting support or "push" from a wholesaler or retailer will be the result of creative selling.

For the most part, however, the salesman will be doing service selling. His main activity will be that of writing up reorders for established customers, reorders of products the buyer needs to replenish. In one sense, this service selling makes the salesman's call more of a friendly visit than a product-promoting conference. Indeed, friendship is a major influence in this type of selling.

Creative Selling Duties. As was just indicated, the typical salesman who calls on wholesalers and retailers with merchandise for resale does not do much creative selling. Prospecting, discovering unfilled needs, and getting dealer "push" were mentioned as challenges to the salesman's creativeness and resourcefulness.

There is, however, one area of selling to middlemen for resale in which creative selling ability is most essential. This is the new-product area. Products can be new in one of two ways. *First*, when the *name* of the product is new to buyers, the salesman must do creative selling in order to elbow his way into a group of brands already known and established. An example would be the entrance on the Pacific Coast market of a product marketed up to that time only east of the Rockies. Or, a different type of example would be a manufacturer's addition of an electric razor to his line of cigarette lighters. *Second*, when the nature of the product is new to buyers, then the demand for creative selling is even stronger. Both electric razors and cigarette lighters, when first offered to retailers, were so different in nature as to be startling — even revolutionary. Middlemen stock new types of products with reluctance; they fear the item may be ahead of its time, or overpriced, or a short-lived fad, or not yet rid of all of its defects. To place such a different type of product on the market is a real pioneering job. Only hard and able creative selling can open new markets.

Service Selling Duties. The big job expected of regular dealer-selling salesmen is that of service selling. Usually the seller and the buyer have been doing business with each other for some time. The products the salesman is handling are generally well known to the buyer and, more importantly, to the buyer's customers. Often the products are well advertised. In these circumstances, the salesman's job is largely one of contact and service in a regular routine. His customers are steady customers. The salesman's task is to keep them steady, to hold on to them. This he does by keeping them stocked at all times with a supply of merchandise that is adequate. So, much of his job is that of writing up reorders after checking the dealer's stock and after looking at the dealer's "want book," if he keeps one. A "want book" is a notebook or set of forms where the retailer lists the items he will soon need to replenish. Thus, while it is true that the service salesman hopes to expand each of his present accounts, his main concern is for continued patronage.

Nonselling Duties. Great variety is found in the number and in the nature of nonselling duties performed by dealer-selling salesmen. Many do about five per cent creative selling and ninety-five per cent service selling, and that's it. Others will undertake certain nonselling duties, either because they think they should or because their companies tell them to. Collecting past-due accounts is such a duty. Hearing and handling complaints is another. Counseling is a broader nonselling duty that may have to do with any of the buyer's problems. Even more general would be the working for goodwill, both for one's company and for one's self.

Selling to Retailers for Wholesalers. This type of salesman works for a wholesale house and calls on three types of buyers: *retailers, business and industrial buyers,* and *other wholesalers.* Our interest at this point is in his selling merchandise to retailers for resale. When he sells to industrial and business buyers, he is, in effect, selling to purchasing agents, and that area of selling is taken up later. When he sells to other wholesalers, nothing is involved that is so different as to demand our attention now. But, a word or two are in order about the wholesaler's salesman as he deals with retailers.

Wholesalers stock thousands and thousands of items. In groceries, the number is often about 10,000; in drugs, 50,000 is not uncommon; in hardware, a figure of 60,000 raises no eyebrow. This means, of course, that the wholesaler's salesman must know *something* about a wide line of products. Furthermore, he can't *push* any specific products to any great degree — he does not have the time. If he works in only a single market, he may have to make as many as fifty calls a day.

In the drug field, a recent survey showed that four out of five retail druggists want advice and assistance from their wholesalers on various problems concerned with retail store operation. The retailers desiring help wanted assistance in moving merchandise through to the consumer. This included mainly sales promotion advice and assistance, and help in training retail store clerks — two major services wanted by about one half of the druggists. Two out of five wanted information about successful promotions of other druggists. About two out of five wanted wholesalers to advise them on what to display and how to display it. Three out of eight wanted their wholesalers to tell them how and where to get special display materials.

Here, according to the survey, are the top five kinds of assistance retail druggists want most:[1]

TYPE OF HELP	% OF DRUGGISTS WANTING IT
Sales Promotion Advice	51.8%
Clerk Training	48.6%
Information About Other Druggists' Promotions	39.0%
Advice on Display Arrangements	39.0%
Advice in Getting Special Displays	36.9%

Above all, the wholesaler's salesman must keep reorders coming in to his firm. Because his products and his prices are close to identical with those of competing wholesalers, he must hunt for some unique extra or plus point to stress. Such may be found in the personality of the salesman himself. The salesman will not do much imaginative fitting of product to buyer. He will not need an outstanding ability to sell. Job security is his if he keeps his territory reasonably well worked.

Requirements. For any creative selling, the salesman will need to be confident and even aggressive. He must be a person of initiative. He will find enthusiasm and resourcefulness to be desirable. It hardly needs to be said that he must know how to use the principles and techniques of effective selling.

Service selling calls for a different set of requirements. Here the demand is for a friendly, a helpful type of person. He will need much energy and durability because his day is long and hard. In the light of the repetitive nature of his calling, he will not last unless his customers find him sincere and dependable. He will need more persistence than aggressiveness. He must grow on and with his dealers.

The necessity for customers' confidence is indicated in these words from an executive of the Optical Wholesalers National Association:

[1]*The Retailer Looks At His Service Wholesale Druggist* (New York, National Wholesale Druggists' Association, 1954), p. 11

In my estimation, the ability to obtain the confidence of his customer
is the #1 requirement of a wholesaler's salesman. His calls are frequent
on the same account so any attempt to "high pressure" is a boomerang
on subsequent calls. A wholesaler's salesman must be more than the
name implies — he must be a business friend, a close-mouthed confidant
of his customers' troubles, and a "fatherly advisor" on quantities to buy,
etc. Any overloading of customers' shelves by a wholesaler's salesman
destroys that #1 requirement — confidence.

Missionary Salesmen

Features of the Job. Missionary salesmen work for manufacturers
and are relatively prominent in the marketing of drug, tobacco, food, and
hardware products. The primary duty of the missionary salesman is
not selling goods directly to buyers. That assignment is given to the
manufacturer's *regular* salesmen. In a sentence, the goal of the manufacturer's missionary salesman is to get his products moving faster and
in larger volume through the use of techniques that are more indirect
than direct.

The most common situation finds a manufacturer's missionary salesman calling on wholesalers to develop greater interest in and support
for the manufacturer's line of goods. Arrangements may be made for the
missionary salesman to tell his story to the wholesaler and his salesmen.
The follow-up might well be for the missionary salesman to travel for a
short time with each of the wholesaler's salesmen, making calls on the
wholesaler's prospects and customers with those salesmen. Another
situation finds the missionary salesman calling alone on retailers who
should or do stock the manufacturer's merchandise. Still another possibility is found in industrial selling. A manufacturer supplying fabricating
materials or parts to other manufacturers might employ missionary
salesmen to keep in close touch with those manufacturers. These salesmen
will work to promote their *customers'* sales, thus increasing their own sales.

Creative Selling Duties. A look at a typical missionary salesman
of a food manufacturer as he accompanies a wholesaler's salesman in
calling on retailers helps us to appreciate the creative selling demanded
of the missionary salesman. The over-all objective of the missionary
salesman is to stimulate business for the wholesaler by writing up a larger
order than the retailer would have bought had the wholesaler's salesman
been calling by himself. Stated in other words, the objective is to improve,
at least for a while, circumstances common to many manufacturers,
namely, the failure of wholesalers to "push" the manufacturer's products.

In order to achieve his goals, the missionary salesman must, in most
instances, get the retailer to stock a larger quantity of the manufacturer's
goods. This can be quite a challenge when the manufacturer is launching

new products on the market. Then, the missionary salesman wants to get the best location in the store for his line and, in that location, to be given excellent shelf position. Finally, the missionary salesman wants as much retail support or "push" as can be obtained. This includes displaying the merchandise, advertising the merchandise, and putting stronger personal selling behind it. Clearly, the missionary salesman must be competent in creative selling.

Service Selling Duties.   Service selling is obviously neither an adequate nor an appropriate assignment for a missionary salesman. He *can*, of course, write up an order for a retailer's needs in his line while the wholesaler's salesman he accompanies is busy with other matters. But then he must move immediately into creative selling or into performing services for the retailer.

Nonselling Duties.   One of the most effective techniques of the missionary salesman is to use the *service approach* to buyers. This is not to be confused with service selling, which, it will be remembered, is nothing more than filling the retailer's requests. In calling on retailers, the missionary salesman has an excellent opportunity to make extensive and effective use of the service approach. He can offer point-of-purchase material to a retailer, even going so far as to change a retailer's window or to build a floor display of his products. He can help retailers with their advertising. He can teach the retailer and the retailer's sales staff about his merchandise, especially how to sell more of it more profitably. If he qualifies as an adviser on management problems, the missionary salesman may analyze some of the retailer's problems and make recommendations. Such problems might involve store equipment, store layout, organization, credit, records, special promotion events, or customer services.

It appears that a missionary salesman must be a "merchandising" salesman and, to some degree, a "management" salesman. If he builds store traffic and sales volume for retailers, if he is able to improve their management, then he automatically builds goodwill, confidence, and profits for his company.

Requirements.   The missionary salesman must be a broadly oriented and a highly competent salesman for two reasons. First, his assignments are varied and challenging. He must be an expert in his product line, he must know more than a little about the buyer's business, and he must be a successful salesman. In other words, he must be good before he is entitled to any of a buyer's time. Second, the buyers seen by a missionary salesman present a special type of challenge. Retailers, upon seeing that a wholesaler's salesman is not calling alone, may immediately become wary, feeling that they are in for a matching of wits with a high-powered specialist. As for calling on wholesalers, getting them to show even a bit more interest in a manufacturer's products is not easy.

SELLING TO PURCHASING AGENTS

Who Purchasing Agents Are

A purchasing agent is responsible for the procurement function in his organization. His authority and his activities will vary from organization to organization depending on what his management thinks the purchasing staff should do. Of the duties he usually performs, the one with which we are concerned is, of course, that of buying. Because he is the person who makes his organization's purchases, he is the man a salesman must see and sell.

Purchasing agents are found in four major areas, one of which is *manufacturing*. A factory making shoes or a mill making steel typically has on the staff a salaried employee whose job is to buy most or all of the products and materials required by the company. Mining companies and public utilities are examples of other types of businesses which can be grouped with manufacturers. A second area is that of *government*, where purchasing is done at the local, the state, and the national levels. A third area is composed of the *institutional market*. Purchasing agents in this area are found buying for colleges, hotels, and hospitals. In the fourth area, the buyers are *wholesalers and retailers* but they buy as purchasing agents when they are buying for use (delivery trucks or cash registers) and not for resale. While some of the following treatment can be applied to all purchasing agents, the discussion is concerned with the purchasing agents of manufacturers.

What Purchasing Agents Buy

It can be claimed that purchasing agents have two expectations when they make purchases. First, they, like consumers, assume that what they buy will deliver the utility or the satisfaction desired. This expectation is universal whether the purchase be of a physical product, such as a desk, or of an intangible, such as storage space. The second expectation involves a more general or less precise hope; the absence of a better designation practically demands that this objective be referred to as *service*.

Tangibles and Intangibles. The specific purchases of purchasing agents can be grouped into six classifications. *Installations* include such capital items as bank vaults, looms, elevators, locomotives, and printing presses. *Raw materials* might be cotton, wheat, lumber, pig iron, or crude rubber. In some instances, the purchase of a basic raw material might be done by a specialist in that product; for example, tobacco for cigarettes might be bought by a tobacco expert and not by the purchasing agent who buys the machines for the factory. *Fabricating parts and materials* go into the finished product and could be tires, paint, springs, batteries, or containers. *Operating supplies* are essential to the functioning of the enterprise and include fuel, stationery, lubricants, wrapping paper, and brooms. *Accessory equipment* could be employee lockers, scales, cash registers, time clocks, or hand tools. *Intangibles* include electric current, advertising, insurance, storage, and transportation.

Service. As was indicated, purchasing agents expect something in addition to the specific tangibles and intangibles they buy, something we called *service*. Prominent here is the matter of *quality*. Purchasing agents expect salesmen to recommend the quality of product that will best serve the buyer's needs. Then, once buying starts, the purchasing agent counts on a uniformity of quality that will continue indefinitely. In many manufacturing processes, even a slight change in quality can disrupt production. In addition to quality, the purchasing agent expects much and qualified *attention* from the salesman and his firm. This may call for a survey and an analysis of the buyer's operations before any specific products are considered. And, after purchase, the buyer expects the seller to make any check-up calls indicated and to be available gladly and promptly if problems arise. Purchasing agents buy *delivery*. Their sources of supply must be dependable lest a delay in receiving some essential parts or ingredients or supplies halt operations. Purchasing agents expect *sound advice* from all salesmen, whether or not any purchase is made. The purchases made by a purchasing office are expected to be reflected in larger profits, and these can result only from an increase in sales or a decrease in costs, or both. So, the purchasing agent is always in search of new products, new intangibles, new vendors, or new methods which will affect sales volume and expenses in the manner desired. Last but not least, purchasing agents want *economy*. Cynical salesmen sometimes complain that the first requirement for selling to purchasing agents is to quote them the lowest price in the market — and if you do that, the business is yours. Of course, purchasing agents want to make the best buys possible; that is what they are paid to do. But they find out quickly that unless quality is correct and unless service is satisfactory, low price is a delusion.

Features of Selling to Purchasing Agents

The Market. Many of the industries for which purchasing agents buy are, in reality, very limited markets. The automotive industry, the aluminum industry, and the cigarette industry are examples of markets consisting of a relatively small number of buyers. Because buyers are few, geographic concentration is common; the result may well be that 85 to 90 per cent of an industry can be found in just a few locations. Where this concentration exists, salesmen have little trouble locating their buyers.

The individual buyers making up the industrial market are experts at buying; the contrast between their purchasing skill and that of the typical consumer is impressive. Purchasing agents are trained thoroughly for their role. In addition, most of them are experienced buyers. They are hard buyers; they are cost-conscious buyers. After all, they are spending the company's money and not their own, and this means that their accountability for their purchases is more serious and strict than that of a consumer buying with his own dollars.

Purchasing agents must be rational buyers. Whereas consumers can gratify some or many of their emotional desires, not so the purchasing agents. Because they make purchases that will be considered good or bad depending on whether profits go up or down, purchasing agents must act only on rational motivation. To do otherwise would jeopardize the buyer's standing within the company. Because advertising and sales promotion are more effective in appealing to a person's emotions than to his reason, they are of limited use to sellers who sell to the industrial market. Purchasing agents are less influenced by these two marketing forces than are consumers or even middlemen buying for resale.

Buying. The nature of the buying done by purchasing agents is interesting. To begin with, their demand is a *derived* demand, being the result of actual or anticipated buying by consumers. If the sales force of the buyer's company is not moving merchandise, then no salesman on earth can persuade the purchasing agent of that company to buy on a grand scale. In the case of capital items, the purchasing agent may not buy at all for years; this makes infrequent purchase a feature for certain types of product. For many industrial goods, the business cycle is a very significant factor. The natural longevity of some items such as railroad cars or turbines can be extended even further by a relatively small increase in maintenance costs. Replacement of such items can be postponed when times are bad.

The fact that certain purchases are made by a *group* of company officials suggests a few other features of the buying process. For example, the *need* decision can originate in one or more of various offices. When a salesman does not know which individuals can request his type of product, and when he does not know the relative influence of the members of the buying group, that salesman does not know whom to ask to see. Suppose he is selling industrial lubricants. How much voice does the production manager have in such a purchase? How about the chief engineer, the plant engineer, the master mechanic, and the superintendent? Or, lest he be overlooked, how much does the purchasing agent have to say about the purchase of the lubricants? Automotive trucks are another product in which several individuals have legitimate and real interest. A common feature of buying groups is their diversity of interests. For example, the sales manager may want to buy from firms to whom he sells or wants to sell. This factor of reciprocity means nothing to the production manager whose main concern is to keep production costs low. In the case of the automotive trucks, a spokesman for the drivers may ask that consideration be given to comfort, convenience, or safety.

Purchasing agents buy from manufacturers, from industrial distributors, from mill supply firms, and a bit from wholesalers. There is much more buying direct from the manufacturer and less use of middlemen than is found in the marketing of consumer goods. Several vendors are usually investigated before a purchase is made.

Selling. Selling to purchasing agents is understandably influenced by the buyers themselves and by the character of their buying. In many lines, the salesman will make few sales, but each will be a large one. Often the salesman can predict quite accurately when a certain buyer will be buying and can even make a shrewd guess as to when he will begin *thinking* seriously about buying. Because buyers can postpone certain purchases for years, the negotiation phase can extend over a long period of time.

There can be great fluctuations in a salesman's sales volume. It could happen that a salesman might not make a single sale in an entire year — for instance, if his line were locomotives and the year one of recession. Price must often be quoted or negotiated when a product is to be built to the specifications of a single buyer. If the salesman's customer is also a manufacturer, that customer can be the salesman's most dangerous competition in the sale of products such as parts. The customer has the choice of making certain parts himself or of buying them.

Often the salesman is extremely active with the account both before and after the actual sale. His first big job in many situations is to sell *need* to the buyer; as has been noted, many industrial products can be made to do for one more year. Where appropriate, the salesman may ask for permission to make a survey of the buyer's circumstances and, if need exists, may ask permission to demonstrate his product, hoping thereby to convince the buyer of his need. After the sale, the *sales*man may find himself a *service*man. He may install or help install the product; he may take care of the product's maintenance. If the buyer's employees must be trained to use the salesman's product, that training may be conducted by the salesman. Finally, the salesman must be a serviceman in helping the buyer solve problems, those involving the salesman's product and other problems, too.

Requirements for Selling to Purchasing Agents

For most selling to purchasing agents, the salesman will need a dual background consisting of his technical specialty plus marketing. Engineering, accounting, chemistry, or electronics might be the specialty to which must be added the selling function and operation. In some lines a person with a marketing background can be hired and taught by his employer as much of the specialized field as he will need. In other lines the specialists or technicians can be hired and given the necessary training in marketing. In any event, there must be much study and learning, much knowledge of the laboratory and factory of the salesman's company, and maybe even a lengthy apprenticeship before a salesman is put on his own in his own territory.

Salesmen need a thorough grasp of what their technical products or intangibles can do for buyers. They need the ingenuity necessary to see how their present products can be adapted or modified to provide better solutions to buyers' problems. And, in regard to those problems, the salesman must be keen enough to spot waste, inefficiency, and unnecessary expense of which the buyer is unaware. This demands an analytical, probing mind and a knowledge of the production, equipment, and operating problems of plants. Thus, the requirements for this type of selling are exacting; the pay is excellent for those who qualify.

SELLING TO PROFESSIONAL MEN

Members of certain professions exert great influence over certain purchases made by their clients or their patients. Architects, for example, when designing homes for their clients are often asked which plumbing fixtures are best or which brand of floor tile is the best to use. Probably few days pass without someone in a dentist's chair asking which brand of dentifrice he should use. Engineers are asked about brands of petroleum products. Doctors have much to say about the purchases of not only their patients but of their local drug stores as well. Clearly, certain professional men are in positions of significance to certain manufacturers because of their practice of *specifying* or *recommending* products for their clients and patients.

One type of selling, then, is that done by a manufacturer's salesman who works to get the goodwill and favorable influence of professional men. In the drug field these men are called "detail men." Their operations will be considered as typical of this type of selling and will be examined briefly.

Detail men are concerned with two groups, members of the medical and dental professions and druggists. The detail man calls on doctors, dentists, nurses, and hospitals, describes how his products answer certain needs of the professions, and leaves samples and literature. The detail man must sell himself and his firm to the doctor, because the prescribing doctor is a key factor in the sale of his products. The detail man must be able to meet doctors and impress them favorably; he must be able to talk intelligently to one doctor or to a group of them about the problems and needs of the world of medicine; he must literally speak their language.

Druggists are the second group with which detail men work. The phase of the job involving public relations and goodwill is about the same here as it is with calling on doctors. The other phase involves actual selling and merchandising. The detail man shows the druggist why the doctors will be prescribing his product and why he, therefore, should have a supply on hand. The salesman works for more promotional support of the prescription department from the retailer. In selling non-prescription drug products, the salesman must try to convince the retailer that it is in his own best interest to give the line more or better display space, more participation in advertising, and stronger support by the salespeople. When he leaves a doctor and calls on a druggist, the detail man must switch from his professional vocabulary to his commercial vocabulary.

The general sales manager of the Norwich Pharmacal Company has this to say about Norwich salesmen:

> In a professional drug company, the salesman is a highly specialized individual. He is not only a salesman who actually sells merchandise to wholesale and retail drug outlets, but he is also sufficiently trained in pharmacy and /or medicine to be able to discuss intelligently the advantages of his products with practicing physicians and registered pharmacists.
>
> In an operation of this type the doctor is the "key" to the movement of products since he originates the prescriptions. Therefore, the salesman of professional products must be in a position to present such products to the individual physician or group of physicians not only with conviction but backed up by a thorough knowledge of the needs of the medical profession.

SELLING TO CONSUMERS

In Retail Stores

Of all types of selling, it is quite probable that the lowest quality of salesmanship is found inside retail stores. It is true, of course, that some retailers employ outside salespersons to sell certain high-priced products; in the case of these salespersons, able and effective salesmanship is a prerequisite to success. Within the store, also, those same lines of products require capable salespersons. But, for the most part, the great bulk of the transactions over the counter are *purchases* rather than *sales*. Typically, the customer seeks out the retail store in which she expects to find what

Performance Appraisal Form

		Out-standing	Above Standard	Standard	Below Standard	Unsatis-factory
Name of Salesman	Date					

PERSONAL DEVELOPMENT IS THE MUTUAL RESPONSIBILITY OF THE INDIVIDUAL SALESMAN AND HIS DISTRICT MANAGER.

I. *Efforts with Physicians*

A. Does effective detailing with all physicians on major products in Marketing Plan.

B. Promptly creates demand for all new major products through effective detailing, seeing the most influential physicians first.

C. Does effective planning and detailing to promote products with specialist.

D. Sells average or above average share of products to consuming physician.

. E. Keeps the Product Reference Set up to date and merchandised.

F. Reminds physicians of the wealth of practical information in *De Re Medica.*

G. Judiciously provides physicians with material for personal use.

H. Keeps informed on current medical developments.

II. *Efforts with Retailers*

A. Strives to sell every retail contact.

B. Checks stocks and gets major share of competitive turnover.

C. Encourages stores to merchandise the Prescription Department.

D. Obtains militant support from pharamacist on appropriate products.

E. Keeps price lists up to date.

F. Reduces to a minimum the time spent in "low potential" stores.

G. Obtains 100 per cent of opening stock orders.

H. Graciously handles complaints and returns in accordance with established policy.

over

IT IS THE JOB OF THE LILLY SALES MANAGEMENT TEAM TO BUILD MEN — THEN SELL PILLS!	Out-standing	Above Standard	Standard	Below Standard	Unsatis-factory
III. *Efforts with Hospitals*					
A. Strives to sell every hospital contact.					
B. Checks stocks and gets major share of competitive business.					
C. Makes friends with key people who can influence specifications.					
D. Has interns and resident physicians on the Lilly team.					
E. Details hospital pharmacist and other personnel.					
IV. *Efforts with Wholesalers*					
A. Encourages wholesalesmen to *sell* Lilly on every call.					
B. Encourages wholesalesmen to have *Lilly Price List* at all times.					
C. Encourages wholesalesmen to check stocks and sell in the Prescription Department.					
D. Encourages wholesalesmen to use the promotion material in the Planned Selling Program.					
E. Encourages wholesalesmen to play an important role in influencing the profitability of their company by selling Lilly.					
V. *Miscellaneous Aspects of the Job*					
A. Completely cooperates in all programs.					
B. Promptly handles paper work.					
C. Judiciously uses promotional aids and supplies.					
D. Shares sales ideas with associates.					
E. Reports on unusual programs of competitors, always giving *facts*.					
F. Uses imagination and creative ability in sales work.					

SPRTD

Eli Lilly Co.

This rating chart gives a complete picture of the job of a salesman selling for a drug manufacturer.

she wants and may even seek out her favorite salesperson. In addition, the customer typically enters the store wanting something or at least favorably inclined toward the possibility of buying. In these circumstances, the inevitable result is that there is much *service* selling, which is nothing more than filling the customer's requests, and little *creative* selling, in which the salesperson uses both imagination and persuasion. Self-service has simplified the retail selling job, making "attendants" out of salespersons and thus has been an influence on the lowering of salaries in this field of selling.

Duties. The selling duties of a retail salesperson can be stated simply. First, he must greet and size up the customer, determining the customer's needs and wants. Next, he selects the merchandise he thinks most suitable in the light of the customer's circumstances. Third, he tells and shows the customer how and why that particular merchandise will best fill the requirements. Fourth, he completes the sale. Then, if it is indicated, an attempt is made at *suggestion* selling — at recommending some product the customer had not asked about. Finally, the salesperson makes a bid for the customer's goodwill so that the customer will be inclined to return for future purchases. During the day, the typical salesperson will deal with many buyers and will make many sales of small size.

Certain nonselling duties are usually assigned to retail salespersons. Integral phases of the sale are such steps as making change, operating the cash register, writing up a sales ticket, and wrapping the merchandise sold. In addition, the salesperson must know the location of stock throughout the store, must see that his own department's stock is always adequate, and must keep his stock in place and his area neat. Many salespersons are asked to take part in taking inventory. It is not uncommon for some retail salespersons to be asked to do some of the store's displays.

Features of the Job. On the plus side, selling in retail stores does not make extreme demands of an individual. This area of selling can be entered and mastered adequately by almost anyone who is attracted to it. Just average amounts of courtesy, tact, patience, and endurance will enable one to get along satisfactorily. The activity offers a measure of security because a store must have employees to serve its customers. There are internal promotion possibilities to such positions as buyer or assistant manager. Retail selling is good preparation for other types of selling, and it is good preparation for marketing jobs other than selling. It is almost a prerequisite to a person's opening his own store.

Probably the largest minus in retail selling is the low starting salary. Another major disadvantage is the poor personnel management found in entirely too many retail organizations. Unreasonable, ignorant, arrogant, and insulting customers do not make the salesperson's life easier or happier. Long hours on one's feet can also do things to one's disposition. Saturday work and evening work may be required.

In Consumers' Homes

While the heading of this section uses the word "homes," the salesman could call on the consumer at his office or place of business, at his farm, or, indeed, the interview could take place in a restaurant over lunch. Because customers do not always visit the sellers' places of business often enough to buy or to be sold, some salesmen take the initiative by looking up and going to see buyers. Such a salesman can be working entirely for himself, for a retailer, or for a manufacturer. He or she may sell intangibles such as insurance, securities, or travel tours. Or, he or she may sell physical products such as automobiles, sterling silverware, appliances, shoes, books, brushes, or cosmetics. Calling may be as mechanical and unscientific as going from house to house, or it could be highly selective and only by appointment.

The housewife looks on house-to-house salesmen both with favor and disfavor, depending on the product, and mainly on the person. The family can make a group purchase with a minimum of inconvenience if the salesman will call at their home at an appointed hour. The housewife can then experiment with and operate certain products under much the same circumstances as in everyday living. Instruction is typically available from the salesman. In addition, the housewife may well feel less under the pressure of time in her own living room than in a retail store. She appreciates the comfort, pleasantness, and economy — no traffic to fight, no dressing up for a trip to the stores, no parking expense.

Of course, most housewives have knowledge of, sometimes even experience with, dishonest and otherwise objectionable house-to-house salesmen. Many have been subjected to the rude behavior or the almost-insulting aggressiveness of high-pressure salesmen and "veterans" with phony afflictions, selling everything from shoestrings to vacuum sweepers.

Certain aspects of selling to consumers on their own ground deserve special mention. One of these is that locating prospective buyers is often a considerable job. Then there is the problem of getting in to see the buyer. Housewives don't *have* to open the door when a stranger rings the bell, and requests for appointments *can* be refused. These two features result in a third — the high percentage of failures where calling is non-selective. Another factor is that in house-to-house or office-to-office selling, the salesman has little specific information about the person he interviews. If a salesman can, for a consideration, get a prospect to hold a "house party" to which other prospects are invited, if he can send out direct mail to a large list and offer an incentive to prospects, or if he can request appointments with individuals whose names he has acquired from satisfied customers, the number of unproductive calls and the amount of wasted time are reduced. Another feature of this type of selling is that the salesman is practically, if not completely, in business for himself. The hours worked and the income received vary from salesman to salesman and from month to month. Also, in this type of selling, many calls must be made every day. Finally, the salesman must often sell the *need* to the buyer before he can sell his *product* to fill that need; he must often establish want or desire where the prospect feels none.

Selling to the consumer in his home demands that the salesman meet certain requirements. He must be a rugged individual with a strong backbone and much intestinal fortitude. The activity has no place for thin skins, weak wills, or easily discouraged personalities. The salesman must work hard and long hours each day. This demands steady control and effective discipline of self. The salesman must be able to find and then to stay in the ideal middle-ground between too much and too little aggressiveness. He will need to be able to meet strangers easily and to make a favorable impression on them quickly. He must capture the buyer's attention almost instantly and convert it without delay into interest in the salesman's product. His selling style must be smooth and persuasive.

The job of selling the products of the Real Silk Hosiery Mills house-to-house exclusively requires:

1. A person who can govern himself. This is a primary requisite, since there is no boss to get him started each morning, and no time clock to punch. A good salesman must be able to govern the use of his time.

2. A person who is in good health and has an abundance of energy.

3. A person with a pleasant, likeable personality, with a pleasant voice and mannerisms.

4. A person with a desire to win. He must have a certain amount of drive and must not retreat before obstacles.

STUDY ASSIGNMENTS

1. Why are wholesalers and retailers entitled to markups on the merchandise they sell?

2. When times get bad, which is a manufacturer apt to cut first and more drastically — his sales budget or his advertising budget? Discuss.

3. Why do some people consider selling to be an insignificant activity that can be performed by almost anyone?

4. When college students discuss ambitions and their careers, few indicate any interest in house-to-house selling. How do you explain this attitude?

5. A missionary salesman working for a manufacturer of floor coverings is expected to get retail salesmen to "push" his line. What are some of the points he could make when talking to a retailer's salesmen?

6. Should a regular, dealer-selling salesman welcome or deplore being given a new, nonselling duty?
7. Two salesmanship students were clarifying their concepts of creative selling. One suddenly exclaimed, "I see something — in *creative* selling, a salesman may be assigned some nonselling duties, but that is not done in *service* selling!" Was he correct?
8. List three ways in which selling to retailers for resale usually differs from selling to consumers for consumption.
9. What do you think is the most striking difference between a salesman and all other employees of the company?
10. For years one has heard that from a wholesaler's or a retailer's point of view "goods well bought are half sold." Is this true today?

CASE STUDY 2A

Ward Long grew up in a small town of 7,500 population located in the deep South. His father worked in the local post office. Ward, the oldest of three children, had two sisters. The section of the country was largely agricultural, and cotton was the main crop. The nearest city of 100,000 population was 100 miles distant.

While Ward was in high school, he got a part-time job working in the second largest drug store in town. Although he started out behind the soda fountain, from almost the very first day, Ward found himself handling sales of just about all of the store's merchandise. When no other employee was available, customers naturally expected Ward to take care of them, whether they wanted toilet items, candy, first aid products, soap, or anything else.

By the middle of his senior year in high school, Ward was a pleasant, courteous retail employee. It was his preference to give customers what they asked for rather than to sell better merchandise or more of it. About this time, Ward began to think that he would like a career in selling, and the type of company he thought he'd like to sell for was one manufacturing a line of ethical drug products. Manufacturers' names like Squibb, Upjohn, and Parke Davis ran through Ward's mind.

QUESTIONS:

1. Do you think Ward Long is qualified to become a detail man for a drug manufacturer?
2. How would that job differ from his drug store job?

CASE STUDY 2B

Mr. Reaves is a salesman for Putt-Putt Golf Courses. He is calling on a Mr. Biggs at a Putt-Putt Golf Course in Jacksonville, Florida. Mr. Biggs has four other courses in Florida, three in Texas, and two in California, for a total of ten courses. He has been buying supplies from the Putt-Putt wholesale establishment, Southern Golf, Inc., for the past two years. On his last visit,

Mr. Reaves sold Mr. Biggs 3,000 golf balls, one hundred tee mats, and four rolls of carpet. This was four months ago. It is now June, and the course has been open for three and a half months. This is Mr. Reeves' first trip to Florida for the year.

Salesman: Good afternoon, Mr. Biggs. It's good to see you again. I believe this is the first time I've seen your golf course this year. You certainly do have it in good shape.

Customer: Thank you, Mr. Reaves. We have worked hard on it, and we are very pleased with the results.

Salesman: I visited your course in Miami about two weeks ago, and it was doing extremely well. Even with that big parking lot of yours, it was hard to find a space for my car.

Customer: The Miami course is doing an excellent business. We might even set a new course record in receipts this season. Our manager down there is doing a terrific job.

Salesman: Mr. Biggs, I would like to show you something that your Miami manager was very interested in. It is our new putter, the "7-11," with a brand new feature called the Pride Grip.

Customer: Mr. Reaves, you know we do most of our business with you because we like your products. But we are almost at the point of being overstocked with clubs right now. If you remember, I placed a large order with you at the beginning of the season.

Salesman: Yes, sir, I certainly do. And I appreciate your business. It makes us very proud to see excellent miniature golf courses like yours using our equipment. And I do realize your position, Mr. Biggs. I just want you to look at this club because it is our newest and best club. I know you are always thinking ahead, and you will probably need clubs for some of your other courses before long.

Customer: Well, I may need clubs later on, but I certainly don't need any now.

Salesman: Mr. Biggs, you will notice (handing him a putter) that this shaft and face are coated with chrome to give a lasting and clean appearance at all times. In the manufacturing process that goes into the making of the 7-11 putter, this shaft and face are dipped into the chrome not just once, as most putters are, but *three* times. This will give it three times the life of regular putters and will prevent the chipping and scraping of chrome from becoming noticeable. This is why we call it the "triple-dipped shaft."

Customer: You mean there are three separate coatings of chrome instead of one?

Salesman: Yes, sir.

Customer: And you are absolutely positive that it will last three times longer than the regular putters now in use?

Salesman: Mr. Biggs, the 7-11 carries with it a two-year Putt-Putt guarantee, fully backed by us. We have never had a 7-11 putter turned in to us and have not heard a single complaint about its performance.

Customer: Well, then, with this supposedly long life, I imagine the 7-11 costs more, doesn't it?

Salesman: Considering the advantages that this putter offers, Mr. Biggs, it is relatively cheaper. I've already mentioned the added life of the shaft. It also has features in the face and grip which give longer life and durability to the club.

Customer: I believe you did mention something about a grip a while ago. What were you talking about?

Salesman: Here is the feature of our 7-11 putter which makes it stand head and shoulders above everything in its field. This is the "Pride Grip." No other putter has this, Mr. Biggs. It is exclusive with Putt-Putt. This is a grip which will come off the shaft when it becomes too dirty or too sticky for play, and it can be replaced with a similar grip.

Customer: That is really nice! I've never seen that before. But how do I know some kids won't jerk it off by accident? I even have some people around here who, I believe, would take something like that off just for meanness.

Salesman: Well, it is not exactly that easy to take off, Mr. Biggs. You notice the tape at the bottom of the grip which holds the grip to the shaft. This has to be cut — like this. (Demonstrates.) Then it has to be worked loose like this. (Does so.) It is not easy for small kids to do, and it takes about half a minute to take one off completely. Besides, this feature is not known outside of the golfing business, so I doubt if you would have any trouble with the kids tampering with the grip.

Customer: What is the purpose of this grip coming off? So I won't have to re-place the whole club?

Salesman: Exactly! You know that the grip gets sticky and dirty long before the shaft and face of the club are damaged. This way — with the Pride Grip — only a part of the club is replaced and you wind up with seemingly a brand new club at only a minimum price — $1.50 per grip. This price is hard to beat.

Customer: What about the price of the whole putter?

Salesman: They sell for $6.50 a piece. That includes everything.

Customer: That's a little higher than the average club, isn't it?

Salesman: Yes, it is, Mr. Biggs, but considering the two-year guarantee and all of its features, especially the Pride Grip, it is a relatively inexpensive club, don't you think?

Customer: Well, I guess so.

Salesman: The grip feature alone would save you the purchase of a new club in a year or so. This club at the present is in great demand. Do you happen to know of any other club that offers as many advantages as our 7-11 putter does?

Customer: No, I don't believe I do.

Salesman: Well, here's what I'd like to do, Mr. Biggs. I know your inventory of clubs is full at the moment, but you will be needing some next season. Let me put you down for five hundred clubs now, and we can send fifty clubs to any course you desire, and you can use them now. It would be on sort of an experimental basis. Look at the response that you receive from your customers, and if you aren't satisfied, we can cancel the order before next season. But I am sure that you will be more than pleased with the performance of this club.

Customer: You mean if I don't like the club, I don't have to take the order?

Salesman: That's exactly right. If you aren't satisfied, the four hundred and fifty will not be charged to you at all.

Customer: But the fifty will.

Salesman: You may even return those.

Customer: That sounds all right to me. But will the four hundred and fifty clubs have to be sent to the same course as the fifty experimental clubs? If so, I can't take them.

Salesman: No, sir. If you wish, we can ship one hundred clubs to five different courses. It's all up to you.

Customer: All right. I'll take five hundred. When do I get my bill? Now?

Salesman: No, sir. You may, if you prefer, but otherwise you won't be billed until after you receive all of your clubs.

Customer: Fine! When can I get my fifty clubs?

Salesman: Where do you want them shipped, sir?

Customer: I would prefer twenty-five shipped to Miami and twenty-five sent to Dallas, Texas, if possible.

Salesman: Well, we can have the clubs in Miami in four days, and the clubs in Dallas within seven to nine days. Will that be satisfactory?

Customer: Fine! It is a pleasure to do business with you, Mr. Reaves.

Salesman: Thank you, Mr. Biggs. It is *our* pleasure.

QUESTIONS:

1. Did Reaves make a sound presentation?
2. Does the sale strike you as being "too easy" for the salesman?

Background for Selling

Part

B

CHAPTER 3

THE MAN FOR THE JOB

In a very real sense, every normal individual, each person in normal circumstances has a "selling" job to do. Everyone wants to "sell" his ideas, his suggestions, his preferred course of action, his point of view. Everyone who must deal with or work with people uses principles of personal selling. There are many instances of a firm's asking *all* its employees to take part in a special promotion of the firm and its products or services, and this includes accountants, credit personnel, and production department employees.

The selling just referred to can be thought of as a form of communication. In it, one person, the seller, sets up for himself the goal of persuading another person to think as the seller does on some issue or matter. The second person, the buyer, joins the seller in his thinking and "buys" the solution to a buyer-problem recommended by the seller.

Before any buyer buys, he must feel a *desire* for something he lacks; he must believe that his circumstances will be improved if he buys. Then, of course, there must be a *product* (or a service) which is the answer to the buyer's desire. The source of the product as well as its price are features of this product. The buyer must have *financial power* before he can buy; this may be either cash or credit. Finally, there must be a *decision* on the buyer's part to make a purchase.

Before buying, buyers usually voice some opposition or display some resistance to the salesman. This is understandable. Perhaps the buyer in question is not aware of his need. Or, he may favor or even be using a competitive product. Most buyers hate to part with their personal cash or their personal credit. No buyer can tell in advance just how happy he will be over a contemplated purchase; each remembers purchases he later deplored. Too, if he buys product A for ten dollars, he cannot have B *or* C, each five dollars. And, he *does* need both B and C, doesn't he? Of course. This resistance and opposition demands from the salesman more benefits, more demonstration, more persuasion, and more reassurance.

Buyers were classified in the preceding chapter which described types
of selling. Briefly, consumers buy for their own consumption; they want
to maximize their personal satisfaction. Merchants buy to resell. Merchants and purchasing agents buy to use in their business operations.
Both merchants and purchasing agents are mainly concerned with maxi-
mizing profits. Unless buyers benefit from their purchases, the purchase-
and-sale transactions are unhealthy.

THE NATURE OF PERSONAL SELLING

When the salesman deals with the prospect, the salesman should
first establish the fact that a need exists which his product will fill. The
next move is to point out to the prospect how he will benefit from the
purchase. And, in one sense, that is all there is to selling.

From this point of view, salesmanship is showing a prospect how he
can get greater satisfaction from the money he spends — it is aiding the
prospect to make wise buying decisions — it is *helping*.

True salesmanship is neither a "game" nor a "racket." In calling
attention to a product and asking the prospect to buy, the salesman is
doing a favor and not *asking* one, for he does not recommend the purchase
unless he has a deep conviction that it will benefit the prospect to buy.
This outlook may be idealistic for it is true that sharp practices are engaged
in by salesmen every day. It is expected that the salesman will tend to
give himself the benefit of any doubts. But, as will develop throughout
this text, the successful salesman is the one who guides his customer's
purchasing in order to benefit that customer.

In performing this buyer-seller function, the salesman sells *ideas*, not
products or services, because the buyer buys *satisfaction*, not merchandise.
A buyer appears to be buying a tire, but he actually is buying safe, low-
cost transportation; the buyer does not buy lamps, he buys lighting; the
insurance policy is, in reality, protection; and the mattress is comfort.
If economy is what the buyer is actually purchasing, the salesman may
need to go so far as to help the customer spend the dollars he is going to
save, to help him spend them securing the satisfactions and attaining the
ambitions he desires.

IS SELLING A PROFESSION?

The *professional point of view* is the feature that identifies the professional salesman. Neither technical skill, nor experience, nor basic
talent, nor size of income are the deciding factors. Instead, the salesman's
attitude is the criterion. If his principle of selling is, "What can I do *for*
my prospects and customers?" he is a professional. If he asks, "What can

my prospects and customers do for *me?*" or, even worse, "What can I do *to* them?" he is less than a professional salesman.

The professional salesman is dedicated to serving the needs and problems of buyers. Because he knows his calling to be a proud one, he is jealous of his own reputation. His basic *honesty* reflects high personal principles as well as the integrity of his company. His initial *interest* in buyers develops into *loyalty* to them. He advises them about their circumstances and about what should be done in the light of those circumstances. He instructs buyers about product features and product uses. The true professional is not content until his customers are happy — even enthusiastic — over what they bought from him. He knows that the buyer, too, must benefit from purchase-and-sales transactions. Only when he sees that this results can he enjoy the long-term associations with customers which are customary in many industries.

The professional salesman recognizes that it is every man's duty, privilege, and pleasure to contribute to the general welfare. He knows that he has a useful, constructive mission in the world of business and that selling, for him, is an honorable profession of service.

A picture of the professional salesman reveals these facts:

1. He possesses a satisfactory amount of basic ability to sell.
2. He consciously chose the selling field and is proud of it.
3. He is loyal to high ethical standards.
4. He is skilled in his work.
5. His knowledge is thorough.
6. He is true to his obligations.
7. He has had actual selling experience.
8. He stays up to date because he never stops learning.
9. His integrity is above reproach.
10. He knows that there is no substitute for hard work.
11. He maintains his self-respect and his independence.
12. He knows that to sell is to serve.

In case some student has become worried that selling benefits only the buyer, it should be pointed out that a salesman's rewards increase as he becomes of greater and greater service to more and more buyers.

Salesmanship is not yet a profession and will not be until the buyer can place the same trust and confidence in those from whom he buys as he does in his doctor and dentist.

CAN SALESMANSHIP BE LEARNED?

Some persons take the position that one cannot *learn* how to sell. This contention is supported by their concepts of, first, the nature of selling, and, second, the nature of individuals. On the first point, the argument is that salesmanship is an art and not a science, and that, because it is not a science, it cannot be taught and learned. On the second point, it is believed that some individuals are born salesmen, while others just are not endowed with the ability to sell and there is little or nothing they can do about it.

It would seem more in line with facts to recognize that there are certain sound principles of selling that are so long-established and susceptible to proof that they cannot be challenged successfully. These principles can be examined and understood in a classroom and can then be proved by pragmatic testing on the outside.

There are two conclusions that are drawn from the concept of the nature of individuals. First, it is true that some persons are not attracted to selling as a profession, and if they did enter the field, they would be miserable failures, whereas, if they undertake some other, more suitable vocation, they can be happy, successful, and worthwhile to society. Other persons are better qualified to enter selling and to become outstanding in that field because of their likes and dislikes, their talents, and their basic natures.

The second and more significant observation is that each group, even the group without "natural" sales ability, can improve the quality and increase the quantity of its sales ability. An outstandingly successful person is not born ready-made that way, be he a farmer, a doctor, a merchant, a manufacturer, or a salesman. Much of his success must be attributed to hard work, practice, and a fierce determination to improve. Even the innate qualities and characteristics of one with an aptitude for selling need cultivating and developing. Companies would not conduct elaborate and expensive sales training programs if the principles of personal selling could not be taught and learned.

There is no implication here that one can study and become a perfect salesman, for such a salesman does not exist. Every salesman makes mistakes, has handicaps he never completely overcomes, and loses sales. Knowledge, however, is conducive to improvement, to a lengthening of the odds for success, to the reduction of mistakes, and to the raising of the salesman's average.

Advantages of College Courses

It is quite possible that more salesmen lose their jobs because of their lack of adequate training than for any other cause. It certainly seems reasonable to assume that a person who enters the field of selling with *no* sales training is handicapped. There are both major and minor ways in which college courses in salesmanship can be helpful.

One major benefit is that the student learns of the need for training in selling. He sees that selling is a demanding, specialized activity for which preparation is necessary. Quickly discarded is the idea that he will automatically succeed because he is a charmer, because his name is well known, or because of his connections.

The second major benefit is that the college course serves as an introduction to selling. The student learns something of what to expect; he will be confronted later by fewer situations that are completely unexpected.

Third, a college salesmanship course can help the future salesman to work more intelligently and satisfactorily with his boss and with the sales training personnel of his company. Because he knows what they are trying to do, he can cooperate more effectively.

Fourth, an appreciation of the value of studying all phases of the selling field, including allied courses, is acquired.

Last of the major benefits is that the college student can acquire in a short time much of the fundamental selling knowledge that has been accumulated by others through years of experience in every field of selling.

As for lesser advantages, the course can help uncertain individuals decide whether or not selling is the proper field to enter. It may help all students to become better buyers. A course in salesmanship makes a student's record more impressive, gives him more confidence in applying for a selling job, and is a valuable adjunct to other business courses.

Limitations of College Courses

Despite the need for and the value of college courses in salesmanship, this type of instruction has limitations, as would a classroom study of swimming, for example. Courses in schools cannot turn out salesmen in the same way that schools turn out typists, mechanics, or bookkeepers.

Because a sales situation involves human beings, and because there are always some differences between any two interviews, prospects, or conditions, the salesman is called on to exercise and demonstrate originality, mental agility, and ingenuity. If this were not true, the job of a salesman would be as simple as that of a robot. Experience is needed as a supplement to give life and meaning to the principles learned in the classrooms. Proficiency in selling can be acquired in no other way. For maximum progress, it would seem desirable to combine study and instruction with experimentation and practice.

Necessity of Continuous Study

It is said that a person need learn to ride a bicycle only once, and that this particular skill, once mastered, remains with that person indefinitely. Be that as it may, it does not hold true for selling. There is no specific time period within which selling can be learned, whether it is a quarter, two semesters, a year, or a decade. The obvious inference is that a salesman can never afford to stop learning, that the minute he becomes complacent, he begins to stagnate and slip. Instead of ever feeling that he has mastered the process of selling and, hence, is entitled to coast, the salesman must pursue a relentless, unending search for new and more effective techniques if he wants to insure success. He must always study people carefully. He must check books and trade papers for whatever may be of value to him. Company material and personnel must be used as sources of selling aids. Observation and practice must not be neglected. Constructive suggestions about changes that will be beneficial should always be welcome. Only by adopting an inquiring, experimental attitude and maintaining it throughout his career can he avoid drifting into mental ruts.

THE SALESMAN'S OBLIGATIONS TO HIS COMPANY

A salesman owes something in two directions: to his employer and to his prospects and customers. This section and the next consider these obligations.

Profitable Sales

From his company's point of view, the salesman's major long-range duty is to turn a profit. The company wants to continue in business, and this will not be possible unless its operation is profitable. It should be mentioned perhaps, at this point, that a related and concurrent aim of the company and of the salesman is to serve their customers well. The salesman best serves his own interests and those of his employer by being of maximum benefit and help to his customers.

Selling at a profit demands that the salesman explore his territory and analyze it in order to find out just how much opportunity is present. Having determined what the area is capable of producing, he proceeds to draft a specific, detailed program for its development, the objective being to build sales and profit up to their full potentials. If a virgin territory is being opened, prospects must first be identified and then converted into customers; in an established territory, the program calls for holding present customers, making them larger customers, and adding new customers.

The young salesman should learn at an early date that profitless selling does not require any salesmanship — anyone can dispose of large amounts of merchandise by reducing the price until the margin of profit has disappeared. The real salesman is the one who maintains prices at a level that returns a profit to his company; by making money for his company, he makes money for himself, too. It may be helpful for the junior salesman to think of his territory as his own personal business, in which case he cannot fail to relate selling expense to gross margin and to strive for a satisfactory relationship.

Although the selling of merchandise at a profit is the primary obligation, it may have to be postponed, on occasion, in favor of promotion of goodwill or building up the customer's desire for the product. Likewise, in an extreme seller's market when merchandise is being rationed or is unavailable to all, the salesman finds his chief concern to be that of keeping on good terms with those he hopes to serve in the future.

Hard Work

In employing a salesman, the company assumes the risks involved in a new employee; the salesman should justify this risk. In training the salesman, the company spends both time and money; the salesman should justify this expenditure. In making the salesman responsible for a part of the company's activities, the company acknowledges belief of a certain capacity and potentiality in him; the salesman should justify this faith.

The salesman goes about discharging these obligations by expending the effort necessary to do a successful job. He must be an efficient manager of himself, always in control, purposeful, active, and he must conduct himself so as to get the greatest possible return from his efforts. His time and energy are budgeted wisely, and there is no wasted motion.

When working at peak efficiency, when keeping fit and busy, the salesman can safely trust the law of averages. This is possible because few relationships are more basically sound than those between calls and interviews, and interviews and sales. If the salesman makes enough calls on properly selected prospects, he will get a satisfactory number of interviews, and from this number of interviews, he will get a satisfactory volume of sales.

Cooperation

Immediately upon joining the company, the salesman should try to fit himself into the spirit of its organization. He must learn as much about the company as he can, not operating details at first, but attitudes and policies. He should be eager to get acquainted with the personality of the firm, to appreciate its aims and ideals, and to understand its methods of doing business and the principles that shape its policies.

Outline for a job description having general application:

Sales:

    Make regular calls.
    Sell the line, demonstrate.
    Handle questions and objections.
    Check stock — discover possible product uses.
    Interpret sales points of the line to the customer.
    Estimate customers' potential needs.
    Emphasize quality.
    Explain company policies on price, delivery, and credit.
    Get the order.

Services:

    Install product or display.
    Report product weaknesses, complaints.
    Handle adjustments, returns and allowances.
    Handle requests for credit.
    Handle special orders for customers.
    Establish priorities, if any.
    Analyze local conditions for customers.

Territory management:

    Arrange route for best coverage.
    Balance effort with customer against potential.
    Maintain sales portfolio, samples, kits.

Sales promotion:

    Develop new prospects and new accounts.
    Distribute home office literature, catalogs, desk pieces.
    Make calls with customers' salesmen.
    Train jobbers' personnel.
    Present survey reports, layouts, and proposals.

Executive:

    Each night make a daily work plan for the next day.
    Organize field activity for minimum travel and maximum calls.
    Prepare and submit special reports on trends, competition.
    Prepare and submit daily reports to home office.
    Collect and submit statistical data requested by home office.
    Investigate lost sales and the reason for loss.
    Prepare reports on developments, trends, new objectives met and new ideas on
        meeting objections.
    Attend sales meetings.
    Build a prospect list.
    Collect overdue accounts; report faulty accounts.
    Collect credit information.

Goodwill:

    Counsel customers on their problems.
    Maintain loyalty and respect for firm represented.
    Attend local sales meetings held by customers.

From Kenneth Lawyer, *Sales Training for the Smaller Manufacturer* (Washington: Small Business Administration, 1954)

Just as soon as he has the "feel" of the company and considers himself, and is considered, a part of it, his obligation is to work in harmony with the rest of the organization so that a healthy spirit of cooperation may prevail. Because the new salesman is in need of instruction, advice, information, and aid, he has every possible reason for cooperating with everyone. The credit manager and the opening of new accounts, the sales promotion manager and the influencing of dealers to use display material, the advertising manager and the letters of inquiry from prospects, the production manager and the scheduling of a rush order — these situations point up the necessity of the salesman's cooperating with the other units of the company.

When the salesmen are considered as constituting one group and all other personnel another, it becomes clear that the two groups are responsible for the welfare of one another, that each depends on the other in a very literal sense, and that if one suffers, so does the other. When each group keeps this fact in mind, cooperation is a natural result.

THE SALESMAN'S OBLIGATIONS TO BUYERS

Fair Treatment

No one, of course, questions the obligation of a salesman to deal honorably with buyers. The relationship between salesman and buyer must be characterized by mutual loyalty, trust, and dependence. The salesman must respect the buyer's position, his policies, his time; in return, the salesman hopes for the buyer's confidence and goodwill. The buyer must certainly be able to count on the salesman to keep secrets and promises. Unethical treatment and undependable behavior will destroy this trust. Deceptive presentations, misleading statements, ambiguous phrases, overstatement, exaggeration, or careless handling of the literal truth are not to be tolerated.

If he is to treat his buyers fairly, the salesman will not sell to one unless he truly thinks that the buyer will benefit adequately from the purchase. Here's a good test: if the salesman can sit in the buyer's chair, assume the role of buyer, and buy what the salesman is offering from across the desk, he can recommend the purchase sincerely and in good faith. Because the typical salesman is an optimist, he tends to have a bias which must be discounted somewhat by prospects. There are, however, pragmatic as well as ethical reasons for the salesman's being frank and fair. Hard, aggressive selling is sometimes necessary because some products and some buyers require it, but to carry this so far that the result is a disgruntled or disappointed buyer is not wise. Hard selling and satisfied customers, however, can coexist.

Hard, aggressive selling is not to be confused with "high pressure" selling, a type of selling which violates the principle of fair treatment. It operates when a salesman offends by letting his personality become too aggressive or offensive, or by stooping to tactics that are unethical, deceitful, or dishonest. High-pressure selling is flagrant when a salesman uses extravagant means to sell something to a buyer which the buyer neither wants nor needs.

Sometimes fair treatment to his customer competes with fair treatment to the salesman's company, as in the case of a complaint or a request for an adjustment. Clearly the salesman is in the middle of a conflict of interests, owing something to his customers and something to his company. There is no rule universally applicable. Whatever the salesman's actions, he must be honest and fair to both; he must do nothing to damage his own independence and self-respect.

Assistance

Because each individual is an assortment of desires with only limited purchasing power, he welcomes any assistance that will enable him more nearly to realize his desires and to provide for his needs. In general, buyers-for-consumption want increased satisfaction, whereas business buyers want to make or save more money. These facts make of the salesman a missionary charged with the responsibility of guiding prospects to a better mode of living or improving the prospect's circumstances to the end that satisfaction or profits are increased.

The position of the salesman must be that he sincerely wants to serve and to help prospects and customers. His being of aid is more than permissible or desirable — it is mandatory.

Since the salesman is going to serve, he must be qualified to serve. If he plans to pose as an expert, he should be an expert; if he wants to function as an adviser on purchasing, he should have adequate information to perform that function.

In fulfilling the obligation to help prospects and customers, the salesman must render whatever assistance he can, regardless of whether the prospect buys or not. Prospects and customers have problems, and they need help in coping with them on nonbuying days as well as on days when purchases are made. Whether there is a large order or no order at all, the salesman should be a friendly counselor with valuable data and advice. Looking after his prospects and customers is the heart of a salesman's job.

THE NATURE AND ROLE OF PERSONALITY

A dynamic personality is one of the basic needs of all salesmen. Complete product knowledge is eminently desirable as are such other features as strict obedience to company instructions, long hours of work, determination to keep up-to-date and accurate records on all prospects, and a mastery of selling fundamentals and techniques. It is quite true that these are examples of things the salesman should try to achieve, but they and other similar accomplishments are not enough. Their effectiveness is at the maximum point only when they are under the management of an individual who is a superior sales personality.

A pleasing personality by itself is not enough. A person's thinking is faulty if he believes that just because he is popular and has an engaging personality, he can sell anything to anybody. The salesman who relies solely on his personality finds himself at a disadvantage the moment he competes with an all-around salesman.

Personality is a broad concept that cannot easily be defined. A sales personality may be thought of as the impression the prospect gets of the salesman. It is the salesman as he appears to prospects. His sales personality is what the prospect likes or dislikes about the salesman as a human being, and, at the same time, it is why the salesman enjoys the approval or incurs the disapproval of prospects. Viewed in this light, superior sales personality, instead of being complex or baffling, is something that can be attained by any normal, emotionally stable person. It does not demand of the salesman superhuman ability, phenomenal intelligence, hypnotic power, classic features, or concentrated charm.

No salesman can afford to be indifferent to or negligent about the cultivation of a superior sales personality, because personality influences prospects. Every impression the salesman makes helps or hurts his chances of making the sale. If the reaction he elicits is unfavorable or negative, or even neutral, the sale will be more difficult.

A superior sales personality, by avoiding the mistakes of an only "ordinary" salesman, by adding a certain distinctiveness to all his own actions, by encouraging the prospect to like him, and by being an unusually good salesman, can make impressions that are favorable and build respect and confidence. Such a salesman never forgets that a buyer prefers to patronize persons he likes, nor does he underestimate the value of personal friendship between the buyer and the salesman. He knows that a warm, helpful, friendly personality is essential for success in selling.

In implementing his program of personality development, the salesman will start with an analysis of himself. Then he will work largely through control and change of habits, because methods of operation, selling techniques, and even attitudes are matters of habit. It is his habit pattern that affects, for good or bad, his prospects and customers, his company, and himself. Superior sales personality is largely the result of certain habits and ways of thinking, certain practices and policies that fortunately can be acquired by experimentation and effort. Of course certain qualities are susceptible to little or no change, as, for example, a person's physical endowments or basic intelligence, but in the main, progress is always possible.

It is not easy to develop a more pleasing personality. Most individuals are reluctant to admit even to themselves that something about themselves is wrong and needs changing. Because such an admission deflates the ego, it tends to be avoided or postponed. Persons with whom the salesman comes in contact are hesitant to point out habits that need correction. The role of reformer is both thankless and distasteful in most circumstances. Then, too, new habits of a detrimental type have a way of insinuating themselves so quietly and gradually that the salesman is usually unaware that they have been adopted until they are a part of him. Once established, a habit violently opposes its own eradication. The complexity and far-reaching ramifications of habit structure by their very nature operate so as to make change difficult.

PHYSICAL FACTORS — VISUAL

The physical image of the salesman is the first one to register on the prospect, and it is possible for it to make an impression on four of the prospect's five senses. In order of impact, these are the senses of sight, hearing, smell, and touch. Because of the strength of the impression on the sense of sight, what the prospect sees must be considered carefully.

Importance of Appearance

Appearance is a big factor in personality, and, as such, it is a big factor in selling. The salesman is a person who poses as an expert, and, in fact, must be one. He must appear to be both trustworthy and able; he must advise with authority. To do this, his appearance must help him instill confidence and respect in the prospect. Nothing could be more anomalous than a shabby, run-down salesman selling a correspondence "success" course.

It should be recognized, then, that the salesman pays dearly for any indifference or inattention to appearance, for such neglect will cost him sales. If he is to *be* a success, he must *look* like one. It is true that a person tends to be accepted at his own evaluation. A personal appearance that is beyond reproach goes hand in hand with success in selling.

Factors That Are Controllable

Ability to sell is not limited to any one physical type. Tall or short, fat or slim, blond or brunet, bald or bushy — each group has its share of outstanding salesmen. It is good that such physical differences are un-important, for one is limited in what he can do about such matters as his build, features, or vision.

The first controllable factors mentioned here are designated as personal factors and include the shave, the cut and grooming of hair, the condition of hands and nails, and the appearance of the teeth. Even the new sales-man knows what is pleasing about these and should need no instruction.

Clothes constitute the second group of controllable factors. As to condition, the requirement is neatness. Clean shirt, pressed suit, and shined shoes bear silent but powerful witness to the attention and care they receive. The individual will want to express his own personality in his choice of clothes but, at the same time, allow his wardrobe to help him do his job. In view of the heterogeneity of the typical group of pros-pects and customers, the generalized advice may be ventured that extremes should be avoided. Perhaps a worthwhile concept is that clothes plus grooming do for a salesman what a product's package does for its product.

Posture and bearing are subject to the salesman's control. They should be positive and confident; sitting or standing, the salesman should display both respect for and assurance in himself. His physical manner should be of such vigor and power that it bespeaks authority and gets attention. Because posture and bearing are revealing, the salesman should see that they are working *for* and not *against* him.

The salesman's walk is the fourth and last factor in this list. It should be an energetic and businesslike walk, with head erect and shoulders back. It should connote authority and purpose and, in a dignified yet un-mistakable way, make it clear that the salesman is out for orders.

The Smile

Although smiling is a controllable matter, as are the two following topics, it is important enough to deserve separate consideration. A warm, flashing, contagious, genuinely sincere smile is of incalculable aid in selling. Indeed, the ideal salesman is a smiling person, one who likes to smile and is constantly finding occasions to do so — one who is not completely dressed for work without his ready, spontaneous smile.

The young salesman is strongly urged to practice his smile until it is without technical flaw. It must never seem sly, artificial, unnatural, or condescending. There should not be too much of it, nor too little. It should include the eyes. Only through practice can he develop the pleasant facial expression that makes for good prospect response.

Some student may be having difficulty in reconciling *sincerity* with *practice;* he may feel that one calls for *being*, the other for *seeming* — that one is *genuine*, the other *counterfeit*. Actually, there is no conflict. There is no cause to accuse a salesman of hypocrisy or to question the artlessness of his smile merely because the smile is without technical fault. You are not one bit less polite or respectful because you practice tipping your hat before a mirror until the gesture is smooth, unhurried, and graceful. The same is true for smiling.

Mannerisms

These are habits the salesman has acquired of which he is not conscious, yet they may distract the prospect's attention or even annoy and irritate him. The salesman may tug at an ear lobe, fidget with his glasses, scratch his head, constantly adjust his tie and collar, or rub his hand over his face repeatedly in the same nervous gesture. He may tap with a pencil, crack his knuckles, chew gum, or even talk with food in his mouth. Wearing fraternity or club insignia might also be included here as undesirable.

The trouble with such mannerisms is that they make concentration harder for the prospect, and in more extreme cases create an impression that is definitely unfavorable. This, of course, hinders making the sale.

The salesman must be constantly on the alert to detect any such mannerisms as these, to the end that he may have complete, conscious control over his physical self. If feasible, he should encourage some associate, his sales manager, or even some long established customer to observe him in action and to suggest desirable changes.

Health

The daily grind of selling makes heavy demands of a salesman, causing him to expend much physical effort and to deplete his reserve of nervous energy. Because appearance depends in large measure on physical condition, health should be guarded.

The sales job is exacting and exhausting. Yet, at all times the salesman is expected to be the personification of vigorous, cheerful vitality. If the salesman is to have the drive he needs, he must watch his physical efficiency; otherwise, he will not exhibit that energy which helps so much in evoking enthusiasm from the prospect.

PHYSICAL FACTORS — NON-VISUAL

The prospect's sense of hearing ranks second to his sense of sight in registering an impression of the salesman. In order for the prospect to enjoy favorable reception, the salesman's voice should be pleasing — clear and well-modulated, easy and warm. Its tone should be both courteous and respectful. Because the salesman's job is that of persuading, his voice needs to be convincing, emphatic, firm, and purposeful.

Since effective expression is his goal, the salesman is obligated to eliminate vocal defects, and then to continue improvement until he has acquired vocal versatility. A monotone is lifeless and boring and will not persuade, and because it will not persuade, it cannot be tolerated. Practice is required until voice, enunciation, and expression are all acceptable.

Distracting and irritating oral mannerisms can no more be permitted than can the visual. An odd-sounding laugh, a nervous cough, an objectionable clearing of the throat, a resort to "ahs" or "uhs" as prefaces to remarks, or a habit of humming or whistling should be completely and permanently eradicated, for some prospects and customers will certainly find these habits offensive.

MENTAL AND MORAL CHARACTERISTICS

The physical salesman is an *external* part of the total sales personality and is usually the first to stimulate the prospect's senses. The *internal* salesman is made up of mental and moral characteristics to which the prospect also reacts. Twelve are considered here.

Optimism

It is impossible to envision a successful salesman who does not have a definite and pronounced faith in his own future. The first thing he is cheerful and happy about is, of course, himself, for he is absolutely confident that he is going to better himself in practically all respects, and certainly in an over-all way, as time passes. Second, the salesman is optimistic about the products he sells, feeling that each óne is an excellent value in its own price class and that, when placed in the proper hands, each will give a thoroughly satisfactory amount of satisfaction to the user. A third source of optimism for the salesman is his company, in that his feeling toward the company is one of enthusiasm. A final matter which calls for a bright view on the part of the salesman is the prospect himself. If the salesman is of maximum help and service, if the product is what it is purported to be, if the salesman's company is everything it should be, and if the prospect cooperates as the salesman expects he will, then the salesman can be nothing less than optimistic about the prospect's future.

Optimism is a characteristic of a success-minded salesman, of a man who, within reasonable limits, does not admit to himself the possibility of failing to reach his objective. In a word, the salesman is a man of vision, faith, and hope. This means that he has eliminated such negative and expensive attitudes as fear and uncertainty. He considers skepticism a luxury he cannot afford. In one sense, the salesman cannot allow himself to be too open-minded, for too great a tolerance on his part would reduce his exuberance of belief and trust in his selling. In similar fashion, too much optimism prevents the salesman from being completely practical.

Before a prospect buys, he must *want*, and, in addition, he must *be convinced* that the contemplated purchase will benefit him. Optimism on the part of the prospect is planted, encouraged, and increased by the optimistic salesman.

It would be fallacious to imply that an optimistic salesman will never get discouraged, that his spirits will never droop, that there will never be days when successive rebuffs by prospects will damage his morale. At such times, the salesman may feel that he has lost his ability to sell; he seems unable to influence any prospects; he despairs of making his quota. During these periods, the prospect is successfully selling negative ideas to both the salesman and himself. He says he does not need anything just now, or that he has no faith in the salesman's company, or that the price is too high, or that some other obstacle prevents the purchase. He is selling "no" to the salesman instead of the salesman selling "yes" to the prospect. The salesman must end periodic slumps as quickly as possible by analyzing them, identifying their causes, and then taking appropriate action.

One possible cause of a low period is that the salesman has been working so long and hard that he has become stale and needs a vacation from selling for a while. Or, at the other extreme, he may not have been working enough. Another move that may work is for the salesman to discontinue being a *salesman* and become a *serviceman*. Maybe the salesman's presentation is at fault in that he has drifted away from the "you" approach. Perhaps his use of his sales material has become careless, or maybe what was once an orderly, coherent story has become disorganized and spotty. A personal reason may be behind the slump, as, for instance, poor health, a run-down appearance, a recital of personal problems, or the absence of a cheery smile. The changes needed under these circumstances are obvious. If the discouragement is caused by low volume of sales, then the salesman must convert more prospects into customers, and present customers into larger customers. A final action that may be helpful to the salesman in regaining the optimism he must have calls for him to sit down and list all the assets he has at his command, and then to go out and make maximum use of them. The results, both from prospects and from within the salesman himself, are usually prompt as well as gratifying, and soon he is selling as well as before.

Enthusiasm

Optimism is not enough — enthusiasm is a "must" item. The neophyte salesman particularly needs enthusiasm, for sincere enthusiasm covers many selling sins. Enthusiasm is a combination of interest and belief, of energy and activity. Every salesman needs a broad curiosity about his products, his prospects, himself, and even matters unrelated to selling. Enthusiasm leads a salesman to become acquainted with his work from all possible angles.

A dominant role in the sales interview is played by enthusiasm in helping secure the interest and confidence of the prospect. A display of encouraging enthusiasm makes a prospect feel that his "yes" will increase his sales, profits, or satisfactions. It is a requisite for eloquence, and, when translated into animated and persuasive delivery, it prevents the sales story from being a dull, insipid recital. If the salesman is to arouse enthusiasm over his proposition in the prospect, the only safe course for him to follow is to carry into the interview so much enthusiasm that it cannot help but become infectious.

The young salesman may be inclined to feel that enthusiasm is something that should be curbed, that restraints should operate to prevent it from being apparent, and that the salesman should always be casual. This view is not sound. Enthusiasm is definitely no cause for embarrassment, and apologies need not be made for it. As a matter of fact, the salesman should consciously encourage it and should practice expressing it in all possible ways. In addition, he should stay responsive to and capable of thrills, for thrills cause enthusiasm, and enthusiasm inspires sales.

The enthusiastic salesman usually finds his enthusiasm extending to fields other than selling. His recreations, his hobbies, his feelings toward his favorite athletic teams or toward his college — these are examples of the proper objectives for his ardor and his active interest. By talking about these interests in a dynamic and even partisan manner, the salesman presents himself to his public as a much more interesting and attractive personality than he otherwise would.

Confidence

Confidence is the result of knowledge plus experience, and for this reason it can be developed and is more easily acquired than optimism and enthusiasm. To a salesman, confidence is a belief in himself, a healthy respect for his own capabilities and powers. It is the motivation that causes the salesman to be not merely *willing* but *eager* to encounter hard-to-sell prospects. To a prospect, the confident salesman is an able fellow who is entitled to some time and attention. Because the salesman is confident, he inspires the prospect to feel that he need not worry after placing an order with him.

Fear is one of the worst enemies of the salesman, and the salesman just out of school finds many causes for fear, including competition, criticism, the future, difficult prospects, inexperience, and the problem

THROUGH FIVE STEPS THE QUALIFICATIONS
NECESSARY FOR SUCCESSFUL SALESMEN ARE JUDGED

	Sales Applicants Checked on 15 Qualifications During 5 Selection Steps				
QUALIFICATIONS FOR SUCCESSFUL McKESSON SALESMEN	SELECTION STEPS				
	Initial Screening	Scored Application	Guided Interview	References Checked	Selection Tests
1. Appearance	X		X		
2. Speech	X		X		
3. Poise & Manner	X		X		
4. Maturity	X	X	X		
5. Knowledge	X	X	X		
6. Experience	X	X	X	X	
7. Intelligence		X	X	X	X
8. Interests	X	X	X		X
9. Initiative		X	X	X	
10. Responsibility		X	X		
11. Work Habits			X	X	
12. Honesty			X	X	
13. Cooperation			X	X	
14. Personal Traits			X		X
15. Health		X	X		X

McKesson & Robbins, Inc.

of making his quota. These fears must be banished and replaced with confidence in his line of products, in his company, in himself, and in his ability to solve prospects' problems. When he gains this faith, the salesman will find his job easier.

Sincerity

Still another requisite of a successful salesman is genuine sincerity. Nothing is so vital to the continued trust and confidence of the prospect as a true, sincere interest in his problems and in his well-being. The salesman who is known to be a high-powered individual determined to sell at all costs, who has concern for his own interests above the interests of his prospects and customers, who makes claims that will not be lived up to, who resorts to half-truths and false information to influence customers, cannot expect to hold customers long.

While it sounds quite commendable and respectable to suggest that a salesman's make-up needs to include sincerity, it is also sound, practical advice. Prospects usually have little trouble in detecting the false ring of an insincere presentation. The salesman cannot hope to make other persons believe that which he himself knows to be untrue. By way of contrast, the sincere salesman, knowing his work to be beneficial to all concerned, finds his persuasive ability increased and his listeners ready to hear him.

Both honesty and loyalty are concomitants of this quality. Because of them, the sincere salesman can be depended on to do the right thing for his prospect, his company, and himself. His sincerity is a particularly valuable asset for the long run, as it operates both to attract new customers and to hold present ones.

Determination

Determination is the will to succeed. It is required to carry out the resolution that both society and the individual salesman are going to benefit by the best possible service that the salesman can give customers and prospects. Since the salesman takes a rather severe buffeting each day, selling is not for the vacillating and weak-willed individual.

The successful salesman is one who is determined to get ahead. His urging, driving ambition makes of him an industrious individual who is willing to work long hours under discouraging circumstances. This same ambition is responsible for his aggressive, competitive spirit and for his pride in wanting to *equal*, then *be*, the best man on the sales force.

Patience and perseverance, parts of determination, do not allow the salesman to give up easily, but, instead, make him stick to his job. The persevering salesman keeps making calls on a certain desirable prospect repeatedly and regularly, one after another, knowing that the first order will come eventually. He knows that the prospect may be testing and judging him on this characteristic and that repeated return calls work in his favor by making it clear that he intends to get some business.

Dependability

Buyers are always in search of elements of certainty in an area which, by and large, is one of perpetual change. One such welcome element is a dependable salesman.

They know too many salesmen who have proved to be unworthy of confidence. Consequently, when a salesman comes along who can be counted on by his customers, he is received with enthusiasm and joy; his number is *not* legion.

The dependable salesman develops and improves his memory until he can be relied on to remember what he should of names, instructions, requests, circumstances, details of the last visit, or other matters. He certainly remembers to keep all promises and appointments he made, and all secrets given him.

The dependable salesman can be counted on to cooperate. When the customer knows for certain that the salesman is working month after month to promote his interests, competition finds the customer furiously loyal to the seller and extremely difficult to wean away.

The dependable salesman is a temperate, moderate person. He recognizes his duty to his customers, and he sees to it that they can always rely on him to do that duty. He will not let golf, drinking, hunting or fishing, cards, civic activities, or any hobby or avocation drain off so much of his energy and take up so much of his time that his customers suffer.

The dependable salesman is truthful. Students know that it is *right* to tell the truth; you are now being told that it is also *profitable*. Unless he enjoys credibility, no salesman can become a success, and the way for him to insure both is to be honest and truthful in his dealings.

Initiative

A salesman with initiative is a self-starter who, instead of being hesitant about undertakings, is both willing and desirous to get action under way. He is essentially a man with ambition who has implemented his ambition with a healthy amount of industry; he thinks and acts for himself and is continuously busy even when not under close supervision. Customers have confidence in him because of the skill and intelligence with which he takes care of them.

The salesman's need for initiative is a dual one. First, his control over the expenditure of his time demands that he be a man of initiative.

Second, the nature of the sales interview calls for initiative in that the salesman needs to control and direct the discussion.

The salesman with initiative is a delight to his company. He can be depended on to be doing something all the time, and he usually manages to do the right thing without being told. He learns to rely on himself, to make his own plans, and then keep in action as he works according to those plans. Furthermore, in his constant search for methods of increasing his value to his company, he is a fertile source of new ideas, suggestions, and challenging questions. Any success he has with experimental techniques or innovations is reported to the company for dissemination throughout the sales force.

Imagination

The salesman is not only kin to the artist; he is indeed a bit of an artist himself in telling stories, painting word pictures, and playing his true role of benefactor to clients. As do all other artists, the salesman finds a prolific imagination a tremendous help; unless his selling is shot through with imagination, it becomes dry, boring, and colorless.

As ideas are his real stock in trade regardless of what the physical product may be, the salesman makes greatest use of imagination when painting word pictures. Consider, for example, an annuity. It is not presented merely as a legal document, nor even as a certain number of dollars each month. Instead, the imaginative salesman paints a marvelous picture of the retirement period of life. He talks of trips and touring, of hobbies and longings to be gratified, of the incomparable feeling of security, of hopes realized. Using his imagination, he is able to translate his product into those exact things which his prospect desires.

Thus, imagination may be considered in the same light as a solution to a problem, or the key to a lock. Recourse to it supplies resources of inestimable value, particularly when the unusual or the spectacular is going to be needed if the salesman is to succeed. The delightful thing about imagination is that it can be developed, that the more it is called on in a search for many and different solutions to problems, the more it improves.

Imagination can serve as a safeguard against imitation, an error into which the inexperienced salesman may fall. Every salesman should strive to be a distinctive, ingenious, imaginative individual and should avoid the conscious and unconscious mimicking of another's manner.

Mental Agility

In addition to the other definitions scattered throughout this text, selling can be described as matching wits with prospects. The obvious implication is that the salesman should have a quick, keen mind, one that will tell him what to say and how to say it on every possible occasion. Only by being alert can the salesman be ready for any eventuality.

This mental agility will be needed if the salesman has built his sales story for one specific individual, but on arrival at a prospect's place of business, the salesman is referred to quite a different person. It is also needed if, after the interview has begun, it develops that some of the salesman's advance information about the prospect turns out to be incorrect, or if something occurs while the conference is going on that completely changes the atmosphere. Finally, in rare instances, the salesman may have started a sentence when he senses intuitively that his original thought will be inappropriate or harmful, and has to revise the ending of the sentence literally in a matter of seconds.

Once the salesman and prospect start talking, the salesman must do some extemporaneous thinking, must be nimble with new ideas, and must demonstrate an ability to improvise.

Control

Of the two different types of control needed by the successful salesman, the *first* is self-control during and immediately after the sales interview. Regardless of the obstacles and adverse conditions he encounters each day, he must at all times control his feelings and emotions and never show any disappointment or irritation. His mien should always suggest an even temper that keeps thoughts and reactions well in hand. In fatiguing conditions or under fire, his poise remains unshaken in order that he may continue to express himself effectively. When he fails to gain his objective, he does not stalk away in an angry mood. Instead, he analyzes the situation, records the salient features of the interview for future reference, removes the memory of the defeat from his mind as completely as he can, and goes on to his next appointment with little or no bitterness or frustration.

The *second* type of control is the salesman's ability to understand and manage his own affairs. The salesman with this ability works out the most effective methods for performing his tasks and then follows them. He concentrates his energies and efforts where they will do the most good. Indeed, he maintains temperate and healthy habits even after becoming a financial success, and this is no mean accomplishment.

There are numerous reasons why a salesman needs to be a *composed* individual. His dealings with his sales manager involve such controversial matters as quota-setting, assigned territory, transfer to some other territory, competition with other salesmen, lost orders, and, worse, lost customers. Then there is the need to do the often unexciting, sometimes irritating, and always time-consuming job of prospecting. Travel scheduling, time budgeting, difficult buyers and difficult incidents — only a composed salesman can maintain control in the face of these.

The exercise of control demands a systematic handling of prospects and customers because each one is a separate problem with circumstances peculiar to himself. Even for the salesman who will never occupy an executive position, the negotiations he will carry on will be many, simultaneous, and heterogeneous. If he is to command this situation — and he must; if he is to acquire and deserve a reputation for managerial ability, stability, and common sense — he has two choices: systematic management or chaos.

Some persons will protest that asking an optimistic, enthusiastic, imaginative salesman to be systematic, too, may be making an excessive demand. They may be right.

Courage

Many sales managers and many more salesmen argue that the most essential characteristic for a salesman to possess is *courage* — sheer, raw courage. Often instead of "courage" they use a more earthy word — "guts." The desire to sell and the enthusiasm needed both evaporate unless based on a courageous, even a venturesome outlook. The true salesman looks forward to his major task, that of influencing the behavior of buyers; he feels a drive to dominate, to lead rather than to follow; he has the will power to keep selling even when frustrated. Courage enables a salesman to be tenacious and persistent. It lets a salesman dare to be frank, or firm, or forceful, and he must often be each of these. Courage can make the difference between an *average* salesman and an *outstanding* salesman who is thrilled by the challenge of competing.

Maturity

The mature salesman is, as the second part of his title implies, a *man*. He has "grown up." He is well adjusted socially, well developed individually, and healthy emotionally. His maturity is reflected in a quiet manner, an independent, confident attitude, and an absence of narrowness. Praise neither turns his head nor blinds him; advice and criticism — even correction — he accepts gracefully.

Another feature of the mature salesman is his recognition of his responsibilities and his willingness to assume them. He is responsible in his territory for his company's sales and profits. He is responsible for helping buyers make more satisfactory decisions and for contributing to their efforts toward greater satisfaction and profit. In working with these buyers, the salesman adopts a positive approach; he tries to build up, not break down.

Maturity makes the salesman think before taking action, and, once the mature salesman has made his decision, he is willing to accept any blame for the results rather than try to avoid or escape the consequences.

The mature salesman is a realist and not a rationalizer. He does not allow himself much time for just hoping or waiting to sell a big order or to acquire a big customer. Of course, he won't rule out wishing and dreaming entirely, but he follows up wishing with working, dreaming with doing.

Discretion marks the mature salesman. He knows when *not* to talk and what *not* to say, and he behaves accordingly. Because buyers know they can trust him, they confide in him; they know confidential information will not be revealed. The salesman demonstrates his trustworthiness in various ways. For example, he is cautious in talking to strangers or even in the hearing of strangers in washrooms, planes, and hotel lobbies; or, he forgoes what little thrill he might experience by "being the first to tell" some bit of information lest such disclosure backfire to the detriment of himself, his company, or some buyer.

Finally, the mature salesman knows how to face the unpleasantness of temporary failure; he knows how to take losing tough-to-lose sales just as he knows how to accept winning tough-to-win ones. When he loses, he does not feel personal ill-will toward the buyer, nor does he display ill-temper or resentment. He does not feel that Lady Luck has turned her back permanently on him, nor that something must be basically wrong with his merchandise, his company, or himself.

An Illustration from Business

These thoughts from Stromberg-Carlson are an appropriate summary for this section on the mental and moral characteristics of sales personality:

> It seems to us here at Stromberg-Carlson that the quality known as "sales sense" is an absolute prerequisite to success — real success — in the field of selling. Sales sense seems . . . to be a combination of common sense, awareness of situations, a fair memory for faces and facts, and a willingness to do what needs to be done to gain an objective. There are many other factors; let's discuss a few.
>
> Personality in selling is a very important and penetrating factor. Salesmanship depends so much on personality that it can almost be compared to the fuel in an automobile engine — or perhaps more aptly to the yeast that causes a loaf of bread to rise. To go way back to the Bible for even another simile on the negative side, a salesman without personality — and by that we mean the desirable or "plus" traits of personality — can be likened to "the salt that has lost its savor and is fit only to be cast out upon the ground."

A salesman needs good health. This is not exclusively true; successful magazine salesmen have operated from sickbeds, wheelchairs, or other handicapped situations, but a good constitution is such an obvious advantage — especially to those who must travel — that further comment is unnecessary, except that radiant good health is an attractive trait that always makes a favorable first impression.

A salesman needs an optimistic, extroverted outlook on life. This again is obvious. A man who doesn't like people and who cannot surmount occasional (or even frequent) discouragement has no business selling. In fact, he will probably end with no business.

A salesman needs a keen mind. He must be able to meet different people and different situations at every hour of the day; he cannot permit himself to think always in fixed patterns or establish a routine approach to his daily problems. Each person he meets for business purposes is standing on his own ground and has established convictions and bargaining points of his own choosing. Our salesman must meet him and convince him on that ground, always remembering the old truism, "A man convinced against his will is of the same opinion still." Reduced to straight prose, this . . . says that you may win the argument, but lose the sale. Possession of a keen mind implies knowledge of product — this is the starting point of all sales. . . .

A salesman needs honesty. Example after example could be cited to show how the tricky, smart, sharp salesman has outsmarted himself in the long run, and how the honest tortoise often comes home in front of the flashy hare. Salesmen who are actually dishonest are few and far between and soon found out. The "operators," the fast-talking push boys, are the ones who stay a few steps in front of the law, or a few steps behind the ethics of good business, and give a bad name to salesmanship wherever they work.

A salesman needs stability and staying power. As hinted above, the race is not always to the swift, and the first time around the course may not yield any brass rings. It's the man who can come back smiling the second and third times with new reasons, new information, new profit opportunities or new satisfaction to be gained from his product, that finally establishes himself and his wares with the buyer. Which does not mean that the wise salesman never knows when to quit and stop knocking his head against a stone wall. He has to learn to recognize a stone wall when he finds one.

These are a few of the personality factors needed by a good salesman, and to them all should be added ambition and loyalty. With no ambition or drive, all the above is beside the point, and with no loyalty he will soon — and should be — working for some other firm, and this will be his continuing fate.

SOCIAL ATTRIBUTES

Thus far in this chapter, the salesman has been two things, a *physical* individual and an assortment of *mental and moral* characteristics. There is a final part, the *social*, which the prospect likes or dislikes. This treatment of the social salesman may seem to be brief, but the feeling here is that only four essential requirements remain to be covered: a friendly nature, social grace, the ability to converse intelligently and interestingly, and poise.

Friendly Nature

A salesman's chances of long-term success are slight if he lacks a definite and pronounced social inclination. He must have a basic liking for people and be eager to meet and know new individuals. He is friendly by nature, and as a result he makes friends easily. Because he enjoys their company, he likes to associate with others.

As an atmosphere of good feeling and friendship usually precedes a sale, the salesman often finds himself becoming a *friend* first, and then a *vendor*. The only lasting basis for friendship between salesman and prospect is the salesman's genuine interest in the prospect and an accompanying desire to help him. To *be liked*, the salesman must *like;* and to know a prospect is to take a long step toward liking him. Knowing and liking the prospect help the salesman in getting information about him, in understanding his problems, in obtaining his confidence, and in working with him.

The salesman encounters all types of prospects in all types of situations. Prospects vary in point of view, age, pattern of living, background, ideals, knowledge, and in many other respects, yet the salesman must be a friend *to* and *of* each. This demands extreme social adaptability.

Social Grace

The mannerly salesman does all he can to make each of his calls a pleasant, enjoyable visit marred by no violation of social custom or the proprieties. He uses tact and diplomacy in arranging and opening the interview, in handling objections, interruptions, and all other obstacles to purchases. His courtesy is in evidence from the moment he enters until he senses that it is time to go. This matter of courtesy deserves special attention, for the prospect notes immediately whether it is present or not, yet the salesman may be unaware of his own discourtesy.

The salesman should be noted for his politeness. Never should he be guilty of such obvious breaches as entering the prospect's office or home with a hat on, or talking with a cigar in his mouth. He is quick to do favors and even quicker to express his appreciation for favors shown him. He is agreeable, interesting, and fair.

Prospects should not be the only ones subjected to and favorably influenced by this social grace. Included also should be clerks, receptionists, secretaries, assistant buyers, and all other lesser personnel who can appreciate the salesman's thoughtfulness, consideration, accommodation, and patience as much as prospects do.

Conversational Ability

In being the good conversationalist and storyteller the salesman should be, his concern centers around four matters. First, the salesman must assume the "you" point of view and talk from that position all of the time. The prospect, in the final analysis, is interested in only one subject, *himself;* his indifference to the salesman, the product, and the company that makes the product is both natural and colossal *unless* they have some bearing on the amount of satisfaction the prospect can enjoy. The "you" point of view requires of the salesman a sympathetic understanding of the prospect's problems and hopes, together with a spirit of tolerance. It also demands that the salesman be a good listener, good enough, in fact, to be attentive to and interested in the prospect's pet topics of conversation.

The salesman's second concern is to make the prospect feel important, and this calls for deferring to and complimenting the prospect. It is quite desirable for the young salesman to be realistic in realizing what compliments are and what they will do. Two bald and blunt facts are, first, that persons like to be complimented, and, second, that a compliment is an effective sales tool. So, the salesman in his conversation will find something to congratulate the prospect about; he will ask for the prospect's advice and opinions; he will be impressed, even amazed by what the prospect has accomplished; and he will hold the prospect's judgment and experience in high regard.

The third concern is to control the conversation with finesse, not appearing to do so. Later on in the text, this control will be pictured as necessary for technical reasons. Here it is recommended for social reasons only, the thought being that by exercising subtle control over the subject matter and direction of the conversation, the salesman prevents clashes, arguments, interruptions, undesirable domination by the prospect, and discussions of unhappy topics.

Fourth, the salesman must guard against overusing certain words or expressions. This practice is deplored for several reasons. For one, it restricts the salesman's ability to express himself graphically and precisely because his limited vocabulary prevents his employing the different shades of meaning found in different words. If he uses the word *look* all the time, he misses the plus values of using such words as *peer, stare, glance, peek, gaze, squint,* and all the other possible synonyms. A second reason is that excess repetition becomes monotonous and annoying. Finally, the salesman who does not bother to equip himself with an adequate vocabulary does not appear very ambitious, thorough, energetic, or intelligent.

Poise

Poise is the characteristic or power which permits a person to be in effective command of himself — physically, mentally, and emotionally. Poise means self-control, self-possession, and self-assurance. It permits one to appear relaxed yet regulated, at ease yet disciplined. There is the strong and impressive implication present that the poised person cannot be easily perturbed or ruffled. The calm, cool, collected manner of that person indicates in no uncertain terms his mastery of the situation.

Nothing is more essential to a salesman's personality than self-confidence, and that confidence permits poise. The poised salesman is recognized immediately as such, and is understandably envied. His carriage and bearing give proof of his selling maturity as well as of his emotional stability. He is the good actor that every good salesman must be. He avoids revealing surprise or impatience or embarrassment. He suppresses any show of irritation or pique as successfully as he restrains his temper. He maintains his composure even when harshly used, he disagrees without being disagreeable, and he loses gracefully when that is unavoidable. At least on the surface, the poised salesman takes criticism or praise, disappointment or success with the same even manner.

Every successful salesman must be forceful if he is to be convincing. No one can deny that good salesmen are emotional and intense persons. This means that a salesman must build some poise into his selling; he must have a checkrein on his impulsive inclinations or his selling will suffer. Poised selling reassures and soothes; it calms a buyer's fears and doubts; it implants faith and confidence in a buyer's mind. Buyers detect and respect poised selling, and this makes it easier for the salesman to direct the course of the interview and the direction of the buyer's thinking. Poised selling is a magnificent recommendation of the salesman, his products, his company, and his suggestions.

How can one become a poised salesman? Junior salesmen acquire poise in several ways. The first step is thorough preparation for a selling career; this is to be followed by painstaking preparation for each major interview. If the salesman knows himself, his products, his company, and his buyers, and if he knows how to sell, he has every reason in the world to feel calm and collected. A helpful device is the rehearsal, in which the salesman runs through a presentation before actually making it to a buyer. Some cub salesmen have discovered that, for them, talking to groups equips them to talk confidently to any individual. Still another resort is simulation, because one can feel some degree of poise just by acting poised. In simulation, control is reflected in quiet breathing, even speech, slow movements, concentrated thinking, and even in brief pauses to get oneself better in hand. Over the long run, a salesman should undertake to develop his presence of mind and a sound philosophy of life. He will recognize that experience will provide in large measure the competence and confidence which result in poise.

STUDY ASSIGNMENTS

1. It is probable that most salesmen spend most of their working hours without direct supervision. What does this demand of the salesman?
2. A company made a survey of its customers asking them this question, "What features or qualities of salesmen do you dislike?" Can you guess the three most frequent answers?
3. When a company is hiring salesmen, it finds interviews essential. Why are written records and correspondence inadequate?
4. "A good salesman can sell anything." Do you agree? Why?
5. Discuss the duties, problems, and pressures involved in the job of selling throughout the phases of the business cycle.
6. A drug manufacturer claims that success in selling for him calls for seven qualifications in each salesman. What do you suppose they are?
7. How far should a salesman go in trying to imitate the personality and adopt the mannerisms of some outstanding salesman?
8. Is aggressiveness an asset or a liability? Discuss.
9. What are the benefits of being a good listener? What happens when salesman and buyer are *both* good listeners?
10. To what extent should a salesman always be a dissatisfied person?

CASE STUDY 3A

Upon graduation from college, Nat Fagan became a sales trainee for a manufacturer of first aid and hospital supplies. The company's sales force was divided into two groups; one group called on drug stores, the other on hospitals. Fagan, following the usual trainee pattern, was assigned to the drug staff. Experience in this work was usually prerequisite to joining the group of salesmen who sold to hospitals.

After two months of training, Fagan was called in and told that the hospital salesman whose territory was Fagan's home state was leaving the company. Fagan was asked if he wanted to replace this man, and, of course, he immediately said that he did. Within 24 hours, Fagan had reported to the regional sales executive under whom he would be working. Here he was told to begin selling in his territory right away. The man who was to leave the company stayed long enough to accompany Fagan for two weeks. During this time, the two salesmen were able to call on about one-third of the hospitals for which Fagan was to be responsible. The salesman being replaced was friendly and cooperative, but his mind was on his new job.

The third week in his new territory found Fagan on his own with two-thirds of his hospitals yet to receive their first call. On each of the first four days of the week, Fagan really pushed himself. At 4 P.M. Thursday he entered the hospital in Salemboro for the first time. All he knew about the Salemboro hospital was that a Miss Ashby did the buying of Fagan's products. He also had a record of the hospital's purchases for the last five years.

Another salesman was in the reception room ahead of Fagan, and the two had a pleasant chat. When the other salesman learned that this was Fagan's first call, he volunteered that Miss Ashby was about 62 years old and seemed to be somewhat of a tyrant. At 4:35 Miss Ashby notified the receptionist to send in Fagan. As Fagan entered her office, Miss Ashby rose from her chair and asked in a tired but accusing tone, "What have you done about my gauze?" This was the first Fagan had heard about any gauze matter, so he explained that he was new, mystified by the reference to gauze, but eager to be helpful. Miss Ashby's reaction to this was to slap the palm of her hand on her desk top and exclaim, "This is just *too* much!"

Miss Ashby had referred to 30 bolts of *uncut* gauze which Fagan's company had sent when her request had been for *cut* gauze.

QUESTIONS:

1. Had Fagan's company fulfilled its obligations to him?
2. What were Fagan's obligations to Miss Ashby?

CASE STUDY 3B

Bill Woodson, a recent college graduate, has just entered the office of R. S. Blakeston, Sales Manager of the Allied Products Company. Allied Products is a regional producer of pumps and parts for both the new and the replacement market. Their conversation follows:

Blakeston: Come on in, Bill, and sit down.

Bill: Thank you, sir.

Blakeston: Bill, I've been looking over your record while you've been with Allied Products and have here your request for a transfer to the Sales Department. Let's see, you've been with us now for five months, haven't you?

Bill: Yes, sir, that's right. For the past four months I've been doing drafting work with the research and development section. I heard that the Sales Department had an opening for a sales engineer, and I decided that I'd like to talk to you about the job.

Blakeston: You've got a degree in mechanical engineering, according to your record, and according to your efficiency reports, you're doing some good work as a draftsman. Bill, why do you think you'd like to go into sales?

Bill: Well, sir, when I first came with this company, since I had been trained as a mechanical engineer, I thought I should take an engineering job. But I've always liked to meet people and talk with them, and I've decided after working for five months that what I really want is an opportunity. I feel that with my background in engineering and my experience here at the plant that — well, I just believe that I could go out and sell Allied pumps. I just feel that there's more opportunity for me in the field of sales than there is in drafting, and so when I heard about the opening, Mr. Blakeston, I made up my mind that I was going to ask you to help me make the change.

Blakeston: Bill, have you ever done any selling before?

Bill: No, sir, only as a part-time service station employee. But Mr. Blakeston, I can learn; I'm sure of it.

Blakeston: I think you could, Bill, but you know some people will never make salesmen, even if they learn every accepted principle of salesmanship. There are others with "natural" sales ability, but this will not guarantee success either. By improving his natural abilities, by practicing the accepted principles of salesmanship, by hard work, enthusiasm, and a determination to get ahead — by these things will the salesman succeed.

Bill: Yes, sir, I know it'll be hard at first, but I feel that I owe it to myself at least to try.

Blakeston: By the way, Bill, what do you think about Allied pumps?

Bill: I believe our centrifugal pump is without a doubt the best-engineered pump on the market today. From an engineering point of view, our rotary pumps are built to last twenty years. I don't think anyone could knock our products.

Blakeston: Good. Glad to hear you say it, Bill, for you know a good sales-man has a couple of important obligations — one of which is to have faith in his company and in its products. Another is to be able to shoot square with his customers; he must be willing to help them with their problems, to sell them the product which will do the job that has to be done. You know, in a lot of respects, the reputation of the company rests on the shoulders of its salesmen.

Bill: Yes, sir, I can see how that would be true, but don't you think a man has to look out for himself sometimes?

Blakeston: You're right, Bill, he has to look out for himself in order to become a better salesman. He has to have principles of decency and a good reputation. People must learn to have respect for him and to trust him. Too, a salesman must also be advancing. It's my belief that a good salesman will not be standing still long; he'll be going right on up the ladder to success. To do this he's got to study, to improve, and to be constantly seeking for new and better ways of doing his job. It's a tough road, Bill, this job of selling.

Bill: But it's a challenge; it's the kind of job that is changing, one that doesn't go stale.

Blakeston: That's right, Bill, a good salesman usually has a challenging, in-teresting day ahead of him. A good salesman will strive to make a profession of his occupation. He must always be seeking to help his customers.

Bill: I think I know what you mean; you're saying that to be a success, he's got to make an actual profession out of his job of serving his customers; almost like a doctor serving his patients.

Blakeston: Right, Bill, and it's a hard and sometimes thankless task. Do you still think you want to sell?

Bill: I do, Mr. Blakeston. I really believe that it's the type of job I want.

Blakeston: O.K., Bill, I'll arrange to have you transferred up here as a sales trainee starting the first of next week.

Bill: Fine. And . . . thanks a lot, Mr. Blakeston.

QUESTION:

Was Mr. Blakeston's decision to transfer Bill Woodson sound?

CASE STUDY 3C

A salesman of the Farmer Supply Company calls on a poultry farmer who specializes in raising broilers for market. The farmer is a man of the old school who is usually critical of new ideas and new methods. As the salesman drives up to the farm, he sees the farmer sitting on the front porch.

Salesman: (Walks up onto the front porch.) Good afternoon, are you Mr. Watkins?

Buyer: Yup.

Salesman: I'm George Norris from the Farmer Supply Company. You sure have a nice looking place here.

Buyer: Thank you. Have a chair; take a load off your feet.

Salesman: I was talking to Mr. Holmes yesterday down at the Holmes Poultry Company. He was telling me that you have a real fine poultry farm and that he buys a lot of your broilers. I thought I'd come by and see if you would give me some tips on raising poultry. My company, the Farmers Supply Company, is always interested in new ideas and how farmers solve their feed problems. Incidentally, what kind of feed do you use?

Buyer: Oh, I use Diamond Brand feed. It's pretty good stuff. They grow it right here in this state.

Salesman: It is good, but have you tried Excel feed?

Buyer: I thought about trying some of that Excel feed, but the price is way too high. Why, last time I went to town it was $6.25 a bag. I pay $5.25 a bag now. Anyway, feed is feed, and if you can save a dollar a bag, then you do.

Salesman: You're sure right, feed is feed, but even more important than feed is meat — meat on your broilers, and money in your pocket.

Buyer: Slow down a minute, young fellow; I don't quite follow you.

Salesman: What I mean is you can increase your dollar profits even though you may pay a higher price for feed. You know that if you buy a good pair of shoes they will probably last twice as long as a cheaper pair of shoes. So in that case it would pay you to spend a little extra to buy the good pair of shoes. Well, it's the same way with feed. It will pay you to spend a little more on Excel feed.

Buyer: How does this Excel feed make me money?

Salesman: Well, how old are your broilers when you take them to market to be sold?

Buyer: Anywhere from 12 to 13 weeks.

Salesman: They will weigh from 2¼ to 3 pounds, won't they?

Buyer: That's about right.

Salesman: All right, it takes you 12 weeks feeding to obtain a marketable broiler with an average weight of 2½ pounds. Is that about right?

Buyer: Yes, that's pretty close.

Salesman: The Excel Company has conducted tests and has had poultry raisers just like yourself test their feed. We found that in just ten weeks the flocks that we tested had attained a marketable weight of 2½ to 3¼ pounds. The average weight for each flock was 2⅜ pounds plus.

Buyer: Now look, Mr. Norris, I've been raising poultry for a long time now, probably from before you were even born. You can't make me believe that.

Salesman: You're right. It really is hard to believe, but do you know Mr. Campbell over in North County?

Buyer: Nope, I don't know him, but I've heard of him. Good farmer. I remember his father. He was a good farmer, too.

Salesman: Well, we conducted one of our tests with him, and he was very much impressed. He has been using Excel feed ever since.

Buyer: What kind of chicks does he use?

Salesman: Rhode Island Reds. He buys them at the Clinton Hatchery.

Buyer: Say, that's where I get mine.

Salesman: Then you could certainly get just as good results as he did, if not better.

Buyer: I still don't see how he does it.

Salesman: He starts them on our starter ration. Then after three weeks he puts them on growing ration, and finally he feeds them broiler ration for the last three weeks. He keeps them closed up pretty tightly so they can't run around and develop their muscles or lose weight. And he keeps Excel feed in front of them 24 hours a day. In ten weeks he is ready to market them. They average 2⅜ pounds, and they are uniform in size, and very rarely do you find any culls or sickly ones. The cockerels have broad, full breasts just like a pullet's, and the pullets are really beautiful.

Buyer: Sounds pretty convincing, but I still don't see how Excel can be that much better than Diamond feed.

Salesman: It is the quality of the feed. In Excel you get a well-balanced ration made only from the finest Midwestern grain — grain grown under conditions which make a grain far superior to those grown in this state. I believe you said Diamond was grown in this state.

Buyer: Yes, that's right.

Salesman: Midwestern grain has little or no inert or non-nourishing bulk. That means that when a chicken eats Excel it will get nourishment out of every ounce. The more nourishment in a feed or the higher the quality of the feed, the more nourishment will go to the body. Then the body will develop faster, and you have a marketable broiler quicker. Do you see the difference between Excel and ordinary feeds?

Buyer: Yes, I see what you mean, but that price is sure high. I don't like the idea of paying for a lot of advertising.

Salesman: What do you mean?

Buyer: Well, you folks have that radio program, the Arnold show. That must cost an awful lot of money to put on, and I don't want to pay for a radio program in my feed, even though I do like Arnold.

Salesman: That's a good point you've raised, Mr. Watkins. You know, Arnold does the work of 50 salesmen in putting the name of Excel before the public. Fifty salesmen sure cost a lot of money, and Arnold saves that cost. I guess if you look at it this way, Excel is even more economical than it ordinarily would be, isn't it?

Buyer: I guess if you look at it that way it does cost less.

Salesman: Using Excel, you can get more nutrition per bag of feed, cut production by two weeks, and still get a broiler that will weigh more and be easier to sell. How many bags of Excel would you need in the course of a week?

Buyer: Well, let's see. Send me about ten bags of starter ration, ten of growing, and ten of broiler.

Salesman: You're making a wise move, Mr. Watkins. I'll have the Excel delivered to you in two days.

QUESTIONS:

1. What did the salesman do well?
2. What did the salesman do that could be improved?
3. What techniques are illustrated in the sale?
4. At what points in the interview did the salesman demonstrate an effective selling personality?

CASE STUDY 3D

The salesman represents The Experiment in International Living, a program that sponsors sending college students to foreign countries for a summer. He is trying to convince the father (and only parent) of a college girl that his daughter would benefit from a trip to France. He has previously talked with the daughter at college, and she is very much in favor of going.

Salesman: Mr. Whittier, I'm Forest Helton, representing The Experiment in International Living. We sponsor a program that sends American college students to foreign countries during their summer vacations. I know that you must be greatly interested in your daughter and her summer program. I'd like to discuss with you the benefits she could receive from our program.

Prospect: Well, that's all very nice, but I think that a trip such as that would be financially out of the question for Leigh.

Salesman: I'm glad you brought that up first. Actually the total cost of the trip, excluding spending money, is only nine hundred ninety dollars. The experience alone will mean as much to your daughter as a year in college, but when you compare the cost of the trip with the expenses for a college year, well, the trip is quite a bit cheaper. A trip like that would mean so much to your daughter, and it's something that she would cherish and remember for the rest of her life. Have you ever considered sending Leigh to Europe?

Prospect: Well, she has mentioned it a few times, but we haven't discussed the idea. Leigh is just too young to be running all over Europe. No doubt she'd like it, but I think she'd enjoy a trip to the beach just as much, or maybe I might send her on a trip to New York.

Salesman: You know, Mr. Whittier, last week, I was talking to Mr. Reynard, Leigh's French instructor. He told me that Leigh is not only a good student, but that she has taken an exceptional interest in the people of France themselves.

Prospect: Yes, that's true. Leigh has never caused me the slightest concern in her academic work.

Salesman: That's why I came to see you, Mr. Whittier. You see, we select all the students whom we wish to sponsor abroad. And since this is an educational experience also, we take only the best qualified students that we can get. Our program is called The Experiment in International Living, and it's a challenging plan for internationally minded people to go abroad and actually get to know the people of a country as well as their language, customs, and history. During the past two decades, The Experiment in International Living has provided over six thousand college students with an opportunity to further their cultural and social education, to say nothing of making hundreds of lifelong friendships. Although we sponsor trips to twenty-two different foreign countries, I feel that Leigh would benefit most from a trip to France, don't you?

Prospect: Well, yes, that's where she said she wanted to go.

Salesman: Not only is the trip a wonderful vacation, but most of the students feel that it adds at least a school year of knowledge to their education.

Prospect: Just who looks after the people after they get to Europe?

Salesman: They are supervised by our trained counselors who stay with the students throughout the summer. After the group arrives in France, it is broken into small units of eight or ten people — each with a supervisor.

These groups are placed in Paris, Bordeaux, Cannes, or some smaller community. Then each student or, in some cases, two students are housed with an approved French family which has a child near the age of the student placed there. It'll be just like visiting a cousin in another state. Leigh will do whatever the French family does, and she'll go where they go, and — well, in short, she'll be just like a member of their family.

Prospect: But you said the counselor would be with them.

Salesman: She will. Members of the group will live within four or five miles of one another, and three times a week the counselor will bring them together to share experiences, plan trips, and discuss their common problems.

Prospect: Trips? Do they get to travel?

Salesman: Of course. Most of the families try to show the students as many of the historical sights and other points of interest as their budget allows, and then at the end of the summer, the students have three weeks to themselves. Many then like to finish their summer on the Riviera or sightseeing in Switzerland and Italy.

Prospect: When does the tour start?

Salesman: The student ship leaves on the tenth of June, and Leigh will be back here in time to have a week or so with you before the start of the new school term. We require a fee of one hundred dollars in order that we might make the necessary reservations for Leigh. Would you like to pay that now?

Prospect: No, I don't think so. I prefer to talk to Leigh when she comes home this weekend and see just how she feels about this trip.

Salesman: Of course, that's certainly understandable. Would it be all right if I came by Sunday afternoon to see you and Leigh?

Prospect: Well, I — sure, come on over about three o'clock.

Salesman: All right, sir, I'll see you at three on Sunday. Thank you very much.

QUESTIONS:

1. What did the salesman do well?
2. What did the salesman do that could be improved?
3. What techniques are illustrated in the sale?
4. List the personality characteristics and attributes exhibited by the salesman.

CHAPTER 4

THE SALESMAN'S COMPANY

The salesman's company itself is an important factor in some types of selling. As examples, in the sale of services or intangibles or in selling to purchasing agents, the prestige and standing of the company, its record of service to its customers, and its policies that affect customers are basic considerations. Indeed, it is not uncommon for buyers to weigh the reputation of the company as heavily as or even more heavily than its product or service. In these cases, the company is understandably interested in seeing that its salesmen have adequate company information. Because the picture that buyers get of the company is the one given them by its salesmen, it is clear that the salesman is in a position to help or to hurt his company.

IMPORTANCE OF COMPANY INFORMATION

Company information can play a positive role in the selling process and thus become a basic selling tool. There may be certain facts or features about any phase of company activity which will carry considerable weight in the prospect's opinion. If the prospect had a problem that the salesman's company confronted and solved earlier, then the salesman may be of specific help in the prospect's present circumstances. Such problems and solutions may concern office procedure, delivery, handling requests for contributions, reviving dormant accounts, or other common matters. Just one suggestion or one bit of advice in such a situation may be instrumental in influencing the prospect favorably.

Being sold on his company prevents the salesman from making the glaring, unpardonable mistake of criticizing his company, one of its executives, or one of its policies to prospects. Such a practice jeopardizes whatever confidence the prospect may have in both the salesman and his employer. Of course, whenever the salesman becomes ashamed of or apologetic about the firm he represents, continuation of his affiliation is clearly unadvisable.

Let it be definitely understood that while company facts are vitally important to the salesman, they are not necessarily essential in the sale of the product; they are a complement to and not a substitute for product data. Company information is more valuable in giving the salesman a background, a frame of mind, and a completeness which he needs than it is in persuading prospects.

Personal Progress

A person's interest in his own promotion is both understandable and keen; because he is engaged in selling, the salesman's thoughts and attention in regard to personal progress are probably greater than average. His promotion will be based largely on his ability to produce at a profit, and this ability reflects his knowledge and understanding of his company's objectives and methods.

With thorough knowledge, the salesman is able to guide his own activities and efforts so as to follow the policies set up by his company. He can protect himself and his company by making no commitments his company will refuse to honor.

Building Loyalty

In Chapter 3 it was indicated that a salesman owes loyalty to his company; it can be repeated here that unless that loyalty is unqualified, success in selling will not be so outstanding as it might be. Extensive knowledge of the company not only supplies a foundation for loyalty, but helps imbue the salesman with a respect for his company.

Before one can be loyal, he must approve, and before he can approve, he must know. Knowledge of facts about operating policies and principles precedes faith in them. Only by knowing the philosophy and ideals in back of his company's operation can the salesman know what to believe, subscribe to, and defend. Loyalty based on this knowledge, and partially a result of it, is essential to conducting a successful defense of the company.

A question has undoubtedly formed in some students' minds as to whether or not this matter of approval needs a bit of qualifying. The answer is decidedly in the affirmative. In many cases, the salesman will not be in wholehearted agreement with every policy of his company. That is to be expected. It is only natural, but it need not undermine loyalty. By analogy, a student can be loyal to his school, his church, his political party, his social group, or even his family, and still withhold his approval from one of its policies.

Developing Personality

In the last chapter, certain characteristics were designated as helpful if not necessary in becoming a superior sales personality. Four of these are developed when the salesman knows his company.

The salesman's *sincerity* will increase and become more effective as he learns about the many things his company does, some expensive and troublesome, to help its customers obtain greater satisfaction and success. And the more he knows about the various experts who are in charge of the company's departments, the more sincere he can be in talking with prospects, for the salesman's knowledge will convey to the buyer greater confidence in both the salesman and his product.

As for *confidence*, it is unlikely if not impossible for a salesman to place his trust in a company unless he knows that company thoroughly. The concern that informs its new salesmen about itself, acquainting them with all significant details, makes a strong bid for their confidence. It shows it has nothing to hide.

If he is uninformed about his company, the salesman may feel a lack of *enthusiasm* that will have an unfortunate influence on prospects and customers. Conversely, if he has unbounded enthusiasm for personnel and policies, he does a better job. For instance, it is impossible for any company to operate for any length of time and not make some enemies; the conversion of these enemies into friends calls for enthusiasm, among other things.

Fourth and last, *optimism* is increased by company information. By learning how his company is constantly on the alert to improve methods, to cut its expenses, to expand, and to make its employees happier, the salesman finds facts which encourage him to be quite cheerful about the future. Knowledge is a forerunner of optimism.

Some cynical student is probably wondering about the salesman who, in learning about his company, unearths facts that do *not* occasion joy. Such a salesman should continue to learn as much as possible about the company, because, in addition to facts that need justification, he undoubtedly will find some that are inspiring. These are the ones he should concentrate on and boast about.

Working with Other Departments

A high degree of cooperation must exist between the sales division and the various other divisions of the company. Efficiency throughout the company is the objective, and it cannot be obtained if one division is poorly informed about the functions of the others. If the sales personnel is ignorant of or uncertain about the operations of the rest of the company, the job of working together for maximum profit becomes more difficult.

Customer Relations

Many prospects and customers never see the president, the sales manager, or any other top executives of the salesman's company. The factory and the home office are photographs, not actual experiences. All the prospects and customers see of the company is its salesman. In such cases, the salesman *is* the company to his customers. In his dealings with these customers, he will be asked many questions about his company and its operation, and he should be able to supply most of the answers at the time the questions are asked.

In extreme cases, the salesman will find himself called on to explain and justify company actions and policies in areas remote from selling such as finance, labor, or factory location. Without a wealth of company information he cannot present his company intelligently and effectively, nor can he explain what it can do for its customers.

Selling the Company

Persons need to take pride in their business affiliations, and the salesman is no exception. Only when he knows his company completely is he in a position to be unqualifiedly proud of his connection with it. The salesman himself first becomes sold on his company, and then he sells the company to prospects and customers. Investors Syndicate of America recognizes this fact when it says to its salesmen:

> The first thing . . . for each man and woman to do is to determine the value of the services we render. You must be sure it's the finest, or you will fail.
>
> If, after a thorough study and search, you can find any contract or any investment more suited for the purpose for which it is sold than these services, then you should not accept a connection with Investors Syndicate. *You must be honest in your conviction, or you will fail.*

The salesman's feeling of pride should be so intense and obvious that prospects and customers cannot fail to notice and be affected by it. If he fails to sell his company to customers, he is working on a strictly personal basis, and that is not sound. It gives competition an opportunity to take advantage of a weakness of omission on the salesman's part.

THE COMPANY'S FIELD OF BUSINESS

This mention of industry is intentionally brief. The rest of this chapter considers phases of company activity which have counterparts in competing organizations. Thus, the salesman might benefit from knowing as much as he reasonably can about each of his competitors. Chapter 9 is devoted entirely to competition.

Before he starts studying his own company, the salesman should acquaint himself with the industry of which his company is a unit. If he has the inclination to explore into industry matters, he can find the study to be nothing less than fascinating. For example, if the industry is part of the broad field of communication, or illumination, or transportation, tracing that field up to the present time could be both challenging and intriguing; it could become an interesting hobby. Similar possibilities are present in narrower fields such as footwear, writing implements, household heating, athletic activities, or jewelry.

The logical starting point would be the beginning of the industry, and this would be followed by its history and evolution. Then the salesman might branch out into his industry's relationship to and dependence on other industries. Knowledge of current developments, particularly those that are being referred to by newspapers or radio, will most certainly be in demand by prospects and customers, as will the activities of the industry's trade association. If the nature of the industry is such as to be affected by current legislative proposals, or by current international events, or by the activities of some outstanding personality, the salesman can count on being asked for the detailed story.

Many individuals will ask the salesman about the future of the industry, simply taking for granted, fairly or unfairly, that, since the salesman is connected with the industry, he should be an expert source of information about future possibilities. He will be expected and encouraged to talk knowingly about trends within the industry and about problems and their solutions. How soon will the rest of the textile industry move south — or will it? Just how large are our oil reserves? When will our supply of lumber be exhausted, and what will we do then? When will synthetic raw materials replace the natural ones? Really, just how much competition is there in the steel industry, or among the meat packers? Even though such questions may be asked flippantly, the response of the salesman can help or hurt.

In certain cases, the size and nature of the industry will be interesting. For instance, the national significance of an industry might be impressive. The number of persons it employs and the volume of its output, both in units and dollars, will interest customers. Likewise, the number of companies making up the industry and the relative rank of the leaders will be found to be essential information. The salesman will automatically learn who his chief competitors are, but he should also know where his company fits into the industry picture, what rank it holds, and what rank it has held in the past.

Whatever the competitive position of his company, there is always an explanation for its being what it is; this may be worth learning. Perhaps less interesting but vastly more important are the reasons *why* buyers should patronize a company so located within its industry. Competitive position, then, is one more company matter that must be translated into a reason for buying.

HISTORY OF THE COMPANY

Origin

There is usually a point that can correctly be considered the origin of any particular business, and the reason for being is the logical point of departure for a study of a company's history. Concerning the business enterprise into which the idea was translated, the significant questions will have to do with *who, when, where, what, how,* and *why.* To these questions the salesman must have correct answers. If the character of the times was foreboding, if the stage of the business cycle urged postponement, if prominent men scoffed, or if the courage and pioneering spirit of the founder were conspicuous, then the story is all the more interesting and inspiring.

This story of the birth of a business, taken from Coty training material, is illustrative:

A Slight Accident

Early in the 1900's, Francois Coty created his first perfume. It was to be a perfume so important that an entire business venture was born at the same time. Mr. Coty's first perfume creation was the beloved La Rose Jacqueminot.

He was then unknown as a perfumer, and his attempts to sell to the Paris stores failed. One day, after being turned away again, he started to walk slowly out of the store, a discouraged man. He was so limp in body as well as spirit that he let slip from his hand his sample of La Rose Jacqueminot. When it crashed to the floor, the perfume department was almost stampeded with requests for "that magnificent fragrance." The store was then, of course, forced to stock the perfume and Mr. Coty was launched on one of the most spectacular careers in business history.

Location cannot be divorced from origin. Many factors influence location, including nearness to raw materials, proximity to markets, abundance of cheap power, availability of satisfactory labor, adequate capital, safety, and the tax burden. Regardless of the present location, the salesman should know why the company was originally established where it was, and why the location now is advantageous.

Early Period

In addition to origin, the salesman should be acquainted with the early period of the company, the period when the struggle was often bitter and the outcome uncertain. The salesman is fortunate who has a picture of the physical plant of the small, young venture, its financial condition, its personnel, its first products, the original territory covered, the type of customers that constituted the market, and just how buying, production, advertising, and selling were handled.

For example, consider the F. W. Fitch Company's first advertising technique:

> In the early days of our business, Mr. F. W. Fitch would not sell our merchandise unless he could make a demonstration in the barber shop and put up a mirror sign or advertising sign. His theory was that unless the barber knew how to use our shampoo properly, he couldn't get repeat business, and, secondly, if the reminder wasn't up there, he would forget the product as soon as his initial supply was exhausted. For years, this was the only means of advertising we used.

This background of a famous advertising character is interesting:

The Arrow Collar Man

> The ARROW collar man was an inspired character created by Charles Connolly, the first advertising manager of Cluett, Peabody, and L. T. Leyendecker, the famous illustrator. Together, these two men not only changed the sartorial habits of the American male, but also changed the American woman's idea about her ideal man. Favored by hero worship from women and emulation from men, the ARROW collar man couldn't help but succeed, and ARROW collars sold by the carload. But that's not all the collar man sold.
>
> Bceause the ARROW collar man was clean shaven, the youth of the land began to be clean shaven, and the razor business boomed. Because his attire was modish, men became style conscious, and clothing stores prospered. Because he once appeared smoking a curved-stem pipe, curved-stem pipe sales soared. He was a great influence. His fan mail came to our factories by the truckload; songs and poems were written for him; playwrights produced shows about him. Thousands wanted his autographed photograph, and even proposals of marriage came his way.
>
> In those days, each month brought forth a new ARROW collar man wearing a new style collar, which appeared in advertisements in every street car in the nation, station billboards, outdoor signs, over five hundred newspapers, and all popular magazines. The reception was immediate, and men all over the country rushed to the nearest store for the latest ARROW collar. Even the women couldn't resist wearing ARROW collars.

Original policies and regulations, now long discarded, are often quaint, sometimes amusing. When used alone, such information becomes a basis for conversation; when used as a contrast to current operations, it is a basis for salesmanship.

Parallel developments in other fields and concurrent events can be related to this early period. Anything unusual or outstanding about economic, social, or political conditions may help to make the story complete. Probably no period of the company's history provides such a fertile field for finding unique, colorful incidents. Early-period events are almost certain to show interesting differences from today's.

Changes

In addition to origin and early period, the salesman needs some familiarity with the changes that have taken place in the company's operations. A change of the gradual type is that of growth, and the fact of growth should be stimulating to both salesman and prospect. Progress that the company has made exerts the same influence. Both growth and progress are suitable topics for discussion between salesman and prospect because of the almost universal fascination exerted by that sought after, fabulous something known as success. Once again, as in the handling of the early period, comparisons can be used to advantage.

Major changes are the milestones that punctuate the company story. They serve as landmarks that identify significant changes in direction or pattern, and, as such, should be known to the salesman. Examples of such major changes include incorporation, adoption of present firm name, mergers, achievement of national distribution, and the launching of a new product.

CURRENT FEATURES

Following up a consideration of company history, it seems desirable to point out three features of the present-day company which the salesman should know and appreciate. These have to do with physical matters, financial matters, and matters of reputation.

Physical Aspects

Nothing is more basic or necessary than for the salesman to be informed about the physical make-up of his company. He must know the various parts that combine to make the complete physical plant. He should know what each part looks like, for he will be asked for exactly that information. In addition, he should understand why each of the component parts is needed and how it fits into the broad picture. Prospects and customers alike will assume that the salesman knows where all of the divisions and branches are located and how they happen to be there.

In many and probably in most cases, the plant or factory or single building will be the physical company. Here, too, as in the case of the multi-plant company, the salesman must try to keep posted well enough to answer the questions that will be referred to him. It will help him to know where the machinery was bought and what it cost, as well as its features and method of operation. Acquaintance, at least, with other equipment, facilities, and holdings, such as mines, office buildings, ships, trucks, and metropolitan offices, is desirable.

The young salesman should understand that these facts about the physical company are of little value unless they are properly presented to prospects. For instance, size is the most impressive feature about most companies, and for this reason it should be expressed in many ways. Size can and should be expressed in terms of daily consumption of raw materials, amount of floor space, daily output, annual output, number of employees, size of payroll, and intensity or extent of dealer representation. Statistics on such matters should be presented in graphic, understandable style. Floor space is not a certain number of square feet, but an area that could contain so many football fields; daily output is not a certain figure, but enough to provide one item for every person in Washington; employees are not so many thousands, but enough to equal the population of some locality the prospect knows.

Financial Aspects

Of the various phases of a company, the financial one has a popular and definite attraction. Fiscal topics enter into the conversation between salesman and prospect easily and frequently, and the prospect is only exercising ordinary caution when he displays an interest in and requests information about the financial condition of a possible supplier. Since this is a common salesman-buyer topic, the salesman must be prepared to answer questions concerning it.

First of all, the salesman needs facts about finances in order to be able to converse intelligently and accurately and to answer the many questions about finances that he will be asked. There is also a second angle. Just as the salesman may discover physical facts that will strengthen his sales presentation and make it more effective, so also may he find potent reasons among the financial aspects of his firm for the prospect's buying.

The salesman should start by learning the financial structure of the company and its banking affiliations. He should find out as much as he conveniently can about past and future financing. Occasionally, he will be asked the identity of the largest stockholder, He should always be aware of what the current reports of the credit agencies say about his company. If the rating is good, the salesman has an effective selling point; he can compare his product and its responsible parent with a competitive product which may soon become an orphan. If the rating is not good, the prospect is more concerned about a product than a current ratio, is he not? All favorable aspects of the financial picture have value. A respectable earnings record, a long string of consecutive dividends, a low interest rate on borrowings, a gilt-edge rating for its bonds, or a generally strong fiscal condition can be pointed to with pride.

Reputation

Every manufacturer needs the active approval of two groups. One of these, the trade group, is made up largely of wholesalers and retailers, while the other is composed of consumers. This is true of the makers of industrial products, even if only to a limited extent, but it is completely and vitally true of those who manufacture for the individual consumer market. The salesman is forced to keep a very sensitive finger on the pulse of each of these groups so that he may know from day to day how his company is thought of by each. If both groups think highly of his company and regard it with favor, their goodwill becomes a very impressive and influential selling tool. Of course, when a manufacturer produces for mass retailers or for wholesalers under their private brands, the consuming public does not know who the manufacturer is. Even in this anonymous state, he must have consumers voting for him with their dollars.

A good reputation with the trade may be indicated in various ways. Among the middlemen handling the merchandise of the manufacturer may be included the most desirable dealers. The buyer-seller relationship between the manufacturer and his better customers may have been established quite a long time ago. If there is a trade association that is well recognized and respected in the manufacturer's field, the membership of the manufacturer might be a point in his favor. If the company is having no difficulty in adding new dealers to its list of customers, that can speak well for its trade reputation. If the salesman's company is a wholesale house or a broker who handles the lines of the better manufacturers, then it is patent that the company enjoys the business esteem of those manufacturers. Finally, the company may be recognized as *a* or *the* leader in its field because it is credited with a large number of "firsts."

The company's standing with the second group, the ultimate consumers, is of greater significance than its trade standing because the public helps influence and may almost determine what that trade reaction will be. If the public has passed through the earlier stages of brand recognition and brand acceptance and has moved on into one of the later stages, brand preference or brand insistence, then the manufacturer has happily solved his most serious problem of reputation. Evidence of continued patronage by the consuming public, or, better still, proof of increased buying, may be emphasized by the salesman as indicating an excellent standing with the consuming public.

While on this subject of reputation, it may be well to remember that there is such a thing as a company's character. This character is difficult to analyze and evaluate, yet it is potent; it is intangible, yet persuasive, and it is definitely a factor which influences sales.

In a word, some sellers are looked on as possessing integrity, stability, and responsibility, and if his company is one of these, the salesman has cause for being intensely proud of his affiliation. He knows that his company's ideals and aims, its principles and policies mean something to him and to his customers. When he can show an integrity of purpose displayed through a period of years, or contributions to progress and social betterment, he can more easily convince prospects that his company will take a particular interest in them, that it will allow them to buy only those items which promise to benefit the buyers.

It is quickly admitted here that obvious, absolute, and universally acceptable proof of company reputation is not to be had. Furthermore, the concept of such an intangible factor as reputation can be absorbed gradually by the salesman as he works for the company much more satisfactorily than the company can describe and impart it to the salesman at the time he comes to work.

PERSONNEL

Who and What

Just as a study of the history of the company started with its origin, in the same way a study of personnel should start with the person or persons who founded the company. Names, background, characteristics, beliefs — these illustrate the information about the founders that the salesman should know. A second group is made up of directors and major stockholders, and about these the salesman should have readily available the names, business connections, antecedents, and the voice each has in the company's management. The top executives of the company comprise a third group. Here the salesman will want to know such business facts as name, correct title, duties, and responsibilities of each person who is considered a major executive. If possible, and in most cases it should not be too difficult, this business information should be supplemented with personal details. As many facts as possible about the personalities of these executives, their pet likes and dislikes, their hobbies, and their eccentricities should be filed away mentally. Interesting anecdotes about the executives should be collected, as well as such specific facts as have curiosity value. The advertising manager may breed and show dogs, the purchasing agent may be a topnotch chef, the production manager may be a weight-lifter.

A fourth group includes those minor executives and other employees who will do the actual handling of the customer's business. The head bookkeeper, the head of the shipping department, the warehouse manager, order clerks, and credit department personnel are members of this group.

The main things to be known about them are names, duties, and the authority of each. A fifth and final group contains any outstanding or unique employees. Persons with whom the salesman should be acquainted include such characters as an engineer of national or international prominence, a famous athlete who recently joined the company, wage earners who have done or can do extraordinary feats, or notable persons who have dropped out of the nation's headlines into obscurity.

Why

There are one personal and several business reasons why the salesman should have knowledge about these five classes. The personal reason is that the salesman's chances of success with the company will increase as his information about company phases, of which personnel is one, grows. He can do more and better work when he knows the persons under whom and with whom he works. Even in small matters, the knowledge is valuable as it prevents his mispronouncing a name, making an assumption that is not warranted, taking a position that proves to be awkward, or introducing a conversational topic that is embarrassing.

Personnel data are helpful in a business way in making more successful the salesman's attempt to personalize his company and to make it distinctive. Such facts give an intimacy of the description of the company that invites the prospect to feel close to the company and to place confidence in it. The prospect gets the impression that the company is manned by able, considerate, human individuals who are eager to help, and that they are the type of honest, intelligent, sincere vendors with whom he likes to transact business.

A second business reason has to do with answering prospect's questions. Both prospects and customers are inclined to feel that the president and any other prominent figures on the company payroll are public property. This attitude is often reflected in referring to the president by his first name or nickname, a practice engaged in no matter how awed the prospect or customer would be if the president happened to drop in. The same attitude is often revealed by the personal questions referred to the salesman concerning top officials — questions about the president's age, the size of his family, or the size of his income. Because the salesman is the company to a buyer, he is naturally expected to have all this information.

Finally, personnel facts are valuable in a business way as conversational material, of which a salesman cannot have too much. That material encourages satisfactory, harmonious, and friendly relations between customers and the company personnel with whom they deal.

In a booklet entitled *The Story of HERSHEY, The Chocolate Town*, salesmen of the Hershey Chocolate Corporation are told about the history of their company and its founder. This typical section from the booklet tells how the chocolate town got its four golf courses:

From the very beginning Mr. Hershey had been imbued with the idea that all work and no play makes a world without balance. In furtherance of this idea he provided unexcelled facilities for boating, basketball, bowling, swimming, baseball, football, and tennis.

In the days when Hershey was more idea than town, it boasted a nine-hole golf course, laid out in the rear of the chocolate factory. But as expansion pushed the factory out in all directions the golf course grew correspondingly smaller. As a consequence, Mr. Hershey, who liked to play a game of golf occasionally, engaged a golf architect to lay out an eighteen-hole course.

The first tee of the course was set on the broad lawn fronting Mr. Hershey's home. It is only a few feet from the edge of a bluff that overlooks Spring Creek, which at this point is hidden under clouds of spray issuing from iron jets, the water pouring from the chocolate factory condensers to be cooled so that it thriftily may be used again.

Although Mr. Hershey had put its waters to work, Spring Creek was also made to do its part for art, preserving a nice balance between utility and aestheticism. Therein it epitomized the life of Mr. Hershey, who, although he had amassed millions and had given the townspeople everything he could think of, decided to give away his beautiful home to be used as a clubhouse, reserving only two rooms for his personal use. At an age when most men prize a home and all a home implies above everything else, he decided to become a boarder.

"The club will be more than merely a place to play golf," he said. "It will be a sort of social center for the people who live in the town and vicinity. I want to cement the community together. We are not like the ordinary town of many diverse interests. We are just one big family. That's the way I like to look at it.

"At first I thought I'd build a clubhouse, but I didn't know where to build it, so I gave my house because it was conveniently located. I spend a good deal of my time in Cuba, and all I want is living quarters while I am in town.

"And because I am not quite sure how the club will be able to make both ends meet, I am going to become the club's star boarder," he further explained.

Later on Mr. Hershey laid out a public golf course on the edge of the park and he built a handsome clubhouse on a craggy bluff overlooking the park swimming pool. It has attained national reputation among public courses, and like the Hershey Country Club golf course, it is of championship calibre. For the exclusive use of Hotel Hershey guests a golf course was built atop Prospect Heights. It lacks sand traps, but even so it is a difficult course to play.

And across the way from the Hershey Country Club a nine-hole juvenile golf course was constructed. It isn't an easy set-up, for its fairways are narrow and there are three water holes and a big quarry hole to drive over. It also has a clubhouse, built like a log cabin, which is particularly effective in the charming rural setting.

ORGANIZATION

The Company

In equipping himself to talk with authority about the business organization with which he is connected, to make the proper start, the new salesman should accumulate knowledge about the corporation itself. Attention here centers on the stockholders, board of directors, executive committee, if any, and the officers. The date and the place of incorporation and the reason for incorporating there should be known. Moreover, it is not unreasonable to expect a knowledge and understanding of the financial structure, including the various types of securities and the corresponding owners and creditors. If there has been either vertical or horizontal integration, the salesman should have the story on it. In the same way, if there are working agreements or other relations with outside business firms, the salesman should be able to explain and defend them.

Departments

Within the company organization, the larger divisions of production, marketing, finance, and management must be known. Moreover, there should be rather complete knowledge of those departments to which the salesman is more or less closely related.

A letter from Eastman Kodak reveals that work assignments are provided for sales trainees in the main office and plant departments. They spend from two weeks to three months in such departments as order, stock, billing, accounting, statistical, market research, and various production divisions — quality control, testing, film processing, etc. The experiences of the sales trainees during these periods provide them with an excellent background for their customer contacts.

In addition to the sales department, the salesman needs an excellent working knowledge of the credit, order, billing, traffic, advertising, sales promotion, personnel, purchasing, and research departments. About each the salesman should understand the functions, the connection of each with other parts of the company, how each is related to his own work, and finally how the departments cooperate and are coordinated. An understanding of each department will give the salesman a fuller appreciation of his own department's function.

While it must be recognized that the salesman should know something about each of these departments, neither the prospect nor the company has the right to expect of him the knowledge of a specialist. He should know what he needs to know about the accounting department, but obviously not so much as the chief accountant. He should know enough about the credit function to operate satisfactorily as a salesman, but not as a credit manager. Clearly, the amount of this type of information about particular departments will vary from company to company.

POLICIES

Determination of policy is a function of top management, not of the salesman nor of the sales manager, yet there are two reasons why each salesman should be thoroughly familiar with his company's policies. The first is that he, as an employee, is interested in the company and curious about policies that affect him. The better he understands, the better he sells. The second reason is that he is frequently called on, in his contacts with prospects and customers, to interpret the company's policy on certain matters, and this explanation can become a strong selling point.

In this treatment of the subject of policies, it is immediately obvious that not all policies are included, for that is neither practical nor necessary. Not much can be gained from inquiry into how the company schedules vacations for its employees or whether it places stores-keeping under the production manager or the purchasing agent. The purpose of this section is to select, *as illustrations*, a few major policies that most salesmen will have to understand, interpret, and justify. The young salesman will not have been out selling very long before he becomes keenly, sometimes painfully, aware of the policies *he* needs to know.

All product matters, including price, are omitted here since Chapter 6 is devoted to them. Students may care to refer to recognized books in the marketing field for a fuller handling of marketing policies and practices.

Market Area

If his company does not market its product on a national scale, the salesman must know why it is available in some area and not in others. Time and time again the salesman will be asked why this is so, and on occasion the question will be put to him in the form of a buying objection. It is clear that the salesman will need an explanation of this particular policy.

Channels of Distribution

In certain instances, the choice of the channel of distribution selected by his company will have to be defended. Perhaps the best illustration of this is that of a manufacturer who sells directly to such mass retailers as chains, department stores, and mail order houses, and at the same time

asks wholesalers and independent retailers to handle the same brands.
Or the manufacturer may skim the cream off his market by selling the
large customers direct or by selling direct in metropolitan areas. The use
of exclusive agencies or selective distribution are less extreme examples.
This is not the place for a discussion of the strong and weak points of the
many channels of distribution available to sellers, and neither is it pertinent
to condemn or advocate the use of more than one channel by a single
manufacturer. All that can be said is that the salesman must be able to
make a case for the channel his company uses.

Credit and Collection

Every salesman, no matter with what company, should understand the
fundamentals that underlie sound credit management. He should comprehend fully the role of the three C's, *character*, *capacity*, and *capital*, and
have a working familiarity with financial statements and credit reports.
He should keep informed of how his company feels and what his company
does about these matters.

An appreciation is necessary of the fact that a credit policy cannot
be sound by being either too conservative or too liberal. The policy
that is too strict may keep bad debt losses down to a very low figure,
but it does so at too great a cost in the form of a small sales volume.
Conversely, the overly lax policy encourages a large sales volume, but
at the same time encourages heavy costs. A firm, middle-of-the-road
policy is the one that maximizes sales *and* minimizes expenses most
satisfactorily.

Credit procedure must be known in its entirety, and it is related closely
enough to credit policy to be taken up at this point. The salesman must
know what the credit manager requires prior to the opening of a new
account, and if the salesman is responsible for any part of this first step
he should be completely clear in his own mind about every detail. He
should know the credit limit of each customer, and in the case of new
customers he needs to remember just what the company wants them told
about their credit limits. Company regulations about selling delinquent
and inactive accounts constitute essential data, as does the action the
company takes in cases in which the customer experiences a financial crisis.

The young salesman should *learn* his firm's credit policy and practice,
then *follow* them. He should never override a company decision with his
own, as a salesman tends to be a notoriously poor judge of credit. This
is only natural because of his optimism and his desire for more sales.
Furthermore, in most cases his company has been operating for years and
has no doubt experimented with a variety of credit regulations. The new

salesman is in no position to challenge this background of experience. He will save himself time and trouble and will get along better with the home office if he follows credit instructions to the letter.

As for the policy on collection, the salesman first acquaints himself with the collection techniques adopted by his company. He needs to be able to explain and defend them to customers who, as a result of an unhappy credit experience with the salesman's company, hesitate to reopen their accounts. He should be prepared to inform new customers of collection policy. If the salesman himself is to do any collecting, he should, of course, get detailed instructions from the home office on how it is to be handled.

Each salesman should be impressed with his individual responsibility for helping his company avoid bad debt losses. As a matter of fact, he will be eager to help keep the total cost of handling credit at a low figure once he realizes how easy it is for this expense to grow and take away from net profit. Some companies take the point of view that a salesman should not ask his company to extend credit to a prospect to whom the salesman himself would not extend credit. A salesman's first and foremost consideration admittedly is to sell, yet he should cooperate with the credit manager as much as he can. He must realize the obvious truth that no sale is of value until it is paid for. Unless the salesman and the prospect agree during the sales interview on a satisfactory method of payment, there exists no solid foundation for future selling.

Reciprocity

One matter the salesman will want to be clear on is that of reciprocity. This is the policy that allows the sales manager to influence the purchasing agent in his choice of suppliers in such a manner that the buying opposition that the sales force encounters is reduced. This is the policy of the company that buys from its *friends*, pronounced *customers;* it is the old game of "You scratch my back, and I'll scratch yours." It is the policy that helps the weak salesman, because it is one reason for buying that the prospect is not likely to ignore.

So long as it does not become vicious, there is nothing wrong about reciprocity. It is perfectly natural for the automobile dealer to buy his groceries from the grocer who buys his delivery trucks from him. But in advanced stages, reciprocity becomes something formidable. It tends to close a large possible market to the salesman whose company allows reciprocity to control its buying. It renders good salesmanship ineffective. The purchasing agent, also, dislikes too much reciprocity because it ties his hands and prevents the most skillful, scientific performance of his procurement function.

Despite the probable fact that most companies disapprove of a policy of reciprocity in principle, the influence of reciprocity is widely felt, particularly in periods of depression. That is why the salesman needs to find out what his company does about the matter. He himself will not be able to do anything about it, since it is a top management matter, but he will know what to expect out in the field. He is fortunate if his company both *buys* and *sells* on merit alone.

Order Handling

This final topic is more of a procedure than a policy. It is a "must" for the salesman to know the route an order takes as it is processed and filled by his company. He should know where the order is received and by whom, where and to whom it is sent for authorization, what records are made of it and for whom, where and when it is filled, and when the shipment begins its trip to the customer. The handling of transportation charges, what is done about back ordering, where stocks are carried and in what amounts, and the billing operation are allied matters about which he cannot afford to be uncertain.

FRICTION BETWEEN SALESMAN AND COMPANY

Occasional friction between the salesman and his company is unavoidable. A glance at the table of contents of any standard textbook on sales management reveals treatment of areas of possible misunderstanding and bases of possible disagreement. The purpose of this section is not to explore *all* types of difficulty between a salesman and his company but to help the student to recognize the general problem of friction by merely mentioning a few.

Communication

The problem of company-salesman communication can lead to friction. More than a few companies, wisely or not, send to their salesmen a voluminous and continuing stream of mailings which becomes a very real problem for some of them. When the salesman is supposed to read all this company mail is a very good question. Before breakfast? While waiting to see buyers? At lunch? After supper? Weekends? It certainly is not easy for a company to require a full day of selling and then several hours of reading that the salesman feels must be done on "his" time.

When company-salesman communication is not coordinated effectively, there may be entirely too many persons in the home office who send out a mailing whenever they feel like it. If two officials send the same message to a salesman, he gets disgusted; if they send contradictory messages, he gets confused as well as disgusted. A problem of this sort is one that salesmen can bring out in company sales meetings.

As for salesman-company communication, the main problem is one of paper work. There are many cases where the salesmen have legitimate complaints against the substance, the number, and the scheduling of required reports. The question of *when* to do paper work is the same as the question of when to read company communications. On the other hand, the home office does have to have certain information that only the salesman can supply, and quite often deadlines are involved in his furnishing it. The efficient salesman realizes this and does his utmost to cooperate.

Credit Management

The way a firm handles its credit and collection can be another cause of friction. A salesman may be required to get and submit credit information before he is allowed to sell to new prospects. Because this job is time-consuming and can put a strain on salesman-buyer relations, it is understandably resented by some salesmen.

Equally understandable is the difference between the credit standards of the typical salesman and the typical credit manager. The salesman sees his hopes dashed by an inhuman statistical robot whose dream of the perfect year is one in which no collection efforts were necessary and no bad debts were charged off. The salesman wants higher credit limits for his customers than the credit manager is willing to grant. The salesman wants orders approved and accepted from questionable accounts. He feels that he is not told promptly enough of *lowered* credit ceilings for customers. It is very discouraging for him to spend time selling a big order only to have it turned down by the credit manager. Full knowledge of company policy will help the salesman avoid this area of trouble, as will proper prospecting.

In the distasteful assignment of collecting past-due accounts, the salesman's commission may be at stake. Certainly some of his valuable time is involved. It is quite possible, too, for the credit manager to scream for money past due from the same buyer to whom the sales manager expects the salesman to make a big sale. Certainly the sales manager hopes the salesman will work to revive accounts inactive because of credit difficulties.

Salesman Versus Sales Manager

There are many problems, issues, or matters which the salesman and his sales manager may not see in the same light. Only a few examples are included here as illustrations. One is the matter of earnings and method of compensation. The salesman may question the basic fairness of the plan, even going so far as to suspect his company of wanting to keep his earnings low and to keep him somewhat off balance and on the defensive. Where the amount of a bonus is determined by the performance of a *group* of salesmen, the top salesman is understandably inclined to be irritated. When a firm makes any change in its compensation method, some salesmen are likely to conclude that it is the firm's intent to maximize its profits at the expenses of its salesforce. Many salesmen feel that they are paid inadequately for non-selling duties.

Close kin to the matter of earnings are two others, those of territories and quotas. Some salesmen claim that their territories are too large; others claim that their territories are too small; salesmen in both groups claim that their territories are too low in potential. Sometimes a salesman is reassigned to a territory he does not want; sometimes he is not given the first desirable territory that opens. Within any territory, the salesman's quota can lead to friction. Is it realistic? Was he consulted when it was being set? Is he penalized, in effect, if he greatly exceeds it? Does it allow him time to *service* his accounts as well as to sell to them? Was allowance made for "house accounts" in his territory? (House accounts are those that are handled directly from the home office, and their purchases are not included in the salesman's commissions.)

Then there is the issue of the expense account. Typically, the salesman considers his allowances too low and reimbursement too slow. Some of the items the salesman includes will be questioned, some will be scaled down, some will be turned down. The "buyer entertainment" item and the "miscellaneous" item are fertile sources of disagreement. The current trend toward closer control of costs contributes to the probability of friction over the expense account.

As a final example, friction can be based on the salesman's image of his sales manager and on his impression of how that sales manager operates. Unless a sales manager is skillful in his use of the "carrot" (rewards, compliments) and the "stick" (penalties, criticism), he may seem to his salesmen to be a temperamental slave-driver, superior and domineering. His supervision may appear to be little more than negative criticism, devoid of any constructive aid. If the sales manager pulls rank on his salesmen instead of encouraging them, then he seems to them to have allied himself with top management and not with his sales force. Sometimes the sales manager cannot be depended upon to live up to his promises; sometimes he plays favorites rather than recognizing *every* job well done. The manager who does not bother to keep his sales force informed, who is not receptive to ideas and suggestions from his men, and who is not attentive to their problems asks for trouble.

STUDY ASSIGNMENTS

1. Most business firms must make use of sales forecasts and quotas in their operations, and typically a firm assigns a sales quota to each of its salesmen. Just what are the purposes of quotas?
2. Should a salesman be given a free hand to run his own territory as long as he shows a reasonable profit?
3. When a salesman for a manufacturer of floor coverings tries to get a retailer to begin handling his line, the retailer often is curious about other stores handling that line. What specific bits of information should the salesman be able to report about retailers who have been stocking and selling his line?
4. Can you think of any good that can come from intracompany friction?
5. Identify five industries where company history and background are valuable to the salesman and tell why. Identify five industries where this information is of little help and tell why.
6. When should a salesman stress his company above his products?
7. Which salesman will need more company information, one selling to wholesalers or one selling directly to consumers?
8. Would you say that purchasing agents who buy for industry pay more attention to the matter of *company* than you do when you buy for personal use?
9. Describe five areas in which ignorance of company policies could easily cause failure for the salesman.
10. What handicaps might you expect if you were to become a salesman for a firm which offers no formal training to new salesmen?

CASE STUDY 4A

Mr. Simms, the salesman, has an appointment with Mr. Webb, the owner of Webb's Men's Shop. Mr. Webb is just entering Mr. Simms' sample room at the hotel.

Salesman: Hello, Mr. Webb. I want to thank you for your courtesy in coming down to inspect the Grifton line.

Prospect: Well, I'm always glad to see you, but as you know I have been pretty well satisfied with our present clothing line.

Salesman: I know, but I'd like to show you what we have. These samples are size 38. Now I'm not a perfect model, but I want to slip several of these on to give you an idea of the fitting qualities. This first coat is our Princeton model. It's our most popular young man's coat. Isn't it well styled?

Prospect: Yes, it is a nice coat.

Salesman: As you see, it is not the extreme continental model, but a conservative Ivy cut with moderately narrow lapels. The length of this coat is 30 inches based on a size 38. The trousers are unpleated with 17-inch unfinished bottoms.

Prospect: Do you consider this your standard coat?

Salesman: That is correct. Now I'd like to show you our more extreme young man's coat, the Romano model. This coat is a bit shorter, and it is a high-style model with a cutaway front. This next one is the Cort model, which is a three-button with soft-roll lapels to the first button. It has a plain, easy back, patch pockets, and a center vent. This is our businessman's coat.

Prospect: Do you make up these styles in a good variety of materials?

Salesman: Yes, indeed, and before I show you any more, I want you to see the intrinsic values in our various types of fabrics, particularly the imported flannels which are exclusive with my company. Also I want you to see our strong line of all-wool worsteds. As you know, many companies buy the same colors and the same materials from the same mills, but the weight of the cloth is much different. I want you to feel this material for yourself.

Prospect: It does have a good feel to it. Mr. Simms, what are the prices of these garments?

Salesman: That is where we feel we have the edge over a great many houses. Our entire line is priced at $41.95 for coat and pants. However, there are certain styles in our line that are made with vests at the same price. I think I am safe in saying that this is not applicable to any other line in the country. We also give a discount, although it is not a cash one. In fact, it is better than a cash discount; it is a time discount. Many manufacturers sell their clothes on net 30 terms, but our company's bills are payable just twice a year, on December 10 and on June 10. And that is so, no matter when the goods are shipped. It gives you plenty of time to convert your goods to cash, and you are not forced to lay out cash for unsold garments.

Prospect: That is very lenient. You know, I have been in the clothing business many years, so of course I'm familiar with your line, but my biggest objection is that your company doesn't advertise, and therefore my customers don't know of it. And after all, it's my customers I have to consider.

Salesman: I agree with you. You say we do not advertise; that is true. We are not attempting to support the advertising media. We merely try to pass on to the retailer the best product for the least amount of money. We would much rather spend money in putting better quality into our goods than waste it on things that will not improve the product. We feel that if we can get Grifton clothes to you at a lower price, you will benefit because you can sell at a lower price. And in the long run we will benefit too.

Prospect: Now, does Grifton set a retail price on its clothes?

Salesman: No, Grifton does not tell you at what price you must sell our merchandise. We think that is your business, not ours. You said you have been in business a long time. Then I know your customers must have implicit confidence in you and the goods you offer in your store. With our line you can make a larger margin of profit. Your customers' confidence in you will help sell Grifton clothes. No amount of advertising could replace that confidence. And you can be safe in putting your personal guarantee on our merchandise.

Prospect: Well, I'll admit you have a good line of merchandise, but I've gotten along pretty well in the past without Grifton.

Salesman: You're right, Mr. Webb. You can get along without Grifton clothes, but as I always say — you can get along better *with* them. We've been in business since 1869, and we're one of the largest in the industry now. And we've done all this with our policy of no advertising. So you see, we must have a superior product. You and I both know that you can't fool a retailer for long.

Prospect: What type of in-stock service does your company have? As you may know, we are able to get additional single replacements from some other firms.

Salesman: And as I'm sure you know, this is a costly process. Grifton has no service of this type, because if we did, then we could carry only staples and it would necessarily raise the price of all the merchandise a good bit. However, I have worked out something even better than an in-stock service. At any time you want a single garment, I will be able to get it for you 90% of the time. If another customer of mine has purchased the suit anywhere in the territory and still has it in stock, he will ship it to you at only $1 above the cost price. This system has worked out successfully and all are cooperative. Doesn't that sound good to you?

Prospect: Yes, that does sound like a good system.

Salesman: Mr. Webb, what I would like you to do is to give our line a trial, and I am convinced that you will think it is the best line in the country for the money.

Prospect: We have already bought most of our requirements for the next season, but I'll give your line a trial. I'll buy only about fifty suits, but that will be enough to give me an idea as to its comparative merits.

Salesman: Thank you, Mr. Webb. I know you'll be highly satisfied with our merchandise.

QUESTIONS:

1. What did the salesman do well?
2. What did the salesman do that could be improved?
3. What techniques are illustrated in the sale?
4. What fault did Webb find with Simms' company?
5. What company features did Simms point to proudly?

CASE STUDY 4B

Larry Penegar entered his senior year of college with an outstanding record of achievement for his first three years. He had lettered in two sports; he had maintained a B average in his courses; as a senior, he would hold a responsible and respected student body office. Larry was popular both with faculty and with students.

As for a career, Larry had selected the field of selling. He did not yet know whether he would stay in *selling* or move into *sales management*, but he assumed that future developments would throw light on that question. Larry registered with the college placement office and, through it, scheduled appointments with recruiters from several companies. Of the seven companies wanting to hire him, Penegar was strongly attracted to two, Langley Adams Company and Macon Mills.

Langley Adams manufactured a long line of soaps, cleansers, and toiletries for consumer use. The products reached consumers primarily through food, drug, variety, and department stores. In addition to the retail line, industrial departments sold a line of industrial products to institutions, government, and business buyers. A foreign division handled export sales and the operation of company plants in other countries. If Penegar went with Langley Adams, he would be placed in the foreign division. All in all, Langley Adams was large, old, able, organized, advertised, and established. The infrequent openings in its foreign division were eagerly sought by graduates of many schools.

The picture of Macon Mills was quite different. It was largely a one-man operation. The company manufactured medium-priced hosiery, under the Macon label, for all members of the family. A sales force of 22 men covered the national market, working on a commission basis and selling to wholesalers and retailers. The salesmen had been hired and trained by Mr. Macon himself; only one was a college graduate. Macon Mills did no advertising. Annual sales were between three and five million dollars. Mr. Macon had started the company on a shoestring. With borrowed funds and the sheer force of his industry, ability, and personality he built the company up to its present size.

At this time, Mr. Macon is sixty-one years old. His only son expects to graduate from another school at the same time as Penegar; the son plans to join Macon Mills. If Penegar were to join the Macon company, he would start as a salesman in the field after two weeks in the home office.

QUESTIONS:

1. What factors favor Langley Adams as an employer?
2. What points could Mr. Macon make in trying to sign up Penegar?

CHAPTER 5

THE COMPANY PROMOTION PROGRAM

In disposing of his products, the manufacturer finds three sales-producing forces available to him. The first, *personal selling*, is the topic with which this book is primarily concerned. Personal selling has been described as a "push" technique because it applies a force back of the manufacturer's products and pushes those products down through their channels of distribution.

The second sales-producing force is *advertising*. Manufacturers may direct some of their advertising to their middlemen, hoping to get new wholesale and retail customers and more volume through their present dealers. And, some manufacturers direct part of their advertising to certain professional groups the members of which influence or control specific consumer purchases; advertising directed to dentists, doctors, and architects is of this type. But by far, most of the advertising done by manufacturers is addressed to ultimate consumers. The nature of this advertising makes it a "pull" technique because its effect is to urge consumers to ask for the advertised brands, thereby pulling those products down through their channels of distribution.

The third sales-producing force consists of a group of auxiliary and facilitating activities labeled *sales promotion*. Found here are the coordinating of personal selling and advertising, certain relations between a manufacturer and his middlemen, and a manufacturer's stimulation of and services to his ultimate consumers.

These three forces have much in common. They all have the same objective — more profitable sales. They all use the same appeals to sell the same products to the same two groups of buyers, the middleman group and the consumer group. They use the same geographic market units and the same market data and forecasts. All three observe the same principles of attacking their common problem of buyer-resistance and converting it into customer-patronage. The three forces are complementary and not competitive; they must be coordinated effectively if the maximum results are to be had from a manufacturer's promotional activities.

Each manufacturer confronts that most challenging problem of constructing what, for him, will be the most profitable promotion program. Can just *one* of the forces do a satisfactory job for a manufacturer? Apparently so. We see a number of manufacturers seemingly happy and prosperous in their use of nothing but advertising. We see a somewhat larger group using personal selling only. They, too, seem to be getting along nicely. Sales promotion does not, however, appear to be sufficient by itself to provide a manufacturer with even the minimum amount of promotion his products must have. What about using two of the three forces? We see some manufacturers adding some advertising to personal selling, or basing their sales hopes on advertising plus some sales promotion, or, finally, selecting personal selling and sales promotion as the promotion pair.

Most manufacturers of medium or large size who sell consumer goods put together promotion programs composed of *all three* sales-producing forces. Each manufacturer in this group believes that he can maximize his profits only if he uses some of each of the forces. Typically, we see a manufacturer communicating impersonally to large groups of buyers through his advertisements, talking face-to-face and individually with certain buyers through his salesmen, and then using the amounts and types of sales promotion he feels he needs. The manufacturer combines the three activities in whatever promotional mixture he deems most effective.

Every salesman connected with a firm is obviously affiliated with a company which considers personal selling essential. Whether his firm also uses advertising or not, the salesman must understand the company's policy and the reasoning behind it. The same holds for sales promotion. Only if he understands the other sales-producing forces, and only if he understands the assignments his company gives to them can the salesman contribute the most to the company's promotion program — and benefit the most from it.

The next few pages are devoted to a consideration of advertising. Then follow several pages dealing with sales promotion. Remember that neither is intended to be an extensive treatment of these topics. Instead, each section is limited to those aspects of the subject that are of most immediate concern to salesmen.

ADVERTISING

Features and Uses

The sales-producing force known as advertising has certain features that are relatively unique in the field of promotion. Advertising is speedy communication, able to tell a seller's story to millions of consumers in a matter of minutes. Advertising is mass communication, the low cost-per-buyer-impression making it quite economical. Advertising is uniform communication, being under the rigid control of the advertiser and not subject to revision without the advertiser's consent. Because advertising is impersonal communication, it is much more easily ignored than is a salesman. This impersonal quality, plus the method of delivery, allows advertisements to get into the presence of some buyers who would be much less receptive to a saleman. In the main, the advertiser must resign himself to paying for some waste circulation; not all persons who see or hear his advertising message will be prospects for his products. Furthermore, the advertiser must resign himself to standard messages rather than tailored, personalized messages; that is the price of uniform communication.

The characteristics of advertising make its most logical assignment that of *pre-selling*. When a manufacturer's advertising pre-sells middlemen on his products, his salesmen have an easier job actually selling to those middlemen. When the manufacturer's advertising pre-sells consumers, he makes easier the selling done by retailers. In pre-selling, advertising introduces products and their manufacturers to buyers. Upon subsequent contacts, buyers recognize the products, their names, and the names of their manufacturers. If this recognition is favorable, buyers will often buy one of the items when that purchase is recommended by a retail sales-person, or suggested by a friend, or sometimes when the advice is seen in another advertisement.

Because of its limitations, advertising is seldom asked to complete sales to buyers. Giving it a pre-selling assignment is much more realistic because such an assignment is more susceptible of achievement. Advertising cannot track down buyers as a persistent, determined salesman can. Advertising suffers from the absence of personal contact and the impact of a salesman's personality. Demonstrations of products are severely limited, both in nature and in the number of media which can accommodate them. Advertising copy cannot answer the buyer's spur-of-the-moment questions. Closing a sale as known in personal selling simply cannot be accomplished by an advertisement.

Relationship to Personal Selling

Advertising and personal selling are each in a position to contribute significantly to the more effective functioning of the other; they are, by the same token, seriously and unavoidably dependent on each other. As was mentioned earlier, advertising pre-sells merchandise. Advertising that invites inquiries from interested buyers can locate prospects for salesmen. Advertising can stimulate demand for the products the salesman sells. Advertising helps to keep sales in balance, whether the problem of balance is among products, among types of buyers, among markets, or among seasons of the year.

Good advertising, then, does a superb job of increasing a salesman's sales power. Because advertising instills confidence in the salesman and endows him with prestige, the results are more interviews, shorter interviews, and more successful interviews. Advertising makes for stronger sales presentations because salesmen get both facts and ideas from their company's advertisements. The presentations sound stronger to the buyer because he hears from the salesman points which he saw earlier in advertisements. A final way in which advertising increases sales power is in helping keep customers sold between the salesman's calls. The advertising seen by buyers during this interval reduces the chance of the salesman's being forgotten.

In return, advertising can expect valuable favors from the sales manager and his staff. First of all, it is the sales force which stocks wholesalers and retailers before an advertising campaign breaks. Then, in a general and continuing way, the sales staff can insist that the company's advertising be sales slanted and contain sales-producing power. This insistence can prevent the advertising from drifting off its only proper course into activities which have other goals. Salesmen are often in a position to supply some of the raw materials of which advertisements are fashioned, materials such as case histories, experiences, testimonials, and product information not previously known by the company. Salesmen may offer suggestions of value about the company's advertising, suggestions having to do with such matters as motivation, media, or message. Detailed, individual pictures of a manufacturer's market may be available only from the company's salesmen, and such pictures often allow advertising to be tailored to some extent to specific markets. Salesmen may be able to report helpful information about how the company's advertising is doing in each market and about how each of the company's competitors seems to be faring.

Types of Advertising

Advertising can be classified by various categories. One basic classification separates product-promoting advertising from institutional advertising. Promotional advertising features the products or services the company offers for sale, while institutional advertising publicizes the company itself and not its wares. Institutional advertising itself breaks down into three sub-groups. That of a *patronage* nature hopes to establish the company as a preferred source of the types of merchandise or services it sells. That of a *public relations* nature is used by a company for the improvement and then the maintenance of relations between the company and its "publics." Prominent in this assortment of "publics" are the company's prospects and customers, competitors and suppliers, middlemen, employees and the labor force, suppliers of capital, government, plant cities, and advertising media. Finally, institutional advertising of a *public service* nature promotes the public welfare. Companies use it to publicize health, savings, safety, conservation, security, education, and the like. It is probable that salesmen are more sympathetic toward advertising that promotes specific merchandise than to advertising that promotes their companies. A third type of advertising is aimed at industrial buyers; a fourth type at certain professional groups — doctors, engineers, or accountants — who serve clients as buying advisers or product experts.

Anatomy of an Advertisement

Appeal. The mechanism which controls a buyer's expenditures is his motivation. When an individual decides what experiences and sensations, what gratifications and pleasures he wants, he establishes his own scale of priorities and his motivation pattern. For ultimate consumers, the goal is described broadly as personal satisfaction; for business buyers, the goal is increased profits. Advertisements (and salesmen, too, for that matter) succeed only to the extent that they translate a product or a service into appeals which will activate the buyer's motivation mechanism. The advertising appeal, consequently, must be chosen carefully and correctly if the advertising is to be effective.

In their search for the appeal to use, advertisers can use guesswork, or imitation, or hunch — or research. A thorough study of products and buyers leads to the identification and selection of the strongest, the most successful appeals. Through research an advertiser can learn what is the most impressive, the most influential satisfaction his product offers. In every instance, the advertiser will make certain to appeal to the self-interest of buyers. He will be particularly happy if research recommends such a basic, primary appeal as sex, comfort, safety, superiority, or approval.

Copy. The most important element in an advertisement is the copy. Its purpose is to increase sales. In the typical advertisement, the copy breaks down into the headline and the text or body copy. The headline shares with the illustration the task of attracting the attention of the group the advertiser hopes to reach. The headline and the body copy share the task of converting attention into interest, the stage in which the buyer begins to relate in his thinking the three matters of need, product, and price. Then, if the copy is successfully persuasive, it causes the buyer to feel attracted to the product — to want it, to wish he had it. In rare cases, sellers use advertisements to move one more step and complete the sale.

In all cases, the copy of an advertisement aims to achieve some reaction from buyers. The advertiser hopes his copy will get the prospect to try the advertised brand the next time he is in the market to buy. That time may be tomorrow — or months from now. Or, the action desired may be the sending in of a coupon, or the making of a telephone call to a dealer. If overt action is inappropriate, then the copy seeks to favorably incline the buyer toward the advertised brand. The copy strives to get a reaffirmation of confidence in the advertised product from present users and a renewal of their intent to remain customers.

As for organization, the copy in an advertisement frequently begins by recognizing or posing a buyer-problem. Unpopularity, financial burdens, overweight, underweight, sleepless nights, impaired hearing, and fatigue are examples. Then, of course, the advertisement recommends the sponsor's product as the best solution to the problem. Benefits and advantages are described, and claims are made and explained. Proof of these promises may be included. Finally, the action the advertiser wants is indicated, and reasons for acting *now* may be added. All this may take much copy — or little. Regardless of length, copy must qualify against the criteria of unity, clarity, coherence, and emphasis. In addition, it must translate a product or a service into benefits and then persuade buyers to accept those translations.

Layout. Seldom does one see an advertisement containing nothing but copy. Perhaps one is entitled to conclude that the "standard" advertisement is made up of a headline, one or more illustrations, some body copy, and the signature — the brand or firm name in prominent type. Just which of these elements will be in an advertisement is a decision for the "visualizer." He conceives the advertisement. Then he goes about arranging those elements, and this step involves laying out the advertisement. Visualization decides that there shall be a headline and an illustration; layout decides whether the headline shall be *above* or *below* the illustration.

Layout makes its own contribution to the success of the advertisement. It supplies a variety of devices and techniques for the use of those individuals who build advertisements — intensity, contrast, isolation, balance, and motion are some. It offers the two variables of size and shape for appropriate uses. It offers two basic types of illustration, the drawing and the photograph. It observes such principles as simplicity, unity, and rhythm. It makes certain that the advertisement appears in good taste and in good proportion. It invites reading.

Typography. An assortment of type faces can be found in the typical shop where advertising copy is set in type. The advertiser's job is to select the face or faces which will help his advertisement be most effective; among his favorites are such faces as Caslon, Bodoni, and Garamond. For special purposes the advertiser can have some of the copy, often the headlines, hand lettered. Advertisers want typography to contribute readability, appropriateness, emphasis, life, and interest. They do not want typography to call attention to itself.

If an advertiser runs his advertising in color instead of in black-and-white, his costs are greater, but color usually makes a more powerful impact. Color adds realism, product and package identification, atmosphere, and quality. Advertisements in color are larger and less common than black-and-white advertisements; as a result, they have greater attention-getting value.

Point-of-Purchase Medium

Those advertising materials displayed by retailers in, on, or at their stores make use of the point-of-purchase medium. "P.O.P." includes window displays, counter displays, floor displays, and materials for wall, ceiling, and exterior displays. In addition, the medium includes some items which are really fixtures and equipment. These are racks, stands, clocks, door handles, store signs, thermometers, and cabinets for the display and sale of merchandise.

The point-of-purchase medium has some interesting and significant features. It provides a manufacturer with his last chance to communicate through advertising with the customer before that customer makes a purchase. And, no memory factor is involved because a decision and a purchase can be made immediately. The medium's circulation is of high quality because many persons reached are close to the buying act — physically, emotionally, and, best of all, financially. The medium is particularly effective in spurring impulse buying and reminder buying. It is a versatile medium, used by retailers for many purposes. Normally, control of the medium is *not* vested in the manufacturer, but, instead, is a prerogative of the retailer; the dealer can install a manufacturer's window display for a week — or he can throw it into the trash can unopened. So, in this medium there is waste which every manufacturer would like to reduce. Point-of-purchase materials back up a manufacturer's advertising in all other media at the most crucial moment.

There is a troublesome problem of distribution in the point-of-purchase medium; it involves the method by which a manufacturer places his materials in retailers' hands. Some manufacturer ship their items direct to each retailer, sometimes in the case or carton with the merchandise, sometimes packed separately. Often this shipment is made only upon the retailer's request. The manufacturer may have invited the request by sending the retailer an advertisement through direct mail or through trade papers. Occasionally a manufacturer makes use of an installation crew. In rare cases this crew would be his own — in most cases it would be a commercial firm specializing in this type of work. The other common method finds the manufacturer asking his salesmen to be responsible for the distribution and use of the materials.

Several factors influence the retailer's evaluation and selection of the point-of-purchase materials he will use. His own inventory conditions are one consideration, urging him to promote fast-moving products — or slow-moving products — or outstandingly profitable products. The materials from which he can choose are another consideration; among these features are size of item, its excellence, its timeliness, and its ease of installation. The identity of the manufacturer can be a consideration; for example, a retailer with a desirable franchise from a manufacturer wants to and must cooperate with that manufacturer. Finally, the salesman calling on the retailer can be a potent factor; it is only natural for a retailer to favor salesmen he likes.

The salesman plays a key role in his company's effective use of the point-of-purchase medium. To start with, he must see that his retailers are stocked with enough merchandise to justify their use of his company's materials. Then he has a continuing job of selling his retailers on the excellence of his company's point-of-purchase program. By getting more retailers to use more of the items for greater lengths of time, the salesman helps his company reduce waste in the medium. The salesman tries to get the retailers to synchronize their point-of-purchase activities with the promotion schedule of his company. He is always trying to get the most desirable locations for his materials. He reports to the company on the use of the various items. He acts as an adviser to the sales promotion manager, commenting and making suggestions on his company's program, the programs of competitors, and the thinking of his retailers.

Here's what the Kraft Foods Company tells its salesmen about their company's point-of-purchase materials:

Display Material Is Costly

A salesman without a technique for handling point-of-sales material is like a violin with a string missing. But techniques employed by some salesmen rate even lower than a stringless violin. Maybe you can spot the type.

Storage Man: This type apparently believes that his truck or car is a big storage bin for all point-of-sale material. He has never been known to put up anything except price cards. Banners and special appetite appeal pieces never get beyond the floor of his car — until he tosses them out as soiled material.

The Ripper: First name may or may not be Jack, but when he gets his hands on point-of-sale material — it's rip . . . rip . . . and rip! His route is marked by torn, tattered, and frayed material. Of course he usually runs out of anything to rip long before he gets to the end of his route.

Buck-Passer: This man really gets the point-of-sale material out on the route. No ripping either. He can't be bothered with a small matter like that. He just unloads the material in the back room of the first store he calls on — he figures they'll find *some* use for it. (And he gripes about being stuck with "small volume" stores!)

The Big Spreader: This one is always looking for more material. He isn't happy unless he can put 10 to 20 banners in one store — even if it's so small he has to overlap his banners. Sales possibilities have nothing to do with his plans. If he sees a blank spot on a wall, he'll cover it even if he has to put up a couple dozen recipe pads.

What these types cost their company in just sheer waste of point-of-sale advertising material must be fabulous. Imagine tossing away a pack of Salad posters at 23 cents each! Or a stack of full-color Salad Bowls at 25.3 cents apiece! Think of the cost of a pile of full color Cheese Trays at 30 cents each or the Miracle Whip blow-ups at 15.1 cents for every one! Even ad reprints average 5 cents apiece.

But an even bigger loss is in sales. Surveys have shown that point-of-sale material builds sales tremendously. But it can't help sell more products lying in an ash can, a backroom, a company vehicle, or plastered a foot thick in a tiny store!

Direct Mail Medium

The direct mail medium consists of a wide variety of items sent by the advertiser to buyers through the postal facilities. Commonly used forms are letters, cards, folders, circulars, booklets, broadsides, catalogs, and order forms. A major use of direct mail by a manufacturer is to communicate with the middlemen, the wholesalers and the retailers, to whom his salesmen sell. Manufacturers who find it desirable to influence certain professional groups or to speak to purchasing agents also find direct mail to be a most appropriate vehicle for their advertising messages.

This medium, like point-of-purchase, has its own peculiar characteristics. Direct mail is too expensive to be employed as a mass advertising medium; that's why it is rarely used when a manufacturer is addressing ultimate consumers. To compensate for the expense, direct mail can be quite selective and can hold waste circulation down to a minimum. Furthermore, this is a flexible medium, offering wide choice of cost of each mailing, frequency of follow-up, composition of each mailing, timing, volume, and geographic area covered. Direct mail is the only advertising medium of a confidential nature. It can reach buyers whom salesmen find difficult to see. Its results can be checked if the advertiser is willing to go to some trouble. There are two problems involved in direct mail — getting and keeping current the desired mailing list and getting the mailing piece read. Salesmen often contribute to both solutions.

Direct mail can do many jobs for a manufacturer and his salesmen. It can locate prospects for them. It can send pre-call information to buyers — or request it of them. It can make appointments. Direct mail is useful in following up a salesman's call and in maintaining contact with buyers between calls. It helps keep the goodwill of customers and helps keep them sold. A reminder use can be made of direct mail. It can be employed in sampling and in answering inquiries. Some salesmen can use it to get actual orders.

Dealer Advertising Campaigns

Dealer campaigns are made up of a manufacturer's advertising to his trade — to his wholesalers or distributors, and to his retailers or dealers who buy and handle his merchandise for resale. This phase of the manufacturer's advertising program is properly assigned to the sales promotion manager for responsibility and execution. The appeals on which trade advertising must be based are quite limited in breadth because wholesalers and retailers buy for resale with a single objective in mind — greater profits. So, advertising addressed to middlemen about merchandise for resale must talk increased sales and reduced costs. Two types of media carry most trade advertising, these being direct mail and the specialized publications more similar to magazines than to newspapers, the so-called business papers. *The Progressive Grocer* and *Furniture Age* are examples of trade papers read by retail grocers and merchants handling furniture. While it is true that the ultimate aim of advertising addressed to middlemen is to increase their purchases of the manufacturer's products, the immediate or short-range hope of the manufacturer is often to get greater use of his promotional aids. The manufacturer wants more retailers to order or accept his window displays, for example, and to install them. Indeed, the advertisements themselves may not talk about selling *to* the middlemen — they may describe all the things the manufacturer is doing to sell the merchandise *for* the middlemen.

A manufacturer's dealer advertising campaign may have a vertical cooperative feature. The manufacturer may encourage his retailers to

advertise the manufacturer's products locally by offering to defray part of
that cost. It is not uncommon for a manufacturer to tell a retailer that he,
the manufacturer, will match the retailer dollar for dollar in local advertising of the manufacturer's line. This offer may be limited to a certain
percentage of the retailer's dollar purchases, 5 per cent perhaps, and
sometimes it is restricted to certain media. In addition to offering to help
pay for local advertising, the manufacturer may make the planning and
arranging of such advertising easy by offering to supply mats for advertisements, suggested copy for radio and television, posters at attractive prices,
and such. The manufacturer's salesman is intimately involved in his
company's vertical cooperative advertising because, as he is usually the
only personal contact, he will be asked to work for greater dealer participation. Too, he will be the one to see that the cooperative undertaking
operates smoothly in his territory.

Retail Tie-in Advertisements

A type of advertising of official interest to and even a partial responsibility of some salesmen consists of advertisements run by retailers featuring
a manufacturer's brand or brands. The last paragraph indicated that
sometimes the cost of such advertising may be divided between manufacturer and retailer. Regardless of who pays the bill, various manufacturers expect their salesmen to encourage and to obtain retail tie-in
advertisements.

The reasons back of this policy are numerous. Greater closeness is
fostered between retailer and manufacturer; the same is true of retailer
and salesman, because the latter has considerable opportunity to become
an adviser and consultant to the retailer. In addition, retailers tend to
put greater than average promotion (displays, quality and quantity of
floor space, personal selling) behind what they advertise; they are more
likely to use more of the manufacturer's point-of-purchase material. New
retailers are more easily signed up as customers. Present retail customers
are easily persuaded to follow the lead of the advertising retailers.

The manufacturer benefits from having his own advertising, be it
national *or* local, backed up and supported by the retailers' advertising.
Copy can be localized to make it more effective; local consumers can
learn *where* a manufacturer's brand can be found. And it just may be
that those consumers read more *local* advertising than they do *national*.
When the advertising retailer is one of great local prestige, some of the
prestige rubs off onto the manufacturer.

After promoting retail tie-in ads, some salesmen call on local advertising media, suggesting that the time may be favorable for them to solicit
advertising from these same retailers.

Consumer Advertising Campaigns

The lion's share of a manufacturer's advertising fund goes to finance consumer advertising campaigns. By their very nature, they are of greater help to the salesman of consumer goods than are other types of advertising campaign. Even though his company may have several consumer advertising campaigns running at the same time, the salesman does well to post himself about them completely. One most basic matter is the theme or keynote idea of a campaign. If the theme is a wise choice, the campaign can be an outstanding success. Conversely, if the keynote idea is weak, inappropriate, dull, silly, or irrelevant — or if for any other reason it fails to reach the buyer's thinking and to stimulate a buying motive, then the campaign is doomed to a mediocre performance at best. It is not uncommon for a company to spend much time and many dollars in trying to identify the keynote idea which will be most successful. Details of this search supply the salesman with information he can use to advantage.

Then there is the field of media. Consumer advertisements are usually found in newspapers and magazines, in the broadcast media of radio and television, on poster panels and other outdoor structures, in, on, and near public transportation vehicles or their stations, and in the two media already mentioned, point-of-purchase and direct mail. In respect to the first six media listed, the salesman needs detailed information including significant statistics. He needs a list of the media in which his company's advertisements will be appearing. He needs to know sizes of advertisements and schedule of appearance. He needs an appreciation of the compromise that is inevitable between size and frequency; if his company runs large advertisements, it must run fewer of them than it could if a smaller size had been selected. Extremely impressive are circulation breakdowns, medium by medium and market by market. After all, a Mobile retailer is interested only in advertising impressions among Mobile consumers — completely indifferent to circulation in Minneapolis!

Advertising Management

In respect to the management of his company's advertising, a salesman needs a limited amount of information about four specific matters. First of all, he cannot afford to be completely ignorant about the *advertising department*. He benefits from knowing some of the individuals in the department on a personal basis. He needs to know the functions which have been assigned to the advertising staff. The attitude of his company toward advertising and the policies it has adopted can, on occasion, prove to be helpful bits of information. The salesman does well to keep current on the thinking and planning going on in the department. Even though his contacts with the department are made most often through the sales promotion department, it is imperative for each salesman to understand precisely what he can count on *from* the advertising department, and what he owes *to* it.

A second area is that of his company's *advertising agency* or agencies. Buyers do not consider unreasonable the questions they might normally ask a salesman about his company's agency. For example, if his company severs relations with one agency and transfers its advertising to another, the salesman can expect at least a few buyers to ask why this was done. Evidence of the agency's skill and competence in the field of advertising can be used by salesmen to good advantage.

Few salesmen can operate satisfactorily without some facts about *how their advertising is budgeted.* Size of advertising fund is, of course, a basic matter here. If salesmen know something about how the size of the fund is determined, that is fine. Complementary information would be the amount and type of advertising done by competitors. Particularly valuable to know are the items or activities which the company *will* or *will not* charge to advertising. Pursuing this one step further, a smart salesman will learn which of the calls he might make on the advertising fund will be honored. Then, perhaps the most necessary of all is a breakdown of the total advertising effort. Each salesman must know how much of the advertising fund will be spent in his territory, by product line, by medium, by time period, by type of advertising campaign, and by market.

A fourth and final phase of advertising management of interest to salesmen is the *measurement of advertising performance.* His company's interest is, of course, understandable. The company wants to know what it got for each advertising dollar it spent. It wants to know what was good and what was bad in last year's program in order to use advertising more profitably next year. Salesmen, too, have an interest in this area. If they know how successful last year's advertising was, they can point with pride and assurance to that achievement. The results of last year's advertising prove the advertising claims the salesman made year before last. His current claims about *next* year's advertising are more credible. He will find himself better able to handle buyer indifference and buyer skepticism. This is not the place to explore or even to describe briefly the techniques of evaluation. Suffice it to say that the determination of the results of advertising is a most difficult and complex undertaking. It is no job to determine advertising costs, but to determine what the advertiser got for his money is far from easy. Fortunate is the salesman whose company supplies him with sound facts on this matter.

Selling His Company's Advertising Policy

A salesman has an obligation to understand his company's advertising policy and to be able to make a creditable case for it. While this obligation applies in some measure to all salesmen, it is of greatest concern to those in the employ of manufacturers who sell merchandise to wholesalers and retailers for resale. Obviously, the salesman's company can adopt either one of two policies — it can do no advertising, or it can incorporate the activity into its promotion program.

Salesmen for manufacturers who do not advertise usually contrast their products with advertised products of higher price, yet they assume, at the very least, equal quality. These salesmen will stress that their lower prices permit wholesalers and retailers to sell their unadvertised lines at lower prices than advertised lines. The salesman may point to a high markup. He may say that his company builds more value into the product with the dollars *not spent* for advertising. He can usually promise wholesalers and retailers greater freedom in pricing the merchandise and freedom from price wars. He may feel that his company has put together a promotion program that is more effective than if some of the promotion funds were earmarked for advertising. Finally, he may claim that his company favors the middlemen and their customers rather than advertising agencies and media.

If his company is an advertiser, the salesman stresses consumer demand, consumer preference, and prestige with consumers. He will brag of uniform quality known to the public, a quality in which the public has complete confidence. In the area of sales, he will stress high turnover and ease of selling, the results of the manufacturer's pre-selling the merchandise for middlemen. He will point out the manufacturer's interest in purchases from retailers — happy purchases — repeated purchases. Store traffic will be mentioned. Reduced expenses will be promised in selling, in markdowns, in advertising, and in inventory. The end result of all these can be nothing but greater dollar profits.

Using His Company's Advertising

A salesman is remiss if he fails to make maximum use of his company's advertising. By reading it, he acquires valuable information and makes possible synchronization between his company's promotion (advertising) and his own promotion (personal selling). His morale can hardly help but benefit from a review of what his company is doing to pre-sell buyers, to enhance brand prestige. He can describe with pride how company advertising works to increase dealers' sales and profits. Because this activity is welcomed by merchants as a topic of conversation, the salesman has a story which helps increase repeat buying by old customers, helps attract new accounts, and helps achieve a larger volume of the tie-in advertising already mentioned. By informing middlemen of his company's advertising schedule, he gives them facts which will help guide their buying.

Salesmen for manufacturers who advertise probably have no more versatile tools available than reprints of actual advertisements. A salesman can mail one with his answer to a buyer's inquiry — an inquiry which may well have been stimulated by advertising. Or, he might mail a copy of an advertisement to introduce himself as he asks for an appointment. Or, he might attach one to a "thank you" note. Advertisement reprints can be used as identification cards when calling on buyers, and as visual aids when putting across a certain story effectively while making a presentation. They can be left with buyers as reminders or mailed to buyers as between-call reminders.

SALES PROMOTION

In the typical company, the activities of the sales department plus the activities of the advertising department do not add up to all the promotion the company uses. Manufacturers need not restrict their promotional activities to personal selling or to advertising, or, indeed, to a combination of these sales producing forces. Most think it desirable to add to these two forces some *sales promotion*. Today sales promotion is a loosely used term. It is used by different individuals to describe different activities. It has one meaning for retailers but another meaning for manufacturers. So, our first job is to delineate the sales promotion function for our use, and this delineation will be one appropriate for manufacturers.

Perhaps there is increasing unanimity in the feeling that sales promotion should consist of three basic areas — three activities that are close to personal selling and to advertising — yet not part of either. One of these areas is performing auxiliary jobs for the sales manager and his staff and for the advertising manager and his staff. In this same area, sales promotion operates as a liaison between the two functions of personal selling and advertising.

Coordination of Selling and Advertising

In its liaison duties, sales promotion serves as a go-between and as a coordinator. The sales promotion manager does *not* coordinate personal selling and advertising from a line position of authority *over* those two. Instead, his rank should be the same as theirs, and his coordinating should be that of an equal.

Selling. Many companies have found that the training of their salesmen should be an assignment given to the sales promotion department. In some cases, the sales promotion manager reports to the sales manager; in other cases, the two report to the same senior marketing executive. Regardless of organization chart, sales promotion would first teach the salesmen about their company, their products, their buyers, and then about how to sell.

It is the sales promotion staff who should teach the company's salesmen about advertising. This project breaks down into three phases, the first of which involves a general explanation of what advertising is and why sellers use it. This orientation provides an understanding and a basis for the next two phases. The second phase is devoted to the company's advertising policies and plans. Here salesmen are told of the role advertising plays in the company promotion program. The various advertising activities are described and then explained. A major aim of sales promotion in this second phase is to "sell" the proposed advertising to the salesmen, getting them enthusiastic and proud over it. The third phase involves the salesman's advertising relations with middlemen. Salesmen will be expected to "sell" the program to wholesalers and retailers in largely the same manner in which it was sold to them. Then, as a part of this third phase of learning about advertising, salesmen examine the advertising problems of their middlemen customers and qualify themselves to advise middlemen on those problems. The advertising portfolio, the salesman's most impressive selling aid when he is talking to a retailer, is put together by sales promotion. Salesmen are taught by sales promotion how to use this tool most effectively in their selling.

Sales promotion may be asked to be responsible for the long range or continuous education and stimulation of salesmen. The sales promotion manager is often in charge of sales meetings and conventions. It is not uncommon for salesmen's contests to be designed and executed by sales promotion. In companies whose missionary salesmen are under the line control of the sales promotion manager, and this is certainly a logical arrangement, the education and stimulation of those salesmen obviously should be duties of the same executive.

Advertising. The sales promotion department supplements and coordinates some of the work of the advertising department. As has been mentioned briefly, sales promotion puts together the advertising portfolios given to salesmen. These contain two types of material. First, copies of future advertisements are included, together with information about media and dates. The second type of material consists of items for use by middlemen, particularly by retailers, including advertising materials a retailer can order for his future use. Examples of these are mats of newspaper advertisements, commercials for the broadcast media, point-of-purchase items, and direct mail pieces that the salesman's company provides for use by retailers.

It is not at all common for persons in the advertising department to be in contact with a manufacturer's wholesalers and retailers. In most cases, the only *personal* contact with them is that of the company's salesmen; so, in the majority of instances, sales promotion handles advertising matters through the salesmen or directly with the customer. Sales promotion tries to solve the advertising problems of middlemen, often transmitting the solutions through the salesmen. The sales promotion department constantly strives to get each retailer to tie his promotion in with the manufacturer's promotion, an arrangement that makes the efforts of both retailer and manufacturer more productive. A successful joint promotion plan may often be attributed to the work of a salesman. If the manufacturer makes a cooperative advertising program available to retailers, its management is a responsibility of sales promotion. The handling of the manufacturer's advertising direct to the trade sometimes falls within the province of sales promotion.

Response to company advertisements are usually sent to the sales promotion department for processing. Those which come from prospects are forwarded at once to the appropriate salesmen for follow-up.

Dealer Relations

A second area of sales promotion consists of certain relationships and certain dealings between a manufacturer and his middlemen. In the area of selling there are problems, questions, issues, and activities for which the manufacturer's sales manager should not be responsible. There are matters relating to advertising which would be awkward and inappropriate for the company's advertising manager to try to handle. Indeed, dealers make requests and have problems in the area of management which by no stretch of the imagination could logically or properly be assigned to *either* sales manager or advertising manager. Relations with middlemen contribute so much to the company's over-all promotion program that they must be given serious and systematic attention — by the sales promotion department.

At this point it may be well to recall that point-of-purchase and direct mail are properly assigned to the sales promotion manager. The justification for placing point-of-purchase under the sales promotion manager is the fact that point-of-purchase materials are a dealer relations matter. As for direct mail, since the great bulk of it is directed at a manufacturer's middlemen, it makes sense to assign the direct mail medium to the department in charge of dealer relations. Direct mail designed by the manufacturer for use by his middlemen is also a part of this assignment.

Counsel on managerial matters is another aid which should be available to middlemen from the sales promotion staff. Retailers should be able to get suggestions and recommendations about store location, layout and equipment, and about organization from the manufacturer's sales promotion department. Guidance should be available for retailers in such operations as buying, pricing, credit, and control. Certainly the retailers should be able to get from this department all the advice and aid they should have in the three promotion areas of personal selling, advertising, and display. Manufacturers may help retailers build up their floor traffic by offering the retailers the use of demonstrators, or the use of an expert adviser who will spend a day or two in a retail store, analyzing customers' problems in the expert's field of specialization and suggesting solutions to them. Clothes, cosmetics, and cooking utensils are examples of such fields.

A final activity of the sales promotion department in its handling of dealer relations is one of stimulating retail salespersons. The dependence of manufacturers on distant, transitory, unidentified salespeople in retail stores is real. If it seems worthwhile, a manufacturer can undertake to do something about this group of retail salespersons. He may publish a house organ for them. His program may include sales manuals, sales training courses, films on selling, and sales instructions given by his salesmen. He may offer retail salespersons PM's (push money) to encourage their support of his merchandise. Gifts, discounts, and contests are other possible elements of a program to stimulate a retailer's sales force. All such activities are handled by sales promotion.

Consumer Stimulation and Services

The third area belonging to sales promotion is made up of certain tactics a manufacturer uses to stimulate his ultimate consumers and of his services to those final users of his products. Manufacturers like to feel in close touch with a considerable number of their ultimate customers, and they want just as many consumers as possible to feel close to them. The various elements which make up this third area of consumer stimulation and consumer services mesh with the other phases of the manufacturer's promotion.

Prominent in this area is the creation of *stimulants* intended to actuate consumers. A by-product of favorable consumer action is, of course, the demand that prompts middlemen to take favorable action in the form of buying. If consumers in great numbers can be induced, for example, to visit retail stores pre-sold on a manufacturer's brand of merchandise, then strong pressure is felt by those retailers to stock or, indeed, to feature that brand. It is not uncommon for the manufacturer to include the retailers in the promotion, as, for instance, when he stages a contest and makes the entry blanks available in retail stores. *Services* consist of a manufacturer's activities intended to make better buyers and happier users of individuals who purchase his wares.

Contests. One tactic guaranteed to provoke some consumer reaction is the consumer contest. The sales promotion manager is responsible for its design. He may schedule simultaneous contests for the company's middlemen and its salesmen. There are many objectives which may be gained by staging successful consumer contests. Likewise, there are many patterns or models along which a contest can be constructed. Some call for wordbuilding, some for slogans, some ask the contestants to add the last line to a poem or a limerick, some are based on puzzles, and many ask for a written statement or letter. Contests pose many problems, such as the type which will be most successful, the period for which the contest should run, the number, nature, and sizes of the prizes, the contest rules, the judging, and the ill-will of losers. If retailers are to have a part in the consumer contest, obtaining their cooperation is itself a problem.

Sampling. A second type of stimulation is the sample. Its virtue rests on the claim that nothing promotes the consumption of a good product so effectively as a trial of the product itself. Like contests, sampling confronts a manufacturer with troublesome problems. Is his product one that can be sampled satisfactorily? How can he determine the optimum size of sample — the size that is neither too large nor too small? Should it be a free offer? If not, what charge should be made? What method or methods of distribution should be adopted? Should retailers be given a role in the project? Retail cooperation is usually most desirable; seeing that retailers are well stocked is usually the first step in a sampling operation.

Premiums. For the many consumers who, at any given time, are close to buying and trying a manufacturer's product, only a small inducement is needed to cause such a purchase and trial. The inducement or bonus may well be, and often is, a premium — something of value given to the consumer at no cost, or at a very attractive price. Premiums can take many forms. They may be items of merchandise packed inside the containers which hold the manufacturer's products. They may be products offered free, or at a small price, with a combination purchase. They may be products which the consumer can get free or at greatly reduced prices if she has made a certain amount of purchases from a seller. Premiums, too, pose problems. Should the manufacturer insist that the premiums be self-liquidating? In other words, should the cash payment required defray the cost of the premium operation? What *is* a provocative premium? How should it be distributed? Should premiums be offered to wholesalers and retailers at the same time they are being offered to consumers? How likely is retail hostility; how can it be avoided? How can maximum middleman favor and goodwill be obtained as a result of a premium offer? These are typical of the questions the sales promotion manager must answer.

Consumer Services. The fourth and last element of sales promotion's consumer program is sometimes referred to as consumer education, but it seems that *consumer services* is a broader and more accurate term. The idea back of a consumer service program is that the better the manufacturer serves his ultimate consumers, the better customers they will be. Education, information, and advice before the purchase teach the consumer how to buy more expertly, and this is an absolute prerequisite to the continuation of cordial relations between manufacturer and consumer. Unless the consumer selects and buys wisely, his or her experience with the manufacturer's product can be nothing but unhappy. Once the prospective buyer becomes an owner of the item, he or she must use the product correctly and care for it properly to get the most out of it. Teaching consumers the use and care of his merchandise is part of a manufacturer's program of service to consumers.

Various techniques can be employed in providing consumer services. Tags, labels, and, indeed, the manufacturer's advertisements can be designed to give the consumer more information about the product. Literature can place valuable facts in consumers' hands. Lectures, training courses, and training schools are suitable for the manufacturers of some products. A speaker's bureau may be feasible. Tours of the plant and consumer house organs contribute to this program. Fashion shows and exhibits may be indicated. Facilities for answering inquiries from consumers, especially those inquiries sent in to the company by mail, are part of a complete set-up to give service to consumers. Such requests can be pre-purchase or post-purchase. Both types give the manufacturer a marvelous opportunity to cultivate consumer goodwill.

STUDY ASSIGNMENTS

1. Many men who sell for manufacturers and wholesalers call on retailers who need and welcome recommendations about their advertising. On what specific advertising problems might retailers appreciate advice?

2. One of the duties of a certain manufacturer's salesmen is to tell retailers of their firm's forthcoming advertising. What specific benefits can result from this?
3. In what ways do personal selling and advertising differ?
4. How does it happen that some successful firms use advertising and no personal selling, others use salesmen but no advertising, and still others use a combination of the two?
5. In what specific ways can a salesman benefit from reading his company's advertisements?
6. What do you consider to be the most basic facts that a salesman should have about his company's advertising?
7. Manufacturers who advertise should "merchandise their advertising." Just what does this involve?
8. When a company's sales promotion department functions efficiently, what specific benefits accrue to the company's salesmen?
9. If salesmen are to be retail management counselors in order to help their retailer customers, in what areas of management must they prepare themselves?
10. How can a salesman get retailers to use more of the promotion material his company provides?

CASE STUDY 5A

Joe Dirkin, salesman for a manufacturer of food products, was depressed because his last ten days had been exhausting and disappointing. When he returned to the hotel he found in his mail a letter from his company's sales promotion manager telling of a nationwide consumer contest which would be announced to the public shortly. Joe groaned and fumed. Why did he have to travel, to call on hostile and chiseling buyers, to have the impossible expected of him? Boy, how *he* would like to run those contests! After a heavy supper Joe went to bed, the contest still on his mind.

The sensation Joe had was of being conducted into the room where the company's directors held their meetings. His guide steered Joe to the head of the table and seated him in the head chair over which was a huge sign reading "Mr. Dirkin — Director of Consumer Contests." Around the table were seated the directors. As Joe looked at them, each seemed to fade away and to turn into a flaming question mark — then the question mark would fade out and change back into a director. This routine continued. The chairman of the board was the first to speak.

Chairman: Mr. Dirkin, your selling days are over. You are now in charge of our consumer contests. You won't mind, of course, giving us evidence of your ability to handle your new assignment. Questions?
Director A: Tell me, Mr. Dirkin, how will you know precisely when we should schedule a consumer contest? I'm anxious to know how you will support any future claim of yours to the effect that we should plan one.

Dirkin: Well, every so often you just feel or sense that it's time for one . . . or maybe all our competitors . . . or maybe sales are falling off . . . or maybe . . .

Director B: Let's get all the questions on the record, and then you can answer all of them at the same time. I want to know what is the best *type* of contest. Will you ask contestants to finish a "I like the product" statement in 25 words or less — or to name a new product or a new trade character — or to write a slogan or a letter?

Director C: I want to know *how long* the contest period should be. For example, do you favor one contest running 10 weeks — or one-contest-a-week for 10 weeks? Why do you prefer the one you do?

Director D: The *prizes* are the element that bothers me. What *is* the best assortment of prizes? Will you ask for *cash* prizes or for *merchandise* prizes? Or, do you know that *trips* make even better prizes? When you offer merchandise prizes, will you use automobiles, or appliances, or watches — or just what? How *many* prizes are best? Is one gigantic prize better than many small prizes? If the first prize is $10,000 should the second prize be $7,500 or $5,000 — or $2,500?

Director E: Being a lawyer, I'm naturally curious as to how you will protect the company against any legal difficulties or problems. What rules will you recommend? How can you insure against law suits? When does a contest become a lottery?

Director F: A related matter is that of judging. Mr. Dirkin, who will judge your contests? How will the winners be announced? Will you investigate the winners of the top prizes? How will you avoid the ill will of losers?

Director G: I'm wondering about promotion. How much promotion do contests need? Doesn't promotion money mean less for prizes? How will you advertise your contests? What is the ideal coverage and the ideal timing for this advertising?

Slowly the figures, the table, and the room faded away. The telephone was ringing to tell Joe that the time was seven o'clock. Joe headed for a shower with a faint smile on his face and an affectionate glance at his portfolio. "You know," he mused softly, "sometimes a fellow doesn't realize how well off he is."

QUESTION:

List the favorable and unfavorable aspects of consumer contests.

CASE STUDY 5B

The Allerton Manufacturing Company made a line of consumer products which reached the public in significant volume through drug stores. Soap, shaving cream, toothpaste, and shampoo were typical of the family of products, and the Allerton brands in these and other product classifications were among the leaders in their fields. The Allerton company was a heavy advertiser in all of the major advertising media; its point-of-purchase material was of high quality. Like all other manufacturers selling through drug stores, the Allerton company wanted as much effective use of its point-of-purchase items and as little waste in the medium as it could obtain.

At an Allerton sales convention, four men who found themselves at the same luncheon table one day were Mr. Lee, the sales training director, Talbot and Burns, two senior salesmen, and a recent college graduate, Tom Hafer, who had just joined the sales force. Mr. Lee brought up the topic of window displays.

Mr. Lee: Well, Talbot, you and Burns have more window displays in the drug stores in your territories than do most of our salesmen. Tell Tom, here, how you do it.

Talbot: There's nothing to it — after you make certain the retailer understands what his windows can do if he's smart in the way he uses them.

Burns: Sure, just about every retailer will listen and go along better once he realizes how costly each square foot of window space is and how much of his sales volume his windows are asked to produce. They've got to do their job in mighty few seconds, too.

Tom Hafer: Then those windows mean a lot to us.

Burns: I'll say they do. They are preferred positions because they are our last chance to influence shoppers. And, they make our ads in other media more effective by repeating the key ideas from those other ads.

Talbot: Another thing, Tom, our advertising messages in the point-of-purchase medium are the only ones to reach a buyer when she can act on her desire of the moment. No other medium speaks when all prerequisites to purchasing are present — customers, money, and merchandise. *Allerton* merchandise.

Burns: And, Tom, when you remember how often our products are bought on the spur of the moment — how many of those transactions are impulse purchases or reminder purchases, then you realize why we salesmen fight for those windows.

Mr. Lee: But, how do you get them?

Talbot: As soon as I know the retailer appreciates his window space, I tell him how good our display materials are. After all, no shopper sees our displays unless the retailer thinks enough of them to use them. So, I talk about stopping power, timeliness, attractiveness, impressiveness, inviting power, and, of course, sales power. I convince him that size of display, the single simple idea expressed in the copy, the features of light and motion (if they are included), the ease of installation, the opportunity to show prices, and the possibility of the suggestion selling of related merchandise all add up to a display he cannot afford to turn down.

Burns: Then there's just one point remaining. That is to convince the retailer that we manage our point-of-purchase advertising efficiently. We find out beforehand what he can use to best advantage. We tell him well in advance what will be available so he can incorporate our displays into his own promotion program. We see that he gets the displays in plenty of time and in the correct amount. We don't bundle up a whole season's displays and send them to him all in one shipment.

Talbot: That's right. The retailer sees that our soundly designed and soundly managed displays will increase his sales, his store traffic, his turnover, and his profits. Those are what he's in business for.

QUESTIONS:

1. What are some of the factors influencing a retailer's choice of which point-of-purchase materials to use?
2. Suggest a few ways in which a manufacturer can reduce the waste in his point-of-purchase advertising.

CHAPTER 6

THE SALESMAN'S PRODUCTS

Product knowledge is a "must." The Vice-President in Charge of Sales of the Hawaiian Pineapple Company expresses an opinion widely held by sales executives when he writes:

> To be a salesman in the full meaning of the word, the individual must be equipped with a thorough knowledge of his product — how it is produced and distributed — and he should be an authority. This does not necessarily mean that he must have technical knowledge or that he needs it — but he must know in infinite detail all there is to be known that is of interest to the purchaser about the product he offers. He must be sure of the facts. Superficial knowledge is always dangerous, and it is particularly dangerous in selling work because it leads to erroneous statements or statements that are misleading.

Product knowledge has a single purpose — to help a salesman become a better, more professional salesman. This means that he needs to collect those facts about his merchandise which will enable him to do a more efficient job than he could do without them.

The greatest single use made of product information is that of showing prospects how and what they will gain by buying. A minor use of product information yet one that is worthwhile is that of supplying facts that have conversational or curiosity value. Such facts may aid indirectly in selling.

What should a salesman know about his products? The following outline indicates how wide this knowledge can be. The rest of this chapter is devoted to discussion of these product facts.

General Information	Physical Product
Origin and history	Sizes and weights
Research and development	Colors, models, design
Major improvements	Place in product line
Identification	Nature, source, cost of materials
Brand name	Specifications
Trade mark	Packaging
Trade character	Method of manufacture
Competitive position	Quality control
Availability or supply	Prices, discounts, terms
Talking points	Profit
Related products	

Product in Operation	*Services*
Uses and applications	Credit
User benefits or satisfactions	Shipping and delivery
Performance potential	Installation
Limitations	Instruction for use
Operation and service	Maintenance
Cost of operating & maintaining	Support
Cost of replacement	

PRODUCT FACTS ARE ESSENTIAL

There is no information more indispensable than product knowledge if the salesman is to do an acceptable job. Proof of this can be had from a quick glance at four angles of selling.

Confidence

One aspect revolves around confidence. It is impossible to imagine a successful salesman who does not know just what his product is and what it will do. He simply cannot get along without being familiar with its capacities, performance, and limitations. Consider just one phase of the sales conference — the demonstration. Before an effective, showmanlike demonstration can be planned, much less executed with professional skill, the salesman must know precisely what he can count on from his product.

In addition to increasing his confidence in the product, the salesman's product information increases his confidence in himself. If he feels that he has full knowledge of his wares, he need not be reluctant to make an appointment with even the most hard-bitten, notoriously ill-tempered prospect. Confidence in product and self sensed by prospective buyers encourages their confidence.

Enthusiasm

The salesman hopes that he can make the prospect see the product as he does, be this a matter of quality, value, dependability, style, profit, or otherwise. To bring this about, enthusiasm is required, because, as we discussed earlier, enthusiasm increases the salesman's effectiveness in convincing prospects. The salesman cannot be fully enthusiastic unless he knows all the good things about his wares.

Professional Selling

As we have seen, both business and individuals buy for use, and business buys for resale. Professional salesmanship shows buyers-for-use how best to use the proper products, and it shows buyers-for-resale how best to merchandise what they stock.

Needs vary among prospects. Mr. A cannot afford what Mr. B can. Mr. C must be able to defend his purchases to his wife, whereas Mr. D is a happy bachelor responsible to no one. Mr. E uses the item for one purpose, Mr. F for another. Now add the fact that products vary. Design, size, or color that satisfies Mr. A may not please Mr. B. In a word, products vary in their capacity to give satisfaction and benefits to buyers.

The conclusion is clear. If our salesman is to sell only to persons who will benefit from buying, and this is how the professional sells, he must have adequate product information so as to be able to match product with need.

This matching of product and need is considered sound by the general manager of Sweet's Catalog Service:

> A good salesman is one who is thoroughly familiar with the product or service he has to sell and who can find out enough about his potential customer's needs to make sales which will satisfy those needs most effectively and economically. Knowledge of why a potential buyer should buy is just as important for a salesman as knowledge of what he has for sale. The good salesman has to have both. At least in selling the technical products, the marriage of the seller's product information with the buyer's need for the product results in the birth of an order. Product information is delivered from seller to buyer through advertising, cataloging and personal selling — each with a different, and dominant, complementary function in the procedure for producing orders efficiently.

Income

A fourth and final angle about product facts involves the salesman's income. Earnings have a way of fluctuating in the same direction as sales volume. Anything that increases sales tends to increase income. The more product knowledge the salesman has, the more merchandise he should be able to sell. More product facts will make the salesman better able to handle excuses and objections. They will help him to convert desire into an actual purchase more often.

CAN SALESMEN KNOW TOO MUCH ABOUT PRODUCTS?

Sometimes an informal discussion develops around the question of whether or not a salesman can know too much about his merchandise. Although a negative answer to the question is obviously correct, additional comments are in order. Two pitfalls in this matter must be considered. The first to be avoided is the mistake of spending too much time in *studying* product features to the neglect of user-benefits. The second is the mistake of *talking* too much about the product and too little about what it will do for the buyer.

Because he is apt to be attracted to and impressed by product features, the beginning salesman is often found spending much time and many words in describing them to prospects. Nothing could be more unfortunate than too much stressing of product features, because nothing is more certain to cause a "so what?" reaction on the part of the prospect. The salesman, instead of selling product features, should sell the effects and results of buying. He should not sell insulation — he should offer economy; he should not sell a new automobile — he should stress the pride of ownership; she should not sell dancing instruction — she should guarantee popularity; she should not sell a black evening dress — she should assure a stunning social success.

Most salesmen cannot carry in their minds every product fact about every item they represent. Catalogues, manuals, and such make any attempt to do so unnecessary. When a salesman represents a wide line or a large family of products, he correctly concentrates on the more important facts of his more important lines, and acquires perfect mastery of the key facts that help him sell.

The proper conclusions, then, seem to be that the salesman cannot know too much about his product and that he does not need to memorize every possible product fact. He must recognize that the greatest danger he must guard against consists of overburdening his talk with so many technical data that either confusion or indifference results on the part of the customer.

Collecting product information is virtually never a waste of time. Sooner or later, the salesman will be asked for, or have an opportunity to use, every bit of product knowledge he has.

PRODUCT HISTORY

Product history has two phases. The first is generic and has to do with product type. Many products have interesting, perhaps fascinating backgrounds that can be discovered by the salesman who takes the trouble to explore. Such a salesman asks: who made or invented the first product of its kind? where? when? how long did it last? what did it look like? what did it cost? how large was it? what was it called? how did it operate? what was the public reaction to it?

Shoes, for instance, were first of the sandal type, then evolved into a bag-like covering, then a boot, and finally a shoe. A study of the evolution of incubators, cooking utensils, or timepieces would undoubtedly disclose interesting developments.

The Hershey Chocolate Corporation is a company which thinks its salesmen should know about the history and background of the products they sell. The Hershey booklet, *The Story of CHOCOLATE and COCOA*, starts with this section:

The Discovery of Chocolate

In the year 1519, Hernando Cortez, the Spanish explorer and conqueror of Mexico, learned from the Aztec Indians the secret of preparing a delicious new beverage. History tells us that the Emperor Montezuma entertained the Spaniards at elaborate ceremonies during which the guests were served golden goblets filled with this wonderfully palatable and refreshing drink.

Thus did the first white man come to know chocolate.

"Cacahoatl" was the Aztec name for the seeds of the tropical tree from which this beverage was produced. The Spaniards contracted this to "cacao" and called these seeds "cacao" beans, a term which we have since Americanized to "cocoa" beans.

The Indians of Mexico believed that the cacao tree was of divine origin. They valued the beans highly, not only as a food, but also as a medium of exchange. We are told that a fair purchase price for a good slave was one hundred cacao beans.

When Cortez returned to Spain, he created great excitement with his new discovery. For many years, the Spaniards refused to divulge the secret of extracting "chocolatl" from the "cacao" bean. Being highly valued as a beverage, the price was beyond the reach of all but the wealthy, who believed that only they should be permitted to enjoy such luxuries. It was through the royal courts that the drink became known in other European countries.

In the eighteenth century, chocolate houses became fashionable in England, and commercial production was begun as the popular demand increased. The first manufacturing process was merely one of making a paste from the roasted and shelled cacao beans since chocolate even then was consumed only in liquid form.

In 1720, Linnaeus, the Swedish botanist, gave the cacao bean its official name, "Theobroma Cacao" which, literally translated from the Greek, is "Cacao, Food of the Gods." Not knowing the diet habits of supernatural beings, we cannot be certain that this description is accurate, but we can say that in chocolate, Mother Nature has provided one of the most delightful flavors in her realm.

The second phase of product history concerns the record of the salesman's particular brand of the product. Here he should be able to trace its development from its beginning to the present. He should know the significant dates of change or improvement and some of the public events that occurred about the same time. Such events include wars, depressions, fashion changes, the appearance of a popular novel, and outstanding accomplishments in sports, aviation, and the like.

Product history is no exception to the principle that each type of product knowledge should be sales-slanted, if possible. It can illustrate and explain such things as product improvement, reduction in cost, and proved performance.

PRODUCTION
Raw Materials

Knowledge of product "ingredients" should help the salesman sell. For this reason, he is not so much interested in collecting a file of facts as he is a working fund of selling ammunition.

Learning what goes into the product starts, of course, with knowledge of raw materials. This includes the source of the materials, their origins, how they occur, how they are located, and how they are extracted and transported. The next thing to learn is the "why" of the company's use of those specific raw materials and why substitutes would be unsatisfactory.

A man's shoe is an interesting study in raw materials. Into it go 300 pieces of material from all over the world. Among the hides and skins used are those from sheep, goats, kangaroos, cattle, snakes, lizards, shark, alligators, seals, pigs, and horses. Quality of hides and skins is affected by the climatic conditions in which the animals are raised, the way in which they feed, their exposure to the elements, and the manner in which the hides and skins are taken from the animals.

Silverware is another case in point. The law requires that the quality of all sterling be 925/1000 fine; so, as a raw material all sterling is of the same quality. This puts all the salesmen of sterling on an equal basis so far as raw materials are concerned.

Manufacturing Processes and Standards

No salesman needs try to know so much about what goes on in the manufacturing part of the business as the production manager, but at the same time he should be well enough posted to do a satisfactory job of selling. Knowledge about this phase of the product gives him more confidence in himself and his merchandise, supplies him with more selling points, invites the prospect to be more confident, and supplies answers to questions that will be asked.

In regard to manufacturing processes, the basic thing the salesman should be able to do is to trace the production sequence, starting with the raw materials and following through their various processes and treatments until they become finished items. An interesting comment on the proper sequence in manufacturing comes from Hickey-Freeman Company:

In the making of ordinary ready-to-wear clothing, the usual procedure is for the manufacturer to decide at what retail price the garment is to be sold ... and then to figure backward to determine how much he can afford to spend for materials, trimmings, and workmanship. The Hickey-Freeman method, on the other hand, is first to experiment and find out the best possible way to make the garment and then to lay out specifications for the maintenance of that standard throughout the years. Thus, Hickey-Freeman Clothes are made up to a standard and not down to a cost.

As a rule, neither prospect nor customer sees the items in production, yet each may want to know many things about how they are made. They may want construction explained in terms of how, how long, where, and why. They may be curious about the hand processes that reflect care and custom attention and about the machine processes that insure accuracy, uniformity, cleanliness, and economy. They undoubtedly will demand details about secret or exclusive steps. For this knowledge, their primary source is the salesman.

Closely related to manufacturing processes are manufacturing standards. Personnel standards are seen in the qualifications demanded of production employees, machine standards reflected in the maintenance each machine gets, inspection standards in the narrow tolerances allowed, and general standards in the amount by which the product's purity or accuracy exceeds that required by law or competition. The inspection policy of Fenestra Steel Residence Casements is described to their salesmen:

1. *Raw Material.* A completely equipped metallurgical laboratory is maintained to analyze samples of all steel received from the mills to make certain that our specifications for low carbon, hot rolled, new billet steel have been followed. Sample sections are also inspected to insure that the thickness and over-all dimensions are within the close tolerances allowed the rolling mill.
2. *Machining Operations.* Cut-off dimensions, location of holes, slots, etc., are carefully checked before production runs are started.
3. *Welding Operations.* Samples of work from the various machines are inspected at regular intervals to guarantee uniformity of welds.
4. *Assembly Operations.* Each casement is inspected for tightness between casement leaf and the frame, fit of interior bars, especially at intersection point, and general over-all appearance.
5. *Bonderizing.* Temperatures (thermostatically controlled) of water, chemical solutions, drying towers, baking ovens, etc., are checked several times each day. Each shipment of paint is analyzed to insure proper proportions of the various ingredients according to our specifications.
6. *Hardware.* Locking handles and sill operators are checked for proper location of holes, operation, and quality of finish. Sets of hardware,

selected at random from stock, are tried on casements to further
assure us that hardware fits and operates properly.

7. *Free Lance Inspection.* Operating under instructions from the Chief
Inspector, free lance inspectors drop in to the various departments
from time to time to inspect the work of the inspectors. The free
lance inspectors assure us that the high quality specifications we set
up governing the manufacture of Fenestra Casements are followed to
the letter and, also, guard against the element of human errors and
and mistakes going undetected by the regular inspector.

If each member of a family of products is manufactured in a separate
plant, the salesman can give this specialization credit for maintaining
the uniform quality of each line. If there is continuous quality control
from raw materials to finished products, the salesman can point out the
resulting protection against defective units. Once again, the reminder is
appropriate that facts about manufacturing processes and standards must
be converted into reasons for buying.

RESEARCH

The two types of product research of interest and value to salesmen
are *manufacturing* and *marketing*.

Manufacturing Research

The salesman needs to know the nature of manufacturing research,
where it is carried on, under whose supervision, with the use of what
facilities, and above all, with what purposes and results. By way of
examples, the company might be experimenting with a new type of machine, a change in manufacturing sequence, other methods of storing raw
materials, more complete utilization of fuel, or the use of substitute raw
materials.

In lines in which design is quite important, the salesman does well
to check on research activities. He can benefit from knowing how many
designs were made and discarded before the right one was created. A detailed account that will impress prospects can be made of the difficulties
encountered in perfecting any one design and of the care, thought, cost,
and responsibility attached to bringing forth a new design that is effective
and useful.

Manufacturing research done by certain outside firms frequently
supplies the salesman with selling points about the product. If the maker
of a line of mattresses has the U. S. Testing Company subject its brand
to the "torture" test, the results may well become reasons for buying.

Still in the line of manufacturing research, the salesman's company
can secure product specifications from some group of experts, from some

outstanding professional personalities, or from some well-known, reputable magazine. The company can go back to its factories, build the product according to the specifications it received, and then tell both the dealers and the public from whence came the specifications.

Gaines Division of General Foods describes its manufacturing research activities briefly in this manner:

> In the hilly country outside of Ridgefield, Connecticut, you will find the Gaines Research Kennels. These large, modern, well-equipped kennels were established in order to provide a place for the actual, practical study of the problems involved in the feeding, breeding, housing, and care of dogs. The kennels work constantly to provide information to Gaines in order that the general welfare of dogs is furthered. These kennels also function to enchance the name of Gaines and to increase its prestige throughout the dog world.
>
> *What Is Being Done.* For these purposes, property was secured, pure-bred dogs purchased, and the kennel staffed with the most able and expert dog men available to us. By feeding our products to our dogs and observing the effects on the dogs' health and general condition, we have conclusive proof that our product is *right.* Continual feeding projects are always being made of new and improved formulas as well as competitive products against the basic formula, which we consider the finest type that can be produced.
>
> *Scientific Food Testing With Pure Breeds.* Our breeding program is conducted solely with pure-breds, because it is only through such breeding that better dogs can be produced. Also, it has been proved that only through the use of pure breeds can scientific food testing be done. With pure breeds, definite characteristics of certain lines can be determined and properly discounted in judging test results, whereas such determination is not possible in cross breeds.

Market Research

Market research, the second type of product research, also can make the salesman's job easier. Information is needed by the salesman about what projects are undertaken and for what reasons, and about whether the projects are executed by the company or turned over to a commercial research organization. The salesman should know as much as he conveniently can about the studies that are made, and he certainly should learn about the findings.

Examples of market research with product significance include the determination of consumer attitudes and habits, acceptance of the package, selection of a brand name, and the identification and evaluation of the market for a new product.

Statistics are needed on the trend of public thinking and on the thinking of the trade in regard to the product. If he sells to wholesalers, the salesman should know what retailers and consumers do and think about his merchandise. If he sells to retailers, he should know what consumers think and do; and if he sells to consumers, he should know how various types of consumers react.

If the manufacturer of a luxury item like an electric blanket, for instance, finds that his largest market is among medium and medium-low income groups, retailers will be more inclined to stock that item. If market research reveals that an electric blanket can be sold to one out of every five purchasers of a mattress or a set of springs, the retailer will be even more willing to handle the blanket.

Use of Research Data

Favorable research results can be used to help sell because they can offer evidence that a product is just what the prospect needs, the best quality for the price. When his company uses tested methods and builds up a store of facts over years of research, the salesman is better able to meet the exact needs and wants of prospects and customers.

As for manufacturing research, product quality can be improved as a result of a continuous research program. Reductions in price can result. Prospects can be assured that a never-ending study of all manufacturing phases is being made and that operating methods and practices are being subjected to ceaseless scrutiny.

Market research influences both buyers who use the product and those who resell. Both groups are pleased to know that the manufacturer is making a popular product year after year, and that he keeps a sensitive finger on the consumer's pulse.

THE PRODUCT LINE

When a salesman is selling a single item, knowing the what and why of his line is a simple matter. When he handles several or many items, the same technique that he uses with the single product applies. This technique consists of identifying the significant points on which he must have facts and then acquiring those facts. Care should be exercised by the salesman selling a broad line of items in learning the acceptable minimum about each item, for he must know his full line before he can present it. Unless he watches carefully, he is apt to postpone learning about the latest addition to his line, and this lack of product information will prevent him from presenting the addition effectively if at all.

The Physical Product

The first thing the salesman needs to know is his physical product. The salesman must be able to describe his merchandise clearly and adequately, demonstrating his familiarity with whatever trade terms or abbreviations there may be. He must know the product's main features and what needs they satisfy.

A good example of product features comes from the pressure cooker field, where the product can be of the outside-closure type or of the inside-closure type. The outside-closure type has a cover that fits over the edge of the pan and locks in position by a series of lugs and flanges. The inside-closure pans have either flexible covers or rigid covers. Both kinds rely on a combination of steam pressure and hooks to keep the cover in place. It would be interesting to know how often salesmen have been asked about the merits of each type of closure.

Patents are another phase of the physical product, and the most valuable are those on features that make the brand superior to all others. Specifications for manufacture are another phase, and two things to know about them are source and quality.

Two final aspects of the physical product concern type and selection. As for *type*, the salesman needs to know what type he should recommend for different purposes. This calls for a knowledge of such things as dimensions, capacity, design, and adaptability. *Selection* refers to choices available to buyers, and it involves models, grades, sizes, colors, styles, quantity per case, minimum orders, and dealer assortments. As used here, type and selection overlap.

Composition of Line

Second in importance is composition of the line. If the salesman happens to work for a spark plug manufacturer who makes only spark plugs and makes them only under a single brand, his line is the one brand of plugs. If his company manufacturers a family of products, the salesman may benefit from knowing which was the original item, the sequence of additions, and how, when, and why each was added.

PRICES AND DISCOUNTS

Prices and discounts are of vital interest to buyers and, consequently, to salesmen, even though the typical salesman's interest is probably considerably greater than his pricing authority and influence. Despite his limited control, a salesman's ideas about prices are of significance — to his company in making pricing decisions, and to himself in justifying and "selling" his prices to buyers. As for the buyer group, the importance of price varies from buyer to buyer and from time to time. Our salesman is not ready to sell if he is ignorant in the area of prices and discounts or even if he feels on the defensive about them.

The salesman should know the pricing philosophy, policy, and procedure of his firm. He should understand why his prices are above the market, at the market, or below the market; he should know the logic back of his firm's price lining, including the individual price levels and the gaps between them. He must be agile in computing prices, and he must know what discretion is his about adjusting them.

List price is of less interest to buyers than is the net cost, delivered, of the salesman's product and of competing products. This fact demands that the salesman be posted on discounts and terms of sale. He must recognize that if his prices are soundly set they will be matched by product utility or satisfaction and that the buyer has no grounds on which to ask for an "extra" discount. These "extra" discounts reduce profits and incur the wrath of sales managers; they can be illegal.

List Price

List prices are printed, published, basic; they are found on price lists, in advertisements, and, most important, in sellers' catalogues. List price can be thought of as the *highest* price because it is usually subject to discounts. These discounts are often printed on separate discount sheets.

Why do sellers use list prices and discounts? When prices are being changed, the seller can have a new discount sheet printed rather than an entire catalogue. The seller can adjust his real prices to various groups of buyers, quoting one group perhaps $20\% - 10\% - 5\%$ off list and another group $10\% - 10\% - 5\%$ off. He may even quote an additional 10% or 5% off to an individual buyer. List price in the catalogue may suggest to retailers what they should charge to consumers, and retailers can show the catalogues to consumers without revealing the retail markup. Competitors may have more difficulty in discovering a manufacturer's prices.

Net Price

When one reduces list price by the discounts applicable, he arrives at net price.

Zone Price

Sometimes a seller divides his total market into a number of geographic areas ("West of the Mississippi," "Southwest," "Pacific Coast") and quotes the same price to all buyers within any one area. These are "zone" prices. Because like buyers in a given zone pay the same freight rate, each gets the product involved at the same delivered cost as every other buyer in that zone.

F.O.B. Price

F.O.B. means *free on board* — on board a ship, a railroad car, a motor truck — at the seller's factory, farm, mill, or warehouse. In other words, the seller defrays any transportation charges *to* the F.O.B. point, and the buyer pays transportation *from* it. It is obvious that F.O.B. prices cause different buyers to have different cost-of-goods figures.

Guaranteed Price

The guarantee here is against certain reductions in the seller's prices. A manufacturer, for example, might agree to protect a customer on price cuts the manufacturer makes after the customer places his order but before the customer takes title to the goods, receives the goods, uses the goods, or resells the goods. Typically, the manufacturer would refund to the customer the amount of the unit reduction for those units the buyer still has on hand.

The guarantee can be a powerful selling point in getting big orders, or early orders, or long-term buying contracts. The guarantee may be a "must" if there is considerable fluctuation in prices. It is risky in that the seller may be forced to cut his prices if *his* competitors cut *their* prices.

Quantity Discounts

These are offered to buyers in return for buying in large volume. They encourage buyers to place large orders and discourage hand-to-mouth, small-scale purchasing. Discounts usually are for single orders but may be cumulative, applicable to a buyer's purchases for a month or even for a year. They may apply to one product — or to two or more of the seller's products.

Quantity discounts permit a seller to share his savings (administrative, production, marketing) from volume operation with the customers who make that large-scale operation possible. This feature, incidentally, makes *cumulative* quantity discounts and discounts on two or more of a seller's products somewhat difficult to justify. Premiums, deals, and free goods are close kin to quantity discounts; they, too, permit price to vary with the amount bought.

Trade Discounts

When a manufacturer sells to different *types* of middlemen, he may offer trade or functional discounts. He groups buyers according to their position in the distribution channel, according to the jobs or functions they perform for him. Status of buyer is the key issue, not quantity bought. Retailers might be allowed $33\frac{1}{3}\%$ on their selling prices, and wholesalers might be allowed $16\frac{2}{3}\%$ on their selling prices. Discounts for each group are intended to cover the typical buyer's operating costs plus an amount for profit.

Cash Discounts

These are incentives that the seller offers for prompt payment for merchandise bought. A common base is the invoice date; a common set of terms is "2/10, net 30." Suppose the order totals $100 and the invoice date is August 1. If the buyer pays by August 11, the seller will accept $98 as payment in full; otherwise, the buyer is obligated to pay the full $100 not later than August 31. Both seller and buyer are said to gain from cash discounts.

Price Control

When a manufacturer exercises price control, the buyer-for-resale is not permitted to determine his own selling prices. This prevents price wars among dealers, and thus encourages small retailers to stock the line. They need not fear being undersold by a larger outlet that can take a smaller profit because of large volume.

If resale price maintenance is a major consideration in the industry of which the salesman's company is one unit, then his company will either decide to cooperate with the mass retailers and the consumers by not dictating resale prices, or it will decide to align itself with the wholesaler-independent retailer group and specify resale prices. Regardless of which side the company chooses, the salesman will be criticized by the opposing side. He should learn the "reason why" for his company's choice and then learn to present that reason convincingly.

BRAND NAME

The young salesman's first interest in his brands is in learning the relationships between or among them. If the premium brand is rated at 100%, the salesman should be able to place correct ratings on the lower-quality lines. The origin or construction of the brand names may be good for a bit of dialogue between salesman and prospect. The Eastman Kodak Company says its product was named in this fashion:

The Origin of The Name "Kodak"

The origin of the name "Kodak" has run the gamut of human curiosity. Romance, mystery, superstition, legend — all have been in the minds of thousands of persons who have tried to guess the source of the name.

As a matter of fact, there is nothing obscure about it. The word came straight from the mind of George Eastman, who coined it.

In 1888 George Eastman designed the Kodak. The photographic inventor also devised the name for his new instrument — devised it by experimenting with the letters of the alphabet in much the same way in which he was accustomed to trying out the various elements of a camera.

The mental processes that went into the name "Kodak" are quite simple. Mr. Eastman wanted a word easily spelled and readily pronounced in English or in a foreign tongue. To that end, he toyed with the the letters of the alphabet until he had arranged the since famous combination of consonants that remain constant and vowels that have no greater vagaries of accent than are found between Kent and Kansas.

Mr. Eastman's own etymology of the word is contained in an interview:

> I devised the name myself. A trade-mark should be short, vigorous, incapable of being misspelled to an extent that will destroy its identity, and — in order to satisfy trade-mark laws — it must mean nothing. If the name has no dictionary definition, it must be associated only with your product and you will cease to be known as producing a "kind" of anything.
>
> The letter "K" had been a favorite with me — it seemed a strong, incisive sort of letter. Therefore, the word I wanted had to start with "K." Then it became a question of trying out a great number of combinations of letters that made words starting and ending with "K." The word "Kodak" is the result. Instead of merely making cameras and camera supplies, we made Kodaks and Kodak supplies. It became the distinctive word for our products.

Terse, abrupt to the point of rudeness, literally bitten off by ice-cutting consonants at both ends, the word snaps like a Kodak shutter.

SALES ANGLES

This last section shows how product knowledge may be expressed as reasons for buying. The section is merely illustrative and does not attempt to be complete.

The salesman of an electric blanket may point out that four new and improved precision resistance elements are employed to insure absolute control. He could, of course, say it more simply.

A pressure pan's features may be translated into four user-benefits: safety, simplicity of operation, convenience, and dependability of performance.

A large, talented designing staff may enable the company to maintain pattern leadership. The superiority in design helps retailers get higher prices.

If his is a one-product company, the salesman will refer often and proudly to the advantages of specialization and concentration in turning out a better product, and he will boast that his item is not a side line or a fill-in. If he is selling a family or line of products, he extols the popularity of his company, the services that a family of products can give buyers, the research that resulted in a well-balanced line, the economies and other benefits of concentrating one's purchases, the possibility of future additions to the family, and the variety that is broader than that of any other manufacturer.

When he has a number of price lines, the salesman can list first the features that all lines have in common, then the additional features that are found only in the premium line.

If his prices are above the market, the salesman points to top quality and reminds the prospect that the lowest-priced item is rarely the most economical, that quality is remembered long after price has been forgotten. He says that his company, knowing that the quality trade includes the most satisfactory customers, will never sacrifice quality in order to be competitive. If his prices are at the market, the salesman points out how he offers a better buy than his competitors. If his prices are below the market, he emphasizes economy, volume, and competitive position.

His price structure may give the merchant a generous markup that will greatly increase profits, and the inducement to take his cash discount may be made irresistible.

Whether or not his company manufactures for private branding, the salesman can show how the policy results in buyer-benefits.

PRODUCT PERFORMANCE

A product is more than just a collection of parts or an assembly of mechanical and technical features. To a buyer, it is a means of solving his problems, of satisfying his wants, of attaining his aims, and of increasing his sum total of satisfaction. For these reasons, the salesman must know what his line will and will not do if he is to be certain that prospects will be helped.

Here are some important product questions to which the salesman should know answers:

What is it designed to do?
How does it do it?
How long will it last?
What care and maintenance should it get?
For what will it substitute?
Who are its proper users?
What caution should be used in operating?
What won't it do?
How can the user insure optimum performance?
How should it be installed or applied?

Carrier

Standard Product Warranty

We warrant every Carrier product to be free from defects in material and workmanship under normal use and service, and we will, within one year from date of original
installation, repair or replace without cost to the customer any part, assembly or portion thereof which shall be returned to our factory, transportation charges prepaid, and
which our inspection shall show to be thus defective. This one year warranty plan does
not apply to any parts not supplied or designated by Carrier. This warranty applies
only to Carrier products installed within the boundaries of continental United States.

CARRIER CORPORATION, Syracuse, New York

Installation Date   Cabinet Serial No.   Compressor Serial No.

Carrier Corp.

**Complete knowledge of his product's warranty or guarantee is necessary if the salesman is to
prevent or handle difficult situations.**

At the risk of being repetitious, the statement is made again that the
saleman must sell what the product will do, not the product itself — because buyers buy future satisfaction, not merchandise.

COMPANY SUPPORT OF THE PRODUCT

Just where and how a company stands behind its wares constitutes
essential product information. There will be reasonable and unreasonable
requests, honest and dishonest claims made by buyers who regret their
purchases.

Product guarantees form one type of company support. Information
on guarantees should include the precise terms of the guarantee, the
mechanics of handling, and, for the salesman's own personal knowledge,
the strictness with which the company observes the letter of the agreement.
Here is the Black & Decker Mfg. Company's guarantee:

> Every Black & Decker product has been carefully inspected before
> shipment, and we guarantee to correct any defect caused by faulty
> material or workmanship. Our obligation assumed under this guarantee
> is limited to the replacing of any part or parts which prove to our satis-
> faction, upon examination, to have been defective, and which have not

been misused or carelessly handled. The complete unit must be returned to one of our factory service branches or to our factory, transportation charges prepaid. We reserve the right to decline responsibility when repairs have been made or attempted by others. No other guarantee, written or verbal, is authorized on our products.

Product service is another type of support. The necessary facts here include the amount, kind, and availability of company service; the details about charges for it; and the time limit for the services.

The handling of defective merchandise is another phase of this subject. Time limits, repairs, credit memorandums, refunds, replacements, proof, and transportation charges are typical of the matters involved.

What the company does about adjustments and returns is properly included in thinking about company support of its product. The returned goods policy of Merck & Company is quoted:

The quality of Merck products is fully guaranteed at the time of original sale. Since chemicals are affected by temperature, light, moisture, improper storage, and other conditions beyond its control, Merck & Co., Inc., cannot be held responsible for deterioration due to such causes when out of its hands. All Merck products from a retailer's stock must be returned through the wholesale distributor from whom originally purchased, subject to the following conditions:

Returnable for exchange or credit:

1. Outdated merchandise bearing an expiration date
2. Quality complaints
3. Faulty containers
4. Merchandise declared to be overstock to be returned subject to valuation on a salvage basis
5. All household products
6. Bilhuber products
7. All specialties

Not returnable for exchange or credit:

1. Products which have spoiled because of age or improper storage and whose quality and/or value are not worth while for remanufacture.
2. Items in unsalable condition because of broken seals or damaged packages. (Damages in transit should be claimed from the carriers.)
3. Merchandise acquired in a fire or bankruptcy sale.
4. Merchandise discontinued from our lines.

NOTE: No returns are to be made to Merck & Co., Inc., by the wholesaler without prior authorization. Such returns, when made, are to be on a prepaid basis and subject to laboratory examination for credit at invoiced or current market price, whichever is the lower.

The salesman's first duty in these matters is to know what his company's policy is and to make sure that every buyer understands clearly and correctly the company's position so that friction will not be caused by misinterpretation. He must also know exactly what his personal authority and responsibility are. Finally, he should transform his company's support policies into reasons for buying.

RELATED PRODUCTS

In learning all he can about what his product will do for its buyers and just how it can be best applied to users' needs, a salesman frequently must acquire information about complementary or auxiliary products and matters.

The man who sells gasoline will need more than a layman's knowledge about tires, spark plugs, batteries, and carburetors. One who sells vacuum cleaners must know rug construction and types of dirt found in rugs. The salesman of furniture needs to have a better than casual acquaintance with accessories of various types. And the paint salesman should be familiar with period furniture. Windows should be sold only by an individual who knows both architecture and construction. Farm machinery, cash registers, systems, and insurance are random examples of other products that make extra demands of the persons who sell them.

TALKING POINTS

Product knowledge is of complete usefulness only when converted into user-advantages. Because a product is only as good as the salesman makes it appear, one of the first things the young salesman should do is to make as long a list as he can of the advantages his product gives buyers. This process enables an imaginative salesman to change an impersonal, inanimate, and inarticulate bit of merchandise into an almost irresistible something that will help the buyer get what he wants.

General Talking Points

Some talking points about some products are capable of such universal application that they can be used by any salesman in presenting a particular product to any type of prospect. Such talking points can be used effectively by manufacturers, by middlemen, by individuals — in fact, by any seller. Here are seven examples of general talking points.

1. The performance of the brand in some famous event. Examples are tires in the Indianapolis 500 mile race, ammunition used by a championship rifle team, or the make of bar bell with which a weight-lifting record was made.

2. The percentage of the total market accounted for by the brand. This could be 6 or 60 per cent and be impressive in either case, if presented correctly.

3. The ratio by which the brand is preferred by experts.

4. The result of the brand's being tested by prominent specialists.

5. The seal of approval of a prominent, respected magazine.

6. Approval of Underwriters' Laboratories, Inc.

7. The versatility of the product. (An automobile fan might clear the windshields of ice and sleet in winter, mist and fog in spring and fall, and cool the car in summer.)

Talking Points for Users

Some talking points particularly interest and influence those buyers who buy to use. Seven examples of consumption talking points follow.

1. The factory-trained service the buyer gets.

2. Sales volume.

3. The number of units sold years ago that are still on the job.

4. Superiority to competition.

5. Identity of prominent users.

6. Total number of satisfied users.

7. Product features that are consumer advantages.

Resale Talking Points

In one sense, the typical middleman is interested in only one matter — how to increase net profit. Despite this fact, the salesman who sells to middlemen quickly learns that the two stories of how to increase sales and how to cut costs are inadequate because they are too general. As a result, the salesman constructs a list of resale talking points of which these seven are examples.

1. Number of middlemen handling the brand.

2. Number of middlemen who have handled the brand profitably for years.

3. Identity of prominent dealers.

4. Safety of investment in inventory. This may be because of great consumer preference, sustained advertising, sound marketing policies, or trade goodwill.

5. Excellent display possibilities of the product.

6. Volume, turnover, and margin.

7. Advertising and merchandising aid.

STUDY ASSIGNMENTS

1. "A salesman's knowledge about his products is not an end in itself, but a means to an end." Comment on this statement.

2. How valuable is a "lifetime guarantee" as a product feature?

3. A salesman with six years' experience in a retail jewelry store joined the sales force of a manufacturer of sterling silverware and began calling on retailer jewelers. What shifts might the salesman have to make in emphasis on product information?

4. There are many well-known brand names. What do you consider to be some features of some of the most outstanding brand names?

5. How does an adequate fund of product information contribute to the salesman's success in controlling the interview?

6. What are the dangers of merely *pretending* to have product knowledge?

7. Comment on salesmen as a source of ideas about new products.

8. In the long run, can a salesman successfully sell a product on which he himself is not sold?

9. Is it advisable for a young salesman to be told what his products will *not* do? Why?

10. How can a salesman go about collecting product information on his own?

CASE STUDY 6

Mrs. Joyner lives in a small city and shops every now and then in one of the appliance-housewares stores there. On her last visit to this store, she was approached by a young salesman who knew little about her except her name.

Salesman: Good morning. You are Mrs. Joyner, aren't you? What can I do for you?

Prospect: Oh, nothing in particular; I'm just looking around. (Examines an egg beater.) Well, maybe I should replace my old egg beater — mine has seen its best days.

Salesman: Then let me show you the new Ajax portable mixers we got in last week. We've sold six already.

Prospect: But I don't need an electrical gadget to beat eggs.

Salesman: Yes, but this mixer is just what women want in a portable kitchen mixer. Years of research and testing went into this appliance. And there's no company in the appliance field more respected than the Ajax firm. Isn't it attractive?

Prospect: Yes, it is.

Salesman: Just look at these features. First, the motor is powerful, though small. It has a governor — offers you twelve speeds — is controlled by that convenient button on the handle you adjust with your thumb. You may not believe it, but that motor gives you speed up to 1000 r.p.m.'s.

Prospect: Oh?

Salesman: And the beaters — two extra large, king-size, full-mix beaters. Nickel chrome, I'll tell you. A thumb-tip push button on the handle ejects the beaters when you want to wash them.

Prospect: Where does one keep this gadget?

Salesman: I'm glad you asked that. The wide-base heel serves as a rest on which you can set the mixer; or it can be hung neatly on a wall; or it can stand on a shelf. Convenient, isn't it?

Prospect: I guess so. What is the price?

Salesman: $19.50 — a bargain, wouldn't you say? Did I mention that a removable, six-foot cord is part of the mixer? A recipe book comes with it, too.

Prospect: $19.50 is more than I care to spend for an egg beater.

Salesman: I know what you mean, but this Ajax will last the rest of your life. Your husband can even mix paint with it.

Prospect: Oh, no!

Salesman: Doesn't hurt it a bit — you just wash off the paint. Mrs. Joyner, this is really a bargain. Which color do you like?

Prospect: One of these regular egg beaters will do for today. Will you please wrap it for me.

QUESTIONS:

1. Criticize what the salesman did.
2. How might his presentation be strengthened?

CHAPTER 7

THE SALESMAN'S PROSPECTIVE CUSTOMERS

Many a salesman must look on his customer group as a reservoir, far from empty but with the drain pipe open and running. Unless the salesman sees that the intake pipe pours into the reservoir a volume equal to the volume disappearing down the drain, the customer group shrinks. Successful salesmen find prospecting unavoidable, week after week, year after year. They must replace customers who die, fail, retire, move away, switch to a competitor's product, cease to qualify financially, or, indeed, cease to be able to use their products to advantage. For products or services bought infrequently, particularly durable, expensive items, the buyer is out of the market — not a prospect again — for a long time.

In addition to *finding* prospects, the salesman needs to *find out about* them. Actually, these two activities overlap because a salesman cannot separate prospects from suspects until he has obtained certain information about them. So, one use the salesman makes of prospect information is in qualifying prospects. It may be observed that the outstanding salesmen spend their time selling to the most promising prospects, whereas weak salesmen try to sell to anybody.

Besides helping to qualify prospects, buyer information helps in selling to those prospects. Effective selling is tailored selling. Unless a salesman has a clear picture of the individual buyer, he can't tailor his selling or make the soundest recommendations. When the salesman adds to adequate product knowledge the desired amount of prospect information, he can plan personalized and individualized presentations.

PROSPECTING

Widely Used Techniques

The first thing for the salesman to do in the way of locating prospects is to make an exhaustive *study of what he sells*. When he has learned what his products will do, the salesman is in a position to draw a rather detailed picture of who could use those products to advantage. For instance, even

151

a cursory study of electric water heaters reveals that there are domestic prospects and commercial prospects. A manufacturer of glass containers finds, as a result of product examination, that he can sell to beverage, dairy, food, pharmaceutical, cosmetic, chemical, and other consumer goods manufacturers. It is not impossible to discover a prospect group which has never been thought of as a fertile field before.

Some *companies* supply their salesman with prospect lists. These lists may have been compiled by the company itself, or a list may represent individuals who have made inquiry of the company. Being supplied by his company with such a list does not relieve the salesman of the duty of using his ingenuity in expanding his list of prospects.

The *endless chain* is a fruitful source of prospects. In using this technique, the salesman asks satisfied customers or former customers to suggest individuals who logically could use the product he sells. Customers are inclined to be most cooperative with the salesman who goes out of his way to do them favors. When a buyer takes obvious delight in displaying his new possession and in receiving compliments on it, the persons making up his audience may quite naturally be prospects.

A slightly more helpful version of the endless chain technique is the *referral*. In the endless chain, all customers do is to supply names of prospects to salesmen, but in the referral technique customers do more. They may give the salesman a card or note of introduction. They might recommend the salesman to a prospect through a telephone call to that prospect, perhaps trying to set up an appointment for the salesman. Or, they might arrange to introduce the salesman to a prospect face to face.

Referrals are much used in selling both products and services. To get them, the salesman usually has only to ask for them. Such requests can be made upon completion of the first sale, on the next call, or after allowing a reasonable length of time for the customer to enjoy and become accustomed to his purchase. Most customers cooperate. Some want their friends to know of the wise purchases they have made. Most feel that their decisions and actions carry weight with their friends and acquaintances.

There are several advantages to referrals. Prospecting time and approach time are minimized, permitting more face-to-face selling time. Appointments are more easily arranged, *and* they are generally with high-quality prospects because the customer's recommendation served as a screening procedure. Finally, the fact of the referral helps support the promises the salesman makes to prospects.

Centers of influence are a source of prospects. These centers are friends (perhaps customers, too) who can and will help the salesman in his prospecting. They have influence over other individuals and information about them; they use both in the salesman's behalf. An office manager, for example, can identify for the salesman of home study courses those employees under him who have promise enough to be good prospects. Lawyers, doctors, ministers, bankers, public officials, and business executives serve as centers of influence on their friends, employees, neighbors, associates, and relatives.

Centers of influence do the job of referral and then some. They may supply all the prospect information the salesman needs. They make appointments and then go on to recommend the salesman and his proposal. They have even been known to be present at the selling interview.

Why do people use their influence in this manner? Sometimes the explanation is personal — perhaps just friendship, or perhaps the salesman returns the favor by helping the center of influence attain *his* goals and objectives. Another possibility is that the center of influence owes a debt of some sort to the salesman. The center may be making a bid for goodwill and patronage for his company.

Centers of influence are encouraged to function for the salesman's benefit if the salesman keeps them posted, fully and currently informed about developments. Like anyone else, centers appreciate favors, friendliness, thanks, and appreciation — from salesmen. They like to know that they have been of aid.

Junior salesmen, sometimes referred to as hostesses, spotters, or even "bird dogs," do specialized prospecting for some salesmen. Automobiles, major appliances, tires, and lines of housewares are suitable products. Housewives who give "houseparties," policemen, waiters, barbers, beauty parlor operators, meter readers, milk route men, and laundry men make good junior salesmen.

Other sellers can be used as sources of information. Contractors and architects can give clues to the sellers of plumbing and heating equipment. A seller of coal stokers can persuade a coal dealer to supply him with a prospect list. In similar fashion, service station operators can pass valuable tips on to automobile salesmen.

For certain products or services, a *manager or employer* may point out one of his employees to the salesman as being a prospect. This is true, for example, of home study courses.

Friends and acquaintances can help by supplying personal leads, either in casual conversation or in conversation directed toward uncovering prospects. If the salesman's friend is also a friend of the prospect, so much the better.

Direct mail may be sent out by the salesman for the purpose of identifying prospects. Such a mailing may be executed by the salesman himself or may be made by his company.

In some lines, the salesman finds it profitable to make *technical surveys* in order to locate prospects. The salesman of lighting equipment will make a study of an industrial plant or of an office to see if lighting needs are being met. Insurance, air conditioning, petroleum products, and home heating are other lines in which the survey has been effectively used in identifying prospects.

Some salesmen can profitably consult various *public records* in their search for prospects.

Directories are a source. A directory of directors, a corporation register, a credit rating manual, a register of advertisers, or even the classified section of the telephone book are examples.

List brokers may have just the list that the salesman needs.

Advertising media may cooperate by compiling prospect lists in their respective localities.

Even *competitors* sometimes help the salesman, usually unintentionally, by disclosing something of their own activities.

Trade papers with their information about new companies, new functions, or personnel changes justify the salesman's examination.

A medium as general as the *newspaper* can frequently be scanned by the salesman with the result that new prospects are located.

A salesman's *observation*, if he is keen and alert, will help him in his hunt. An alert tire salesman spots bald tires on a parked car and identifies a prospect through the license number. When an insurance salesman sees ground being broken for a house, he needs no better clue.

Some salesmen use the *cold canvass* in their search for buyers. This technique is also called *cold prospecting*. The salesman locates prospects by contacting persons who may or may not be prospects and about whom he knows little or practically nothing. He then eliminates those who are not prospects. Often the salesman can do nothing to pave the way for his call on a person whose name he does not know; his sales work must be done after meeting the customer.

Usually the salesman starts by knowing the type of individual to whom he can sell. Next he finds how and where that type of person can be found. Then he talks briefly to many persons so as to identify those who are real prospects.

House-to-house selling is a prime example of cold canvassing. Another is the "working" of an office building from top to bottom in selling, for instance, a correspondence course.

Illustrations from Business

Here are remarks from the makers of some well-known products to their salesmen about the "why" and "how" of locating new prospects.

From the training material of Carrier Corporation:

Finding the Prospect

You should organize your work and build a list of prospects from:

The neighborhood bank.
Present users.
Architects, contractors, builders.
Telephone and business directories.
New car registrations of owners of higher-priced automobiles.
Main street businessmen's association (or similar organization).
Friends and acquaintances.
Building permits, construction reports.
Members of various clubs, such as

Rotary, Kiwanis, Lions, Chamber of Commerce, and country clubs.
A local letter shop's list of larger income tax payers. (See "Mailing Lists" in the classified telephone directory.)
Various supply houses which deal with air conditioning markets.
The "cold canvass" method.
The utility companies.
Old files of prospects and propositions.
Other sources used in the past.

From the Pittsburgh Plate Glass Company:

Established customers provide most of the business for the future. But you will lose some. They die, go out of business, or move out of the territory. Just to hold your own, you must continuously put new, active accounts on the ledgers. You make a net gain only when you get more new accounts than you lose in old ones.

The plus business comes from two sources: from established accounts and uses; from new accounts and new applications. Obviously, if you are selling five or six of our glass and paint items to a customer who regularly buys a dozen more from others, you will try hard at every opportunity to increase your share of his business. Likewise, you will have a list of live prospects who are known buyers, but who get their supplies elsewhere; and you will work on them regularly and persistently.

Then, there is the big undiscovered field — buyers of our types of products who may be unknown to you — unknown because you failed to inquire, neglected to use imagination, and just did not think about them.

And again there is plus business to be had in promoting the use of our products in places where they are not now used: glass instead of metal, wood, marble, brick and other materials; paint where finishing materials have not been regularly applied.

NEED FOR AND USE OF PROSPECT INFORMATION

The professional salesman has two objectives. One is to be of maximum help and service to prospects and customers; the second is to be financially successful. These two goals cannot be divorced because in a sense they are two ways of expressing a single ambition. It is difficult if not impossible to picture a salesman who does an outstanding job of taking care of his prospects and customers, yet whose income is low. The converse is also true.

If the salesman is to convert prospects into customers and then develop those customers to the greatest possible degree, he must have prospect information. The more complete and comprehensive the information, the better the salesman can serve the persons he calls on and make his efforts produce.

Qualifying the Prospect

The first use the salesman makes of prospect information is in selecting out of a group certain individuals who warrant the salesman's future attention. Perhaps the larger group can be called the "suspect" group. Some of the persons in this group will deserve the salesman's time and sales efforts; others will not. Suspects are those who do not qualify *now* for sales attention, but may in the future. The smaller, deserving group becomes the "prospect" group because the salesman determines that each member needs his product, can finance the purchase, and has authority to buy. The Penn Mutual Life Insurance Company qualifies a prospect to its salesman as one who:

1. Has need for life insurance.
2. Can qualify medically and morally.
3. Can pay for life insurance.
4. Can be approached by you.
5. Is the right type for you.

In qualifying the prospect, the salesman will check first those angles which are key matters for his product. The major consideration may be location or credit rating or freedom to buy on the part of the prospect. In other cases it may be a matter of age or vocation, of ownership or marital status.

It should be mentioned here that many prospects do not know their wants and needs until they have been shown and that most prospects are not ready to buy until some salesman makes them ready. Furthermore, criteria change. This fact requires the salesman to keep informed on new trends and developments, on the changing demands of various age, sex, or income groups, on the appearance of new markets, and on new uses for old products.

Regardless of time, place, product, or criteria, the process of qualifying the prospect provides the salesman with the answer to a single question, "Should I spend any more time on this particular person?"

Visualizing the Prospect's Needs

A second use of prospect information is to picture the prospect's problems and requirements. The Ralston Purina Company helps its salesmen by pointing out areas of prospect problems in which a salesman must be helpful:

Products: He must be thoroughly informed about the products which we make, and he must be able to give genuine help to his customers in their farm management.

Profits: He must be a competent financial counsellor to his dealers. Unless he can teach the firms that handle our Purina products how to be sound financially, he will never have successful outlets for the sale of our products.

Plant: He must also be able to advise our dealers on how to arrange their buildings and warehouses conveniently, efficiently, and with good sales facilities.

Promotion: Then he must be able to teach his dealers how to advertise and market their products in the modern way.

Personnel: Finally, he must be competent in helping his dealers to hire the right kind of people, pay them a fair working wage, and make it worth their while to improve themselves.

If the salesman is to help the prospect buy, he must have a grasp of the prospect's current situation in sufficient detail. He cannot fit his offerings to the prospect's needs until he knows what those needs are. Prospect information identifies and describes those needs. It reveals why the prospect needs the product and how he should apply it so as to solve one of his problems.

Increasing Sales Effectiveness

A third use of prospect information is in making sales efforts more productive, and the applications here are many.

Because facts enable the salesman to weed out those persons who are not prospects, fewer wasted calls and fewer costly call-backs are made. Prospect facts help in securing interviews, too, and with the right persons. Less time during the first calls need be given over to the job of collecting prospect information, and thus more time is available for selling.

It impresses a prospect when a salesman can discuss his specific problems on the first visit. When the salesman shows that he has spent time, effort, and perhaps money in acquainting himself with the prospect's circumstances, the salesman makes a strong bid for attention, interest, and even confidence. He has a sound justification for taking up some of the prospect's time, and he invites the prospect to open up and supply facts which could not be determined prior to the call.

Prospect information helps in the selection of the most promising approach and appeals. It makes the salesman better able to anticipate objections and to overcome them skillfully before they are voiced. For example, if the prospect has a hard and fast commitment to another vendor, the salesman can handle this difficult circumstance more satisfactorily if he knows about it in advance.

The salesman's presentation is stronger because of what he knows about the prospect. He can talk in actualities which are arresting and tailored rather than in vague and impersonal generalities. By examining the prospect's problems from the very first contact and showing what his product will do, the salesman makes his story easy to follow, understand, believe, and act on. The more the salesman knows about the prospect, his problems, and his hopes, the more expertly can he fit his product into the picture, the more convincingly can he show how the product will be of benefit.

The salesman must often be a friend before he can become an advisor. Indeed, one of the salesman's first objectives is to be accepted by the prospect as a friend, because buyers prefer to buy from persons with whom they are friendly. Frequently, because of advance prospect information, a more friendly atmosphere can be created in which the salesman and prospect can become acquainted.

Respecting the Prospect's Wishes

A fourth use of prospect information is concerned with information of a general nature that applies to practically all prospects. This information answers the salesman's question, "What does the prospect expect of me, and what must I avoid doing?" Knowledge that is deposited in this fund of facts guides the salesman in his effort to please the prospect and to avoid annoying or irritating him.

Any set of recommendations will probably need to be adjusted in the light of such matters as the stage of the business cycle, nature of the product, type of prospect, characteristics of the salesman, and section of the country. Each salesman will certainly want to compile a list of "do's" and "don't's" that he finds, from experience, he should observe.

The Flintkote Company classifies prospects and tells what each group wants. Local industrial accounts constitute one group of prospects:

> These companies usually have a purchasing agent or maintenance engineer whose word is final in the selection of materials to be used. Be sure to learn which man is the one you should see. On your first call, ask the superintendent or other executives to direct you to the man who is interested in what you sell.
>
> The approach to the purchasing agent or the maintenance engineer should be on a strictly informative and businesslike basis. One very effective way to establish a profitable contact is to offer to make an inspection of the roof, with no obligation to the prospect. Make your report freely and frankly. If everything is in good condition, say so. If something needs to be attended to, make your recommendation very

specific. Whatever the case may be, use the inspection as an opportunity to find what else needs to be done for which you can supply materials.

This is what the man in charge does and does not want in a sales representative who calls on him:

1. He wants the sales representative to be thoroughly conversant with his line and to submit factual information.
2. He wants the sales representative to realize that he buys on the reputation of the product and the standing of the company producing it and according to the plant's requirements.
3. He doesn't want the sales representative to break down sales resistance or to tie him up when he is busy.
4. He wants the sales representative to realize that he will not be influenced by high pressure sales tactics.
5. He doesn't want the sales representative to attempt to sell him anything which has not been tested under actual service conditions.
6. He wants the sales representative to call on him only when he has something of interest to talk about.

Caution Against Overemphasis

After all this attention to the desirability — yes, even the necessity — of prospect information, perhaps it may be well to recall that prospect information is merely a selling aid. In many cases, the salesman will have opportunity to collect or to use little or none of it. This will often be true in selling to merchants for resale. So, it is suggested that the salesman not spend a disproportionate amount of time in getting ready to sell. He does not get orders signed while digging up prospect facts.

TYPES OF PROSPECT INFORMATION

Most salesman need two types of information about prospects, *personal* and *business*. The amount of each required for a satisfactory job varies, as do the specific items. One salesman may find that he will use little or no business information in selling to housewives. Another salesman will be helpless in qualifying prospects unless he knows whether or not they are parents.

Personal information refers, of course, to facts about the individual whom the salesman interviews. The salesman may be hoping to sell something to the individual himself, or the individual may be the purchasing agent or buying representative of the company that employs him. Obviously, the salesman will need and make use of more personal information in the first instance.

Business information consists of facts about the company or institution with which the individual buyer is connected. Once again, the salesman may be hoping to sell the individual as an individual, or he may be selling

Prospects Like the Salesman Who:

1. Exhibits thoughtfulness and consideration in scheduling his calls.

2. Keeps appointments and promises.

3. Conducts his business efficiently and then leaves promptly.

4. Has authority for any commitment he makes.

5. Knows prices and terms, and quotes them in a clear, understandable, complete manner.

6. Tells a concise, coherent, well-organized sales story.

7. Can answer all questions he should be able to answer.

8. Displays genuine interest in helping the prospect better himself.

9. Continues to be interested even after changing a prospect into a customer.

10. Makes the prospect feel important.

11. Respects confidences, beliefs, and intelligence.

12. Refrains from going behind or over the head of the prospect without the prospect's knowledge.

13. Does not allow himself to become too familiar or too aggressive.

14. Keeps friendship and business in their proper places.

to the company through the individual employee. The salesman will need and make use of more business information in the second instance.

It is the salesman's duty to build a list of facts which he can use to maximize his sales effectiveness. The items listed below should appear on most lists. An illustrative application of each "personal" factor is given.

Personal Information — Objective

1. *Name.* This includes initials, spelling, and, most important, pronunciation. Because the average person loves his name, enjoys hearing it, and shudders when it is mispronounced, the salesman should call the prospect by name frequently and correctly during the interview.

2. *Age.* The insurance salesman probably needs this most of all.
3. *Birthday.* Remembrance on this day builds goodwill.
4. *Home address and phone number.* Racial origin and income classification may be revealed by street address.
5. *Ownership.* Ownership of specific items, such as houses or automobiles, is of direct concern to some salesmen.
6. *Education.* By knowing this, the salesman may avoid embarrassment or may have a good conversational topic.
7. *Background.* Same as No. 6.
8. *Purchasing power.* This is one aspect of ability to buy. The other is listed in No. 14.
9. *Marital status.* Sometimes this is basic enough to be a qualifying criterion.
10. *Family data.* Included here are such items as names, schools, interests of wife and children, and anniversaries.
11. *Social circle.* A mutual friend or a satisfied customer may be found in this group.
12. *Reputation.* Knowing what people think of the prospect helps the salesman in making plans.
13. *Membership and affiliation.* Here are included the fraternal, club, political, and religious ties.
14. *Job.* Items needed include company name, job title, nature of work, responsibilities, approximate salary, training, experience, years with the company, and years on the present job.
15. *Daily routine.* This may help in arranging an interview.

Personal Information — Subjective

1. *Character.* Knowledge of his character may be necessary in qualifying the prospect.
2. *Beliefs.* These must be handled with caution. The prospect is entitled to some beliefs, such as political and religious, and these should be respected. Any attempt to change a prospect's belief requires delicate maneuvering.
3. *Mental type and quality.* The sales presentation must be attuned to the prospect's quality of comprehension.
4. *Traits.* These are clues to motivation.
5. *Interests.* The salesman who knows what the prospect's interests are has a more detailed picture of the prospect, and he also has some good conversational material.
6. *Hobbies and recreations.* Information about these may help break the ice on the first call, particularly if both the salesman and the prospect have the same preferences.

7. *Tastes.* On these pegs, compliments can be hung.
8. *Likes and dislikes.* The former are to be cultivated, the latter left dormant.
9. *Problems.* The salesman's duty is to point out solutions to these.
10. *Aspirations.* Prospects should be aided in their efforts toward attaining their goals.

Jan	Feb	Mar	Apr	May	Jun	Jul	Aug	Sep	Oct	Nov	Dec	

CLIP TABS. EXCEPT BIRTH MONTH OR AGE CHANGE

NAME			AGE	DATE OF BIRTH	AGE CHANGE
Louis S. Hudson			39	3/12/22	9/12
OCCUPATION *Office Manager*		WIFE *Alice M.*			DATE OF BIRTH 11/25/26
BUS. ADDRESS *312 E. Main St.*	PHONE *1920*	CHILDREN *Susan E.*			12/20/49
		John R.			8/17/52
RES. ADDRESS *374 Maple Ave.*	PHONE *3283*	*Paul J.*			7/15/55

INSURANCE OWNED

	BEST TIME TO SEE *After 6 PM*		APPROX. INCOME $*9000*		MORTGAGE $*17,500*			
AMOUNT	COMPANY	PLAN	PREM.	A.S.Q.	ISSUED	BENEFICIARY	SETTLEMENT	DIS. INC.	W.P.	D.I.
10,000	*NSLI*	*Term*	*22.80*	*Q*	*6/10/43*	*Wife*	*Option*	—	—	—
10,000	*ONMLI*	*Ord*	*61.20*	*Q*	*9/15/48*	*"*	*Cash*	—	—	—

REF. BY *Geo. Robbins*   DATE *3/11/61*

INS. OWNED WIFE CHLDR

AMOUNT	COMPANY	PLAN	PREM.	A.S.Q.	ISSUED	BENEFICIARY	SETTLEMENT	DIS. INC.	W.P.	D.I.
2000	*MELI*	*20 pay*	*16.56*	*Q*	*3/46*	*Husband*	*Cash*	—	—	—

DATE	RECORD OF CALLS			SEE AGAIN
	REASON FOR CALL	PLAN PRESENTED	RESULT	
3/12/61	*Referred*	*Pref. Risk*	*No decision*	*3/27/61*

REMARKS - PERSONAL INTERESTS
Likes fishing, boating

PRINTED IN U.S.A.   J.H.M.L.I. CO., BOSTON, MASS.   FORM 531RB

Above are the front and back of a card showing the basic prospect information desired by salesmen of the John Hancock Mutual Life Insurance Company.

Business Information

1. *Name of company.*
2. *Type of business.*
3. *Size of business.*
4. *Location and most efficient routing to get there.*
5. *Product line.*
6. *Markets served.*
7. *Organization.*
8. *Type of management.*
9. *Credit rating.*
10. *Prominent executives and other key men.*
11. *Policies.*
       Distribution — Sales — Advertising and merchandising — Product — Purchasing — Relations with vendors.
12. *Pertinent routines and procedures.*
13. *Terminology.*
14. *Major income and expense items.*
15. *Competition.*
16. *Previous experience with salesman's company.*
17. *Problems.*
18. *Future prospects.*
19. *Where, how, when, why, and by whom his products will be used.*
20. *Volume possibilities.*
21. *Frequency of purchase.*
22. *What the prospect now does about the salesman's type of product.* Competitive line now bought — Why — How long from present supplier — Prices paid — Type and duration of present contract or commitment — Salesman's products now bought or in use in case salesman is new — Attitude toward salesman's line and line now used — Dollar volume of purchases in this field.

An Illustration from Business

An executive of Sherwin-Williams Company says:

The subject of "What a Salesman Should Know About His Prospect" can be covered very simply and completely by replying that he should know all there is to know about his prospect! I have always felt that the better posted a salesman is about his prospect before he calls, the better chance he has of fitting his presentation and his proposition to the needs of the prospective customer.

For example, I cannot imagine one of our salesmen being able to make an intelligent, constructive presentation of our paint line to a paint store or hardware store prospect without knowing something about the prospect personally. He should know:

How long the prospect has been in business.

What his success has been in his present location.

The extent of his trading area and his market potential.

About how much volume he does.

What his credit rating is.

What other paint line or lines he is carrying now.

Whether he is buying from a jobber.

From which shipping point he gets his paint.

If he has a hardware store, whether he operates a separate paint department or whether the paint is just thrown in with the rest of his stock.

Whether he has someone in charge of his paint department.

Whether he does any painter business.

What kind of an advertiser and merchandiser he is.

What his customers think of him, and how he stands in the community.

There may also be other factors which a salesman would be wise to investigate prior to calling on his prospect. For example, the prospect may have a silent partner or stockholder who is connected with some other paint company, or he may be hooked up with some cooperative buying group, or some such situation. A little personal information such as the prospect's habits, hobbies, pet likes, and dislikes, etc., is helpful to know in advance of a call so that the salesman knows what to capitalize on and what to avoid.

If the salesman is well posted and has this general information, any one of the above points might come in mighty handy in making the sale, whereas the lack of all or some parts of this general information may mean the loss of the sale.

We have a great many salesmen calling on us here in the Cleveland office, and I have observed on so many of the calls that they know relatively little or nothing about our business. To put it another way, the occasional salesman who makes it a point to find out something about us and our business has a big advantage in getting an interview, and particularly in being welcome on his second or third repeat call. The buyer just doesn't have time these days for the salesman who undertakes a "shot in the dark."

For example, I know certain publication advertising salesmen who never think of calling unless they have a message which is usually carefully prepared after they have made a number of calls on our dealers or have made field or market surveys. Sometimes they take photographs of our dealer stores or bring in other interesting information from the field which invariably warrants our time and attention. This is constructive, creative salesmanship which is bound to impress the buyer with the fact that the salesman knows not only his own business but knows something about your business as well.

SOURCES OF PROSPECT INFORMATION

The following list of sources of prospect information is not grouped into sources of personal and sources of business information because most sources listed can supply both types.

Direct Sources

1. The *prospect himself*, by mail, by telephone, or in person.
2. The *family* of the prospect.
3. *Friends* and *acquaintances* of the prospect.
4. *Persons in the prospect's company*, especially the receptionist, secretaries, and the prospect's boss.
5. *Vendors* selling to the prospect, usually noncompetitive.
6. *Customers* who buy from the prospect.
7. The prospect's *competitors*.
8. The prospect's *bank*.
9. The *salesman's company*, provided there have been previous contacts.
10. *Windfalls*. Here the salesman gets information from some unexpected, unsolicited source. Such acquisitions can be thought of as accidents or coincidences.

General Sources

1. *Chambers of Commerce*.
2. *Directories and registers*.
3. *Trade associations*.
4. *Rating agencies*.
5. *Official records*, as in courthouses.
6. *List brokers*.
7. *Newspapers, magazines, business and trade papers*, both news stories and advertisements.
8. *Publicity releases* of the prospect's company.

Observation by the Salesman

Personal observation, perhaps the most valuable single source of prospect information, is sometimes scheduled to be done prior to the sales interview. The salesman may need to inspect and analyze the situation and to collect and classify the facts before he is ready to recommend. For example, the great majority of furnaces are sold during the second half of the year, but this does not mean that the salesman is idle during the spring. It is then that he qualifies prospects by making surveys.

In other cases, where surveys have not been made, the securing of an immediate order is not the only objective of the salesman. He makes use of the sales interview to explore in many directions. His personal observation, operating every minute from the time the prospect's home or place of business comes into view, corrects and supplements his advance information, which too often turns out to be incomplete, superficial, obsolete, biased, or even incorrect.

The Penn Mutual Life Insurance Company challenges its salesmen to:

Interpret what you see and hear each day in terms of life insurance by using your head. Four instances should make clear this method:

1. If you saw a delivery van unload a baby carriage in front of a home around the corner from where you live, would it mean anything to you?
2. If, on your way from the train to your office in the morning, you overheard one man say to another, "I've just moved my office to the new Bond Building; the old place got too small," might it mean anything to you?
3. If the man in the next office sells his Ford and buys a Lincoln, would it mean anything to you?
4. Suppose you heard of a man or woman who has just received a promotion, profit, or a substantial gift or legacy. Would that have any business significance for you?

Suggestions About Sources

1. Sources should be selected for their simplicity, adequacy, promptness, and economy. The telephone and the mail inquiry recommend themselves in many situations.
2. There should be no snooping. When persons find that they are being investigated, and they often do, they tend to resent it.
3. When the prospect is a middleman who will resell the salesman's merchandise, there is less need for an elaborate fact-fund about him.
4. The salesman should always be hunting for new methods of getting prospect data that will make his selling less difficult and more productive.

PROSPECT INFORMATION IN TERMS OF GROUPS

The individual prospect is the smallest and most basic unit in the salesman's territory because his territory, in the final analysis, is nothing more than a certain number of persons, with a certain amount of purchasing power and a certain inclination to buy, who need his product. For each of these prospects, the salesman will want to fill out a record card. This card will provide for the compilation of the specific prospect facts that the salesman has found he needs if his selling activities are to be successful. Continuous revision keeps these cards up to date.

While it is true that the salesman properly thinks of his territory as a number of individual prospects, even a cursory examination of his prospect cards usually shows that these individuals naturally fall into groups, with each group having common characteristics or features. So, in addition to thinking about his market as consisting of individual prospects, a salesman frequently must recognize his need for prospect information in

CONCENTRATION OF BUSINESS
BY SIZE OF ACCOUNT

Av. Mo. Purchases Per Customer	% Customers	% Sales Volume	% Calls
Under $10	85%	29%	68%
10.01 — 20.00	5%	6%	6%
20.01 — 40.00	5%	10%	12%
40.01 — 100.00	4%	18%	6%
Over $100	1%	37%	8%
Total	100%	100%	100%

This table, taken from experience, not only illustrates the concentration of business with a relatively few large customers, but it also shows up the all too familiar pattern of dispersed sales effort — too much attention to smaller accounts, too little attention to larger accounts. Adequate prospect information is essential if a salesman is to spend his time most effectively.

terms of groups of prospects. Classifying the total prospect group into a small number of markets and combining similar individual prospects into homogeneous groups makes for efficiency and convenience of handling, thinking, and developing.

The salesman will group his individual prospects into classifications appropriate and useful for his own needs, and he will collect for each class the prospect data that he finds worth while for his own purposes. One classification might be according to *geography*. Each state or each city might constitute a separate group, or, an urban-rural breakdown might be indicated. A second classification might be according to *type of retail outlet*, separating, let us say, drug from department stores, or chains from independents. *Class of trade* is a third possibility; examples include merchants or industrial buyers, banks or manufacturing establishments, and groups that use the product for different purposes. A fourth basis could be *desirability of account*. Customers could be rated on such matters as prominence or volume or cooperation. *Size, purchasing power*, and *vocation* are other bases of classification.

PROSPECT INFORMATION IN TERMS OF
THE ENTIRE TERRITORY

Just as the salesman needs prospect information in terms of individual prospects and in terms of homogeneous prospect groups, he sometimes must think of his sales area as a single prospective market, as a marketing entity which his prospects and classes of prospects have united to form for him.

The salesman must have certain market information in terms of that one unit. He must keep abreast of all territory-wide trends and developments such as population shifts, changes in total income, and other factors that affect his sales potential; he must ask whether his territory contains any neglected markets; he must stay informed of general conditions throughout his area. He must study and understand the characteristics of his territory, its physical make-up, transportation facilities, attitudes, economic foundations, types of inhabitants, and all other significant features.

STUDY ASSIGNMENTS

1. What are the strong and weak points of the "cold-canvass" call?
2. Make a list of types of centers of influence for an insurance salesman.
3. Would you recommend any cautions to a salesman in respect to his collection and use of information about buyers he has not yet seen?
4. In prospecting for additional wholesale customers, what wholesale-prospect characteristics are of interest to the manufacturer?
5. Wholesalers have their own prospecting duties — prospecting for retailers. Are retail-prospect characteristics for wholesalers the same as the wholesale-prospect characteristics for the manufacturer?
6. What are some steps a salesman can take in identifying the dominant buying influence in a large company?
7. What are some limitations or problems the salesman might encounter if he uses the prospect as a source of information about himself?
8. Where can a salesman get information about his company's inactive accounts?
9. Describe five sales situations where much *personal* information is essential to the salesman's success. Describe five where much *business* information is more essential.
10. Do the principles of qualifying the prospect apply in selling to customers of long standing? Why?

CASE STUDY 7A

Early in December a man walked into the Johnson Furniture Store, not seeming to know just what he wanted. Mr. Adams, a salesman, noticed the man's entrance and walked over to greet him. Adams could not recall ever having seen the man before. He judged the shopper to be about 30 years old and from the middle or low-middle income group.

Adams: Good evening, sir, how do you do?
Customer: Fine, thank you.
Adams: May I show you something?
Customer: I'm not just sure — I don't know what I want.
Adams: I don't believe I've had the pleasure before of meeting you. (Extends hand.) I'm Mr. Adams.

Customer: (Shaking hands) My name is Harris.

Adams: Do you live here, Mr. Harris?

Customer: Yes, we recently moved here. We live out in Starmount.

Adams: That's a lovely development. I'm sure your family likes it.

Customer: Yes, my two youngsters and my wife think it's nice.

Adams: Who are you with, Mr. Harris?

Customer: I'm an assistant professor at the university here.

Adams: Well, you're certainly with a fine school. Many of your associates are among our best customers. Dean Anderson was in here earlier today doing a bit of Christmas shopping. By the way, can I be of help to you with *your* Christmas buying? Have you selected a gift for your wife?

Customer: No, I guess that's why I came in here.

Adams: Do you have anything particular in mind?

Customer: No, I want something nice but not too expensive.

Adams: About how much do you want to spend?

Customer: Well, not too much. I simply can't afford to spend a lot. Moving here and getting settled have strapped me.

Adams: Does your wife have a toaster?

Customer: No. But aren't they high?

Adams: Here is one of our cheaper models, the Speedy toaster. Of course, you may not like it. Think your wife would?

Customer: Well . . .

Adams: I know what you're thinking, Harris, you want to know how much it is. It's $13.95. Is that too steep?

Customer: I guess not. What about the quality of the toaster?

Adams: Don't worry about the quality of the toaster. It's worth $13.95. Take my word for it. Think it will do?

Customer: I would want any toaster I buy to last.

Adams: Then how about this DeLuxe Master-Toaster. Fully automatic. All you have to do is drop the slices of bread in. The toaster thinks for itself. Suppose your wife would like it?

Customer: How much is it?

Adams: $29.50.

Customer: That's more than I can afford to put into a gift.

Adams: Then suppose you look around for something cheaper while I wait on those folks who just came in.

Adams walked over to greet a couple who had entered a moment or two earlier. Harris looked at the toasters a moment and then left the store.

QUESTIONS:

1. What did the salesman do well?
2. What did the salesman do that could be improved?
3. What techniques are illustrated in the sale?
4. How successful was the salesman in obtaining information from the prospect?
5. Can you spot a significant turning point in the interview?

CASE STUDY 7B

The J. H. Reid Company is a wholesale firm whose salesmen call on hardware retailers and other retailers who handle hardware. A credit department and credit facilities are included as part of the Reid wholesaling operation. Up until the first of this year, salesmen of the Reid company had not been asked to assume any credit duties because the credit manager had been following a procedure which did not call for participation of the company's sales force. Early this year, however, the credit manager proposed an innovation — he wanted the salesmen to begin submitting a credit report when sending in initial orders from new customers.

The credit manager felt strongly that the salesmen should represent the entire company, not just the sales department, and that they should be primarily concerned with net profit, not just sales volume. The credit manager was of the opinion that new orders could be approved or disapproved more quickly if accompanied by a credit report written by the salesman. Moreover, he hated to see a salesman spend time working on a prospective customer who would later be denied credit.

The Reid sales manager was skeptical but not hostile. He wondered how willing his salesmen would be to spend time in an activity which could irritate or even infuriate prospective customers. He wondered if a salesman's makeup was as suitable for credit work as it was for selling. What changes would have to be made in the sales training program? Would the salesmen's reports be sound — or slanted? Would the salesmen be reluctant to report unfavorable information about prospects? Would they *refuse* to assume credit duties? Would they be serious about or indifferent to their new assignment? Would the salesmen feel their selling handicapped and their earnings jeopardized?

The credit manager reassured the sales manager by promising him that the salesman's credit report would be of slight inconvenience. Only a few factors would be included in the report because it would be only one of several sources of information about retailers. Furthermore, the factors would be limited to those easily checked by salesmen. He reminded the sales manager that the salesman was the only company representative to interview retailers face to face, the only personal contact with retailers, the only employee to observe personally a retailer's store, stock, and staff. He asked the sales manager to agree to asking salesmen to be the eyes and ears of the credit department.

The final decision was to adopt the plan recommended by the credit manager. Immediately, the sales manager and the credit manager scheduled a conference to draft the credit report form.

QUESTION:

What factors should be included in the credit report?

CHAPTER 8

CONSUMER MOTIVATION

In the last four chapters we noted the information a salesman must have about his company, its promotion program, its products, and its prospective customers. Once this knowledge has been acquired, the salesman is ready to explore why consumers spend their money as they do and what consumers get for their expenditures. In other words, now is the time to start a study of consumer motivation.[1]

NATURE OF CONSUMER MOTIVATION

A study of consumer motivation is a study of why consumers have the attitudes they do and why they act as they do; it seeks an explanation of *why* consumers buy what they buy.

What Is Motivation?

Every normal person is a self-interested individual who experiences *drives, urges, desires,* or *wishes* which influence his attitudes and his actions. His motivations "push" a consumer into actions which he considers likely to gratify his needs. Thus, *motivation is the mechanism which controls behavior*, including *buying* behavior. It is a key which permits an understanding of a consumer. It includes those influences, attitudes, and considerations which determine consumer choices and cause consumer purchases. It reflects an inside urge, an inadequacy calling for corrective steps, an emptiness demanding to be filled, a problem in need of solution.

Needs Versus Wants

Every consumer has an assortment of *needs*, many needs. If we define need as the capacity to use a product or service to advantage, then all consumers are in a state of need, whether they live in a country with a high standard of living or in one with a low standard of living. In this

---

[1]See also C. A. Kirkpatrick, *Advertising* (Boston: Houghton Mifflin Company, 1959), Chapter 7, "Benefits Which Appeal to Buyers."

171

frame of reference, all consumers "need" more than they now own or consume.

The countless needs a consumer feels cause tensions which annoy and irritate him. Because he does not like them, the consumer wants to make these tensions disappear. So, the consumer feels driven to gratify his needs in order to escape from the tensions which result from those needs.

Needs are the basis and origin of *wants*. Needs lead to feelings of incompleteness, to awareness of the lack of something beneficial. The sequence is this: certain *needs cause wants*, and the more intense *wants become* active and influential *desires*. Within the framework of our present thinking, consumers are seen as *buying what they want*, not what they need. Their *needs*, in this sense, are far more numerous than their *wants* and far greater than they can afford to indulge.

The consumer can be said to want to *have*, to *be*, and to *do*. He wants *to have:* a better job, pleasure, money, more time, possessions, friends. He wants *to be:* safe, proud, slimmer, appreciated, superior, creative, attractive to the opposite sex. Among his wants *to do* are these: to rise on the social ladder, to feel needed, to keep up with the Joneses, to live an interesting life, perhaps just to live, to enjoy approval, to express affection.

In another classification, the consumer is pictured as an individual with four powerful wants — for sex and love, for security, for new experiences, and for recognition.

The salesman's undertaking is to convert certain *consumer-needs* into strong *consumer-wants* for his specific product. He creates wants by making consumers realize the urgency of certain of their needs. Often the consumer wants only because some salesman called his attention to needs of which he was not aware. The salesman, then, detects and establishes need, moves the consumer from a state of need into a state of want, and develops want into active and immediate desire.

MOTIVATION RESEARCH

Although buying motives may be and often are foolish, wrong, illegal, in poor taste, or unworthy of social approval, they are always present and responsible for voluntary purchases. In marketing, a feature of the 1950–60 decade was the considerable interest in motivation research, commonly referred to as "MR," the objective of which is to identify and evaluate the motives back of consumer purchases. The term "motivation research" is a misnomer, actually, because what is referred to is psychological research. Practically all MR makes use of certain tools, techniques, and procedures largely from the fields of psychology and sociology.

Some consumers do not know why they spend their money as they do, and some consumers do not tell the truth about why they buy what they buy. Motivation researchers claim that they can discover the *real* reasons back of consumers' purchases, the real explanation of consumers' attitudes and actions. Salesmen welcome any and all increases in the fund of knowledge about consumer motivation and buying behavior.

MOTIVATION AND BUYING

The fundamental, insistent wants which cause purchases constitute the motivation of interest to us. Every voluntary purchase is the result of the functioning of one or more buying motives. This is true even though the purchase seems impulsive and unplanned — even though the purchaser does not admit or even know just why he or she bought the item purchased. Thus, buying motives control a consumer's spending; they select what types of satisfaction a consumer buys with his dollars because they reflect what he considers worth obtaining. Buying motives, indeed, dictate how many dollars a consumer saves, how many dollars he spends, and what he buys with the money he spends.

The consumer is a baffling individual. He would rather be happy than logical. He prefers products which make him look good and feel good over products the purchase of which he can defend coldly, objectively, unemotionally. He and he alone decides the types and amounts of satisfaction each product delivers to him. When he pays $5 for product "A," he automatically implies (a) that he sees more satisfaction in "A" than in "B," "C," or "D," each costing $5, and (b) that he prefers to have product "A" rather than to save the $5.

Individuals do nothing that is not tinged in some manner with their own personal interests. We do those things that offer us some personal advantage. The motives that actuate us go back to our own selfish concerns. This is true even of a gift to a beggar. Of course, this does not mean that altruistic acts are ignoble; they are not ignoble, for they give pleasure to others. The point made here is that in the final analysis persons act to benefit themselves.

The way a buyer thinks and acts can be summed up in what may be termed the law of self-interest. This law states that a buyer makes a purchase only to improve his circumstances. His interest is not in the salesman, the salesman's company, or the salesman's merchandise, but instead it is in himself and in his own personal well-being. Essentially, the buyer buys nothing but advantages; he buys to satisfy one of his desires or to get some particular benefit he wants. Even outstanding features or qualities of the product must be translated into desired, advantageous results before there will be a purchase.

It may be well to recognize at this point that a consumer encounters a most serious difficulty when trying to satisfy his many desires. Gratification can usually be had only by buying some product or service, and the typical consumer has far more desires than he has dollars with which to satisfy them. His desires compete among themselves for attention and gratification. As a result, one product or service may have to satisfy, at least to some extent, two or more desires.

Instead of a physical product, the purchaser sees the satisfaction of a desire. The individual consumer buys not a hat, but compliments from his friends. Gasoline to him is transportation to the beach, and a corsage is feminine approval. For the purchasing agent of a factory, the purchase of industrial lamps is really a reduction in the number of accidents, lower personnel turnover, and increased efficiency. What the merchant buys will increase dollar profit by increasing sales or reducing costs.

We may try to rationalize about it, deny it, escape it, ignore it, camouflage it, or hide our heads in the sand from it, but the ancient and ubiquitous query in the mind of almost every prospect is, "Yes, but what do *I* get out of it?"

Variation In Buying Motives

Motivation is a personal, individual matter. Each consumer, selfish and self-centered, sets up his own goals and values, his own targets and aspirations. Each decides, subject of course to his limitations, what he wants from life and then pays life's prices for those particular satisfactions. Almost any student can be the best dancer or the best bridge player in his group — if he or she will pay the price. More students would make straight A's if the price were not so high!

Each consumer determines which benefits and advantages he wants to enjoy personally, then he buys those products and services which promise those chosen benefits. The skeptical, selfish questions with which each consumer confronts salesmen are: "What will your product (or service) do for *me?* What do *I* get out of the purchase?"

At any one moment the buying motive or motives back of a buyer's most accute, most intense desire constitute that buyer's strongest drive, and this is the drive the salesman hopes to put to work in his behalf. Very quickly the young salesman discovers that buying motives vary in strength and that this variation can be of a *person-to-person* type or a *time-to-time* type.

Person-to-person variations in buying motivation reflect the fact that no two individuals are alike. Each sets up his own goals and scale of values, as we have said before. *Hereditary background* is one factor that helps explain why A's buying motives are different from B's. *Personality* and *capabilities* are two more factors, each quite close to the matter of heredity. *Training* and *education* are two influences that cause A's hopes

and values to be unlike B's. *Experience* to a major degree causes A to love
what B loathes and to detest what B desires. *Environment*, too, is a force
that helps shape a buyer's decisions about what is essential or desirable,
and what is unnecessary or irrelevant. *Social status* is today recognized as
a significant influence on what a specific consumer elects to buy and not
to buy. Finally, *occupation* and the *income* therefrom are powerful determinants of buying behavior.

The strength of any one buying motive, then, varies from person to
person. For example, consumers with great purchasing power are under
less pressure to make *economical* purchases than are persons in modest
financial circumstances. Also, consumers differ in respect to the composition of the *combinations* of buying motives which cause certain purchases.
Two individuals can buy completely identical automobiles or refrigerators
or insurance policies — but the motivation of Buyer A will not be identical
to that of Buyer B.

Even the same individual buyer, however, experiences changes in his
motivation pattern from time to time. His *age* is obviously a variable that
affects what he wants to do and what he can do. *Season of the year* affects
and changes what buyers consider desirable, with the Christmas season
probably being the outstanding example. In a broader way, the *phase of
the business cycle*, whether times are good or bad, can permit buyers to be
spendthrifty — or force them to spend thriftily. A change in *marital
status* usually changes a man's buying pattern because there has been a
change in the control mechanism. *Immediate circumstances* can make a
big, bold spender out of what is normally a meek little mouse. Even so
slight a change as that of the buyer's *mood* can alter his feelings and,
through them, his buying.

The salesman's job is all the more challenging and complicated, then,
because Mr. A buys insurance from *fear* while Mr. B buys it out of *affection*
for his family; Mrs. A buys dresses early in the season in order to be
distinctive while Mrs. B buys late in the season for reasons of *economy*.

Universality In Motivation

Just as there is some change and difference in the effectiveness of buying
motives among prospects or between certain days, there is also some
permanence and universality. The young salesman will find that a pattern
of buying motives exists and is rather well established, that most prospects
want the same things that others want. This helps to instill confidence
in the less experienced salesman. He comes to realize that there are five
or six appeals or motives that will satisfactorily take care of ninety per cent
of the prospects he sees. As soon as he can stimulate those motives, he is
prepared to talk to the majority of prospects. Furthermore, by con-

centrating on how better to satisfy those five or six wants, the salesman recommends himself as an increasingly important factor in the prospect's buying decisions.

Motivation Is Complicated

Not only does the salesman find much variation in motivation, but also he discovers that motivation is complicated, partially, of course, because of the variations just discussed. Because it covers the whole field of human relations, values, and dreams, motivation cannot be simple. Drives overlap and intermesh. Several drives may well be back of a single purchase. Then, as has been hinted, any one product or brand can easily be (and usually is) a different "image" to different consumers. In theory, at least, it is possible that a salesman calls on no two customers who buy his product or service for precisely the same reasons.

It is probable that your last two purchases of shoes were triggered by two different patterns of motivation. Incidentally, can you explain just why you bought each pair — each *particular* pair — from that particular store — at that particular time — at that particular price?

The most hard-boiled, scientific purchasing agent will buy an expensive electric range for no other reason than the fact that his wife wants it. Some women buy a certain make of range because they would not be caught dead using the same make as a neighbor. At the same time, thousands of ranges are sold to women on the recommendations of other women.

Perfectly normal people are sometimes thrown off balance by the act of purchasing. The prospect may refuse for two or three years to buy something, then, for some unknown reason, he decides to buy it, and he wants it *now*, experiencing all the reactions that salesmen love. Every student reading this should be able to confirm these facts by making an honest analysis of some of his own recent purchases.

Consumers make some purchases for frivolous or even base reasons. Certain products they buy are "illegal, immoral, or fattening." But, irrational behavior delights in and may even demand rational support or camouflage. The consumer needs to protect his privacy and his pride; he needs logical, decent, proper, socially acceptable reasons to offer to those who question his purchase — or even to himself.

So, what the consumer does is dream up (or accept from the salesman) excuses for his attitudes and respectable explanations for his behavior. He acquires *rationalized* motives to match and mask his *real* motives. A consumer may know his real motivation and not be willing to reveal it, resorting to rationalization; or, he may not be aware of the fact that he is indulging in rationalizing.

CONSUMER CLASSES

Social Stratification

Most studies of consumers stratify them into five groups. In looking from top to bottom, one cannot escape an implication of status, of superior and inferior, of upper and lower. The top class is often termed the "upper" class and contains "old" families, certain business and professional persons, and a high proportion of college graduates. Next is the upper-middle or semi-upper class. Here again are many college graduates, also small business men and certain professional men. Third is the lower-middle group. Many of these are high school graduates, some are blue-collar workers, some are self-employed. Fourth is the upper-lower or working class. This level is made up of clerical workers and skilled wage-earners; it is by far the largest of the five groups. Some of those in the fourth class are high school graduates. The fifth and bottom position is occupied by the lower-lower group which is in contrast to the upper-lower (the fourth) group. Here are the unskilled workers who must spend just about all they make for basic necessities. Education only as far as grammar school is common.

What determines which social level one occupies? Financial ability to buy is one important influence, but no longer is it thought to be the sole determinant. Amount of money and the source of that money are two phases of financial ability to buy. Occupation is a second important influence. Education is the third important influence. Three other influences sometimes mentioned are type of house occupied, neighborhood, and number of generations of United States ancestry.

Within any one of the five classes, consumers tend to have the same goals, hopes, attitudes, preferences, and customs. Because their values are the same, persons in a particular class tend to be alike in respect to taste, and because taste is identical, buying decisions and buying behavior tend to be uniform.

Effects on Consumer Spending

The consumer is an individual — and a member of a social stratum. As a consumer, he has a "self-image," and this picture is always a part of him. Because it is his concept of himself, a self-image is highly subjective. When he contemplates buying, the consumer feels inclined to buy products, brands, and services which are in harmony with his self-image; he wants his purchases to qualify for *self*-approval.

As a member of a social class, the consumer finds himself wanting *social* approval as well as self-approval; he wants his purchases to reflect his social class and to merit the approval of his group. To start with, he tends to save and to spend the same portions of disposable personal income as does his group. His group has arrived at what it considers the most desirable compromise between its desire for many products and services and its desire for many dollars. Our consumer tends to adopt this group ratio as his personal ratio. Then, when spending the dollars he elects to spend, the consumer feels the influence of his class in deciding what to buy, what not to buy, which stores to patronize, and which not to patronize. Interestingly, the consumer feels "right" or "correct" with certain products as possessions and "wrong" with others. He feels at home in some stores but clearly out of place — a stranger — in others.

Income was once thought to dictate social status and to determine buying decisions and patterns. Now sellers are recognizing that consumer income changes more quickly than do consumer buying habits — that sometimes social status can be a stronger influence than income. A young doctor may earn the same amount of money as a truck driver, but his buying pattern will not be the same. Assistant professors do not buy what carpenters buy, even when they earn as much. When a salesman is collecting buyer-information, he should include facts about the buyer's sociological level or class.

KINDS OF BUYING MOTIVES

How many buying motives are there? There is no general agreement on how many basic buying motives there are nor on terminology. It is possible to hold that each individual is motivated by a single basic desire — to maximize his satisfactions. There are at least three pairs of motives, each of which has its own advocates who claim their two motives to be all-inclusive: (1) the desire to possess and the desire for approval; (2) the fear of loss and the hope of gain; (3) the enjoyment of pleasure and the avoidance of pain.

Some sellers hold that there are four buying motives: (1) profit and economy, (2) comfort and convenience, (3) health and safety, (4) pride and prestige. Others would add a fifth — the need for affection.

Three Types of Buying Motives

Persons who have been active and prominent in motivation research of the consumer see that consumer responding to three types of buying motives. *Physiological* motives include sex, comfort, hunger and thirst, and the drive to maintain life. *Psychological* motives, largely subjective, are exemplified by pride and fear. *Sociological* motives are closely related to social status, present and desired. Consumers try to chart the proper course between conformity to their present group and the need to be distinctive. They seek prestige. They emulate their "betters." They are anxious to hold on in their present stratum and/or to climb in status.

Of course, consumers must buy in the light and within the limitations of their respective buying power. Their purchases are made in a climate of unavoidable economy.

Primary Versus Selective Motives

Primary considerations are those that are involved in a consumer's choice of *type* or *kind* or *class* or product. The issue here is *what* shall be bought. When a consumer begins to toy with the idea of buying a boat *or* a foreign automobile, a swimming pool *or* a piano, primary motivation is at work. Primary considerations can lead a consumer to buy a sofa rather than some shrubbery, a wafflemaker rather than a coffeemaker. phonograph records rather than perfume, or a suit rather than a watch, A salesman must check to see that a consumer has some interest in becoming an owner of a camera before he starts pointing out the unique features of his brand of camera.

Selective considerations dictate the consumer's choice of brand, source (manufacturer and/or retailer), or of salesperson. The issue here is *which* — not *what*. The consumer's primary motivation has functioned with the result that he or she has just about decided to buy a certain type of product. Now selective questions arise. The product of Manufacturer A or Manufacturer B? Brand C or Brand D? From Retailer E or Retailer F? From Salesperson G or Salesperson H?

Product Versus Patronage

Another classification of buying motives separates product motives from patronage motives. When *product* motivation is operating in strength, the consumer is inclined to make some specific purchase because of the physical or psychological attractiveness of the product. The product appeals to him, perhaps because of one of its elements, features, or characteristics. Design, color, size, performance, package, or price can be the basis of product motivation.

Patronage motives have the same relationship to sellers that product motives have to products. Sellers are manufacturers, wholesalers, retailers, and retail salespersons. Sellers appeal to consumers on such bases as services, location, assortment, personnel, reciprocity, and price. Note that price can be either a product feature or a patronage feature.

Positive Versus Negative

When a salesman promises pleasure and satisfaction to consumers, the salesman is using *positive* appeals; he is implying that his product or service will help the consumer do, be, or get what he wants. The salesman stresses experiences and sensations consumers want; he pictures goals that are inviting and pleasant. Positive appeals can be powerful because they focus on the satisfactions consumers desire. Positive appeals can be persuasive because consumers prefer to identify themselves with what is pleasant and desirable.

When a salesman pictures what consumers want to get rid of or want to avoid, he is using *negative* appeals. He is presenting his product as a means of preventing pain, loss, risk, embarrassment, mistakes, unpopularity, worry, drudgery, or unhappiness. Negative appeals are just the reverse of their positive counterparts; the salesman can stress *pleasure* (positive) or the *prevention of pain* (negative); he can stress *safety* — or the *avoidance of danger*. In a sense, all negative appeals are appeals to consumer fear. They are often quite effective when the consumer is unaware of his need, a need the salesman's product will fill.

Emotional Versus Rational

For a long time it was thought that purchases are either emotional *or* rational in nature — that they are irrational, unstudied, and impulsive or well thought out, analyzed in advance, and planned. This older school of thought, for example, classified as *emotional* any purchase made for reasons of pride, sex, or emulation; the same school deemed *rational* those purchases made for reasons of economy, durability, or efficiency, to name a few. A basic assumption of this older school of thought was that purchasing agents, buying for business, institutions, and government, made nothing but completely rational purchases.

A more up-to-date, more realistic conviction seems to be that consumers make very few purchases that are 100% emotionally motivated. Another feature of modern thinking on the emotional-rational dichotomy is the increased awareness of the difficulty of separating the irrational from the rational. Just what is an *emotional* purchase? Just what is a *rational* purchase? The best answer seems to be that the answers are largely subjective. Suppose a consumer joins a country club. In all probability, aren't there both emotional *and* rational reasons back of his action? Suppose a boy decides to give a girl a present and then shops the stores thoroughly and systematically. Is his purchase emotional or rational, or both? Suppose a girl buys an expensive suit in the hopes of landing a coveted job; or, suppose she buys an expensive party dress in the hopes of getting or holding a husband. And even our purchasing agent — is he a rational robot when buying a huge electrified outdoor sign to go on the factory roof, or when he makes certain purchases mainly because certain other firms make them, or when he favors one salesman over another because of friendship or personality?

Perhaps we are influenced to conclude that the consumer studies, weighs, and analyzes some purchases more than others. In practically all instances, he and she want their purchases to *appear* to have been made rationally. As has been observed earlier, for the more irrational purchases the consumer has little or no difficulty in rationalizing.

Acquired Versus Basic Wants

Acquired wants are *learned* wants. They are secondary wants, not so clearly defined as basic wants. Consumers have to develop these acquired wants and to appreciate the satisfactions they involve. Consumers have learned to value such satisfactions as these: economy, information, cleanliness, efficiency, profit, curiosity, convenience, quality, dependability, beauty, fashion, and durability.

Basic wants are almost completely universal among consumers. Normal persons are born with these wants or with the capacity to develop them. They include physical, psychological, and sociological needs most of which are either in constant operation or else recur frequently. Basic wants tend to get more uniform treatment from consumers than do acquired wants. Consumers spend many dollars buying satisfaction for their basic wants.

How many basic wants are there? There is not agreement on the number. Ten are commented on briefly below.

Approval. Consumers need two types of approval, self-approval and social approval. Self-approval calls for a wholesome respect for self with a minimum of regret and remorse. Social approval comes from family, friends, associates — even strangers. The consumer wants these individuals to look with favor on what he is, has, and does. He does not want from them any criticism, ridicule, or lack of notice; instead, he hopes to be accorded recognition and even admiration. Desire for social approval puts strong pressure on the consumer to conform, to imitate, and to observe conventions rather than to violate them.

Comfort. Consumers want to be comfortable. They want to avoid pain, strain, and physical exhaustion. Comfort can be affected by temperature, humidity, hunger, thirst, extent of space, noise, degree of softness, and accuracy of fit.

Food and Drink. This is often referred to as the "appetite" want. We want what we eat and drink to taste good, to look good, to smell good, and to feel good. Food and drink are often associated with health, with the consumer's preference for variety, with hospitality, with entertaining, and with social activity.

Mastery Over Obstacles. The normal consumer wants to win, to make good against odds, to be a hero. He will undertake difficult projects because they offer challenge and competition. He is ambitious to move up, to get ahead, to better himself. He considers success to be the reward of accomplishment and achievement.

Play and Pleasure. Here are the ideas of amusement, of frolicking about, of sports and games, and of devoting oneself to having fun. Some consumers play and get pleasure by traveling; some resort to golf, or cards, or tennis; some enjoy just relaxing. Some consumers prefer to *do;* some prefer to *watch* others do.

Safety. Consumers want to be safe from danger, fear, pain, and want. They want to prevent loss, to reduce accidents, to protect somebody or something, even to avoid risk and responsibility of making decisions. The frantic and almost universal search for "security" is a manifestation of our unwillingness to grapple with uncertainty. We want safety for ourselves, for other persons, for our possessions.

Sex. This basic want is both physiological and emotional. Normal consumers want to love and to be loved by members of the opposite sex. Their sex drive is a powerful force that makes them want to be attractive to the other sex.

Superiority. The consumer needs to be proud of what he is, what he has, what he has done, what he can do today. He needs actually to be superior to others in some area and to feel that superiority. By excelling over the crowd, by being above average on some score, he makes a bid for attention, praise, and even envy. Because superiority endows one with a certain prestige, that one is more likely to be recognized as a person of consequence. Most of us think of ourselves as "Very Important Persons"; most of us want to be "somebody" in a social way.

Survival. Have you ever known a single person who was ready to depart this life? Are *you?* An interesting and true observation is that "nearly everybody wants to go to heaven, but hardly anybody wants to die." So, we want to continue living even into old age. We want to retain our health or regain it if illness, accident, or disease has impaired it.

Welfare of Loved Ones. Let's assume that most husbands and wives love each other, that parents and children love each other, that boys and girls love each other. Some consumers contribute to the happiness of loved ones from a sense of privilege, others from a sense of duty. Some consumers want appreciation, some want to obligate others; some want gratitude, others want reciprocity.

KNOWLEDGE OF BUYING MOTIVES

Nothing is more essential in selling than knowing what the prospect wants. Human nature being what it is, effective selling has to be based on, and must be responsive to, personal motivation. The salesman finds it necessary to study buying motives until his understanding of them is a part of his subconscious mental processes. His information must be assimilated to the point that he does not consciously use any rules, as he would in referring to a guidebook or a roadmap. Constant analysis of the prospect's point of view, plus practice, will enable the better salesman to use buying motives unconsciously and automatically.

Why Essential to Salesmen

The more knowledge he has about different buying motives, the more qualified the salesman will be to sell. He must know, and know how to appeal to, more motives than influence any one prospect. He must be in a position to stimulate every motive, to arouse every desire that might influence *any* prospective buyer. The ideal is for the salesman to be able to project himself into the prospect's circumstances, to determine what motives will influence the prospect toward buying, and then to be able to set those motives in action.

A recommendation to young salesmen is that they promptly, thoroughly, and continuously absorb all product advantages of their goods and classify them according to buying motives. This procedure will provide a supply of talking points for each motive. When the salesman knows what the prospect wants, what he will expect of the product, and how much the prospect will hope to profit from his purchase, he can emphasize the specific advantages of his merchandise which will appeal to that prospect. His sales story will be more complete and of sounder construction.

Product Features Versus Buyer Benefits

It is vital that a salesman understand the difference between *product features* and *buyer benefits*. Product features are of two types: (1) elements or qualities of the product itself, or (2) features or details of the salesman's proposal which can contribute to the buyer's satisfaction. The first type includes what a product *is* or *has* — raw materials, parts, manufacturing processes, grades, colors, sizes, design, packaging. The second type includes what the salesman offers or does — credit, delivery, service, sound advice, friendliness. The term product features, thus, includes certain "sales features."

Product features supply, make possible, support, or prove the benefits, advantages, and satisfactions the salesman promises to buyers. Indeed, a salesman has no other reason to call attention to product features.

The nature of buyer benefits has already been mentioned. They are the satisfactions delivered either by the product itself or by the salesman who sells it. And, even at the risk of seeming repetitious, let's once more recognize that consumers don't buy products, they buy satisfaction; consumers buy what products and services will do to them and for them; consumers buy *benefits*.

The relationship between product features and buyer benefits is now clear. Buyer benefits are gains, gratifications, utilities, and advantages; buyer benefits originate in, come from, are possible only because of product features. Buyer benefits are the effects of product features; product features cause buyer benefits.

What is a pair of shoes? Largely a combination of appearance, comfort, and economy. What is a suit? Largely a combination of style, appearance, comfort, durability, suitability, and economy. What is a refrigerator? Largely a combination of pride, protection, pleasure, utility, and economy. What is an automobile? Largely a combination of pride, protection, pleasure, utility, comfort, and economy. Note that *economy* is the only benefit common to all four.

Buyer benefits must not be confused with product features. Above all, they must not be treated as though they are interchangeable. The reason for this is that product features are weak in getting buyer attention, buyer desire, buyer purchases. Consumers are *not* interested in product features, but they are interested in what product features *do for them*.

WORKING WITH BUYING MOTIVES

A salesman should set up a definite program aimed toward the more effective handling and use of buying motives, because only through constant study and practice can he achieve proficiency. The reading and understanding of trade papers, sales training materials, advertisements, and books on psychology should be part of this program. Planned experiments and deliberate practice should be included, for they have no satisfactory substitutes. Most important of all, an extremely sensitive finger must be kept on the prospect's pulse in order to keep current on what he wants.

Identifying Buying Motives

It is not difficult to figure out the salesman's first concern with buying motives. He must identify them. If the salesman can get a picture of the way each buyer rates and evaluates his desires as of the moment, then he has a guide to that buyer's motivation. If the salesman can learn what each buyer wants and how badly, then he has discovered the key to each selfish buyer's purse. If, then, our salesman finds the pattern of buyer motivation working in this buyer's thinking, he has the answer to why this buyer spends his dollars as he does. Specifically, our salesman needs to know (a) which motives are in control of the buyer's spending, (b) the relative strength of each, and (c) what features and advantages of the salesman's product will appeal most to the buyer in the light of (a) and (b).

To sell George Brown what George Brown buys
You must see George Brown through George Brown's eyes.

How does a salesman go about discovering a buyer's motives? After he has studied his product from A to Z to find what types of utility, benefit, advantage, value, and satisfaction that product delivers, he consults the more-or-less standard lists of buyer's desires to find the universal needs and wants that his product answers. This first step gives the salesman an idea of the motivation of the typical buyer to whom he will be selling. Second, he investigates each buyer in advance. One of the main purposes of this preliminary exploration is to determine as much as possible about the motivation of individual buyers. Third, all during his interviews the salesman will STOP — LOOK — LISTEN. He will observe each buyer with a keen and constant eye for clues to motivation. He will ask the buyer questions. He will analyze and interpret all the buyer's comments in the light of buying motives. Fourth and finally, the salesman will rely heavily on experimentation, research, and experience. He must try many appeals, see how they work, and then file away in memory or written records his conclusions.

Implanting Them

There will be occasions when the salesman finds himself confronting a buyer in whose motivation pattern some changes must be made before there will be any purchase. In some of these cases the buyer sees no need to attach importance to one or more motives the salesman's product answers or satisfies. For example, some individuals think that certain forms of comfort and convenience are for sissies — *not* for *them*. In other cases, buyers will be giving too much weight to motive Y and little or none to motive Z. For example, economy might be overstressed and recreation understressed.

Where the buyer's spending control mechanism is faulty or unrealistic, the salesman's first duty is to teach and educate. He must make clear to the buyer that a different motivation pattern is preferable to the ones he now obeys. Only if the buyer "buys" the new set of motives is he apt to buy the salesman's product.

Exciting Them

Having discovered or implanted the buying motives that recommend the salesman's product to the buyer, all that is left for the salesman to do is to fan the flames of those desires until they induce the buyer to buy. In one sense, it is fair to say that the main duty of a salesman is to exercise and stimulate buying motives. The motives to be excited, of course, are those which seem most powerful in that buyer's scheme of affairs and are best satisfied by the salesman's product.

The salesman excites the buyer's motives by pointing to product features that deliver the types of satisfaction the buyer wants. If a woman prospect wants more time to spend with her children or her club, then the salesman stresses that spare time is just what an electric dishwasher supplies. If the salesman lists the advantages his product gives to buyers, and if he then supports each claimed benefit with specific details or characteristics of his product and proposition, he will get his share of sales.

Now for a word of caution. The most expert, intensive exciting of buying motives will do little good unless directed at *dominant, powerful* motives. One story has it that Lifebuoy soap was for years billed as "The Health Soap." Sales volume was respectable but not huge. When the manufacturer began to feature Lifebuoy as the answer to "BO," sales volume zoomed. In this instance, it would seem that the motive of the desire for popularity or acceptance was stronger than the desire for good health.

Classifying Them

Classification of buying motives is possible only after time and study have been consciously devoted to analyzing the prospect and the product. There are three excellent reasons why a salesman must classify buying motives, and the first is for ease of handling. As has been discussed, each prospect is a wondrously complex mechanism composed of many individuals rolled into one. And because he is many individuals, he has many wants — so many, in fact, that they cannot be handled in the mass. Before a salesman can grapple with such a broad assortment, he must classify them for practicable, convenient handling.

Second, classification is necessary so that the salesman can construct a complete sales presentation. All salesmen, particularly the younger ones, like to feel that they are fully equipped to do their jobs, to feel secure in the knowledge that they are not vulnerable because of some error of omission. A salesman's automobile is defective if a cylinder is missing; his story is deficient if a chapter is missing. Stories are checked for completeness against a classification of buying motives.

Third, a salesman should sell more effectively after he has classified buying motives. Prospect A is a puppet to buying motive X, whereas Prospect B, unaware that such an urge exists, worships buying motive Y. The automobile salesman, demonstrating the same make and model to three prospects, finds the doctor, the housewife, and the clergyman looking for and seeing three different cars. So, by classifying buying motives and by knowing what each buyer is hunting, the salesman provides himself with many arrows for his quiver, and he has a much better idea of where and how to aim.

Using Classification — An Example

Before looking at an illustration of just how a salesman makes practical use of classified buying motives, let's recall three facts. Buyers are persons with limited purchasing power and unlimited needs who make purchases *because*. They make only those commitments which they think will get for them the greatest number of things they want. They expect specific utilities and satisfactions from each product they buy.

Our prospect is a person who has tentatively decided to build a house, and our salesman, young and inexperienced, sells heating installations. The salesman properly thinks along these lines:

What type of building is this prospect going to put up?
What does this type of prospect want from a heating installation?
What services does my unit provide?
Can my unit help the prospect spend his dollars to his greatest satisfaction?
What should the prospect know about my unit before he makes his buying decision?

Next, the salesman consults the list of buying motives that operate on a person who is building a home for himself. He finds that these are some of the considerations that can and do influence the selection: approval, cleanliness, comfort, convenience, economy, health, imitation, ownership, play, and safety.

The heating installation must be translated into these buying motives before the prospect can evaluate it correctly. So, the salesman asks himself, "How will my unit guarantee comfort, economy, health, safety, and the other things to the prospect?" Regarding economy, the salesman establishes these facts:

1. The monthly fuel bill will be low.
2. Insurance rates on the house will be modest.
3. There will be no half-burned fuel.

4. Cleaning costs will be low.
5. Medical expenses will decrease.
6. The capital outlay will be small.
7. Maintenance will cost little.
8. Little space is needed.
9. The life of the unit will be long.

When the salesman has followed through on each of the other buying motives in this same way, he has the story he needs to make an effective presentation to the prospect.

STUDY ASSIGNMENTS

1. When selecting benefits to feature, should the salesman pay more attention to the *buyer* than to the *product?*
2. Suppose you went to work for a manufacturer of home freezer units. Into what satisfactions would you translate your product when talking to a housewife?
3. What consumer satisfactions can be found in a pair of shoes?
4. Should a salesman ever try to change a prospect's buying motivation? Why?
5. Can a salesman translate his product into too many different types of satisfaction? Explain.
6. Describe how two buying motives can conflict with each other as a buyer contemplates a purchase.
7. Give five examples of purchases which buyers might well wish to rationalize.
8. What elements or features are present in rational buying that are not found in emotional buying?
9. Should a salesman appeal to prospects' reason more than to their emotions? Is it unethical to appeal to emotions? Is it more effective?
10. A salesman for an agency selling an automobile in the low-price field leaves his job to go with an agency handling one of the high-priced cars. What changes are indicated in the buying motives to which the salesman will have to appeal?

CASE STUDY 8A

A young man has just entered the luggage department of a large department store. As he stands looking uncertainly at some luggage in front of an American Traveler display, a salesgirl approaches him.

Salesgirl: Isn't that a beautiful piece of luggage? We've just heard that American Traveler won the Fashion Award with this design at the New York show only last week.

Prospect: Yes, it is nice, but I don't quite know what I want. . . . I'm looking for something for my wife's birthday, and I just can't seem to decide on anything.

Salesgirl: I know that she would love to have something like this. This is one of the finest bags made in America today, and what's more it's also the lightest. And you know, that's definitely a fact to consider in buying a bag for a lady.

Prospect: Well that's true enough, but I don't want to get something that's going to be falling to pieces in a week or two.

Salesgirl: You won't have to worry about that with an American Traveler bag. Look! (Puts bag on floor and stands on it.) This bag will easily hold two hundred pounds! Here, you stand on it.

Prospect: No, that won't be necessary. It looks pretty sturdy.

Salesgirl: It is. Look at this cut-away section. (Picks up a model and shows him.) Notice that the bag is constructed of a laminated plywood which has been moulded to a solid one-piece frame. I don't know much about moulding plywood, but you can see how this has been moulded right to the frame, and look at the corners. Notice how an extra thickness has been moulded there for reinforcement. This all means that American Traveler has produced a bag that is the strongest and lightest high-quality bag made.

Prospect: It does look pretty strong. But what's that covering? Is that some sort of imitation leather?

Salesgirl: Oh, no sir! This piece of luggage is covered with Lyn-Weave Permanite which is guaranteed to be resistant to scuffing, staining, peeling, scratching, and chipping. (At this point, salesgirl takes out a key and "strikes" it across the bag.) See! Not a scratch. And here's another good point. This bag is not only waterproof, but it's washable. That's a feature which appeals to all women.

Prospect: Seems to be built pretty good. But that sure is a funny shape, I think. Why is it wider on one side than it is on the other?

Salesgirl: Well, sir, that is the exclusive design of American Traveler. If you've ever noticed your wife packing, she usually has several wide items to go in like shoes and bottles. By making the bag higher on one side than the other, American Traveler has been able to provide a space for these wide items. This permits you to pack your other things flat, where you'll have less wrinkling and crushing That's another reason why this bag was designed to be tall and narrow. It's also much easier to carry, doesn't bump against your leg when you're carrying it.

Prospect: Oh, yes. Now that's nice.

Salesgirl: Here, try it. (Buyer takes bag and walks a few steps with it.)

Prospect: Yes, that certainly is an advantage, especially if it's heavy. Let me take a look at how this handle is put on. You know, I bought a bag one time, and I had gotten no further than the railroad station when the handle pulled right off that thing!

Salesgirl: I don't think that you'll ever have that trouble with this bag. The handle and locks are moulded right into the frame of the bag with a metal-base plate back of each one of them.

Prospect: Is that lining loose on one side?

Salesgirl: Oh, no. That's another feature of American Traveler bags. These two full size pockets have a detachable plastic lining which is completely waterproof. That's in case some of your wife's cosmetics should ever get broken. In this waterproof pocket, it couldn't ruin the rest of her clothes.

Prospect: Say, that's nice, I bet my wife would really appreciate that.

Salesgirl: I'm sure she would. Which color do you think she'd like? This line comes in three beautiful colors — grey, green, and tan.

Prospect: I think she might like this tan the best. But, you know, I was just thinking of what you said a few minutes ago. If this luggage is guaranteed not to crack or scuff, why has it got that binding around it?

Salesgirl: Here, I'll show you. (Picks up cut-away model.) Notice what's between this binding and the bag itself. That's live rubber! That gives a cushion to make this bag virtually shock and travel resistant.

Prospect: What is the price of these bags, anyway?

Salesgirl: The prices in this line run from $15.95 to $52.50, depending on which pieces you select. When is your wife's birthday?

Prospect: It's next Wednesday, but I really don't think . . .

Salesgirl: We could have it gift wrapped and delivered to your home anytime you say next Wednesday. And you're going to be a very proud man, I'm sure, when your wife sees her present.

Prospect: Do you suppose they could bring it out about six, so I could be there?

Salesgirl: Of course, we'd be glad to. Would you rather pay for this now, or charge it?

Prospect: Maybe I better wait until later on in the week, since I'm not sure just which pieces I want to get.

Salesgirl: I think this overnite case and this twenty-six-inch pullman would be just the thing to start a set with, and then you could add other pieces at Christmas and special occasions.

Prospect: Well, I suppose I might as well as long as I'm here. Do you really think those are the best pieces to get?

Salesgirl: They're our two best sellers and are just the thing for a woman on a weekend trip.

Prospect: Well, all right then. (Salesgirl takes out charge book.) You can charge that to Robert Hinckley. I live at 1920 Westwood Place. Now are you sure it'll be there?

Salesgirl: Yes, sir, I'll make the delivery ticket out right now. And thank you. Mr. Hinckley. I'm sure your wife is going to enjoy her new American Traveler luggage.

QUESTIONS:

1. What did the salesgirl do well?
2. What did the salesgirl do that could be improved?
3. What techniques are illustrated in the sale?
4. List the motives to which the salesgirl appealed.

CASE STUDY 8B

This sales interview takes place in a furniture store in a medium-sized town. The prospect is in the middle income group, and he has just purchased a table lamp. He is starting to leave the store.

Salesman: Before you leave, sir, let me show you this new appliance we have just received. This is the new Ajax Combination Sandwich Grill and Waffle Iron, one of the most convenient and useful appliances we have.

Prospect: It seems to be nice, but I don't need anything like this at the present time.

Salesman: Perhaps you are right, but I'll bet your wife would like to be able to grill sandwiches or fry foods and do many other small cooking jobs right at the table without having to bother with heating up the range, wouldn't she?

Prospect: I suppose so.

Salesman: Well, she can do just that with this combination appliance. She can just set it on the table, plug it in, and in a very few minutes it is ready for cooking. Whatever you want, you can cook on this grill. You can make delicious waffles and sandwiches, and not only that but this top portion (Salesman lifts top back.) may be opened and you have two cooking surfaces for frying bacon, hamburgers, eggs, and many other foods.

Prospect: That's nice.

Salesman: You see this dial here. (Salesman points out the dial.) This enables you to set the temperature you want, and a thermostat on the inside maintains that temperature. This feature will give you quick heat and an even distribution of heat over the entire cooking surface. With this controlled temperature, you can be assured that food will be properly and thoroughly cooked. There will be no half-cooked or unevenly cooked food or food waste from burning. You know how important this is, don't you?

Prospect: Yes, I guess it's pretty important.

Salesman: I'll bet your wife would enjoy these features, wouldn't she?

Prospect: I imagine she would.

Salesman: Wouldn't you like to take this home with you? It certainly would be a wonderful surprise for your wife.

Prospect: Oh, this is just another gadget. I don't think I really need this.

Salesman: I'm sure your wife would like it. Women can see the advantages of an appliance like this even better than men can. She is the one who has to prepare the food and cook it. You know, this appliance is made by the Ajax Company. They make some of the finest appliances in the country.

Prospect: Well, this is all very interesting, but I must be going now. When did you say my lamp will be delivered?

Salesman: You should have it by next Thursday at the latest. But let me tell you just a little more about this sandwich grill and waffle iron combination. Ajax scientists and engineers have specified only the best materials for its manufacture, and this, coupled with Ajax craftsmanship, brings you an appliance which is modern, attractive, and which will give you years of excellent service. How would you like to own this?

Prospect: I suppose I might like to, but I can't see where it will do me too much good.

Salesman: Just look at this modern design and the attractive chrome. This would certainly be an asset to your kitchen. Your wife would be proud to own it, wouldn't she?

Prospect: She has plenty of gadgets now, and another one would just clutter up the kitchen.

Salesman: Wouldn't you like to have those delicious waffles in the morning?

Prospect: A waffle iron doesn't cost as much as this thing, does it?

Salesman: No, but this appliance can also grill sandwiches or fry hamburgers or eggs. This combination appliance will give you maximum service and enjoyment. It will pay for itself many times in the enjoyment and service you will receive from it over its long life. Why not let me put it on the same bill with your lamp? I could have them delivered at the same time next week.

Prospect: No, thanks, I'm not interested.

Salesman: You wouldn't believe it but this combination appliance costs only $21.50. And it is certainly well worth its price. I'm sure your wife would love to own it. A modern kitchen should really have one of these appliances. May I send this to you with the lamp?

Prospect: Sorry, I don't need the grill-waffle iron. I'll expect the lamp by next Wednesday or Thursday. Be seeing you. Goodbye.

QUESTIONS:

1. What did the salesman do well?
2. What did the salesman do that could be improved?
3. What techniques are illustrated in the sale?
4. To how many buying motives did the salesman refer?
5. To which other motives might he have referred?

CHAPTER 9

THE SALESMAN'S COMPETITION

Whenever a product is invented or a service designed and then sold profitably, a prediction involving no risk whatever is that competitive products and services will appear. And, in a general sense, this it not totally unfavorable. One good effect is that it keeps the originator on his toes. Another is that this original seller gets help in building a market for his new type of product and in informing and educating prospects about a better answer to one of their needs or problems. A third good result is that buying decisions are more easily and readily made once buyers can compare several products of the same type.

Salesmen must accept competition. After all, if there were no competition, there would be no need for salesmen. Salesmen must accept the facts that (a) these are days of great product standardization and (b) few, if any, brands are superior on *all* counts. Salesmen must see that the plus points of brand "M" are the minus points of brand "N," and that "N" is superior in areas where "M" is inferior.

The most promising approach to an effective handling of competition is a search for something that is different. Each salesman needs something unique, something exclusive, something only he can offer. He hopes to find this something in the product he sells — low price, patented part, most attractive package. Otherwise, he must hunt for the something in some aspect of his company's operations or in something he personally can supply in greater amount than can any competing salesman. In the final analysis, the salesman hopes to present a proposal or proposition which, in its totality, is different *and therefore most desirable* from the buyer's point of view. This is particularly indicated if the salesman's product is relatively high in price; here he must present the overall concepts of total cost, worth, and value.

Two features of competitive selling are worth mentioning. First, a salesman must do unto competitive salesmen what he must not allow them to do unto him — he must woo prospects away from them. Second, the salesman must cope with *direct* competition (Ford vs. Chevrolet) and *indirect* competition (new automobile vs. vacation trip).

IS KNOWLEDGE OF COMPETITION DANGEROUS?

Sometimes the opinion is expressed, occasionally by salesmen, that it is dangerous for a young salesman to know too much about his competition. Indeed, there are a few sales managers who assert that they want their junior salesmen to know as little as possible about competing products. This attitude is explained and defended by two fears. First, if a young salesman learns very much about his competition, he may develop a fear-of-competition complex. Second, the salesman may do unwise things in his collection and use of these facts.

These fears do not seem sound. As for the former, if the salesman is a person who, in learning about competition, will develop a fear-of-competition complex, if he will be unduly impressed by competition's good points and qualities, if he is apt to get an exaggerated idea of what his competition is and what it is doing — then his success as a salesman is in serious doubt.

The second fear actually cannot correctly be charged against the salesman's knowledge about competition, for what the critics have in mind is the salesman's misuse of his time or his selling efforts. The critics fear that the young salesman may be inclined to spend too much time hunting competitive weaknesses when that time should be devoted to studying the merits of his own product. His selling efforts are misdirected if channeled into a condemnation of competing products for their weak points instead of into an explanation of what his product does for buyers.

As a matter of fact, a person entering the field of selling is going to find out about competition in any event. He will need such information, and, in addition, he cannot avoid collecting it in his daily work. A vice-president of the Penn Mutual Life Insurance Company, realizing that the acquisition of facts about competition is inevitable, says:

> If a salesman has faith in his product and in his employer, his enthusiasm should carry him over the reefs of the average competition. By faith, we do not mean mere credulity, but a belief based upon careful examination of the product as useful, well made, and sold at competitive prices. In establishing this faith, the salesman naturally would have to examine other products, and that in itself would give him a knowledge of competition.

Since this is true, instead of being frightened at the thought of learning too much that is good and bad about competition, the smart individual collects and uses competitive information in a purposeful, premeditated manner.

PROPER ATTITUDE TOWARD COMPETITION

One feature of the salesman's attitude should be a *respect* for his competition. In many fields and lines, one brand of product is just about the same as the others, and prospects know this. Furthermore, any real competition must, of necessity, involve companies, salesmen, and products that have both good points and good friends. A prospect may have a deep admiration for a competitive company, or he may have a warm feeling for a competitive salesman, or he may think so highly of a competing product that he buys or uses it. In view of this, it is a mistake to show lack of respect for competition before the prospect. The wiser thing to do is to show respect for all competitors by giving them credit for having something to sell. A respectful consideration for competition is one of the suggestions of a sales manager for Exide Batteries:

> ... it behooves any salesman to know all he can about his competitors and their products so as to be able to guide his own selling efforts. Particularly is it desirable never to underrate a competitor. What to do about the competitors is a matter which varies to some extent but, sub-stantially, it would seem . . . that the most important thing is for a salesman to remember at all times the fact that he is selling his own company's products and that the advantages to the customer in buying them should be emphasized.

A second characteristic is *fairness.* The salesman lowers himself in the prospect's estimation when he does or says anything that smacks of unfair treatment or unfair criticism of competition. Resentment may be particularly strong when there are no defenders of competition present, or when a direct comparison requested by the prospect is not made fairly and squarely. All questions and comparisons call for a clean, honest handling, for a "Let's put all the cards on the table and see just what is what" treatment. Such fairness gives the salesman two things: the good feeling that results from operating ethically, and more enthusiastic cus-tomers.

A third phase of the salesman's attitude toward competition should be that of *disinterest.* At the same time that he shows his respect for competition to the prospect, he should also make it clear that his time is too valuable to be used discussing competition. His brief answers to questions about competition indicate that he is enthusiastically interested in his own wares, and unconcerned about others. His position is that he has a proposal to make that will be good for the prospect, and he, the salesman, intends to speak positively of that proposal — not negatively about other brands or makes. Indeed, his product has so many buyer-advantages that he is forced to restrict his conversation to them. When competitors' barbs are relayed by a prospect, the salesman registers amusement and tolerance as he brushes them aside with a terse "That's the penalty of leadership," or "Whoever is in first place makes the best target."

Confidence is a fourth and final essential of a proper attitude. It is the factor that prevents fright, anxiety, or irritation; it is the comforting knowledge that the salesman has nothing to fear from any fair comparison. If there is something his product does not have, then that something must not be necessary. His confidence translates into an aggressive enthusiasm that automatically puts him on the offensive and competition on the defensive. His products offer so many advantages to buyers that he can graciously and generously acknowledge that a competitive item is excellent in one respect, or perhaps even in two.

WHAT TO KNOW ABOUT COMPETITION

It appears that data on competition cluster around two matters, *product comparison* and *selling activities*. The third subdivision of this section deals with *sources* of such information.

Product Comparison

The first and most essential thing for the salesman to know is how his product stacks up against competing products. After mastering the facts about his product that were discussed in Chapter 6, his next step is to learn all the strong and weak points about competitive brands and makes. In taking this step, the topics included in Chapter 6 can be used as an outline or guide, thus eliminating the need for any specific or detailed consideration here.

Just as the salesman concentrates on the salient and significant features of his own merchandise, so does he identify and study the outstanding features of other products. At the same time that he is collecting all the facts he conveniently can, he ranks them in order of importance and directs his expenditure of search-efforts accordingly.

The most helpful procedure for the young salesman is to write down a list of every strong point, every user-benefit, every advantage his product has or provides, and then make a second list of any handicaps or limitations. If this second list is too long, perhaps our salesman should consider changing lines. After covering his product thoroughly in these two lists, the next thing to do is to draw up a similar pair of lists for each item in competition with his product. He then has a complete summary of all points of strength and weakness on each product in that particular field.

Competitors' Selling Activities

Competitive Salesmen. The first thing to know about competitive selling activities is who the competitive salesmen are. Personal facts about the man who represents a competitor might include his name, background, where he lives, his interests and tastes, his avocations, and the social circle within which he moves. Business facts might include the length of time he has been with his company, what he did before that, his various jobs with his present company, how long he has been in his present territory, and how and about how much he is paid.

More specific and relevant information about the competitor's representative concerns his sales personality. His personal characteristics are worth knowing. His concept of the duties and responsibilities of a salesman, as well as his pattern and method of operation, should be enlightening and valuable. How his prospects and customers rate him as a salesman, what they like and dislike about him, and the extent to which they consider him a personal friend as well as a source of supply are bits of information which can be used to advantage.

By way of example, if the competitor's salesman relies too heavily on friendship to hold his present customers (who, of course, are prospects of our salesman), his relationship with them and his control of them is not secure. Such a situation invites our salesman to move in with more quality, more service, lower prices, or better selling, because these are the things that will get and hold customers away from competition. And our salesman should keep an eagle eye on himself so he will not fall into the same trap that caught the competitive salesman. Friendship is fine, but he must not depend on it.

The more similar or even standardized the product line is, the more the emphasis shifts away from merchandise features and toward the salesman himself. In some lines, the product can be bought on the buyer's specifications from two or more vendors of equally satisfactory standing and at the same or approximately the same price. In such cases, the purchaser has little to base his choice on except differences in competing salesmen. Hence, our salesman needs to know *whom* as well as *what* he is selling against.

Competitive Presentations. In the presentation made by any competitor's representative, our salesman is particularly interested in two things: *what* was said and *how* it was said.

The proposition offered by the competitive representative is the *what* that our salesman needs to know, and the first consideration here is the product recommended to the prospect. Our salesman must determine whether or not the item recommended adequately meets the prospect's requirements, being neither too little nor too much. If the item is unsatisfactory on either score, the question is whether or not the prospect thinks that it is completely suitable. In view of competitive recommendations, with what should our salesman counter? The price quoted by the other

MINUTE MAID CORPORATION

WEEKLY SALES REPORT

YOUR NAME

DATE

TERRITORY No.

CITY

Retail	TOTAL CALLS	TOTAL ACCTS. SOLD	NEW ACCTS. OPENED	NUMBER OF ACCOUNTS STOCKING																	
				ORANGE		G. F.	BL.	TANG.	LEMON			LIME	GRAPE		PINE	TNGO	ORE ADE	MIXERS			
				6 OZ.	12 OZ.				6 OZ.	12 OZ.	5¾ OZ.		6 OZ.	12 OZ.				34 OZ.	76 OZ.		

| INFORMATIVE REMARKS GUIDE: | BY ITEMS | | | | | | | | | | | | | | | | | | | | |

R E M A R K S

A. MINUTE MAID
   Sales
   Price
   Position

B. COMPETITION
   Price
   Position
   Sales Effort

C. PROMOTIONS
   Suggested
   Current & Results
   Competitions' & Results

D. COMPARE WITH COMPETITION
   Ad Support
   Cabinet Display
   Distribution

E. Number of Accounts
   called on this week
   not regularly contacted?
   Results

F. OTHER

Minute Maid Corp.

The significance of competitive activities to Minute Maid salesmen is indicated in this report.

representative, as well as terms, deals, allowances, and any "special" or "inside" angles, should be learned.

A second phase of the *what* of competitive presentations involves what is said about the competitive item and about our product. Particularly desirable is information about the product-points stressed. Which features of his product does the competitive representative accent? Which does he not mention? What word-of-mouth publicity is he giving another's products throughout his territory? Does he take a dim view of some feature of those products? If so, can that view be converted from a drawback into an effective buyer-advantage?

A third and final phase of *what* the competitive representative says is made up of his most effective and successful reasons and maneuvers. For each individual prospect, our salesman benefits from knowing those features of competitive proposals that have strong appeal. Similarly, the features which most often impress prospects in general are good to know. Add to these persuasive features the closing appeals that frequently take orders away from our salesman, and the result is a collection of data that better enables our salesman to select and emphasize the features of his proposition which will counteract and counterbalance competitive features.

The second part of the competitive presentation concerns *how* the representative tells his story and is important because the more our salesman knows about the type of presentation made by each representative, the stronger his own can be. The aids that are used, the models, samples, charts, catalogs, reports, survey findings — all of these are parts of how the story is told. If demonstrations are used, especially when they are impressive, our salesman cannot afford to be uninformed.

Intra-territory Matters.   Intra-territory matters form another segment of competitive selling activities. One territorial matter of interest to our salesman is the total amount of business in his line in his area. This figure, best thought of in terms of annual dollar purchases, is the 100 per cent quantity of which our man wants a satisfactory share. So, he wants to know the dollar total and how it is divided among the various vendors. Trends and relative standings are significant because they point out which vendors are gaining ground at whose expense.

Treatment of prospects and customers is a second territorial matter in which our salesman should be interested. What are competitors' calling habits and schedules, and how complete is their coverage of the area? Is any competitor too confident — even smug — about holding his good accounts? What other mistakes is he making in handling customers whom we would like to have? Which of *our* customers is he working on hardest? Which of our customers is he most likely to take away from us?

Finally, there are certain spheres within each of which our salesman should know what competition now does and plans to do. For example, present practices about delivery or billing should be known. The amount and kind of advertising, sales promotion, and merchandising effort the area is receiving should be matters of knowledge. Any changes scheduled for the future involving, perhaps, geography, personnel, product, or price policy should be learned about as promptly as possible. Price cutting is something the salesman must always know about.

Sources of Information

Although it is always possible that a salesman may not be able to get some bit of badly needed information about his competitors, there are several sources that will, in most cases, prove to be helpful. The advertisements of competitors are one such source, and they are particularly worthwhile in regard to product facts. Other salesmen, with his own company or with another, noncompeting company, frequently can supply valuable knowledge. For certain consumer products, comparison shopping and trials are practicable. For the fortunate salesman, his company will distribute whatever information it considers desirable or essential. For example, the salesmen who sell Nibroc Towels find this list in their company's training material:

Some Weaknesses in Competitive Towels

Have poor absorbency.	Same towel used many times.
Lack wet strength.	Container holds fewer towels.
Come apart.	Manufacturer is unknown.
Do not dry efficiently.	Time dispenser frequently
Have harsh, rough surface.	out of order.

News stories are a minor yet sometimes fruitful aid. The salesman's own keen observation can prove to be an extremely significant servant in the search for competitive data. Last and most important of all is the prospect himself with his revealing comments, actions, and questions.

In its *Basic Notes on the Armstrong Line*, a manual for wholesaler salesmen, the Armstrong Cork Company includes this section:

Competitors

The resilient flooring industry has attracted a large number of manufacturers. There is plenty of competition on practically every Armstrong floor and wall product.

This section will tell you nothing about the fine points of competitors' merchandise. It merely gives you a summary of Armstrong's competition.

Here are three cautions about competitors:

The time you spend talking down a competitor can be spent to better advantage talking up Armstrong.

Whenever you mention a competitor by name in your sales presentation, you give him a free plug. He appreciates it. The dealer naturally says to himself, "This competitor must be good. He's probably a thorn in this salesman's side. If he were not, this salesman wouldn't be talking about him."

If you must refer to a competitor in a sales interview, "another manufacturer" sounds a lot better than "competitor" or the competitor's name.

Linoleum Competitors. There are five other domestic manufacturers of linoleum. All of the linoleum manufacturing plants are located in the East except one plant that is located on the West Coast.

Felt-Base Competitors. Armstrong has nine competitors in the felt-base manufacturing field and most of them have their plants in the East. All except one make both roll goods and rugs. Only four make 12' wide felt-base, 6' and 9' being the standard widths with the other companies.

Asphalt Tile Competitors. There are about ten other companies in the United States that make asphalt tile. Several of these companies have more than one plant, and the plants are located generally in the East, the Midwest, the West Coast, and near the Gulf Coast.

Rubber Tile Competitors. Twelve other manufacturers compete with Armstrong in the rubber tile business. These producing plants are pretty well scattered all over the country. Some of these companies also make sheet rubber which is used for flooring.

Cork Tile Competitors. The competing companies who make cork tile are not so numerous. There are only two other manufacturers, both of whom are located in the East.

Manufacturers of "Plastic" Floors and Walls. There are many plants of all sorts, sizes, and characters that make some kind of "plastic" floor or wall material. Most of the major producers of resilient flooring make a "plastic" floor or wall product.

Summary. You have plenty of competition . . . about 50 companies with a total of some 60 producing plants.

USEFULNESS OF COMPETITIVE INFORMATION

Knowledge of competition provides the salesman with a broader background for the intelligent handling of his job of selling. It helps him orient himself in his territory. Knowledge of what he is selling *against* complements his knowledge of what he is selling. Part of this background is the appreciation of and respect for competition acquired in the process of learning and as a result of it.

The salesman's confidence increases, directly in his merchandise and indirectly in himself and his company, as he learns more about competition. Certainty breeds confidence; the young, fearful salesman is robbed of his power to convince and to persuade if he is uncertain about competition.

Facts about competition help in formulating the sales approach and the presentation; they keep the salesman from being in the dark about the competition he confronts. By comparing his product with competitive products, he identifies the points of superiority that will make the most successful story, and the same comparisons that convince him can be used to convince prospects. It is, incidentally, a "must" that the salesman know the most influential three or four ways in which his product excels if he is to convince the prospect of the benefits that will be received by buyers. The prospect can grasp, believe, and remember four points of superiority better than fourteen.

Information about competition makes easier the salesman's task of getting his product introduced into the prospect's stream of thought. If the prospect has never before bought the type of product in question (examples: insurance, pianos, power mowers, or air conditioning), then it is both possible and desirable for the salesman to know more about his own product and the other brands under the prospect's consideration than the prospect does. Because he knows the differences among the brands, the salesman is more successful in explaining them in a way that interests and satisfies the prospect. On the other hand, if the prospect has used or is using a competitive brand, he is acquainted with its characteristics, features, performance, and merits. His knowledge and his thinking are in terms of that brand. The more the salesman knows about that brand, the more gracefully and effectively he can introduce his brand into the prospect's thought pattern. International Harvester reminds its salesmen that prospects who now use a competitive product may know more about it than the International Harvester man.

> Keep your objective in mind — selling your own product — and keep your prospect's attention on that product. Mention of the competitor's product turns attention from your own.

> If it is necessary to discuss the competitor's product, be fair. Admission that competitors also make good machines will do your cause no harm. You must show the prospect offsetting advantages of Harvester machines.

> Do not attempt a detailed analysis of the construction and operation of a competitor's machine unless you know what you're talking about. The prospect may be the owner of a competitor's machine and know more about it than you do.

> Never knock the competitor's products or methods. Sell your own instead.

Knowledge of competition prepares the salesman for whatever the prospect may think, say, or ask. The salesman cannot afford to be surprised by criticisms or claims voiced by prospects — he must know the correct from the erroneous — he must have the right answer ready when the prospect makes some point that competition stresses.

Competitive data permit the salesman to protect his prospects and at the same time to fulfill his obligations to his own product. He must assume that competitive salesmen will suggest standards and criteria of judging which will show off their respective products to advantage. So, at the same time he is protecting his prospect and discharging his duty to that prospect, the salesman guarantees his product a fair break and looks after his own personal interests by suggesting bases of comparison which do justice to his own particular brand of merchandise.

The more he knows about the subject of competition, the more successful the salesman is in keeping it out of the discussion. By not letting it creep into the conversation, the salesman forestalls competitive arguments, avoids clashing points of view, and prevents a waste of time for both the prospect and himself.

Selling against strong competition takes more tact, judgment, and control than any other phase of selling. Every product, every salesman, every company has its good points. Each salesman will stress those points. The prospect buys from the salesman who convinces him that his product will provide the greatest net amount of satisfaction. One company helps its salesmen do just that with sales clinchers. The makers of Fenestra Steel Residence Casements say:

Sales Clinchers Aplenty

in FENESTRA'S advantages over . . .

Double hung windows.   Wood casement.   Other steel casements.
In the following pages we are giving you powerful sales ammunition.
This is factual information . . . advantages over competition that old
hands at the business have used for years to boost sales.

1. *Easy to Open.* Fenestra windows open at a finger's touch.
2. *More Fresh Air and Better Control of Ventilation.*
3. *Easier . . . and Safer . . . to Clean.* Less window washing.
4. *More Daylight.*
5. *Finer Appearance . . . Inside and Out.*
6. *Better Screens . . . on the Inside.* No fitting. No painting. Easy
     to put up or down. Easier to store. Longer life — less main-
     tenance.
7. *Better Protection from Prowlers.*
8. *Reduced Heat Loss.*

WHAT TO AVOID

Because competition is, at best, a difficult matter, some suggestions
about what *not* to do should be helpful.   If the errors listed here are
avoided, the handling of competition will be less risky and costly.

1. Do not include any reference to competition in constructing the sales
presentation, because it is not sound strategy to recognize it in that manner.
In putting his story together, the salesman should be like the runner who
eyes the tape, not the other runners.

2. Never initiate the subject of competition.   If it is to be mentioned, let
the prospect make the first reference.   Furthermore, the salesman should
not compare his product with another unless the prospect demands it.
Neither should he discuss competition except to answer a direct question.

3. Do not stray or be maneuvered away from the primary task, which is
to explain what the salesman's product will do for the prospect.   Stay
on the track.   Do not be dragged into a discussion of competitive topics.
Remember that it is never desirable to discuss competition even though
it is sometimes unavoidable.   A company that feels strongly about this
matter, the Pittsburgh Plate Glass Company, includes this statement in
its training material:

> Competition is a business stimulant and a challenge to the members
> of a right-thinking organization. Pittsburgh Plate Glass Company is an
> aggressively keen and worthy contender for its share of available business,
> and wishes to merit and maintain the respect of its competitors as to its
> high ethical standards. It is our policy not to discuss competitors with

the trade, but instead to discuss our company, its products, and service. Your objective is to sell our products on their merits, not to disparage competitors' products.

4. Have no ambitions to win mud-slinging contests. Most prospects can be trusted to detect and resent any disparaging remarks made by competitive representatives. Mud-slinging is best met with user-benefits.

5. Never make a statement about competition before checking its accuracy.

6. Do not expose flaws in competition in the hope of selling thereby.

7. Don't welcome gossip. If you must listen to it, don't repeat it.

8. Never, *never* criticize competition. Criticism can be interpreted as "knocking," and that is considered poor sportsmanship, which in turn is poor salesmanship. In addition, the prospect knows that the salesman is not impartial and for that reason the prospect has difficulty in believing him. Finally, the prospect may like, have faith in, or even use the other brand or make. He will resent any belittling of it. Of course he may not, but if he chooses to defend his opinion or action, a discussion may be extended when it should not have been allowed to develop at all.

STUDY ASSIGNMENTS

1. "The penalty of success is competition." Discuss this statement.
2. Suggest some rules for a salesman to observe when a buyer demands that he compare his product with its leading competitors.
3. Should a salesman be pleased to learn that several of his competitors have a lot to say about him and his merchandise? Why?
4. Selling trucks is a very competitive business. In order to compete successfully, into what buyer-advantages should a salesman translate the trucks he sells?
5. Comment on the salesman as a source of information about competition for his company.
6. Describe three situations in which a salesman can put to good use information about the selling done by competitive salesmen.
7. Draft a few rules, principles, or bits of advice about handling competition. Assume that you are addressing them to a young man who has just been given his first sales territory.
8. List some ways in which a salesman's ignorance about competition can handicap him.
9. Point out two or three specific ways in which "knocking" a competitor can do damage to the salesman doing the knocking.
10. "Build a better mousetrap and the world will beat a path to your door." Is this the best answer to competition?

CASE STUDY 9

Sam Jones, one of our salesmen, has come up with a new idea in selling to chain stores where, right now, our leading competitor is outselling us ten to one. Our company's policy is to spend little money on advertising and sales promotion, and to pass this saving along to the customer.

Sam went into a chain store last week and noticed that our competitor's product was displayed prominently in the store, while ours was limited to just a couple of rows on the shelf. Sam asked the store manager why our brand wasn't displayed more. The manager told him that our brand sells only 200 cases a month while our competitor's brand sells 2,000 cases a month and that they advertise a lot and we don't.

Now, Sam is pretty good in arithmetic. He told the store manager that he could make him some money using some elementary arithmetic. Since our company doesn't advertise much, we have lower selling expenses. We sell for $9.75 per case, while our competitor sells for $9.96 per case; that's 21¢ cheaper per case. Sam checked and found that our brand returns the chain store $14.50 per case by selling @ 2/29¢. Our competitor returns the store only $10.50 per case since it sells @ 2/21¢. That means the store makes over $4.00 more on each case of our goods sold.

The chain store is making $4.75 per case gross on our goods and only 54¢ per case on our competitor's. Sam showed the manager that 200 cases of our goods would make the store $950. The chain sold 2,000 cases of our competitor's goods, and that made them a gross profit of $1,080. To make this additional $130 profit, 1,000 per cent more merchandise had to be handled (200 cases of our goods × 1,000% = 2,000 cases of competitor's goods). Sam told the chain store manager how the overhead costs involved in handling 2,000 cases against 200 cases would probably wipe out the higher gross profit figures.

Sam then explained that if the store were to purchase 200 additional cases of our brand and add two rows to our brand display, the store could gross $1,900 on our goods. Sam knew that our brand could be sold very easily if we had additional display space.

So, by this little exercise in arithmetic, Sam Jones showed how our chain store sales could be increased:

	OUR BRAND		RIVAL BRAND
Return per case @2/29......	$ 14.50	@2/21.	$ 10.50
Cost per case.............	9.75		9.96
Gross profit per case........	4.75		.54
Cases sold................	200		2000
Total gross profit...........	$950.00		$1,080.00

If the store took 200 additional cases of our goods and 200 fewer cases of our competitor's goods, then the "Profit Chart" would look like this:

	OUR BRAND		RIVAL BRAND
Return per case @2/29......	$ 14.50	@2/21.	$ 10.50
Cost per case.............	9.75		9.96
Gross profit per case.......	4.75		.54
Cases sold................	400		1,800
Total gross profit..........	$1,900.00		$ 972.00

QUESTION:

Do you consider Jones' arithmetic convincing?

Part

C

The Selling Process

CHAPTER 10

PLANNING THE SALES STORY

A salesman needs a plan for each call he makes just as a motorist on a cross-country tour needs a road map. At all times, each needs to know where he is and where he is going.

Many "no sale" calls can be traced to a salesman's dependence on a prayer instead of a plan. To check on this, what happened the last five or six times you were some salesman's prospect? How many of those salesmen had planned to sell to you? How many made you feel inadequate, in regard to his product or service, in your present situation? How many merely visited with you, perhaps in a somewhat aimless fashion?

Planned presentations beat hit-or-miss, extemporaneous presentations. When planning, the salesman learns about each prospect as a person — his personality, experience, and motivation — his circumstances of the moment — his attitudes toward the salesman's product and competing products — his peculiarities, problems, and hopes. The salesman seeks the best approach to use in adapting his goods to each individual buyer. He identifies probable objections and drafts plans to overcome each. He plans a presentation which is both believable and complete enough to close the sale. He plans to establish buyer-need and to show how utility and satisfaction outweigh price. In a word, the salesman plans for a purchase to be made.

EMPATHY — A PREREQUISITE

Before starting upon selling careers in the field, it is worthwhile for salesmen to get some notion of what *empathy* is and to grasp the significance of the role it plays in selling.

What is empathy? Webster says it is "imaginative projection of one's own consciousness into another being." In selling, then, it is the salesman's understanding of the buyer's viewpoint — it is seeing matters as the buyer sees them — it is the salesman's causing himself to feel as the buyer feels, even his feeling *for* the buyer. The empathic salesman treats each buyer in a considerate manner. His capacity for empathy permits the salesman to be sympathetic to the buyer's preferences and prejudices, perceptive to the buyer's attitudes and beliefs, sensitive to the buyer's hopes and fears, receptive to the buyer's ideas and reactions, and appreciative of the buyer's objectives and values.

When empathy is operating, the salesman thinks in terms of others, not just himself. He gives the buyer no impression of conceit, superiority, condescension, criticism, irritation, or impatience. Instead, the salesman's sincere question is: How can I help this buyer get what he wants most?

Being an empathic salesman is an art. It is an ability a salesman must acquire and master if he is to realize his full potential. This takes time, planned practice, experimentation, and experience. A salesman should want to perfect his skill in this area until his attempts to understand each buyer are automatic.

Empathy contributes to a salesman's success in several ways. It helps make salesman-buyer relations pleasant. It fosters greater understanding of the buyer by the salesman, thereby helping the salesman sense the buyer's mood of the moment. Empathy tells a salesman when he should be aggressive and when he should be more restrained, when he should talk and when he should remain silent, even whether he should joke or be serious. The empathic salesman is more accurate than his non-empathic competitor in interpreting what a buyer says and does; he knows more often whether buyer-resistance is serious or sham and when and even how to attempt to close the sale. Because he can operate on the buyer's wave length, the empathic salesman "feels" how his sales story is registering in the buyer's thinking. Empathy encourages the buyer to be frank and sincere with the salesman, to reveal instead of to conceal. It encourages the buyer to welcome and even to look forward to subsequent visits with the salesman because the buyer considers him an ally and a friend.

THE PREAPPROACH

In planning the sales presentation he will make to a specific buyer, the salesman must do some preliminary work usually referred to as the *preapproach*. Prerequisite to our examination of the preapproach is a brief review of the selling process.

Steps in Selling

It is generally agreed that a salesman makes a sale by leading the buyer through five steps. The salesman must get the buyer's *attention*, arouse the buyer's *interest*, stimulate the buyer's *desire*, secure the buyer's *conviction* that he should buy, and, finally, get *action* from the buyer in the form of a purchase. The story or presentation the salesman plans should be constructed so as to have these five effects on buyers.

Attention. The salesman must get and then hold the buyer's complete and undivided attention if a sale is to be made. This is not always easy because a buyer is a mass of problems, interests, thoughts, and things to do, and his attitude is, "I'm not interested in you or what you are selling. I don't need your product." Often a buyer will close his mind and not give his attention to the salesman because he is afraid of being sold.

Interest. A buyer can be said to be interested in the salesman and in the salesman's products when he becomes willing to hear more of the salesman's story. The best start the salesman can make toward arousing the buyer's interest is to use effective attention-getters, because they help shift attention into interest. Also quite effective are the salesman's expressions of interest in the buyer. Because all buyers are greatly interested in themselves, salesmen should plan to talk about buyers' interests — their hopes, problems, possessions, family, accomplishments, and such. The result of this approach is to encourage the buyer to link together, in his thinking, his need, the salesman's product, and its price. When the buyer does this, he is interested.

Desire. The way to sell is to present a story that will make the buyer *want to buy* the salesman's product. Because an individual wants a product or service only if it will do something he wants done, the first step in stimulating desire is to establish a need or a want. This requires much tact if, in effect, it asks the buyer to admit that he has been careless or ignorant, or that decisions or purchases made earlier by him were mistakes. The second step, of course, is to get the buyer to agree that he would like to have the salesman's product because it seems a desirable answer to the need or want. This desire must become intense before there will be a purchase.

Conviction. A salesman has succeeded in this fourth stage when the buyer admits he should buy. The buyer now sees a problem or situation about which something must be done. He agrees that the salesman's product will do the job better than any other product. The buyer now sees the price of the product to be a reasonable price — when related to the satisfaction he sees resulting from the purchase. In a word, the buyer is now convinced that the product will be worth more to him than the figure on the price tag. No longer is the buyer bothered by doubt; he agrees he should buy.

Action. There can be only one act that will make the salesman's undertaking a success, and this, of course, is a purchase by the buyer. When the buyer's conviction is of sufficient strength, he makes a purchase, and the salesman has made a sale.

In the light of these steps comprising the selling process, one seems entitled to claim that the first objective of the salesman's story is to create buyer-unhappiness with his present circumstances and buyer-dissatisfaction with his present consumption pattern. This has been accomplished when the buyer agrees with the salesman (a) that he, the buyer, has an unsolved problem or need about which something must be done, or (b) that he, the buyer, has a problem or need that is receiving attention *but not the best* attention. Next, the buyer must accept the salesman's recommended solution to the problem. This is the salesman's product. When the buyer recognizes his lack and sees that much of what he wants can be found in the salesman's product, he is ready to buy. The salesman's story is the tool that sells merchandise.

Nature of the Preapproach

The preapproach is the salesman's preparation for the coming sales interview. To be more specific, the preapproach is the salesman's finding the basic problem which the salesman's product will solve for the buyer, and then planning how best to concentrate on the problem and its solution when talking to the buyer. The preapproach gives the salesman so clear and detailed a picture of each buyer that a personalized story can be built for each one. While the major emphasis is on the salesman's getting himself ready emotionally, mentally, and physically for the call, there will be certain instances in which the preapproach includes some preparing of the *buyer* to hear the sales story. In every instance, the purpose of the preapproach is to insure the best possible odds for a successful sale.

A salesman does the great bulk of his preapproach study and analysis before he ever sees the buyer or even asks to see him. The first step in the preapproach is to identify buyers. This step was described in Chapter 7 and was called *qualifying the prospect*. The second step, the largest of three, is the collection and study of information and the planning of the sales story. The third and final phase of the preapproach takes place during the first few minutes of the salesman's call on the buyer. During this introductory period, the salesman can requalify the prospect, he can verify the facts he collected about the prospect, and he can expand the information he obtained in his preapproach.

Information Needed by Salesmen

The facts in almost universal demand by salesmen can be inferred from a glance back to Chapter 7 and a glance forward to the next five chapters. A primary area includes the problems, needs, and wants of the buyer; also in this area would be any circumstances and relationships that bear on the salesman's undertaking. A complementary area involves which product or products to recommend and the quantity to suggest. The buying philosophy and practices of each prospect should be determined, as well as any personal peculiarities, preferences, and prejudices. If other persons will have something to say about the purchase to be recommended, they should be identified.

Then there are matters pertaining to the actual sales interview. The salesman must determine what seems to be the most persuasive and irresistible story. He must figure how best to get in to see the buyer — where, and when, and for how long. He must find out which are the most controlling buying motives of the buyer, what buyer-benefits to stress, and which satisfactions and goals are of greatest interest to the buyer. The salesman will need to know what type of demonstration will be of greatest influence and through which of the buyer's senses he should try to communicate. The salesman will be particularly aided if he can determine in advance the objections and resistance he will most probably encounter. Finally, he must try to predict which type of closing should be made.

Benefits of Thorough Preapproaches

Sales interviews should be preceded by adequate preapproach activity for several reasons, some of which have already been suggested if not discussed. In launching on a preapproach, it is not only desirable but also essential for the salesman to consider his future sales presentation from the buyer's point of view. Certainly the salesman must see, think, and feel as the buyer does before he can succeed in getting the buyer to see, think, and feel as the salesman does about the salesman's products. In a somewhat oversimplified view, the salesman can base his story on hunch, impression, or habit — or he can build it of and base it on ascertained facts. A preapproach makes it unnecessary for the salesman to take too much for granted. His strategy and tactics can be fashioned against a background of knowledge. Less often will the salesman find himself surprised or in a difficult spot, because his preapproach reduces the number and range of operation of unfortunate contingencies.

Thorough preapproaches result in more interviews of higher quality with better prospects. Those interviews get off to good starts because the salesman can justify his request for some of the buyer's time with specific, individualized reasons why the buyer should see him. The salesman knows what each buyer wants and, consequently, can skillfully interpret his product in terms of those wants. The story the salesman tells reveals unmistakably the planning that went into it, the planning of appeals to emphasize, of product features to stress, and of demonstrations

PLANNING GUIDE FOR SALES INTERVIEWS

PLAN YOUR PURPOSE
THEN
PLAN YOUR INTERVIEW
BY OUR 4

INTERVIEW ELEMENTS

Salute
- *OPENING*
- *START*
- *FLASH*
- *GET FAVORABLE ATTENTION*

Excite Interest
- *MAKE CONTACT*
- *GET TO LISTEN*
- *BUILD BRIDGE*
- *USE BENEFIT*

Let Go
- *WITH CLEAR PROPOSITION*
- *WITH BENEFITS, EXPLANATIONS, PROOFS*
- *WITH "FOR INSTANCES" (SUCCESS STORIES)*
- *ASK QUESTIONS (CHECK TEMPERATURE)*
- *ANTICIPATE OBJECTIONS*
- *HANDLE OBJECTIONS*
- *HANDLE QUESTIONS*

Loop Thru
- *"SUGGEST" THE WAY*
- *"SUGGEST" A CHOICE*
- *GET SOME ACTION*
- *LAND ORDER*

CHECK AFTER INTERVIEW
WHAT POINTS CLICKED?
WHAT POINTS NEED STRENGTHENING?
WHAT ARE MY NEXT MOVES?

USE AND REUSE WHAT WORKS FOR YOU!

Standard Brands, Inc.

This planning guide is used by Standard Brands salesmen.

to perform. The excellence of story and the thorough preparation of the salesman increase his confidence; they also invite the confidence of the buyer and help convince him of the salesman's interest and competence in making recommendations. Preapproach work results in sounder selling and in shorter, more successful calls.

THE FIVE BUYING DECISIONS

General Considerations

No purchase is ever made, be the product a candy bar or an automobile, until the buyer has said "yes" to five questions. Because the five affirmative answers result in a purchase, the salesman's basic job in any sales situation consists of identifying which of the five decisions are missing, and securing a favorable verdict on each. Once the five assents have been obtained by the salesman, the prospect buys.

These are the five admissions a prospect must make before he will buy: that he has a definite *need* for certain advantages, benefits, or satisfactions that he does not now enjoy; that a specific *product* is the best answer to that need; that a specific *source* is the best one for him to patronize; that the *price* is acceptable; that the *time* to buy is now.

There is no standard sequence in which prospects make the five buying decisions. This means, for example, that *source* may be selected or *price* determined before *need* is admitted. Similarly, prospects observe no time schedule in making the decisions. Seconds or months may elapse between any two decisions. These two uncertainties make it possible for a prospect to have made one or more of the decisions before the salesman comes into the picture and to make the remaining decisions in whatever order he chooses.

If you run a classified advertisement in a newspaper saying that you want a baby carriage, sellers start with Buying Decision No. 1, *need*, already made in their favor. If you have been wearing ABC brand shoes for years and have no intention of changing, then Buying Decision No. 2, *product*, is settled at least for the time being when any shoe salesman starts talking to you. If you have been buying your clothes at the BCD store for years and plan no change, Buying Decision No. 3, *source*, is already made. If you have decided that X dollars is the right amount for you to spend for a suit, then that much of Buying Decision No. 4, *price*, is settled before you see the salesman. Finally, if you walk up to a retail salesman and say that you must have a birthday gift, Buying Decision No. 5, *time*, clearly has been made.

Salesmen cannot assume that each prospect really means what he says relative to the buying decisions. The prospect may say that he has n time to spend in listening to the salesman when what he actually does not have to spend is money. Much of the time, however, the prospect will make a comment or ask a question that throws light on the missing buying decision. He certainly feels no need when he sincerely observes, "My car is only three years old; it's certainly good for two years more." He objects to product when he exclaims, "Venetian blinds? I loathe them!" His feeling about source must be changed if his reply is, "But I've bought all my insurance from Mr. A." He is sneering at price when he asks, "What's it made of, gold?" And, finally, he refuses to make the time decision when he dismisses the salesman with, "See me next week."

By ascertaining quickly which buying decisions are missing — and these are the ones that must be won before he can close the sale — the salesman avoids wasting time on any matter which the prospect has already decided in the salesman's favor. He also avoids expounding on a topic that needs no expounding and thus reduces the risk of irritating or antagonizing the prospect. In finding out how the prospect feels about the five buying decisions, the salesman will lean heavily on two techniques. He will *analyze* the voluntary comments of the prospect, particularly his objections, and he will *sound out* the prospect, indirectly if possible, on each matter.

Buying Decision No. 1 — Need

The dictionary tells us that *need* is a condition demanding supply or relief, that it is a lack of something useful or desired. It is also a feeling of inadequacy; it is the restlessness that results from dissatisfaction with the present state of affairs. It is desiring what you do not have; it is the conviction that you are not enjoying maximum personal satisfaction. It is the desire to have or to be more.

In most cases the feeling of need will have to be planted and nurtured. It is not the salesman's proper job to condemn a prospect for what he wants or to try to dissuade him from buying something the salesman thinks he should not have, unless the proposed purchase will harm the prospect. The line that separates those purchases the salesman should oppose from those he should encourage is a very debatable one.

If the prospect is not conscious of a need, the salesman must do a tactful job of educating to establish the presence of the need. The prospect's conviction and admission of need must be sincere or else later in the interview he is likely to object to price, time, product, or source.

Let's see how a salesman for a realty firm secured this first buying decision. The prospect was a man trying to sell his house himself before leaving to take a job in another locality. Prior to calling on the prospect, the salesman had opportunity to inspect the house from the outside and to chat with the contractor who built the house. When the salesman called in person, his knock on the door was answered by Mr. Carpenter, the prospect.

Salesman: Mr. Carpenter, my name is Morgan. I'm with Belmont Realty. I'd like to talk to you about your house.

Carpenter: Come in, Mr. Morgan, I'd like to sell it to you.

Salesman: I'd love to have it, but let's talk about the advantages of your having us sell it for you.

Carpenter: Talk's cheap and I don't mind talking, but I don't want to waste your time. I don't need any help selling my house. Of course, it would be convenient, I guess, but I don't need you badly enough to pay your commission.

Salesman: Are you having pretty good luck showing it?

Carpenter: Maybe I could be luckier, but I guess everything will be all right.

Salesmen: How many people have you had look at the house?

Carpenter: Well, not enough people, I guess. There were two men who came by, but they weren't really too interested. And then there were three other men who came by with their families.

Salesman: Were they really interested or just riding around?

Carpenter: They seemed interested enough at the time, but I haven't seen them or heard from them since; and it's been almost a week now.

Salesman: Wonder why they didn't come back?

Carpenter: I don't know. You're in that business, you tell me.

Salesman: There could be a lot of reasons. Maybe the house wasn't what they wanted; maybe other customers came by and you weren't home; maybe the price is too high or maybe too low.

Carpenter: Too low? I didn't think that ever happened and if it did, it would just be buyer's good luck, wouldn't it?

Salesman: It might be. But haven't you noticed how a low price scares people off?

Carpenter: Maybe you've got a point there.

Salesman: Have you thought of the risks you are taking if the price isn't right?

Carpenter: Well, I could either lose or make more money than I should.

Salesman: Not only that, if the price is wrong you scare people away. If it's too high, people will be scared away from dealing with you any more, and you'll have to lower the price and maybe take a loss.

Carpenter: Yes.

Salesman: And if the price is too low, people think they aren't getting quality. Right?

Carpenter: Right.

Salesman: Then you'd have to raise the price, and it's hard to raise the price on someone, don't you think?

Carpenter: I guess it is. Nobody's going to do it to me.

Salesman: And you can't do it to them either. When you list your house with Belmont Realty, you don't have to worry about your house's being priced wrong.

Carpenter: Why is that?

Salesman: Because we are experienced in this business, we know the neighborhoods, we sell houses like yours often, and we know what people are willing to pay for a house like this one. How much have you been asking for it?

Carpenter: I think I should get $19,200 for it.

Salesman: How did you arrive at that figure?

Carpenter: Well, I've got $16,000 in it and I think I ought to make a 20% profit on it. Isn't that about as good a way to figure it as any?

Salesman: Mr. Carpenter, that's one way to figure it. But what you have in the house doesn't really have much to do with what you can sell it for, does it?

Carpenter: What do you mean?

Salesman: What you get for the house depends mostly on what someone is willing to pay for it, doesn't it?

Carpenter: That's true, I guess. Well, if you were going to arrive at a price, how would you go about doing it?

Salesman: I've already come to a price, and I'll tell you how I arrived at it.

Carpenter: O. K.

Salesman: First, I did some thinking about the neighborhood. This thinking is based on my years of experience — I've sold over 300 houses in the fifteen to twenty-five thousand dollar range. Then I talked to Jim Lyon who built the house. Jim's a good fellow, and he told me about how you just insisted on ceramic tile instead of plastic tile, how you had to have plaster instead of wall board, and he also showed me the plans.

Carpenter: He told you right. This is a quality house.

Salesman: And a high-quality house should bring a high-quality price, shouldn't it, Mr. Carpenter?

Carpenter: Of course it should. What did you decide it should be priced at?

Salesman: I will list it for you at $19,900.

Carpenter: This is sort of a shock to me. Why is it $700 higher than I had priced it?

Salesman: Because we are in this business, and we keep up with the market so that we can price our clients' houses at market prices so they will be sold fast. How long have you been trying to sell the house?

Carpenter: I put my sign out about two weeks ago.

Salesman: Can you afford to have just three customers look at the house in a two-week period? How long before you'd planned to leave Chapel Hill?

Carpenter: Well, I have to be in Baltimore March first. That's a little better than a month.

Salesman: What had you planned to do about selling the house when you are in Baltimore?

Carpenter: I guess I was going to worry about that problem when I came to it. I guess I would have ended up letting a real estate man sell it for me, even though I do hate to pay his commission.

Salesman: But have you thought how you would be tying the real estate man's hands behind him?

Carpenter: No, I hadn't. What do you mean?

Salesman: Well, it's mighty hard to sell a house if the public thinks it's distress merchandise. Also, you can get a better price for a house by showing it with a family living in it.

Carpenter: Oh?

Salesman: It's a fact, Mr. Carpenter. A house doesn't look so good when there's no furniture or people in it, and customers can't picture themselves living there. They just aren't as attracted to the house. Often the price has to be lowered to sell it. You want to sell it before you have to lower the price, don't you?

Carpenter: Of course. I don't want to cut the price and then have to pay for your commission, too.

Salesman: This happens all too often to people who try to sell their houses themselves and find they can't. Mr. Carpenter, being a realtor is as much a profession as being a doctor or a lawyer. You know that doctors won't do professional work on themselves.

Carpenter: Certainly.

Salesman: And you know what they say about a lawyer who defends himself?

Carpenter: That he has a fool for a client.

Salesman: By listing your house with us, Mr. Carpenter, you eliminate three big fears, and that is well worth our commission.

Carpenter: What are those?

Salesman: Taking a loss, selling ineffectively, and legal redtape. Mr. Carpenter, this house is a big investment of yours, isn't it?

Carpenter: Yes, a lot of my net worth is tied up in this house.

Salesman: It's a shame to see fine young people not able to buy a new house when they get to a new community. People are judged by their houses, aren't they?

Carpenter: They shouldn't be, but I guess they are to a large extent.

Salesman: Do you want to move into an apartment house when you get to Baltimore and then have to wait until this house is sold to buy a new house?

Carpenter: No. Of course not.

Salesman: Let me list your house so we can free your investment and you can go to Baltimore and move into your own new home.

Carpenter: Well, I still think I can sell it myself, before I leave.

Salesman: But you might have to cut the price. I don't want this to happen to you.

Carpenter: I don't want it to happen either, but what have you got that I haven't got?

Salesman: Clients who want a house are my main asset. Right now, I have the names of 15 people who are actually looking for a house in this size and price range. These are *bona fide* prospects, not just people riding around. Don't you want the house to be seen by people who can afford it?

Carpenter: They'll have to arrange their own credit; I'm not in that business.

Salesman: We're not in that business exactly either, but we do know people who are, and we can get a buyer together with a bank so that you can get your money out of the house.

Carpenter: That would be a help.

Salesman: Another advantage is that we will show the house only by appointment. You don't have to worry about keeping everything bright and shiny all the time. We'll give you a call before coming out so that you can have the house ready to be seen.

Carpenter: You're probably right.

Salesman: Mr. Carpenter, let me protect your net worth for you by going ahead and selling this house for you before you have to leave for Baltimore. By signing this contract, I can have customers here to look at the house day after tomorrow.

Carpenter: Maybe you are right. I guess I do need you to sell this house for me.

Buying Decision No. 2 — Product

Once need has been established, the next step is to show how our salesman's *product* fits and fills that need. Products appear to be bought for one of two purposes, to be used or to be resold. If the prospect is buying to use, and this includes using as a gift, the salesman points out the many satisfactions (safety, comfort, economy, approval, affection, prestige, and such) desired by the prospect and found in the product. Practically all buying for resale is done with one objective: greater dollar profit. Here the salesman points out how and why the product will make more money for the prospect. So the physical product and its features are not what a person buys; what he does buy is satisfaction. This second buying decision finds the prospect agreeing that our salesman's product best supplies the satisfaction he requires.

In the following example of how a salesman obtained the second buying decision, the prospect, a Mr. Brown, has a home, a wife, and three children. He is shopping for a floor polisher, and, at this moment, is in conversation with a Sears-Roebuck salesman.

Salesman: Mr. Brown, let me point out some of the outstanding features of this Sears Twin Brush Floor Polisher.

Prospect: Well, we certainly are in the market for a polisher but just can't decide. This scrubbing by hand is murder. But we are pretty interested in the brand sold by the store across the street. It seems to be a pretty good polisher and to have all the necessary equipment.

Salesman: I'm sure it is a fine polisher, and, as you say, doing the job by hand is very hard and really doesn't do the job right. Do you know what equipment comes with our polisher? As regular equipment you get one rug scrubbing attachment, two Bakelite-backed scrubbing brushes, two Bakelite-backed polishing brushes, two snap-on lambs wool pads, and two snap-on felt pads for buffing.

Prospect: That seems to be standard equipment on *all* polishers. What makes your brand so special? I really want to compare brands so that I will be sure that I am getting the best.

Salesman: I certainly don't blame you for that, and I'm very anxious to show you all the features of our polisher, Let's outline some of the important features that you would like in a polisher, one that would suit your particular needs. Certainly you would want one that will be easy to operate, one that will save time, one that will do a variety of jobs, one that is durable, one that is attractive, and one that will be serviced quickly if need should arise. Do you agree that these are the features you are looking for in a floor polisher?

Prospect: Yes, that seems to cover about everything.

Salesman: Fine. Now let's take these one at a time and see how this Sears polisher fills these requirements. First, we said that a floor polisher should be easy to operate. Let's check some of the features of this polisher which fill this requirement. First of all, the polisher weighs 21 pounds; this means that you get plenty of weight for scrubbing and waxing without having to apply pressure yourself. It also means that it is easy to lift and store if your storage space is off the floor. In addition, this polisher comes equipped with wheels for easy moving from room to room. Just flip down the wheels and it rolls easily from place to place.

Prospect: Doesn't that seem to be a bit heavy? Most of your competitors' models weigh somewhat less.

Salesman: Most of our competitors' models do weigh less. I believe they run about 14 to 18 pounds. We feel that through experimentation we have hit upon the ideal compromise for efficient work *and* easy handling. The weight of this polisher gives you controlled pressure for cleaner floors and better shines.

Prospect: I guess that much weight would do a better job, and 21 pounds isn't too much to lift when the need arises.

Salesman: Also, this polisher has a built-in light. It helps you see into those hard-to-see nooks and corners, and it helps you see those areas or spots you may have missed in the middle of the floor. I'm sure that you have scrubbed or waxed a floor only to find later that there are several spots you missed. This light helps you locate them.

Prospect: The light probably costs more than it's worth.

Salesman: Notice where the polisher's switch is located on this model, directly below the fingers when the handle is grasped for use. There is no stooping or bending because the switch is always in a handy position; starting and stopping are quick and easy.

Prospect: But your polisher has two brushes instead of one like some polishers I have looked at.

Salesman: These two brushes rotate in opposite directions, making the polisher more stable. You don't have to use force to guide it and hold it in position as you do with a single-brush polisher. Just try this and see how easy it is to handle.

Prospect: Ummm.

Salesman: Another feature which makes this polisher so easy to operate is the manner in which the brushes and pads are attached. You see, these scrub brushes slip down on these shafts, and this clamp is moved into place, and the polishing pads snap on, just like fastening your coat. You notice there are no other tools to bother with.

Prospect: But will these clamps and snaps hold the brushes and pads in place? Won't they always be coming off?

Salesman: I'm sure you will find that these clamps and snaps hold the brushes and pads. We have never known of brush or pad to fall off. Also, you don't have to be too easy around furniture with this polisher. Of course, I don't mean that you would want to go banging around in a reckless, haphazard manner, but these long-lasting vinyl bumpers prevent scars and dents in regular, everyday use.

Prospect: That looks good; it's impossible to keep from hitting furniture. But there is one thing I like better in the other model, the cord rewind.

Salesman: Yes, that is a feature that many people seem to admire, but let's compare the two machines. First of all, on the cord rewind there is more chance of the mechanism's fouling up; when this happens you can't get the cord in or out so you have to do without the polisher during the repair period. Now with our polisher, all you have are two simple winding hooks, nothing to get out of order and give you trouble. When you get ready to operate the polisher, simply release the top winding hook. This lets all of the cord out for immediate use. This cord doesn't get in your way because the brushes just push it aside if they touch it. There is nothing for the cord to get caught on. Then, when you are finished with the polisher, you simply rewind the cord on the two hooks, and it is ready for storage. Isn't that simple and efficient?

Prospect: Well . . . .

Salesman: Now let's move to the area of time saving and see what features this polisher has which save time. First on the list of timesavers is the two-speed action. Most other polishers have only one speed. With these two speeds you have controlled speed. Low speed is for scrubbing so that the polisher doesn't splash all over everything. Or, if you find some especially stubborn spot, you can move aside some of the water and use the fast speed. The faster speed can be used for waxing and polishing so as to give you a better, longer-lasting shine. You know that in order to get a really good protective coat of wax you must get the wax down into the wood; the friction caused by these rapidly rotating brushes creates heat which helps soften the wax and get it down into the wood. So, you see, with these two speeds you can really get the job done in a hurry.

Prospect: That may all be very true, but with the large single brush you can cover more area.

Salesman: Because this polisher has two seven-inch brushes, you get a full fourteen-inch path at each stroke. To equal this coverage with a single brush would mean getting a machine which is too large for household use — one that would be very hard to handle. And at high speed these two brushes cover quite a lot of area because they are seventeen per cent faster than this polisher's closest competitor. We mentioned another time-saving factor a few minutes ago, these snap-on brushes and pads. In only a few seconds, you are ready to go to work.

Prospect: Maybe.

Salesman: Now we come to the really great feature, the area in which this polisher really excels. We said that you needed a polisher that would do a variety of jobs. Just what kind of floors do you have in your home?

Prospect: We have hardwood floors in four rooms, tile in two rooms, and carpet in two rooms.

Salesman: That sounds very nice. Now let's see how this polisher will satisfy your needs. This polisher will scrub the hardwood and tile floors and wax them with the same two brushes; you polish with these two polishing brushes. Then, without removing these brushes, you simply snap on the lambs wool pads or the felt pads for buffing. Now for another star feature of this polisher. I suppose you send your carpets out to be cleaned, don't you?

Prospect: Yes, that's right.

Salesman: Well, with this polisher there is no need for that. Just attach this rug-scrubbing attachment, put some rug cleaning compound on the rug, and you can do a professional job yourself, right in your own home. Doesn't that sound great?

Prospect: Yes, it does, but are you sure my wife and I could do that?

Salesman: Certainly you could! It is just as easy as using the polisher for scrubbing or waxing. Now just a couple of other advantages. As optional equipment you can get a wax and water dispenser so that you don't have to stop to pour your water or liquid wax on the floor, you just release it as you need it from the dispenser. Also, as optional equipment, you can get a reconditioning or sanding kit. With it you could refinish your own floors. Tell me, Mr. Brown, have you ever seen a polisher as versatile as this one?

Prospect: Well, I don't know.

Salesman: And this polisher is as durable as any you can find. The polisher is not made out of light, flimsy plastic but of high-impact, metal zamac which resists wear and tear and breakage. The handle is made of a high grade of steel, rectangular in shape to resist bending and breaking. And the brushes are made of Bakelite, a highly break-resistant plastic material, and the bristles are made of 100% Tampico.

Prospect: Those materials do suggest a very durable polisher.

Salesman: Let's don't forget, either, that this polisher comes in two very attractive colors, Desert Sand and Dusk Pearl. So, this is a very attractive as well as an efficient polisher. Another important thing to remember is that if you should ever need service on this polisher, quick, efficient, and reasonable service is as near as your Sears store.

Prospect: Well, I just don't know. I still can't decide. It sounds good, but some of the other polishers have some good points, too.

Salesman: I'm sure they do. But let's review the facts we have gone over. First, the polisher has all the features which make it easy to operate: proper weight, wheels, spotlight, position of the switch, twin brushes, snap-on brushes and pads. Second, it has the features which are time saving: two speeds, large seven-inch brushes, and an easy method of attaching the brushes and pads. Third, it can do a great variety of jobs — scrub, wax, polish, buff, spread its own wax and water, and even recondition your floors. Fourth, we found that it is very durable, made of the best quality material. Fifth, we found that it is quite attractive. And, last, we found that if it should ever need service, it is as close as the Sears store.

Prospect: You know, I've made up my mind. I believe your polisher is the one for me.

Buying Decision No. 3 — Source

From the prospect's point of view, *source* may involve one, two, or three matters. The first is the salesman himself. The prospect must approve of the salesman in every purchase. A second type of source involves middlemen. Individual consumers give approval to retailers by patronizing them, and the customers of other middlemen, notably wholesalers, do the same. The third type of source is the manufacturer. He must be accepted as being satisfactory before purchases are made from him. A combination of three sources is involved and must be approved in the sale of a national brand of a household appliance by an outside salesman for a department store.

The product involved in our example of winning the *source* decision is a Lion Electric Company vaporizer. It is used mainly to produce steam in order to relieve breathing difficulty; it can also warm baby bottles. The prospect, an experienced drug store proprietor, has stocked and sold a competing vaporizer in the past in another market. If he puts vaporizers in his new store, he is inclined to return to his former source of supply at the manufacturer level. The interview opens.

Salesman: Good morning, Mr. Ball, I am John Taylor, representative of the Lion Electric Company. I would like to talk to you for a few minutes about carrying the Lion Electric Vaporizer as a regular item in your stock.

Prospect: Good morning, Mr. Taylor, I am glad to meet you.

Salesman: Mr. Ball, I understand that you were the manager of a large retail drug store in the eastern part of the state and that you have a reputation for being a highly successful business man. As a result, you decided to go into business for yourself.

Prospect: You're right about my going into business for myself, but as for being successful — I don't know.

Salesman: I understand that you are not carrying any vaporizers in stock presently. Is that correct?

Prospect: That's correct. We have been open for only two months and have not been able to stock the store completely with all the necessary merchandise. You know, it's a real job opening a new store and trying to stock all the items one needs. I have been running around like a chicken with his head chopped off. I'll be glad when we get settled.

Salesman: I certainly know that you will. I don't believe that I could do such a job. It's too much for me to handle. By the way, you are familiar with the Lion Electric Vaporizer?

Prospect: Only to the extent of knowing it's on the market. I have never carried the L. E. Vaporizer in stock before. I was carrying the Val Vaporizer in the store I used to manage and was very much pleased with its sales performance. As a matter of fact, I had thought about carrying the same vaporizer in this store.

Salesman: Mr. Ball, judging from your past sales and managerial performance, I know that you are a well-qualified retailer and that you naturally carry only the best merchandise in your store. That is just the reason for my being here today. I would like for you to carry the Lion Electric Vaporizer in your store.

Prospect: I haven't had any experience with the Lion Electric Vaporizer and don't know what its sales performance would be. I have had experience with the Val and know that it is accepted by the consumers as being a reputable product.

Salesman: I certainly understand your point of view. The Lion Electric Company is a name that is known and accepted by everyone. It is one of the nation's largest producers and manufacturers of appliances. Lion Electric has the most advanced and modern research facilities, the most qualified and trained scientists, and plenty of "know how." By the combination of these facilities we are able to produce the best, the most profitable in electrical appliances. We know what consumers want and supply this to them through our appliances. We have a reputation that can't be disputed, and we stand behind every single item we produce as being the tops in technological improvement. Don't you think that you might benefit by carrying a product that is associated with such a reputation as that of the Lion Electric Company?

Prospect: Well, you have a good point there, and I'll agree; but I can imagine that by dealing with such a large company as the Lion Electric Company they would expect me to order several dozen vaporizers at one time. I don't have that much capital nor the storage space that it would take to stock vaporizers. As for Val, I know that I can order from them in much smaller quantities which better fit my needs.

Salesman: I am glad that you brought that point up, Mr. Ball. The Lion Electric Company is just as aware of this inventory investment and storage problem as you are. As a result, the Lion Electric Company took it upon themselves to devise means by which the retailer would be able to carry the L. E. Vaporizer in his stock and yet not be compelled to fight this inventory and storage problem. My company has made arrangements with selected drug wholesalers throughout the nation to stock and distribute the L. E. Vaporizer to retailers along with their other drug merchandise.

Prospect: Are you trying to say that a wholesale drug house is carrying an appliance that should be carried by appliance distributors?

Salesman: Yes, that's right. The Lion Electric Vaporizer is an item that is closely associated with drug stores because of its nature. As a result, better economies would be achieved by distributing such an item through the same channels which distribute its related products. Since you buy your drugs from drug wholesalers, why not buy your vaporizers from the same source?

Prospect: Mr. Taylor, I can imagine the type of service I would get if buying such an item through the wholesaler! They are the hardest people to deal with. I don't believe that I would be interested in carrying the Lion Electric Vaporizer if I had to buy it through a drug wholesaler.

Salesman: Mr. Ball, service is just what you would be getting, and much more than if you bought directly from the manufacturer. The reason for this is that the wholesaler is advantageously located near you. Why, you have a wholesaler within fifteen miles of your front door! This proximity enables the wholesaler to give you efficient and fast service. Time is the most important factor nowadays, and when there is the opportunity to cut time down to hours instead of days, then it seems only natural that we do so, and that is just what the wholesaler is doing for you — cutting down the length of delivery and storage time in rendering service to you.

Prospect: What do you mean by cutting down the length of time? Do you mean that I would get fewer deliveries by buying from this wholesaler you are talking about?

Salesman: Oh, no! I am sorry if I was not clear. What I was trying to say is that the wholesaler would be able to give you *more* deliveries. In fact, you would be able to get deliveries each day. The wholesaler in Durham delivers to Chapel Hill on Monday, Wednesday, and Friday, and the Raleigh wholesaler delivers on Tuesday, Thursday, and Saturday. So you see, there is daily delivery to Chapel Hill which enables you to phone in an order whenever you need to replenish your stock, and within hours you will have a new shipment of vaporizers at your front door. Going back to your inventory investment problem, this daily feature would enable you to maintain a minimum stock requirement of say — about six vaporizers. As vaporizers sell and you get down to your last vaporizer, all you have to do is call the wholesaler for a new shipment, and within hours your vaporizer stock will be replenished. Now that really is fast and efficient service, isn't it?

Prospect: Yes, that does sound like fast service, but I still don't think I'd be interested in carrying the L. E. Vaporizer. What kind of guarantee do I have that the wholesaler will take care of warranties and returns of defective vaporizers?

Salesman: The Lion Electric Company warrants to the purchaser of each new Lion Electric Vaporizer that any part thereof which proves to be defective in material or workmanship within one year from the date of original purchase will be repaired or replaced free of charge. The Lion Electric Company has authorized the wholesaler to replace any defective vaporizers returned to him by his retailers, at no cost to the wholesaler. This feature is passed along to you, the retailer, and you can likewise pass it along to your customers. Whenever a defective vaporizer is returned to you by one of your customers, you can replace it with a new one, and the customer will be more than pleased because he has immediately received a new vaporizer in place of his defective one. Actually, you are benefiting from this in *two* ways. First, there is no cost to you in replacing the defective vaporizer, and secondly, goodwill has been established with the satisfied customer who would surely tell all her friends about the wonderful service she received from your drug store. Don't you agree that a satisfied and happy customer is the best advertisement that you can have?

Prospect: Well, that certainly is an added advantage that I never received when buying direct from the Val Company. It took about two weeks to return defective vaporizers to the service center and then get them back to the customer, and of course during this time the customer was far from happy about the whole deal.

Salesman: Would you like to carry six vaporizers as your minimum stock requirement?

Prospect: Hold on a minute here. I haven't said that I was going to carry your vaporizer in my store. How do I know that they will sell?

Salesman: Mr. Ball, the sales performance of the Lion Electric Vaporizer has been outstanding, and the demand for it is increasing steadily. The Lion Electric Company has a promotional campaign that is very effective. We are currently advertising in the *Ladies Home Journal* and *Good Housekeeping* magazines. Also, we have prepared most attractive and eye-catching point-of-purchase displays. They are terrific! I'm ready to set one up in your window right now at no cost to you whatsoever. This is another service that the Lion Electric Company provides for its retailers.

Prospect: You can't tell me that you will *personally* build a window display for my store!

Salesman: Yes, that's right. It won't cost you one red cent. The Lion Electric Company likes to help its retailers in every way possible. By helping you, they are helping themselves. Let me tell you about the Standard Drug Center over in Raleigh. They had been carrying a competitive vaporizer for the past several years and were receiving only average sales results. Six months ago I sold them on the advantages of carrying the Lion Electric Vaporizer in their store and I also set up a window display for them. Well, I was over there just last week, and Mr. Brown, the manager, told me that his sales from the Lion Electric Vaporizer had doubled the sales performance of the other vaporizer over the same period of time. Now isn't that proof enough that the Lion Electric Vaporizer is a popular product with the consumer?

Prospect: Yes, I suppose so; but I had been buying from a very reputable and reliable wholesaler in the eastern part of the state and I was very pleased with his service. Of course, he doesn't sell this far upstate, but he recommended several wholesalers in this area that he thought would give me the same service which I received from him. I have already started doing business with them, and I don't have any intentions of changing wholesalers just to get one who is carrying the L. E. Vaporizer.

Salesman: Mr. Ball, I certainly understand your position. Would one of these wholesalers that you referred to be the Durham Wholesale Drug Company with a branch outlet over in Raleigh?

Prospect: Yes, it is! How did you know that?

Salesman: The Lion Electric Company likewise likes to deal with wholesalers who are reputable and reliable; therefore, we, too, have chosen the Durham Wholesale Drug Company to handle the L. E. Vaporizer. So, you see, there will be no necessity for you to change wholesalers just to have the extra advantage of carrying the L. E. Vaporizer in your store. I will be happy to call them up right now and place your first order for L. E. Vaporizers to be delivered to you this afternoon.

Prospect: Are you going to set up the window display this morning also?

Salesman: I will be more than glad to do so. How many vaporizers would you like for me to order for your stock requirement?

Prospect: Let's see — I'll take six to start with.

Buying Decision No. 4 — Price

The fourth buying decision is made by the prospect when he agrees that the *price* of the salesman's product is acceptable. This feature of price is closely related to need and product. Only after the prospect is clear on those two matters is he able to relate the satisfaction that the product will afford him to the product's price tag, and to compare that amount of satisfaction with satisfaction which could be bought with another product for the same amount of money. The greater the satisfaction and value the salesman has built up, the more easily and promptly the prospect is able to approve of price.

In the following interview, our salesman recommends an irrigation system to a farmer who raises tobacco. The farmer's opposition is based largely on his belief that the installation costs too much. The salesman hopes to win the *price* decision. As the presentation begins, the introduction and preliminaries are over.

Salesman: I see you have a nice, large pond; have you ever considered putting in an irrigation system?

Buyer: Yes, I have thought about it, but those things cost too much money. I can't afford one.

Salesman: How many acres of tobacco do you grow each year, Mr. Sigman?

Buyer: Thirteen acres last year, but my allotment has been cut to nine for next season.

Salesman: Your goal of course will be to make the maximum amount of profit possible from your nine acres. Correct?

Buyer: Certainly.

Salesman: Well, there is no denying that an irrigation system does cost a lot to purchase. However, if I can show you how you can pay for one in approximately two years with a minimum of approximately eight additional years in which to realize further profits, then the price would seem more reasonable, wouldn't it?

Buyer: Yes, but I believe you are dressing that thing up a little. The fact that you said it will take *approximately* two years to pay for it shows that.

Salesman: I know it's hard to believe that you can recover the cost of a system like this in such a short time, but let me show you how it can be done. I said it would take *approximately* two years to pay for it because we cannot tell for sure how much your system will cost —

Buyer: You mean you are trying to sell me something, and you can't even tell me how much it will cost?

Salesman: That's right, Mr. Sigman, because we engineer the Rex Rain system to fit *your* particular needs. We do not sell a system considered to be adequate for the *average* needs. If we did, it would be more than some men need and less than others; this would result in unsatisfactory operation. When you buy a system from us, you can be sure it fits *your* requirements. Let's assume that your system will cost $3,000. Now, how much fire insurance do you carry on your buildings?

Buyer: Well, I have $9,500 on the house, $6,000 on the barn, and $500 on the garage. That makes a total of $16,000.

Salesman: How much are your total premiums a year?

Buyer: I believe the total is about $148.

Salesman: Mr. Sigman, by investing an extra $15 you can buy a fire hose which will fit on the pipe for your irrigation system — thus saving 50%, $74 a year, of your total premiums.

Buyer: I see. The insurance company will figure I'm a better risk.

Salesman: That's right.

Buyer: That helps of course, but you've got a long way to go to make up that high price of $3,000.

Salesman: Yes, I know, but here comes the big item. According to figures published by the Department of Agriculture, irrigating tobacco results in an average increase of $210 per acre in income. If you raise nine acres next year, the total increase in revenue would be $1,890. That's a substantial increase, isn't it?

Buyer: It certainly is, but where did the Department of Agriculture get those figures?

Salesman: Here's a copy of the report, Mr. Sigman. The Department of Agriculture made a survey covering the last five years and, as you can see, $210 was the average increase per acre.

Buyer: That's a surprising amount. I had no idea it would be that much.

Salesman: If we add this to the savings on insurance, it will give us a figure of $1,964. This amount will enable you to pay for the irrigation system in two years with a $928 margin. Then you will have eight years in which to use your system and realize an increased profit of $210 per acre or $1,890 per year. That will certainly help you get the maximum profits from your crops, won't it?

Buyer: I guess you're right, Mr. Wilkins. I'll tell you what — if we don't get enough rain this spring, I'll give you a call about getting an irrigation system.

Salesman: Mr. Sigman, you can't afford to wait to buy one until it gets too dry. By the time you could get it delivered and installed, you could lose a large part of your crop.

Buyer: I certainly don't see how I can afford to own one if we have enough rain. It would just be sitting around here, and I wouldn't get any use out of it.

Salesman: It does look that way on the surface, but let's take a close look at the benefits you can have by buying it now. First, by buying it now you can start your savings on fire insurance immediately. Second, as you know, the major aluminum companies were on strike last spring, and this has resulted in an increase in the cost of pipe for aluminum irrigation systems. Prior to the strike we stocked quite a lot of this pipe and, consequently, are able to pass along to you a saving of 6¢ per foot for a total of approximately $150.

Buyer: All that sounds good, Mr. Wilkins, but I still hate to think of spending. $3,000 for something I'm not even sure I'll need. That's just too much money.

Salesman: I'm sure I don't need to tell you, Mr. Sigman, that even if we do get enough *total* rainfall next spring and summer, the quality of your crop is very likely to suffer if the rain doesn't come *at the proper intervals*.

Buyer: Yes, but the question in my mind is whether the quality will suffer enough to warrant my buying an expensive irrigation system.

Salesman: According to the figures I showed you from the Department of Agriculture, it has more than paid many other farmers, Mr. Sigman. As I stated before, this report covers the last five years. If you will recall, the rainfall for those five years was about average, but the use of irrigation still resulted in an average increase of $210 per acre. Since this is true, even if we have an average rainfall for the next ten years, you will still be able to pay for your system in approximately two years, realizing an additional profit of $210 per acre for a minimum of eight more years. This would make a total increase of $15,120 after paying for your system.

Buyer: That all sounds good, but I'm still not convinced.

Salesman: Mr. Sigman, you stated before that you are paying $148 a year for fire insurance, isn't that correct?

Buyer: Yes, that's correct.

Salesman: Do you expect your buildings to burn down?

Buyer: Well, I certainly hope not.

Salesman: Then why do you insure them?

Buyer: For protection of course. If they should burn, I don't want to have to shoulder all of the loss.

Salesman: Then let's consider your irrigation system as insurance against crop failure. If we do have a dry season, then you won't have to worry. That would be good insurance, wouldn't it?

Buyer: It would be good insurance, all right, but it would be too expensive.

Salesman: On the contrary, it wouldn't cost you a cent.

Buyer: How do you figure that?

Salesman: Well, if the increased profit from your crops pays for your system in two years, then it will be giving you free insurance, won't it?

Buyer: Yes, I guess it would at that. There is still one big problem, Mr. Wilkins. What am I going to do with all that equipment this winter? I haven't any place in which to store it.

Salesman: You could very easily store it in the loft of your barn.

Buyer: No, I couldn't either; that's filled with hay.

Salesman: Well, how long is your garage?

Buyer: It's about twenty-four feet long.

Salesman: Since your pipe is only twenty feet long, you could store it overhead in there.

Buyer: Wouldn't it be too heavy?

Salesman: No, it wouldn't. The pipe is very light in weight because it is made completely of aluminum. The pumping unit could be put in the barn with the tractor. That will take care of your storage problem, won't it?

Buyer: Probably.

Salesman: What will be the most convenient time for me to have a man come out to measure your fields?

Buyer: I guess tomorrow morning will be all right.

Salesman: That will be fine. And I'll figure up your requirements and come out to see you next Monday morning. Will that be suitable?

Buyer: Yes, that will be fine.

Salesman: Then I'll see you Monday; thank you very much, Mr. Sigman.

Buying Decision No. 5 — Time

When the salesman makes a bid for the *time* decision, he is attempting to close the sale. When the decision is an affirmative one, the prospect buys, and the salesman has made another sale.

The prospect finds specific reasons for accepting the salesman's recommendations in conflict with pressures and fears urging him not to buy. He wants the salesman's product because it will give him something he desires, but, if he buys it, he will not be able to buy other items he would like to have.

Sam Smith is in an office supply store where a salesman has shown him a Remington Portable Typewriter. Smith is a college senior and expects to go into graduate school next year. He is married, and his wife works as a secretary. Smith has been thinking about purchasing a typewriter. He needs one, he can afford to buy, and he likes the one he has seen, but he does not want to buy now.

Prospect: Well, I don't know. This looks like a good machine, but I just don't know about buying now.

Salesman: You told me that you need to type papers for some of your classes, didn't you?

Prospect: Yes, that's right, but I don't have too many, and I can usually get them typed for me or rent a typewriter. Either way, the cost doesn't amount to much for the little work I have to do.

Salesman: I agree, but when you are in graduate school you'll have a lot of typing to do, especially for your thesis and for all those reports and book reviews.

Prospect: That's right, I will, but I don't think I need to buy a typewriter just for that.

Salesman: But before you get out of school you will be writing companies for job interviews, and you'll always be writing personal letters. Just think how much nicer it is to receive a typewritten letter and how much easier it is to read.

Prospect: You're right about that. In fact my handwriting isn't all it could be.

Salesman: What I'm trying to show you is that a typewriter is something you can and will use all your life — not just while you are at school.

Prospect: I hadn't thought of it that way. I guess there would be plenty of opportunities to use it after school, but I am still not sure I want to buy. Let me think about it awhile and let you know in a few days.

Salesman: Sam, why don't you think it over right here, right now so if you think of any more questions I can answer them for you.

Prospect: Well, I was thinking that perhaps I need a standard typewriter rather than a portable.

Salesman: Sam, this Remington Letter-Riter has only four characters less than the standard office typewriter. It does not have the plus or equal characters, but they are not used much in letter writing or in school work. The numeral *one* is not on here, but the lower case "l" is used for that. In fact, many office typewriters don't have the numeral *one* anyway. There is no exclamation mark either. But the most important fact about this machine is that it is portable. It is easy to carry and easy to store. You wouldn't want to leave your typewriter out all the time, would you?

Prospect: No, I wouldn't be using it every day so I wouldn't need to have it out all the time.

Salesman: If you had an office typewriter, you would just about have to leave it out because storing it would be such a problem. So you see, Sam, the machine for you is a portable, not an office size. Don't you agree?

Prospect: I suppose so.

Salesman: Well then, Sam, let me just close up this machine here, and you can take it with you. (Salesman starts to close the case.)

Prospect: Hold on, I still haven't made up my mind to buy this typewriter. I think I ought to look around awhile before I decide.

Salesman: It is smart to compare before you buy. But, Sam, I can tell you truthfully that you cannot find a better machine than the Remington Letter-Riter. It has features that just aren't found on other portables. Take Remington's patented ribbon changer. It makes changing the ribbon much simpler. In addition, we have right here in this store a complete line of supplies and parts for the Remington. We have everything you will need for your Remington.

Prospect: That's good to know. When I do get ready to buy I surely will come back to you and probably buy this Remington, because I really do like it.

Salesman: I have known a lot of people, and I am sure you have, too, who put off buying something they needed for one reason or another. These people end up never buying the product that they need, and therefore, they never get to enjoy the advantages and savings. The most important thing is for you to start owning your typewriter *now* so you can begin to enjoy the advantages now.

Prospect: You are probably right, but I think I will wait a while before I buy. I just don't want to jump into this.

Salesman: Is there something about this typewriter that is not clear? If there is, I will be glad to go over it with you. I want to be sure that you understand all about it.

Prospect: It's not that. I understand everything about the typewriter. As I said before, it seems to be what I want. I like its features, and when I get ready to buy, I will come back to see you.

Salesman: I appreciate that, but my job is that of salesman, and when I know that someone needs something I try to sell that product to the person. You will agree that you need and can use a typewriter, won't you?

Prospect: Yes.

Salesman: You should not wait another day before you buy. If it is something that you need, then you should buy it now. If you needed food in the house you would buy it, wouldn't you?

Prospect: Yes, but that's not the same thing.

Salesman: I wonder — maybe it is. If you needed a new pair of shoes and didn't get them, you would be cheating yourself. It is the same with a type-writer. You need it, and by not getting it you are cheating yourself. Do you agree?

Prospect: Oh, perhaps.

Salesman: Good. Now would you like to take *this* one (salesman points to typewriter on the counter) with you?

Prospect: I did say I agreed with you, but I didn't say I was going to buy. I still want to think about it awhile.

Salesman: Let's get back to school work a minute. Do you type every class assignment that you have to turn in?

Prospect: No, only if it is some sort of term paper or report, and even then I don't always type the short ones.

Salesman: Did you know that the use of a typewriter on all your assignments can improve your grades as much as 25 per cent?

Prospect: No, I didn't. How do you know? That sounds kind of hard to believe.

Salesman: An impartial survey was made about a year ago which included students all the way from junior high school through college. Students who didn't use typewriters started to use them, and their grades in some cases improved as much as 25 per cent.

Prospect: That sounds good. I'm always looking for a way to improve my grades, but I don't think it would help me this semester because so much of it is already gone. I will probably be ready to buy by the time the spring semester gets started.

Salesman: But if you bought now you could start enjoying the other advantages tomorrow.

Prospect: Thank you for taking so much time showing me the typewriter, but I am not going to buy now. I am going to have to go because I have some other things to do.

Salesman: Sam, do you mind if I ask you exactly why you don't want to buy now?

Prospect: Well . . . I want to talk it over with my wife. You see, she has worked as a secretary for the last three years, and she can tell me from her experience how typewriters rank.

Salesman: I think that is a very wise idea. If anyone would know a good typewriter, she would. But I think I can save you trouble. The Remington has a very wide acceptance in the field of office typewriters. Why, just last week the local Globe Company bought five new Remingtons for their office. I think that speaks well for Remington, don't you?

Prospect: Yes, I guess it does.

Salesman: You can't find a better typewriter than the Remington. Let me fix this one up for you to take with you.

Prospect: Gee, I don't know. I really hadn't planned to buy one yet. Maybe I still better talk to my wife about it.

Salesman: If you brought this home with you today I am sure your wife would be surprised and pleased. I know she will be able to use and enjoy it often, won't she?

Prospect: I don't know. She gets all her work done before she comes home. I have never heard her say that she needed to do any at night.

Salesman: I wasn't thinking about her work but about letters she writes, and if she is like my wife she is probably writing one every day or two.

Prospect: I never thought of that. She does write letters to her parents and mine and to several of the girls she went to school with.

Salesman: Just think, if you took this home with you, she could start enjoying the advantages herself at once. It will save her time in writing her letters also. You would want to do something to help your wife, wouldn't you?

Prospect: Of course.

Salesman: Well, this will do that for her and for you also. Just think, starting tomorrow you won't have to worry about renting a typewriter or finding someone to type for you. You would like that, wouldn't you?

Prospect: Yes, but . . .

Salesman: Sam, you can't afford to wait. Remember that you will be cheating yourself by not buying now. You have agreed that you need a typewriter and can use one, haven't you?

Prospect: Well . . . yes.

Salesman: You have also agreed that this Remington is the best typewriter that you can buy, haven't you?

Prospect: Perhaps, but I'm still not sure I want to buy *now*.

Salesman: Don't forget that your wife will be able to use this also. It will help her write letters faster and more easily. You do like to take home things that will help and please your wife, don't you?

Prospect: Yes.

Salesman: You would want her to start enjoying the ease and advantages of a typewriter as soon as possible, say tomorrow, wouldn't you?

Prospect: I suppose so.

Salesman: Well, in that case you should get a typewriter right now. Would you rather have this one or one that is still boxed up?

Prospect: Well . . . I guess one that is still boxed up.

For the salesman, the fifth buying decision is a test. He succeeds or fails as he gets or fails to get agreement to this question. If the prospect has said yes to the first four buying decisions but refuses to approve this fifth suggestion of the salesman, then the salesman knows that one of the four agreements was phony. He must start all over again.

ADOPTING THE PROSPECT'S POINT OF VIEW

Let the Prospect Be King

One of the first questions confronting a salesman as he approaches his task of constructing a sales presentation is where the emphasis should be placed, or, in other words, what element of the sales situation should receive the most attention. Should the sales effort be centered on the prospect or on the product? The answer is clear — the prospect. All prospects want recognition and appreciation because they all are proud of something they *are*, or *have*, or *did*. One is reminded here of the man who, as a gag, sent one-word telegrams to ten of his acquaintances. The one-word message was "Congratulations." Eight of the ten thanked the sender promptly and warmly, some of the eight being a bit modest. The eight thought the sender had learned of some one of their recent achievements or honors.

Letting the prospect be king requires that the salesman give him the position of prominence and that he fashion his own thoughts, words, and actions accordingly. It means locating the prospect's problems and finding solutions for them. It calls for the salesman's putting himself in the prospect's shoes and chair to see things through the prospect's eyes.

What is involved here is sometimes called the "you" point of view. The salesman will reflect this attitude in his story by his frequent use of the word "you." This attitude puts the salesman in step with the prospect and keeps him there. It forbids the salesman to preach to the prospect about product, company, or self, or to expect the prospect to accept and apply the preachments. Far too many salesmen are far too anxious to acquit themselves creditably as makers of good speeches, and, as a result, they construct speeches for their own ears instead of for their prospects. A final phase of the "you" attitude consists of putting a strong service flavor into each story; instead of selling to the prospect, the salesman helps him to make a purchase decision.

Letting the prospect be king is absolutely essential if first things are to be first and the spotlight is to focus on what it should. The cold, blunt truth is that product excellence, company prominence, or the salesman's ambition are not in themselves reasons for buying. The prospect's indifference to each of those three is colossal — unless one of them affects *his* interests.

The prospect's interest and faith in the product are most easily captured by giving him the number one spot. Letting him play the prominent role (but this does not mean letting him dominate the conduct of the interview) invites his confidence. He is led to feel that the salesman is sound because the salesman placed major emphasis on *him* instead of on the product or on his own views. Prospects will accept recommendations only from salesmen who recognize their situations sympathetically and specifically and then prescribe for them.

Letting the prospect be king is not impractical theory nor madcap altruism. It is the smartest and most profitable long-range policy.

How Prospects Look Upon Products

In the construction of a sales story, the salesman must remember that the efficiency of a product, its inexpensiveness, or its style appeal mean little to a buyer until he sees how these features affect him. As the salesman gives his sales story, it is the satisfactions the product will or will not bring that enter the purchaser's mind.

The satisfaction that a buyer buys must be a personal satisfaction. A retailer prospect cares little for what Brand X does for retailers in the mass, just as the consumer is little moved by what it does for John and Jane Doe. The individual prospect wants a product that fits into his own personal, selfish, different-from-all-others pattern.

Let the Prospect Talk

It should be axiomatic that the salesman's adoption of the prospect's point of view demands that he plan for the prospect to do some of the talking during the sales interview. Each prospect has his own ideas, doubts, questions, opinions, and objections. The more a salesman knows about the prospect's views and attitudes, the most completely he can identify himself with the prospect and with the prospect's interests and ambitions. By intentionally arranging to do some listening, the salesman insures the prospect a chance to take part in the interview and to express his opinions.

Prospect participation in the conversation helps the salesman in several ways to understand and adopt the prospect point of view. First, an unfettered exchange between prospect and salesman can be had only if the prospect tells the salesman what is on his mind. This he is encouraged to do without reservation if the salesman is tactful, receptive, and a respecter of confidences. Second, the polite, courteous salesman who listens to the prospect's ideas and opinions is well liked and held in high regard by the prospect. The prospect feels that the salesman demonstrates good judgment by listening, and this makes him feel that the salesman understands him. Indeed, this is true. Third, by talking *and* listening, the salesman keeps a close check on the prospect's thinking. He can tell what the prospect takes exception to and what he accepts. Fourth, the prospect's comments provide the salesman with clues and facts which enable the salesman to adapt and revise his story so as to best personalize it. Last, conversation helps the salesman to recognize early in the interview the buying motives which seem to be dominant. It is around these that the salesman will construct his story.

THE "CANNED" STORY

The question of whether a memorized sales talk is superior to an extemporaneous one is controversial. Some companies insist on one method while other companies prefer the other. Much writing and discussion has been directed at memorized sales stories, usually called "canned" presentations. The canned story is a standardized story that a salesman memorizes word for word and delivers exactly as memorized. In its extreme form, a single story is memorized literally from beginning to ending. In a less extreme form, the salesman memorizes story elements or sections but uses some discretion in deciding which sections to include and which to omit from the story he tells a specific buyer.

There are strong arguments in favor of canned stories. One is the logical assumption that they have been well constructed. This, of course should be the case because the builder of the story can test the component parts, identifying and eliminating those that are weak. The wording and phrasing of the canned story should be superior to those the typical salesman would use when he tells his story in his own words. Another argument is that the scientifically sound construction of the story supplies confidence to salesmen, particularly to beginning salesmen. There need be no fear of awkward pauses, nor of uncertainty, nor of any frantic groping for what to say and what point to make next. Instead of these dreaded possibilities, the salesman can concern himself with other matters because he has a track to run on; he can pay more attention to his delivery of the story, to the handling of the product, to the buyer's surroundings, and to the apparent reception his story is getting, There should be fewer objections to bother the salesman because of the completeness of his story. All important points are included, and they are arranged in the strongest possible sequence so as to make buying easy in all cases and irresistible in many. Carefully built canned stories avoid two undesirable extremes — superfluous repetition and inadvertent omission. Another significant point is that the memorized story is favored by some very large, very successful companies.

The canned story is wide open to criticism on several scores. It seems neither unfair nor inaccurate to claim that it is simply out of the question where a salesman makes frequent calls on the same buyers month after month. It appears equally unusable for salesmen who handle a really wide line of products. It does not seem appropriate in situations which, for some reason or other, are unusual or peculiar. The inflexibility of the story makes it unrealistic in at least three respects: (1) it does not recognize that a buyer can be completely ignorant about the product, or violently hostile toward it, or impatiently ready to buy; (2) it does not recognize the motivational differences which are present in a group of buyers; and (3) it does not recognize the differences among sales interviews — differences such as length, place, or atmosphere of interview. Its lack of originality can bore, and its rigidity can cause irritation and resentment. Because the salesman does not have to tailor his story to fit each buyer snugly, his mental growth is discouraged and the development of his imagination is handicapped. Countless recitals of the same story are apt to lead to a delivery that sounds mechanical and listless. Customers will find the story standardized and dull. Monologue may gradually move in to such a degree that most interruptions force the salesman off his track. Finally, the good salesman may find himself handicapped by working for a company that has difficulty in attracting the better grade of salesman.

There are both advantages and disadvantages to the canned story. Perhaps the most effective solution to the controversy lies in a combination of the canned and the original presentation. It is highly desirable that young salesmen go through the first phase of the memorized story, the committing to memory of a complete sales presentation. Even if they find that they do better in actual selling by setting the script aside and talking extemporaneously in their own individual styles, the memorized story provides a safety reserve to fall back on, if and when it is needed.

THE STORY PLAN

The Story Plan Itself

The position of this text is that what a salesman needs is not a memorized story but a *story plan*. This story plan is, in a sense, a program which appropriates all the good that it possibly can from the memorized story, yet tries to avoid the canned story's defects. The story plan is an outline, in considerable detail, of the complete story that the salesman is competent to tell. It is an agenda of the points the salesman will make, unless, of course, a change is demanded. It is a framework and schedule of the main features of the salesman's most effective presentation. The story plan has a single purpose — to enable the salesman to make a sale.

The construction of a story plan calls for a salesman to identify and then to memorize in four areas. First, he will identify and memorize the buying motives that he can stimulate with telling effect, as, for example, economy.

Second, he will identify and memorize for each buying motive the ways in which the prospect will enjoy that particular benefit. For example, a product can be economical to buy, to operate, to service, or to replace.

Third, he will determine and then memorize the most potent sequence by which the buying motives can be appealed to and excited. In some cases, this can be done best by making a memory scheme of the initials of the buying motives that the salesman selects to compose the framework of his story. For example, the code word for a household appliance might be C-A-S-H-E-D, as:

    Comfort
        Approval
            Safety
                Health
                    Economy
                        Durability

Fourth and last, he will experiment until he has discovered any key phrases and key sentences that have proved valuable in forestalling objections or in describing what the product will do. These he will memorize.

The story plan, thus, is the raw material of which the salesman's actual presentation is fashioned. In itself, it is a standard story, and as such it will fit the typical situation in the same way that a memorized story fits. As a matter of fact, the standard story embodied in the story plan will be told without change unless conditions demand some revision. When, however, circumstances put pressure on the salesman to adapt and tailor the story a bit, then the story plan proves to be superior to the memorized story in that its elasticity provides for just such situations.

The more the story is personalized, the more convincing and persuasive it will be. If prospect "A" places great importance on comfort, the salesman will concentrate on that particular buying motive; if prospect "B" ranks economy as the most desired feature, the salesman translates the same product into economy for prospect "B" and emphasizes economy instead of comfort. Personalizing the story, of course, demands of the salesman the ability to diagnose accurately and to modify skillfully on short notice; otherwise, the salesman had best stick to the standard story.

Why a Story Plan Is Needed

Nothing successful, from an automobile to a chocolate cake, can be made without a design, plan, blueprint, schedule, recipe, formula, or pattern. Regardless of how the salesman feels about the memorized story, he cannot avoid the duty of organizing his presentation. If organization is lacking, there is a loss of cumulative strength. If the presentation is random, the prospect is confused. Because erratic selling is unsound selling, the story must be planned intelligently. No interview is adequately planned if conscious, calculated study has not been given to the organization of the story.

The resistance or objections that a salesman encounters form a pattern that is almost statistically constant. Out of each group of one hundred prospects successively interviewed, probably forty will object to the product's price. Twenty, perhaps, will always want to "think it over." Because opposition from prospects shapes into a pattern, a patterned story must be built if that opposition is to be successfully forestalled.

A well-planned and organized story enables any salesman to make a more favorable impression than would otherwise be possible. For the nervous junior salesman, the story plan will save him from being asked to play music without a score. For the brilliant junior salesman, the plan prevents the presentation of ideas in a rambling, disjointed manner that can produce only unpredictable results. Instead of *hoping* his salesmanship will achieve the desired results, each salesman must know how to *make* it do that. This requires planning.

The Story Plan in Operation

When adopted and put in use by the salesman, a story plan such as described here has several outstanding advantages. It is freely granted that some of these features can be found in some memorized stories.

The basic story is a sound story. No strong points are omitted; there is no repetition or backtracking unless the salesman so intends; and there is no overemphasizing or underemphasizing. The order is logical and clear rather than slipshod.

The story can be tailored. This permits the product to be described in terms of the hopes and dreams of each individual prospect. Because the salesman can construct a complete, specific story for each prospect he sees, his presentation is more impressive and persuasive. The job of tailoring the story delineates an area wherein the salesman's initiative, imagination, and resourcefulness can operate and grow. These abilities are always needed in unusual situations, of which there are many.

The salesman tells the story in his own words. As a result, he delivers a natural story and not one that is awkward or artificial. Because he is telling his own story, he is not a mere mouthpiece for someone else. He can take advantage of personality traits and abilities peculiar to himself.

The salesman's task is made easier than it otherwise would be. When he has a story well in hand, he can concentrate on prospect reaction and watch for indications of how his story is being received without any sacrifice of effectiveness. Control is less of a problem because he knows where he is going. Less time is wasted.

Finally, the systematic story pays off in dollars and cents.

A Minority Point of View

A few sales managers do not look with favor on a planned sales presentation. Because some students may go to work for companies which hold this view, this attitude is presented.

These sales managers do not think it advisable to outline a sales talk, offering as a basis for their feeling the fact that no two calls are alike. They do give each salesman information about product, prospects, and how his company operates, and they may even indicate points to be brought up in the interview, but there they stop.

If the salesman is intelligent, fully conversant with his merchandise, posted on current market conditions, and if he strives for a close personal relationship with his prospects, this, it is felt, is sufficient for the interview. Experience, they say, will enable the salesman to handle interviews satisfactorily. One sales manager of this group wrote that he considers selling similar to swimming; he puts a salesman in a territory and tells him to go to it. The salesman, he claims, will pick up the knack of story telling.

This text is in violent disagreement with the point of view just expressed. Instead, a strong recommendation is here made that the young salesman write out several complete presentations, revise and improve them, and then memorize the best. Rehearsing in this manner puts a strong story in his hands until the day when he can do better by improvising. Even if the memorized story is never delivered, it inevitably renews and increases his own belief in his product, and this conviction will be present in whatever story he does tell.

STUDY ASSIGNMENTS

1. What essential features should characterize the story a drug manufacturer's salesman plans to tell doctors?
2. Do you know of a "one best way" to establish *need* in a buyer's mind?
3. When planning their sales stories, many salesmen count on considerable use of the prefatory phrase, "As you know, ..." What good does this do?
4. Some salesmen do very little planning of the sales stories they tell. Where, when, and how might this be reflected?
5. Must the salesman always spend time and effort in winning each of the five buying decisions? Why?
6. Why should a salesman spend a considerable amount of his working time in *getting ready* to talk to buyers?
7. Certain products are sold successfully by canned sales stories. Can you find features or characteristics which are common to these products?
8. The prospect is king, yet the salesman's job is to lead him to do what he wants him to do. Explain this paradox.
9. A salesman sells tires to a service station operator with one presentation but drafts an entirely different one when selling the identical tires to a purchasing agent. Why? How would the two stories differ?
10. "Successful selling starts with making prospects dissatisfied with present conditions." Is this a good starting point for the sales presentation?

CASE STUDY 10

Hospital organization and operation conspire to pose a most difficult problem for salesmen selling medical equipment and supplies. The heart of this problem lies in the question of buying influence and buying authority. There is no standard pattern. In general, the same job titles are found in all hospitals, but the responsibilities and the significance of the jobs vary considerably. This circumstance affects a salesman particularly in: (1) determining the sequence in which he should try to see individuals, and (2) building a presentation which will influence several individuals, each of whose dominant buying motives differ from those of his associates.

One individual who has a voice in the purchases made by a hospital is the *purchasing agent*. If a hospital is large enough, or if it considers procurement important enough to bestow this title on a person, the odds are that the purchasing agent is a major buying influence. Another person to consider is the *administrator*. His important job of managing the institution explains his interest in purchasing. The *director of nurses* is a key person in many hospitals; sometimes she is assigned certain buying duties. The *operating room supervisor* is in a strategic spot. Her favor and her disfavor are not to be taken lightly.

Finally, there are the *doctors*. Their concern for their patients and for their own personal activities and advancement understandably urges them to concern themselves with what the hospital buys.

QUESTIONS:

1. How can a salesman who is selling medical supplies to a hospital identify and rate the buying influences involved?

2. What is the probable interest of each buying influence in purchases made by the hospital?

CHAPTER 11

GETTING AND OPENING THE INTERVIEW

Having planned his sales story, the salesman's next concern is to tell it to the buyer for whom it was built. Before the story can be told, the salesman must (a) be with that buyer in a physical, face-to-face sense and (b) have permission from that buyer to make his presentation.

If one considers selling to consist of four types of activity, namely, *preapproach, approach, demonstration or presentation,* and *close,* this chapter deals with the approach. For some ideas on the nature of an approach, here is a section from the sales training material of United Air Lines.

The *approach* is of great importance for it will determine to a great extent your future association with a prospect, including: (1) how receptive the prospect will be, (2) whether your close will be difficult or easy, (3) how welcome you will be on succeeding calls.

The objective of the approach is to determine who needs our service and to insure a presentation to an interested individual, or one who can become interested.

Many sales experts agree that the first thirty seconds is the most important part of the approach. In fact, Jack Lacy says that the first thirty seconds is the most important time you will ever spend with the prospect as long as you know him.

Before getting in to see the prospect, you first must "sell" yourself to his secretary or receptionist. She must be on your side, or you will never see the prospect, and the bigger the prospect, the truer the statement.

A good immediate impression can be made by a fine appearance and attitude. You must be appropriately and neatly dressed and convey a sense of poise and dignity. Your greeting should be warm and sincere, but not familiar or patronizing.

Introduce yourself and company, and present her with a *readily available* business card, asking for the prospect. A most accessible place for your cards is in the breast pocket of your suit coat.

Remember the way you impress the secretary/receptionist will make her an invaluable ally or an adversary of equal import.

When you get in to see the prospect, he, too, must react favorably to your appearance and manner and be made to invite you to tell your complete story.

Several things at this point will influence his impression of you:

(1) Watch where you place your hat. Leave it in the reception room if possible — otherwise on the floor next to your briefcase —*never* on his desk.

(2) It is dangerous to wear a lapel pin, other than your United Air Lines service pin; e.g., an Elks button may be a red flag to this man, since he may have been unsuccessful in gaining Elks membership. . . .

(3) Do not sit down until he invites you to; if the invitation is not issued in a reasonable length of time, it is proper to ask if you may do so.

The approach must accomplish several things to lay a good foundation for a successful presentation. You must progress through the following steps in this order:

(1) Neutralize the thoughts which were in his mind.

(2) Establish the idea you wish to sell.

(3) Get his interest in your proposition.

SECURING THE INTERVIEW

Whom to See

In many areas of selling, the question of whom to see is readily and automatically answered. This is particularly true in selling to ultimate consumers. On the other hand, in some business selling a real problem does exist in identifying the person who should be seen. For example, does the credit manager of a corporation specify the typewriters his stenographers use, or does someone else?

The man the salesman prefers to deal with in a large organization, first of all, is the person most influential in the purchase of the salesman's product, but this does not mean that he is the person easiest to see. Second, this individual has time to hear the salesman's story. Third, the person has the authority to make the purchase or to approve it. Fourth. he is able to grasp the benefits that will accrue from buying. Finally, he is the one most vitally and intimately interested in the advantages to be gained from making the purchase.

When in doubt about whom to see, a good rule seems to be for the salesman to call on as high an executive as possible. If the executive sees the salesman, that's fine; if he refers the salesman to someone else, the salesman possesses a good entree. Once in a while the solution is as simple as asking someone in the organization, "Can you tell me who buys your typewriters?"

When to Call

Very little help can be given the college student in a textbook about the matter of timing or scheduling calls. About all that can be said is that the salesman should try to tell his story during the time of year, month, week, and day that the prospect is most nearly in a receptive frame of mind. It should not take much time or ingenuity for the young salesman to learn what the "best" hours are for his particular line of merchandise. He can quickly learn that certified public accountants are extremely busy from January 15 to April 15, that merchants may be less busy between one and three in the afternoon, that professional people may be best approached between eight-thirty and ten in the morning before their professional day starts, and that low-salaried prospects perhaps should be seen at home soon after the evening meal.

Handling Barriers

A "barrier" is a person who is paid to see that his employer's time is not wasted. Barriers are supposed to keep salesmen from reaching the employer when such a meeting could not benefit the employer. They are the switchboard operators, receptionists, secretaries, junior employees, partners, and even members of families. Their story frequently is that the prospect is out, busy, not interested, not open-to-buy, or not available. They may or may not ask the salesman to leave pamphlets, catalogues, or booklets and may or may not ask him to call again. It should be emphasized that the job of the barrier is to bar only the salesmen who do not qualify for some of the prospect's time. They are instructed to admit any salesman the prospect should see, which means any salesman who probably would benefit the prospect.

In handling barriers, the salesman needs to use imagination, resourcefulness, and ingenuity. He also needs to cultivate the goodwill of all minor employees, for such goodwill constitutes an asset that can result in the salesman's securing helpful information about prospects. For example, the secretary just might tell a salesman who had made a favorable impression on her when her employer will next be in the market to buy.

Absolutely no tricks are warranted in gaining admission, because they are remembered with resentment. A bit of curiosity is perfectly legitimate, but deception is not. For example, to crash a gate on the pretext of being a market researcher or a schoolmate of the prospect when such is not the case is clearly unethical and usually fatal to the salesman's chances.

Here are some suggested techniques for penetrating barriers:

Deliver a Requested Item. If the prospect has written to the salesman's company for information, samples, booklets, or such, the salesman can take the inquiry and the item requested and use them as a passport to get in to see the prospect.

Depend on the Company Name.   Some companies instruct their salesmen calling on retailers to open the interview with, "I am John Jones with the XYZ Company." These companies say that the mention of the company name is frequently enough to insure getting some of the prospect's time. Other companies, of course, instruct their salesmen not to mention the company name or the company business to a barrier in order to save that information for the prospect himself.

Disclose Little.   Sometimes as a last resort, when the barrier is adamant, the salesman may find it necessary to reveal part of his mission and objective to the barrier and count on the barrier's letting the salesman in or selling the prospect on the idea of the interview. In this connection, a young salesman must guard against getting the jitters and blurting out his entire story to the barrier. Instead, he should limit himself to speaking generally of "lowering costs" or "increasing profits" rather than giving the barrier any other information. The salesman should point out that he needs data that only the prospect can supply. Sometimes the advice of the barrier can be asked to advantage.   Again, the salesman may have success with some such statement as "I won't need but a couple of minutes, and my suggestions will be profitable."

Promise Another Call.   Sometimes, when turned down by the barrier, the salesman can profit from saying, "Then I will call again tomorrow. Mr. Prospect will be in, I assume." If this brings the prospect out today, that, of course, is fine.

Display Command Presence.   Some companies instruct their salesmen to announce their presence in such words as to impress the barrier into allowing the interview. Two examples are "Mr. Salesman is here to see Mr. Prospect," and "Please tell Mr. Prospect that Mr. Salesman is here to see him."

Make an "Entrance."   The theatrical entrance is recommended by some companies and is apparently used with success by some salesmen. Here the salesman opens the door in a positive manner, strides from door to receptionist in a fashion calculated to impress, removes his hat only upon getting to the receptionist and not before, and thus conveys the idea of importance and authority before he speaks. This stage entrance fits in with the command presence announcement.

Be Obvious in Expecting Cooperation.   One of the soundest ways of coping with barriers is to make certain of the good appearance and the confident, pleasant manner that constitute an effective passport. If the salesman looks and acts as if he is the type of salesman that the prospect should see, then the chances are that he will be seen. His obvious conviction that he has a story valuable to the prospect is his best insurance of admission. By acting successful, by expecting to be welcome, by being prepared physically and mentally to be welcome, he helps to insure an interview.

Limit Waiting Time. If the salesman has to wait in a reception office, his chances can be hurt if he waits too long. Not only does he lose prestige, but, of course, he also loses productive selling time. Incidentally, any waiting time can be used to review the presentation he hopes to make and the answers to the objections he expects.

While the above-mentioned techniques will be helpful on occasions, there is nothing more basic or effective than collecting and analyzing as much information about the prospect as possible. The more advance information the salesman has, the better the odds are of |his seeing the prospect.

BUYER ATTENTION — A PREREQUISITE

Necessity for Attention

Before taking up the salesman's problems of opening his sales interviews with buyers, perhaps it is well to review some basic truths about attention. Our initial recognition is that no salesman can influence or persuade buyers unless those buyers listen to the salesman's presentation. So, the salesman's first undertaking is to get a buyer to "attend." This means that the salesman must get into the buyer's mind and thinking, and that is no easy task; the competition for the buyer's attention is intense. Yet, unless the salesman breaks successfully into the buyer's stream of thought, he can seldom expect anything but failure, because few persons can pay close attention to two matters, topics, objects, or persons at the same time.

An analogy that seems sound is that of an instructor and a class of students. Unless the instructor gets a student's attention, he can be of little aid to that student. No matter how brilliant the instructor's comments are and no matter how challenging and informative are the discussions he leads, until he has students' attention, he is sorely handicapped in his objectives of helping students to learn, to grow, and to think. If students are reading or writing letters, studying for a quiz, working crossword puzzles, looking at a paper, or frantically trying to dash off an acceptable written assignment for next period's class, they cannot take in much of what is going on about them.

If the buyer is to understand the full significance of the salesman's story, he must be attentive. The salesman must have possession of the buyer's undivided attention if he is to obtain and hold control of the interview so effectively that the buyer looks only at what the salesman does and listens only to what the salesman says.   If the buyer tunes the salesman in, adjusts himself mentally, physically, and emotionally to receive the salesman's message, and if he is willing to grasp the meaning of what the salesman has to say, then the salesman has the buyer's attention.   In such circumstances, the salesman has an excellent opportunity of getting the buyer to travel with him along the marked route to a purchase and a sale.

Mechanical Techniques

There are two types of technique for getting a person's attention. This section gives brief mention to methods usually put in a single group or classification and labeled *mechanical* methods of attracting attention. These can be thought of as physical stimuli to attention; they are what one can *use* (in contrast to what one can *say*) to get attention; they are "how" techniques.   Adaptations of these methods are a challenge to salesmen.

Color.   Colors speak a language all their own; red is exciting, blue is restful, and black is tragic. School buses, curbs denied to parkers, and caution lights are orange because of the high visibility of this color from a distance.   Color affects a buyer's emotions and his judgments. His reactions can be strongly favorable — or just as strongly unfavorable. Color lends distinctiveness.

Size.   Unusual size attracts attention whether the item in question be quite large or quite small.   The presence of elephants in the circus parade suggests that large sizes are used for emphasis more often than are small sizes.   Dowagers may invite envious attention to their large diamonds and to the small watches they wear.   An actress wanting to attract attention may affect a Peke — or an Irish wolfhound, a Pom — or a Great Dane. A very large house or an extremely small one will stand out when every other house on the block is an average-size home.

Intensity.   This element or quality relates to the strength, the power, or the force of a stimulus.   In the area of sound, we have, for example, the police whistle and the fire truck siren.   In the broadcast media of radio and television, we have the entire range of sound effects. In the theater, certain plays have widely known high points or climaxes that grip the attention of the audience and hold it breathless.   In the area of lighting, we have spot lights, stop lights, flood lights, and the sun's blinding brilliance.

Motion. Motion is eye- and attention-catching. Students wanting to attract the instructor's attention make hand motions to achieve their purpose. When a retailer's window contains a display which incorporates motion, that window is much more successful in drawing attention than are competing windows containing motionless displays. Motion can be actual or suggested in pictures.

Contrast. If the tendency in regard to size is to make something *larger*, then in contrast the idea is to make something *different*. Variety is one expression of contrast. Sometimes a "before" photograph is placed alongside an "after" photograph; sometimes the current model of a product is shown with an older model; often the giant and the midget of an athletic squad are posed side by side, and the corny caption often says something about "the long and the short of it." The effect of contrast can also be obtained through the use of contrasting colors.

Isolation. In this technique, some item is set apart from other items — off by itself. The isolated element stands out from the other elements. If you ride in an elevator or in a bus with just one other passenger, you normally notice more about him or her than you would if the elevator or bus were nearly full. If you must wait for a line of automobiles before crossing a street, no one automobile receives your attention as it would if it were alone. Isolation removes other bids for attention. Spoken phrases can be isolated by preceding them — and then following them — by short periods of silence.

Position. Certain positions possess greater attention value than do other positions. Individuals at the head table and the person to the right of the hostess get a generous amount of notice. Occupants of theater boxes or the front and center of the stage are prominent. A corner location for a store and the counter space next to the cash register command premiums because they are preferred locations. Back covers of magazines and head-on sites in outdoor advertising are superior positions.

Interest Techniques

The second technique for attention-getting is usually referred to as the *interest* method. It involves the nature of the message delivered to the person whose attention is wanted. Just as mechanical techniques were referred to as "how" techniques, interest techniques can be termed "what" techniques.

One of two possibilities, and by far the major one, is to make a specific appeal to a specific need or want or to a specific individual. The most interesting person the buyer knows is himself or herself. The problems of greatest concern to a buyer are his own personal problems. References to an individual's self, hopes, desires, and circumstances are powerful attention-getters.

The second possibility is to approach a person with some matter of universal interest. Because people are interested in other people, one can refer to other individuals — individuals who are prominent, perhaps, or respected. News, current events, local happenings, matters of common concern at the moment — these attract attention. Once the salesman receives a prospect's attention, however, that attention must be directed quickly to the buyer's needs and wants which the salesman's product will fill.

THE SALESMAN'S FIRST OBJECTIVES

There appear to be three main goals that the salesman should have in mind during the first few moments of the interview. These are to make a good impression, to survey the situation, and to stir the feelings of the prospect.

Making a Good Impression

Making a good impression is eminently desirable because it helps in making a sale. In addition, salesmen who will be making subsequent calls on the same prospect stand to benefit from favorable first impressions.

His initial impression is better if the salesman succeeds in establishing, by manner and attitude, the fact that he is frank, sincere, competent, and anxious to help. He needs to convince the prospect that he is personally interested in the prospect's problems and their solution, that he wants to help the prospect get what he wants.

By inviting and inspiring the prospect's confidence, the salesman puts him in the mood to discuss and explain his problems, and this frequently must be done before the salesman can attempt to ascertain the prospect's needs. The prospect must have confidence in the salesman and his propositions before he will accept them. He must feel that the salesman is both honest and well-informed.

Surveying the Situation

The first phase of a survey or analysis of the situation involves qualifying the prospect, and this step was described in Chapter 7. If the person on whom the salesman is calling can use the product to advantage, then he is a prospect and is entitled to the salesman's time and efforts. If he cannot use the product, the salesman should tell him so. If those who are not prospects are identified quickly, the salesman obviously has saved time. If a suspect turns out to be a prosepct, there is the question of whether the prospect realizes his need. In getting this information, the salesman may need to ask questions and encourage the prospect to talk.

A second phase of the survey is sizing up the prospect's whole self — mental, emotional, and physical. This early appraisal will influence and guide the rest of the interview. The salesman will observe and measure the prospect because, by so doing, he gets clues as to what type of person the prospect is and what he is thinking. The saleman who is trained and alert will continue to follow throughout the entire call the prospect's reactions as expressed in looks, tone of voice, and movements.

This second phase of the survey is closely related to a very interesting question: Can prospects be "typed" successfully? Probable the greatest difficulty about attempting to classify individuals results from the fact that each one can be in a different mood on the salesman's successive calls. And woe to the salesman who has typed a prospect as a Caspar Milquetoast and gives him the Caspar Milquetoast treatment on the day he is feeling and acting like Fearless Fosdick!

A third phase of the survey calls for the salesman's quick inspection of the physical surroundings when the interview is at the prospect's home or place of business. These external furnishings are indicators of such important matters as purchasing power, taste, interests, and, above all, needs. A word of caution is that appearance cannot be taken as conclusive proof of anything. Speech, clothing, address, atmosphere, and appearance can be misleading and misinterpreted.

A fourth and final objective of the survey is to determine, as accurately as possible in a very short time, what the prospect really wants, and this, of course, is a matter of buying motives. Identification of the dominant desires of the prospect, of the active influences that make him spend his money as he does, will help in finding a common ground on which prospect-problem and product-solution can be related to each other. Indeed, unless the most effective buying motives are quickly found out, the salesman runs the risk of dismissal or, at least, apathetic listening from the prospect.

Stirring the Prospect's Feelings

Another major objective of the salesman in the opening moments of the interview is capturing the undivided, favorable, and relevant attention of the prospect. If the attention is unfavorable, the salesman has created another block between himself and a sale; if it is not relevant, the prospect feels tricked, and that is bad. Unless, then, the salesman secures the right attention, his position is weak because he does not have control, and control of the interview is essential to his success.

Having secured the necessary attention, the salesman is next ready to start arousing interest, and this he does by relating his product to one of the prospect's needs, problems, or hopes. The prospect experiences a bit of stimulation because an answer, the product, is being recommended to one of his insistent wants. He becomes an attentive listener to the salesman's story. He has become curious enough about whether or not the salesman's product is a superior solution to one of his problems to hear the salesman. Indeed, the prospect feels that both the visit and the proposal are important to him.

THE SALESMAN'S ATTITUDE

Optimistic Confidence

If the frame of mind most needed by the salesman in the first moments of the call can be described briefly, it might be tagged as being optimistically confident. This attitude is reflected in the salesman's being relaxed and feeling the equal of the prospect. And the good salesman has many reasons for feeling confident. He knows what his company has done and is doing. He knows how his product has helped other buyers in the past. He knows that he has made of himself an authority — an expert in solving prospects' problems. He knows there is no occasion for fear or timidity because he knows more about his product than the prospect does. In a word, he has a sincere belief in the ability of his company, his product, and himself to help the prospect.

Viewed from another angle, the salesman's attitude is one that assumes that he will be welcome, that his story will be heard, that the prospect will realize the desirability of the product, and that a purchase will be made. These are the assumptions that prevent the salesman from being defeated before going in.

It sometimes happens that a salesman feels severely handicapped because he is not a friend or even an acquaintance of the prospect, or because there are no reciprocal connections. Confidence can be bolstered by such a salesman's remembering that it takes sound selling and sound service to get and hold customers. Prospects will listen to any salesman who has a concise, logical, well-planned, helpful story to tell. Furthermore, prospects tend to be flippant with and not take too seriously those salesmen whom they know quite well.

Correct thinking reminds the salesman that he is conferring a favor on the prospect, not asking a favor — that the prospect needs the salesman as much as the salesman needs the prospect. Because his mission is to help, the salesman has no justification for feeling other than optimistic.

Things to Avoid

This feeling of optimism must not lull the salesman into expecting the prospect to be ready to buy. Instead, it must be accompanied by an assumption of prospect-ignorance and prospect-indifference. Otherwise, the prospect would be getting in touch with the salesman, and the salesman's job of getting the prospect ready to buy would vanish.

A second mental slant that cannot be permitted is that of indifference. Young salesmen, particularly, often force themselves in ruthless fashion to be casual and even unimpressible. This pose of never being surprised or enthusiastic can easily result in a spiritless, dispassionate opening that loses sales. Prospects seldom accept a product with greater enthusiasm than the salesman demonstrates.

A third error is the other extreme from the one just mentioned, an attitude of anxiety. Tautness can be just as fatal as indifference, for it alerts the prospect's caution and diverts his attention from the sales story.

The salesman should never impress the prospect as being:

Affected	Confusing	Offensive
Apologetic	Critical	Pessimistic
Argumentative	Eager	Pompous
Awkward	Familiar	Sarcastic
Careless	Hurried	Thoughtless
Condescending	Nervous	Vague

Westinghouse reports on a research job intended to find out more about how salesmen affect and impress buyers. One question asked buyers was, " What do you most dislike in the general manner of any salesman who has called on you?" Included in the answers were the following:

He was too darn nonchalant. His lounging, slouchy manner seemed to imply he didn't think I was a particularly important person.

His eyes were shifty and evasive. I didn't like the way he kept them narrowly slitted.

His eyes were unfocused and dreamy. I didn't like their blank stare. I didn't like the phony way he smiled. It was either a forced smile that made him look like a pained ant-eater . . . . or the kind of a half-smile you see on the face of a baby about to have a gas burp.

His whole manner was that of an order hawk rather than that of a fellow sincerely trying to help me. I got the impression that my order to him meant the same thing a scalp means to an Indian.

I didn't like the bored, impatient way the salesman listened when I talked. His manner seemed to say: "For Heaven's sake, will you ever pipe down and let a *smart* man talk."

I didn't like the liberties he took in my presence, like placing a soiled hat on my papers, balancing a lighted cigarette on the edge of my desk . . . . and then, later on, knocking its ashes off into the little jar that holds my paper clips.

I didn't like the pompous, bombastic way in which he orated his sales talk. He spoke to me as if I were a public meeting.

I didn't like the inquisitive way his eyes roved over my desk during the interview.

He fingered his lips as he talked, so his words sounded like someone drinking coffee out of a moustache cup.

I didn't like the presumptuous back-slapping way he breezed into my office and took the initiative in shaking my hand.

The salesman's manner implied he was a wiser, better man than I.
He was full of nervous mannerisms that distracted my attention.

I didn't like the salesman's obvious attempts at flattery. He impressed me as the kind of fellow who cultivates your friendship because later on he may need a blood transfusion.

The salesman's manner was too oily, too clever. My reaction was: "I don't want to play poker with *this* city slicker!"

He was too synthetically pleasant. I like a salesman to be sunny . . . . but I don't want to get freckled.

TO MAKE APPOINTMENTS OR NOT

In the entire field of selling, there are, at one extreme, some salesmen who find the selling-by-appointment technique impracticable if not impossible. For instance, appointment making is not easily adaptable to house-to-house selling and to much selling in retail stores. At the other extreme, there are salesmen who sell only to persons with whom they have appointments. Certain salesmen in the insurance field, certain missionary salesmen, and certain salesmen selling to purchasing agents supply us with these examples. between these two extremes there is a large group of salesmen who can, if they wish, make some use of appointments to see specific buyers. Undoubtedly, more salesmen can make profitable use of the technique than do. Appointments are easier to arrange with *customers* than with *prospects*, and for *subsequent* calls on buyers than for *first* calls.

Drawbacks

There are three major contingencies which discourage a salesman as he contemplates the use of the appointment technique. One, of course, is the risk of refusal. It's so easy for buyers to put the salesman off — to postpone any commitment — to say "no" to the request. Salesmen know that many buyers who will *not* sign up *will* see the salesman if he shows up in person. A second drawback is the risk of being late for the appointment. A schedule of appointments injects a rigidity into a salesman's movements that can be frightening. There is no completely satisfactory method for a salesman to handle tardy appearance for an interview. Third and last is the possibility of not being able to keep the appointment at all. Whether the cause be illness, rerouting, or travel trouble, the chance of not being able to show up at all for an appointment is disturbing.

Advantages

On the other side of the ledger, appointments result in benefits to buyers as well as to sellers. Appointments give buyers greater convenience in seeing salesmen because the buyer can schedule the calls so that they will be most convenient for him. Purchasers appreciate the salesmen's consideration and thoughtfulness in not wanting to catch them at unfortunate moments. In addition, each buyer is allowed to get ready for a salesman's visit. The buyer can do any surveying or checking he cares to; he can have facts and questions ready; he can confer and arrange. These advantages are particularly helpful when the buyer is already a customer of the salesman.

Appointments benefit the salesman in several ways. The granting of an interview by the buyer further qualifies him for the salesman's efforts. Appointments eliminate the salesman's having to face assistants of the buyer and having to convince them of his right to some of the buyer's time. This is a great boost to a salesman's confidence, particularly if he is a young salesman or if the buyer is hard to sell or see. Sometimes the salesman can reveal some of his business in such a manner as to whet the buyer's curiosity and interest. Sometimes the salesman can impress the buyer with his enthusiasm, concern, and determination; some salesmen have been known to ride with a doctor as he makes his nightly round of calls, or to accompany a buyer on a short railroad trip just for the opportunity to tell their stories. Appointments allow the salesman to arrange for the minimum amount of time he needs with each buyer. They flatter the buyer; he is being approached by a salesman who recognizes the value of time — the buyer's time and the salesman's own time. The request makes an event — a *scheduled* event — of the call. When the salesman has an appointment, the buyer *expects* him, receives him on a higher level, and gives him a better hearing. The buyer, in effect, has agreed to listen courteously if not sympathetically to the salesman's story. Finally,

When to Telephone

To save time and build prestige with a replier, it is usually best to arrange for an appointment by telephone. Because timing of the call can be as important as what you say, here, based on the experience of many sales-men, is a schedule of the best time to call various prospects:

Prospects	Best Time To Call
Chemists and engineers	Between 4 p.m. and 5 p.m.
Clergymen	Thursday or Friday
Contractors and builders	Before 9 a.m. or after 5 p.m.
Dentists	Before 9:30 a.m.
Druggists and grocers	Between 1 p.m. and 3 p.m.
Executives and business heads	After 10:30 a.m.
Housewives	Between 10 a.m. and 11 a.m.
Lawyers	Between 11 a.m. and 2 p.m.
Merchants, store heads and department heads	After 10:30 a.m.
Physicians and surgeons	Between 9 a.m. and 11 a.m.; after 4 p.m. Some between 7 p.m. and 9 p.m.
Professors and school teachers	At home, between 6 p.m. and 7 p.m.
Public accountants	Anytime during the day, but avoid Jan. 15 through April 15.
Publishers and printers	After 3 p.m.
Small-salaried people and government employees	Call at home.
Stock brokers and bankers	Before 10 a.m. or after 3 p.m.
Prospects, at home	Monday nights between 7 p.m. and 9 p.m.

Mutual of New York

appointments save the salesman's time and energy, reducing wasted activity and getting the salesman more as well as better interviews.

Suggestions

Every salesman should determine for himself what use, if any, he should make of the appointment technique. He can do this only by studying how he might use direct mail, telephone calls, and face-to-face requests for future interviews. Much time must be spent in analysis, composition of requests, experimentation, practice, and improvement because all of these are necessary. The further in the future the salesman requests appointments, the more appointments the salesman will succeed in getting. Salesmen must guard against the mistake of trying to deliver their sales stories over the telephone. A simple method of appointment arranging is the announcement card or note telling the buyer the date of the salesman's forthcoming call; literature may accompany the card or note. In a few cases, a mutual friend will go so far as to make the appointment, although normally friends prefer to limit their cooperation to an introductory card, or, indeed, to an anonymous identification of prospects. If the salesman can make the appointment for *his* office or place of business, it is especially beneficial to him. There he can bar interruptions, permitting speedier calls. There he can introduce the buyer to products, facilities, and individuals if such are appropriate. In addition to these factors, there might be a psychological advantage accruing to the salesman; if the buyer joins the salesman at his *place*, maybe he will be inclined to join the salesman in his *thinking*. His role as an invited guest may influence his buying reactions.

TAILORED VERSUS STANDARD APPROACH

One of the first questions arising about the salesman's opening is whether he should use a tailored approach or a standard approach. A strong case can be made for the tailored approach. For one thing, no single approach fits the individual personality of each salesman. In the second place, no standard approach fits all prospects, particularly where there are considerable differences between and among prospect groups. For a third reason, no single approach fits all situations. It is obvious that because of these differences a sound argument can be made for acquiring and using varied approaches. Without doubt, it can be claimed that a salesman's effectiveness increases as he uses approaches that are interesting and colorful and not stereotyped. No one can successfully challenge the fact that a formula cannot be constructed that will work equally well in all situations.

The standard approach can be defended with equal vigor. It can be and usually is an approach to which conscious and careful attention has been given to its development and, as a result, it is a tested and proved technique. A second plus of the standard approach is that results from using a single opening are much more predictable and uniform. A third point in its favor is the fact that the standard approach is comforting and calming to young salesmen. For them it is a safe and satisfactory technique, as it prevents their making mistakes in attempting to tailor the opening. A final point in favor of the standard approach is that its use requires no mental agility, nor even the attention of the salesman, thus allowing him to observe and analyze the situation more completely.

It is not easy to reach conclusions about the tailored approach versus the standard approach. It should be observed that each salesman should realize the advantages and limitations of each. Furthermore, there is no reason why each salesman should not experiment and find out for himself which approaches work best for him under most conditions. If it seems desirable, he can then try to develop a "best" approach for each prospect classification (doctors, politicians, policemen, grocers, or mothers), or he may consider it desirable to experiment with approaches that tie in with current news events (World Series, Fourth of July, or two days before payday). Each salesman should try to construct at least one *service* approach and one *selling* approach. The service approach starts off with the offer of a favor to the prospect in the hope of getting his goodwill. The main presentation will be made at some later date. In the selling approach, the salesman gets down to brass tacks immediately and thus saves time. This is most effective when the salesman knows the prospect.

Of course, the company employing the salesman may prescribe verbatim his opening remarks, in which case all this discussion is purely academic.

PRINCIPLES OF APPROACH

Here are some principles of approach that will be sound in most instances:

1. Make maximum use of advance information. When the salesman knows the needs, the interests, and the most impelling aspirations of the prospect and skillfully recognizes these in his opening remarks, he will be more apt to get to tell his complete story. The prospect is inclined to listen to the entire presentation because he sees immediately that his circumstances and problems have been considered.

2. Never call "just to be calling." There should be a definite reason and a definite goal for each call. This requires that the salesman have a well-thought-out plan and a specific objective in calling. He should start moving toward this goal from the very first moment.

3. Ask questions if necessary. In many cases the salesman will need data he was unable to get prior to the interview. For this reason, he will find it perfectly proper, permissible, and helpful to ask tactful questions.

4. Give out what prospects should absorb. Attitudes and enthusiasms are contagious. Instead of radiating gloom, the salesman should exude cheerfulness, optimism, and reassurance.

5. Secure control at the beginning. The salesman wants to secure control of the interview and to hold that control throughout his visit.

His approach should connote authority. Of course, the salesman needs to be subtle in leading the prospect around to the salesman's way of thinking.

6. Keep in step with the prospect. The salesman must synchronize his thinking and his conversation with both the direction and the speed of the prospect's thinking. The two individuals must think about the same matters at the same time.

7. Observe the law of self-interest. All prospects are motivated by self-interest; they know of nothing so interesting and so important to them as themselves. For this reason, the salesman will do and say those things which will appeal to the prospect rather than things which might appeal more to him. The proper point of view for the salesman is the "you" point of view.

8. Promise a buyer-benefit early. Because of the crucial nature of the first few seconds, the salesman will usually find it desirable to promise a benefit to the prospect within the first few moments. This is because the prospects listen only to those salesmen who promise advantages to them. So the salesman wants to appear immediately as one who will help or advise or improve or instruct or serve.

9. Make the prospect feel important. Compliments make excellent openers and if a salesman cares to go to the trouble, he can always find something on which he can sincerely compliment the prospect. The salesman makes a good impression by being impressed by something the prospect is or owns or has done.

10. Show sincere interest in the prospect's welfare. One of the best ways to get accepted is to have and show a sincere interest in being of benefit to the prospect. Both by attitude and expression the salesman can clearly indicate that he desires to know the prospect better so as to be able to help him more.

11. Like and be liked. The salesman should ever strive to be a personable individual. He should be easy to talk to, informal, agreeably disposed, and pleasantly mannered throughout. He should be a tactful person, thoughtful of the prospect's feelings and ideas and prejudices. He will not antagonize but instead will approach with understanding. Above all, he will not upset the prospect. As for courtesy, the salesman will observe what is ordinarily accepted as good behavior. He will practice those little courtesies that mean so much until they are a part of him. Particularly in the presence of discourtesy will he always be courteous.

LAST-MINUTE CHECK

Four matters are entitled to a final check by the salesman just before the interview. The first of these is *physical self.* His appearance was discussed in Chapter 3. Punctuality in keeping appointments secures the prospect's confidence and makes the salesman appear dependable.

A second matter to check is *mental self.* Here the salesman will want to remind himself that the prospect's business is very important to him and that the prospect should be made to feel that he is a very important person. Our salesman must assume that he will be courteously received and that he will be listened to with interest. He repeats his intention of liking the prospect, and this practice gives him a warm glow of friendliness to accompany and complement his personal appearance. The salesman is prepared to do the prospect a real favor at any moment the prospect indicates his willingness to buy.

Equipment constitutes the third item to check, and it should be checked for completeness first of all. Whatever the salesman needs should be there, be this a matter of vital facts, figures, diagrams, pictures, samples, testimonials, price lists, sales manual, advertising portfolio, contract forms, even names of such persons as the receptionist, the prospect's secretary, or the prospect himself. At the same time, the salesman will want to hold down bulk as much as practicable. By so doing and seeing that none of the equipment is dog-eared or dirty, the salesman will succeed in looking and acting like more than a peddler. All equipment should be arranged for quick reference and easy handling, placing at the salesman's fingertips in instant availability all selling tools required. If there is anything special for that particular prospect or if anything was requested by or promised to him, the salesman should be sure to see that the prospect receives this special attention.

A final item to be checked is the *plan* for the interview. The salesman should plan to make every minute count toward achieving his objective, and his objective, of course, is turning his prospect into a customer. He will review what seem to be the best buying motives to stimulate, the best procedure to use when doing this, the proposal he expects to make, the points which ought to be stressed, the proof to be offered, the prices to be quoted; and, above all, he will plan to ask for the order.

THE FATEFUL FIRST FEW MOMENTS

A sale can be broken down into four steps from the prospect's point of view and into four different steps from the salesman's point of view. Before he buys, the prospect has to give his attention to the proposition, he must become interested, he must become convinced, and finally, he must decide to buy. As for the salesman, his first step can be termed the *preapproach*, and this consists of getting prospect information as described in Chapters 7 and 10. The salesman's second step can be termed the *approach* and consists of his getting the prospect's attention and interest; there is little of the sale proper in this second step. The salesman's third step is called the *presentation* and in it the salesman converts interest into conviction. Step number four is the *close*, at which time the prospect makes a favorable decision and becomes a buyer.

What this amounts to is that the salesman first sells himself to the prospect, then he sells the prospect on granting the interview, and finally he sells the product. The salesman cannot continue through this series unless he makes a favorable impression quickly and achieves control of the interview.

Immediate Favorable Impression

The first thirty to sixty seconds of an interview often determine the outcome, and, because of this, it is essential that the prospect's immediate reaction to the salesman be favorable. Indeed, it can be said with some truth that the salesman's first ten seconds and first ten words either do or do not get for him a hearing. Within this brief period the prospect decides to give the salesman his attention and time or else his mind moves elsewhere.

Salesmen realize that we all tend to judge strangers on the basis of our first impressions; and they further know that they themselves must be accepted personally because prospects cannot separate a salesman from his proposition. If a salesman does not impress the prospect, it is difficult for his proposal to do so.

An immediate favorable impression is difficult for the salesman to achieve when he shuffles in and squints, scowls, blinks, stammers, smiles artificially, or laughs in a forced fashion. By way of contrast, a favorable impression is made when he is natural and gracious, pleasant, agreeable, tactful, serious, enthusiastic, and convincing.

Control

The salesman's start cannot be considered satisfactory unless within the first few seconds he begins to achieve control of the situation. This control is necessary because the salesman wants to guide the prospect's mind through the four steps of the buying process. The problem is that of leadership and unresented direction; it is the problem of guiding, of staying ahead, and of teaching. Incidentally, control is most easily secured when the salesman has made it obvious that the call is a gesture of sincere and personal interest.

THE INTRODUCTION

Formal or Informal

The first matter to be handled once the salesman is in the presence of the prospect is whether or not there should be a formal introduction. A formal introduction is executed when the salesman, on entering the prospect's presence, states his name or states his own name together with the name of his company. Earlier, when the salesman was talking to the barrier, he had to give his name, but he may have preferred and may have been able to postpone revealing the name of his company. When he meets the prospect, however, the choice more often seems to be between the formality of stating his name and his company's name, or the informality brought about by omitting both.

There is no pat answer to the question. Instead, to introduce himself or not is often optional for the salesman. Many times the introduction is the accepted and the only thing to do. For example, in the South and West many retailers and many individual prospects more or less expect a formal introduction from the salesman, and they react unfavorably if it is omitted. On the other hand, circumstances may argue against an introduction. For example, salesmen making house-to-house calls might not bother with a formal introduction. The same course might be followed by salesmen calling on retail prospects who see so many salesmen daily that they must (or think they must) eliminate all time-consuming non-essentials. Finally, the formal introduction might be dispensed with when a salesman is calling to generate, retain, or increase goodwill, and his company's identity is far more important and significant than his own.

Every salesman needs to establish a feeling of friendliness and confidence, a mutually sound relationship, and if the section of the country, the type of prospect, the type of sale, or, indeed, the salesman's own company suggests or demands an introduction, then there should be one.

The formal introduction is straightforward. It allows the prospect to concentrate on what the salesman has to say instead of wondering who the salesman is. Furthermore, it puts the prospect at ease. It may be expected by the prospect. The salesman's company may insist on it.

Arguing against the formal introduction, one can say that it is more important to put a "need and answer" feeling in the prospect's mind, or to put a sample in his hands. In addition, the introduction might detract from the demonstration which follows. It takes up time. Desired or favorable curiosity may be created if it is omitted. Indeed, in one sense, why should a prospect care who the salesman is? Or, why should he become excited by learning that his visitor is with the ABC Company?

The Handshake

Probably the salesman's handshake is accepted by prospects as correct and appropriate in more cases than it is resented. The safe rule here seems to be: Don't offer your hand, but be ready to accept his. If the prospect is not a handshaker, no shake should be forced on him. If there is a handshake, avoid the two extremes of vise and fishtail.

OPENING THE CONVERSATION

The preceding section pointed out that a formal introduction might or might not constitute the salesman's opening of the interview. The first few remarks which follow such a formal opening, and these would be literally the salesman's initial statements in cases where the formal introduction is omitted, are extremely vital. Here are some sound principles of opening the conversation:

1. Reflect for a moment during the first few seconds and the first few glances around. For one thing, a last-minute change might have to be made in the approach. Secondly, this moment of reflection lets you organize your thoughts. Finally, the moment allows a last-second check to insure that the opening remark is going to be appropriate.

2. Wait until the prospect's complete attention has been secured before making the opening statement. Without such complete attention you would be attempting to do the impossible, namely, to influence one who is not hearing your story.

3. Do not, in most cases, ask for specific permission to tell the complete story. For instance, you might need a minimum of forty-five minutes to make a complete presentation, yet, if you ask for forty-five minutes of the prospect's time, too often he would refuse it. Maybe it is best to start a story — then sell the prospect on the full interview *only* if he tries to shut it off too soon or asks at the beginning, "Will this take more than five minutes?"

4. Get down to business promptly. Don't hang around talking innocuous nothings just because the prospect permits it.

5. Make voice and speech letter-perfect. A voice that is clear, lively, pleasant, and properly modulated prevents an ineffectual monotone. As for speech, it must not be hesitant or awkward. Enunciation should be proper, and the rate of speech should be moderate.

6. Have a standard opening. For "cold" calls when you have no information about the prospect, it's best to have and use a standard,

tested opening broad enough for all situations. One possible refinement of this is to have a predetermined approach for each prospect type (grocers, doctors, housewives), to be varied only as suggested by the conditions encountered at the moment of the meeting. While you should memorize and practice this until perfect, your delivery must still be lively, fresh, and enthusiastic.

7. Tailor the opening, if possible, making maximum use of your prospect information. State a definite, specific, accurate, personal, or at least individualistic reason why you are calling. This reason should be a buyer-benefit.

8. Record how successful or unsuccessful each opener is. From such a record can be constructed a list of good openers and those to be avoided.

9. Assemble a repertory of case histories to use as openers. In selling to buyers-for-resale, merchandising ideas make marvelous openers. For this reason, ask yourself on each call, "What is this merchant doing that is new or better or different or particularly effective?" Check displays, stock arrangements, selling techniques, merchandising efforts, advertising, and sales promotion in search of outstanding experiences. Usually the customer is proud to relate the details about his outstanding activity or effort, and you will usually find that such a story is gratefully received by other prospects whom it will help.

10. Accompany the spoken opener with the most appropriate physical presentation. If possible, show the prospect something quickly, because approximately 80 per cent of the impressions that enter his mind enter through his eyes.

11. Put yourself into the position of the prospect. Ask yourself, "If I were the prospect, what could a salesman say or do to interest me — to make me welcome him? Where do I need help or advice?"

12. Have something constructive to offer the prospect.

13. Tie in promptly with something the prospect consciously or unconsciously desires, believes, is interested in, is curious about, or suspects. Then at once offer the prospect some personal advantage.

14. Talk to the prospect about himself, because he loves himself. This puts him at ease and prevents suspicion, resentment, and opposition. The prospect thinks, "This salesman chose to talk to me about me — what excellent taste he has!"

15. Avoid irrelevant topics. They are practically always very poor openers because the interest or curiosity they arouse does not focus attention on your proposition.

16. Never embarrass the prospect or even go so far as to put him on the defensive.

17. If personal likes, dislikes, hopes, and other such matters are to be exploited, they must be handled indirectly and unobtrusively, lest you appear to be "polishing the apple."

18. Don't open on any topic that allows the prospect to take a pessimistic attitude. If the government is considering action which may affect the prospect unfavorably, if a potent competitor is just beginning to be felt, if the weather has been unkind, if sales volume has been disappointing — you will find these subjects treacherous.

19. If a question is to open the conversation, do not allow it to be abrupt or personal nor to alert instinctive resistance.

20. In showroom or on-the-floor selling, the prospect often gives the salesman a clue. Let the prospect alone for a moment or two, and he will disclose his interest. What he stops and looks at provides a topic for opening the conversation.

21. The opener is specifically provided for you if a lead has been given to you or if the prospect made an inquiry of your company.

22. After the opening sentence or two, stop to get the prospect's reaction. If there is no comment, or a polite yet obviously formal comment, no interest has been aroused. If the reaction is clearly good or bad, you know where you stand. If the prospect will not disclose what his reaction is, then you must ask questions in order to find the lay of the land.

Conversation Openers

Here are some examples of ways to open a sales interview.

1. Show the prospect something and start talking about it. Approach with a current advertisement of your company in hand, and use it as a topic of conversation; or, if the prospect is an advertiser, one of his advertisements could be used for the purpose. Your opener could be either a comment or a question.

Example: "Have you seen this new material we are now making into automobile seat covers?"

2. Render some "free" service to the prospect, and let that favor be the basis for opening a conversation. This can be done easily by salesmen who sell to retailers, and often no authorization or permission will be needed. Where the prospect must approve in advance, the offer of the service or favor can be the opener.

Example: "I'll count your empties."

3. Point out current conditions right at hand which you can be helpful in improving. Usually this help will be in the form of the product you are selling.

Example: "I notice that juries around here have recently been awarding plaintiffs large damages in personal liability suits. You know, this could happen to you."

4. If a single buying motive is discovered to be predominant, appeal to it in the opening remark.

Example: "We know that you fleet owners don't buy tires, you buy economy, and my tire is the one that gives you the most transportation for your dollar."

5. Refer to some personal interest of the prospect. When the salesman knows the prospect, he is in the best position for opening up immediately on the prospect's personal interests and aspirations.

Example: "I believe I saw your picture last week — you pitched for that softball team that won the championship."

6. Find something on which the prospect can be sincerely complimented, and use the congratulations as the opener. Remember that no one gets too much praise.

Example: "I would like to be one of the first to congratulate you on your promotion."

7. Ask the prospect a question. Tactful questioning is permissible, particularly in ascertaining a prospect's needs; but if questions are to be used, certain rules should be observed. Do not apologize for asking the questions. Do not ask too many questions. Ask personal questions only when they are absolutely necessary. Do not ask for information the prospect can't supply. Do not collect vague, general information, because it is of little or no value.

Example: "Have you checked how the recent revisions in the Social Security laws affect you?"

8. Make a statement or claim. To business prospects, the claim will usually have to do with reducing expenses or increasing sales so as to make profits greater. If the salesman prefers, the claim can be striking or

challenging so as to jolt the prospect and make him think.

Example: "A few minutes of your time could be worth $250 to you."

9. Within a limited area, dramatic or curiosity-arousing openings are both permissible and effective. These have a dual value in that they usually secure complete attention from the prospect, and secondly, they encourage the prospect to ask for illumination.

Example: Salesman touches lighted match to material that looks inflammable and asks, "Ever see anything like this before?"

10. Relate a near-by case history. The experience related can be either favorable, describing something that the prospect wants, or unfavorable, showing something the prospect wants to avoid.

Example: "If you have been in business long enough to have a good many inactive accounts, you will be interested in what a manufacturer quite similar to you did about reviving his."

11. Where the prospect has requested something from your company or where the prospect made a request of you on your last call, open the conversation by saying, "Here is what you wanted."

Openers to Avoid

Among the worst, absolutely inexcusable openers are these:

"Hot enough for you?"
"About ready to give us some business?"
"What's new?"
"What do you know?"
"How's business?"
"I would like to interest you in a money-making proposition."
"Just happened to be out this way and thought I'd drop in."

FOUR COMMON FIRST-CALL DIFFICULTIES

One difficulty commonly encountered on the first call is that the *prospect's fear of a stranger* puts him on guard and causes his frame of mind to become defensive. His uneasiness in the presence of one whom he does not know makes him suspicious, particularly if he has been the victim of some fast-talking stranger in the past. Some prospects think such things as, "Salesmen do not tell the truth," "Salesmen are biased," "Salesmen hide the weaknesses of their wares," "Salesmen will not tell the complete story," "Salesmen think of their own welfare."

A second difficulty is *getting a full hearing.* Thirty minutes may be needed to tell the story, yet only ten are granted. If the prospect specifically tells the salesman he can have only so many minutes, and if that amount of time is hopelessly insufficient, the salesman may feel forced to spend at least part of his time allotment in "selling" the worthwhileness of the longer interview. Seldom can a thirty-minute story be condensed into ten minutes and still be effective. If the time needed cannot be obtained, then the salesman should ask for a later appointment. This shows the prospect that the salesman means business, and he may reconsider and grant the full time.

A third problem is the *prospect who says that he is busy*. This means that the salesman must earn some of the prospect's time, and this is best done by having a generous supply of helpful ideas and suggestions. Few prospects are too busy to listen to those. Sometimes the prospect who says he is busy is merely stalling. To minimize stalling, it is desirable for the salesman to have a businesslike behavior and manner. His air should mark him as a man who values his own time and hence that of his prospect — a man who is considerate of the problems and demands of the prospect.

If the prospect *is* too busy, try for a later appointment. When the prospect is preoccupied, the salesman's story obviously is not going to register. The salesman should then offer to return, "selling" the prospect on the desirability of proper conditions for the interview.

A fourth difficulty at the conversation-opening stage is a *prospect who sincerely claims that he is not interested*. Here it is that the salesman must remember that each and every prospect is interested in something and that his job is to find the prospect's major buying motives.

Sometimes in cases of uncertainty, the salesman can ask for a very few minutes in which to determine whether his product can be of any aid, and, consequently, of any interest to the prospect. The salesman should assure the prospect that little of his time will be taken.

It is inexcusable to be arrogant or impertinent in the face of this obstacle of disinterestedness. Once in a while it might be permissible to meet this type of resistance with an aggressive, independent attitude, but that is a risky course to follow.

EXAMPLE OF OPENING AN INTERVIEW

This example of how one interview was opened is supplied by a skillful salesman and a keen student of salesmanship, Mr. T. B. Creel. The incident took place while he was selling cash registers.

A textile manufacturing concern operated two commissaries for its workers. There was a commissary rush hour each day about the time the mills closed. The salesman made five trips to survey the operations during these rush periods. Because the commissaries had no cash registers, service was slow, the company was not getting all the money customers paid, records were not complete, and the commissary staff was larger than it needed to be.

The persons to be seen were the company's treasurer, commissary manager, and secretary. These three met once a month. On his first contact with them, the salesman told them he was making a survey of cash handling in the commissaries and would like to report back at the next monthly meeting. During the next thirty days, he sent all his findings to his home office where a tailored proposition for the textile concern was constructed. This proposal showed exactly how service could be speeded up and how expenses could be reduced.

At the time of the return call, the mills were running only three days a week. Nobody was in a buying mood. The mill executives suggested that the salesman call later when the mills were running full time. Hence, the salesman knew his opening remarks would be crucial. They were:

> I understand that the mills are running only three days a week and that this has probably reduced commissary sales. The way cash is now handled in your commissaries wastes between twelve and fourteen dollars a day. If the mills were running six days a week, sales would increase and your commissaries could better afford that waste. But that amount out of your present sales volume is more than you can afford. I'm going to show you how you can save it.

Cash registers were bought for both commissaries.

STUDY ASSIGNMENTS

1. On several of his first contacts with buyers, a new salesman who had replaced a salesman who had been fired met immediately with criticism, sarcasm, and mild insult. What should he do?
2. How can a salesman obligate a buyer to listen to his presentation? Do you think he should ever do this?
3. Does the buyer size up the salesman at the same time the salesman is sizing up the buyer? Explain your answer.
4. What can a salesman do while waiting in a large reception room to see a buyer?
4. What specific factors influence the "first impression" a salesman makes?
6. How important are the atmosphere and the surroundings in which the interview is held? How can they help or hurt the salesman's chances of making a sale?
7. One hour after giving his name to the receptionist, a salesman is still waiting to see a buyer. What should he do?
8. If the prospect's secretary tells the salesman that the prospect does not make appointments with salesmen, what can he do?
9. Describe how each of five other departments of the salesman's company can help him open his interviews successfully.

10. Draft three replies for a salesman who is told by a buyer, "I don't have much time right now."

CASE STUDY 11

A representative of an encyclopedia publisher is going from door to door in a residential neighborhood. He does not have any leads. The area may be described as a lower middle-class neighborhood.

Salesman: (Walks up to the door and rings the bell.) Good evening. I am Mr. Palmer. I'm with the advertising department of the American Press of Chicago. We're out in this neighborhood gathering some information for our own use, and we thought possibly you could help us. Could I step in and chat with you a moment? (Makes motion as if to enter.)

Prospect: Well, all right, come in.

Salesman: Thank you. What is your name, sir?

Prospect: Jack Smith. Have a chair. Don't mind the mess the place is in. My wife is out for the evening.

Salesman: Mr. Smith, as I told you, I am with the advertising department of the American Press of Chicago. As you probably know, we are the owners and distributors of the famous World Reference Encyclopedia. But fortunately the company didn't send me out here to sell you a lot of books.

Prospect: Oh, that's good. For a minute there, I thought you were going to try to sell me a set of encyclopedias.

Salesman: Our advertising department is making a study to find out the best way to help our salesmen, and we have found that the best thing we can have is satisfied users of our books. If we can give our salesmen names of people in this area who have written us letters of recommendation on our set, then, as you can see, this would be a great help to a salesman in selling to other people. And in order to obtain these letters of recommendation the company has decided that in addition to our advertising on radio and television we would put some of our advertising money into merchandise and place our complete ten-year program in a hundred thousand homes all over the country where the people would cooperate with us by writing us one of these letters of recommendation. Mr. Smith, if my company were to spend some of its advertising money in placing one of these sets in your home, would it be something that you would use and appreciate?

Prospect: Well . . .

Salesman: You see it wouldn't help us much from an advertising standpoint if you were to recommend the set and yet not like it.

Prospect: Now how much did you say this set is going to cost me?

Salesman: Oh, I'm not selling this set. My company is just placing it with people who will review the program for us and write us a letter of recommendation after they have had the program about sixty or ninety days. Do you think that if the company were to send you one of these sets in about two or three weeks it would be something that you would use and appreciate?

Prospect: Certainly, if it doesn't cost me anything.

Salesman: Let me show you our program. (Reaches into his briefcase and takes out his papers — shows the prospect a broadside on the encyclopedia.) This is the binding on the set. It's five times more durable than leather, and it won't crack or scratch. Isn't it beautiful? And we send you a supplement every ninety days so that your encyclopedia will never be more than three months old. In addition to that we let you have access to our library research center for a period of ten years, which means that at any time in the next ten years you can write to our research center to get information on any subject under the sun.

Prospect: That sounds pretty good. But it seems to me that this will cost something.

Salesman: This service is worth $25 a year, and for ten years that would be $250. The supplements to the encyclopedia cost $10 a year, and for ten years that would be $100. Altogether, with the encyclopedia, the whole set and service comes to $579.50. Now we'll just mark it paid in full and charge it off to advertising, just as if we took the $579.50 down to the local paper and spent it for a full-page ad.

Prospect: Well, that's mighty nice of you to give me this set. I sure will appreciate it.

Salesman: We're very happy to give you this set, and all that we ask you to take care of is the postage that it takes to ship the program to you. In this area that amounts to only $4.95. We also ask you to take care of a small service charge that we find necessary to maintain the program properly over a ten-year period. And after a very careful survey, our auditors have told us that this amounts to $15.95 a year. We ask you to write us a letter after you have had the set for about sixty or ninety days. Can we count on you to write us a nice letter?

Prospect: Now did you say that this is going to cost me $4.95 postage and $15.95 a year?

Salesman: Mr. Smith, the only purpose of my call is to get your letter of recommendation. That service charge is only incidental. Can we count on a letter from you?

Prospect: I suppose you can.

Salesman: All right, sir. If you will just O.K. this card, we will send you the program in about ten days or two weeks. (Hands Mr. Smith an acceptance card.) Would you prefer to use my pen or yours?

Prospect: (Takes pen from salesman.) Thank you. (Looks at card and signs his name.)

Salesman: Fine, Mr. Smith. We'll just mark the whole $579.50 paid in full and charge it off to advertising. Now we only ask you to take care of the postage and a small service charge. But I'm sure you don't want to obligate yourself for a period of ten years, and anyway we certainly couldn't afford to keep books on such a small amount. So what we ask you to do is to lump the whole ten years together and take care of it in a more reasonable length of time, like six or eight months, or even a year. And for those people who will cooperate with us to that extent, I am authorized to give them either this $35 solid walnut bookcase which holds the complete program or this $30 atlas. (Shows pictures of both items.) Which of these do you prefer, sir?

Prospect: I believe I'd better take the bookcase, since I don't have any place to put the set.

Salesman: And what length of time did you want to take, Mr. Smith, six months or ten months?

Prospect: Well, how much would that be a month?

Salesman: That depends on how many months you want to take.

Prospect: Maybe I'd better take the year.

Salesman: That will be fine, Mr. Smith. That way it will amount to only $13.50 a month, and then we'll put you on our mailing list for the balance of the ten years. Is that agreeable?

Prospect: I suppose that will be all right.

Salesman: Now I am authorized to do one other thing for you, Mr. Smith. If you would like to make a deposit of as much as three or four months in advance, I'll give you either the atlas which you didn't choose a moment ago or this $49 set of classics. (Shows pictures of each.) Which of these do you prefer, sir?

Prospect: Well, I'd just as soon not pay anything down tonight.

Salesman: This will be your only chance to get this offer, and you may as well get some benefit from your first payment.

Prospect: Well, how small a payment can I make?

Salesman: Why don't you give me $25.

Prospect: Oh, that's too much; I couldn't give you that much.

Salesman: Well, how much could you give me now?

Prospect: Well, $10 would be tops.

Salesman: Mr. Smith, I know we can count on a good letter of recommendation from you, so I'm sure my company will let me accept $10 as a first payment from you. Would you want to give me cash or write a check?

Prospect: I guess I may as well give you the cash. (Hands him the money.)

Salesman: Thank you, Mr. Smith. You should receive the program from us in about two weeks or so.

QUESTIONS:

1. What did the salesman do well?
2. What did the salesman do that could be improved?
3. What techniques are illustrated in the sale?
4. What is your reaction to Palmer's methods of getting and opening his interview with Smith?
5. Was Palmer's selling of the "high pressure" type?

CHAPTER 12

TELLING THE STORY

This chapter presents the *advantage-proof-action* plan for telling a sales story, makes suggestions about the actual delivery of the story, and identifies certain problems which may arise while the story is being told.

ADVANTAGE-PROOF-ACTION TECHNIQUE

We have already learned that buyers are interested in themselves. They are concerned with their own circumstances. They want to get a greater sum of satisfaction for the dollars they spend; they want to get, to be, and to have *more*.

We have also found that the way to get a buyer's attention and interest is to promise him *advantages* or benefits. Because most buyers are somewhat inclined to doubt salesmen's promises, salesmen usually find that they must support their promises and claims with *proof*. Then, to make certain that the buyer both understood and accepted the proved promise, the salesman tries to get *action* from the buyer in the form of an agreement or a commitment. The final agreement of the buyer is, of course, that he should make a purchase immediately.

Advantages

Elsewhere in this book is the statement that persons do not buy merchandise but, instead, buy satisfaction. That is true. Our observation here is that satisfaction is composed of many separate advantages. It is both convenient and effective for the salesman to classify the advantages he is going to state, and this is best done according to buying motives. Viewed in this light, an advantage is an appeal to and a stimulation of a buying motive.

For each buying motive the salesman plans to excite, he will collect as many advantages as he can. One of the buying motives an automobile salesman appeals to is safety because safety is one part of the total satisfaction a person acquires when he buys a car. The salesman gets the concept of safety working hardest for him when he builds up in the prospect's mind a huge mass of safety satisfaction. This is done by piling one safety advantage on top of another — the braking system providing one type of safety advantage, body construction providing its own version of safety advantage, shatter-proof glass, the lighting system, the high degree of visibility, the tires, and all the other automobile features that provide the driver with safety.

Advantages appeal to the self-interest of the prospect. They do this by painting word pictures with the prospect in the center, pictures of what the prospect wants intensely, or what he wants intensely to avoid. The advantage invites the prospect to imagine, as vividly as he possibly can, the thrill, the pleasure, and the satisfaction he will derive from the salesman's product. It fills the prospect with a vision of how he is going to enjoy the benefits of the product. It influences the prospect by getting him to dream of how he would feel and be if he bought. Finally, the advantage visualizes for the prospect what the product will do for him and just how he will profit from buying it.

Principles of Stating Advantages. Here are some sound suggestions about how to state advantages.

1. Relate what a person buys (advantages) to why he buys (buying motives). The most effective way to do this is to match the product's most outstanding features or qualities with the prospect's strongest buying motives in that product classification.

2. Make the advantage personal by fitting it individually to each prospect. Housewives are members of a somewhat homogeneous group, but each housewife wants the salesman to talk to and about her — not about housewives in general.

3. Explain to the prospect just how he will qualify for and actually receive the promised advantage. This may demand some description of technical phases of the product's operation.

4. Do not depend on the prospect to translate the product into what it would do for him. Do not stop at merely pointing out the product's exclusive features. Instead, state the advantage, and picture what it means to the prospect in such an appealing way that the prospect feels that he must have it. Sell the prospect, not the product.

5. Work on one buying motive at a time, and do not leave it until it has been handled satisfactorily. Under this one buying motive, do not move from one advantage to another until the first advantage is accepted. The retail sales person selling a suit may choose to appeal to the buying motive of appearance and may talk of weave, color, and texture as con-

CONVENTIONAL DEFINITIONS
OF HIGH-PRESSURE SELLING

There are so many different concepts of high-pressure selling that the simplest way to portray them is to list the various categories into which they fall:

1. Forceful persuasion, dominance, aggressiveness.

2. Lack of remorse, failure to consider prospect's needs, dishonest claims for product.

3. The opposite of factual selling.

4. One writer distinguishes between high-pressure and aggressive selling (a distinction on moral grounds).

5. Causing purchase of excessive quantity, or purchase of unneeded merchandise.

It is obvious from the above listing that high-pressure selling has no common and specific meaning. It is used loosely and means different things to different persons.

MEANING OF LOW-PRESSURE SELLING

Some of the meanings attached to low-pressure selling are:

1. Letting the customer make up his own mind.

2. Creating value for the customer.

3. Creation of demand by customer.

4. An opportunity to buy.

5. Less pressure than high-pressure selling.

6. The opposite of high-pressure selling.

High-pressure selling is not the answer to competition.

The above ideas on high-pressure and low-pressure selling are those of Cash and Crissy in *A Point of View for Salesmen* (New York: Personnel Development, Inc., 1957). By permission.

stituting one advantage. As soon as the prospect's acceptance of this advantage has been secured, then the salesman can establish a second advantage composed of workmanship, style, and cut. A third advantage, fit, can next be introduced.

6. Be polite about and show respect for competition. Never include in the advantage any reference to competition which might offend the prospect or work in any manner to your disadvantage.

7. Make no claims of advantage that cannot be proved.

8. Dramatic work pictures can do heavy duty for those who sell services and intangibles. A personal, human-interest picture can be painted to show the prospect after buying the product. The prospect wants this picture. Or the picture can show the prospect without the product — a picture of something the prospect wants to avoid.

9. Make the advantage definite and specific instead of general. Telling the prospect that a product will "make money for you" or that "not having this product will cost you money" is far less graphic and effective than measuring those gains or losses in dollars and cents. It is better to say, "You should net $18 a week from this line," or, "This product will reduce your food bill $11 a month."

10. Have a large supply of advantages, and do not hesitate to state them. If the prospect knew all of them, he would be hunting you with money in hand.

11. Use different methods of stating the advantage, because variety helps the salesman just as a good change of pace helps a pitcher. You should be constantly on the alert for new techniques of presenting advantages, and, in this search, your own imagination should prove to be a fruitful source. These examples illustrate three ways of stating the same advantage:

A. Ask a question that challenges the prospect: "Did you know that you can arrange to receive $200 every month after you are sixty?"

B. Make a plain statement that promises the prospect something: "This plan will pay you $200 every month after you are sixty."

C. Ask an "iffy" question: "If I can show you how you can get $200 every month after you are sixty, you'd be interested, wouldn't you?"

Sources of Advantages. Because a prospect's expenditures are dictated by his buying motives and because each of his buying motives may require the stimulation of many advantages before it exerts significant pressure on the prospect to buy, the salesman will need many advantages and will want to know where to find them. There are two main sources.

The *prospect himself* is the most productive single source of the advantages the salesman will need. The first step for the salesman to take here is to study human behavior and motivation, placing special emphasis on the buying motives that are mainly responsible when a prospect thinks about, investigates, buys, and is happy with the salesman's type of product. A second method of using the prospect as source of advantages is that of analyzing the advance data the salesman has on the prospect. The salesman tries to place himself in the prospect's position and then decide what motives will cause that particular individual to buy. A third and final way of learning from the prospect what advantages to use is through observation. Before and during the interview, the salesman has a marvelous opportunity to observe the prospect in his surroundings. He can talk with and even question the prospect, thus gaining much information about the prospect from what he has to say. If the salesman requests and gets permission to make a survey of the prospect's situation, observation identifies the advantages the prospect will enjoy if he buys.

The *product itself* is the second source of buyer-benefits. Other product sources of buyer-benefits include advertisements, material supplied the salesman by his company, and comments from members of the distribution channel.

These sources cannot be consulted, drained of whatever advantages are found, and then ignored. Instead, the salesman must continually refer to them, and his analysis and use of what is gleaned from them must never cease.

Proof

The first step in the advantage-proof-action technique secured the prospect's attention, aroused his interest, and kindled a desire for the product. This second step has as its sole objective convincing the prospect that the purchase should be made.

Skepticism must be expected from prospects. They cannot be asked to believe without proof, and for this reason the salesman must have proof for all claims and assertions made. Conviction is the big problem, as the salesman must prove the verity of each claim convincingly and conclusively. He must prove each advantage to the prospect until the prospect knows that he can attain and make good use of that benefit.

General claims of excellence are weak and can hardly be expected to appear to the prospect as legitimate grounds for buying. Concise facts are more interesting than vague claims, and hard, specific evidence excels generalizations. Prospects prefer to prove the advantages to themselves, but, where this is impracticable, their second choice is disinterested, impartial authority to support the truth of the salesman's claims. Six useful types of proof are listed.

Logical Reasoning. Logical reasoning appeals to the prospect's judgment, common sense, experience, and observation. It is one positive form of proof if the product does not permit demonstration. It can be forceful and easily grasped if it is kept simple, clear, and direct. Logical reasoning has two limitations. It will seldom overcome prejudice, defective thinking, or emotional feelings; its use is limited by the intelligence and mental capacity of the prospect.

The simplest form of logical reasoning is a direct oral statement made by the salesman. This is a weak type of proof because it consists of words only. It is somewhat stronger when coming from a salesman with extensive knowledge of and experience with buyers' problems. A second form of logical reasoning is a printed statement. The prospect may accept this more readily than an oral statement from the salesman because of his inclination to believe the printed word more than the spoken. A third type of logical reasoning is found when the prospect and the salesman sit down together with pencil and pad and "figure out" how the prospect will fare if he buys. This third version is superior to the unsupported claims found in the first two versions of proving a sales point.

Company-Supplied Proof. The salesman's company may supply him with a variety of types of proof. First, his company may have run tests, the results of which the salesman can use to support his claims. Second, if his company operates under a guarantee, another form of proof is available. Third, in talking to middlemen, the company's advertising support may be used as evidence of the market for the product. In talking about advertising support, the salesman will find it desirable to know the number of dollars earmarked for advertising, the media to be used, and the total circulation of those media, both national and local. He will find that tear sheets are more convincing than proofs. A fourth example of company proof consists of any statistics supplied the salesman by his company, as, for instance, data on dealers or consumers. A fifth and final example of company proof could be the findings from a survey that the salesman himself made of the prospect's circumstances.

Independent Research Findings. This third type of proof consists of data secured from outside and, hence, impartial sources. One example would be the results of an analysis of the salesman's product, together with an account of the experiments conducted by an independent com-

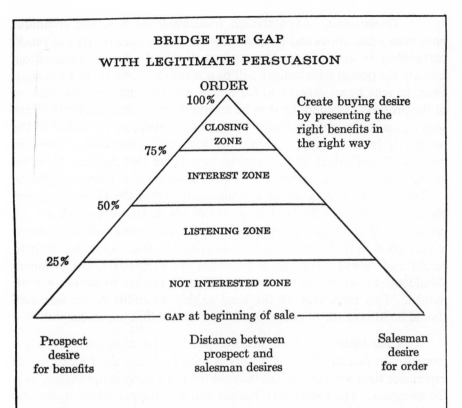

BRIDGE THE GAP

WITH LEGITIMATE PERSUASION

ORDER

100%

CLOSING ZONE

75%

INTEREST ZONE

50%

LISTENING ZONE

25%

NOT INTERESTED ZONE

GAP at beginning of sale

Create buying desire by presenting the right benefits in the right way

| Prospect desire for benefits | Distance between prospect and salesman desires | Salesman desire for order |

There is an old legal phrase applying to contracts, "There must be a meeting of the minds." Likewise, regarding your sales.

From a purely selfish standpoint there always is an initial gap between your desire for the order and the prospect's desire for what he wants.

Maybe you like roast beef, but if you expect to catch fish you feed them what they like to eat.

The successful salesman avoids talking about what he wants and instead emphasizes what the prospect will get. That's how he bridges the inevitable and initial gap.

United States Gypsum Co.

mercial testing laboratory. A second example might be the results of market studies made by some unrelated company as, for instance, the pantry polls or consumer preference studies made by newspapers or magazines. A third example consists of statistics a salesman has acquired to strengthen his case such as the probability and expectancy tables of insurance companies, or the sales and expense figures for department stores collected by some impartial agency.

Testimonials. Even though testimonials as a selling technique have been joked about and abused, they are still an effective type of proof, particularly in cases where the product does not allow demonstration. Usually the person who testifies will be a member of one of three groups. First, he may be an expert and for that reason demand the consideration of the prospect. Second, he may be a prominent person, usually from the society, sports, or entertainment world and, as such, be the object of the prospect's hero worship.   Third, the testimonial may come from an "ordinary" individual, the reasoning here being that because he is an everyday individual like the prospect, his testimonial is more acceptable.

The obvious beauty about a testimonial is that the prospect cannot challenge or argue with laudatory statements made by consumers.   A printed testimonial, particularly one with "before" and "after" pictures, is very good in that it requires little imagination and almost no effort to accept and believe.   Because testimonials are so effective, the salesman should try to get one good customer in each market to supply a testimonial.   This takes care of the local angle.   In addition, the salesman should build up a file of every type of testimonial that proves helpful.

Case Histories. Case histories are not far removed from testimonials. In essence, the case history is built around a third party whose experience the prospect believes because the third party is not biased, as is the salesman. The third party bought and was happy. Once again, the prospect cannot argue with success.

As in the case of testimonials, the histories can be built around an expert, a famous customer, or an ordinary customer.   In the majority of cases, it is best to use a customer as much like the prospect as possible. If he is a local customer, one the prospect knows and can even telephone for verification, then that's all the better, provided his being a customer will not alienate our prospect. By having name, address, and pertinent data, the salesman proves that the subjects of the case histories are real and not just creatures of his own imagination.

Once again, "before" and "after" photographs are extremely appropriate in relating a case history. The salesman should collect case histories for every possible situation and objection.

Demonstration. Where practicable, the best type of proof that a salesman can use is that supplied by his product itself. It is based on the principle that "seeing is believing."

The demonstration of the product shows how it is built and what it will do. One form of demonstration is a visit to a current user of the product. A second form is the sample which the salesman can place in the prospect's hands. A third is the sale on approval. Very close to this are trial offers and trial orders. Finally, and most effective of all, is the placing of the product in the prospect's hands and letting him experience what it does for him. Demonstration will be discussed in Chapter 13.

Action

The action the salesman wants is agreement. He wants the prospect to concur with his own conviction that the prospect should have the product. He wants the prospect to see the product as he himself does — the answer to one of the prospect's problems. He wants the prospect to accept his reasoning and agree with his conclusion.

Specifically, the salesman first wants the prospect to agree with each point he made and to accept each advantage he presented and proved. Then, the salesman wants a "yes" to each of the five buying decisions, including, of course, the decision to buy immediately. If the salesman is to succeed in getting what he wants, each of the prospect's agreements must be voluntary decisions that are made without reservation.

Getting some form of action early from the prospect helps to make the prospect "action-minded" from the very start of the interview. This is good, because otherwise the act of purchasing might strike him so strongly as a brand-new idea at the end of the interview that he might be frightened into refusing to act. Getting him in the habit of agreeing with the salesman makes his final "yes" just another "yes." Commitment after commitment soon gets the prospect to a point where it is easier to go ahead and buy than to turn back. So the salesman will start off in the direction of a sale and will tolerate nothing more than momentary breaks in his inexorable, onward movement toward that sale.

When a prospect withholds his agreement, the salesman knows that more advantages are needed.

How to Get Action. Action is secured by asking questions all during the interview. Questions will be constructed so as to secure from the prospect a favorable commitment to each point and advantage. Even in the case of the difficult prospects, the salesman will usually continue to ask questions until the prospect says something that can be interpreted as a "yes."

By asking frequent questions, the salesman observes one of the cardinal rules of selling, and that is to take up a second point or advantage only after the prospect has accepted the first one. Occasional violation of this rule is permissible when a prospect feels lukewarm toward a particular advantage, not caring especially whether he gets it or not. In such cases, the salesman will attempt once or twice to get a commitment, and then move on.

In his periodic checks on the prospect, the salesman is ever alert for a strong, enthusiastic agreement on an advantage, for that is a signal to the salesman to try at once for a commitment on the buying decision on which he is then working. Whenever there is a strong, enthusiastic agreement on one of the buying decisions, that is a signal to try to close the sale.

Here are a few questions that can be used to advantage:

"Don't you?"
"Don't you agree?"
"You like that, don't you?"
"Isn't it?"
"Isn't that true?"
"Isn't that right?"
"That's worth while, isn't it?"
"That's what you want, isn't it?"
"Can't you?"
"You'll enjoy that, won't you?"
"Your friends will certainly enjoy this, won't they?"
"Your girl will enjoy that, won't she?"
"A 10 per cent increase in sales sounds good, doesn't it?"
"You'd like to cut delivery costs 17 per cent, wouldn't you?"

Cautions. A salesman should always be ready for unfavorable action by having some reserve selling ammunition ready. He must never run out of advantages. If beauty, comfort, performance, and economy fail to sell the automobile, he can still talk dependability and safety.

Any attempt to get action must be so executed that a negative response will not bar the salesman from continuing to sell. The salesman must not allow the door to be shut in his face.

Agreement should not be requested in a "trap" manner. Instead, what is desired is the confirmation of a sound conclusion that two individuals arrived at by a free discussion of mutually recognized facts.

Finally, agreement must be strong and sincere, especially in the case of the first buying decision, *need.* Until this type of agreement is secured, the salesman must continue to add more advantages.

PRESENTING THE STORY

Consideration for Prospect

Because the prospect knows his caller is a salesman from whom a story must be expected, the salesman should start his story early in the interview. The prospect resents the salesman's killing time on weather, sports, politics, unnecessary conversation, and needless stories.

As for the salesman who "just visits" for a while with the prospect, perhaps he should let the prospect choose his own friends. All of this argues for the salesman's getting down to business promptly, and, after telling the story, leaving promptly.

A salesman must be careful not to offend prospects by the manner in which he tells his story. He is irritating when he interrupts one of the prospect's questions or objections. If he follows up by arguing or contradicting, this not only antagonizes the prospect but also makes him defend his resistance. That is not smart selling.

Any tactics that the prospect considers objectionable are to be avoided. That includes pestering, wise-cracking, dictating, begging, or being too persistent. It includes the use of profanity and vulgarity. The salesman should keep a respectable distance from the prospect by refusing to be too forward or too familiar. At the same time, he must not be the aloof, high-and-mighty type of person who talks *to* his prospects rather than *with* them. Prospects do not care to be overwhelmed with the salesman's personal opinions either on products or on such controversial subjects as labor unions, religion, politics, or the danger of war. Such opinions had best be expressed only when the prospect requests them. Attacking the prospect's present choice of product or arbitrarily making a decision or selection for him are unreasonable and inexcusable presumptions.

The salesman's assumption in telling his story should be that his main objective is to serve the prospect. This attitude will be reflected in his concern over the prospect's affairs and in his sensitive response to the prospect's interests. Adopting the role of an interested friend, the salesman will strive for the prospect's goodwill by being agreeable and by demonstrating courtesy and tact. Anything that annoys or upsets the prospect puts him in a frame of mind that works against rather than for the salesman.

Words Are Tools

A salesman needs a large vocabulary, and he must be able to use it effectively. If he has a generous command of words, he can choose from a wide assortment and select for his use those most appropriate. Thus, the words with which he expresses himself can be more impressive as well as more precise. Concepts, ideas, and suggestions can be expressed in a concise manner, and greater conciseness contributes to greater success in influencing the thoughts and actions of buyers. While it is true that a salesman should appeal to more than just the buyer's sense of hearing, one can, nevertheless, contend that words are a salesman's basic tools — they are what he depends on most heavily in his communication with buyers.

TO ALL CUTLER-HAMMER SALESMEN and DISTRICT MANAGERS

SUBJECT: SALES REMINDER #18
           CUSTOMER RELATIONS (#1 SIZING UP THE PROSPECT)

YOU CAN'T BUY IT...

IT CAN'T BE GIVEN TO YOU...

YOU MUST *Earn* IT...

WE'RE TALKING ABOUT YOUR MOST VALUABLE ASSET...

J·A·K

Salesmen use a great variety of language on prospects--None of it the kind you may be thinking about! But, some salesmen still use the wrong language--language over the heads of their audience.

Few housewives care about the kind of gears in a waste disposing unit. The motor horsepower or the kind of electricity is so much Greek to them. Papa may be interested, but mama wants to know if even she can use it, is it noisy, and will it get out of order. She also wants to know when she can get the product. "Benefits of Use" language that is easy to understand (straightforward stories told in simple language--not "talking down" language) is the kind that makes sales.

The engineer wants "use" language, told in technical words that he understands. His Purchasing Department wants a somewhat different language, perhaps just as technical, but including delivery dates or availability of stock.

Add to these different "languages" the difference between individual prospects, and it is evident why good salesmen are good linguists.

The most successful salesmen study their prospects and customers very carefully, tell their story in language to fit the prospect, and steadily earn a backlog of GOOD WILL.

F A Wright

F. A. Wright
Sales Manager
District Sales

Cutler-Hammer, Inc.

Salesmen are reminded of their use of words, of their need for a broad vocabulary, and of the necessity to tailor their stories.

In those types of selling where buyers' backgrounds, intelligence, and education are above the average, the need for an outstanding vocabulary becomes more urgent. In those areas, a salesman needs to set himself apart from ordinary salesmen because his buyers are not ordinary buyers. Instead, such buyers are highly sensitive to and responsive to the salesman's speech. Buyers of this type have nothing but contempt for salesmen such as the one whose extreme for everything is the word *hell* — the weather, for example, was hot as hell — or, cold as hell. By way of contrast, a large stock of words lets a salesman describe the weather as sweltering, broiling, melting, scorching, and sizzling, or bleak, biting, nippy, cutting, and bitter. The better his mastery and use of words, the better a salesman sells.

Delivery of Story

The rate of delivery of the sales story must be adjusted to the prospect's speed of thought and his ability to comprehend. If the speed of delivery is either too fast or too slow, then the salesman is in danger of losing the prospect. If the salesman rushes his presentation by talking too fast, especially if the prospect is a slow thinker, some of his points will not register and will not be understood. If he talks too slowly for the prospect who is frequently impatient, nervous, and restless, the prospect's attention will roam. The salesman's more common error is to talk too fast because he knows his story so well from having told it so many times; yet, this very story is new to the prospect. Although speed of delivery can and should be varied for emphasis and for variety, the flow of the story can be so smooth and clear that salesman and prospect stay in mental step with each other.

The salesman's delivery should be animated and not monotonous. The same emphasis and variety mentioned in the last paragraph, each of which is desirable and even essential, demand that the story be told in a lively manner. By dramatic use of pauses, by executing accompanying gestures, and by changing the pitch and volume of his voice, the salesman is able to maintain more successfully a pace that sparkles.

A confident delivery is a valuable asset. The poised salesman in his presentation makes an impression that is characterized by assurance, smoothness, and finesse. His is a competent story told by a competent person. His confident delivery leans heavily on tone of voice and enthusiasm. His objective is to develop a tone of voice that will convince and persuade, a vigorous expressive tone, one in which authority is evident. The sincerity in his voice can mean and do as much as the words he speaks. The enthusiasm the salesman wants is not mere breezy cockiness; it is that enthusiasm born of deep conviction. This is the type of enthusiasm that will influence and activate.

The story should be simple and complete, with positive, affirmative statements of what the product will do rather than negative statements of what the product will not do.

Industrial salesmen who sell Westinghouse products to purchasing agents are warned that they must become good public speakers if they are to acquire top skill in selling. This conviction is held despite the fact that a Westinghouse salesman usually does his talking sitting down and to an audience of one rather than to an audience of one hundred. When Westinghouse asked several hundred purchasing agents for suggestions on speaking to pass on to its salesforce, these four developed:

Talk . . . don't orate!

Listeners of today dislike speakers who "make speeches." That holds good for all kinds of public speaking . . . . and applies with *double* force to a sales presentation.

So, when you lean forward in your chair to begin a sales talk, or rise from it to face a purchasing committee, beware waxing oratorical, like a political stump speaker.

Instead of talking to your customer as if he were a public meeting, talk to him *conversationally* . . . . with the same shirt-sleeve naturalness of voice that you'd use chatting with a neighbor over a backyard fence.

Talk earnestly!

In your desire to avoid oratorical bombast, make sure you don't overshoot your goal and talk lifelessly.

Instead, get into your voice, right along with freedom from affectation, a fire-alarm quality of deep earnestness which conveys to your customer the unmistakable impression that you *believe* what you say . . . . believe it to be *true* . . . . believe it to be *important*.

If you fail to talk with sufficient earnestness, your customer is likely to infer that you, yourself, are unimpressed with what you're saying . . . . that you wish you could go out for a beer without waiting to hear the end of your own sales talk.

Talk at a moderately brisk average speed!

According to purchasing agents, nine salesmen out of ten talk too haltingly rather than too rapidly.

Instead of violating the maximum speed law of understanding, they block thought traffic — block it with a sluggishness of delivery that after a time becomes exasperating . . . and *particularly* exasperating when the "word whisker" *er* clutters up every pause between words:

"You see . . . er . . . integral with the hood of the . . . er . . . AK-10 street light there's a . . . er . . . bug-proof breather arrangement that

... er ... that prevents a vacuum forming should the ... er ... luminaire suddenly get cooled by ... er ... rain."

If you were a customer on the receiving end of that kind of delivery ... you, too, might become annoyed.

To avoid such annoyance, make your average speed of delivery a moderately brisk 160 words a minute.

And, when you DO pause, pause CLEANLY ... without that customer-maddening *er ... er ... er*!

Make sure that every word you speak can be heard!

This fourth recommendation may seem pretty obvious to you . . . . but note it just the same.

Often a salesman becomes so deferential in the presence of a customer he considers particularly important that he fears raising his voice to the level of easy audibility.

Don't YOU make that mistake. When you talk to a Westinghouse customer, speak *up*! Mumbling in your beard is a poor way to register customer respect.

Register it, instead, by the general courtesy of your manner and by your willingness to listen attentively when your customer is talking.
But when YOU talk during a sales interview, no matter how important the customer is, talk loudly enough to be heard without effort.
Bear in mind that no customer likes to "pay" anything . . . not even attention.

So speak UP ... and, at the same time, speak CLEARLY.

Two-Way Communication

Interviews work out to be more satisfactory for both the salesman and the buyer if both take part. So, it is desirable for the salesman to encourage each buyer to enter into the interview and to contribute *his* ideas, *his* questions, and *his* reactions. When the salesman succeeds in developing the interview into a conversation, he is able to draw the buyer out because he has succeeded in getting the buyer to express himself. To be sure, it is not always difficult to get buyers to talk; some of them are more than willing — they are anxious and determined to state their views to salesmen. It is wise for a young salesman not to monopolize the conversation when the buyer is expertly informed and qualified in buying, as, for

The Uses of Silence

A well-timed pause, as many salesmen know, can be the most effective part of a sales presentation. Silence at the right moment can help:

To get a prospect to participate in a demonstration by asking a question or making a comment.

To get a prospect to make a buying decision.

To dramatize a product by centering attention on it exclusively for a few seconds.

To allow a particularly important sales point to make an impression on a prospect's mind.

To create a change of pace, especially with prospects who have heard presentations by several other salesmen.

To allow a prospect's associates to influence him if they appear to favor a product.

To dramatize a period of time, such as the one minute per operation a certain machine might save.

Reprinted with permission from the October, 1959, issue of *The American Salesman.*

example, are many purchasing agents. In such circumstances, it is not uncommon for the buyer's years of experience to outnumber by far those of the young salesman. The salesman who finds himself in this position has an excellent opportunity to acquire valuable information, and he has a much better chance of making a sale if he encourages the buyer to talk. Part of being a good salesman is being a good listener.

A strong recommendation can be made for salesmen to achieve what has been referred to as the art of listening. When a salesman has become an expert in what may be called *creative silence*, he lets his silence help him sell. He accomplishes this by making his manner of listening active and dynamic. He seems eager to hear the buyer talk on any subject. He appears to be quite interested in the buyer's statements, even to the extent of giving the buyer the impression that he, the salesman, is absorbed in what the buyer is saying.

The proper amount of buyer-participation is difficult to define and just as difficult to control. The buyer who talks too much is just as much a problem as the buyer who says little. Somewhere between these two extremes is a satisfactory balance. Even while he is listening, the salesman's facial expressions, his movements, and his actions can, at least to a degree, influence how much the buyer talks and can guide what he says.

What does the salesman gain by seeing that buyers take part in the conversational phase of the interview? Some of the benefits have already been suggested. In addition, the salesman gains some goodwill because he is being well-mannered and polite. Among the buyer's comments will be some with which the salesman can agree enthusiastically — urging the buyer, in turn, to find points in the salesman's comments with which he, the buyer, can agree. The salesman gets information he can use to advantage because, as the buyer talks, he reveals his thoughts and his feelings, and his concerns of the moment. The salesman spots the buying motives of many buyers as well as their objections; he can proceed in the light of these. Buyer-interest and buyer-desire are invited, and it is not unknown for buyer-conviction to result, in part, from the buyer's selling to himself. The salesman gains some analyzing and planning time while a buyer talks. The fact that the salesman listened to the buyer somewhat obligates the buyer to hear the salesman. Some buyers may even expect salesmen to listen to their views and opinions as part of the price of getting an order. Finally, talking buyers are expansive buyers, apt to disclose, intentionally or otherwise, what they want and even how the salesman can help them get it.

Not all successful salesmen encourage questions and comments from prospects, preferring to present their entire proposals without interruption. This does not seem to be so sound a policy as that of welcoming questions and objections from the prospect. When the prospect expresses his views, he is giving the salesman an indicator which measures the progress the salesman is making, because it shows what the prospect is thinking. When the prospect takes part in the conference, his interest is greater and more easily held. His answers to the salesman's questions supply needed information. These same questions can be used to challenge the prospect and to plant ideas in his mind. If the prospect is so agreeable as to make the salesman suspicious about the penetration and actual acceptance of the story, such questions as these are helpful:

"Just where can my product help you most?"
"Which concerns you more, increasing your sales or lowering your expenses?"

The fact that the salesman arranges for and achieves dialogue rather than monologue gives variety to the presentation. Most important of all, dialogue makes it possible for the salesman to get agreement as he goes along, leaving no gaps in acceptance that could turn out to be fatal.

Use of Questions

There is an art to asking questions just as there is an art to listening to a buyer's conversation. Tactful questioning can contribute much to the presentation of a sales story in both strategic and tactical ways. Strategically, the salesman can use questions to help him discover what satisfactions a buyer needs or wants which his product delivers. He can phrase questions to help a buyer recognize what he needs, or even recognize what he wants. Questions can contribute to a more enjoyable, pleasant visit; answers to them will identify the matters which a salesman can discuss with propriety and profit *and* the topics which he should avoid or at least handle with extreme caution.

There are several tactical jobs questioning can do. It is the simplest way to insure the two-way communication discussed in the preceding section, assuring dialogue and preventing monologue. It can be used to recapture a buyer's attention and to arouse his interest. As has been hinted earlier, questions can be used to get much needed information from buyers; answers are revealing even if incomplete or, indeed, inaccurate. A salesman can check on the clarity and understanding of his story through the use of questions. He can, by asking questions, get on record a buyer's agreements, and these must not be assumed nor taken for granted. Questioning is a smooth method by which the salesman reveals what *he* thinks — and what he thinks the *buyer* should think; the salesman can introduce a question with, "Don't you think that . . . ?" Many buyers will accept the salesman's ideas and consider them their own. Finally, buyers appreciate and are impressed by questions about their views, ideas, attitudes, and opinions. Such questions make buyers feel important.

Headlining

All prospects are not equally interested in the same advantages or motivated by the same desires. Yet, selling is easiest when based on interests that are most intense for each particular prospect — when the salesman can make his major appeals to the prospect's dominant buying motives. Equipped as he is with a hugh collection of product facts and their buyer-benefits, the salesman feels the need for some method of selecting the major points and advantages he should stress. Particularly where he knows little about the prospect, the young salesman often concludes wistfully that if he only knew what the prospect's problems and motivation are, he would have the key to the sale. He knows that he is able to pile up point after point in telling his story; but, he feels with even greater certainty that he could well use a smaller number of telling strokes — selected shafts that will find the center of that particular bull's-eye.

The tactic known as headlining may be what the salesman is hunting. In headlining, he absorbs, masters, and even memorizes a two- or three-sentence summary for each major advantage. Then he opens his story with a quick, impressive summary of the chief benefits of his proposal and spotlights the major reasons for buying in brief, outline form. For example, he might give a thumbnail sketch of what his product will do and mean in the areas of appearance, accuracy, ease of operation, safety, and economy of operation. As he runs over all of the product's major appeals, he observes, listens to all remarks from the prospect, and analyzes the situation for clues as to which appeals to stress.

The salesman is hoping to strike a responsive chord or to draw a comment from the prospect. He wants the prospect to look at the head-lined preview of the salesman's story and to perk up in such a manner as to indicate the sections of it he wants to know more about. The salesman hopes the prospect will select the topics for the ensuing conversation just as he glances over the front page of his newspaper and decides, from the headlines, which story he will read first, which he will read next, and so on.

When the salesman strikes fire, he plugs those features of his product that tie in with the interest he has aroused. He slants his story toward the prospect's wishes and toward the services and benefits the prospect wants. He builds up many advantages and offers much proof in the areas of those buying motives which have been pointed out to him as being "special" to that prospect.

Rehearsing

A quick yet painless way to become proficient in presenting a sales story is to rehearse. Cheerleaders and clergymen, politicians and debaters, public speakers and actors — all know the value of rehearsals. These persons will assure salesmen that running through a sales story, out loud, is the best preparation and training they know to acquire poise and confidence. Salesmen are advised to write out a sales story, and then read and re-read it, editing, revising, and improving it on each trip through. Then comes the rehearsing. At first this can consist of nothing more than reading or speaking the story aloud. Next, the salesman can talk to himself before a mirror. After this, he can talk some kind-hearted member of his family or an accommodating friend into giving him an audition. Or, he and another salesman can take turns playing the role of salesman and buyer. Eventually, the salesman will progress to the point where he can rehearse a presentation in his mind; this permits him to rehearse in a variety of places and circumstances.

Certain matters should get particular attention in the rehearsals. One such matter is the salesman's manner of speaking. The objectives here should be correct pronunciation, pleasant tone of voice, clear enunciation, proper inflection, and a change of pace which lends variety and emphasis to the presentation. Another matter, closely related to speech, includes the key words and phrases which, after being tried and tested, prove to be effective. A third matter is that of the extremes which should be avoided. Anything *over*done or *under*done, be it emphasis, enthusiasm, contrast, speed, or length of story, handicaps the salesman. Finally, mannerisms must be abandoned because they annoy, they distract, and they monopolize the buyer's attention or, at least, make a strong bid for it. These mannerisms include such actions as sniffing, pointing a finger at the buyer, pounding on the desk or the palm of the hand, tapping a foot, or cracking the knuckles of fingers.

DIFFICULTIES AND OBSTACLES

External Interruptions

One of the most troublesome experiences encountered by all storytellers is interruption. The external interruptions a salesman must cope with are usually of three types. The prospect may get a phone call, he may be called away from the interview, or he may be visited by someone else — a member of his firm, a friend, a customer, some other salesman, or a member of his family.

These external interruptions are unfortunate because they break the flow of thought by calling the prospect's attention to other matters. They reduce the cumulative force of the salesman's story. They consume the salesman's time. They give the prospect an excuse for ending the interview or for not buying.

In every case, the salesman should use this break for a quick mental review of what he has done, both right and wrong. This will enable him to plan the rest of the interview soundly.

When the prospect resumes the interview, the salesman should not act as though nothing had happened, for that would be too abrupt a resumption in view of the fact that the prospect has been away, physically or mentally, or both. Instead, the salesman should summarize the points made prior to the interruption so as to remind the prospect of the ground that was covered, check the prospect for understanding and attention, and then resume the sales story.

For lengthy interruptions, particularly those from which the prospect seems to return in a worried or distracted frame of mind, or with a manner which seems to say that something went wrong, the general rule is to make one try to regain control and continue the presentation. If unsuccessful, the salesman should make an appointment for an early return call, leaving the prospect, if circumstances warrant, with a new point — one on which the salesman can open the interview when he returns. When external interruptions are either too long or too numerous, a later appointment is usually advisable.

It is frequently possible to avoid or certainly reduce external interruptions. The shorter the salesman's story, the less time there is for interruptions. The salesman will be less bothered by interruptions if he calls during hours that are not the busiest for the prospect. Sometimes the salesman can request an appointment of "ten free minutes." In other cases, the salesman may be able to get the prospect into his own world where the salesman himself is in control. This may be the salesman's car, his office, his home, his favorite eating place, or even the golf course. Sometimes a direct, courteous request to go to a place of quiet, the prospect's office perhaps, is often sufficient. Finally, if the salesman can convey to the prospect the thought that he will not start what is going to be an important interview until circumstances are favorable, he may secure consideration and cooperation.

Interruptions by Prospects

Although all of Chapter 14 is devoted to handling the most troublesome form of prospect-interruption, the *objection*, brief reference to interruptions by the prospect seems desirable at this point.

Every question from the prospect interrupts the salesman's story, whether the question be a request for information, an objection, or one that constitutes a willful attempt to derail the salesman from his sales talk. There are, obviously, two broad methods of handling a question — to deal with it at once or to postpone answering it. If the salesman elects to handle the question immediately, he should do so with firmness and conviction; he should be brief, yet satisfy the prospect. He will resume his story immediately after he has checked with the prospect to make certain that his reply was satisfactory.

If an instantaneous answer to the prospect's question would, for any reason, be awkward for the salesman, then he should try to postpone handling the question. Particularly if the question is, in reality, an objection, the salesman may find it desirable and possible to delay an answer with some such reply as:

> "I'm coming to that."
> "I'll take up that point in a minute."
> "Yes, I can see your point."
> "Yes, I'll cover that later."
> "Perhaps you're right."

He will then resume his presentation.

We know that the salesman's story should be built about his product's advantages rather than the weaknesses of competitive products, for this construction makes his story more persuasive. If the prospect insists, early in the story, that the salesman's product be compared with a competitive brand, perhaps the brand the prospect then owns, then the comparison should be executed immediately and fairly. At once the salesman will proceed to build up the advantages of his own brand.

Price should be kept in the background in the initial stages of the interview. Price in itself is never high or low. It is a relative factor that depends on what the buyer gets; it is important only in terms of value. No prospect can judge price fairly until he knows what the product will do for him. And a price quoted too soon always sounds high because the salesman has not had time to build up much value. For these reasons, an early inquiry about price should be sidetracked, perhaps with such a diverting question as "Which model fits your needs?" or "What size are you thinking about?"

The Difficult Prospect

Sometimes our salesman encounters a prospect who is difficult to handle. Six causes of difficulty are mentioned.

Inattentiveness. When the prospect's attention wanders away from the story, the salesman should try at once to determine the cause. It may be that the story is so vague that the prospect cannot or will not spend the effort required to follow it. It may be that the salesman is failing to interest the prospect because of what he is saying or because of how he is saying it. It may be that the prospect's attention is intermittently yet irresibly drawn to other matters. Whatever the cause, something must be done.

One possible course of action is to mention the prospect's various wants, if the salesman knows them, in the hopes of finding a clue to the prospect's most powerful buying motives. A second and somewhat similar possibility is to summarize what the product delivers, all the while looking for clues. Third, the salesman may need to startle the prospect and revive his attention by enthusiastically presenting something new — a new angle, a new slant, a new case history, or a new advantage. Fourth, proof that is more spectacular than any yet used may be offered. Fifth, the salesman may pause in his storytelling until the prospect's attention returns. Sixth, in serious cases when the prospect is too inattentive, the salesman may frankly ask for his attention. Finally, if none of these techniques results in capturing the prospect's attention, then the only resort left is to ask for a later appointment.

Silence. Being met by silence is not so serious as it seems, because if a prospect listens, he can be sold. The proper procedure is to feed advantages and proof slowly to the prospect and to make sure that he is listening. If questions such as "That's true, isn't it?" are interspersed frequently, the salesman is taking necessary and positive action to open up and draw out the prospect. An occasional question which cannot be answered by "yes" or "no" will help the salesman check the progress he is making.

Indifference. One of the most exasperating hurdles a salesman has to take is indifference. The difficult job here is to convince the prospect of his need, yet not let him know he is on the road to buying. To do this, the salesman must keep the interview informal, free, and frictionless. He must make the interview a casual dialogue as though two individuals happened to get together for a few minutes. Ignoring the prospect's apparent indifference, the salesman will continue to add advantage to advantage.

Indecision. The salesman confronts indecision when his prospect is so uncertain and afraid that he hesitates and postpones the purchase. Here the salesman must take the initiative by demonstrating firm, friendly guidance. Questions will be asked so as to build up a series of commitments from the prospect. By taking a positive, decisive attitude and by showing that he knows what should be done, the salesman helps the prospect decide and make up his mind. Case histories are a very effective form of proof here. A close will be selected that will not frighten the prospect and will make his buying painless.

Skepticism. Skeptical prospects are usually persons who have been deceived themselves or who know persons who have been deceived. They should not be taken too seriously because they are not as tough as they appear.

Instead of making the skeptic back up his bark, a better course is to go ahead with the sales story and to keep piling up facts backed up by a generous amount of clear, trustworthy proof. By being intentionally conservative and by using understatements, the salesman makes it difficult, if not impossible, for the prospect to voice disagreement. Above all, the salesman will need to keep cool, refusing to argue or dispute and ignoring prejudiced and vitriolic remarks.

Hostility. Whenever the salesman encounters a prospect who is decidedly antagonistic, he must correct that attitude for two reasons. First, such an attitude can hurt the salesman's company and the salesman, and, second, once the erroneous opinion has been corrected, the salesman has a good customer. The worst possible course of action the salesman could take is to argue; the prospect will naturally defend himself, and even though his mistake is proved, he will usually be too irate to buy. Instead, the salesman should listen sympathetically and silently, thank the prospect for telling his story, and promise the prospect he will investigate and make things right.

STUDY ASSIGNMENTS

1. A salesman can deliver his story at too fast or too slow a rate. What are the results of these mistakes?
2. Are there any general guides for a salesman in selecting the testimonials and case histories to use in selling to a particular buyer? Explain.
3. What might make a salesman suspect that his sales presentations are characterized by too much talking and not enough listening?
4. Midway in a sales interview, the buyer is called out for about ten minutes. What might the salesman do during those minutes?
5. A salesman for domestic heating installations knows his models technically from A to Z. Into what six advantages might he translate product features?
6. Are there products which must be sold through appealing to the prospect's emotions and others which must be sold through appeal to reason? Give some examples and tell why.
7. Can a salesman be too polite in dealing with buyers? Discuss.
8. Point out the excellence of the case history as a form of proof.
9. The prospect should feel that he *bought*, not that he was *sold*. Do you agree? Explain.
10. As a salesman tells his story, he can count on being asked questions by buyers. Should he postpone his answers? Explain your answer.

CASE STUDY 12A

A representative of the National Chemical Laboratories Company is making a call on a large factory that produces wool fabric. The factory uses large steam irons in a pressing operation. This is a follow-up call on selling a boiler compound used to treat boilers to keep them from forming scale, corrosion, and rust on the inside walls and tubes. The salesman in his first call obtained the permission of the purchasing agent to speak with the maintenance engineer, who was directly in charge of the boiler. After talking with him, the salesman found that the company was using no boiler treatment and that the boiler was building up scale. At the rate scale was forming, the boiler needed immediate treatment. The salesman obtained samples of the scale, boiler water, and city water to take to the laboratory for his company's chemist to analyze and to recommend treatment. After obtaining the analysis and recommendations of the chemist, the salesman is returning to convince the purchasing agent that he needs to treat his boiler.

Salesman: Good morning Mr. Taylor. I'm Bill Ball of the National Chemical Laboratories Company. It's nice to see you again.

Purchasing Agent: Well . . . . Ball, have a seat.

Salesman: Thank you for letting me talk with Mr. Westbrook, your engineer, about your boiler the last time I called.

Purchasing Agent: Yes, he told me what you had to say. He's under the impression, and I am, too, that we don't need to spend any money on boiler treatment. That boiler is practically new.

Salesman: Yes, I can't blame you for wanting to save on your boiler costs; that's exactly what I plan to help you do.

Purchasing Agent: Look, Ball, we paid $18,000 for that new boiler. It's one of the best made. I don't think it needs any chemical treatment.

Salesman: That sure is an expensive boiler, and it should last you a long time. How long did you use your last boiler?

Purchasing Agent: I don't know, about 10 or 15 years. Anyway, what has that got to do with it?

Salesman: Why did you have to junk your old boiler?

Purchasing Agent: It was costing too much to keep it running, and it just didn't operate efficiently.

Salesman: Your maintenance man said your old boiler was a Queen City.

Purchasing Agent: Yes, it was.

Salesman: We have customers still using Queen City boilers who expect many more useful years from them. Of course, they use our treatment. Mr. Taylor, I can show you how to increase the life of your boiler, avoid costly repairs, and reduce your fuel bill.

Purchasing Agent: How?

Salesman: Our chemist ran an analysis on your water supply and on water from the boiler that had been used. These are the results. (Takes laboratory report from case along with sample of scale from within the boiler.) The tests indicate that your feed water, the raw city water that goes into the boiler, has 40 parts per million hardness.

Purchasing Agent: What difference does this make? The boiler is operating without any trouble.

Salesman: You have seen what hard water does to household sinks and pipes.

Purchasing Agent: Yes, it causes rust, and will stain porcelain sinks.

Salesman: This is almost exactly what hard water does to your boiler. Try to picture your boiler set-up. You use the same water over and over, or your water bill would be outrageously high. The hot water is circulated from the boiler to all your radiators, your big steam irons, and then back to your condensate tank. The condensate then feeds back into the boiler. You lose steam when you operate the steam irons, thereby concentrating the amount of calcium and magnesium hardness in the water. Now take a look at this report on the used water from the boiler. You will note the hardness is 120 parts per million, enough to form this hard scale. (Shows purchasing agent sample of scale.)

Purchasing Agent: This came from my boiler? (Holds up scale.)

Salesman: Yes, sir.

Purchasing Agent: Exactly why did this scale form?

Salesman: The hardness is precipitated into the form of a salt when water is heated and put under pressure. The scale formation is due to the crystallization of these salts immediately adjacent to the heating surfaces. As this scale becomes thicker, your fuel bill increases.

Purchasing Agent: Why?

Salesman: You not only have to heat the heating surfaces of your boiler, but also the scale that covers these surfaces. Have you noticed any increase in your fuel costs?

Purchasing Agent: I would have to check the records to see, but it does sound logical. But even if the fuel bill has increased, I'm sure the extra fuel isn't costing us enough to warrant using your treatment.

Salesman: What about the repair cost it will save?

Purchasing Agent: Such as what?

Salesman: Your maintenance engineer said he has to replace the water tubes from the condensate tank to the boiler about once every quarter because they become corroded and stopped up. He said it costs about $40 each time he replaces these pipes. At four times a year, this amounts to $160. You won't have this cost if you use our treatment.

Purchasing Agent: It still doesn't save enough to pay for the treatment.

Salesman: Can you take a chance on the state boiler inspector's closing down your boiler because of excessive scale on its heating surfaces? Just think of the lost production this would cause.

Purchasing Agent: Why would the boiler inspector do this?

Salesman: The scale will cause not only heat loss but also overheating of the boiler metal and consequently tube failures. The scale acts as an insulation holding heat within the tube metal. When this heat reaches a certain point the boiler could possibly explode.

Purchasing Agent: I don't think this will ever happen.

Salesman: It happened at Seashore Packing Company not long ago. The fireman was lucky not to have been in the boiler room. You can't afford such an accident. It might cause loss of life as well as monetary loss.

Purchasing Agent: Are you trying to frighten me into thinking I need your product now?

Salesman: No, sir, but you should know the facts. Do you have insurance on your boiler?

Purchasing Agent: We have some, but it is about to expire.

Salesman: When you bought this insurance, didn't the insurance agent look in your boiler before he wrote the policy?

Purchasing Agent: Yes.

Salesman: I doubt very seriously if you can renew this insurance at the present time because of the scale formation. Insurance men are stricter than state inspectors. You do agree you need boiler insurance . . . don't you?

Purchasing Agent: Yes.

Salesman: If you use our compound we will assure you that your boiler will pass the insurance inspections *and* the state inspections.

Purchasing Agent: I'll worry about that when it's time for these boys to inspect my boiler.

Salesman: Mr. Taylor, when was the last time you were in your boiler room?

Purchasing Agent: Couple of months ago, I guess.

Salesman: You wouldn't be aware of your boiler unless your steam presses or heat went off, now would you?

Purchasing Agent: Probably not.

Salesman: You *are* well aware of those knitting machines out in the plant aren't you?

Purchasing Agent: Yes.

Salesman: If those machines needed lubricants or parts, you wouldn't hesitate to buy them — would you?

Purchasing Agent: Of course not — they are our bread and butter!

Salesman: Yet your boiler cost as much as one of those knitting machines, didn't it?

Purchasing Agent: Well . . . . . . yes.

Salesman: Don't you think you should protect your investment in the basement just as you do your investments in the plant?

Purchasing Agent: Yes.

Salesman: Now don't you agree you need this compound?

Purchasing Agent: I don't know . . . I . . . . we can get along without it.

Salesman: Remember now — we check on your boiler every six weeks and obtain a sample of your boiler water. This water is analyzed, and you are sent the results. On the bottom of this sheet (holds up water analysis sheet) you see a place for comments. In these comments we recommend whether you need to increase or decrease the amount of treatment being fed into your boiler. We also make recommendations concerning blowdown.

Purchasing Agent: What is blowdown?

Salesman: This is when your fireman ejects or drains portions of the water from your boiler.

Purchasing Agent: This sounds like a waste of water to me.

Salesman: The blowdown removes some of a boiler's concentrated water so that it is replaced with feed-water, thus effecting a general lowering of concentrations in the boiler. If you don't have a regulated blowdown schedule, scale builds up much faster.

Purchasing Agent: Does my fireman know about this?

Salesman: He probably blows your boiler down periodically, but it is impossible for him to do it properly without first performing a chloride test.

Purchasing Agent: That guy doesn't know chloride from pure water.

Salesman: This is why most concerns need professional help concerning boiler blowdown. If your boiler is blown down too often you are wasting fuel and water. If not blown down enough, the efficiency of the boiler is impaired.

Purchasing Agent: I see . . . . . .

Salesman: Getting back to the report we send to you each six weeks . . . . we will perform the necessary test and recommend a regulated schedule of boiler blowdown. How does this sound?

Purchasing Agent: It sounds O.K., but . . .

Salesman: Now, don't you agree you need this boiler treatment and service we are offering because it will increase the life of your boiler, cut costly repair bills, assure you that your boiler will pass state, and insurance inspections reduce your fuel consumption, and provide a regulated blowdown schedule.

Purchasing Agent: I guess we do need it, since you put it that way.

QUESTIONS:

1. What did the salesman do well?
2. What did the salesman do that could be improved?
3. What techniques are illustrated in the interview?
4. What types of proof did the salesman offer to support his claims?

CASE STUDY 12B

The salesman is selling Royal typewriters. His prospect is the owner of a small business, a retail store. The salesman had 'phoned the prospect previously and obtained an appointment. The scene is the prospect's store.

Salesman: Good morning, Mr. Wells. I'm Jack Harper from the Royal Typewriter Company. I spoke to you on the 'phone yesterday.

Prospect: Oh, yes, that's right. Won't you sit down here? It's kind of quiet around here now.

Salesman: Thank you, sir. I'm glad to see that you have one of our typewriters sitting over there. You've certainly taken fine care of it.

Prospect: Yes, indeed. That's a real old timer that I bought when you were probably in grammar school. It's a bit shopworn now, but it still clacks away. I've had it ever since I started my business here.

Salesman: You and the Royal Company started out just about the same time then, and you're both going stronger than ever now. I wonder if you have seen the new Royal typewriter. It has 32 new features which make it the world's number one typewriter and make it the most time- and labor-saving machine ever intvented. Here is a picture of our brand new office machine.

Prospect: Oh, I don't want anything like that. I was thinking of something a little bit smaller.

Salesman: Then our portable model would suit your needs better. See, this is a picture of the portable. This model is especially convenient. It's extremely light and easy to move from place to place, yet it has all the features and does all the work of an office model. I have a portable outside in my car. I'll show it to you. Be back in a minute. (Goes outside and returns with the portable.) See how easy it is to carry. This case has special padding and clamps which prevent damage to the machine while it is being moved. This molded handle makes the machine as easy to pick up and carry as an over-night bag. And look inside; isn't it well-designed and nice looking?

Prospect: Yes, it does look quite nice. You know, I'm not the world's fastest typist. I don't know if I could handle one of these new machines. I'm sort of used to my old one.

Salesman: Mr. Wells, if you can handle one of the old ones, you'll have no trouble at all with these new ones. Here, I'll show you what I mean. This space bar fits right into the frame of the machine to make your typing easier and more comfortable. Doesn't this look a lot easier than your old machine?

Prospect: Yes, it does.

Salesman: I'm sure you have often fretted at your present Royal and wondered why there was not some easier way to get down at the keys for cleaning and to change ribbons. Now, this Royal portable has the perfect answer to that problem with the exclusive *Time-saver Top.* This allows full and easy access to all the inner parts of the machine. And when it's closed, it provides a guard against dust. See how it works. (Demonstrates on the model.)

Prospect: (Works the top on the model.) Yes, that is a very good idea.

Salesman: Now, do you see this little lever?

Prospect: Yes, what is it?

Salesman: That's the Royal touch control indicator. It is one of the finest features of this machine. It enables you to adjust the tension of the keys to suit your own typing style, whether it is hard or gentle. And when you type for long periods of time, it is sometimes relaxing to change the tension from time to time. You have your choice of adjustments; there are nine variations to suit all styles of typing.

Prospect: That's mighty fine.

Salesman: Let me slip a piece of paper in the machine. See how easy it is to put in. And the paper lines up straight. That's one thing the old machines never seemed to do right.

Prospect: Yes, I always had trouble with that.

Salesman: Here, just try out the feel of this machine. Type on it just like you do with your old machine. (Prospect types.) Notice the finger form keys. They're designed to cradle your fingertips for more comfort and easier typing. How does that feel?

Prospect: Yes, the keys really do fit your fingers. Say, this is a peppery little gadget, isn't it?

Salesman: That's a good way to describe it, Mr. Wells. Notice this magic margin, exclusive with the new Royal. Now, just a flick of the finger and you have exactly the margin you want in no time at all. You automatically set your margin merely by releasing this key and sliding the carriage to the desired position. This gives you perfect margins with no effort at all. Compare that with your old machine.

Prospect: This is really quite a typewriter. I didn't realize they had changed so much in in the last few years.

Salesman: Don't you think that this Royal portable would be a fine machine to own? I can have one delivered to you tomorrow — or would you prefer this one right here?

Prospect: Oh, this machine is nice; I can't deny that. But I don't think I want to buy just yet.

Salesman: Your old typewriter is not getting any younger, and you want a new one. Now is a good time to buy and take advantage of all the benefits of this new Royal — benefits such as the magic margin, finger form keys, and touch control indicator.

Prospect: Well, I suppose you're right, but I'm a little hard-pressed for cash right now. How much does this model sell for?

Salesman: If you're short on cash, and we all get in that position, we can arrange easy credit terms for you.

Prospect: Oh, no. When I buy something for myself I pay cash, or I don't buy at all. That's the way I do business. What does this machine cost?

Salesman: Our production methods have enabled us to reduce our price to $85.

Prospect: Well, I don't know about Royal. Your service on typewriters isn't too good. In order to get mine fixed I have to send it to the shop just to get an estimate of repair costs.

Salesman: That is only because your present machine is over nine years old. Those old models require special attention and general estimates are hard to make. For all models less than nine years old, I can leave with you today a complete list of service prices for all repairs you might find necessary. However, you won't have any trouble with this new Royal portable for many, many years. These new machines are built to last. Would you like me to send you this model?

Prospect: Well, I don't know if I should buy now.

Salesman: Just look at this new Royal. You have finger form keys designed to cradle your fingertips and bring you the best in typing comfort. Look at the beauty of this portable. It will be the envy of everyone who sees it. And you will have the new speed spacer built right into the frame, eliminating all obstructions to rapid spacing. And look how easy it is to arrange your margins. Just move the carriage to where you want the margin, flick the magic margin lever, and the margin is set. Altogether this is the world's first truly modern typewriter, and it is tailored to fit your own individual needs here and at home. You said you would prefer not to buy on credit. Would you rather pay cash, Mr. Wells, or do you want to write a check?

Prospect: Well, I guess I may as well buy now. I'll give you a check.

Salesman: Good. Would tomorrow afternoon be soon enough to deliver it?

Prospect: Yes, that would be fine.

QUESTIONS:

1. What did the salesman do well?
2. What did the salesman do that could be improved?
3. What techniques are illustrated in the sale?
4. How many genuine agreements did the salesman get from the prospect?

CHAPTER 13

DEMONSTRATING WITH SHOWMANSHIP

Demonstrations can be used for many purposes. They can be constructed to demand and capture the interest of the prospect and move on toward desire, conviction, and, hence, action. They are particularly effective in achieving conviction. They show what the product will do for the prospect. They prove to him that the product is *the* solution to one of his problems. They prove the salesman's points by presenting external evidence to back up his assertions.

Demonstrations illustrate the salesman's story and confirm, verify, and substantiate it. They make the story sink in and stick. They translate words into action. They give the prospect the experience and thrill of ownership. They can be used to teach the prospect how to use the product or, if he is a merchant, how to sell it. Finally, they can be real time-savers because one simple demonstration can often be the equal of a flood of oral eloquence.

WHY BUYERS LIKE DEMONSTRATIONS

Buyers like demonstrations because they prefer to trust their own five senses rather than a salesman's promises. They would rather taste than be told how something tastes, rather touch than be told how something feels, and see how a product works rather than hear a description of the process. When the buyer takes part in the demonstration, his participation gives him something to do for himself. He learns by experience what the product will and will not do, and how to operate and use it properly.

Demonstrations are popular because they permit a buyer to understand the salesman's product and proposal *quickly*, thus saving the buyer some time and reducing the wordage to which he must listen. He understands *painlessly*, not having to fight and think in order to follow and grasp what the salesman says. He understands *proudly* in well-conducted demonstrations because his vanity is tickled by the speed and ease of his comprehension. The demonstration reduces the salesman's story to simple terms. It converts talk into action. It translates mental ideas into physical activity and general concepts into specific, concrete form.

WHY SALESMEN LIKE TO DEMONSTRATE

Salesmen like to demonstrate because demonstrations make their sales stories more effective. Clearly, when the salesman makes contact with a buyer through two or more of the buyer's senses, his chances of selling are greater than if he reaches only one — the sense of hearing for the transmittal of words. The impressions the salesman makes are deeper and more vivid. The points he makes are remembered longer because they penetrate further. Buyer-belief is more certain because the buyer's grasp of the product and its advantages is firmer. The buyer is shown the satisfactions that will be his with the products, and the manner in which he learns of the satisfactions is convincing.

Demonstrations are helpful both in starting the buyer out on the road to buying and in carrying him well down that road. They reach out and grab the buyer's attention, quickly develop it into interest, and usually increase the buyer's desire for the item. This is true because, for many products, the demonstration is one of the quickest and surest ways to prove buyer-need. Demonstrations also are marvelous in achieving conviction; they convince buyers better than words because they are a much stronger form of proof. Especially is the sense of sight a powerful channel through which to communicate to buyers. Some authorities have claimed that the eye is 22 to 25 times as powerful as the ear in transmitting impressions to buyers' brains.

Opposition to buying is reduced by effective demonstrations. The buyer's attention is focused on the buyer-benefits that are to be had. The buyer cannot deny what the salesman is demonstrating. The salesman does not seem to be *selling* — just operating, explaining, and showing. The buyer feels that he and the salesman are allies and partners in executing and watching the demonstration. As a result, there are fewer interruptions of the troublesome, unwelcome type.

Finally, demonstrations make for strong, effective selling. They simplify the salesman's job, giving him more time and more confidence. Not only can they be used to impress, startle, and even amaze buyers, but they also can serve as a home base to which the salesman can steer buyers whose attention is prone to wander. It is difficult to quarrel with the claim that every sales story ever composed can be strengthened by the addition of demonstrations.

WHEN AND WHAT TO DEMONSTRATE

Demonstration can be used by the salesman at any time. Chapter 11 indicated that the salesman may use demonstration to open the interview.

Usually those openers are only partial demonstrations and are employed only to get the prospect's complete attention. The demonstration most often follows some introductory selling talk; it is usually accompanied by its own oral presentation.

Salesmen must be able to demonstrate *every* product feature that *any* buyer finds interesting. In addition, salesmen must master several methods of demonstrating the *outstanding* points of their products. This is not to say that salesmen should go through their entire assortment of demonstrations on every call. In using a more effective plan, the salesman learns the buyer's exact needs and interests — then concentrates his demonstration on the product's features that most closely relate to that particular buyer's needs and interests. To demonstrate every feature with equal emphasis ignores two basic truths: (1) product features are not of equal importance; (2) buyers are not alike. Assume Buyer A is mainly interested in *safety* while Buyer B is more influenced by *comfort*. If our salesman embarked on a long demonstration of comfort, "A" would become restless and inattentive and probably would start dreaming up objections to buying. In other words, if no purchase results from the demonstrations of the first few features, then the salesman can, if he deems it wise, move over into other demonstrations of other features.

ADVANCE PREPARATION

There is need of much advance preparation if the demonstrations are to be powerful, polished, and persuasive. The perfect demonstration calls for a perfect plot, perfectly planned. It must be conceived and constructed carefully and thoughtfully, because planning here is of equal if not greater importance than it was in planning the story. What the salesman is planning is a standard demonstration of maximum excellence which will be followed faithfully, unless there is a specific reason for deviation.

The first responsibility of a salesman who is to conduct a demonstration, then, is to have a *plan*. This involves deciding what to demonstrate and what to omit. The salesman will need to determine the points that his demonstration is to make and their most effective sequence. It involves finding the best standard sequence of steps to be followed when the salesman is able to learn little or nothing about his individual buyers that would aid him in "tailoring" the demonstration. The sequence should be memorized. The amount of emphasis each step deserves must be determined, and the timing of each must be scheduled. If the buyer is to take part, questions of *how*, *what*, and *when* must be settled.

Any *products* to be shown, operated, or used in any manner should be inspected before they are exhibited. If a product is supposed to work in a certain fashion but fails to do so, such failure can easily be fatal to the salesman's chances of making the sale. If some items are exposed to the buyer's view too often, or under harsh conditions, the appearance of those items should be checked periodically to make sure they look fresh and presentable. Even the best salesmen can not sell a product that gives a poor appearance.

Often the *buyer* must be prepared in advance for what is to happen. If possible, his curiosity should be whetted and his anticipation increased until he is anxious to see at least certain phases of the demonstration. He should understand adequately what is being done or what is to be demonstrated. Frequently this means that the salesman must brief the buyer on *what*, *when*, and *why*.

The usual demonstration is accompanied by some explanation and description. So, a *sales talk* should be composed prior to the demonstration to point out the buyer-benefits being shown. Such a talk not only keeps the buyer from being in the dark but also helps persuade him to buy.

Time and *place* of demonstration are left frequently to the salesman's choice. The salesman hopes that both hour and site will work for and not against his purposes.

In the automotive field, by way of example, planned demonstrations are far superior to unplanned ones. The rule is to give only a brief demonstration in the showroom or at the prospect's home before the main demonstration, the ride. This ride is carefully planned by the salesman by deciding where to go and the sequence of situations he wants to encounter. He plans what to do and what to say in each set of circumstances. The prospect is not put behind the wheel until keen anticipation has been aroused. The salesman almost always drives the car for the first three or four miles. During this part of the demonstration, the salesman follows a planned route that will take in country, hills, city traffic, and straightaway. The car used as the demonstrator will be immaculate and in perfect mechanical condition.

Finally, the salesman sometimes wants to make use of other *persons*. Either he wants them present, or he would like to use products they bought from him earlier, or he prefers to use their experiences. In such cases, arrangements should be made well in advance.

PRINCIPLES OF DEMONSTRATION

Don't Tell When You Can Show

The first principle of using demonstrations is that the salesman should never *tell* a prospect something when he can *show* him the same thing. Showing includes sending messages to the prospect's senses of sight, touch, taste, and smell. There are many reasons why the wise salesman appeals to the prospect through his sense of sight. Not less than four fifths of an individual's impressions and knowledge reach him through this sense. Things seen are considered more reliable than things heard. This fact is recognized in a negative way by the common saying, "Don't believe anything you hear and only half of what you see." Speed of grasping is greater when the prospect sees *and* hears. The prospect remembers what he sees longer than what he hears. Indeed, it is difficult to find serious fault with the maxim, "One picture is worth ten thousand words."

Demonstrating to one of the senses other than the sense of hearing should be done as much and as often as possible. Appealing through them is more subtle in that he sometimes can be *shown* what he would resent being *told*. In demonstrating, the salesman seems to be explaining and experimenting rather than selling, and this invites the prospect to relax his buying defenses. Demonstration allows the product to do its part of accomplishing the selling job by appealing to whichever sense or senses are most appropriate.

The product is not the only item the salesman can show to the prospect. Maximum use should be made of visual aids that help to picture the proposition. Examples of visual aids are these:

Accessories	Figures	Photographs
Advertisements	Graphs	Pictures
Blackboards	House organs	Portfolios
Booklets	Letters	Posters
Cartoons	Lights	Recordings
Charts	Manuals	Samples
Cross sections	Maps	Sand tables
Diagrams	Models	Signs
Drawings	Movies	Sound-slide films
Easel pads	Parts	Swatches

Cover Every Product Feature

The standard demonstration should include every vital feature of the product. Three specific dangers of omission are worth mentioning. First, the feature omitted may be of particular interest to the particular prospect. Second, competitors may be stressing their comparable feature in talking to that prospect. Third, competitors may be telling the prospect that this particular feature of theirs is more outstanding.

If the salesman's company provides him with an outline of a suggested demonstration, the odds are that it omits nothing important. Company plans are usually well tested, they are usually the sum of many brains, they usually represent the organized experience of the company, and they often are the cream of successful field trials.

Here are the general suggestions the J. I. Case Company makes for any demonstration. All sales personnel are expected to study these ideas and to discuss them in sales meetings scheduled for that purpose.

DEMONSTRATION INSTRUCTIONS

1. Inspect the work to be performed prior to agreeing to demonstrate.

2. Arrange for a specific time for demonstration and see that the maximum number of interested prospects and personnel will be available at the specific time for the demonstration.

3. Lubricate, adjust, and work the equipment before the demonstration without any prospects or interested people observing.

4. Have a skilled, experienced and qualified operator to demonstrate the tractor and equipment, an operator who knows the equipment and knows what it will do.

5. Actual demonstration:

   A. Have two participants in attendance:
      (1) The operator (qualified).
      (2) The salesman, who will direct the demonstration and explain the various features and advantages of the equipment and its performance.

   B. The initial part of the demonstration is the unloading of the tractor or equipment from the trailer. If a Case trailer is being used, do not do this until the group is assembled.

   C. Give a short explanation of the features of the tractor such as:
      (1) Its weight in relation to power.
      (2) Its clearance.
      (3) Power on both tracks when turning and our Terramatic Power Shifting Transmission in those models which have them.
      (4) The advantages of the anti-friction lower track wheel bearings.
      (5) The advantages of the method of mounting our dozers and loaders.
      (6) The advantages of our unitary loader frame — direct pushing cylinder.
      (7) The advantages of having a dozer or loader close to the tractor.
      (8) The advantage of our torque tube in the tractor and how we push or pull from this torque tube, the backbone of the tractor.
      (9) The advantages of our pushing position and our powered bucket.
      (10) Our cylinder design, packings, etc., interchangeability.
      (11) Terratrac Backhoe — Foot swing strength, alloy pins, bushing quick removal.

D. Both participants should have a card with each operation listed on it in the sequence in which they are to be performed. The salesman should tell the operator what to do and direct the demonstration, and when any particularly outstanding feature of work is performed, the demonstration should be stopped and this explained. At some time during the demonstration, the operator should be told to proceed for five minutes without stopping. This should be announced to the crowd. At the end of the five-minute interval, he should stop so that the crowd can see the work performed in this . . . interval, whether it be loading trucks, bulldozing, or digging a ditch with a backhoe. During this operation, the operator should make every move count. Take a full cut, all the tractor will handle without slowing down excessively. It is better to take a shallow cut, make a complete pass without stalling and clutching than it is to try to take too big a bit and then to stop in the middle of the pass.

E. The concluding demonstration (particularly with loaders) is the loading of the tractor onto the trailer, showing how easy and simple it is. The tractor should then be left on the trailer.

6. Length of demonstration.

A *half hour* should be adequate for the demonstration. The success of the demonstration depends on knowing what you're going to do and doing it. Do not allow anyone else on the tractor until after the first fifteen or twenty minutes and you have definitely and effectively shown the outstanding performance of the equipment. Never allow operators who are not familiar with the equipment to operate it without first explaining the operation and the handling of the controls. It is good and desirable to have operators sit in the seat of the tractor and turn the tractor slightly from side to side so they can see how easily it steers and handles, but inexperienced people or smart alecks should not be turned loose with the tractor.

A *half hour* of properly prepared and conducted demonstration will show more and be equal to a day of disorganized work. Customers who want to see the tractor work a week or so are more interested in getting work done than they are in seeing the equipment work.

Those who sell to merchants have a dual job in covering every product feature. They need to demonstrate all the benefits that will accrue to the retailer as well as the benefits that will accrue to the retailer's customers. In other words, the salesman's demonstration to the retailer is not complete unless it demonstrates how to demonstrate.

Make the Sales Talk Interpret the Demonstration

One of the first things a salesman must learn to do is to talk while he is demonstrating — to synchronize a spoken message with each phase of the demonstration. An accompanying sales talk is necessary primarily because it permits the salesman to continue his selling efforts. This is particularly desirable because the prospect cannot and must not be depended on to interpret the demonstration for himself. A second purpose served by this sales talk is to prevent awkward pauses or periods of silence.

The initial part of the talk that is built to go with the demonstration normally precedes the demonstration proper. The purpose of this preliminary part of the talk is to build up the demonstration in the prospect's mind, sell him on the idea of a demonstration, and, it is hoped, arouse his desire for a demonstration. The main body of the accompaniment takes product facts and converts them as they are demonstrated into advantages of owning and using the product. These advantages should make a very strong impact on the prospect because any spoken claim is instantaneously backed up by product performance.

Make the Product Look Its Best

Demonstration should display merchandise in its best possible light. This calls for staging the demonstration where and when it will be most effective. Every distraction that will compete for the prospect's attention should be eliminated. He must be permitted to give the product his undivided attention.

The merchandise should be tested in advance to see that it will work perfectly. The demonstration should get off to an excellent start because the salesman and his product need to make a good impression from the very first moment. The pace of the demonstration must be maintained so as not to allow enthusiasm to wane.

Nothing is more basic in showing a product off to best advantage than that the salesman's performance be of professional quality. Young salesmen should practice giving demonstrations phase by phase and point by point until everything is done perfectly and naturally. The awkward salesman is not convincing; the polished salesman tends to get the order. Even a talented actor spoils an otherwise fine performance by clumsy use of props; the expert salesman, drawing the obvious parallel, practices until he can do the demonstration blindfolded, thus insuring a competent, sure, smooth, and poised demonstration.

Make the Demonstration Clear

Since one purpose of the demonstration is to clarify what the salesman *says*, care must be taken that it does just that. The salesman starts off by making sure that the prospect understands the purpose of the demonstration. The salesman will demonstrate only one point at a time in order that the prospect can completely absorb each. Brevity is another aid in making the demonstration clear, provided completeness is not sacrificed. Still another idea is not to attempt too much in any one demonstration. Displaying too many products or making too many points or doing anything to excess invites confusion. Clarity sometimes demands that the *salesman* do something rather than depend on the prospect to do it, for example, figuring out costs or savings with pencil and pad. In some circumstances it may be desirable or even necessary to repeat a demonstration several times.

Make the Demonstration True to Life

It is not enough for the salesman to point to each part or accessory of the product and name it. Instead, he must show why each was provided, and what each means in the day-to-day use and operation of the product. This can best be done if the product is demonstrated in circumstances of actual use. When conditions and atmosphere are realistic, the prospect's feeling of confidence is increased.

Tailor the Demonstration

No automobile salesman would demonstrate a car to a spirited college student in the same fashion as he would demonstrate it to the student's prim aunt. Instead, he fits his demonstration to the prospect by dwelling on those characteristics and features which are or seem to be of particular interest to the prospect. In other words, the salesman slants his demonstration by dramatizing those buyer-benefits that each prospect can relate intimately and individually to himself. When any setup or installation is to be used for the demonstration, one should be selected that is as nearly like the prospect's circumstances as possible.

In some ways the salesman does with the demonstration exactly what he does with his story. He plans it in advance and then modifies it only when such modification will make it fit the individual prospect more snugly. The tailoring job includes such auxiliary matters as scheduling it to suit the prospect's convenience, determining its length in the light of the same consideration, and executing it at the proper rate of speed. Incidentally, the salesman is usually inclined to go too fast because he has run through so many demonstrations.

Put the Prospect into the Act

A basic feature of demonstrating is to let the prospect take part and do as much as possible, even permitting him to execute the complete demonstration where possible. This allows the prospect to sell to himself. Indeed, the product and prospect working together can often do more to bring about a purchase than can the salesman by talking to the prospect. Here is an illustration of this principle from the training material of Nibroc towels:

> *Strength Test:* Tape Nibroc and competing towel together with cellulose tape. Wet a strip on each towel. Have prospect take hold of one towel and another person the other towel. Have each pull evenly. This will prove comparative strength in use.

If the salesman uses props that the prospect can examine, take in his own hands, and manipulate, the prospect becomes better acquainted with the product's features and remembers them longer. In handling the product and working it or working with it, the prospect acquires first-hand knowledge; he experiences the "feel" of ownership. When he participates and does so satisfactorily, he feels a glow of personal achievement. For this reason, he, not the salesman, should throw the baseball at the pane of shatterproof glass.

Get Prospect Agreement Throughout

After demonstrating each individual point, the salesman should check with the prospect to see that he "saw" what was being shown and that he accepts the demonstration as satisfactory proof. This is the same principle that was established in the salesman's telling his story. The salesman gets agreement all down the line as the demonstration proceeds and thus puts the prospect on record as finding in the product what he needs and wants. As in telling the story, the salesman's object is to make a sale, not a complete demonstration, so, after any very enthusiastic agreement, the salesman may try to consummate the sale.

Maintain Control

Control must rest with the salesman during the demonstration for largely the same reasons that were suggested in connection with telling the story. Two angles deserve mention. First, it is dangerous to turn the product or any visual aid over to the prospect if such a step allows him to determine the course of the demonstration, or if it lets him decide what will receive his attention. An example of this is the prospect who is allowed to leaf through a portfolio or catalogue when his attention should be on what the salesman is doing. Second, by maintaining control of the situation, the salesman can prevent the prospect from making mistakes or errors that might humiliate him. An extreme illustration of this is the prospect who breaks the salesman's sample as a result of impulsive and uncontrolled handling.

Control can best be maintained by having a standard presentation and by telling the prospect when he is to take part, exactly what he is to do, and what he may expect.

Stick to the Demonstration

Occasionally a salesman drifts into the habit of wandering away from the demonstration proper and its objectives. It is not good for him to tell the prospect what he did last weekend, or tell local gossip or stories that he heard here and there, or give his own personal views and opinions on matters that are not connected with the sales interview and demonstration. Instead, his conversation should relate either to the advantages being conclusively shown by the demonstration, or, in cases of waiting time, he should review buyer-benefits.

Be Appreciative of Cooperation

When a salesman of installations demonstrates, he often uses units that have been bought and installed by previous prospects whom the salesman has converted into buyers. This might be true, for example, of a heating plant for a house.

When such is done, several rules should be observed by the salesman. First, he should inconvenience his customers as little as possible, calling them well in advance, choosing a satisfactory time for the visit, and not staying too long. Second, the customer should be put to no expense. Third, the salesman himself should do all he can to get things ready for the demonstration, and then put them back the way he found them. Fourth, he should express sincere and generous appreciation for any testimony his customer gives the prospect and for his customer's answering any of the prospect's questions. As a matter of fact, it is desirable for a salesman to encourage his customer to talk during the demonstration or examination because the prospect knows the salesman is biased, but he accepts the customer as being an independent third party.

Follow Up Vigorously

At the conclusion of the demonstration, no pause or let-down or hesitation should be permitted. The time of climax is at hand. In most cases, the salesman will want to exhibit a bold attitude, face the prospect, sum up the demonstration, and try to complete the sale then and there. If the prospect wavers, the salesman should return to his sales story.

SHOWMANSHIP

What Showmanship Is

The story the salesman tells consists of words and talking. The demonstration has just been described as the dramatization of the sales story. *Showmanship* is dramatization of the demonstration. In its mildest form, it is nothing more than stepped-up demonstration. In more advanced form, showmanship is what makes a demonstration sing, dance, or take the prospect's breath away. Showmanship permits a demonstration to be staged properly and impressively as though it were a theatrical performance, and it makes the demonstration picturesque instead of allowing it to be ordinary and commonplace.

What are some examples of showmanship? When a salesman writes up his orders with a fountain pen 18 inches long, he is using showmanship. If he hammers or jumps up and down on his product to prove its toughness, he's a showman. If he does no more than list reasons for buying with *black* pencil or ink, and then list the buyer's objections in *red*, he is using showmanship. Corks, thermometers, matches, coins, hourglasses, magnets, magnifying glasses — all these are useful to showmen. Mystery, challenge, and the spectacular are also useful. Handling the product with obvious respect and admiration is showmanship.

From the salesman's point of view, showmanship is a flair for the dramatic that enables him to be an unusual salesman. It keeps him from doing what the ordinary salesman does — the usual thing in the usual way. Showmanship is adding something extra. It is making each call an occasion. Showmanship is the salesman's imagination translated into his use of action, curiosity, and suspense.

Purpose of Showmanship

The purpose of showmanship is to make the demonstration more effective. Showmanship enables facts to be presented or actions to be executed in such an unusual way as to secure attention, increase prospect receptivity, make proof more spectacular, and thus bring about conviction. Showmanship makes a definite and decided impression on the prospect's emotions. Since the prospect buys with both emotion and reason, a message with emotional appeal can be just as persuasive as a statement of fact. Appealing to the prospect's emotions is not taking advantage of him, because he would not be a prospect unless he were likely to benefit from purchasing our salesman's product.

Two additional and minor uses of showmanship are to entertain the prospect while prescribing for his needs, and to demonstrate to merchants the showmanship they can use to secure sales.

USING SHOWMANSHIP

Handle the Product Impressively

In most cases the salesman will handle his merchandise with much and obvious respect as he demonstrates it. He will show that he holds his product in high esteem — even affection. He will exhibit loving care as he takes samples out of their cases, treating them as items of great value. He may flick imaginary dust off a sample or examine and test it two or three times before he considers it ready for the prospect's scrutiny. A salesman may handle an automatic pencil with great care to show the retailer that he knows and appreciates its value. The pencil may be displayed wrapped in velvet like the finest silverware. Every gesture of the salesman will be a *studied* gesture. By putting the pencil on a psychological pedestal, any discussion of obstacles becomes a secondary matter.

At the other extreme, if toughness is one of the outstanding features of the product, the salesman may handle the product in the roughest manner conceivable so as to show it off effectively. If the product is glass and unbreakable, it can be bounced against the wall.

Professional execution is needed for showmanship as much as for demonstration, but in a greater degree.

The salesman and his calls are similar to the Broadway actor who plays the same role convincingly night after night. The salesman must put on a convincing performance for each prospect.

Use Props

Showmanship can be evidenced in the selection of the props themselves. For example, showmanship is the objective of the salesman who decides to take along and use a blow torch, a thermostat, or scales.

Similarly, the character of the everyday items that the salesman uses may reveal showmanship; for example, his letterheads, his business cards, or his written proposals may be beautifully printed jobs that fairly reek of quality.

In addition to the selection or design of the props to be used, the handling or use of them also offers a field where showmanship can be helpful. The performance demanded here needs no further comment because it is the same described in the treatment of demonstration.

Tailor Showmanship to Fit You

Much of the salesman's thinking and talking must be tailored to the prospect. This is even true of showmanship, to a limited extent, but the major tailoring job in the area of showmanship is fitting it to the salesman himself. Two salesman can be quite successful and yet not be able to use the same type of showmanship. If one attempts to use showmanship unsuited to or inappropriate for himself, the result can be ghastly, and will certainly be disappointing. Instead, each salesman must experiment until he has identified what he can use in the area of showmanship that will be in harmony with his own personal chacteristics.

Use Showmanship Where Most Useful

Defined in its broadest sense, some form of showmanship can be used in almost any product classification and by almost any individual salesman. There are, however, certain areas in which showmanship is more suitable and effective than in others. First, new products will benefit more from showmanship than will old products. This is true because the sale of a new product demands a change in the prospect's pattern of thinking before his buying pattern changes, and, as this is a big job, showmanship helps.

Second, specialty products offer more and better opportunities for the salesman's imagination to be translated into showmanship than do staple items. This must not be interpreted as meaning that the selling of staple products disallows the use of showmanship. Third, intangibles need showmanship more than do physical products. Fourth, circumstances which permit the prospect to take part in showmanship, as in demonstration, are more promising. Fifth, as price and quality increase, so does the possible use of showmanship. Sixth and last, there is less use for showmanship in selling to purchasing agents and merchants than in selling to ultimate consumers, and less for wholesalers than for retailers.

Be Cautious

Lest the student be carried away by the idea of showmanship — and the idea *is* both fascinating and intriguing — let these cautions be examined. First, showmanship is no substitute for a thorough preparation for selling that includes product information, prospect information, and the principles of selling.

Second, showmanship must not be tawdry or gaudy, insincere or undignified, because it then not only fails to convince, but it also boomerangs against the salesman. Third, showmanship must be used only to get sales, and not to show off. If the salesman learns to write upside down so as to enable a prospect seated across the desk to read (and this is a good gag), what he should learn to write are orders. His showmanship must not call attention to itself or in any way distract the prospect's attention from buyer-benefits. If the *only* reaction to an advertisement is the comment, "What an interesting and clever ad," then the advertisement has failed. In similar fashion, if a prospect's only reaction is, "What a card, what a showman that salesman is — always up to something," then the salesman has shown off himself instead of his product. Fourth and last, showmanship must be in good taste. Salesmen used to employ all sorts of attention-getting devices, sometimes bordering on trickery. However, putting drama into the demonstration does not demand or even allow methods that are too extreme. Circus tactics and flamboyant gestures are not necessary, nor are trick gadgets and hocus-pocus. Slapstick and medicine-show tactics are taboo. The salesman himself should be neither pompous nor gaudy in dress. He should realize that the days of the brass buttons, the derby hat, the elk's tooth, and the red carnation have gone forever.

SALES MANAGERS' ATTITUDES ABOUT SHOWMANSHIP

It seems desirable in concluding this section to relay to college students the three attitudes found among sales managers toward showmanship. A first group consists of sales managers who want their salesmen to have nothing to do with showmanship. Instead, all they ask, as they phrase it, is sound thinking and a sound, businesslike presentation. They want a salesman to appear to the prospect as an earnest individual who knows his business thoroughly and is keenly interested in his customers' welfare. Some of these managers feel that both advertising and sales promotion need showmanship but personal selling does not.

Sales managers in the second group are only mildly enthusiastic about the use of showmanship. They feel that some salesmen possess the flair and that others do not. They observe that some very successful salesman get along nicely without any particular knowledge of showmanship or dramatics. They feel that showmanship is helpful but not essential. They argue that some salesmen cannot develop it, no matter how much they train their voices or practice gestures before mirrors. In addition to being hard to learn, it is hard to teach. Whereas showmanship may be an asset to a natural showman, it becomes a questionable practice for an amateur or inept salesman who can often get satisfactory results only from hard work plus long hours. These sales managers prefer personality development, initiative, and forceful character instead of showmanship.

Most sales managers are found in a third group which considers showmanship a priceless ingredient in a good salesman. They say that a sales presentation without showmanship is merely a recitation without color — that it takes showmanship to make the sales story stand up and walk. They consider showmanship one of the most important phases of a salesman's activity, largely because advertising, TV, and radio have accustomed people to expect dramatic presentations. These sales managers contend that prospects react more easily to showmanship; hence, dramatized selling is essential.

STUDY ASSIGNMENTS

1. Halfway in the salesman's demonstration, a buyer reaches over, gets one of the salesman's portfolios, starts looking through it, and tells the salesman to continue. What should the salesman do?
2. Most salesmen have found from experimenting that demonstrations are more effective if the buyer takes some part in them. What might the buyer do?
3. Almost every salesman can devise some sort of a "pencil and paper" demonstration. Why should he?
4. Under what limitations or handicaps does a salesman work when making product demonstrations to groups rather than to one buyer at a time?
5. How can a salesman's attempts to use showmanship handicap his efforts to make a sale?
6. It is clear that demonstrations are of great help to salesmen. Are there ways in which those same demonstrations benefit buyers?
7. One of the questions that often arises in connection with the demonstrating of products is whether the buyer should be allowed to handle the item. What are the advantages of such handling?
8. What are the dangers of leaving a product with a prospect for a "free" trial period?
9. Should a salesman of golf equipment be an expert golfer? Why?
10. How can a salesman go about developing his showmanship ability?

CASE STUDY 13

The owner of a specialty shop for children has already become acquainted with Mrs. Brown, who came into the shop to buy a suit for her baby boy. Mrs. Brown mentioned that she would like to see some strollers.

Salesman: Now I believe you said you would like to look at some baby strollers?

Prospect: Yes, I just want to look, not buy. I already own one.

Salesman: Then you must be thinking of purchasing it for a gift.

Prospect: No, it's not for a gift. If I look, it's just for me. But I certainly don't want another one like the one I have.

Salesman: Would you mind telling me what you dislike about your stroller?

Prospect: Well, it's all right for the baby, but it's so inconvenient for me. I don't know, it's just hard to handle. I believe I would be just as well off if I carried Johnny in my arms.

Salesman: Then you are really looking for a stroller that was designed with both the baby *and* the mother in mind. Is that right?

Prospect: Yes, that's about it.

Salesman: Well, believe me, Mrs. Brown, you're not alone in that search. Mothers demand a stroller that provides them with maximum convenience as well as comfort for their children. Now let me show you a stroller that is first choice with mothers everywhere. This is it — Folda-Rola, a stroller you'll enjoy using.

Prospect: You say this is the first choice of mothers everywhere. What's so different about this stroller?

Salesman: I imagine Johnny's comfort and safety come first as far as you're concerned. Folda-Rola is designed for the baby. Now notice this floating seat. See, it really does float. There is no framing to hold it down. This is how Johnny can go over the bumps with ease. The back and sides of the seat are made of sturdy canvas. See how high and strong they are?

Prospect: Yes.

Salesman: That will give the baby the most comfort and support. Now this canvas seat is removable and washable. That's very useful, isn't it?

Prospect: It sure is with that boy of mine.

Salesman: Now for safety, the seat is real deep and this strong plastic safety strap can be used. But the best safety feature is this long wheel base. It gives the stroller plenty of stability and makes it almost impossible to tip over the stroller, Now this Folda-Rola will help your Johnny to walk. Let me show you. Just remove this sanitary feeding tray and the footrest (demonstrates). See, it takes just a couple of seconds. Isn't that easy and fast?

Prospect: Yes, I've never seen one like this.

Salesman: These are just a few of the ways Folda-Rola was designed with the *baby* in mind. Of course, I haven't mentioned the attractive beads, the arm rests, and some of the other features. But Folda-Rola was not designed with only the baby in mind.

Prospect: What do you mean?

Salesman: Well, it's easier for *you* to use. See these large rear wheels? They are designed to take the curbs and steps with ease. And the front wheels swivel around completely. That makes the stroller easier for you to steer. Watch me turn these front wheels (turns the wheels). I guess I don't have to tell you how convenient this large market basket will be. Notice how easily I can snap it on and off (demonstrates). Now this telescopic handle was designed for mothers both short and tall. By turning this little thing here, you can adjust it to any height you want. This should be right for you. (Fixes handle.) Try it.

Prospect: Yes, that's about right.

Salesman: But the best thing about the Folda-Rola is the way it folds. Let me show you (demonstrates). With just a flick of the finger and a downward push, the handle snaps under the beads. Now you notice I did the complete operation with one hand. This means you'll be able to fold or unfold the stroller while holding Johnny. That's certainly designing with the mother in mind, isn't it?

Prospect: It sure is. That's about three times faster than I can fold mine. It really is quite compact when it is folded.

Salesman: Well, Mrs. Brown, that's one of the many conveniences of Folda-Rola. You can tuck it behind the door or under the bed or in any out-of-the-way space. I imagine with your other stroller being so bulky and hard to handle you don't go as many places with Johnny as you'd like to.

Prospect: I never stroll him any farther than the supermarket. My husband has the car all day, so we stay pretty close to home.

Salesman: You know, Mrs. Brown, it was for mothers like you that Folda-Rola was designed. The fellow who designed it got tired of having his wife wrestle it into and out of the car when they traveled. So he decided to design a stroller that would be light and would fold up easily. This Folda-Rola is the result of his idea. Here, feel for yourself how light it is.

Prospect: Gosh, it is light. How much does it weigh?

Salesman: The actual weight is 10 pounds, 12 ounces, just a little more than a newborn baby. So you see, Mrs. Brown, this means you'll now be able to go more places and do the things you've wanted to do. I really believe that you'll discover that wherever you go or however you go, Folda-Rola can go along too. I know you're going to want one of these Folda-Rola strollers. Don't you think you would like this one?

Prospect: Well, it certainly would be nice to have one, but I think I'll get along for a while with the one I have.

Salesman: Don't you think the Folda-Rola has more advantages than any other stroller?

Prospect: Yes, but I don't see how I could afford to own two strollers.

Salesman: That, Mrs. Brown, is the beauty of Folda-Rola. You see, not only was it designed with both the baby and mother in mind, but also the *father's pocketbook.* The price is only $16.95. Now that's a low price for such a high-quality stroller, isn't it?

Prospect: Well, frankly, I did think it would be more. I think I'd like to talk it over with my husband tonight.

Salesman: You know that he'll want you to have a stroller that is so comfortable and safe for the baby and convenient for you. I'm sure that he would be happily surprised if you brought this Folda-Rola home tonight. Or I could send it out to your house if you would like.

Prospect: Well . . . I guess he would say it was all right, and it certainly would be more convenient. I will take it.

Salesman: Would you like to pay cash or use a check?

Prospect: I'll write you a check. I think I'll take the Folda-Rola with me now. I want to surprise my husband.

Salesman: Thank you, Mrs. Brown. I know he'll like it, and it will certainly be more convenient for you.

QUESTIONS.

1. What did the salesman do well?
2. What did the salesman do that could be improved?
3. What techniques are illustrated in the sale?
4. Which principles of demonstrating did the salesman observe? Violate?

CHAPTER 14

HANDLING OBJECTIONS

Because an individual's wants are unlimited and his purchasing power is limited, a salesman meets resistance from prospects in his attempts to sell. This prospect resistance may be active or passive, expressed or implied. In any event, it is of basic significance because it is why the prospect does not buy at once. Viewed from a different angle, prospect resistance is a test of skillful, effective salesmanship. In everyday selling, a salesman encounters resistance which acts as a bar between him and a sale. It is this resistance that this chapter considers.

The opposition that the salesman finds tends to be of a *product* type or of a *prospect* type. In the first category are all of the dislikes the prospect has for the product. He may not care for the size or the color; he may look upon the manufacturer of the product with disfavor; he may feel the complexity of the product too great for him or the price too high. Prospect-type opposition involves the prospect's need of the product. Here the prospect may be unaware of his need, in which case it must be pointed out to him; he may be reluctant to agree that the salesman's product fills that particular need; and all too frequently he refuses to admit that he should buy *now*.

The hostile statements or objections made to the salesman may or may not be the real barrier which is preventing the purchase. Rather than admit that he feels unable to afford the product, the prospect may tell the salesman that the color is wrong. Rather than admit that he is a procrastinator who shrinks from making a decision, the prospect may plead that he first must talk things over with his wife. Hence, one of the salesman's first objectives is to identify and isolate the real reason that the prospect refuses to buy.

The objections a prospect voices are extremely helpful. They are, viewed in one light, merely his way of asking for more information and of pointing out the area that needs more illumination. As requests for information, they present the salesman with opportunities to expand his story of what the product will do for the prospect and why the prospect should have that product immediately.

WHY BUYERS OFFER OPPOSITION

All salesmen meet buyer resistance and opposition. Indeed, neither selling nor salesman is needed where these two factors are not present because, in those circumstances, buyers *buy*. Success in selling consists of disposing of buyers' resistance. There is nothing more basic in selling than for the salesman to resign himself to buyer resistance in the forms of silence, questions, and objections. Since opposition will be a problem so long as a salesman sells, it is well for a salesman to learn all he can about it and to become skillful in handling it.

Much resistance is the result of the buyer's not knowing enough about his needs and about products that might answer those needs. He must have more information before he can grasp the salesman's ideas about need and product. He needs more understanding of his needs and of the benefits the salesman promises before he can appreciate the salesman's product for what it really is and does. Sometimes the information a buyer has is not accurate. Sometimes there is not enough of it. So long as the buyer remains ignorant, his motivation will remain weak.

When a buyer does not understand a salesman's story, that buyer will probably offer opposition to buying. Such difficulty is clearly the salesman's fault. He should have snared and held the buyer's attention. He should have told such a clear story that the buyer easily understood it.

Buyers are reluctant to change their habit patterns. They work themselves down into ruts and prefer to stay there. They adopt a way of life and stick to it, repeating the same actions time after time. They are not interested in making a change. For some buyers, the voicing of objections has itself become a habit. These buyers give all salesmen at least some token opposition whether or not they are going to buy.

Some opposition is presented in order to check on the salesman's knowledge of his product and on his ability to answer objections. Sometimes the buyer is really asking for justification for the purchase he wants badly to make. Or, at the other extreme, he may be trying to justify *not* buying now.

Personal preference and prejudice can cause buyer resistance. Differences of opinion exist in buyers' minds about the quality and suitability of various products. Some buyers believe that certain competing products are superior to the one every salesman is selling, and such beliefs cause opposition.

Finally, buyers are often afraid to buy. They fear the product may not perform as the salesman claims, or that the salesman will benefit more from the transaction than they will. They fear that soon after the purchase they will see a new product and wish that they had waited to buy. Every buyer has had each of these three experiences. By opposing purchase suggestions, the buyers hope to get rid of the salesman without buying. Or, they hope to avoid buyer obligation, which so often leads to a purchase. In any event, fear of future contingencies produces hesitation and opposition.

After glancing at these causes of objections, it should be clear that an objection does not mean that the prospect does not need the product or that he does not want it. The prospect objects in the majority of cases because he lacks information. He may be unconscious of a need that the salesman's product will fill, or he may need help in justifying the purchase, either to himself or others. Particularly will he want satisfactory answers to hurl at those who criticize the purchase or who demand an accounting for it. Furthermore, he wants assurance that what he is doing is right, and this frequently means that a doubt of his must be dispelled by the salesman with facts or suggestions.

OBJECTIONS SHOULD BE WELCOME

Instead of being liabilities, objections can be turned into both assets and opportunities by the skillful salesman. First of all, selling is made easier when the prospect objects, because the prospect who talks to the salesman is easier to deal with than the silent prospect. When a prospect refuses to take part in the conversation, the salesman is in the dark about the impression he is making, about points that are obscure and need amplification, about facts to stress, and about buying motives to excite. The dangerous objections are those not disclosed. Second, objections indicate that the salesman is making some progress. A sound generalization is that the objecting prospect is the interested prospect, that he is beginning to experience desire, and that he is giving thought to the salesman's story. A third reason that objections should be welcome is that their successful handling increases a young salesman's confidence. Fourth, each objection gives the salesman one more peg on which to hang reasons for buying. Finally, objections throw light on the prospect's thinking. By underlining the buying decisions that are missing, they indicate what is needed before the salesman can close the sale. For these reasons, it should be clear that the salesman need not wilt when confronted by objections. It is probably safe to say that 90 per cent of all sales are made after the prospect has voiced an objection.

Because he is going to welcome objections, the salesman will find it profitable to cultivate certain attitudes and abilities. He will be courteous so as not to antagonize the prospect. He will develop respect for objections. Poise will be found desirable in order to avoid becoming annoyed or flustered, rattled or confused. Tact will be helpful in preventing the manifestation of anger or exasperation. All in all, what the salesman needs most is a sympathetic understanding of what an objection really is.

Instead of fearing objections, then, the proper reaction of a salesman is that of welcoming them. This means that he will encourage the prospect to speak what is on his mind. He will treat all questions and negative statements as requests for information. He will use objections as a map and compass for his future course.

EXCUSES VERSUS OBJECTIONS

Before a salesman can close a sale, he must identify any real obstacle that stands between the prospect and a purchase, and then remove it from the prospect's mind. All too frequently, apparent obstacles are only excuses. Those that are excuses merely waste a salesman's time if he handles them directly and in detail. If the salesman answers one, then the prospect thinks up another.

What Is an Excuse?

An excuse is insincere resistance offered by a prospect; it is not the real obstacle to his buying. Sometimes it is an attempt to dismiss the the salesman. Sometimes the prospect is rationalizing his resistance to buy, as, for example, when he hates to admit that he usually buys a lower price-line, or that he does not have the authority needed to buy, or that he has no money with him. Sometimes the excuse is only a buying defense erected by the prospect who feels that he should offer some resistance even when he knows that he is going to buy. On occasions when the prospect displays an amazing lack of interest in the salesman's answer to the objection, the prospect's spoken resistance was probably no more than a mere buying defense. Stock criticisms are often voiced by prospects. They either repeat what they have heard from someone else, or they want to see how the salesman answers them, or they do not care to take the time to analyze themselves in order to identify their real resistance.

How to Identify Excuses

Unfortunately, there is no single test which will quickly and surely separate excuses from objections. Two different buyers could indicate resistance to purchasing by using exactly the same statements, yet in one case the resistance would be an excuse, while in the other it would be an objection. A salesman must learn that to detect excuses he must depend on his own keen observation, on his own shrewd interpretation of each buyer's words and manner, and, broadly, on experience. The acquisition of greater skill in solving this problem of identifying *excuse* opposition is comparable to many other kinds of progress in personal selling — it can come only as a result of much trial and many errors.

There are two techniques which help a salesman to cope with this problem. Although neither is foolproof, each is worth mastering. The first technique is that of tactful questioning; the second makes use of what is best described as the parallel track answer.

Tactful Questioning. The salesman's use of questions was recommended earlier in connection with his telling of his sales stories. The same basic tactic, questioning, is just as strongly recommended in the handling of opposition or resistance, particularly so in the salesman's attempts to determine what is excuse and what is serious objection. So often a buyer lays down a smoke screen by voicing some token reluctance to buying — he wants to save face, or to feel important, or to help rationalize some other purchase he knows he will soon make. Questions help the salesman get behind this smoke screen and probe for any serious objection the buyer has concealed. When asked skillfully, questions can help a buyer clear up his thinking and arrive at a sound decision. By including questions the answers to which the buyer must agree with, a salesman sometimes can help a buyer realize that what seemed to be a valid reason for not buying is nothing more than an excuse. Questions give the salesman facts, and no salesman can deal successfully with resistance unless he has correct and adequate information about the nature of that resistance.

The "Why" Question. The word *why* is one of the salesman's strongest allies. It is absolutely essential in his vocabulary. This one-word question helps clear up the issues between salesman and buyer. It gets the buyer to indicate where he stands. It subtly recommends to the buyer that he think more seriously about the salesman's proposals. Qualified prospects are attempting to mask their real convictions when they make such statements as these:

I'll talk it over.   I'm satisfied.
I'm not interested.   I'll think it over.
I can't afford it.   I'll let you know.
I'm too busy to talk.   I'm well fixed just now.

These are excuses. By asking a *why* question, the salesman often learns why the buyer feels as he does or answered as he did. The salesman must identify the real barrier before he can decide intelligently how to proceed.

The Additional Question. If a salesman strongly suspects that the buyer's voiced resistance is a mere excuse, there is much merit and little risk in asking the buyer to reveal his *real* reason for not buying. A buyer may, for example, be using a respectable excuse to hide a prejudice or attitude he prefers not to reveal. On the other hand, he may be raising a dummy barrier to cover his ignorance or his inertia. In such cases, the salesman is not interested in tampering with the buyer's feeling or belief as expressed in the excuse — but the salesman *must* change the buyer's thinking on the hidden objection. So, the salesman asks, "Mr. Buyer, is there any other reason in addition to the one you mentioned — any additional reason for your wanting to wait?" Another version that has been used successfully is, "Isn't there something else, too, holding you back?" Buyers do not seem to resent such questions. In an amazing number of instances, buyers will reveal their other, their *real* explanation for refusing to buy.

The Parallel Track Answer. In addition to tactful questioning, there is another method of separating excuses from objections, a method which also permits a salesman to make some strong sales points. Suppose that a buyer asks the salesman a hostile question or makes an unfavorable comment about some specific matter. If the salesman believes this resistance to be in the nature of an excuse, and if he chooses to reply to the buyer with a parallel track answer, the salesman will not answer the exact resistance voiced by the buyer. Instead, he will comment on a sales point quite close to the buyer's opposition. He answers on a *parallel* track — not on the *same* track.

Here are some examples of parallel track answers. A buyer complains about a product's design; the salesman answers by talking about the raw materials that go into the product. Another buyer disapproves of the stand the salesman's company takes on labor unions; the salesman answers by describing the company's labor force — how skilled the workers are and what fine craftsmanship they build into the company's products. Still another buyer finds fault with the price of the salesman's product; the salesman replies that he is glad the buyer brought up the matter of price and suggests that they review what goes on back at the factory — the place where the matter of price actually starts. Sometimes a buyer accuses the salesman's company of running weak advertising; the salesman replies, "Let me tell you about our advertising agency, the folks who build those ads for us. They are the brains and the imagination back of our advertising." A final example involves the *product* decision:

> *Buyer:* I'm not interested in your Ajax make of electric razor — I understand the Acme razor gives a closer shave.

> *Salesman:* Mr. Buyer, let me tell you some news about our Ajax electric razors, news that my company just sent me. The American Testing Lab — you've heard of it — has just run an exhaustive set of tests and has found that the typical shaver can actually give himself a

closer shave with the Ajax electric shaver than he can with a *blade!* That's the kind of close shave you want to be able to give yourself, isn't it?

Throughout the parallel track answer, the salesman acts as though he is answering the real question bothering the buyer. He asks for agreement whenever such seems appropriate. At the conclusion of the answer, the salesman asks for general agreement and implies that the buyer's opposition has been handled to the buyer's satisfaction.

What Is an Objection?

An objection is the *real* reason the prospect has not said "Yes" to one of the five buying decisions. It is in the nature of an indicator that points to the buying decision still missing. The objection signifies interest because it is valid and true; it must be handled to the prospect's satisfaction before he will buy.

HOW AND WHEN TO HANDLE OBJECTIONS

Just as there is no single, speedy test which will separate objections from excuses, there is likewise no single technique for coping with either. In one sense, every excuse or objection should be handled. This does not mean that each should be answered, and most certainly it does not mean that the excuse or objection should be featured. Each of the general methods now listed will be effective in some situations. Unless otherwise specified, throughout the rest of this chapter the word "objection" will be used to include both real objections and excuses.

Future Handling

Ignore. It is not always necessary to answer an objection immediately. Instead, the salesman may choose to *disregard* the objection the first time it is made. In passing up the objection, the salesman can make no comment at all, simply appearing not to hear it, or he can say "yes" with no change of facial expression, and continue his presentation.

Ignoring the objection is one way of separating the real from the artificial. If the prospect's objection was a trumped-up excuse used just to change the subject or just to interrupt the salesman's story, it probably will not be mentioned again. Indeed, if it was phony, there is no reason for the salesman to answer it.

In some cases, the prospect gets the idea that the objection was not important enough to register on the salesman or to impress him. By not stopping to handle it, the salesman keeps the objection from appearing to be a big issue and thus tacitly suggests that it not be brought up again.

Sometimes when an objection is raised, the salesman can ignore it and immediately make his recommendations on the quantity and price he thinks the prospect should order, being careful to suggest larger amounts or higher price-lines than the prospect will buy. This encourages the prospect to switch from his first objection to objecting to the quantities and prices recommended.

There is one thing the salesman can count on when he ignores an objection — if the prospect is serious he will repeat his objection.

Postpone. Postponing the answer to an objection may help the salesman in more ways than one. Resistance, when set aside for a few moments, often evaporates. Also, the delay allows the salesman to establish more buyer-benefits before taking up a negative, hostile matter, thus reducing its significance. Finally, by postponing the handling until some later moment, the salesman maintains control of the interview and is confronted by the obstacle at a time of his own choosing. As has been mentioned, the postponement must not resemble evasion.

Admit Ignorance. When the salesman does not have an answer for an objection, he should acknowledge his lack of information. To admit ignorance *occasionally* is amazingly effective.

Immediate Handling

Direct Answer. For some salesmen, for some prospects, for some objections, and for some situations, an immediate, direct answer, complete yet compact, is the proper method of handling. It is unfortunate that these circumstances and occasions cannot be described in sufficient detail so that they can be recognized by salesmen. One big advantage of this technique is that it convinces the prospect of the salesman's sincerity. In addition, it prevents any inference of evasion or inability to answer. A third advantage is that when quick, deft handling is accompanied by courteous and intelligent consideration, it frequently kills objections before they establish themselves in the prospect's mind. A further point is that once the prospect realizes that his objection was really no objection at all, he can concentrate completely on the rest of the salesman's story. Lastly, quick and final handling keeps the salesman out of by-ways and off the defensive.

If the salesman knows the prospect to be opinionated, easily angered, or narrow-minded, a bold denial or a head-on clash may be entirely too risky to use. Whenever one is used, smiles and tact are essential to success.

Indirect Answer. This method of handling objections is probably the most widely recommended, the most widely used, and the most effective. It is versatile, flexible, and safe. Basically, it involves two steps. The first is for the salesman to agree with the objection with some such remark as "That's true" or "Yes," and the second is to follow up with "but" or "however" as a point of departure into a different area for consideration, an area that leads right back into the salesman's selling story.

The salesman's "Yes" implies an attitude of respect for the prospect's viewpoint, and the "but" suggests that the salesman has certain related facts which may not have come to the prospect's attention. The salesman agrees with the prospect as far as he can, admitting that there may be some truth in what the prospect says, and then he points out some other factors which must be considered. After giving some ground in opening his reply, the salesman tactfully proceeds to show how the prospect's particular case is different.

On occasion, the salesman, instead of agreeing with the prospect's entire statement, will choose to agree with only part of it, showing that, when all facts are considered, the soundest conclusion is not exactly the one drawn by the prospect. Instead of arguing, the salesman tries to show that the prospect's conclusion does not apply in this case.

No prospect likes to be told that he is wrong and then be corrected in a blunt fashion. He thinks of himself as being wooed by the salesman, and expects the salesman to go out of his way to be nice. In many cases, the prospect will even want the salesman to be impressed by his shrewd and rugged opposition.

The principle of this technique is, naturally, that concession on the salesman's part will influence the prospect to be more receptive. The beauty of it is that by expressing his understanding of the prospect's position, the salesman encourages the prospect to listen to him.

SOME TECHNIQUES FOR HANDLING OPPOSITION

Fail to Hear

As was pointed out, this works best on *excuses*. It should not be used if the salesman knows the buyer's resistance to be genuine.

Compare Products

When the buyer is mentally comparing his present product with the salesman's product, or when he is comparing some competing product with the salesman's product, the salesman himself may make a complete comparison of the two. He lists the advantages and disadvantages of each. He will take care to see that the buyer, in his thinking, is comparing the salesman's product with the correct competing product.

Give a Case History

Here the salesman describes the experience of another buyer, much like the buyer to whom he is talking. The tactic is the same as that mentioned in the "proof" part of advantage-proof-action in Chapter 12.

Demonstrate

A product demonstration is a terrifically convincing answer to a product objection. The salesman lets the product itself refute the buyer's opposition. He reminds the buyer that the proof of a pudding is in the eating.

Guarantee

Often a guarantee will remove resistance from the buyer's mind. Guarantees reassure buyers that they can't lose. The advertising copywriters know this and use it when they headline "Corns Gone in 5 Days — Or Money Back."

Ask Questions

The value of the *why* question in separating excuses from genuine objections and in probing for hidden resistance has already been mentioned. The same question is useful in disposing of objections. Probing or exploratory questions are excellent in handling *silent* resistance. They can be worded and asked in a manner that appeals to the buyer's ego. In making the buyer do some thinking and giving him the job of convincing the salesman, questions of a probing nature get the buyer's full attention.

Show What Delay Costs

A common experience of salesmen is to get seemingly sincere agreements to the first four buying decisions of *need, product, source,* and *price,* only to find that the buyer wants to wait a while before buying. In many such cases, the salesman can take pencil and paper and show conclusively that delay is expensive.

Admit and Counterbalance

Sometimes the prospect's objection is 100% true and real, and that's all there is to it. If cheaper substitutes can be had, if other colors or sizes are available in competing products, or if our salesman's product weighs less (or more) than other similar products, those may well be facts that both buyer and salesman know. The only course of action for the salesman is to agree that his product has the disadvantage or handicap that is obvious. Immediately, however, the salesman can direct the buyer's attention to the many plus points and advantages which are so successful in overshadowing this one disadvantage that they make our salesman's product still the best buy. The salesman does not *remove* the opposition — he *overbalances* it with good points.

Hear the Prospect Out

Buyers may object mainly for the opportunity to describe how they once were victimized by the salesman, or by his predecessor, or by his company. They may think they have been wronged. On the other hand, buyers may have ideas and opinions they want to express. In some instances they want to talk about themselves — or, perhaps, just to talk. The technique recommended for this type of resistance or barrier is that of sympathetic listening. Once the buyer has talked himself out by unburdening what was on his chest, he is usually easy to handle.

Don't Overdo Point-Blank Denial

To contradict a buyer, to tell him immediately that his claim is not true may prove the salesman's sincerity, faith, and knowledge, but it's very risky as a selling tactic. Many successful salesmen never use it, and no good salesman uses it often. Persons just don't like to be contradicted, even when they are wrong. Above all, they don't want to be contradicted and proved wrong by someone who wants to trade *something* for *money*.

Denials are blunt and, hence, irritating. One can come closest to justifying them when the objection is false, or when the buyer's information is limited or sketchy. In using them, the salesman must be diplomatic, he should lead up to the denial in a gradual, pleasant way, he must smile, and he may well elect to use a light, even a kidding manner.

Admit Ignorance

Buyers can ask questions which salesmen can't answer. For the salesman to admit, "Really, I don't have the answer to that question" gets excellent buyer-reaction because it underlines the salesman's frankness and honesty. Buyers are attracted to that type of salesmen. There must not be too many of these answers, and the salesman should always offer to dig up the answers for the buyer.

Offer a Trial

When buyers are afraid to buy now, that fear can often be dissolved by offering the buyer a trial of the product. Let him take the product,

STEP 1   LISTEN THRU -- DON'T INTERRUPT -- BE INTERESTED!
- because - a. WE LESSEN THE OBJECTION BY LISTENING - "DEFLATE" IT.
     b. LISTENING ALLOWS BUYER TO "LET OFF STEAM" - "RELIEVE PRESSURE."
     c. LISTENING IS A COURTESY - COMPLIMENT TO BUYER.
     d. LISTENING PREVENTS AN ARGUMENT - INTERRUPTING PRODUCES ARGUMENT.
     e. LISTENING PROVIDES US WITH "TARGET TO SHOOT AT."
     f. LISTENING MAY PROVIDE US WITH NEW PROSPECT INFORMATION.

STEP 2 -A-   USE A "CONVERTER STATEMENT" -- WE CONCEDE BEFORE WE CONTEND --
WE PRECEDE OUR "BUT" WITH "BUTTER."
- because - a. IT AVOIDS A "CLASH" OR "COLLISION OF MINDS."
     b. IT COMPLIMENTS, FLATTERS THE BUYER AND HIS THINKING.
     c. IT "BUILDS HIM UP" RATHER THAN "SHOWS HIM UP."
     d. IT QUIETS HIM - DISARMS HIM - HE "LOWERS HIS DUKES."
     e. IT CREATES A "RECEPTIVE" RATHER THAN "BELLIGERENT" MOOD -
       CALMS HIS FEARS AND REOPENS HIS MIND.

- O R -

-B-   RESTATE OBJECTION IN OUR OWN WORDS, BUT IN THE FORM OF A QUESTION
BEING ASKED BY BUYER.
- because - a. AN OBJECTION INVITING AN ARGUMENT IS CONVERTED INTO A QUESTION
       INVITING AN ANSWER. WE ANSWER RATHER THAN ARGUE.
     b. THIS FURTHER COMPLIMENTS THE BUYER AND HIS OPINION.
     c. THIS FURTHER CLARIFIES AND SECURES MUTUAL UNDERSTANDING OF THE
       QUESTION.
     d. FURTHER "DEFLATION" TAKES PLACE.
     e. BUYER'S SELF-ESTEEM IS UNHURT WHEN WE ANSWER HIS QUESTION
       INSTEAD OF PROVING HIM WRONG.

STEP 3   SUBMIT THE SOLUTION -- IF POSSIBLE, USE SOFTLY CITED TESTIMONY OF
A NEUTRAL THIRD PARTY AS A "COLLISION CUSHION."

SOLUTION ALMOST ALWAYS AVAILABLE THRU:
   SUCCESS STORIES   OTHER EVIDENCE
   MORE BENEFITS   NEW DATA   OTHER CONVINCING PROOF

USING THIRD PARTY (SUCCESS STORY) AS "CUSHION" -
     a. AVOIDS AN ARGUMENT -
     b. KEEPS BUYER'S MIND OPEN -
     c. SAVES BUYER'S PRIDE -
     d. MAKES IT EASIER FOR BUYER TO CHANGE HIS MIND -
       OBJECTION LOSES FORCE WITHOUT BUYER LOSING FACE.

TO COMPLETELY OVERCOME OBJECTIONS - WE MUST:
     a. KEEP OUR TEMPER ON ICE - QUICKEST WAY TO "COOK OUR OWN
       GOOSE" IS WITH A "BOILING" TEMPER.
     b. COMPLETELY ANSWER AND SATISFY BUYER.
     c. CONVERT THE OBJECTION TO OUR ADVANTAGE.

STEP 4   HAVING OVERCOME THE OBJECTION AND PROVIDED WE HAVE GOTTEN SOME
GOOD BENEFITS ON THE "BUYER'S SCALE" -- WE

"SUGGEST" ACTION BY THE BUYER

IF ACTION IS NOT FORTHCOMING, WE "GET BACK ON THE TRACK" BY
CONTINUING OUR PLANNED PRESENTATION FROM THE PLACE IT WAS
INTERRUPTED BY THE BUYER'S OBJECTION.

(right margin, vertical:) CODE NO. TF - 32 - B23   PAGE NO. 1   TECHNIQUE FOR HANDLING "BUYER'S OBJECTIONS"   SALES TRAINING CONFERENCE   FLEISCHMANN DIVISION

Standard Brands, Inc.

use it for a week, and then, if unhappy, return it and go back to his former ways of doing things — if he can. Very often after a week's use of a product, the potential buyer comes to regard it as a necessity.

Make It Boomerang

Once in a while the salesman can take a buyer's *reason for not buying* and convert it into a *reason for buying*. This takes expert handling lest the buyer be made to feel that he's too dumb to know one from the other. Here are two stock examples:

> *Buyer:* I'm too busy to see you.
> *Salesman:* That's why you *should* see me — I can save you time.
> *Buyer:* I can't afford your product.
> *Salesman:* You can't afford the danger and risk of being without it.

Use the "Yes, . . . but"

By far the best technique for handling most resistance is the indirect answer known as the *Yes, . . . but* method discussed earlier under "When and How to Handle Objections." Here are two examples:

> *Salesman: Yes*, I can understand that attitude, *but* here is another angle for you to consider.
> *Salesman: Yes*, you have a point there, *but*, in your particular circumstances, other points are involved, too.

The beauty of the *Yes, . . . but* method is that it avoids argument and friction. It does its job without offending or irritating. It respects the buyer's opinions, attitudes, and thinking. It operates perfectly where the buyer's point does not apply in his particular case.

PRINCIPLES TO OBSERVE

Clarify

Before attempting to answer any objection, the salesman must have a clear understanding of just what the prospect meant. A difficult problem is presented when the prospect has a real objection yet will not disclose it, hiding behind such excuses as "Not interested," "Not in the market," or "No time to see you." One way to get this information is to urge the prospect to talk himself out and to air fully what he has on his mind. Another resort of the salesman is diplomatically asking *what, where, who, how,* and *why.* A third course consists of alert, continuous observation until the real objection is identified.

It is often desirable for the salesman to restate the objection. This assures the prospect that his difficulty is understood. It gives the salesman a few seconds in which he can try to analyze the objection and determine what might be the best method of answering. Also, a brief restatement in the salesman's own words can be fair to the prospect and still allow the salesman to maintain better control of the dialogue and the thinking.

Classify

Genuine objections keep buyers from buying. The act of buying requires the buyer to make five affirmative buying decisions, as reviewed in Chapter 10. Putting these two thoughts together we see that objections point to the negative buying decisions. In other words, the salesman can tell from the type of objection which buying decisions are still to be made in the salesman's favor. Thus, as soon as the buyer seemingly raises genuine opposition to buying and the salesman feels that he understands just what the buyer is thinking, the salesman will see which buying decision the objection involves.

Need. Some objections clearly indicate that the buyer does not recognize any need or that he does not want to admit the existence of need. In other cases, the objection implies a belief on the part of the buyer that he has no needs that demand immediate attention.

Product. Some buyers show, through their resistance, that they believe competing products are better than our salesman's product. Similarly, the buyer may decide that the services that go with competing products are preferable to the services our salesman offers. Resistance of this nature indicates that the salesman has not successfully established buyer-need and then fitted his product and its accompanying services to that need.

Source. Opposition to source usually implies a lack of confidence and trust in the seller. It may be that the buyer does not have complete faith in the salesman as an individual, or it may mean that he has doubts and suspicions about the salesman's company. On occasion, prejudice causes trouble here.

Price. Objections to price mean that the salesman has not built up an acceptable amount of value or satisfaction for the price he is quoting. More selling may be needed on the buying decisions of *need* and *product*.

Time. Difficulty here can mean only one thing — the salesman must get more enthusiastic, more solid agreements on the first four buying decisions.

Maintain Control

Every salesman needs to recognize and acknowledge to himself that there are some prospects who will hide behind a host of objections which must be treated calmly. This necessitates control. The salesman's job is to take the prospect by the arm, slow him down, bring him to a mental halt, slowly turn him around, and then get him thinking in the same direction as the salesman.

The salesman easily loses control if he stops talking after answering an objection, or, worse, asks if there are any other questions or matters causing the prospect difficulty. That is simply asking for trouble. Instead of pausing, a better course of action is to resume selling immediately. This does not outlaw the practice of checking with the prospect to see that he understood and agreed with the salesman's answer.

Don't Argue

To argue is fatal. If the salesman wins the argument, he loses the prospect's goodwill, and, of course, if he loses the argument, he loses the sale. Because it is hopeless to antagonize someone and, at the same time, try to influence him favorably, it is never wise to take issue with prospects. Even when the salesman is right he runs a great risk in contradicting the prospect. Rebuttal by the salesman intensifies opposition, and prospects have an unfortunate way of becoming arbitrary when they lose a debate. Instead of arguing, it is far more effective for the salesman to blanket the prospect with questions so as to divert his thoughts and to bring out the weakness of his objection.

Be Diplomatic

Every objection is a challenge to the salesman in that the tendency may be for him to put the prospect on the defensive by making him justify his position. The prospect may not care to do this or may not be able to. Being forced to reverse his position offends his ego. When the prospect is in error, backing him up in a corner from which there is no honorable or face-saving escape usually results in antagonism and resentment.

Challenge, contradiction, or direct attack increase prospect opposition no matter how sound or logical the salesman's answer is. Whatever seems important to the prospect, even though silly and trivial, will help to shape his decision and, hence, must be handled with care. The salesman must so maneuver that the prospect can gracefully reverse himself without appearing ignorant or weak-willed.

Never should the salesman disagree with the prospect in such a manner as to offend. It is for this reason that "wisecracking" or any flippant or belittling answer is dangerous. A second form of disagreement that must not be allowed is the flat, blunt statement to the effect that the prospect is completely wrong. A third mistake is to make the matter in question a personal one in the "I'm right because I know more about it than you do" fashion.

Diplomacy requires the salesman to be conciliatory and to respect each prospect's self-respect and self-confidence. It demands that the salesman remove incorrect beliefs tactfully and replace them with true ones.

Fit Answer to Prospect

Because the salesman must give the objecting prospect a new opinion or concept which he can accept as a substitute for one of his former opinions, the salesman's chances of success are increased if he molds his answer to fit the prospect. There is a definite parallel between this tailoring job and the tailoring of the opening of the interview or the story.

Fitting the answer to the prospect consists of two phases. The first is the matter of the salesman's making certain that he understands the prospect's real difficulty and of convincing the prospect of that fact. This involves nothing more or less than a meeting of the two minds.

The second phase consists of phrasing the reply in whatever manner and words the prospect seems to prefer. Indeed, it must be remembered that the prospect's painful chore is to abandon an idea or belief which has clearly become untenable and then embrace a new one. This argues convincingly that answers will be more logical and persuasive if constructed in line with the prospect's own personality. There can be no good reason for handling the "It costs too much" objection in the same way when talking to a professional baseball player as when talking to a housewife. Their activities, their interests, their ambitions — even their vocabularies differ so widely. Similarly, well-informed prospects can be influenced by an explanation that would be over the head of a rather ignorant prospect. The rule must be that the prospect instead of the salesman guides in shaping the reply.

Don't Magnify

Objections should be minimized and not magnified. This is best done by handling each objection clearly and cleanly. If handling consists of answering it then and there, the salesman should go to no greater length than is necessary. He should check to see that the prospect understands and agrees and then immediately leave the objection. In saying just enough to dispose of the objection to the prospect's satisfaction, the salesman avoids dwelling on it and thereby exaggerating its importance. Any answer that is unnecessarily long, any explanation that goes into too much detail, encourages the prospect to overrate his idea.

At the other extreme, an attempt at complete avoidance can magnify the objection. If the prospect feels that the salesman cannot answer, or has been scored on, or even that the salesman is concerned, then he attributes more significance and more seriousness to his objection.

Two final ways of building up the objection are trying to destroy it or stamp it out by sheer force and returning to it later in the interview.

Capitalize the Objection

The salesman's assumption should be that an objection indicates a sincere interest and that, because of this, it can and should be used as a means of advancing the sale. He should be genuinely glad that the prospect brought up his particular objection, and he will frequently find it advantageous to tell the prospect that he *is* glad about it.

The principle is that never should an objection just be answered; the objection should be used constructively to bring out as many buyer-benefits as possible. In this way, each objection is used to bring the purchase closer. The salesman converts the objection into a reason for buying and capitalizes on it by translating it into a positive, specific justification for the purchase.

Two examples will illustrate how the salesman turns the tables on the prospect by taking an objection and transforming it into a reason for buying. In the first instance, a salesman for a home study course is told by the prospect, "But I don't make enough money to be able to take your course." The salesman's immediate rejoinder is, "That's why you need the course so much; with it, you'll make more money." In the second example, a retailer objects that there is not enough sidewalk traffic in front of his store to justify his buying some expensive window display equipment. The salesman comes back by saying that the absence of the equipment is responsible for the light sidewalk traffic.

In taking advantage of an objection, the salesman may deem it expedient to clarify some or all of the sales points he has already made. A second thing he might do is to review all of the advantages his product offers along the line of the particular objection. For example, when a prospect complains of high price, the salesman points out all of the many plus-points the buyer will enjoy, thus making the price seem extremely fair. Or when the prospect complains that the product is too small or weighs too little, the salesman immediately explains and stresses each advantage that results from his product's size or weight. A third method of cashing in on the objection is to offer more facts to the prospect. A fourth technique is to identify and isolate the buying motive that gave rise to the objection and then build up on that one motive as many buyer-benefits as possible, securing the prospect's agreement to each.

In capitalizing an objection, the salesman should never pause or hesitate after handling it. He should never strike an "ask me another" pose. Instead, he should do one of two things immediately. First, he will attempt to complete the sale at once if, in his own best judgment, he feels that the prospect is close enough to buying to warrant such an attempt. Usually, every time an important obstacle is removed, the salesman should try to consummate the sale. If a trial close is attempted and does not succeed, or if the salesman feels that it is yet too early to attempt to close, then the second course of action is recommended, which is to return to constructive selling. By moving on from his answer to additional selling points, the salesman helps to edge the prospect's objection out of his mind by inserting new plus-points.

List Objections and Answers

The objections commonly encountered in any one line of selling will seldom exceed ten or twelve. No more valuable suggestion can be offered than that junior salesmen list the objections they meet most often and write, in their own language, answers to each. Testing will then sort out the answers that are most effective.

PREVENTING OBJECTIONS

The best solution to objections is to prevent them. In the first place, this strategy keeps the prospect from doing any negative, unfavorable, or contentious thinking and talking. Second, his voicing of an objection at an awkward or regrettable moment is avoided. Thus, the salesman robs the prospect of any defensive objection which he might plan to conceal until the conclusion of the interview, at which time he would unveil the objection and use it as a justification for ending the conference without buying. Third, prevention makes more time available to the salesman for use in presenting a full, complete story. Fourth, the salesman appears completely fair in cases where he himself raises and answers an objection, or just weaves an answer into the presentation. Fifth and most important of all, the prospect is prevented from taking a position. Once an individual states what he thinks, he feels pressure to stick to his commitment and to defend it. He hates to appear easily influenced, to allow his mind to be changed with little trouble. That is too close to admitting that he was wrong.

How to Prevent Objections

The best plan to keep out objections calls for constructing and telling a complete story, a story that includes all the information the prospect will need. As is pointed out in the training material of Lever Brothers:

OBJECTIONS CAN'T HINDER A SALE...

... IF YOU DISPOSE OF THEM *in* YOUR SALES TALK!

The better sales talk you give, the fewer objections you will have. If you are getting a lot of objections from dealers regarding your plan, remember the trouble is not with the plan — it is with you. If you are getting a number of objections from dealer after dealer, there is something wrong with your sales presentation.

Then, in telling the story, the salesman should check with the prospect to insure that each point made is clear.

The salesman will note and list the most frequent and most troublesome objections encountered in his interviews. He will work into his original story the most effective answers to these most common questions, complaints, and criticisms. These answers should be in the form of positive selling points. Especially to be included in the original story will be strong plus-points about product features which competitive salesmen discount. When competition indicates to the prospect that it fails to be impressed by some aspect or characteristic of the salesman's product, competition is probably planting an objection or at least a doubt in that prospect's mind. It is this type of product feature which must be covered fully and favorably in the main story.

The clearer, more logical, and more complete the story is, the less important a prospect's objections seem to him. If his attention is monopolized by the huge mountain of plus-points and the very small pile of minus-points, the prospect will be inclined to consider the objections he planned to make far too insignificant to mention.

Although the rule is to anticipate objections and handle them in the main body of the story, there is one exception. If the salesman has a terrifically impressive and effective answer to a certain objection, he may omit from his original story all reference to that particular topic. Then, if the prospect voices that objection at the end, the salesman can give his irrefutable answer and try to close the sale.

If a salesman meets too many objections, call after call, his story may be vague, defective, and in need of overhauling.

EXAMPLES OF HANDLING OBJECTIONS

The final section of this chapter consists of examples of objections that are frequently encountered and answers that will, at times, be appropriate and successful. The objections are divided evenly among the five buying decisions.

Four things should be remembered. (1) The list is constructed of common objections, but it should not be considered complete, nor even as consisting of the thirty-five objections most often met.

(2) There are more than thirty-five techniques of handling objections. The use of the testimonial, for instance, is not included below, nor is the showing of a product report made by an independent commercial testing company. Each salesman has to assemble and master the assortment of techniques needed for his own use.

(3) Some techniques of handling are so adaptable that their use need not be restricted to just one objection, or even to just one buying decision. For example, relating a case history might be used in attempting to secure the prospect's affirmation to any of the five buying decisions.

(4) The quotations below are not all exactly true to life. Technical, detailed realism was sacrificed if and when such liberties seemed to make the point clearer for classroom use. Only as much of the salesman's reaction is included as is needed to show its general direction.

Buying Decision No. 1 — Need

Example No. 1.

Prospect: "But this Super De Luxe tire of yours is priced much too high for my store."

Comments: Prospects are frequently wrong in this belief. There are many points our salesman can make in reply. The prospect is under-stocked, not overstocked, if he makes no play for the quality market. The higher dollar markup can be stressed. Proof of de-mand can be offered. Because the public considers the Super DeLuxe a leader, it will give the store prestige and easy selling. The tire is a challenge to the prospect's pride and ego. One of the best ways to increase profit is to build up repeat buying by cus-tomers who will pay a reasonable price for good quality. And no manufacturer has learned how to make good quality merchandise at low quality prices.

Technique: *Point out a new market.*

Salesman: "Some buyers here are going to have the best, even if only for exhibitionism. Such individuals are preferred customers because of the truth of the old saying that quality is remembered long after price has been forgotten. This Super DeLuxe tire will get for you some profitable additional business that is now going to another store."

Example No. 2.

Prospect: "I'm not interested in a new furnace."

Comments: This can mean that the prospect is not willing to make the sacrifice that buying would demand. It may mean that he is unaware of his needs, or uninformed about what the salesman's product will do for him. It may camouflage a lack of product understanding on the part of the prospect, or a lack of ambition. Often it is a mere excuse.

The "I'm not interested" comment definitely cannot mean that the prospect is not interested in health, wealth, popularity, econ-omy, comfort, safety, convenience, and the like. So the salesman's job is to find where product-satisfaction touches and stimulates one or more of the prospect's buying motives.

Technique: *Relate product to prospect's buying motive.*

Salesman: "Of course you're not interested in a new furnace — but you are interested in economical heating, aren't you?"

Example No. 3.

Prospect: "Really, I don't need to handle another line of canned soup."

Comments: Prospects often do not know that they lack something. It is risky to take issue with them over whether they need the salesman's product. Instead, the salesman should feed examples to the prospects, relating the experiences and case histories of impartial, similar third parties. Prospects can be counted on to recognize the similarity between their own needs and those of the salesman's satisfied customers. Need must be established before any other consideration can be discussed seriously.

If an individual cannot use the salesman's product to advantage, he does not need it and, hence, is not a prospect. When a salesman has the misfortune to spend time on a person only to find that need does not exist, then the only thing to do is to start a search for a person who *is* a prospect.

Technique: *Case History.*

Salesman: "Before you make that decision a permanent one, let me tell you about another grocery store very similar to yours. Its owner decided to take on our line, even though he, like you, was not certain he was doing the right thing. Today, he is enthusiastic over our line because of the profit it nets him."

Example No. 4.

Prospect: "My customers don't ask here for toys."

Comments: When a retailer tells a salesman that he will handle his merchandise only after there is a demand for it, he is usually just trying to get rid of the salesman. It may not be too far away from the truth to say that no retailer has or can become a successful merchant if he waits until he gets calls before he will stock a product. His more progressive and aggressive competitors would take and hold too much of the local market. Because of the influence they enjoy with their customers, and because their advice is asked, retailers can and do move brand-new items.

The "boomerang" technique converts an objection into a reason for buying. It demands skilled handling and a friendly manner. It should be used sparingly; it can deflate the prospect's ego by making him appear wrong or almost stupid if the salesman implies that the prospect cannot tell the difference between reasons *for* and reasons *against*.

Technique: *Boomerang.*

Salesman: "No demand? Certainly not! You get no calls for toys because your customers know your drugstore does not stock them. They'd ask for them if you carried them. There's 'no demand' because you don't have toys."

Example No. 5.

Prospect: "I've never owned an electric stove."

Comments: If the salesman qualified the prospect, then the prospect needs the product, and it is the salesman's job to persuade the prospect to see his need. Where the salesman is calling to the prospect's attention a new or different type of product, he will have to demonstrate need positively and beyond question. One of his best bets for succeeding in establishing need is to contrast the prospect as he is now with how much happier he will be with the more numerous and better satisfactions provided by the salesman's type of product. The prospect must be led to agree that modern, far-sighted individuals must adopt the new methods called for by progress and development.

Technique: *Comparison.*

Salesman: "Then it's high time you considered making a change.   You'll never know what you've been missing until you try one.   Let's look at some of the differences you can expect."

Example No. 6.

Prospect: "I'm not in the market for any more insurance."
Comments: When a buyer takes this position, he is indicating that he sees no reason to take any buying action. He implies that he has examined his circumstances and feels that he has covered all his requirements.
Technique: *Agreement and diversion.*
Salesman: "Of course not.   If you were, you would have come to my office instead of my coming to yours.   But you have been thinking some about retirement, haven't you?"

Example No. 7.

Prospect: "Despite everything you told us, my wife and I have decided once and for all NOT to put in a swimming pool."
Comments: No big-league baseball player has ever batted 1.000 for a season. Similarly, no salesman makes a sale to every prospect he qualifies and sees.   Often the salesman will not know exactly why he was unable to make the sale.
Technique: *Admit defeat gracefully.*
Salesman: "Thank you so much for your time.   Goodby."

Buying Decision No. 2 — Product

Example No. 1.

Prospect: "I don't have much confidence in this stepladder.   It's so light I don't see how it could be safe."
Comments: Frequently, all a prospect needs is proof.   Logical proof is of certain value; testimonial proof is usually more effective; demonstration proof of what the product will do is the perfect answer where practicable.   Almost nothing removes doubts so completely as letting a product itself answer an objection, particularly if a test can be designed in which the prospect participates.
Technique: *Demonstration.*
Salesman: "You stand on any rung, and then I'll add my weight to yours. It will easily support the two of us."

Example No. 2.

Prospect: "Don't talk to me about that make of car!   The last one I had was a complete lemon.   I'll never buy another one."
Comments: When a prospect is bitter toward the salesman's make or brand, the salesman has a difficult job.   He must be conciliatory and in harmony with the prospect, yet he dare not appear disloyal to his own company and its merchandise.   Sometimes the salesman can point to product changes which make the prospect's criticism no longer valid.   Sometimes the changes have been not in product

but in circumstances, with the same result. Sometimes the salesman should encourage the prospect to "get it off your chest" by sympathetic listening. This process allows the prospect to rid his system of resentment by letting off pressure, and to unburden himself before an audience by airing his complaint completely. At the same time, this performance aids the salesman in two ways. It obligates the prospect to listen to the salesman's reply, and it provides tips and clues as to what that reply should be.

Technique: *Sympathetic listener.*
Salesman: "Tell me all about it."

Example No. 3.

Prospect: "Radio is okay, but I prefer newspapers."
Comments: The "indirect answer" technique was mentioned earlier in the chapter. The salesman agrees — then goes on to point out differences. He gives ground — then brings in a new thought.
Technique: *Yes, . . . but.*
Salesman: "Yes, I agree with you and the many other retailers who feel that newspapers are a good advertising medium. However, in radio, you won't be competing with another ad on the same page, you can schedule your message for any hour of the day, and the human voice is more persuasive than the written word."

Example No. 4.

Prospect: "I've heard that your fire extinguishers sometimes explode."
Comments: This technique, already commented on in this chapter, will seldom work if the objection is a valid bar to buying. Its chances are better where the objection is trivial, or heckling, or obviously an excuse.
Technique: *Ignore.*
Salesman: (Somewhat puzzled) "I never heard that before."
(After slight pause) "Now let's see how easy it is to use it."

Example No. 5.

Prospect: "To be truthful, I had in mind buying a better trunk."
Comments: Sometimes the only sound, sensible, and safe thing to do is to admit the merit of an objection, and then prove that this one minus-point is overwhelmed and rendered inconsequential by a host of plus-points. The prospect finds himself amazed and disarmed by the salesman's agreement — by being told that he has a point, or that there is something to what he says. Then the principle of compensation begins to operate, with the prospect's attention being directed to the advantages that more than counterbalance. The salesman makes no attempt to remove the objection; he shows that the one small sacrifice is eminently worth making.
Technique: *Admit and minimize.*
Salesman: "True, this trunk is not of the very highest quality that can be had. But the quality is indeed adequate, the trunk is durable and very roomy, and just think of the savings my low price gives you."

Example No. 6.

Prospect: "I stock the brand made here in the city and can substitute it when customers ask for your brand."

Comments: When a salesman recommends that a retailer begin stocking and selling his brand, seldom does the salesman have in mind recommending that the retailer discontinue handling any brand he now sells. Attempts to substitute don't always succeed; they can be expensive.

Technique: *Raise questions about substituting.*

Salesman: "The local brand is fine. Don't drop it. Just add *my* brand so you can make more money by serving those consumers who prefer it. *Some* of our consumers seem determined to have our brand and probably don't like to have their judgment questioned."

Example No. 7.

Prospect: "I don't know why I should buy genuine parts from your company when I can get non-genuine parts cheaper."

Comments: Motor trucks and farm equipment are two product lines in which the manufacturer's genuine parts encounter competition from parts made by other firms. Often the equipment manufacturer is at a competitive disadvantage pricewise.

Technique: *Imply that price reflects quality.*

Salesman: "What kind of a guarantee do the makers of off-brand parts give you? Are they as interested in quality and performance as they are in sales volume? Are their engineering standards as high as ours? Has a defective non-genuine part ever failed and caused you an expensive repair job?"

Buying Decision No. 3 — Source

Example No. 1.

Prospect: "Your company is too small."

Comments: Sometimes a diverting move benefits the salesman. One way to switch the prospect's mind away from his objection is to pass the conversational ball to him in the form of a question. The salesman can use the question to make certain that he has a clear understanding of the nature of the prospect's resistance and thus knows where more selling is needed. It makes the prospect commit himself, and that can be revealing. If the objection was a careless, spur-of-the-moment impulse, the salesman's question will discourage any more opposition of that type. Sometimes the salesman finds rumor, envy, or propaganda back of the objection. He will need to be tactful in cases where the prospect finds that his statement was foolish or pointless and not a valid objection.

Technique: *Question.*

Salesman: "Too small for what? How is it too small? Why?"

Example No. 2.

Prospect: "I hear your mill is deserting New England and moving South."

Comments: When the salesman does not have an answer, he should not try to stall or bluff, because sooner or later he will get caught, and that has long-lasting effects. A bald, quick admission impresses prospects favorably and, consequently, helps get and retain their confidence.

Technique: *Admit ignorance.*

Salesman: "I don't know about that because the big boys don't consult me on such matters. Whether it's true or not, our line of textiles will continue to be an excellent buy."

Example No. 3.

Prospect: "I'm going to add a line of electric razors, but I don't know which make it will be. I can't see much difference in razors, prices, or margins."

Comments: What a manufacturer does to win new consumers is always good news to retailers.

Technique: *Merchandising aid.*

Salesman: "Rather than talk about selling my brand *to* you, let me describe the advertising and merchandising aid my company supplies to sell my line *for* you."

Example No. 4.

Prospect: "I've been giving all my business to the ABC company for years and see no reason to change now."

Comments: Prospects who are fiercely loyal to their present suppliers are excellent customers (and hard-to-get ones) because of just that characteristic. Friendship between buyer and seller frequently is a feature, and a very difficult feature it can be for the salesman as he hunts for concrete, clear proof that the buyer should take on a new vendor. Incidentally, the prospect's feeling shows plainly that he thinks our salesman, our salesman's company, and our salesman's product are no better than those he now supports. The problems involved in buying from friends, the healthful effect of competition on present suppliers, the importance of not being dependent on a single source of supply, the desirability of a wider inventory, and the relatively greater importance of product over maker are possible lines of approach. Intelligent salesmanship demands that the salesman find why the prospect is so loyal and why he prefers to deal with the ABC company.

Technique: *Advantages of diversification.*

Salesman: "That's fine, because ABC is a good company. You might find, however, that if ABC had a bit of competition, you would stand to benefit. And the danger of putting all your eggs in one basket is something to think about."

Example No. 5.

Prospect: "I've heard that your company is going to lose the XYZ account over in Charlotte, and that the XYZ folks don't think much of what's happening. Is that true?"

Comments: The bald, flat denial of an objection should be included in the salesman's collection of techniques, but, because it is so risky, it should be used only by experienced salesman, and even then, only seldom. If what the prospect thinks or claims is completely untrue, if the destruction of the objection can be done quickly and to the complete satisfaction of the prospect, and if the salesman takes pains to remain pleasant, smiling, and controlled, then a diplomatically executed correction may be the right answer. When a salesman immediately shows the prospect to be in error, he proves his own sincerity but encourages argument — he increases the prospect's confidence but invites disharmony.

Technique: *Immediate refutation.*

Salesman: "Just a minute there, please. Someone has misinformed you. We are as solid as ever with XYZ. Call them up and ask them about it right now, at my expense, if you care to."

Example No. 6.

Prospect: "I don't like to buy from *big* manufacturers!"

Comments: In Example No. 1, the buyer argued that the salesman's firm was too small. *Now* a buyer claims that a salesman's firm is too large. He may or may not be serious. He may or may not have had an unhappy experience with a large supplier.

Technique: *Redirect attention from seller to buyer.*

Salesman: "Mr. Prospect, I don't know a single small manufacturer who stays small from choice. Let's forget size for a minute and talk about how much money we can help you make."

Example No. 7.

Prospect: "Sure, I split my buying six ways. I don't want all *my* eggs in the same basket."

Comments: For many buyers, the number of sellers from whom to buy a single product can be a troublesome question. The salesman has his own version of the answer. In order to break in, he recommends dispersal; once in, he recommends concentration — with *his* firm, of course.

Technique: *Summarize advantages.*

Salesman: "Yes, you buy from six of us — about $10,000 a year from each of us. This is not big business for any of our firms nor for the six of us salesmen who call on you. If you bought all your requirements from me, just look what that would do for you! You'd be one of the firm's most important customers and entitled to our most favored treatment. You'd be *my* most important customer and get extra services from me. Then think of the higher discount bracket you'd be in — reducing your buying prices. Just one statement to check and pay — just one salesman to see."

Buying Decision No. 4 — Price

Example No. 1.

Prospect: "That is entirely too much money to pay for a vacuum cleaner."

Comments: It is always well for the salesman to build up just as early as he can a large mass of value against which the prospect can measure price. The larger the mass and the lower the price, the more attractive the ratio seems. The salesman should never apologize for a high price. Instead of taking the defensive, he should point out how modest the price is in relation to what it buys. Some prospects relax a bit when they are told that instead of spending money, what they would be doing is making an investment. Other prospects like to be told that what they save will pay for the item. Purchase price is often minimized when reduced to small amounts by, for example, contrasting a pack of cigarettes with $500, or a four-cent stamp with a home study course.

Technique: *Spread cost over life of product.*

Salesman: "You can count on using this machine for a minimum of ten years. This means that the cost to you is a very modest sum of twenty cents a week."

Example No. 2.

Prospect: "I like this one fine, but I think it costs more than I can afford to pay for a television set."

Comments: Prospects frequently talk as though they must limit their examination to lower price lines even when the salesman well knows that the more expensive can easily be financed. One area recommended for more effort by the salesman is the quality area. He can point out that a quality product deserves a quality price, that his product is constructed according to high quality specifications, and that lower prices, for cheaper quality, can always be found.

The salesman may move completely away from the matter of price and drive toward getting the prospect familiar with the product, used to the product, and so dependent on the product that he will not give it up. Although the salesman may say that the prospect is not obligated to keep the item, and that may be technically true, he knows that some feeling of indebtedness will result in most cases.

Technique: *Free trial offer.*

Salesman: "Probably the best place to make that decision is in your own home. I'll send it out on trial for a few days at no obligation to you."

Example No. 3.

Prospect: "I'm afraid I'll never have $500 to spend for a fur coat."

Comments: So-called "easy" terms of payment need no comment as an exceedingly effective answer to large price. Features stressed are low down payment, small periodic payments, long pay period, low charge for the privilege, and, in general, the philosophy of paying out of income.

Technique: *Installment terms.*

Salesman: "You don't need $500. You can buy on our liberal budget plan and pay only a small amount each week while you are wearing and enjoying your coat."

Example No. 4.

Prospect: "You know I can't afford that."

Comments: Even though the prospect's idea is silly, ridicule of it may make the salesman appear to be unsympathetic. Ridicule is dangerous unless the salesman knows the resistance to be a stall or an excuse, or unless he has facts which disprove the prospect's statement. There is one type of ridicule mild enough for occasional use. With it, the salesman turns the prospect away from his objection promptly by suggesting that the prospect can't be serious, that he was mis-informed or heard some false rumors, or that he is joking.

As mentioned in Chapter 7, if a person actually cannot swing the purchase in any manner, then he does not qualify as a prospect.

Technique: *Ridicule.*

Salesman: "Really, how can a man who owns a big house and several auto-mobiles say things like that?"

Example No. 5.

Prospect: "Before we use up any of each other's time, let me get straight on one thing. How much will a cash register cost?"

Comments: It is neither desirable nor possible to ignore the fact that price is a tremendous obstacle for the higher-priced products. The sooner the salesman has to take up the topic, the greater the handicap for him. When he has to quote a rather high price early in the interview, it seems all the higher because he has not had time to describe all that the product will do for its user. The more firmly the salesman establishes the need-and-answer recognition and the more buyer-benefits he explains before referring to price, the more price becomes a detail.

Technique: *Postpone.*

Salesman: "I have them from $50 to $2000, so I can't quote a price to you until we see what model you need."

Example No. 6.

Prospect: "The Star Manufacturing Company quoted me a price that's lower than yours."

Comments: Few objections are encountered more often than this one. It may be true — or false. The items involved may be identical, or they may differ in quality and/or quantity.

Technique: *Stress value over price.*

Salesman: "I'm not surprised. They know better than anyone else what their product is worth. You *are* more concerned with *value* than with initial *price*, aren't you?"

Example No. 7.

Prospect: "The price of your tire is just *too high!*"

Comments: Every price is too high — until related to the benefits, advantages, and satisfactions it represents. Assume brand A costs twice as much as brand B. That makes brand A seem high, but what if it delivers three times more than does brand B?

Technique: *Talk over-all cost instead of initial price.*

Salesman: "Let's look at it this way. If tire cost is to be determined accurately, it must be in terms of performance — in terms of service received. The price of a tire when you put it on one of your wheels does not mean much. That price is high or low only when the time comes for that tire to be taken off and replaced with another tire."

Buying Decision No. 5 — Time

Example No. 1.

Prospect: "Check with me thirty to sixty days from now."

Comments: Several replies may be made to the prospect who hopes to minimize risks by postponing his decision. In the past, he has undoubtedly delayed buying, sometimes to his regret. Perhaps assortments are widest now or prices apt to rise soon. Certainly there will be more time to fill the order carefully. Time will be saved for both prospect and salesman by ordering now, and the time of each is precious. The prospect's judgment is best when facts are freshest. Indeed, will things be any different forty-five days hence?

Technique: *Guarantee against price decline.*

Salesman: "At this moment you have our entire Christmas line in mind more completely than will be the case later on when business becomes hectic. You can order this far in advance with perfect safety because we will take care of you in the event we make any future price cuts.

Example No. 2.

Prospect: "I can't place an order for your set of books without consulting my husband, and he's not here right now."

Comments: This is often just an excuse; it is often a stock trick for getting rid of a salesman. If either of these seems to be the case, the salesman should continue to try to close the sale with the one prospect. If the prospect seems sincere, the salesman can ask to see both prospects. Never should the salesman count on or even allow the wife to explain the proposal to her husband, or someone to relay the proposition to his partner for a decision. This is because the wife or partner lacks facts, enthusiasm, incentive, and ability to sell.

Technique: *Ask to see both prospects.*
Salesman: "Then I'll call back when you both are here, if I may. Will 7:30 tonight suit you?"

Example No. 3.

Prospect: "I guess I'll have to wait till next year to have my house insulated."
Comments: One way to try for an immediate purchase is to describe and emphasize the enjoyment that begins with possession. This enjoyment usually consists of added satisfaction or added savings or both. By comparing costs now with what they would be if the product is bought, the savings can often be used to justify the purchase. The line of reasoning that "You're paying out enough to have it, so you might as well get it" can be effective. Whenever possible, specific figures in dollars and cents should be used instead of generalities.

Technique: *Show what waiting would cost.*
Salesman: "That means six months of winter between now and the time you would insulate. If we take the minimum savings figure we agreed on, $11 a month, the delay will cost you not a cent less than $66 — even more if fuel prices move upward."

Example No. 4.

Prospect: "It might be nice to install a new lighting system, but I guess we'll have to make out a while longer without it."
Comments: This type of resistance is very close to that found under Buying Decision No. 1 — NEED. The prospect may not be convinced of the desirability of the salesman's recommendation; he may need more "You have a problem and I the solution" talk from our salesman. The inadequacy of the present circumstances must be stressed side by side with what the product will do for the prospect.

Technique: *Proof obtained from survey.*
Salesman: "I would not feel right if I left you without emphasizing that each year my company's engineers examine hundreds of retailers' lighting facilities. The survey we made of your store convinced us that your lighting requirements should have immediate attention."

Example No. 5.

Prospect: "I'd better think this over."
Comments: This may come from a postponer of decisions. It may come from one who was not actually sold on his need of the product. Some of the salesman's points may not have been clear to the prospect, or may have been misinterpreted by him. Technically, the objection is more of an evidence of inadequate interest than it is a real

objection. The salesman may elect to move for an immediate close by finding out what it is the prospect wants to think about and handling it then and there. In this event, the advantages of buying now will be stressed. If unsuccessful in this attempt to close the sale, the salesman may choose to leave with the prospect a check-list against which the prospect can test the brands he has under consideration. Because the list is drawn up for comparison pur-poses, it will certainly include every characteristic or feature that is smugly exclusive with our salesman's product.

Technique: *Review of plus-points.*
Salesman: "Okay, here are the main facts you will want to remember about my offer."

Example No. 6.

Prospect: "My future is not clear enough to justify my starting such an investment program."
Comments: Every buyer has known this feeling. Just what *is* one entitled to start today, in the light of future possibilities?
Technique: *Understand and reassure.*
Salesman: "Few trips are taken, Mr. Prospect, for which the traveler can see his destination and be assured of reaching it — before the start. And every trip, even one around the world, must start with a first step."

Example No. 7.

Prospect: "Yes, that's the policy I want, but let's button things up in a couple of months, not today."
Comments: When buyers are quite close to the act of buying something they should have, they simply must not be allowed to delay. In this instance, postponement of purchase does jeopardize a family's future. It is a fact that a man can be insurable today but not tomorrow.
Technique: *Make buyer afraid to postpone buying.*
Salesman: "How fine that you have decided what to do about your need! I'm glad you plan to increase your protection. It would be a shame, of course, for your family to miss out on this $20,000 if something happened to you — when only $\frac{1}{6}$ of the annual deposit is involved. You *do* believe you can pass the medical exam *now*, don't you? Many men in this city would gladly pay and pay dearly if they could qualify physically for life insurance. When could our doctor see you to get the information we need in order to make you a firm offer?"

STUDY ASSIGNMENTS

1. When he is answering an objection, are the salesman's attitude and manner as important as his answer? Why?
2. The text says that objections should be welcome, and it also says that they should be prevented. Reconcile these two ideas.

3. Why is a concealed objection so troublesome? What can be done about it?
4. There are few if any salesmen who have never been told by buyers, "But your price is entirely too high!" What might a buyer really mean when he uses this phrase?
5. If a retailer objects to dropping Brand C and replacing it with your brand, how might you convince the retailer that he should, assuming that you definitely have the better product?
6. After the first swing through his territory, a young salesman knew that he needed some help in distinguishing between excuses and serious objections. What would you tell him?
7. Is it always desirable for the salesman to restate an objection in his own words before answering it?
8. Suggest some answers a salesman might use when a prospect says, "Frankly, I'm not interested in your product right now."
9. Can a salesman take the objections he hears over a period of time and on them build an effective presentation? Discuss.
10. Which do you think are the three most difficult objections most salesmen encounter? Why?

CASE STUDY 14

A salesman of the Fiberglas Insulation Company calls on a home owner, Mr. Bennett. Mr. Bennett's house is a two-story frame. The time is afternoon of a hot midsummer day. It is Wednesday, Mr. Bennett's afternoon off from work.

Salesman: (Knocks on the door.) Good afternoon. Are you Mr. Bennett?

Prospect: Yes, I am.

Salesman: I'm very glad to meet you, sir. I've heard some very nice things about you from Mr. Elder. In fact, he gave me this to give to you.

Prospect: (Takes the letter that the salesman gives him.) Oh, it's a letter of introduction. You are Mr. Stanton?

Salesman: Yes, I am. I'd like to help you in the same way I helped Mr. Elder.

Prospect: Won't you come in, Mr. Stanton? (Mr. Stanton enters the house and sits down with Mr. Bennett.) How did you help Mr. Elder?

Salesman: I cooled his house 12 degrees and saved him up to 35% on his fuel bill.

Prospect: You what?

Salesman: Well you see, Mr. Bennett, I'm with the Fiberglas Insulation Company. I can show you how I can save you money and yet make your house cooler.

Prospect: Well, under ordinary circumstances I would be glad to talk with you about it, Mr. Stanton, but right now I am pretty busy. I brought some work home from the office with me this afternoon, and I have to finish it before supper.

Salesman: I'm sorry that I called at such an inconvenient time, Mr. Bennett, but I'd be more than happy to call again tonight, say around eight o'clock.

Prospect: My wife and I already have plans for tonight.

Salesman: Well, how would it be if I stop by your office tomorrow morning?

Prospect: I'm afraid I'll be pretty busy down at the office tomorrow. Why don't you just leave me some of your literature, and I'll call you in a few days after I've looked it over.

Salesman: Right now you're sitting here sweating. It must be ninety degrees outside. How would you like to be cool — right in this room?

Prospect: Sure, I'd like that.

Salesman: Well, I can cool this room for you, and I can do it within three days and at a reasonable cost.

Prospect: Oh, no. Air conditioning is too expensive for me.

Salesman: Mr. Bennett, you're absolutely right. Air conditioning is too expensive. But do you realize that by insulating your home at a fraction of that cost you can cut the interior temperature of your house down as much as fifteen degrees during the summer months? Why, that means this room would be somewhere around 75 degrees. That would certainly be comfortable, wouldn't it?

Prospect: Yes, it would.

Salesman: Another thing about insulation, there is no upkeep to it. Once your house is insulated with Fiberglas, it is protected for life. Don't you think your wife and children deserve this comfort at home while you are downtown working in an air-conditioned office?

Prospect: Well, I guess insulation would help, but I don't want a bunch of workmen tramping through my house with all their equipment. It's just too much trouble.

Salesman: I agree with you, but our applicators never enter your house at all. You see, all their work is done in the attic and on the outside. Let me show you a diagram of how this works. (Takes out a booklet and shows it.) The men applying the insulation simply carry a long hose up through the attic window. The insulation is blown through the hose by a special machine on the truck. The Fiberglas is then distributed in even, six-inch layers over the attic floor. To insulate the walls, our men simply remove one or two clapboards and blow the material into the openings. The men are always very careful when they do this so there will be no visible trace that a board has been removed. The whole process takes only a few minutes. Isn't that simple?

Prospect: Yes, but your insulation gives a house a funny, chemical odor. A friend of mine had his house insulated recently, and it has smelled funny ever since.

Salesman: Ah, Mr. Bennett. That is one of the advantages of Fiberglas insulation. It is completely odorless. You know that glass has no odor. Well, Fiberglas is made from the same materials that glass is. Do you think you would like a completely odorless insulating material in your house?

Prospect: Well, I would if I were going to insulate my house now, but I don't think it's worth it. The summer will be over in another month or so, and then I won't have to worry about the heat.

Salesman: Yes, Mr. Bennett, you won't have to worry about the summer heat, but more important, you'll have to worry about the winter heat and the dollars you'll lose.

Prospect: What do you mean, winter heat?

Salesman: I mean the heat your furnace gives out and then goes straight through the uninsulated walls and ceilings of this house, and right into the open air, where it is lost forever. How much was your fuel bill last winter?

Prospect: Oh, about $100.

Salesman: You paid $100 for $65 worth of heat.

Prospect: How do you figure that?

Salesman: Well, approximately 35% of fuel value is lost in uninsulated homes; 35% of $100 is $35. That means $35 worth of heat was lost, and only $65 worth was used. How would you like to have that $35 now?

Prospect: Well, it would be nice to have, naturally. How much would the insulation cost me?

Salesman: Let's see now, a house of this size . . . I could do it for you for $345.

Prospect: Wow! That's a lot of money. I know I can get it cheaper than that at the Ajax Insulation Company.

Salesman: The Ajax Company is a good company, Mr. Bennett, and they might possibly be able to offer you a slightly lower price. The only catch is that they can't insulate your house with Fiberglas. Fiberglas is worth more than the few additional dollars that it costs to install it. When you buy a pair of shoes, you don't always buy the cheapest pair you see. That's because the quality of one pair may make it a better buy, even at a slightly higher price. Well, that's the way it is with Fiberglas insulation. You want quality for the price. Fiberglas is completely fireproof. It will never settle and leave too thin a layer in later years. It will not rot or become food for vermin. It can be applied easily to your house with no damage. Fiberglas will help cool your house in the summer and save on your fuel bill in the winter. Mr. Bennett, what day would be convenient for you to have the work done?

Prospect: Well, frankly, Mr. Stanton, I would rather wait a few weeks before I definitely decide on this. I don't want to rush into it.

Salesman: If you had insulation now the temperature in this room would be 75 degrees, and also you would have saved $35 on your fuel bill last winter. Insulation is certainly worthwhile. And Fiberglas is the best insulation for you. Why sweat in the summer when you can be comfortable? The money you save on fuel in the winter will pay for the insulation over a period of time. Shall I have the crew come over tomorrow to insulate or would you like to be here when they do it?

Prospect: I guess I'd like to be here when they do it.

Salesman: How about Saturday, would that be O.K. with you?

Prospect: Yes, that would be fine.

Salesman: Then if you'll sign this order form, I'll make all the arrangements for you.

QUESTIONS:

1. What did the salesman do well?

2. What did the salesman do that could be improved?

3. What techniques are illustrated in the sale?

4. Classify the buyer's objections under the five buying decisions.

CHAPTER 15

CLOSING THE SALE

The *close* is the final stage of the sales interview proper. As the fifth and final "yes" to the five buying decisions, the close is the last act of the five-act drama. It is the climax of the salesman's presentation and selling efforts. When the salesman's closing attempts are successful, he makes a sale; the buyer makes a purchase as he accepts the salesman's diagnosis and prescription — and acts. The salesman has told his story, he has demonstrated his proposition, he has disposed of resistance, and now he wants the buyer's order or purchase.

While the close is technically the last phase of the salesman's performance, the salesman actually starts closing the moment he starts the interview. Although we speak of the *salesman's* closing the sale, actually the *buyer* closes the sale because he is the one who consummates the purchase.

WHAT THE CLOSE MEANS

When a salesman closes a sale, he succeeds in his original undertaking. The buyer's agreement to purchase from the salesman is proof of the salesman's success. The amount of study and preparation, the number of calls made, hours worked, buyers seen, and stories told — not these but the number of *profitable sales made* is the acid test of the salesman. Anyone can dispose of merchandise by cutting prices or giving concessions. Persons who close sales profitably are salesmen — those who do not are merely talkers.

WHY CLOSING MAY BE DIFFICULT

Some difficulty experienced at the close may have been caused by circumstances that existed prior to the close or by some of the salesman's earlier activities. If the salesman does not do a good job in making his preapproach, he will be handicapped in his attempts to close. If he does not do a good job of opening the interview, he will probably have trouble in closing the sale. If he tells a weak story, he will find that closing is not easy. This story might be weak because the salesman lacks sufficient information about the buyer. Or, the weakness may be in the story's failure to get the buyer enthusiastic, or even interested. Of course, the delivery of the story may be defective. Sometimes, too, the salesman's mistake is that of recommending the wrong product. Sometimes his demonstrating is faulty, or his handling of objections inept. Sometimes he just talks too much.

If the close itself is weak, that will make closing difficult. If the salesman makes a ceremony of the close, he frightens the buyer. If the salesman himself is afraid, that, too, frightens buyers. No feeling of excitement must be communicated to the buyer because that suggests to him that the salesman is somewhat green and inexperienced, and buyers are a bit reluctant to buy from salesmen of that type. In the same fashion, any appearance of being flustered, any awkwardness in the handling of the physical phases of the closing procedure, or any suspicion of anxiety alerts the buyer's cautions. Successful closes are jeopardized if the salesman fails to steer a middle course between too much and too little aggressiveness, and between giving the impression of too much and too little indifference. If the close is unfortunately worded or ill-timed, the salesman's goal is attained less often.

PROSPECT'S ATTITUDE TOWARD CLOSING

Usually the thought of buying is both alluring and alarming to the prospect, something to embrace yet something to shun. By definition, he would not be a prospect unless he would benefit from buying; consequently, he quite naturally wants the product. On the other hand, he also wants many other things; he can't have them all; and he can't prove in advance that he will not regret his decision. It is this negative aspect of the prospect's attitude that should always concern the salesman.

Reluctance to buy is normal, expected, and understandable. The prospect feels the urge to play safe, to conserve his purchasing power, to avoid making a commitment. He hates to make a decision; he resents "being sold" something; he suspects a bit of kinship between buying and being defeated. Fear and doubts are obstacles between him and any purchase. He is inclined to postpone action because, who knows, there may be a better offer tomorrow.

The prospect does expect to be asked to buy, yet, he does not like to buy if it demands imagination, initiative, and courage.

ASSURING THE PROSPECT

It would seem that what the prospect needs most is *assurance*. His confidence in his decision-to-buy must be great enough to override his

doubts. If the salesman is to be of help to the prospect in this matter —
if the salesman is to be a successful salesman — he must think, do, and
say the right things.

Thoughts

The young salesman sometimes finds mental hazards building up about
the process of closing; he feels anxiety over the possibility of getting a
"no" from the prospect. Uncertainty and fear insist on invading his
thinking. As such feelings are contagious, they can be fatal, because the
attitude of the salesman influences the decision of the prospect. Such
negative thoughts, spawned by the imagination and usually exaggerated,
must be banished.

The correct frame of mind calls for the presence of self-confidence,
a reasonable amount of aggressiveness, and the absence of excessive
tension. Confidence is necessary because usually a certain thing cannot
be done unless the person involved thinks it can be done. The aggressiveness is needed because more sales are lost by fainthearted salesmen than
by eager ones. Too much tension is bad because it reduces proficiency and
control. Athletes known as "money players" or "good in the clutch"
prove that some individuals do better under some strain.

It is reassuring for the salesman to remember that when he qualified
the prospect, he removed what is probably the biggest barrier between
him and the sale. He can recall that he has prepared himself to sell that
particular prospect, that the prospect needs the product, that he will
benefit from buying, and that he wants the product and is able to buy.

Actions

What the salesman does can be a help or a handicap as he assures the
prospect that he is doing the right thing by buying. The salesman will
carefully guard against any display of excitement or anxiety as well as
any act that betrays doubt on his part. A confident manner implies that
the salesman has made many sales — that orders are no novelty to him.
His casual, matter-of-fact behavior is comforting to the prospect.

Words

What the salesman tells the prospect is as important in this process of
assuring as are his thinking and his actions; perhaps more so. This is
because the prospect wants to be told things that will dismiss his indecision, he wants to hear the comforting news that he is doing the correct
thing in buying, and he wants to have his desires confirmed, his needs
corroborated.

In his conversation, then, the salesman will remove from the prospect's shoulders as much decision-making as he can. This is accomplished by the salesman's talking as though the decision to buy has already been made. He will make positive, constructive recommendations instead of contingent or provisional suggestions. He will describe what is going to happen *after* the prospect has bought, and not what will happen *if* he buys. He will declare, "My product will (not would) do thus and so for you." He flatly states, "When (not if) you get this product . . ."

The salesman strengthens the prospect's resolution to purchase by telling him he is demonstrating common sense — that he is making no mistake — that he can feel proud of his action. In addition, he will remind the prospect of the trustworthiness of the salesman himself and the integrity of the salesman's company.

In some situations, the prospect will feel an acute need for reasons that he can use in explaining and justifying his purchase to other persons. These can be reviewed from the sales story and case histories.

GETTING AGREEMENT ALL ALONG

In Chapter 12, "Telling the Story," the suggestion was made that understanding and agreement be secured from the prospect as the salesman makes his various points. This significant practice should be continued throughout the close.

Unless the prospect concurs with the salesman's analysis and recommendation, no attempt at closing will be successful. Until the prospect gives assent and approval to the advantages he will gain by buying and to the reasons that he should buy now, he will refuse to buy. Furthermore, if he goes along with each benefit as it is presented, he must logically accept the aggregate of the benefits at the end by agreeing that the only thing for him to do is to buy then and there.

What the salesman does specifically is sprinkle his presentation with questions which can hardly be answered sensibly except with assent. Nearing the close, the questions tend to be separated by shorter time intervals. Sample questions are:

> Your wife will be surprised and thrilled, won't she?
> It would be a shame to let all this basement space of yours go to waste, wouldn't it?
> This item certainly will reduce your fuel bill, won't it?
> Ours is the most liberal guarantee you've seen, isn't it?
> A sensible, straight-thinking person has to consider that possibility, doesn't he?
> Beautiful, isn't it?

The use of such questions is helpful because each earlier agreement reduces the magnitude of the final agreement — the final decision becomes just one (the last) of a number of decisions. The prospect will not be surprised and shocked by the unexpected appearance of an attempt to close.

CLOSING CLUES

Closing clues are the signals flashed by the prospect indicating that a close should be attempted by the salesman. They alert the salesman to the fact that the prospect may be ready to buy. The salesman who closely observes and studies the prospect and the prospect's reactions can learn to spot closing clues, although, of course, he can never be 100 per cent accurate in his diagnosis.

Most buyers give some indication when they are close to the act of buying. As a matter of fact, there may be several of these clues or signals in a single interview. This is possible because a buyer can get close to buying, then draw away, and then, once again, be on the verge of making a purchase — all in the same interview. Because these buyer-reactions show that the buyer is ready for the salesman's attempt to close, they are extremely valuable to salesmen. Nothing is more important in closing than for the salesman to learn to spot these signals and to act on them.

Physical closing clues consist of actions and movements. The buyer may nod unconsciously, his facial expression may soften and relax, or he may examine or handle the product in a manner that clearly indicates he just about considers it his. A nod, a shrug of the shoulders, the prospect's putting his glasses back in their case, a facial expression of decision, a relaxing of the body, and the extinguishing of a cigarette are examples.

Spoken closing clues may be *comments* or *questions:*

My present machine *does* need repairs quite often.
This shoe certainly does feel good on my foot.
Yes, your product certainly is a beauty.
I don't like this color.
That's a lot of money to have to borrow.
I'd have to have it by Friday.
But I don't think our engineer is in today.
I've got no business even thinking about buying now.
And your guarantee is for two years?
When would this start?
How much time does it take?
Could you bill me next month?
When could I get delivery?
Is that all the margin you can allow me?
And just what does this cost? (This is a closing clue only when asked
well along in the interview.)

TRIAL CLOSES

Trial closes are closing attempts by the salesman to see if the buyer is ready to make a purchase. They sound the buyer out — they take his buying temperature — they count his buying pulse. Trial closes ask the buyer to buy, but they are constructed in such a way that they are fool-proof. If the buyer's response to the trial close is favorable, the salesman goes ahead at once and tries to complete the sale. If the buyer's reaction clearly shows that he is not yet ready to buy, the salesman's cause has not been hurt; trial closes are constructed so that a negative reaction from the buyer does not endanger the salesman's chances of ultimate success. Indeed, trial closes that fail almost always do the salesman some good because of the information they uncover.

The trial close serves three purposes. First and foremost, it is a safe and simple way of asking the prospect to buy. If it succeeds, it can result in an immediate purchase. Second, it is an inoffensive check on how the prospect is thinking. Is he reacting favorably? Is he convinced yet? Is he ready to buy? The trial close sheds light on these matters. Finally, it protects the salesman by guiding him. It prevents the fiascoes that can result from attempting a final close before the prospect is ready.

Types

Oral trial closes are usually phrased in the form of questions. The question usually calls for a decision on a minor point or on some detail; usually it asks the buyer to make a choice. Here are sample questions:

> How soon will you be ready to start on this?
> How do you want this handled?
> Which model do you prefer?
> What initials will you want engraved on the watch?
> When can our doctor check you over?
> What bank do you deal with?
> Where is this to be sent?
> Do you prefer cash or terms?
> Will you want this gift-wrapped?
> You'll want this next week?

It takes only a glance at these examples to see that if the buyer gives a direct answer to the point, he has actually if not technically said, "I am now making a purchase." Had the question asked, in effect, *whether* he was going to buy — and then been answered in the negative, the salesman would have found himself in a bad situation. When the questions are constructed by skilled salesmen, the buyer cannot make an answer that ends the interview by shutting off further selling by the salesman.

Form 103 300M 5-24-46 13718		E·R·SQUIBB & SONS, NEW YORK							
		This order is taken subject to acceptance either at our home or branch offices and is also subject to the TERMS OF SALE published in our CURRENT TRADE LIST. No deviation herefrom may be made by any representative.—E. R. SQUIBB & SONS.							

Short order blank used by Squibb salesmen.   *E. R. Squibb and Sons*

Physical trial closes are those in which the salesman starts to execute the physical phases of the sale without asking permission to do so. He could pick up a charge book and start to write up the charge ticket, he could do the same with an order form if selling to a retailer, he could start wrapping the product, or he could pick up the item being considered and start with it toward the buyer's automobile.

When a trial close, either oral or physical, fails to cause a purchase, the salesman asks himself why the buyer is not yet ready to buy and then goes to work on what he diagnoses the difficulty to be.

Suggestions About Use

In his use of trial closes, the salesman must not alert the prospect's buying defenses. Instead of asking for a decision on the major issue at that time, he will by-pass it in favor of a lesser decision.

Also, the salesman must never close the door to more discussion or make it possible for the prospect to do so. If the salesman thinks he detects a closing clue, executes a trial close, and then finds that it was not a clue, he wants to be able to resume his sales story. Indeed, no trial close is acceptable which might block the salesman from making a return call. A prospect's circumstances or attitudes can change overnight.

Finally, the salesman must always have on tap more talking points, additional reasons for buying, and new benefits and advantages to describe. He must never allow his reserve fund of facts-that-persuade to become exhausted.

WHEN TO CLOSE

Closing starts the moment the interview begins. And that is when the idea of an eventual close should be firmly planted in the prospect's mind. As a matter of fact, the major part of expert, successful closing is the preliminary work — the paving of the way in the early stages of the sale. If a sound presentation is made from the outset, and if the prospect gives complete assent to the points the salesman makes, the close will almost take care of itself. Thus, the salesman should consciously start moving toward a close the moment he opens the interview.

When to Attempt the Close

A sound rule for closing is to do it as early as possible, for more sales are lost by trying too late than too early. In this connection, it is well to remember that the salesman's objective is to close a sale — not to present a complete sales story just because he has one prepared.

A closing attempt made too early will find one or more of the five buying decisions missing. If, however, the salesman talks past his first closing opportunity, he may lose the sale by not having closed when the prospect was favorably inclined.

Salesmen used to think that only *one* magic moment ever occurred during any one interview and that at that exact time the salesman had to make an attempt to close if he was to make a sale on that call. This magic moment was usually referred to as the "psychological moment." It was the one time during that particular session when the buyer would buy.

Authorities on selling now believe that the psychological moment is nothing but a myth. They believe that there may be several "high spots" of buyer-desire and buyer-conviction during the conversation between buyer and salesman and that purchase might easily be made at any one of them. Buyer resistance and opposition are at a minimum at these points, objections are not raised, and the buyer seems sold on the salesman's proposal. Should the salesman not complete his sale the first time the buyer is ready to buy, he may work the buyer back up to buying pitch later and close the sale then. The salesman might even miss on the first, second, and third high spots, but be successful in closing the sale on the fourth one.

These good closing spots may come at any time. Even if the salesman thinks he feels one early in the interview, he should make a trial close because, as was pointed out in the last section, a trial close that does not work need not do the slightest bit of damage. There is no reason in the world why a salesman should tell *all* his story if the buyer is ready to buy part way through it.

The general rule, then, is for the salesman to make a closing attempt (a) whenever the buyer implies that he is close to buying, or, (b) whenever the salesman infers that the time to sell is at hand. Needless to say, experience is a great help in learning to sense when the conditions for closing are most favorable.

Specifically, a salesman does well to execute trial closes:

When the buyer gives him a closing clue.

When the buyer gives hearty and enthusiastic agreement on one of the selling points or one of the salesman's leading questions.

When the buyer accepts proof of advantage in a convinced, decided manner.

When the salesman has just completed an impressive demonstration of his product.

When the salesman has disposed of some buyer-resistance in a devastating way.

Whenever buyer-desire seems most intense and buyer-conviction seems strongest.

How Many Attempts May Be Made?

There can be no single answer to this question. Generally, the young salesman should make himself try to close more than once on every visit unless there is an exceptional reason for refraining. That will not be often. On most calls, more is to be gained than lost by trying several times to close. More sales will be made, less ground will have to be covered a second time, and fewer interim orders will be placed with competitors. The Penn Mutual Life Insurance Company is one of the companies that have definite views with respect to how often their salesmen should try to close. Their words are:

During every organized presentation there should be at least three attempts to close. Put in more, if necessary. This will not be difficult if you assume your prospect is going to buy.

TECHNIQUES OF CLOSING

No closing method or specific technique is effective in all cases. No matter how natural, unobtrusive, and usually successful is the close he attempts first, the salesman may be forced to resort to others before finally making the sale.

TO ALL CUTLER-HAMMER SALESMEN and DISTRICT MANAGERS

SUBJECT: SALES REMINDER #17
           CLOSING: TYING THE PACKAGE TOGETHER
                      OR "ASKING FOR THE ORDER"

Interesting stories about the late Henry Ford are legion. I recently read one that is worth telling many times, and emphasizes again the infallible maxim, "Always ask for the order."

When Mr. Ford purchased a very large life insurance policy for himself, the Detroit Newspapers blazoned the fact in headlines, since the amount was so large and Mr. Ford so prominent.

One of the articles was read by an old friend of Mr. Ford who happened to be in the insurance business. Being completely surprised by the purchase, since he had not heard Mr. Ford was in the market for insurance, this friend went to see Mr. Ford and asked him if the story was really true. Ford replied that it most certainly was.

The friend asked why the policy wasn't bought from him since he was a personal friend and had been in the insurance business for many years. Henry Ford's simple reply was, - "You never asked me."

After you have properly handled all other steps in the sale, can you think of a better way to close than "Ask For The Order"?

F. A. Wright
F. A. Wright
Sales Manager
District Sales

Ask the prospect to buy; then, ask him again.

Cutler-Hammer, Inc.

No salesman closes all his sales. It must be pointed out, however, that the mark of an outstandingly successful salesman is the high percentage of sales made in difficult situations. Mediocre salesmen get orders from prospects who are ready and waiting to buy; the masterful salesman is able to sell almost anyone who qualifies as a prospect.

Eleven methods of closing that have proved their worth follow.

Closing on a Choice

In all probability, this technique is the safest, the most often used, the most versatile, and the most successful. For these reasons, it should be the first closing method mastered by the young salesman. It is also referred to, incidentally, as "closing on a minor point," the "double question" method, the "selection" close, and the "split decision."

The salesman takes for granted that the prospect is going to buy, but, at the same time, the salesman knows that the prospect is reluctant to concede, in effect, "Yes, you win — you've sold me — I'll buy." So what the salesman does is to ignore and avoid the major buying decision, which is to buy or not to buy, by posing a minor decision for the prospect to make.

The position of the salesman is one of complete indifference and impartiality, because the choice he offers the prospect is so contrived that either selection will be equally satisfactory to both buyer and seller. It is the salesman's duty to see that the two options are of equal utility and suitability.

Closing on a choice is particularly appropriate when the prospect is having trouble making up his mind, because it narrows the choice down to two. This makes the process of choosing less complicated, and, hence, less confusing. The device is also good when a young salesman is reluctant to press for a close.

Specifically, what the salesman does is to ask the prospect which of two products the prospect prefers. The difference between the two may be a matter of model, color, size, material, or some other product feature. Either alternative means a purchase. The salesman frames the choice, and the prospect makes the choice. Then the prospect is complimented on his choice, and his decision is strengthened by the salesman's assurance that his selection was sound. The salesman next attends to the physical details of closing. In using this method of closing, the salesman asks such questions as these:

> Do you prefer the full color assortment?
> Which model do you like better?
> Will one package be enough?
> Which do you think you need, the table model or the floor model?

Assuming the Close

This popular and effective method of closing differs from the first in that here both salesman and prospect have a single specific product in mind; both are thinking about the same model, color, size, material, and price. The prospect may have narrowed the field down to the one product, or the salesman may have selected the most appropriate item for that particular prospect. If the salesman does the selecting, he is completely responsible for seeing that what he recommends is right.

Assuming the close is both a logical continuation and a result of the salesman's doing and saying things throughout his presentation that indicate that the major question is settled. The closing question assumes the prospect's acceptance of the salesman's recommendations and inquires only about some minor point that is not a product matter. Two examples bring out the difference between these first and second techniques:

Choice: Do you prefer the blue car or the gray?
Assumed: The 4-door blue sedan is the model you'll find most satis-
              factory. How much do you want to pay each month?

Specifically, the salesman will do a number of things in executing this type of closing attempt. He will imply ownership and cultivate a feeling of possession on the part of the prospect. This is accomplished by demonstrating the product as though it were already bought and owned, by speaking of the product as belonging to the prospect, and by teaching the prospect how to use his new possession.

He may infer consent and immediately open his order book to write in the prospect's name and address. Or he may open his order book and let the prospect see his name already written, the salesman having done this before the interview.

Thus, the salesman shows that he thinks his job consists of clearing up details and coming to agreement on minor points. The question he asks and the choice he presents are quite similar to those used in the "choice" close, with one exception — his question now is on an auxiliary matter such as delivery, and not on the product. This similarity will be obvious in these sample questions:

How do you prefer to pay?
How much do you want to pay as a down payment?
How do you want this shipped?
When do you want this to become effective?

Incidentally, assuming the close is effective in cases of chronic indecision, it is dangerous if the prospect is positive and belligerent and recognizes what the salesman is doing; and it won't work at all if the prospect is unconvinced.

The Single Feature

Once in a while a prospect will be particularly anxious to get one special feature or quality in a product. Or once in a while a product will have a feature or advantage that competition cannot match, perhaps a matter of design, a method of operation, or a manner of construction. In both situations, the single feature close may be the best method for the salesman to use. The first refrigerator to defrost itself, the first automobile with the motor in the rear, a home in the most elite section of the city, the product made by a company whose reputation is unequalled in the industry — these are examples. Indeed, the prospect's personal confidence in the salesman himself could be a deciding single feature in making the purchase.

If the prospect does not fully appreciate the feature, then the salesman turns the spotlight on it and relates just what the feature means to and will do for buyers. The salesman's enthusiasm over the feature is characterized by respect and showmanship. His aim is to persuade the prospect to buy solely because of this one feature.

If the prospect does appreciate the feature, the salesman agrees with the prospect's point of view, commends him on it, emphasizes how his brand or item excels on that score, and then attempts a close. Reassuring the prospect that his attitude is right helps to build up confidence in timid prospects.

Disposing of the Single Obstacle

Sometimes a prospect gives real and honest agreement to every point the salesman makes except one, and that one difference of opinion prevents the purchase's being made *now*. Perhaps everything is right except price; perhaps the prospect feels obligated to buy from some other vendor; or perhaps the prospect fears the cost of operating the product or his ability to operate it. Whatever the single obstacle is, it prevents the purchase from being made.

The first thing the salesman does is get the prospect to agree that the objection raised is the only thing holding up the purchase. He asks, "Is that the only reason we can't do business? There's nothing else standing in the way?" Otherwise, answering the specific objection satisfactorily will not close the sale; there will still remain in the prospect's mind the true bar to buying — a basic doubt, a lack of serious intent, or an absence of conviction.

The salesman must dispose of the objection cleanly, fully, and conclusively by explaining why that buying block is only imaginary and not real. Strong, positive proof is often required.

The final step is the closing of the sale. As he starts to write up the order, the salesman remarks, "That *was* the one question, wasn't it; then I think we can go right ahead. You prefer the modern style in blue, don't you?" He will have to judge whether or not he will need specific agreement from the prospect, the acknowledgment that the objection has been explained away. This step will be omitted whenever possible, lest the prospect feel that he is being asked to lose face by reversing his stand.

Three illustrations show how this plan may work:

A prospect has agreed to all buying decisions except the last one, that of *time*. His excuse is that he must have the approval (permission) of his wife before signing on the dotted line. And he is telling the truth when he says that only that obstacle stands between him and buying. The salesman goes to the wife, sells her on his proposition, reminds the prospect of his previous promise, and closes.

A middle-aged businessman will not buy a plane because he thinks he is too old to learn how to fly it. That is the only bar. The salesman's job is to convince him that he is mistaken. This he does by amassing proof. He presents case histories; he introduces the prospect to pilots who learned to fly late in life; he shows figures to support his contention; he takes the prospect up in a plane and demonstrates that the prospect is not too old to learn how to fly.

A bookkeeper in an office needs a couple of courses offered by a local evening school. He puts the salesman off by saying that his boss sometimes asks him to work at night. The salesman establishes clearly that this is the only barrier, he clears with the boss, then enrolls the prospect.

Reviewing the Five Decisions

As was pointed out in Chapter 10, no one makes a purchase until he is positive that he is in need of something, the product will fill the need, the salesman is the proper source, the price is satisfactory, and the time to buy is now.

One course the salesman can follow in winding up the sale is to check back on these five decisions and get approval on each one. Until the prospect actually buys, only one conclusion can be made — agreement is still missing on one or more of the five points.

If such is the case, the salesman brings in additional facts, he makes more demonstrations, and he supplies more convincing proof on the missing decision until it is made affirmatively.

Summarizing the Benefits

After the salesman has covered most of the benefits which he thinks will appeal to the prospect, he may sense that the moment has come to try to close the sale. A method of closing that may be effective, especially when the prospect would have to defend any purchase to his family, friends, or employer, is a review, in summary form, of each advantage the salesman has mentioned. The collection of advantages may, by its very size and composition, be impressive enough to persuade the prospect to buy now. If any one or two of the benefits seemed to be of particular interest to the prospect as each was first described, then those should be stressed in the summary.

This summary, which must be made simply and without formality, may be prefaced by some such remark as, "Let's review the benefits I've mentioned so I won't forget any that might be of special interest to you."

The salesman will ask the prospect for agreement on each benefit so that if there is an objection to one it can be disposed of immediately. Piling one agreement on top of another strengthens the salesman's position. As mentioned earlier in this chapter, this procedure makes the final and vital "yes" less terrifying to the prospect.

When there is complete agreement, the salesman assumes that the prospect is ready to buy and goes about the mechanics of winding things up. He may or may not observe, "Now, after considering all these advantages, I'm positive you feel the need for this product." He may or may not ask for instructions or information on some detail.

Changing Pace

Some situations demand that the salesman not allow the interview to continue any longer in the same pattern or vein. Trial closes may have been tried without success and the atmosphere may be less cordial than when the salesman entered. A change is clearly called for.

The first thing the salesman does is quit talking about his proposition and switch the conversation to some safe, neutral topic. This may be accompanied by closing the order book, placing the model or sample back in its case, and preparing to leave. The salesman appears to have given up the sale.

The purpose of all this is to reduce any tension felt by the prospect and to invite him to relax his buying defenses.

Then, in a casual, almost accidental manner, the salesman remembers one point he has failed to mention, and he now presents it with "Oh, by the way, I was about to forget one other thing you might like to know." If the prospect does not object — and frequently he is not prompt in objecting because the new tack takes him by surprise — the salesman enlarges on that point by presenting additional facts and then tests the prospect with another close. If he makes the sale, well and good; if not, he continues his presentation until stopped.

DO'S

Do display a friendly manner at the close, even though there is disagreement. This helps to avoid arguments.

Do be sure to have all materials and equipment that will be needed. Misplaced order blanks, obsolete price lists, and dry fountain pens can lose sales.

Do realize that begging for a sale makes you and your offer look bad; it also disgusts the prospect.

Do ask the prospect to "OK" or approve the order rather than sign it.

Do make buying as easy and painless as possible.

Do try for privacy at the close. Telephone calls and third parties distract.

Do study each prospect like a baseball pitcher studies each batter. Then pitch to his weakness.

Do lead the prospect to think of himself as the owner of the product from the very beginning of the interview.

Do put the order book and pen in a conspicuous, convenient spot long before attempting a close.

DON'T'S

Don't let the prospect know how much the sale means.

Don't be apologetic, particularly in quoting price.

Don't make written or even oral promises unless authorized to do so.

Don't make a ceremony out of closing lest the prospect become frightened.

Don't give the prospect an excuse or an opportunity to back away from the purchase.

Don't ever ask the prospect for the buying decision in such a way that he can answer with a "no," for that closes the door.

Don't make it difficult for the prospect to complete his purchase quickly if he cares to do so.

Don't let the prospect miss seeing that you expect him to buy.

Don't make it easier for the prospect to refuse than to buy.

Using the Emotional Close

Sometimes the sales interview runs along satisfactorily through the first four buying decisions but encounters difficulties on the fifth. This is quite understandable. The first four decisions are easy for the prospect to make because no final action is asked of him. The fifth, the decision to buy *now*, is more difficult in that it requires the prospect to commit himself.

When the salesman runs back over and gets agreements on the four questions of *need*, *product*, *source*, and *price*, yet cannot close the sale, he may find the emotional method effective.

There is greater chance of success if the prospect is a person who dreads to act, who prefers to vacillate. Furthermore, sufficient spade work must have been done already by the salesman in making a strong presentation of his story.

In using the emotional close, the salesman personalizes his closing appeal by intimately relating his proposition to the prospect's emotions and feelings. He now tries to cause an impulsive or instinctive reaction, having been unable to persuade the prospect to take a deliberate, calculated step. Since the prospect won't buy with his head, he is urged to buy with his heart — the salesman stimulates such buying motives as sex, fear of death, rivalry, pride, affection, and self-esteem. Inept handling usually causes resentment. Here are two examples of this strategy.

> A solicitor for contributions to the Community Chest approaches a prominent industrialist and plans to get a larger donation than the industrialist expected to give. The solicitor decides to appeal to the desire for approval. He pictures the industrialist as a prominent citizen, a leader in the community, one who is looked up to and respected, and a person of significant influence in that his lead is watched and followed by hundreds of less conspicuous folk. Because of this, the industrialist has a special responsibility to set a good example. By so doing, he will enjoy the good will and enthusiastic approval of the community.
>
> A seller of fire insurance, unsuccessful thus far in trying to sell a certain prospect, decides to use *fear* to close the sale. He observes that the prospect has not needed to call on any protector yet, and the salesman hopes he never will. But one cannot forget old man Bell. He had not needed coverage until last week — and he had none. With a long sad face and an unctuous quaver, the salesman reminds the prospect that "Bell's tragedy could happen to you."

"Standing Room Only"

Persons want what other persons want and what other persons have. They want anything that is hard to get. They want what they can't have and what they shouldn't have. Persons want things so other persons can't have those things. This is the reasoning back of the SRO close.

Sometimes the salesman challenges the prospect in a smooth, inoffensive way by implying that the prospect may not be able to handle the product, or qualify for it, or get in under some wire. In reply, the prospect grits his teeth, unleashes his blood pressure, and swears he *shall* have the item, in an effort to show up the salesman.

Sometimes the salesman bribes the prospect, telling him that for the last time, a "free" tie goes with each suit bought, or "free" accessories with each instrument purchased.

Sometimes the salesman frightens the prospect by pointing out that only one item is left. Probably it will be gone tomorrow. When will the next shipment arrive? Heaven only knows.

Whenever a salesman tells a prospect that a price increase is due next week, that the medical examiner turned down one of the prospect's friends when he applied for insurance, that supply is becoming tighter, or that a premium offer expires Friday, he is using the SRO strategy to hustle the prospect into buying.

This device should be held in reserve until late in the interview, because it weakens the salesman's position and story. There is a temptation to use it unethically.

The Direct Appeal

Because this is a risky technique, it should be used only in extreme cases. Even then the salesman will wait until late in the interview, calling on a direct appeal as a last resort. He is hesitant about making a direct appeal because, if it fails, he will find it awkward, if not impossible, to switch back to his presentation. Seldom can he then say, "Oh yes, let me mention one or two other points that will interest you."

Before this course of action is tried, the prospect should be obviously interested and seem to be partially convinced that he will benefit from the purchase. The salesman and his company must enjoy an established standing with the prospect. In most instances, the prospect will have said "no" several times to the salesman.

What the salesman does is to build up the reputation, reliability, and prestige of his company and of himself. He then insists that the prospect be guided by the salesman's opinions and predictions and buy because of them. The salesman himself makes the decision to buy, and any question he asks is merely for information.

In effect, here is what the salesman says:

> I've explained this product and how it will benefit you as best I can. You understand the product and what it will do for you. You need it. You have safely followed my recommendations in the past. You can do so now. If there are any questions remaining, let's clear them up now. Otherwise, suppose we go ahead.

Here are sample wordings the salesman might use:

Shall I draw up the contract now?
When shall I send my man over to take the measurements?
I'll send your order in today.
I'm glad you appreciate what my product will do for you; now I need
some information for my report.

This is how a salesman might talk to a wholesaler when the salesman's
company has just come out with a new product:

Mr. Wholesaler, my company has spent two years and $200,000
designing and testing this new item. We know it is right, we know it will
make money for you, and we know you will not be taking any chances
with it. You and I have been doing business for five years, and you
know I've never given you bad advice. I can't afford to run any risks with
you now. Because I know this is a good deal, I'm going to include one
dozen cases in this order of yours.

The Special Concession

Buyers like bargains and "free" merchandise. Buyers get a thrill from
forcing a salesman to replace his original proposal with one more attractive to them. And, salesmen have been known to allow for possible
future revision of offers by starting off high enough so they *can* come down
a little if they must.

When he uses the "special concession" attempt to close, the salesman
offers the buyer some special inducement for acting at once. The most
common inducement is the *cut in price* that a salesman makes, dropping
down from the figure he quoted originally. Or, in some lines of selling,
the salesman might offer something "free" to the buyer; he might give
housewives one "free" unit with each purchase of five units, or he might
offer retailers one dozen "free" with each ten dozen bought. Instead of
free goods, the salesman might offer a *premium* free or at a very low price.
The automobile salesman might offer to fill up the gas tank if the buyer
buys now; he could also, of course, raise the trade-in allowance. In
selling to wholesalers or retailers, there may be some *allowance* the salesman can give buyers, usually if they buy certain minimum quantities now.
An advertising allowance equal to 5 per cent of purchases would be an
example. Finally, the *trial order* is an inducement in that the salesman
backs off from trying to sell the normal or standard amount and agrees
to settle for a smaller quantity — the trial quantity.

Any special concession should be saved until the very last moments of
the interview, and even then there are dangers in its use. The buyer may
keep pressing for — may even demand — *more* concessions once the salesman starts offering them. Too, the buyer may begin to wonder about the

value and the desirability of the product if concessions must be made to make sales. Concessions reduce the seller's profits. Finally, the salesman must not get caught playing favorites among his buyers.

POST-SALE BEHAVIOR

After the interview, the salesman always remembers to thank the prospect for the consideration he was given and tries with his parting remarks to leave the prospect kindly disposed toward him and his proposition. He makes certain that the prospect has his name, address, and phone number, as well as some literature or other material about the product. If it is convenient, as he leaves, the salesman may find it desirable to visit a moment with the receptionist and any other employees whose acquaintance would be an asset. Not only are the employees of a prospect a source of valuable information and suggestions, but they also confer with the prospect and are depended on by him for recommendations. A letter to the prospect may be helpful after the call.

On No-Sale Calls

When the sale is not closed on a particular call, and if the prospect deserves and is to get another visit, the salesman should spend the final moments of the interview in building up goodwill. He secures any needed information so as to be able to present a more appropriate, tailored, and beneficial proposal later. He repeats his determination to be of greatest possible help to the prospect. He inquires if there are any facts he might get or any favor he might do for the prospect before the next call. He makes certain that he expresses warm and sincere appreciation for the time the prospect has given him. In a word, he paves the way for a good return visit.

Immediately after leaving, the salesman begins to prepare for the return call. He jots down everything he learned about the prospect so that he will have a record to review before calling again. He summarizes just what took place in the conference. He lists any mistakes he made and notes possible means of correcting them. A matter which he must not overlook is that of the objections encountered. Here again, thoughts may come to mind while the call is still fresh about how better to handle such obstacles. Buying decisions should be classified into two groups, those made in the affirmative, and those still missing. The salesman must note and file away prices quoted, deliveries promised, or any other commitments he made to avoid possible misunderstanding or failure to fulfill in the future. Finally, he must enter the call-back date on his calendar.

THE "U" CHECKER

General

Did "U" — Refer to "Customer's Sales Record Card" Before Interview?
— Have Pertinent "Customer Information" and "Call Data" Posted on This Card?
— Have Good Contact with Buyer?_____ Key Personnel?_____

"Salute" Step:

Did "U" — Display Good "Customer Knowledge"?
— Capture Buyer's Respectful Attention?
— Put Buyer At Ease?
— Have Buyer's "Confidence"?
— Spend Too Much Time on "Small Talk"?

"Excite Interest" Step:

Did "U" — Secure and Hold Buyer's "Interest"?_____ Quickly?_____Slowly?_____ Easily?_____With Difficulty?_____
— Use, "I – Me – We" to Excess?
— Use, "You – Your – Yours" Effectively?
— Talk in Terms of "Benefits" to Buyer?
— Show Buyer Our Product?_____ Effectively?_____
— Use Other Visual Aids?_____Effectively?_____

"Let Go" Step:

Did "U" — Submit a Clean, Concise, Worthwhile "Proposition"?
— Make it Completely Clear to Buyer?
— Submit "Benefits" in "Full Course Dinner" Style?
— Display Good "Product Knowledge" in "Explanations"?
— Support "Benefits" with "Proof Points"?
— Use "Success Stories"?
— Use Other Forms of Proof?
— Make "Benefits" Outweigh "Cost"?
— Ask Questions — "Check Temperature"?

Did "U" — Meet with "Buyer's Objections"?
— "Listen Thru"_____ "Interrupt"?_____ "Side-Step"?_____
— Use "Converter" Statement?_____ Convert into "Questions"?_____
— Convert "Objections" to your Advantage?
— Cover Them to Buyer's Apparent Satisfaction?

DATE ISSUED 1/15/55

REPLACES 4/1/52

CODE NO. TF - 32 - B2

PAGE NO. 1

THE "U" CHECKER

SALES TRAINING CONFERENCE

FLEISCHMANN DIVISION

(Continued)

THE "U" CHECKER

"Loop Thru" Step:

Did "U" — Ask for Specific Action_____Confidently?_____
Hesitatingly?_____

— Use the "Suggest" Technique?

— Use the "Choice" Technique?

— Use Some Other Specific "Closing" Technique?

— Handle "Last Minute Objections" Successfully?

— Handle "Brush-Offs" or "Stalls" Successfully?

— Catch a "Buying Signal"?

— Ask for Business on "Favor" or "Give Me a Break" Basis?

— Get Desired Action?_____In Full?_____
In Part?_____

— Ask for "Too Much"?_____or "Too Little"?_____

— Improve "Trade Relations" as a Result of This Call?

— "Keep Your Temper on Ice" Throughout?

If "U" Did Not "Land It," What in Your Opinion was the Reason or Reasons?

_____

Service:

— Did You, During Your Sales Interview Discuss —

Sales Promotion Plans,

Publicity,

Trade Paper Adv., or

Other Fl. Service

That Would Be Beneficial to Buyer?

_____

Did "U" Evolve or Use a "Sizzle" — "Sales Technique" — "Tested Selling Idea" that Should be Reported to the Home Office, Sales Training Department?

The causes of failure to sell must be handled in some systematic fashion if the number of failures is to be reduced. Possibly the simplest method of doing this is for the salesman to start a check list which will indicate precisely the deficiencies that resulted in his inability to close each prospect who failed to buy. The assumption here is, of course, that the salesman's product and price are satisfactory and that the prospect has a real need and can buy. Sooner or later such general headings as these will appear on the check list:

Appearance was at fault.
Lack of interest on my part.
Preparation for the interview was insufficient.
Did not ask the prospect to buy.
Could not answer questions about the product.
Was guilty of irritating the prospect.
Exhibited a lack of confidence.
The story was too long, too short, poorly arranged, poorly told, difficult to follow, or difficult to believe.
Did not anticipate and handle objections.
Did not question the prospect intelligently nor follow his reactions closely.
Approach and appeal were unfortunately chosen.
Never really awakened prospect interest.

When the Prospect Buys

If a seller is to avoid ill will, complaints, demands for adjustments, cancellations, expense, and unfavorable word-of-mouth publicity, his customers must use the products they buy, like them, and continue to buy them, if the purchase is of a recurring type. The salesman must understand this for a very personal reason, namely, the size of his income, often determined by the amount of repeat business his customers give him. For this reason, the time to start converting a first-time customer into a regular, satisfied one is just after the first sale has been made.

The first thing, of course, is to thank the prospect for the purchase that made him a customer. This should be sincere, yet crisp, and must never be allowed to become casual. A compliment can be paid the prospect on his good judgment, and he can be assured that the product will live up to expectations.

A second thing is to try to make certain that the prospect will use the product to maximum advantage. Because his participation and often his cooperation are essential to a satisfactory use of the item, the prospect should be completely clear as to what he must do with it in order to benefit most. If appropriate, he should be impressed with the importance and necessity of following directions and with the continued service the seller makes available.

LOST ORDER REPORT

Gaylord Boxes

Name_____Buyer_____

Street Address_____City_____Rating_____

Kind of Boxes quoted on?_____
                                            (Corrugated or Solid Fibre)

Quantity_____Price Per M_____Total Amount of Order_____

_____

_____

_____

_____

To whom was the order given?_____

Did you quote on the same kind of boxes and according to the same specifications as your competitor's?

_____

Did you see the box the customer is now using?_____

State your reasons for losing the order._____

_____

_____

How can we help you with this account?_____

_____

_____

When do you expect to make another call?_____

Has the above firm ever bought from us?_____When?_____

Was he satisfied with our boxes and our treatment?_____

_____

Date_____Signed_____

Gaylord Container Corp.

By analyzing why an order was not obtained, both the salesman and his company benefit.

A third thing is to see if any other sales possibilities are at hand. If the salesman is handling a family of products, perhaps he has other items that might benefit the customer. Or he may observe that opportunities for more business will be coming up in the future. Or the customer may allow the salesman to take "before and after" pictures to use in other solicitations. Or the new customer may be asked to help the salesman by agreeing to be a source of testimonials. Or, finally, he might be able and willing to supply the names of, and other facts about, persons who are prospective buyers.

The time immediately after the first sale is the right time to begin to learn as much as possible about the former prospect who is now a customer. Hence, just as he keeps a file on all prospects, the salesman must also keep an individual, detailed record of each customer. All transactions should be recorded on this record, as should a list of all products bought. These records are virtual gold mines of information, and should be studied thoroughly, systematically, and often. For example, they reveal which items the salesman sells with ease, and which he sells with difficulty; they indicate what buying decisions have been troublesome; they supply clues as to what revisions or adjustments are needed.

Finally, here is a thought on order writing. Extreme care should be used in writing up the order. Errors are bad, particularly on the first order, because they prevent the seller-buyer relationship from enjoying a propitious beginning. Omissions are bad, too; an example is forgetting to get any data that will be called for by some department of the company, for instance, the credit department. In writing up the order, the salesman may ask the prospect several questions, even though he knows the answers to them. This helps to keep the prospect from being idle and from wondering if he did the right thing in making the purchase. As a matter of fact, it lets the prospect help close the sale. As the salesman fills in the order blank or sales contract, he may repeat the terms or figures he is writing. This prevents awkward periods of silence and eliminates possibility of misunderstanding between seller and buyer over quantity bought, price, delivery date, method of shipment, and such. This time of writing up the first order is most suitable for making certain that the new customer knows the terms of the seller and also understands that it is to his advantage to live up to them.

CALL-BACKS

Scheduling Call-Backs

There will be times when a prospect refuses to commit himself, either because he is actually unable to do so, or because he is unwilling. Before giving his final decision, he must secure the permission of someone for the purchase, he must see about arranging certain matters that are involved in the transaction, or his policy is to sleep over a purchase before making it. Regardless of the reason, the prospect postpones buying for what is to him a real and justifiable cause. When the salesman is certain that the prospect is determined in his decision to delay, the only thing to do is to suggest a later visit.

By recognizing that many sales require more than one call and that prospects frequently enjoy chatting with salesmen, the experienced salesman leaves gracefully as soon as he is positive that another call will be necessary. This enables him to avoid antagonizing the prospect by pressing for a decision today, and, at the same time, minimizes the time he spends and wastes in pleasant but ineffectual conversation. The salesman has decided, of course, that the prospect is worth the future call; he goes through the process of making this decision because he knows that no prospect is worth an indefinite amount of time.

The best plan is to agree then and there on a definite time for the next meeting, at which meeting the salesman hopes to review the buying decisions already gained, obtain favorable decisions on the missing ones, and close the sale. The specific appointment for the call-back has a number of advantages. First, it avoids a waste of the salesman's time by insuring that the prospect will see him. Second, the salesman can suggest a date for the follow-up conference which will fall as near as possible to the next time the prospect will be in a position to buy. Third, the move calls the prospect's attention to the interest of the salesman, his expectation of getting the order, and his desire to be of service. Fourth, the prospect feels irritated and imposed on if the salesman calls too often, and he may feel slighted and neglected if the calls are infrequent. These impressions are avoided by making definite arrangements for the follow-up. Fifth, more of the prospect's interest is retained, because he can look forward to a second, scheduled visit from one who wants to help him. Finally, the appointment may mean that the prospect will arrange to block out 'phone calls, visits from associates, and other interruptions during the next conference, thus giving the salesman his undivided attention.

A bit of showmanship may be in order here. The salesman may elect to take out his notebook and carefully enter the new appointment, assuring the prospect at the same time that he will be back at the selected hour. This impresses the prospect with the seriousness of the salesman and may help to influence more prospects to live up to the arrangement.

In some cases, where a number of calls usually precedes the sale, a salesman may violate a sound principle of salesmanship in order to insure a definite and welcome return visit. He may tell an incomplete story on some call, or he may postpone handling an objection with the promise that he will think it over and have the answer on his next trip.

Handling Call-Backs

Call-backs must not be allowed to become casual. Instead, they demand, deserve, and must be given special preparation. In getting ready for his next visit, the salesman should carefully review his prospect card and should refresh his memory about what took place at the previous meeting. If he promised to bring back something to the prospect such as information or samples, he should check to see that he has them. In addition, because time has passed since the two talked things over, which means that the prospect's attention has been called to many matters in the interim, the salesman must be prepared to renew and revive the prospect's interest and to re-establish contact; he cannot expect the prospect to remember all that was said on the last call. Indeed, in some instances the prospect may even have become negative. Pressure, then, is on the salesman to take the prospect some message that is new, important, and promising. If this is done, a very grave mistake can be avoided — that of allowing the prospect to realize that the call-back is just routine. Two other types of call-backs are as indefensible as routine ones: the call-back that is made to salvage time already spent on that prospect with no success and extremely improbable future success, and the call that is made only because the salesman knows the prospect.

In executing the call-back, the salesman must offer a justification or reason for his repeat visit. One possibility is to report on what he promised to do for the prospect. A second possibility is to present the justification as news. Whenever new facts of value to the prospect are used as an introduction to the call-back, the chances of a friendly welcome are good.

Specifically, the salesman must use speed in getting the prospect's interest and in placing the interview on firm ground by quickly launching the subject selected for initial discussion. That subject should usually be a new approach. From then on, the salesman will personalize his talk, show particular interest in the prospect's problems, make a dialogue of the interview instead of a monologue, and offer definite advantages to the prospect as on any first call.

Sometimes a salesman is forced to the conclusion that he is just not the person to sell a particular prospect. His calls are pleasant but not profitable because of his inability to complete the sale. Yet, the prospect is friendly and seems to be almost ready to buy.

As a last resort, the salesman may bring a new personality with a fresh viewpoint into the picture, usually his boss. This calling in of a pinch hitter has two possible merits. First, the prospect is presented with a different individual and with a different manner of presentation, the impact of which may be sufficient to bring success out of stalemate. Second, the prospect tends to be flattered by the fact that the salesman considered him difficult enough, and his business desirable enough, to call in a higher sales executive. This action must be handled with tact so as to avoid any semblance of high-pressure tactics.

STUDY ASSIGNMENTS

1. Is there a single "best" moment in every sales interview for making a strong closing attempt?
2. How does an expert salesman go about making it difficult for a prospect to refuse to buy?
3. Describe how and why a salesman should get agreement from the prospect throughout the presentation.
4. Why is "better too early than too late" sound advice on closing a sale?
5. Trial closes reveal whether or not the buyer is ready to buy. What more specific bits of information may they disclose?
6. What can a young salesman do to avoid being, or at least seeming, too anxious to close the sale?
7. Why is closing on a choice such an outstanding method to use?
8. What are the three most important things a salesman can do after making a sale?
9. If a prospect agrees generally to what the salesman says but does not buy or give any specific explanation for his action, what can the salesman do?
10. A major manufacturer of office machines demands that its salesmen learn a standard presentation and demonstration for one of its lines but lists several closings from which the salesman can choose. Why?

CASE STUDY 15A

Sales are often made and new items introduced in an area by a factory representative. In this case, a factory representative is working a wholesaler's area, and he is going to attempt to persuade the prospect to stock a new brand of cigarettes. The representative has just entered a small neighborhood store.

Salesman: Good morning, sir, (extends hand) I'm Frank Weaver, representing the Federal Tobacco Corporation.

Prospect: Harry Browning. Pleased to meet you. (Shakes hand.)

Salesman: You've got a nice-looking shop here, Mr. Browning. Do you mind if I look over your stock and check our brands?

Prospect: No, not at all; go right ahead.

Salesman: Thank you. (Salesman goes behind counter, straightens, arranges and rotates the stock of his firm.) Say, looks like you're pretty well stocked up on all the regular brands.

Prospect: You know how smokers are, they've got to have the brand they smoke and nothing else.

Salesman: No question about that. By the way, Mr. Browning, do you have on order any of the new Eden cigarettes?

Prospect: Eden? Is that the new filter tip that Federal is making?

Salesman: Yes, sir. It's a new concept in cigarette making. We've been more than two years in the perfection of Edens. It's a king-size cigarette, with both a filter tip and a cork tip. With the trends toward king size and filter tips, we feel that Eden cigarettes are going right up to the top in the cigarette field. They have what the public is demanding.

Prospect: I don't know, I'm of the opinion that there are too many brands of cigarettes on the market now. Why, I know that I've got cigarettes right there on that shelf that I'm going to lose money on. I just don't think I'd be interested in putting in another brand.

Salesman: We realize that there are many brands on the market and that a lot of them are slow sellers. But now you take Knights, for example; back in 1955 and 1956, a lot of retailers didn't want to stock those, but in the past several years, Knights has become one of the leading king-size cigarettes.

Prospect: Yes, that's true enough, but it took it a couple of years to get there.

Salesman: We're going to push this new Eden a lot faster. We're shooting for a definite place among the six leading brands within two years. Federal is behind this brand 100%, and, starting next week, Edens are going to be advertised on all radio and television shows which are now advertising Stars. At the same time, we're going to saturate the East with newspaper ads. We're going to create a lot of interest in this new cigarette, just for the purpose of getting people to try them out of curiosity. You're going to have people walking right into your own store asking for them. Mr. Browning, I'd like to leave you a supply so you'll be able to take care of those customers.

Prospect: I just don't feel like taking on any more new items. Besides, I don't have enough space to display them. If I start getting a lot of calls for them, then I'll make some arrangements to stock them.

Salesman: Mr. Browning, if you wait until you start getting calls for them, then you're going to lose a lot of the initial business. You have the only tobacco shop in a six-block area, and if your customers have to go elsewhere for the brand they want, then you're going to be losing sales on some of your other items also. We can take care of the space problem. I have with me a nice counter display which will not only attract the customers' attention but will take care of your space problem. I'd like to set one up for you.

Prospect: Well, maybe I should have a few; what do they sell for?

Salesman: They wholesale for $1.85 per carton, which is a few cents higher than the major regulars, but it is under the price that you've been paying for other king-size filter tips. Suppose I put in ten cartons for you?

Prospect: Let me see, that would run $18.50. I don't know; that's a little more than I'd want to put into a new brand.

Salesman: You take no chance on a loss with this product, Mr. Browning. You've been dealing with the Federal Tobacco Company for many years, and you know that we stand back of everything we produce, so you won't have to worry about taking a loss on these Edens.

Prospect: You people really seem to be sold on these things, so I guess I can go ahead and get ten cartons.

Salesman: Fine. I'm sure you'll be glad you did. If you'll sign this order, I'll step out to my car and get your display. (Salesman hands order to buyer and goes out to car; he returns with several posters.) Mr. Browning, I've got something else here you'll be interested in. I'm going to set up two of the posters in your tobacco department. (Sets up posters.) How's that?

Prospect: Sure, that's all right.

Salesman: When I was out in the car, I picked up this price card that you might want to put up. It lists all the cigarette brands with a space beside them for you to enter the price. I thought you might like to have one.

Prospect: Fine.

Salesman: Here's something else you might be able to use to your advantage. They're inventory control sheets where you can keep a record of just what stock you have on hand and how old it is. Most of our customers have found that it saves them a lot of stockroom counting.

Prospect: Say, that's all right. It's nice of you to give me these things.

Salesman: You're perfectly welcome, Mr. Browning. We like to deal with customers like you, and we want you to know that we appreciate your business. (Picks up hat.) It's been a pleasure talking to you, Mr. Browning. I'm sure your regular wholesaler will take care of your needs for Edens and the other Federal products, but if at any time we can be of service to you, just drop us a note, and we'll be glad to help you in any way we can.

Prospect: Why, that's very nice of you, and thanks . . . thanks a lot. (They shake hands and the salesman leaves.)

QUESTIONS.

1. What did the salesman do well?
2. What did the salesman do that could be improved?
3. What techniques are illustrated in the sale?
4. How many attempts to close did Weaver make?

CASE STUDY 15B

The prospect is the owner of a dry cleaning store, and the salesman is a representative of the advertising department of one of the two local newspapers. The scene is the prospect's store.

Salesman: Good morning, sir. How are you?

Prospect: Hello. Don't I know you from somewhere?

Salesman: Yes, sir, I've been here once before to see you. Remember, I was telling you how I could help you to improve your business?

Prospect: Now I remember. You're the advertising man from *The Globe*.

Salesman: I have a plan here that will help you to increase your business. Remember, last time you were telling me that just about everybody and his brother are going into the dry cleaning business.

Prospect: They seem to be opening up all over town. It's already cut into my business. I have a good place here, and people know me, but still there's only so much business to go around.

Salesman: I know what you mean, Mr. Phelps. I've seen your truck around town with that slogan about courtesy. And I've heard around town that your clerks are very courteous. That's all part of your plan to sell the public on using your service, isn't it?

Prospect: Yes, it is.

Salesman: That is just why advertising is so important. It lets people know about your service.

Prospect: I don't need advertising. I offer courteous service and prompt delivery, and I do excellent work here. People know that, so advertising won't matter at all.

Salesman: You're perfectly right about your service, Mr. Phelps. I agree with you completely. No amount of advertising would help you if you didn't give such good service. But if you were to use advertising in *The Globe*, more people would know about and be able to take advantage of your fine service.

Prospect: Listen, young fellow, people don't read those ads. You know that.

Salesman: Let's put it this way, Mr. Phelps. Some people don't read ads, just as you say. But many, many people *do* read the ads. Certainly you are interested in those people, and with a *Globe* ad you can tell them about your service and get them to try it out. Why, you probably saw that cigarette ad in yesterday's *Globe*, didn't you?

Prospect: You mean the one on the back page?

Salesman: Yes, that's the one. Well, up to 25,000 people in the surrounding ten-mile area saw that ad. How would you like this number of people to see an ad about your store?

Prospect: Now, hold on. I can't afford any big ads like that one. I'm not a big cigarette company, you know.

Salesman: We have all sizes of space. Naturally, you wouldn't want anything that big. One of our smaller spaces would better suit your needs.

Prospect: Yes, sir, you're right. I don't need any of those large ads. But small ads are no good. Nobody ever looks at those little things. That would just be a waste of my good money.

Salesman: Did you know that small newspaper ads reach more readers at lower cost per reader than do large ads? Why, you've heard of St. Joseph Aspirin, haven't you?

Prospect: Yes.

Salesman: Well, that's a national organization, and yet they have always used small space effectively. And look at all the local businesses that use small space. Just take a look at today's paper (shows him the paper), and see how many local businesses are advertising. Now you know they wouldn't do this if it didn't pay. And I can tell you, they are all satisfied with our service. What type of ad do you think would suit your needs best?

Prospect: Well, let's see .... No, I don't think advertising in your paper can do my business much good. There's just so much business to go around, and that's all there is to it. No amount of advertising will make any difference.

Salesman: Let's take a look at the retail picture. Now you know that some stores receive a much larger share of the market than others. That is because they offer the best service and quality and because they tell people about it through a planned advertising program. Such companies survive and prosper, while others fall by the wayside. Now, we know that you have excellent service and quality, but not enough people in town know about it. Now,

I can run a nice-sized ad in the Thursday paper, or would you rather have me run it in the Friday paper?

Prospect: Well, Thursday would probably be better, that is, if I decide that I want to run an ad.

Salesman: Yes, that's a good choice. Newspaper advertising is the best way to serve your needs for a basic advertising plan. When something is printed, a person can read it as many times as he wishes, and after awhile the name of your store will become imprinted in the person's mind. Now, I've been giving a lot of thought to your advertising problem, and I'd like to show you this series of layouts. You'll notice this uniform border. This will help to tie all your ads together and remind the reader that he has seen your ads before. What size do you want me to run for you? (Shows sample sizes.)

Prospect: Well, how much is this one?

Salesman: We can run this one twice a week for four weeks for only $50.

Prospect: That's just a little too steep for me. Sorry, young fellow, I don't think I'll buy any newspaper advertising just now.

Salesman: Now is just about the most important time for you to start advertising in *The Globe.* With competition getting stiffer, you're going to want to get a larger share of the business. Newspaper advertising to the 25,000 readers of *The Globe* will help your business. At our prices you get your message across to the most people at the lowest cost to you. Now is the best time to get your advertising plan started. Perhaps you would like this smaller-sized ad or maybe you'll just want to try it out for three weeks instead of four. How does that sound?

Prospect: Why don't you come by next week, and I'll let you know?

Salesman: If you place an ad with me today, you can take advantage of our special program. Today is the very last day that we make the offer of running a free ad for every five you buy. In other words, if you run a series of five ads, we will run a sixth one for you at no extra cost. If you'll just authorize this right here (opens order book), I'll take care of all the details for you.

Prospect: Well, all right. I'll just take this small one, though.

Salesman: That will be a good start on your advertising program. (Hands prospect his pen and gets signature.) I'll stop by again after a couple of your ads have been run in the paper. Then we can discuss how we can meet the other needs of your advertising program.

Prospect: All right, I'll see you then.

Salesman: Goodbye.

QUESTIONS:

1. What did the salesman do well?
2. What did the salesman do that could be improved?
3. What techniques are illustrated in the sale?
4. How many closing clues do you find in this interview?
5. Which closing techniques did the *Globe* man use?

CHAPTER 16

WORKING WITH CUSTOMERS

When a salesman's operations are viewed over the long run, two stages are noticed. In the first stage, the salesman deals with *prospects*, individuals who can and should buy his product but don't. This first stage comes to an end when a prospect makes his first purchase and becomes a *customer*. The second stage finds the salesman dealing with his customers. Just as the salesman drafted a program to make a customer out of a prospect, he needs to plan a program for serving and selling to that customer.

You remember that some salesmen sell to wholesalers and retailers for resale, some sell to business buyers for commercial use, some sell to and through professional men, and some sell to the ultimate consumer. Working with their customers has a separate set of meanings and demands for each of these four groups. In this chapter we stress the selling of merchandise to wholesalers and retailers for resale. Some of the principles and techniques from this area can be adapted to others, particularly selling to business buyers for commercial use.

The rewards of working systematically with customers are well worth the effort. Such work helps hold customers, and, as salesmen will tell you, it's easier to *hold* them than to *get* them. Such work includes seeing that the customer benefits to the maximum extent from his purchases and is helped by the salesman in various ways. Repeat sales are a reward, as are increased and expanded sales volume. Customers are a fruitful source of leads on new prospects. If they are happy customers, they give the salesman, his products, and his company favorable word-of-mouth publicity. It is quite likely that *customers* deserve and get far more of the typical salesman's time and thought than do *prospects*.

FIRST RETURN CALL

When a prospect has become a customer by making his first purchase, the salesman is justified in scheduling an early return visit to see that his new customer is getting along all right. On this visit, after complimenting

389

the customer on his choice, the salesman should check to see that his company filled the order correctly and satisfactorily and that the customer is using the product in the proper manner. Instructions about use and maintenance may be repeated and any questions answered that have come up since the sale. Should anything have gone wrong, this early return gives the salesman an opportunity to nip complaints in the bud by exhibiting a sincerely sympathetic attitude, finding out just what went wrong, and by taking appropriate action. He will then follow up to see that the corrective steps are taken. The call should also be used to continue to sell the customer on the benefits and satisfaction he will enjoy. Finally, the visit may line up the customer for future purchases and may result in obtaining a testimonial or proof of performance or some leads and pre-approach information about new prospects.

FREQUENCY OF SUBSEQUENT CALLS

One of the early decisions to be made concerns how often the new customer will be visited by the salesman. Calling on him too frequently wastes selling time and money and might cause the customer to become irritated. In addition, the informed customer recognizes that too many calls are being made, and this tends to make him question the judgment and managerial ability of the salesman. If the calls are scheduled too far apart, again there may be difficulties. The customer resents, and rightly so, being given inadequate service and, as a result, begins to wonder about how much dependence he can place on the salesman and his products. Furthermore, occasional and infrequent calls are an invitation to competition to move in and take the account.

Classification of Customers

In scheduling calls, one of the first facts to be appreciated is that no one interval between visits will fit all customers; some will demand and deserve a short interval between calls while others will require fewer calls. These circumstances call for a grouping of customers. Three or four classifications should be adequate for most situations. The classifications below illustrate the principle:

A group: Most important customers. Called on once a month. Entitled to attention of high executives when necessary.

B group: Good substantial customers. Called on every other month. Expect and should get considerable attention from salesman.

C group: Less profitable customers. Many are small. Many spend more with the salesman's competitors. Called on twice a year. Some mail solicitation.

D group: Least valuable customers. Small, weak, and expensive. No calls. Handled entirely by mail.

A second fact to be appreciated is that a large number of small customers account for a minor part of the salesman's total sales. As a matter of fact, a generalization is that "twenty per cent of the customers account for eighty per cent of the sales." Many sellers find that their experiences approximate this pattern. The problem here involves the other eighty per cent of the customers. Deciding what to do about them is not easy.

Calling on Small Customers

Some of the small accounts will eventually grow into the "A" group. No seller wants to cut off one of these accounts just because it is small and perhaps is being handled at no profit under current conditions. If he does, he will have a difficult if not impossible task trying to recapture it after it joins the competition. Of course, many of the small accounts will become even smaller and eventually disappear. Also, right or wrong, most sellers are reluctant to give up a customer to a competitor. Yet, the profitableness of a customer *today* must be considered. No salesman can continue indefinitely to call on a small customer whose patronage does not result in *some* profit. So, the two forces in operation are today's volume and tomorrow's possibilities versus today's cost of handling the account.

Here are some suggestions as to what might be done about small customers:

1. Service no account buying less than a certain amount. (While this may work toward eliminating unprofitable customers, it sends some customers to competitors. If the minimum figure is for single orders, then a problem is created with respect to small, emergency orders from good customers.)

2. Adopt a service fee for small orders. (Both establishing and collecting such a fee are difficult.)

3. Establish a system of quantity discounts.

4. The seller and his competitors can act jointly (and legally) to see that small customers pay their way.

5. Educate small customers about the costs of handling small accounts.

6. Raise the size of the average order through better selling.

7. Classify small customers into two groups, the promising and the unpromising, and give the former most of the time and attention available for small customers. This available time will be determined by such factors as how many of these customers the seller has, how often they are in the market to buy, how often the seller can do a favor for the customer, and how often the salesman has current, important information to give.

The best policy for the salesman would seem to be to work with small customers in an effort to develop them into large ones and to continue this until he is convinced that he will not be able to effect this growth. There will be many exceptions to this general rule.

The salesman must realize just what "B" and "C" accounts mean to him. "A" accounts are fine and desirable, but they should not be serviced to the neglect of the "B" and "C" groups. These two groups are needed for bread-and-butter volume and may account for as much as one third of total sales. Too, almost all "A" accounts were at an earlier time "C," then "B," accounts. If the salesman wins out over competition at the "C" or "B" level, he will be better able to take care of himself when the buyer becomes an "A" account. The natural mortality in any group of accounts is a final justification for intentionally devoting a certain amount of time to "B" and "C" customers.

In servicing "B" and "C" accounts, the salesman must do every-thing he can to insure ease of buying for the ultimate consumer, because that consumer will be doing business with a merchant who falls short of top grade ability. In making arrangements so that the public can buy easily, the salesman tries to get the "B" or "C" account to do those things that will make selling at retail as automatic as possible, things that will enable the merchandise to come as close as possible to selling itself. To this end, the salesman tries to see that the items the merchant has constitute a balanced stock, and that they are so displayed that they invite the public to examine them, handle them, and try them if possible. Time is spent telling and retelling the merchant why he should feature the merchandise in both window and store display. Any specific selling tech-niques that have proved their effectiveness are passed on to the merchant or his sales force for use. In a word, the salesman does his best to help the "B" or "C" account make sales. Periodic reference to his customer records will tell the salesman the degree of success he is enjoying with any one customer and will guide him in allotting his time more profitably.

HOLDING THE ACCOUNT

Frequently a salesman will have spent much time and money in calling on a particular prospect before getting an order from him. Just as fre-quently he does not gross enough on the first order to equal the expense he has incurred up to that time. Indeed, in some cases, the salesman will need to sell three, four, or even more orders to the customer before he has earned enough money to equal the development cost of that account. If the customer switches to a competitor, the salesman will have to replace him at further cost of time, effort, and money. All of this translates into a basic rule that the salesman must not let accounts get away from him. He must hold on to them. Except for the relatively few salesmen who sell products that are purchased only once in a lifetime (houses, education, certain jewelry items, and insurance are somewhat but not completely of this nature), the salesman looks to repeat orders for his income. This explains the emphasis on the salesman's seeing that the customer gets started right; on the salesman's being sure to keep a sensitive finger on the prospect's pulse, as it were, as he changes into a customer; and on the salesman's doing what he can to keep the customer's enthusiasm at a high level.

Somewhat in this same connection, the salesman must understand that for the long term his interests and those of his customer are the same, that he prospers only to the extent that his customer prospers. Certainly, there will be a narrow zone within which the customer tries to out-maneuver the salesman, and the salesman counters by trying to prevent this. But this zone cannot be very broad. If the buyer buys too shrewdly, the seller must give up the account for lack of profit, and the buyer must establish a relationship with another vendor. If the salesman sells unwisely, the buyer finds conditions not to his liking and takes his business elsewhere. By seeing that his sales are ones which are profitable to both buyer and seller and serving his customers so that they can operate in a satisfactory fashion, the salesman helps to insure repeat orders and helps to hold his accounts.

Because a satisfied customer is hard to take away from his present source of supply, and because his personal standing with his customers is so important, the salesman should be very careful in handling all transactions and contacts with customers. He should win and keep their complete confidence in his honesty, judgment, and discretion. He should not ask favors of customers except in emergencies, and this holds good for such small matters as cashing checks and extending credit.

The salesman must be constantly on the alert for any signal that might mean that all is not well between buyer and supplier. One type of sign is *financial*. A customer's total sales may begin to drop, his purchases from the salesman may become smaller, or some change of financial policy may be made. Any of these moves calls for the salesman's scrutiny because any one of them may affect him. A second type of signal is *personal*. If the customer becomes ill, if he is increasingly influenced by someone unfriendly to the salesman, if he shows less attention to or interest in his business, if he is out of his office more than he should be, or if his associates handle more of the business than formerly, the salesman should prepare for future possibilities. Finally, *outside happenings* may change good customers into poor ones or even former ones. Legislation, obsolescence, physical changes, such as the rerouting of a traffic flow or the appearance of new and keen competition, may foretell changes that the salesman must include in his calculations. These three types of occurrence are mentioned because of their possible influence on holding an account.

As part of his annual analysis of his own past performance, the salesman should study each account he acquired during the previous twelve months and make definite, individual plans for holding it. The same should be done for each account he retained throughout the year. And each account lost during the period should be examined in detail. In establishing the cause of the loss, it may be found that the merchandise did not sell well in a certain area, that the dealer failed to handle the line properly, that something was wrong with the product, that the dealer's margin was inadequate, that the vendor company gave poor service, that the salesman was at fault, or that something else was responsible. Once the cause has been identified, an appropriate program to regain desirable accounts should be begun.

The salesmen of Nibroc Towels are told this about holding accounts:

Holding the Account

Regular contact with each account is excellent insurance against losing a customer.

In order to do an intelligent job in follow up, it is necessary to know the frequency of purchase. If an account buys 25 cases every 30 days, it will prove profitable to contact the account prior to the expected date of purchase.

Give the customer another reason for using Nibroc Towels. There are many different appeals which can be used to do this. It will make the account more solidly Nibroc and will lend purpose to your call.

Keep him sold. Sell new key people in the organization on Nibroc Towel service.

Ask about plans for new washrooms and new locations. Check for possible points where Nibroc Towels are not used at present. These may be within the local organization itself or in its branches. Additional volume may be there for the asking. Customers appreciate interest in their problems.

Keep him supplied with the proper number of dispensers.

Think service, and the account will stay on your books, and the steady flow of dollars to your pocket will continue.

INCREASING THE ACCOUNT

It is not enough for the salesman to get an account and hold it. He must increase it and expand it to its full potential. His first aim is to secure *all* of the customer's business in the lines he sells, never allowing himself to become satisfied so long as he enjoys only a part. The next objective is to develop the account until the customer is buying and selling (or using) as much as can be expected. In attaining these goals, the salesman persuades the customer as soon as possible to designate his company as the regular source of supply, to get in the habit of buying from him and his company, and to think of those two when ready to buy. This helps to insure sales volume month after month and to enable the salesman to get that customer's business even between calls.

There are several excellent reasons why developing each account should be important, the first and strongest of which is additional income from additional volume. Second, so long as a customer divides his buying between or among vendors, the salesman remains in considerable danger of losing out. That is a disturbing risk. Next, less time should be required, in most cases, to build up the volume of customers than to get the same dollar increase from converting prospects into customers. Fourth, in lines of business where retailers place one half to three fourths of their orders by 'phone or mail, the top salesmen are top because of the many orders that are sent in to them. The salesman here wants and needs that business because he cannot live on the orders he gets personally on his calls. Fifth, since the salesman and the customer know each other, it should be comparatively easy for them to do additional business. Sixth, if a customer ought to be buying the salesman's complete line but buys only a part of it, he is not completely supplied, and he should appreciate the salesman's suggestion-selling that shows him how to provide for his requirements more adequately.

Obstacles

There are obstacles that make the increasing of accounts a real job. One may be the salesman's mental attitude. If so, he usually fears that he will offend a customer or maybe even lose him by trying to get more of his purchases. This mental hazard is not warranted; the answer to it is smooth, tactful selling. A second obstacle is inadequate product knowledge. The remedy is simply for the salesman to know enough about his merchandise to effectively recommend the right items in the right circumstances. A really serious obstacle is the reluctance or even refusal of a buyer to change his habits of thought and action. Some buyers divide their purchases to keep a check on the prices of various vendors. Others do this in an attempt to insure a source of supply should something happen to any one supplier. Others do this in an effort to stock the fastest-moving items and brands. Reciprocity influences still others. Certain buyers feel obligated to certain sellers. Others believe in the principle of loyalty to present sources. All these can be powerful pressures on buyers against switching their patronage from current sources of supply; and while the salesman is working to change these established patterns, other salesmen are just as fiercely determined that their customers shall not desert them.

It is only fair to add here that frequently, for one of the reasons mentioned or because of some other influence, the salesman is never able to secure what he or his sales manager consider to be their "fair" share of a customer's total business. This does not excuse the salesman from estimating his "realistic" share in each case and then making plans to obtain it.

Specific Suggestions

The list below is of suggestions and specific techniques that may prove successful in increasing the dollar volume of a customer's purchases. All of the methods included will not be appropriate in every situation, but each will be effective for certain customers on certain occasions.

1. Be systematic about the development program or do not bother with it. A carefully thought out master plan is needed for increasing sales volume, and this over-all program should consist of separate, definite campaigns for building up the business of each individual customer, tailored to fit his particular situation.

2. Try to make some progress toward the ultimate goal of maximum potential volume on each visit.

3. Sell the customer on the idea of becoming a preferred customer of the seller. Every seller has good customers and those who are not so good. When he is in a position to do favors for some, he naturally selects the customers who are most valuable to him, and they are usually the ones who buy the most from him.

4. Identify merchandise that the customer does not carry but should. Then talk to him about the popularity of the line in that classification, how easy it is to sell, the size of the potential market, and how his dollar profit will increase.

5. Keep the customer's business balanced. For every $100 of shirts he sells, he should sell a certain amount of ties, or for every thousand gallons of gasoline, he should sell so many dollars worth of accessories. Any current lack of balance should be called to the customer's attention, and proper steps should be taken when next year's quotas are discussed.

6. Keep eyes and ears open for signs that the customer needs to replenish his stock of an item that he buys from someone else. When the customer is in danger of running out of that particular product, with the resulting cost or loss, he is most apt to listen to your warning and to act on it by letting you rush an order through so that the stock will not become exhausted.

7. Offer a sound merchandising idea, perhaps involving allied selling, ensemble selling, direct mail advertising, or a telephone selling campaign, along with an increased or expanded order. The customer will be much more inclined to buy. The salesman who sells *for* his customers has no trouble selling *to* them.

8. Whenever you have a special offer or deal in your assortment, use it in enlarging the customer's purchase. Place emphasis on the lower price, the larger discount, the more liberal trade-in as a competitive device, and the deadline, if there is one. Translate the additional volume into advantage to the buyer.

9. Mere persistence is crude and ineffectual. Intelligent cultivation is required.

10. Some customers buy one or two items from a salesman but order a broad variety of products from some other vendor. This calls for a careful scrutiny of the numbers making up the broad list and the corresponding numbers in your own line. It may be that you can find one thing, or even more, which makes an item so clearly and impartially a superior buy that the customer must agree that he should buy it rather than the one he is buying. This superiority may be a price, patented feature, frequent or prompt delivery, or completeness of line. These superior buys may serve as opening wedges in securing a competitor's business.

11. Relate the new, recommended line to what the customer now buys. He has less mental difficulty giving the recommendation fair consideration if the new product is related to the known one.

12. When a new item is placed in your line, approach the customer from a new angle, and you may make an additional sale. Show what the product is, what it will do for the customer, and how it will affect that customer's competition. If there is special promotion behind the new item, the proposal will have greater appeal.

13. If the customer is a "split dealer," handling competing brands or buying from competing vendors, sell him on the desirability of handling a single line. Stress savings in transportation, risk, record keeping, and investment, and then talk of improvement in prestige, profit, assortment, quality of selling, turnover, and buyer-seller cooperation. The second job is to get the customer to choose *your* line for concentration and calls for pointing out the ways in which your proposition is better.

14. If there is no possibility of expanding the customer's order by the inclusion of new product lines, there may be a chance of increasing it. This may take one of two forms. First, quantity may be increased where the customer has been neglecting the line and has not built it up to its potential volume. Such a customer may need to devote only a little more attention to the line's possibilities, or put a little more advertising and

selling effort back of it, or give it a little more or better display space in order to increase sales greatly. Second, you may successfully engage in "trading up" if a substantial demand is present in the customer's market for quality merchandise.

15. Giving excellent service on the business the customer places with you is, in a silent yet convincing manner, recommendation that you be entrusted with a larger share of his business. It may be somewhat risky to suggest openly that you deserve more.

16. Always be tactful and sometimes casual. By treating reference to additional buying as an afterthought, as a "by the way, that reminds me" matter, you keep the customer from retreating behind too effective a defense.

17. It is a mistake to be too conservative or too aggressive. The overly conservative salesman, motivated by excess caution or fear, errs by allowing his competitors to go after and get orders that he could have had. He easily convinces himself that he should wait until the atmosphere is more promising before suggesting additional buying. The overly aggressive salesman is equally at fault. In his excessive haste to effect changes and realignments, he can easily close doors in his own face, permanently. Too often he is determined to write up a huge order without proper consideration and study of the customer's needs. Follow a moderate course by being patient but progressive, holding what you now have and taking over other items and lines gradually.

18. Do something on each call that will better cement the buyer-seller relationship. While the nature of this move may be suggested by reference to the customer's record, probably the most versatile type of favor is imparting some valuable market information. Advertising suggestions, successful selling techniques, methods of speeding up collections, notice of future price changes — these are examples.

19. Whenever possible, plant an idea with the customer when leaving. This gives him something to consider, to mull over in his mind until the next visit, and, if it was a happy choice, he may be ready to act on it then. After planting a seed for additional purchases, don't stay away so long that a competitor gathers in the harvest. Delivery calls may be used to check on how the idea is developing.

As somewhat of a summary, the final suggestion is that the salesman should identify what there is about him, his company, his products, or his proposition that distinguishes him, in a favorable manner, from his competition. If he finds no differences, he should create some. Then, he should devote major emphasis to these exclusive points, because by so doing he finds that his message is most effective and his impression most favorable.

SECURING CUSTOMER SUPPORT

Up to this point we have been discussing aid and assistance in one direction — from seller to buyer. Now it is time to examine and evaluate the customer as a possible source of help to the salesman.

The phrase "customer support" is used to describe the most desirable and sought-after service the buyer can render the seller. At the start, the individual is a prospect and nothing more. Next he is prevailed on to place his first order and become an account, usually small and not very profitable, perhaps neutral or maybe a little skeptical toward the seller. As the account increases in size and confidence, it gradually moves into the customer class. Only one further step remains in the process of development, and that step is taken when the customer becomes an enthusiastic, loyal customer. The seller then enjoys customer support.

In this relationship, the customer is actively and enthusiastically in favor of the salesman, his company, his products, and his service. The customer sees that the salesman's line of merchandise is always stocked in adequate volume, is favored in the display treatment given it, and is pushed by personal selling as much as practicable. In one sense, the customer and his employees actually sell for the salesman. Most important of all, the customer looks on the salesman as more than a peddler, viewing him instead almost as a partner.

The customer asks the salesman's opinions on a variety of matters, some broader than just the salesman's line, and often relies on the salesman's judgment rather than his own. Because he considers the salesman an expert, he depends on him, respects him, and is inclined to follow his advice. It should be unnecessary to add that the salesman must be good to qualify for and deserve this relationship.

How to Obtain Customer Support

Here are a few possibilities for obtaining support from customers.

1. Frequent contact, even if only a reminder postal card, is desirable.

2. Make each visit an occasion by always having a good, new reason for calling, such as a new product, model, sample, plan, or bit of information. Don't ever tell the customer or even give him the impression that you "just happened by," or "just dropped in to see how things are going." In contrast, by indicating that a special call is being made, you make every impression a favorable one, flatter the customer, and encourage his cooperation.

3. Do as many favors for the customer as possible. Any help, sound advice, valuable information, or personal assistance obligates the customer

just that much more, and by implication asks him to reciprocate by increased patronage and support.

4. Show the customer how he will benefit by giving you his support and loyalty. It may be that some policy of your company helped the customer to weather a price war, to maintain his margin, to cash in on a special event, or such. Or you may show actual figures that prove how other customers have increased sales in the past by synchronizing their efforts and tying them in with those of your company. Finally, always point out how the customer will gain by cooperating in the future.

5. Develop an agreeable, pleasant personality, and then use it. You want to be on a friendly basis with the customer and with the customer's employees, taking a personal interest in them, cultivating them, knowing their activities, and complimenting them. A friendly relationship, not undue familiarity, is the goal.

6. Serve the customer's best interests by taking thorough care of him, by giving wise guidance and helpful service, by deserving, getting, and holding his trust, and by being a friendly counselor. The customer should never have to ask about something new or wait for something due. Such things as being too busy to help him, going over his head for a decision, divulging information he gave in confidence, must not be done.

7. Wherever practicable, locate customers and prospects for your customers.

8. Never stop accumulating knowledge, particularly about your products and the art of selling.

9. No customer should ever be given cause or opportunity for losing his enthusiasm. Don't allow anything to happen which would encourage him to begin questioning any of his five buying decisions.

10. Be more than just a salesman. Be posted on your field not only locally, but also nationally and internationally. Be able to interpret and justify your company's decisions and policies. Your grasp of general business conditions, causes, and trends must expand continuously. To the maximum extent possible, be a dependable source of current information about such matters as collections, advertising, and legislation. Finally, to the customer be a sincere friend who wants to be of all possible assistance.

How Customers Help Salesmen

Customers are interested in businesses similar to their own, in their objectives, their problems, the solutions they try on those problems, and their general operation and circumstances. The information they demand may be about such general topics as advertising, store arrangement, reviving dormant accounts, speeding up collections, or getting more sales power from the sales force. Or it may be about the salesman's line of merchandise, how it should be displayed and advertised, what assortment is most profitable, new uses for the products, or new selling techniques. The salesman is a very convenient medium for the exchange of such information. On the other hand, when he picks up from a customer factual proof to use in his sales presentation, or gets names and backgrounds of new prospects, he has been done a very definite favor.

In encouraging the customer to aid him, and in benefiting therefrom to the maximum amount possible, the salesman will need to use resourcefulness, originality, and initiative. With some customers he will play a game, each seeing which can give the other the more desirable story. Other customers will become valuable sources only after being challenged, or even discounted, in good spirits, as possible suppliers of any worthwhile news. Still other customers will react as desired when complimented, or when recognized in some pleasing manner. Regardless of the methods used, the salesman further cements buyer-seller relationships as he draws on his customers for material he can use.

We mention here six types of helpful information that customers can give salesmen. The first is "case histories" — experiences customers have had which are of interest or value, but which did not involve any particular problem. One merchant put X brand of tires on his delivery trucks, got so much mileage out of them, and was delighted. Or, an individual provided for his child's education through insurance. Or, a retailer installed a certain system of lighting in his store with gratifying results.

Second, solutions to common problems may be passed along. A retailer revised his business hours and a wholesaler installed a new system of stock control, and each change was an improvement. Or, a manufacturer tried a new series of collection notices, or wrote what he thought was potent copy for an advertisement, and was unhappy with the result.

Testimonials are a third type of valuable information. The customer may describe voluntarily all that air conditioning has done for him. The salesman may write a conservative, appropriate statement for use over the customer's signature on the customer's letterhead. A slightly different kind of testimonial, one that the salesman can construct without having to obtain anyone's permission, is a list of his customers.

Fourth, a list of references may consist of customers. Prospects sometimes like to talk to individuals who have bought and used the item under consideration, feeling, no doubt, that this source may be more unbiased and impartial than the salesman. Many customers enjoy being given as references.

Fifth, new uses for the product may be furnished or pointed out by customers.

Finally, customers may supply the names of new prospects for the salesman to investigate and cultivate. In some instances, background information may supplement a name and address. Or a letter of introduction may be volunteered by the customer in special cases. Once in a long, long while, the customer will make an appointment for the salesman with the prospect.

INFLUENCING CUSTOMERS' MERCHANDISING POLICIES

The Objective

In this section, the word "merchandising" means advertising, display, and personal selling. One characteristic of the better salesman is that he is able to help shape and guide the merchandising activities of his retail customers and, by so doing, ultimately to help determine retail merchandising policy.

It must be emphasized at this point that when a salesman begins trying to influence a customer's policies, he is attempting a job that requires the quintessence of skill, tact, and diplomacy. In an over-all way, the object of such influence is to maximize dollar profits for customer and salesman. In more detail, the salesman wants the customer to believe in advertising and to use it. He wants the customer to handle the full line and to maintain adequate stocks at all times. This permits balanced sales, including sales of the higher priced, high-profit items. The salesman would like every customer's place to be a model of enthusiasm and efficiency, a show place where display and pleasing appearance are exploited most profitably, in this atmosphere the salesman's merchandise being the most preferred, favored, and pushed — to the extent that the retailer can afford to push a single line. In working toward these goals, the salesman learns from customers what they should and should not do, thus collecting valuable case histories and "before and after" data to use in his sales presentations.

Obtaining the Objective

One starting point is a continuing study and analysis of a customer's orders. Once a pattern has been identified, it can be compared with that of the most outstanding customer in order to locate weak spots. A second approach is for the salesman to persuade the customer to plan and schedule his merchandising activities to tie in with and to take full advantage of the complete promotion program of the salesman's company. Along this line, the salesman should convince the customer of the desirability of using all available company promotional material that is suitable for him to use.

The salesman may get the retailer to encourage suggestion selling and trading up, increasing the amount of the average sale and the average selling price per item. Too, the salesman tries to get the customer to do an effective advertising job, both for his entire business and for the salesman's own merchandise. The salesman should never be too important or too busy to lend a hand in setting up displays, dressing windows, or doing other merchandising jobs. Finally, he needs to make constructive suggestions that will help insure profitable operation.

Advertising

Before attempting to influence a retailer's advertising policy, a salesman should check to see that he is clear in his own mind about (1) advertising in general, (2) about his company's advertising, and (3) about his customer's advertising problems.

On the first point, he needs an appreciation of the role advertising plays in the process of distribution, and he should understand just what it is, what can be expected of it, and what not to expect of it. Some worthwhile thoughts on this matter come from Mr. George B. Brown, an executive of a large advertising agency:

> Advertising is a force little understood by the public as a whole. What is more surprising is the fact that few salesmen understand the limitations of advertising as it relates to the products they sell and to their own jobs. Perhaps the reason for this general lack of understanding stems from the fact that most sales managers and advertising managers, aside from telling the sales force what advertising will be used to support them, seldom outline the "reason why" for advertising. For years, there has been a considerable amount of loose talk about advertising *per se*. It is a standard axiom that "it pays to advertise." Actually, the records are heavily laden with the names of now defunct companies who *blindly* believed it paid to advertise. As a matter of fact, advertising is a waste unless it is done right — and unless it enjoys certain prerequisites, such as: (1) good products, (2) fair prices, (3) adequate discounts, (4) adequate packaging, (5) correct distribution, (6) strong sales force. Advertising can do its job efficiently only when it can do so in a state of balance. Salesmen must not look upon it as a mysterious force that of and by itself creates business giants. Indeed, I suspect the record would show that advertising — badly executed and without the proper prerequisites — can accelerate a company's death. It is imperative, then, that salesmen fully understand the limitations of advertising and that they not expect it to be a 20-ton bulldozer which will knock down all the hurdles for them.
>
> A second point which salesmen should clear up in their own thinking is just what is the purpose of advertising. We have all heard that "advertising sells goods" and that advertising is "salesmanship in print."

Actually, advertising does not specifically sell goods (except direct mail). Advertising's basic function is not that of salesmanship in the literal sense, but rather is that of conveying ideas about products (or a point of view) so that people will have a favorable mental attitude toward the product or the idea. This is true whether advertising is used to support the sale of steamrollers or aspirin tablets. Advertising basically, then, is nothing more than a means of conditioning someone else's mind and is perhaps one of the strongest educational factors at work today. Since advertising does not "sell goods" but rather tries to form favorable mental impressions, the salesman must realize that his job is to capitalize upon the job which advertising does. The salesman must be prepared to follow through on the job advertising starts.

At times the salesman will need to be able to defend advertising as a selling tool, especially as used by his company, and to explain to non-believing, nonusing customers how they may be handicapping themselves. The objection voiced may be that advertising costs too much; that it is not needed because the customer was "born and raised here, has been in business in this location for twenty-five years, and is known by every-body"; that advertising is the manufacturer's responsibility; that the retailer is too small to use advertising effectively; or that the retailer ran an advertisement once without results. In explaining and then recom-mending the use of advertising, the salesman will probably suggest that previous efforts could have been deficient, or that too much was expected, or they were sporadic instead of continuous. His strongest move may be to show the customer the total potential demand within that customer's trading area, and then ask how the customer proposes to get his share.

On the second point, his company's advertising, the salesman must first know what company policy is and how to justify it. Troublesome customers will take one of two positions. The smaller, less enlightened ones will criticize the company that advertises extensively, claiming that those dollars should be spent instead in giving wider discounts to dealers. The other position is that the company should do such a complete adver-tising job that dealers will not need to do any. Regardless of company policy, regardless of customer questions and criticism, the salesman who has a sound understanding of advertising has no trouble in replying with appropriate answers.

In regard to his company's advertising, the salesman must have com-plete information about current and future advertising efforts. He must know what campaigns are running, which media are being used, how large the budget is, what the results are, new campaigns scheduled, and the answers to many other questions both pertinent and irrelevant. It is usually easy to secure the attention and interest of customers by showing them actual advertisements in current media.

A final phase of this second point, company advertising, concerns what the company will do for and with customers in an advertising way. If the company identifies its dealers in certain of its advertisements, if mats are supplied, if a cooperative arrangement operates between company and customer, if direct mail pieces with or without the dealer's imprint can be had — all such facts are of interest and value to customers.

Pillsbury Mills tells its salesmen these things about its advertising:

For over half a century your company has been one of the largest and most consistent national advertisers in the grocery products field.

It has always believed that fine quality products must be widely advertised to be widely accepted.

And the main reason for the present nation-wide acceptance of Pillsbury products is the fact that their quality and usefulness have been advertised steadily, year after year, to housewives throughout the country.

Today, your company's yearly advertising expenditure runs into millions of dollars.

Powerful Pillsbury advertisements appear regularly and frequently in all major advertising media — magazines, newspapers, and radio.

And every new medium, such as television, which comes into prominence, is studied with a view to its possible inclusion in the Pillsbury advertising program.

Pillsbury advertising is tremendously effective because it is based on factual information.

Extensive research and analysis go into determining the basis on which the strongest appeal to the consumer can be made.

Product, market, sales coverage, merchandising possibilities, and media — all are carefully studied before any advertising is produced.

And, as the advertising appears, continuing studies are maintained to measure its effectiveness in building consumer acceptance for the product advertised.

The value of this advertising, *to you*, cannot be stressed too strongly.

The third point on advertising concerns the customer's advertising problems, which usually shape up in a pattern similar to that of most advertisers. The usual sequence starts off with setting up a budget and objectives. Retailers will want to know what other similar retailers do about these two problems. Next is the matter of prospect identification, including prospect description, trading area delineation, and prospect enumeration. Third is the question of media selection. Selection of message follows. Fifth, plans are announced to all personnel in an effort to keep them informed and to secure their cooperation. Sixth is the execution of the plan, the actual running of the advertisements. Attempts to get publicity may or may not be made at this time. The last step is to attempt an evaluation of the entire effort.

On each of these phases, the salesman must be willing and competent to advise his customer. Then and only then is the salesman in a position to encourage the customer to use advertising in adequate volume. His plea will be for a well-balanced, continuous program, and not just advertisements for the salesman's products. The strongest recommendation will be for continuity. Until the retailer realizes that advertising is not a luxury for prosperous times to be denied when volume drops, that it must not be scheduled according to his whims or to the persuasiveness of advertising salesmen, that it must be undertaken with full knowledge of the fact that its effectiveness is reduced when turned on and off like an electric light — he is not ready to advertise.

Display

The term "display" as used here has two meanings. The first is non-product and includes window displays, interior displays, point-of-sale material, and any other dealer helps of this type. In its second sense, the term refers to whatever location and display is given the stock of merchandise itself by the retailer.

The significance and potentials of good display should be recognized by both the salesman and his retail customer. In extreme cases, the difference between strong and weak display could mean the difference between black and red ink. The retailer certainly must place a correct evaluation on what his windows can do in the way of inviting and enticing prospects inside. Indeed, with the public buying what it sees, and with the growth of self-service, the merchant must go in for display in a serious, careful manner.

The importance attached to good display by manufacturers is clearly indicated by their competition for prominent positions for their respective brands and point-of-purchase items, positions that will increase sales and profits. Some, perhaps most, prefer favorable store position over mention by the retailer in newspaper or handbill advertisements, or radio or television commercials. One result of this is that merchants receive from manufacturers too much display material, too much that is not suited to their circumstances, and, consequently, is never used. Incidentally, this is a partial explanation of why distribution of such material through a salesman is popular, even though the salesman feels that he is being imposed on. If the merchant gives permission to the salesman to erect a display, he is likely to leave it up a while; if the material comes to him in the mail, it is easy for him to put it in his storeroom and forget it — or throw it away.

Salesmen should check continuously to see that their retailers are using display as an extra sales force, first of all in a store-wide way, and, second, for the salesman's line of products. This frequently means that in his daily work the salesman must first sell the retailer on the general idea of calculated display, then on the use of *his* material, and then on placing it in a preferred spot, such as near the wrapping desk, the cash register, the elevators, or the entrance. Tactful persistence is more than permissible; it is necessary, and the justifications are many. The salesman may point out how expensive his display is, how attractive it will look, what it will do to turnover and sales, how proud the retailer will be of it, why so few retailers are being offered it, how well it was rated when tested, and how much it will increase profits. These points and more may be especially useful if the retailer is asked to defray part of the cost of the display piece or to buy a minimum amount of goods in order to get the item. Salesmen of noncompeting, complementary products sometimes join together to promote a combination display. For example, sugar, cereals, milk, coffee, and tea might be featured in a single cooperative display. They are products that are closely associated, but they do not compete with one another.

A salesman has two very definite obligations in promoting display. One is to keep the retailer completely informed about what is available and on what terms, what he should use, and how he should use it to get best results. The second is to know at all times what his retailers actually do about general display and about displaying his products. By rating his customers as outstanding, average, and unsatisfactory, to use three classifications, he can give any one the treatment that is appropriate, thus avoiding wasting money on poor merchants, or neglecting good ones.

The Kraft Foods Company is one of a large group of companies whose products benefit greatly from good position in retail stores. Kraft sent this message to its salesmen:

Sell 'em with Shelfmanship

Eighty-seven per cent of all grocery sales are made from shelf positions. This means that shelfmanship coupled with salesmanship will move more goods.

It stands to reason that the salesman who works on his shelf-stock sales will sell more in every store.

Basically there are two ways to increase shelf sales:
1. More shelf facings
2. Preferred position

This sounds easy. But how does the grocer look at it? "Shelf space should be considered as rent, an expensive overhead item that should not be made costly with slow-moving merchandise," said the manager of a market in Encino, California. . . . And he's right. Any grocer who thinks about it will agree that shelf space has to be considered as rent.

The good salesman — the shelf-made salesman — has a real opportunity to drive this point home to every customer troubled by decreasing markups and disappearing profits. Once your customer sees shelf space as rent, half your battle is won.

Your second step is to make it clear that **profit and turnover** . . . go hand in hand. Many grocers unconsciously consider margin alone as a basis for allotting shelf space, but . . . percentages don't pay the rent. Profit is not margin. Profit is margin multiplied by turnover.

Now if you can prove that the products you sell have the highest margins and also are leaders in turnover, you've got it in the bag — more shelf facings and preferred shelf position.

Personal Selling

A manufacturer is keenly concerned about the quality and direction of the retail salesmanship encountered in stores by the general public. He knows that the ultimate consumer must be made into and then kept a satisfied, repeating buyer; yet the manufacturer, instead of coming in contact with this individual himself, must depend on some retail sales-person to handle his interests at this final stage in the distribution process. In this sense, the salesperson in the retail establishment is the representative of the manufacturer and is so considered by some of the public. If it were practicable, the manufacturer would have his own employee present and available to handle each final buyer, but since that is obviously impossible, he tries to obtain the kind of representation from the retailer's employees that most nearly approximates the ideal.

There is a second, broader phase of the manufacturer's interest in retail salesmanship. He wants his retailers to be healthy and profitable so that they qualify as excellent outlets for his merchandise. The merchant who is progressive, outstanding, and making money is the one who will, in all probability, sell a better-than-average amount of merchandise for the manufacturer. Hence, the manufacturer's first step is to influence the merchant to raise the quality of salesmanship in a general way, so that the store becomes a better store. His second move is to help get more sales power from the retailer's sales force for his own lines.

The salesman must be extremely tactful in broaching the matter with the retailer. One of the better methods of bringing to the retailer's mind the significance of his employees' salesmanship is to ask about the training program in operation, thereby calling his attention to the subject and setting the stage for further discussion of it. A second method is to note what happens when a retail salesperson meets a retail prospect in an actual sales situation, and then use the observations as an opener for the conversation. Or the salesman may show the retailer or one of the sales-persons how his product should be demonstrated to a prospect. Still another possibility is to pass on to the retail organization all ideas, sugges-tions, or techniques that have proved effective in other stores or markets.

As a matter of fact, one of the most valuable possessions a salesman can have is a fund of simple selling secrets, of product facts translated into reasons for buying. He should always be on the alert to discover new selling tactics that retail salespersons have tried and found good so that he can be of greatest possible help to his customers. If his company provides training materials or manuals, his task is to see that they are used. Throughout his efforts to raise selling standards, if the salesman's attitude is helpful and not critical, his efforts will more often meet with success.

CUSTOMER MANAGEMENT MATTERS

Curiosity and accumulation of knowledge cannot be limited to merchandising matters, first, because advice and information will be asked on other problems, and, second, because conditions in other fields which need to be changed should be recognized. Because these management matters vary in nature and complexity, all that is suggested here is that whenever the salesman is confronted with a question to which he does not have the complete answer, a new field for study has been identified. Typical of management problems are those related to cash discounts, personnel turnover, credit, stock control and turnover, buying, and interior arrangement and layout.

HANDLING CUSTOMER COMPLAINTS

One problem that may as well be prepared for in advance is the complaint of a dissatisfied customer. Some salesmen, very definitely in the minority, work for companies that have a separate division to handle all complaints. This policy has been adopted because of the feeling that harmonious salesman-customer relationships are too valuable and hard to win to be exposed to the risks that must be borne when the salesman is the first person to handle a complaint. Because it is somewhat awkward for a salesman to have to turn down a customer's request for an adjustment when company policy clearly dictates a refusal and then try to sell that same customer, the salesman may feel that he should not be asked to handle complaints. Yet, in most cases, that is the rule, mainly because the salesman is the one company individual who comes in contact with the customer, the one who knows most about the customer and the circumstances in question, and the one the customer looks to for satisfaction. The salesman will need two things. The first is information (the easier of the two for the young salesman to obtain) related to product, company, customer, and competition. The second is experience.

The salesman must, of course, prevent complaints to the maximum extent possible, and he must handle those that are voiced as skillfully as he can. The first step in prevention calls for sufficient knowledge about the product and about the customer's needs so that the salesman can guide the customer in his buying, recommending only those items which will do the jobs to be done, and even refusing to sell if only disappointment and dissatisfaction can result. A second step is to make certain that customer and salesman think alike about the product to be purchased and what it will do, the two of them being in agreement as to just what the other expects and believes. Product misunderstandings usually lead to strained relations. Third, the salesman should describe in whatever detail is needed the policies and routines of his company. The customer should know in advance how inquiries are handled, how mail orders are treated, the specific procedure for dealing with complaints, and what the company's position is on such matters as claims, allowances, damaged merchandise, credit terms, and returned goods. Finally, much will be done toward holding complaints down to a minimum if the salesman carefully keeps all promises he makes. If he says he will pick up merchandise that does not sell, he should pick it up, and with no hesitation. If he promises delivery by Wednesday, the goods should be there by Wednesday.

If a complaint cannot be prevented, then it must be handled by someone. And whether it be reasonable or unreasonable, justified or not, a delicate treatment is usually necessary. For example, the salesman will be trying to hold the customer's patronage even though the complaint is perfectly justified, and he will try to keep both goodwill and business if the requested adjustment is refused.

At the very start, the customer must be made to know that the salesman is determined to be completely fair and to give the customer every courtesy and consideration. There must be no indication of doubt or suspicion in the salesman's mind. At the same time, the salesman must reassure the customer of his faith in his company, thus encouraging the customer to accept the company as one that does the right thing by its customers. Where the salesman or his company is at fault, admission of that fact should be made at once and followed by a promise of prompt and satisfactory adjustment.

Another helpful measure is to let the complainant talk until he has talked himself out. What the salesman does is to constitute a sympathetic audience for the customer as he lets off steam and demands satisfaction. Throughout this performance, the salesman is collecting information and opinions and is withholding his thoughts until he has all the facts.

Still another principle is that the salesman himself should handle the complaint if possible, for several reasons. This is the quickest solution and therefore quite desirable. Correspondence, with periodic occasions to get angry all over again at the perpetrator of the alleged injustice, is avoided. Furthermore, the salesman makes a favorable appearance and a bid for increased confidence by taking hold and handling. Referring the matter to some company official tends to magnify its significance.

If the salesman is unwilling or unable to handle the complaint, he should explain his position clearly to the customer. Next, he should review company policy with the customer and outline company procedure of handling, assuring the customer of prompt and proper attention, and following it up so as to know at all times where the matter rests.

Complaints can sometimes be used to strengthen the seller-buyer relationship. This is not always possible, of course, because complaints do and will continue to result in a complete rupture of established buying habits. In some instances, the salesman can make the complaint work for him rather than against him. The technique calls for selling himself and his company as being fair and reliable, convincing the customer that he has received and will always get honest treatment and a square deal. A particularly golden opportunity to increase goodwill presents itself when the adjustment made is more liberal than the customer expected or would have made to one of his own customers.

REGAINING LOST CUSTOMERS

Customers who used to buy but who do not buy at the present time may well be good prospects. Of course, if their needs or conditions have changed so as to make a product no longer of use to them, they are not prospects. When customers discontinue buying because of dissatisfaction, or because a more persuasive competitor took them away, perhaps it is worth while to try to get them back as customers. After all, they *do* know the merchandise, the company, and, in certain instances, the salesmen.

Each case should be examined to see *why*, *how*, *when*, and *to whom* the account was lost. The answers to these four questions will point out the tactics that should be adopted in attempting to regain the account. Usually, many of the techniques of handling complaints are equally appropriate and effective here.

CREDIT AND COLLECTION

Companies differ in their methods of dealing with credit and collection, some making extensive and others making slight use of their salesmen in the handling of these functions. Be that as it may, there are few if any salesmen who can afford to be indifferent to or uninformed about credit management. For the salesman who is used as a source of credit data and as a collector, these thoughts on credit and collection are usable in the same way as are facts about product uses, and for others they provide background information.

SALESMAN'S
REPORT OF COMPLAINT

Sales Office _____

Complaint No. _____

Always make out this form, whether you write a letter in addition or not. Make out in triplicate, keep one copy, and mail two copies to your Sales Office.

Name of Firm _____ Factory Order No. _____

Address _____ Car No. _____

_____ Made at _____

Please fill in carefully all the information requested below. SEND IN SAMPLES WHENEVER POSSIBLE. NOTE IDENTIFICATION on bundles containing defective boxes.

NATURE OF COMPLAINT: _____

_____

_____

_____

_____

_____

How many boxes or what percentage were defective? _____

_____

Were they all found in a few bundles, or scattered throughout all bundles? _____

_____

Is customer storing, handling, packing and sealing properly? _____

_____

How many sample boxes did you send in? _____ When? _____ How _____

What was IDENTIFICATION on bundles containing defective boxes? _____

What does customer request? _____

_____

What is your recommendation? _____

_____

Salesman's Signature _____

Office _____

Two copies sent

to: _____   Date _____

Gaylord Container Corporation

Form used by Gaylord Container Corporation salesmen in reporting complaints.

No sales transaction can be considered successfully terminated until payment in full is received. The wise salesman quickly translates this to read that in the long run he can sell only to those persons who pay their bills and that sales opportunities decline hand in hand with a decrease in collections. In extreme cases, customers are lost through unsatisfactory,

Johnson MOTORS   **FINANCIAL QUESTIONNAIRE**

Date _____

Please complete and return to Credit Department, Johnson Motors, Waukegan, Illinois.

①   State _____ City _____

Firm Name _____

Street Address _____

Is this your principal place of business? _____. If not, give name and address of headquarters. _____

_____

②   Is your business a sole proprietorship? _____ Partnership? _____ or corporation? _____.

Type of business? _____

Have you had any previous experience in the outboard or marine field? _____. What is your best estimate of

annual motor sales? _____ How much of your business will outboard sales and service represent?

$ _____ % _____

③   Do you finance your business? _____

Bank _____ Finance Company _____ Other _____

Floor Plan _____ Other _____

Do you finance retail sales? _____ Bank _____ Finance Company _____ Other _____

_____

If not presently financing or floor planning, what arrangements do you plan to make?

For Wholesale _____ For Retail _____

④   Johnson Motors' policy is to ship C.O.D. or sight draft against bill of lading Net, payment due within ten

days of date of invoice.

Name and address of banking connection for sight draft _____

_____

Name of bank official with whom you transact business _____

Other banking connections _____

⑤   Are you rated in Dun and Bradstreet? _____ Please give names and addresses of three companies

you presently do business with: _____

_____

Please attach latest financial statements.

Signed _____

FORM #CR-8   Position _____

Johnson Motors

This form is completed by new customers

inefficient handling of the credit function, and the departure of those customers is frequently all the sadder because of the resulting increase in bad debts. Since one cause of bad debts is the failure to watch the operation of an account closely, the recommendation here is that the

salesman should keep informed about the financial health of his customers, especially those who do not pay promptly. He should do all he
can to keep them liquid, to encourage them to take all cash discounts,
and to impress on them the desirability of maintaining a good credit
rating. Keeping the customer enthusiastic and profitable reduces the
collection problem.

Some salesmen are asked to collect past-due accounts and some are
able or are allowed to sell to certain customers only after collecting,
thereby bringing those accounts back to a current condition. Hence,
some observations are in order about collections. The saying that short
credit makes long friends is both old and true. It suggests that each
customer be started off in the right way, that the groundwork for prompt
collection be laid at the time of the first sale. During this first sale, the
salesman quite properly has collection in mind as he shows the customer
that punctual payment is expected and implies that the customer undoubtedly makes promptness a habit. This definite agreement on intention
and expectation at the beginning of the buyer-seller relationship is a basic
principle of sound collection and reduces the number of slow accounts.

Collection requires the salesman to use methods that are courteous
yet firm. Although collection attempts do not need any apologies, they
should be executed with good manners. Being firm does not mean being
hard, obnoxious, offensive, or tough; it does not mean pressing the matter
so far that the customer is lost. Firmness is required lest the salesman
appear weak; that must never be allowed. Although the salesman himself
would prefer to go easy on the delinquent customer, he has to remember
that seldom does he make a friend of any customer by permitting laxity
in payment. The more he encourages the customer to delay paying, the
more apt he is to lose the customer's respect and friendliness, especially
when the time for final settlement arrives.

Promptness is another desirable feature of the collection method. The
hardest amount to collect, and the one which will ultimately result in the
largest write-off debt, is the amount that has been owed the longest.
In addition, the older the debt becomes, the more probable it is that the
customer will switch his patronage to some other vendor. These facts
mean that the salesman cannot delay in putting his collection plan into
operation once its need is clear.

There are many collection approaches that have proved effective.
One that may be used to advantage is the commercial angle where the
salesman points out that his company has bills to meet and needs funds
with which to pay. Another is for the salesman to ask the customer why
he does not include a payment on his account with the salesman's company
when he is paying some of his other creditors. The business or barter

approach reminds the customer that they agreed to an exchange of merchandise for dollars, that the seller turned over the merchandise in good faith, and that the buyer should perform his part of the transaction. A fourth approach is moral, appealing to the customer's sense of honor and obligation. A fifth possibility is to bring some pressure to bear on the customer. These are only examples of the assortment of collection techniques the salesman should amass, remembering all the time that all must be used with tact and common sense.

HOLDING MEETINGS

Some salesmen will never have occasion to hold a meeting in connection with their selling activities because of the nature of their sales transactions, as, for example, those selling automobiles or insurance or home insulation. Other salesmen will conduct meetings, but, before so doing, will be trained specifically and thoroughly for that job, and will then be supplied by their companies with everything needed, even "extemporaneous" remarks. This section on holding meetings is included not particularly for the benefit of these two groups of salesmen, but, instead, to help the person who, when he begins selling, will need to work with his customers by scheduling and conducting meetings without much assistance from any source. In his case, the meeting will be *his* idea and *his* job. In addition, it will acquaint college students with some of the phases of the role that may be assigned to salesman-held meetings.

In most cases, the audience will be composed of one of these:

A wholesaler and his staff.
A retailer and his staff.
A group of wholesalers.
A group of retailers.

When the meeting is with a wholesaler or a retailer and his staff, the staff may be limited to sales employees.

The decision to hold meetings is a serious one and not to be lightly made. Before deciding in the affirmative, the salesman must recognize that the project will take time, money, patience, effort, and thorough planning. He must understand that turning over a suggested program to a wholesaler or retailer for execution is hopelessly insufficient, that he himself will have to help, promote, direct, follow up, and do much of the actual job. Still, meetings can be extremely worth while.

Purposes

The broad purpose of any meeting is to increase profits for the salesman and his company by increasing the volume of sales and profits on merchandise that moves through the salesman and his customer. But this general objective can take a variety of shapes in that any one meeting might be arranged for one of many specific purposes. Each salesman must see what uses he can make of meetings and then prepare for them. The following list contains some popular pegs to hang meetings on. It does not attempt to include all possible topics.

Customer Matters:
　　　How to get new customers.
　　　How to hold customers.
　　　How wholesalers build up retail accounts.
　　　How to handle "A," "B," and "C" accounts.
　　　What to do about small orders.
　　　How to revive dormant accounts.
　　　How to determine the customer's needs.

Product Matters:
　　　How merchandise should be demonstrated.
　　　The manufacturer's support and promotion plans.
　　　Why persons do and should buy Brand X.
　　　Problems and methods of users of Brand X.
　　　How to launch a new product.
　　　A study of Brand X's competitive advantages.

Salesmanship Matters:
　　　A review of selling principles.
　　　How to prove product claims.
　　　How to handle objections.
　　　How to get the five buying decisions.
　　　How to close.
　　　How consumer advantages are superior to product features.

Principles to Observe

These are some principles concerning holding meetings which have proved their soundness:

1. Meetings should be scheduled where they will do the most good. This raises the question as to whether they should be given for strong or weak customers, and the answer in most cases is for the strong ones. The feeling is that the better accounts — the ones which do the most outstanding selling jobs — are the ones entitled to benefit from the time and money spent on meetings. Furthermore, the return to the salesman and his company on their expenditures will be greater than if spent on weak customers. Small, backward customers may need help more, but progressive customers will make greater use of assistance.

2. Have a definite reason for the meeting and publicize the reason beforehand. Chances of success are brighter if members of the group know the purpose of the gathering and recognize the benefits they can

derive from it. Describing in advance how the meeting will mean dollars to them and how they can adapt the ideas picked up at the meeting to whatever products they handle helps sell all prospective attendants on being present.

3. Every effort should be made to schedule only one topic for each meeting. The advantages are shorter meetings, greater unity, more complete treatment, and increased understanding.

4. Each meeting should bear the imprint of the salesman's own personality, differing from one held by another salesman in the same way that the two salesmen differ. Each salesman should capitalize on his own particular abilities, background, and knowledge, as well as take advantage of his own personality and of his friendship with and knowledge of members of the group. Once again a caution is in order that this must not be carried to such length that the intrinsic value of the original plan is lost.

5. Timing is so important that a timetable is essential. Because the typical person attending the meeting will be there only at some inconvenience to himself, and because he becomes annoyed, exasperated, and even infuriated at having to wait, the meeting must start on time. It should continue according to schedule, too. This can be done only if a running check is kept on the passing of time and an adjustment is made when necessary to permit prompt adjournment. Of course, the salesman should try to schedule the phases of the meeting and direct them so expertly that the end of the program and the time limit occur simultaneously.

6. The group should never be made or permitted to feel that limitations, restrictions, or prohibitions have in effect been placed against freedom and spontaneity of action, against one's right to his own opinion, or against one's privilege of being himself.

7. Stay in complete control of the meeting. The group must always be aware of the serious purpose of the program and must not be allowed to get out of order. Discussion must be kept within bounds and confined to the topic scheduled. No one or two individuals should be permitted to monopolize the floor, nor should discussions be allowed to degenerate into disputes.

8. Get the meeting off to a promising start. The opening remarks should be complimentary, giving the group a pleasant feeling of wellbeing, and asking, in a subtle way, for attention and cooperation.

9. A judicious use of humor improves the meeting.

10. The tempo of the meeting must not be allowed to drag. True, there is some danger of traveling too fast, and that must not be done, but the more serious danger is that of killing interest and enthusiasm by moving along at a snail's pace. Pauses are awkward. Slow, clumsy transition from phase to phase actually invites persons to leave, mentally if not

physically. Interest is maintained by keeping things moving, by a skillful use of change of pace.

11. Make it as easy as possible for the audience to understand and retain the message. This may call for distributing helpful printed material to the individuals, such as an outline of the meeting, a summary of the major points made, or a word-and-picture treatment of recommendations. Sometimes, especially when films or dramatic presentations are used, this matter of being clear and obvious involves three steps. First, the group is given an adequate explanation of what the objective of the meeting is and of what is to follow; second, the program is executed; third, a review or summary is immediately made.

12. Make maximum use of audio-visual aids and demonstration props. These include such things as easels, cards, charts, diagrams, blackboards with chalk and erasers, the product itself, tear sheets of ads, models, movies, and slides.

13. Take pains to encourage quiet persons to take a part in the exchange of ideas and experiences. Meetings conducted on a discussion or conference basis have much in their favor. By participating, individual members closely identify themselves as being part of the meeting.

14. In the round-table type of meeting, an atmosphere of friendly informality must be quickly established. Members of the group must sense that their ideas and contributions are wanted and expected. A short series of general questions, such as asking what product is advertised by a certain TV star, or who is the trade character for a certain brand, may be used to put the group at ease and to start it cooperating.

15. Group projects can be extremely worthwhile. The salesman may choose some dominant buying motive, perhaps economy, and ask those present to build up a list of appeals based on that motive, such as economical to buy, to use, to service, to trade in, and so forth. Or a session might be devoted to the construction of a sales presentation.

The purpose of the meeting is to teach and help, not to embarrass. There should never be any sarcasm, ridicule, or biting criticism by the salesman.

Specific Preparation

Thorough preparation is always needed for the scheduled meeting. To be safe, the salesman should be so well prepared that he will be able to carry the complete load if necessary, not requiring any particular assistance from anyone or even being dependent on the presence of any certain person.

If the salesman's company supplies the plan, adequate time should be spent reading and studying it so that the complete program is mastered in detail. The meeting group quickly and correctly recognizes whether or not time and thought have been spent by the salesman in getting ready for the gathering, just as a college student does about a lecture. It might not be a bad idea for the salesman to glance through his company sales manual sometime prior to the meeting just to familiarize himself with the selling techniques and suggestions included there.

Any standard schedule such as a company might supply often needs to be revised and tailored to fit local conditions. This must be done carefully and well in advance. Adaptation may make the difference between success and failure, and it must be executed in such a fashion that the resulting program is appropriate and smooth.

Regardless of source of meeting plan, extent of alteration, or the excellence of the salesman's memory, a definite written schedule of a complete program should be made in advance, and it should name a specified day, place, and hour that were selected so as to maximize the chances of success. The written schedule will outline what matters are to be treated, how much time will be devoted to each phase, and the method of treatment, including the props to be used. Particular preparation is needed for meetings where group participation will require some flexibility in handling and fitting the meeting to the time schedule. Incidentally, the salesman should rehearse with props until he handles them professionally. If such a schedule is not established and agreed to prior to the meeting, the salesman will frequently experience postponements, absence of key individuals who were to take part in the program, lack of coordination, and even failure. The junior salesman may be relaxed instead of nervous if he writes out his opening remarks, a list of questions for discussion, and his closing thoughts, but he should do no more reading to his audience than is absolutely necessary.

If, after the salesman has defined the complete job to be accomplished, it appears that a considerable amount of time will be required, several short sessions should be scheduled rather than a few long ones. To maintain a high degree of interest throughout a long meeting is difficult if not impossible.

Before the meeting, a collection should be made of case histories, experiences, and other happenings from in and around the locality where the meeting is to be. For instance, a new sales technique that was originated near by, or the experience of some local merchant who tied his promotion efforts in with those of the manufacturer to his gratification, gets and holds the interest of the group. Facts and figures, impartiality, and tact are needed in using such information.

A final precaution, something never to be omitted, is to make certain that everyone concerned knows the time and place of the meeting.

BUILDING GOODWILL

Salesmen need and want the goodwill of their customers. What is goodwill? When does a salesman have it? A salesman enjoys the goodwill of his customers when they have faith and confidence in him personally and when they respect his competence and integrity as an adviser. He enjoys their goodwill when they like him, when they think well of him, and when they broadcast these complimentary opinions. Customers of goodwill are a salesman's "fans." They are his enthusiastic press agents and supporters. They give the salesman every possible break.

It is clear why salesmen work so hard for the goodwill of their customers. The first sale is often made only after goodwill has been won. Repeat sales will not be forthcoming unless the customer feels goodwill toward the salesman. A customer's account cannot be increased to its maximum potential without his goodwill. Then, finally, the customer's continuing support, loyalty, and cooperation will not be so great as they might have been unless there is goodwill.

How does the salesman get goodwill? As mentioned elsewhere, nothing is so essential as a program of helping his customers. Helping them in business ways will increase the customer's sales, or reduce the customer's expenses, or both. Helping them in personal ways results in the customer's securing for himself more personal satisfaction.

Goodwill is invited when the salesman lets himself be guided by the customer's interests and goals. The salesman learns the customer's circumstances and takes a position in sympathy with them. The salesman makes sound recommendations only, and then he takes pain to see that the customer understands fully what the results will be if he buys and if he does not buy. The dependability of the salesman in this area of recommending is complete and unquestioned.

The salesman invites goodwill by his ethical conduct. He keeps secrets and promises. He is fair and honest. He demonstrates the fact that the Golden Rule is good business as well as good behavior.

Finally, the salesman invites goodwill by liking each customer personally. This he learns to do by knowing and understanding him and by being a real friend to him. The salesman shows his liking in many ways. He appreciates any favors by a customer, and he is prompt to repay in generous measure. He asks the customer for advice, opinions, and suggestions. He takes time and effort to adopt the customer's mood of the moment, respecting the customer's right to feel differently on different calls. He supplies the customer with related and unrelated information, keeping the customer well posted on the latest happenings in various fields. He may entertain certain customers on certain occasions. At Christmas, birthday, and anniversary times, the salesman will certainly remember each customer in appropriate ways. He will congratulate the customer on the birth of a baby, and he will mail a "get well soon" card when the customer is ill. All this takes time, but it is well worth the effort.

STUDY ASSIGNMENTS

1. What are some steps a salesman can take to reduce danger of losing customers to competitors?
2. Are there times when a salesman should refuse to sell to a buyer who wants to buy and has the money with which to pay?
3. Sometimes when a salesman for a manufacturer of furniture presents his new lines to a retailer, the retailer wants to trade a line he has been carrying for one of the new ones. How should the salesman handle this?
4. Why is it shortsighted to sell a customer more than he should buy? Is this ever justified?
5. How can a salesman persuade a retailer to give his products better position or shelf space in a store?
6. How would you go about convincing a wholesaler to use your company's merchandising aids and mailing pieces for his retail customers, as a tie-in with your company's national advertising?
7. Describe how the salesman operates as both a collector and a dispenser of merchandising service.
8. Is the customer always right? Give examples of unjustified requests from customers. Why should such requests be turned down right from the start?
9. Generally speaking, should a salesman try to adjust customer complaints himself, or should he refer them to the home office?
10. Describe a sales situation in which holding a meeting would be very advisable.

CASE STUDY 16A

A salesman for the Bear Manufacturing Company calls on a garage owner in a medium-sized town. Bear makes and sells a nationally known line of automotive equipment featuring wheel balancers, front end alignment equipment, ramps, and frame straighteners. The prospect owns some Bear equipment now, and the salesman has called on him several times in the past two or three years to service this equipment. The time is the early afternoon, and the place is the prospect's office next to the garage.

Salesman: Good afternoon, Mr. White. How are you today, sir?

Prospect: Fine, fine. How are you? Have a seat.

Salesman: Thank you, Mr. White. I just thought I'd come by and check your equipment to see if all our Bear products are in good order. You know our company has a policy of working with customers to make sure they are satisfied with the service they get from our equipment.

Prospect: Yes, that's one of the things I like about your company. You are very helpful. Let's go over to the shop, and you can look around.

Salesman: Before we go, how about telling me about your front end department. I hear that you have more business in that department than you can handle. Is that right?

Prospect: Yes, it is. I've been doing about six front end jobs a day, and I guess I turn away at least five or six more. And they usually land up at my competitors' garages. But I just can't handle the business now. My place isn't big enough.

Salesman: It's a shame you have to let all that business get away from you. You sure could use another Bear front end machine, couldn't you?

Prospect: Oh, I could use it all right, but as I say, I have no place to put it, and anyway the one I have still does a pretty good job.

Salesman: That piece of equipment is about fourteen years old, isn't it? You know, those old Bears are mighty reliable. I imagine it has paid for itself a hundred times or more. Now, you know how Bear stands behind its equipment and always tries to help its customers. Well, Mr. White, I think I can help you to solve your problem.

Prospect: How's that?

Salesman: From what you tell me, you are already losing as much business as you actually handle in your front end department. And this means that you are losing as much money as you are making. If you had the kind of equipment that could do the job, you would be making this extra money. The Bear Company now has a product that just meets your needs. It's the brand new "Telaliner." Have you heard of it?

Prospect: Oh, yes, I read about it in one of the trade magazines.

Salesman: Well, the Bear "Telaliner" will modernize your entire department without expensive alterations. This new wheel alignment machine makes the work easier for your mechanic, since there are fewer parts to the machine and because its operation is very simple. The "Telaliner" does your wheel alignment work with absolute accuracy. Here's a picture of this modern equipment (takes out a picture of the "Telaliner"). Best of all, this machine will increase your ability to handle front end work from six per day to twelve. How would you like to double your business in this type of work?

Prospect: How much are these machines?

Salesman: Well, you can double your front end business for only $972.

Prospect: Wow! That's plenty. Doesn't the Elder Company sell a machine just like yours for only $700?

Salesman: Yes, Mr. White, they do sell a machine that looks like the Bear "Telaliner," but that's all. Bear offers the only machine of this kind that features completely automatic operation. And our price includes shipping charges, free installation, and a ninety-day guarantee. In both money and service, we make up this price difference to you.

Prospect: Nine hundred and seventy-two dollars is a lot of money. I'm afraid I just couldn't afford it right now.

Salesman: I can understand how you feel, Mr. White. That is a goodly amount, but it's actually very little when you come to realize what a difference it can make to your business. Let's do a little figuring. Here, would you like to handle the arithmetic while I talk? (Hands prospect a pencil and paper.) Let's say you do ten jobs a day with the "Telaliner." That's a conservative figure. At an average of $6 a job this would gross you $60 a day. Isn't that right?

Prospect: Yes, and five days a week would make $300 a week.

Salesman: Then at $300 a week this "Telaliner" can pay for itself in a little over three weeks. That's amazing, but it's true as you can see. The expected life of this machine is ten years. That means with fifty weeks of operation in a year you'll gross $15,000 a year and in ten years $150,000. So a price of $972 certainly is a solid investment, isn't it?

Prospect: Looking at it this way, it certainly is.

Salesman: You've used Bear equipment for over 14 years, and you have been satisfied, haven't you?

Prospect: Yes, I have.

Salesman: Then, Mr. White, you know that your future is safe when you deal with Bear. The longer you wait to take advantage of this opportunity, the more business you'll be losing. That business will only go to your competitors, and that isn't good for you, is it?

Prospect: Of course not.

Salesman: Then would you like your Bear "Telaliner" delivered at the end of this month or would you like it around the 15th of next month?

Prospect: Well, I don't know. I've been thinking about building an addition to this shop and remodeling the whole outfit. I need more space for my front end department anyway.

Salesman: I'll be glad to help you plan your front end department and give you the advantage of Bear's experience in setting up this department.

Prospect: Why, that's mighty nice of you.

Salesman: Not at all. Bear believes in giving its customers the best in service and advice. And whether you expand or not, you are going to need the Bear "Telaliner." I can get your shipment by the end of the month, Mr. White. Or would you rather get delivery around the middle of next month?

Prospect: Let's make it next month. I'll be in better shape then.

Salesman: (Takes out order book and writes out order.) Mr. White, when the "Telaliner" arrives, drop me a line, and I'll be down here to help you install it. If you'll just authorize this, I'll have the "Telaliner" on the way.

Prospect: (Signs order blank.)

QUESTIONS:

1. What did the salesman do well?
2. What did the salesman do that could be improved?

3. What techniques are illustrated in the sale?
4. What do you conclude when you examine closely the Bear salesman's figures?

CASE STUDY 16B

The Dorn Manufacturing Company makes a line of consumer products sold mainly through food stores. The company is a leader in its field and is respected generally.

Dorn is a strong national advertiser, concentrating its effort in 40 magazines, three of which are *Life, The Saturday Evening Post,* and *Ladies' Home Journal.* The company also uses radio, television, newspapers, and car cards. Dorn salesmen call on wholesalers and retailers. The salesmen are paid a straight salary; they can look forward to raises and to transfers to higher-paying territories.

Last year the Dorn company management made a rather thorough investigation of its marketing performance. As part of the research, a classification of customers' orders was made on the basis of size of order. The findings were most surprising. Seventy-five per cent of the orders were clearly in the "small order" class, and only 25% were of medium and large size. The controller's office was asked to compute the average cost of handling an order. When the average cost figure was determined, the Dorn management immediately knew that at least 15% and probably 20% of the orders it received and filled did not gross enough to cover this average handling cost. In other words, the company lost money on one sixth to one fifth of the orders its customers placed.

At the next annual sales convention, a session will be devoted to this small-order problem. Obviously, improvement in this area will not be possible without the cooperation of the company's salesmen.

QUESTIONS:

1. Why do manufacturers receive so many small orders?
2. How can Dorn defend the acceptance and filling of orders which are so small that they must be handled at a loss?
3. What can the Dorn company and its salesmen do to cope with the small-order problem?

CHAPTER 17

SELF-MANAGEMENT

These ideas from a top executive of Ekco Products Company set the stage for our study of self-management:

It has been my experience that the key to successful selling is *advanced planning.* I have yet to see the salesman who takes a systematic approach to his work whose record has not surpassed that of the glib talker, or the party thrower, or the one with a book full of contacts, or any of these dying species of salesmen.

Advanced planning to the successful salesman has the same components of a good newspaper lead to the successful newsman: it should tell who, what, where, when, why, and how.

There is a special significance attached to planning for the salesman whose sample case unfolds like a cornucopia. This is the case with salesmen for Ekco Products Company, world's largest manufacturer of nonelectrical housewares. Ekco manufactures more than 3,000 housewares items .... Add to this array of goods the fact that sales are made in open stock, sets, and an on-going variety of display assortments.

Each salesman is responsible for selling a plethora of goods in a wide range of price points. The challenge ... is telescoped by the complex nature of distribution of goods. Distributed nationally, Ekco merchandise is sold to housewares, hardware, and many other types of wholesalers, to drug, variety, supermarket and grocery chains, to department stores, etc.

Add to this the time required for company sales meetings, customer sales meetings, national and regional shows, and it becomes increasingly evident that his success rests on his ability at detailed planning.

The nucleus of his programming is the Pre-Planned Call Report, Itemized Sales Record and Dealer Call Program. Systematically adhered to, these keep him consistently "on top of" his selling situation . . . letting him know what he is selling and to whom and in what areas he can revise his approach.

Each salesman submits his Pre-Planned Call Report a week in advance. This enables him to decide which customers he will call on each day of the week, what he will try to accomplish and what sales "tools" he will need.

While this type of planning still allows flexibility for a change of plans and unexpected calls, it accomplishes: greatest value from every customer call, most efficient use of time, and most economic routing. These are followed with weekly accomplishment reports.

Ekco salesmen also maintain itemized sales records on a limited number of key accounts which produce the greatest sales volume. This enables the salesman to record the actual number of calls made to important accounts in relation to the proper number of calls based on past purchases and future potential.

Sales records to accounts not classified as key accounts are maintained but in less detail. However, the value of the itemized sales record is two-fold. First, it gives the salesman immediate reference to customer inventory and buying data — particularly as related to new items. Also, it simplifies the transfer of accounts between salesmen.

The third important phase is the Dealer Call Program. Not enough can be said about the importance of such a program to a consumer goods manufacturer who does not sell direct. It is, after all, at the retail counter where the real test of the entire merchandising-marketing program comes.

It has been our experience that an effective and continuing program of dealer calls by Ekco men produces much faster distribution of new goods on the retail counter. Also, it has been found that in most cases the Ekco salesman is more capable of selling display assortments — the most effective housewares merchandising device — than the average wholesaler salesman.

And, in a less direct sense, such a program provides a good tool for learning the needs of Ekco retail dealers and for getting the pulse of the consuming public. It is these areas to which we must orient our manufacturing and merchandising programs. It therefore becomes essential to have a systematic dealer call program.

However, with the thousands of retail outlets for Ekco merchandise in many trade categories, it is not possible to reach all consistently by salesmen's calls. Thus, the Dealer Call Report provides for rating the dealers to determine future advisability and frequency of calls. An appraisal of retailer inventory is also quickly ascertained with this form.

Self-management becomes meaningful only through skilled, detailed and organized advance planning. Integrated with a systematic program of customer calls, dealer calls, and proper sales records, it leads to greater rewards for the salesman and the organization he represents.

THE SELF-MANAGED SALESMAN

What He Is

If someone could show us a picture of a self-managed salesman, what would we see? We would see a self-controlled, organized person who studies his situations, constructs a program of action, and then puts his program into operation. A self-managed salesman *thinks* clearly, *plans* in an orderly fashion, and *works* systematically. He delights the heart of his sales manager because he requires so little prompting and supervision.

In similar manner he pleases his customers because he can and does guard his integrity and dependability, the basis of all successful selling.

Why and How He Gets That Way

Every salesman must manage himself well if his future is to be satisfactory and successful. Regardless of the individual, his product, his company, the size of his territory, or the type and number of his prospects, sane personal management is essential to profitable selling. Indeed, the salesman is one businessman who confronts and is confronted by his "boss" — the prospect — continuously while he works. In view of this situation, it is easy to see why the capacity to control, manage, and direct oneself separates the strong salesman from the weak.

To become a controlled, self-managed salesman, one must "plan his work and work his plan." The objective in so doing and, in fact, the single most important idea in this chapter is *spending more time with buyers in face-to-face selling*. This objective can be gained only if all selling activity is directed most effectively. It demands that the efforts the salesman exerts be soundly planned and constant and that his work be systematically done according to a program or schedule.

In the final analysis, there are only two ways to increase sales volume. First, the salesman can do more selling, and, second, he can do more effective selling. The self-managed salesman who puts method into his selling attacks on both fronts. He arranges to put in more hours each week and month talking with prospects, and he is always trying to raise the quality and effectiveness of his selling. Of course, the more a keen salesman increases the quantity of his selling, the more he automatically raises its quality.

There are both financial and psychological reasons for self-management. The over-all financial reason boils down to a matter of higher earnings. The self-managed salesman spends the maximum amount of time with buyers and as a result is in a position to maximize sales. Furthermore, he minimizes his nonselling time, his misdirected efforts, and his expenses. His self-management encourages and enables him to keep his selling costs at a satisfactory figure, for he is well aware of how basic his expenses-to-sales ratio is. His demonstrated capacity to direct and manage recommends him for promotions. He becomes more familiar with more phases of his job as he studies and plans. Planning allows any salesman to keep busy, and can be used to force lazy salesmen to stay busy. Absence of control means that the salesman works at far less than his potential efficiency. This justifies the contention that lack of system and absence of method are great robbers and that the salesman who tries to sell without using them is literally stealing from himself.

HOW TO GET READY TO SELL

1. Know Your Customer

a. Determine present and potential purchases—what he can use from you
b. Determine financial status—credit rating
c. Determine what competition sells—type of competition
d. Determine selling practices—merchandising practices
e. Determine buying characteristics—personal likes and dislikes
f. What does he think of Oscar Mayer & Co.—its products?
g. What are his problems?
h. What will Oscar Mayer merchandise do for him?
GET THE COMPLETE STORY

2. Know What You Sell

a. Know company policies—manufacturing processes
b. Know all products—dealer advantages
c. Know service advantages
d. Know all prices
YOU CAN'T SELL IF YOU DON'T KNOW

3. Plan HOW You Will Sell

a. Consider quality—price and service of competition—quantities sold.
b. Fit selling features to customer needs
c. Include samples — handbooks — demonstrations — sales promotions
d. Determine amounts — fill needs but don't overload
e. Determine what you will say and how you will say it
TALK THE CUSTOMER'S LANGUAGE

4. Set Up A Schedule

Decide who to call on — when to do it
ADHERE TO A TIME TABLE

5. Work by Plan

a. Stick to objective
b. Follow up results

Consider All Facts—Plan Your Work Work Your Plan

Oscar Mayer & Co.

The well-managed salesman scores high on these five points.

Then there are psychological benefits resulting from being a well-managed salesman. There is the personal satisfaction of achievement which results from doing a job well. There is more pleasure and less worry. In a broad sense, self-management gives him a feeling of self-assurance and of security. The well-managed salesman has more time for his private life. He commands the respect of his company, of prospects, and of customers. Finally, he is of definite service to society by helping buyers find better solutions to their problems — by doing them the favor of showing them how to increase their net satisfactions from living.

A person becomes a self-governed salesman, then, by straight thinking, sound planning, and orderly work. This means that he begins to set up and operate according to budgets — budgets for his sales, his time, his energy, and his expenses. He starts slanting all his activity toward a single goal, that of spending more and even more time in the presence of buyers, selling to them by helping them to buy. And he now concentrates his efforts on those accounts, both prospect and customer, which hold out the greatest promise of profit.

Planning and working give the salesman command of himself. They are both in the reach of any student who is determined to build his future on them rather than on hunch, luck, or personality.

THE SALESMAN AND HIS TIME

The Value of Time

The most valuable possession of a salesman is his time. Because it is the most important item a salesman spends, it should be valued, conserved, and used carefully. Otherwise the salesman finds his situation described in the famous want ad of Horace Mann, "Lost, yesterday, somewhere between sunrise and sunset, two golden hours, each set with sixty diamond minutes. No reward is offered, for they are gone forever."

A salesman does not rank very high, nor does his future look bright, unless he controls and manages his time so as to make maximum use of it. The salesman who appreciates the value of his time spends it according to a single principle — to maximize sales volume and minimize selling costs in helping prospects buy. Every salesman has exactly the same amount of time, twenty-four hours a day. One difference between the star salesman and the bottom salesman is the way each values and uses his time. The star salesman demonstrates his superior ability to spend time wisely and profitably by spending more time in the presence of buyers.

One of the quickest and most penetrating ways for a salesman to realize the value of his time is for him to compute some costs. Let him figure out what one hour of his time is actually worth, or how much it costs him to make a call, or how many days he must work each month before he has paid his expenses and begins to work for himself. If he remains unimpressed, then let him figure how much he loses in dollars if, during a year, he wastes one half hour a day, or what it costs him to talk to a prospect for ten minutes.

The most precious time is that spent helping prospects buy. Yet, many surveys show that many salesmen spend more time in traveling, or more in paper work, or, indeed, more in waiting to see prospects. As a matter of fact, it seems reasonable to generalize that in most lines of selling, only a minor part, often only one sixth, of the working day is spent with prospects. If face-to-face time with prospects can be increased, sales can be increased.

A publisher of business and industrial publications makes these interesting comments and computations about industrial selling:

> A survey by FACTORY magazine reveals that the average industrial salesman spends 500 hours a year on actual customer contacts. A. H. Fensholt, President of the Fensholt Company, says, in a booklet titled

"Mechanized Selling," that industrial salesmen average about a hundred minutes a day in actual selling. And Col. Charles M. Piper reported some years ago in PRINTERS' INK that salesmen average somewhere between two and three hours per working day in the presence of customers.

On the basis of those findings, the 50% figure indicated as actual time spent in the presence of customers and prospects may seem a bit high. It is, of course, in many cases. But, in the opinion of SALES MANAGEMENT and other authoritative sources, it is representative of the capacity of the salesman who is hitting on all cylinders — i.e., the man who makes maximum use of his working hours.

First, let's get the total working time. Deducting Saturdays, Sundays, holidays, and a two-week vacation period, there are 244 "working days" per year. (For example, $244 \times 8 = 1952$ hours of "working time" available per salesman per year. Most surveys indicate that the alert industrial salesman converts his luncheon period into selling time. Therefore, our 8-hour day represents the generally accepted ideal.)

How do salesmen use this time? Surveys show that the average salesman spends 12% of his time on reports, paper work, sales meetings, and a hundred and one other time-consuming chores. He spends 38% of his time traveling and sitting it out — waiting for interviews. He spends 50% of his time face to face with customers and prospects . . . which means 976 hours for actual selling.

The industrial salesman handles an average of 488 accounts. (A survey by FACTORY on 2500 salesmen representing a cross section of ten fields of industry reveals an average of 488 customers and prospects per salesman, and three individuals per plant who have to be sold.) If he called on them twice a year he could spend ONE HOUR with each company. This allows 20 minutes per person, twice a year.

Or, let's see what one company discovered when it investigated how its top-flight salesmen spent their time. The company clocked those salesmen from the time they left their homes in the morning until they returned at night. The figures below tell the story:

Activity	9 A.M. - 5 P.M.	Before 9 and After 5	All Day
Travel	2¾ hrs.	1½ hrs.	4¼ hrs.
Waiting	¾	—	¾
Selling	3	—	3
Administrative	½	1	1½
TOTAL	7	2½	9½

Call average: less than six calls per man per day

Duties of the Salesman

One of the salesman's first steps toward managing his time is to classify his business activities and to find out just what he is doing in regard to each. These activities will be either *selling* or *nonselling*.

Selling. The selling activity consists of showing prospects why they should buy, and consists, in the main, of demonstrating and explaining. Because there are no magic formulas, and because no two interviews are exactly alike, this activity demands that the salesman have and use imagination, creative ability, and resourcefulness.

Nonselling. The nonselling activities will vary from case to case, but they do contain certain duties that all salesmen face. *Traveling* is an activity few salesmen can avoid; it includes travel to prospects, to customers, to the home office, and to the salesman's home. *Waiting* to see prospects cannot be eliminated. *Service* to customers, such as dressing their windows or training their salespersons, is often expected of those who sell to retailers. *Handling adjustments* is sometimes assigned to salesmen. So is the job of *collecting.* Salesmen may drift into or be expected to do a certain amount of *visiting* with prospects or their employees. *Public relations* may occasionally call a salesman away from selling. It is not impossible for *market research* to consume some of his time. *Prospecting*, including both locating and learning about prospects, is a nonselling function most salesmen must engage in if they are to replace lost customers. *Planning* is necessary if the salesman is to have a definite objective for each call, each day, each product, each prospect, and each year. *Paper work*, including correspondence and record keeping, is a chore that cannot be evaded. Finally, *self-development*, both physical and mental, is a necessity.

Handling Nonselling Duties

The first angle that must be considered concerns which nonselling duties are to be assumed. This, of course, is a useless question for those salesmen working for companies which prescribe in detail what they expect their salesmen to do. For the nonsupervised salesman, experience and not a textbook must dictate the choice of nonselling activities because of the varied nature of selling.

A second angle involves the amount of time that should be spent on each activity. It is not too difficult, if he really wants to, for the salesman to keep an adequately accurate record of how much time he is spending on each of the functions he has decided to perform. Such a record will identify quickly where he is spending too much or too little time. Nonselling business activities can be justified only if they provide the salesman more time with prospects and more productive selling techniques. Each such activity undertaken by the salesman must be reflected later in a better sales record.

By selecting the nonselling duties carefully and by devoting to each its own proper amount of time, the salesman achieves the optimum ratio of selling time to nonselling time. His days and weeks are complete because they are in balance. His activities and efforts are planned so as to insure maximum accomplishment.

Budgeting Time

No salesman has enough time. It is equally true that every salesman finds time to spend for what he wants. Yet, the salesman's first, unstudied choice of what he will do with his time may not be the best choice. The answer? He must budget each day's hours if he is to spend them most effectively.

If a salesman comes upon a good prospect unexpectedly, it is fine to be able to talk with him for a while. If a salesman wants to treat himself to the luxury of a ball game or a show, it is good to be able to afford it. If prospects or customers insist that a salesman spend some social minutes with them, it is nice to be able to accede. When selling activities vie with nonselling activities, it is good to know that the latter are not getting more of the salesman's time than they should. Because a salesman spends time just as he spends money, it is possible for him to save up minutes just as he saves up dollars. If a salesman wants to be able to do all these things, yet not appear rushed to meet a deadline, he must budget his time.

Although a "budgeted day" will be suggested in some detail later in this chapter, it may be worth while to introduce a few examples of basic budgeting matters here. A salesman starts with the amount of time he considers available for budgeting. Then he lists all the requests that will be made on that amount of time. He thinks of how much time he should budget for selling, and how much for each legitimate, approved nonselling function. He thinks of how much time he should spend on each market he covers, and how much with each prospect and customer composing that market. He thinks of each individual day in the week, earmarking the best hours for selling, and night or weekend hours for paper work and routine. He sets up danger signals to warn him if and when he drifts into spending too much time in such activities as personal matters or in building goodwill. He remembers that delaying his first selling attempt until mid-morning and quitting work in mid-afternoon are expensive habits. He not only limits the lunch hour to an hour, but he also uses it in qualifying or selling prospects. He particularly guards against the insidious siren of procrastination when he has reached his quota for the month before the last day of the month.

Off-the-Job Time

What a salesman does with time that is spent neither in selling nor in nonselling business activities is, in one sense, his own personal affair.

As is true of many types of careers, however, most of those hours will influence a salesman's selling career, even if only indirectly.

One question that arises in this connection concerns how active a salesman should be in his community. Unfortunately, there is no simple answer. It would appear that each salesman must determine for himself to what extent he can and should take part in civic and community affairs and then participate accordingly. Should he be a joiner? Would organizations just waste some of his limited time? Would they help him find prospects? Is membership for him a desirable hobby? Is he morally obligated to help see that certain organizations continue to operate successfully? Each salesman must answer these questions for himself in terms of his objectives and ambitions.

A second question asks if the way a salesman spends his off-the-job time affects his selling. The answer is affirmative; most sales managers are convinced that a salesman's private life can have an important bearing on his success. Both his character and his reputation help determine whether or not he enjoys the respect and confidence of his customers. The salesman should be careful about where and with whom he is seen. When in public, his conduct should show that he knows that prospects, customers, or references may be present. He should select types of entertainment and recreation that can damage neither him nor his company. Rather than destroy, his recreation time should "re-create."

PLANNING THE WORK AND WORKING THE PLAN

Benefits of Planning

Every salesman wants to call on just as many promising prospects as he possibly can. In addition, he wants to spend the maximum amount of time in face-to-face selling and the proper amount of time in non-selling business activities. Many companies ask and expect their salesmen to average a minimum number of calls each day or each week. One very large company, for example, wants its salesmen to average twelve interviews each complete working day. These objectives cannot be reached without planning; the salesman must organize his work in advance.

Here are some benefits enjoyed by salesmen who plan their work:

Systematic planning starts with a study of the salesman's problems and objectives. This is helpful because it makes the salesman more completely acquainted with his job by revealing that job in detail.

By directing his efforts, the salesman can concentrate on the most promising prospects and markets so as to do a more thorough, more successful job.

Controlled calling insures that a salesman distributes his time to best advantage. It prevents his spending time on persons who cannot use his product to advantage, and it results in his seeing five prospects three times each rather than one prospect fifteen times.

Planning minimizes lost time, and lost time makes it easier for competing salesmen to take over a salesman's accounts. With planning, a salesman avoids wasting a valuable half hour or so each morning deciding where, when, and how to start his day.

Laying out his work in advance relieves the salesman of having to dash about at a furious rate of speed. Such exertion has an unfortunate effect both on the salesman and on his buyers.

Planning provides consistency of action because plans lead to policies.

Planning extends and applies to the technical phase of selling which was referred to as "telling the story." Consequently, the quality and effectiveness of the presentation will increase.

Mistakes and oversights are reduced by systematic planning. Some errors may creep in, but they are quickly detected.

The law of averages works for the salesman who plans. Such a salesman can tell you how many sales he will make from one hundred calls, and he is the salesman who arranges to make the greatest number of calls.

Three cautions are in order about planning. First, occasionally a salesman thinks that he is wiser than his company and that rules are for others to follow and for him to break. He steers according to his own hunches and ideas, ignoring or even scorning the planning his company does for him. He feels that he knows more than his company about what to do about handling his territory. Second, there should always be a plan, and it should be executed in most respects and in most situations. But no plan does or can replace judgment and common sense. Third, because no substitute has yet been found for hard work, hard work will continue to be demanded even of planners.

Objectives

While it is true that a salesman should strive to do a variety of things, he thinks primarily of making a minimum number of calls and of achieving a satisfactory volume of sales.

As for the calls, a salesman should at all times be contacting three groups of individuals. Present customers make up the first group. Second is a group of prospects who have been solicted but not yet sold. The third group consists of new prospects who have just been located but who have not yet been solicted. Each of these three groups should get exactly as much time as it is entitled to — and no more.

```
      DO I HAVE A PLAN FOR—
 1. Keeping the right attitude.
 2. Self-improvement (Always be ambitious, but keep
    your ability one step ahead of your ambitions).
 3. A plan for working my territory to avoid lost
    motion and to save time and energy.
 4. A plan for calling on accounts.
 5. A good relationship with the doctor's nurse
    and/or secretary.
 6. Getting the doctor's attention.
 7. Seeing the better prescribers often.
 8. Stressing the "Benefit Points."
 9. Keeping the doctor's attention.
10. Closing detail or sale.
11. Presenting the sample at the right time.
12. Expressing gratitude.
13. Getting others to work for me.
14. Holding old business while getting new business.
    (Here is where so many fail, and one day you
    realize that what was once yours is now someone
    else's.)
15. Keeping up with purchases by accounts each
    quarter.
16. Starting a re-detail in a different manner so
    that the doctor will not cut me off.  (Never
    make the mistake of thinking a doctor remembers
    everything you told him on your last visit.)
17. Exhibiting enthusiasm motivated by a sincere
    conviction.
18. Keeping up with what competition is doing.
19. Knowing my doctor's prescribing habits.
20. Asking for the order.
```

This is a checklist of one of the leading salesman of the Upjohn Company.

Because the salesman's main concern is usually to make large customers out of medium sized customers, and medium sized customers out of the small ones, the salesman properly spends more time with the customer group than with either of the prospect groups. As for the second group, it contains prospects with whom and on whom some time, thought, and dollars have been spent, yet from whom no orders have come. The goal here is to devote major attention to the most promising prospects. A definite amount of time should be spent each week working with the third group in hunting for future business from prospects not yet contacted. It is this third group that replaces the customers that are lost each year for various reasons. Only by setting up goals for each group and then scheduling that number of calls each week can the sales-man be sure he is devoting the proper amount of time to each classification. As an example, one well-known company expects its salesmen each day to call on three present customers, three prospects who have already been called on, and three new prospects.

The second goal toward which the salesman is working is sales volume. This type of goal is a quota and may be set up in terms of dollars or in merchandise units. Regardless of which base is used, units or dollars, no quota figure should be selected that is unattainable. Quotas can become mockeries and cause much harm if they are so absurdly high that they defeat the salesman before he starts. The best quota is one that forces the salesman to work if he is to make it, yet is attainable if he does work. Such quotas can be established only after the potential market in the salesman's territory has been evaluated. Because conditions change, continuing flexibility is an essential feature of any sound quota; too much flexibility, of course, is as bad as no flexibility. For the long term, a sales-man's budget performance is satisfactory only if he makes a profitable showing.

ROUTING

Routing is coverage. If we consider the aim of the salesman's strategy to be to maximize sales at the most profitable point, then the salesman turns to "working the plan" when he undertakes to route himself soundly and systematically. There is little use in setting up calls and sales goals unless the salesman follows through by moving about his territory accord-ing to a sound, systematic schedule.

The salesman properly looks on routing as a challenge to his executive ability and to his capacity to manage. The importance of routing stems from the fact that many salesmen have considerable authority over their movement. Their responsibility, their independence, and their power to select are often great.

As an introduction to routing, let's review a bit of geography. After weekly or monthly quotas have been determined for dollar sales, unit sales, calls on customers, old prospects, and new prospects, the question is *where* can the salesman look for fulfillment. The answer, of course, is that he is completely dependent upon the potential demand in his area in trying to make his quotas. Whatever programs and timetables he fashions to attain his goals can be constructed only in terms of the geographic area he covers and what it contains.

Size of Territory

The size of the territory may be determined by some salesmen on an individual basis, but the great majority of salesmen will have specific, clearly delineated sales territories assigned to them. In any event, it may be well to mention briefly some of the factors that influence size of selling area. The total number of prospects is one of the most basic of these factors. The buying habits of these prospects are a second important influence. Location of prospects in relation to transportation facilities makes up a third determinant. The best frequency-of-call schedule is a fourth factor. How often the salesman will be called back to the home office and for how long is a fifth consideration. Competition, that ubiquitous opponent who sometimes makes your decisions for you, is a sixth factor. Finally, there is the potential dollar demand present in various markets.

Regardless of the size of the area and irrespective of who determines it, the boundary lines must be clear in the salesman's mind. Those lines embrace the salesman's problems and his possibilities. They contain his job with its duties and responsibilities. They specify the exact area in terms of which he must plan and operate.

Breakdown of Area

Those salesmen who cover a number of cities or a number of states face the problem of organizing their sales territories in the most manageable, profitable manner. This calls for dividing the territory into smaller sections or sub-areas. In this sense, the salesman's geographic responsibility is for a number of individual markets or trading areas. He thinks, plans, and works in terms of the several trading areas that make up the whole of his territory. Even a "city" or "local" salesman is forced to think of his single city market as being made up of different sections or districts of the one city.

By breaking down the large unit into a number of trading areas or districts, the salesman finds it possible to draft an individual, tailored program or plan for working each. These several plans are combined and coordinated in such a way as to allow the salesman to work each smaller area and the entire area systematically. Because his territory is organized as an assortment of separate trading areas or sections, it is possible for selling activities to be fitted and adapted to each market. Because he analyzes and operates in terms of the smaller, more convenient units, the salesman can more promptly and accurately estimate the need for his products; he can be more sensitive in detecting the appearance of any new market or of any new conditions which will affect him. His knowledge of his total territory is more complete and thorough because it is collected in terms of smaller units. Because he knows his territory well, he can move about in it more economically and profitably.

Benefits of Sound Routing

Well-planned routing raises both the number of calls the salesman makes and the ratio of selling time to nonselling time. Futile calls are fewer. The well-routed salesman sees the maximum number of buyers when they are most ready to buy. His sales territory is worked in a logical, planned, and controlled manner, and his coverage is thorough.

Good routing insures that the salesman covers his territory according to plan. It permits him to strike the balance he desires between intensive and extensive coverage. When routing permits the prospect to anticipate and expect the salesman's call, there is more chance that the prospect will see the salesman, will be ready to see the salesman, and will require less of the salesman's time. Sound routing reduces traveling costs. Finally, routing can help the salesman make a better showing against the performance standards he or his company uses for control purposes.

Principles of Routing

Here are some things to do and to remember in order to accomplish the most efficient routing.

1. Study and know your geographic selling area thoroughly. Plot your cities or markets on a map, and trace the most economical ways to get to each. Then do the same type of mapping for all prospects and customers to be contacted within each city or market.

2. Routing should provide you with the greatest possible amount of face-to-face time with the most profitable buyers; therefore, routing in a straight line is usually desirable because it shortens the distances and permits more calls.

3. Strive to conserve time and money. If you call in a hit or miss fashion, skip and jump, zigzag or crisscross, backtrack, or make long jumps between calls, you are being inefficient. Your intent should be to spend the amount of time in each market that each deserves. Travel should be short, quick, safe, certain, and inexpensive.

4. Conserve yourself as much as possible. Unnecessary or irregular travel depletes both your physical and emotional reserves. By making your travel as effortless as possible, you protect your effectiveness.

5. If you do work other than selling, such as collecting, strive for a routing plan that is the most satisfactory compromise.

6. A valuable concept is that of "optimum coverage of each neighborhood." You move in this direction when you ask yourself, "What else can I possibly do on my way to, while in, or on leaving that particular district or town?"

7. Make up the routing plan for the most suitable future period; often this will be the coming week. This practice allows you to designate a "mail-in" or "telephone-in" point for use by your company, your prospects and customers, and yourself.

8. In some lines, buyers should be able to expect and count on a salesman's calls, certainly as to day and often as to approximate hour. This calls for establishing a routing sequence that will be repeated at regular intervals. When leaving a buyer, you might indicate approximately when you will next call.

9. To whatever extent possible or necessary, you should route yourself to suit the pleasure of your prospects and customers. If the day or hour of your call is inconvenient or inopportune, you are working against additional resistance. This means that it might be possible, in certain cases, for you to spend more time in travel, see fewer prospects and customers, yet find that the time spent in face-to-face selling has increased in effectiveness.

10. Experiment is essential to successful routing. Only through trial and error can the best routing be determined.

THE DAILY SCHEDULE

If the salesman routes himself carefully but does not follow up routing by mapping out a program for each day's activities, he stops short of a necessary step. If the salesman's time is to count, if he is to spend the greatest possible amount of time in the presence of buyers, then each selling day must be a planned day. The plan or schedule operates as an efficiency device. It gets the salesman off to work at an early hour and keeps him on the job for a full day. It reduces time waste.

Elements of the Schedule

The program for the day must be fashioned to allow the salesman to attain his objectives. Four basic factors or elements determine the final make-up of the program: (1) the number of calls the salesman hopes to make that day on present customers, old prospects, and new prospects; (2) the sales volume in dollars or units which the salesman hopes to attain on that day; (3) the number of hours the salesman plans to work that day; (4) a combination of the energy, the ambition, and the industry of the salesman. In brief, what the schedule does is take the working hours, earmark them by duties to be performed, allot the selling time to customers, old prospects, and new prospects, and assume that the activities planned will produce the sales volume budgeted for that day.

The calls that the salesman makes will be "planned" calls. He knows specifically what he hopes to accomplish on each, he has a plan or outline for each interview, and he has all the material he will need neatly packed in prospect folders that are arranged in the order of the planned calls. In addition to the selling calls, there will be included in the day's schedule any "in-between" contacts with customers and prospects. These are calculated contacts that are sandwiched in between selling calls and may be made by mail, wire, 'phone, or even in person. The PTA meetings or the civic club luncheons are examples of situations which permit non-business personal contacts that can help business.

The salesman will need to experiment to find out what the hours should be. Also, he will determine by trial and error whether selling at lunch, in the evening, and on Saturday are profitable for him. Appropriate allowance must be made for holidays and for any vacations he takes.

Principles of Schedule Building

The schedule for each day should be constructed around the most important prospects and customers for that day. These principles will help you to set up a practical and efficient daily schedule.

1. Set a time for each of the most important calls for the day. Examples of important calls are calls on buyers who are ready to buy, buyers who you know to be accessible during this trip but who may be out of town or otherwise unavailable during the next trip, buyers with whom the salesman has appointments, and buyers the salesman was instructed to see. Then spot minor calls around and between the major calls.

2. Have a definite, single time to start each day's work. This hour should be early and should be strictly observed. Instead of being misled by the faulty advice never to call at a prospect's office until he has read his mail, some salesmen benefit from meeting the prospect in his office when he arrives.

3. Do not stop until the jobs scheduled for that day have been done, else you will complicate the schedules that follow.

4. Plan a full day's work for each working day. This concept of a standard day's work is extremely important because it defines how much

the salesman should accomplish during a typical day in the way of number of calls, sales volume, or an earnings figure. Only a substandard performance can be achieved if the salesman makes no calls before 10 in the morning, none between 11:30 and 2, and none after 4 in the afternoon. It is only the young or fearful salesman who waits until 10 o'clock "to let the prospect get his day started," and who quits calling at 4 o'clock "because the prospect will be in a hurry to go somewhere." One of our largest companies defines its full work day as running from 8 A.M. to 5 P.M. with one hour for lunch. The first sales story should start at 8 A.M.

5. Lay out more than the usual day's work if necessary to stay busy and make the quota. Some salesmen schedule one third more calls than they expect to make so as to have a margin of safety; if they hope to make nine calls, a satisfactory quota for the day, they put twelve on the schedule. Then, if the interviews go faster than usual, or if some of the buyers are out, the salesman still keeps busy.

6. Lay out the calls in sequence.

7. Appointments, where practicable, are worthwhile. They help reduce pointless calls, waiting time, and the average length of the call. Appointments at an early hour (8 to 9 A.M.) and at a late afternoon hour (4 to 5 P.M.) help keep the salesman on the job all day.

8. Allow enough time for each duty and each call so as to minimize departures from and disruptions of the schedule.

9. Devote the most productive hours of the day to selling to buyers. This activity deserves top priority in the scheduling process. Schedule routine jobs, paper work, and service functions for other hours.

10. Insofar as possible, construct the schedule according to the needs and wishes of the prospects and customers.

11. Do the preliminary draft of the schedule for each day of the coming week (or two weeks) as a final phase of routing for that period. The final versions should be written out on the preceding night.

12. Pay careful attention to the elapsed time per call. This is a fundamental matter. The number of minutes spent with each prospect needs careful interpretation — a high figure may be either good or bad.

13. Make each day more productive by substituting mail or telephone contacts for personal contacts where possible. Of course, duties must not be slighted or neglected by depending upon telephone or mail to do things that should be done in person. It is possible, however, to use direct mail to *hold* and even to *get* some business while you are in other markets. It is also possible to make good use of the two to deliver advance notice of calls in those cases where such notification would increase the probability and the quality of interviews.

FLEXIBILITY IN ROUTING AND SCHEDULING

There must be a certain amount of flexibility in the program the salesman plans for covering his territory and for talking to buyers. Indeed, the salesman must try to be prepared for anything and everything because changes and cancellations in both travel and calls, often on short notice, are inevitable. Schedules must be revised to fit emergencies, and lost time can and must be made up. Adjustments are to be expected, for no plan can or should control the salesman to such an extent that he adheres to it blindly, regardless of developments. Transportation delays, broken appointments, indisposition of the salesman, and inability to get away from buyers on schedule are typical causes of changes in plans. As a matter of fact, a salesman may want to step up his efforts, activities, and calls just after making a big sale because his ability to sell is at a peak at that time.

There are several methods of providing the needed amount of flexibility. Probably the first and most important is for the salesman to have the right attitude toward unavoidable revisions. Flexibility is a frame of mind, and one begins to achieve it when he starts cultivating his ability to improvise. A second step toward flexibility is realization that minutes can be moved about within a time budget in the same way that dollars can be shifted around in a financial budget. Minutes can be temporarily borrowed today from today's paper work allowance, used for selling to buyers, and then replaced tomorrow. A third method for a salesman to stay flexible is always to be easily reached by prospects, customers, and his own company. A fourth suggestion is that alternate plans be set up in case there should be unexpected spare time. By having a second choice if prospect A is out of town at 10:40 on Tuesday, the time of the appointment, the salesman can avoid a waste of time. Second choices might consist of such activities as canvassing for new prospects, calling to see if a dormant, marginal account can and should be revived, making call backs, or even catching up on paper work.

A different approach would be for the salesman to reduce his need for flexibility. If a salesman calls on buyers rather infrequently, he may find that an advance notice of his call will reduce time spent in reception rooms and also reduce the number of fruitless calls. If the salesman concludes that a mailing which gives the date and approximate hour of the call should precede him, he should determine when the buyer should receive it and should then mail it on schedule. Until he gets the feel of his job, the junior salesman may be wise to allow a generous amount of time for each call. By so doing, he will not be asked to squeeze a twenty-minute story into ten, nor will he have to 'phone ahead so often to reschedule an appointment. Incidentally, notifying buyers if appointments cannot be met is a *must*, particularly where the buyer is counting on the salesman to have or do something for him on the next scheduled call.

USING THE TELEPHONE

Certain buyers, particularly retailers, like to buy by telephone for reasons of speed and simplicity. Certain products, especially staples, can be sold successfully by telephone. Many manufacturers and retailers have achieved worthwhile results from their telephone selling programs.

Because a salesman must work for a certain degree of economy both in his time budgeting and in his expense budgeting, he is remiss unless he investigates or even experiments with the telephone as a supplementary selling tool. And, it seems reasonable to suspect that few salesmen use their telephones to the maximum extent. For a few salesmen, of course, telephone selling is the *sole* form of selling.

Many salesmen can benefit from spending one hour a day in telephoning, especially in dull or off seasons. That hour can easily result in more hours each week in face-to-face selling to buyers. In addition to this effect on *quantity*, the hour can easily raise the *quality* of that face-to-face time.

Features

Two-way telephone communication is virtually unrestricted. The salesman can call any buyer anywhere, at an hour of his own choosing, on about any day. Because geography is no limitation, the number of calls possible during a day is high. Because communication is two-way, understanding between salesman and buyer can be speedy.

The telephone puts all salesmen on the same competitive footing physically. Size, looks, bearing, and appearance don't count. The buyer cannot dislike what he cannot see. The salesman's voice is everything; the salesman does not need to *look* good, but must *sound* good.

Contact by telephone is almost instantaneous; this means a salesman can send urgent information to whatever group of buyers he needs to reach. Sometimes the salesman finds it easier to get through a switchboard operator than through a receptionist-barrier of some sort. Some buyers, often consumers, will talk on the telephone when they will not *see* a salesman. Because prestige usually gets prompt handling for their long distance calls, salesmen typically do not have to wait to talk with distant buyers.

To a great degree, telephone calls are as private as they are personal. Privacy is not always to be had when a salesman calls in person; and, telephone calls are more personal than letters.

Even though very few salesmen find telephone calls a complete sub-stitute for face-to-face calls, most salesmen are well advised to remember the difference in costs. There are salesmen whose typical call in person costs twenty times as much as their typical telephone toll call. Telephoning permits more effective market coverage than would otherwise be possible. Because it is relatively inexpensive, telephoning lets a salesman get in touch with important buyers often, particularly between personal calls.

There are some limitations or handicaps, however, The fact that the salesman's impression is determined solely by what he says and how he says it has negative as well as positive implications. Regardless of his physique, almost every salesman can make effective use of his physical presence and personality. And, just as the buyer cannot be impressed by the physical salesman, neither can the salesman observe the buyer, his reactions, his expressions, or his circumstances.

Another handicap is the buyer's disinclination to give the salesman much time. Consumers won't listen so long over the telephone as in a retail store, although this fact may reflect differences in degree of interest. Purchasing agents, too, may be inclined to listen fewer seconds than they do in face-to-face contact. This particular handicap is more understandable when one remembers that the buyer is asked to grasp the salesman's message quickly without the help of any visual aid.

Uses of Telephone Calls

Brief discussions of some common uses of the telephone in selling follow.

To Make Sales. Salesmen sell regular orders by telephone. They telephone buyers to increase orders mailed or 'phoned in by trading the customer up or by the suggestion selling of related or timely merchandise; some manufacturers and wholesalers have a policy of trying to add to a retailer's order *one* item that retailer now buys from competition. Sales-men make telephone calls to land follow-up orders, and to move odd lots, job lots, end-of-season merchandise, and discontinued items.

Salesmen sell hard-to-see buyers and impulsive buyers by telephone. They telephone buyers to encourage them to take buying action now, especially after a first personal call which went well but did not end in a purchase. In such calls, the salesman can repeat, confirm, and support what he said in person. Or, while in a buyer's office, the salesman can telephone a happy customer for a testimonial. Retailers telephone con-sumers inviting them to make store visits — and buy.

To Make Appointments. A major use of the telephone by sales-men is for making, confirming, and rescheduling appointments. The advantages of having appointments are many. They reduce travel time, waiting time, and correspondence time. They raise the quality of calls by preconditioning the buyers; furthermore, when a buyer agrees to an appointment, he admits that he is a prospect. The request for an appointment is a courteous gesture, implying value of the buyer's time and prestige of the buyer himself. By balancing his working days with appointments, the salesman is able to cover more territory, make more calls on buyers, and give more service to customers. Sometimes the salesman can get some buyer-information when 'phoning for an appointment, but he should not try to do any selling.

Almost every salesman can experiment and, by trial and error, develop approach patterns which will get for him a worthwhile number of appointments.

The telephone call requesting an appointment may be preceded by a mail communication. After he has made the appointment, the salesman may drop the buyer a confirming note, asking the buyer to mark his calendar.

To Deliver News. The telephone helps a salesman keep his buyers posted on matters involving products and prices, promotion and policies, because it permits instant contact. Some news is *good.* Maybe a manufacturer is launching a major advertising effort; his retailers will be happy to hear about it. Maybe a price rise is imminent, but buyers can place orders now at the present price. Maybe emergency service is being offered to some buyers hit by fire, flood, or tornado. Maybe delivery can be made to an impatient buyer earlier than originally promised.

Telephone calls transmit *bad* news, too. Strikes or other developments may cause orders to be delayed. A good customer's request for some favor or exception may be turned down by the top management of the salesman's firm. If certain ordered items cannot be shipped, the salesman may telephone to tell the buyer that they have been back-ordered and when he may expect them.

To Cultivate Buyers' Goodwill. Telephoning can be used to keep a buyer-seller relationship on a personal, friendly basis. A call can introduce a salesman to a new purchasing agent, for example, before the salesman's first visit in person. Salesmen can telephone to congratulate and compliment buyers on honors, awards, promotions, and achievements. Salesmen can thank buyers for first interviews, for first orders, for testimonials, referrals, and case histories. Telephone calls let the salesman inquire how things are, keep in touch, check up on customer service. The fact that a salesman takes the time to telephone — especially long-distance — flatters most buyers. Of course, telephoning can be overdone, and it then becomes annoying to buyers. The salesman must find the happy medium if he is to rely on telephone contacts as part of his selling schedule.

To Handle Problems. Studied use of the telephone will forestall some customer problems and will reduce their total number. When certain problems arise, the smart salesman considers telephone communication as a possible course of action. When a written complaint or a cancellation comes in, a telephone call may be indicated. Even some written inquiries deserve to be answered in this manner. Certain collection matters can be handled by telephone better than by letter. Calls can reveal why a good customer quit buying; they can be effective in reviving dormant accounts; they can be made to get approval for a substitution in an order. Indeed, in handling "problems" with a customer, the personal touch of a telephone call can very often get quicker and more satisfactory results.

To Make Contact with Home Office. Salesmen can telephone their home or district offices to get information instantly, to clear proposals, to get decisions, to get backing and support. When in a buyer's office, for instance, a salesman can impress the buyer by telephoning a request for some buyer-favor, or by arranging for the buyer to talk to an engineer, the production manager, or the credit manager.

To Do Prospecting and Preapproach Work. Cold canvassing from a directory is possible by telephone. Customers can be asked for leads. Salesmen telephone to qualify prospects, to build a prospect list, and to get data needed for buyer-evaluation. Calls can identify the real prospects on a company mailing list and can spot those open to buy or seriously considering a purchase. Salesmen selling to business firms make use of the telephone in identifying buying influences.

How Telephoning Affects Routing

Some salesmen have incorporated the use of the telephone into what they call "skip-stop" routing. Here's a simple example. A salesman has 20 markets in which he must make some personal calls. He constructs two swings or circuits. On his first swing, he visits all *odd*-numbered markets — 1, 3, 5, 7, 9, 11, 13, 15, 17, 19 — but telephones certain buyers in *even*-numbered markets from the closest odd-numbered market. On his other swing, the salesman reverses his pattern. He visits all even-numbered markets — 2, 4, 6, 8, 10, 12, 14, 16, 18, 20 — and from them telephones buyers in the odd-numbered localities.

Other salesmen build their routes on "key" towns. Under this plan, a salesman divides his markets and his buyers into two groups: (a) those deserving personal calls, and (b) those which must be handled in a manner more economical of time, dollars, and energy. Telephoning is that manner. Individual customers and markets in the second group are reached by telephone when the salesman is in the closest key town. It is not unusual for a salesman to telephone certain small buyers who reside *in* key towns; neither is it unknown for a salesman to alternate telephone calls with personal calls in his handling of certain accounts of modest size.

Skip-stop and key-town routing contribute to more effective self management. They permit greater flexibility; they make more convenient the soliciting of new accounts and more economical the servicing of marginal accounts and their markets. By permitting a salesman to keep in touch with out-of-the-way markets, they make for more efficient coverage of his territory.

The Telephone Voice

The most important element in his telephone communication is the salesman's vocal delivery. Remember, the buyer can do no lip reading nor can he observe the salesman's facial expressions. In achieving a voice that "smiles," the salesman can benefit from listening critically to (and learning from) radio. He can record a presentation and then play it back, and he can ask family and friends to tell him how he sounds over the wire. He can learn from actors, too, because he needs to deliver his lines as impressively as they deliver theirs. A bit of urgency is permissible when urging action, and much confidence is helpful in inviting respect.

Speed of delivery can be varied for emphasis, and pauses can be interspersed for both emphasis and variety. As for volume, the ordinary conversational tone is best. Some contrast in volume will prevent monotony, but at all times, the salesman's voice should come in strong and clear. Some salesmen believe it effective to step up volume and enthusiasm after calling the buyer by name for the first time.

If pitch of voice is high, the listener tends to tire and to become irritated. If pitch is low, reception may be difficult and voice not pleasing. As was true of volume, *normal* pitch is best.

Enunciation should be natural, clear, and distinct so that the buyer "gets" every word. The salesman should speak directly into the transmitter with his mouth close to the mouthpiece, facing it directly. He should not talk with gum, cigarettes, or pencil in mouth.

Opening the Telephone Conversation

In practically all instances, the salesman should open his call by quickly identifying himself (name, company, brand) and then follow with the reason for the call. Immediately the salesman should give the buyer a reason for staying on the wire rather than ending the conversation; this reason may involve curiosity or information of interest and benefit. It is virtually impossible for the salesman to get to the point too quickly because, by revealing his goal, he may prevent the buyer's losing interest and hanging up the receiver. Sometimes there is something to which the salesman can tie his call. This may be a letter he sent the buyer earlier, some communication from the buyer, the last personal call, the buyer's last order, or even an earlier telephone contact. A pleasant, cordial, courteous manner from the very start helps make a favorable impression.

In business calls, the switchboard operator often tells a salesman that she will ring the buyer's secretary. The proper tactic when speaking to the secretary is for the salesman first to ask confidently to speak to Mr. Buyer, then to identify himself. The secretary not only "gets" the salesman's name better but also is prevented from taking control by asking the salesman who he is. If the secretary asks the salesman what he wants to talk to the buyer about, the salesman should tell her but not in detail. Otherwise he runs the risk of irritating and alienating the secretary and of not being put through to the buyer.

Other Suggestions

Most principles that are sound for face-to-face selling are equally sound for telephone communication. Here are some examples. Telephone calls should be made at times convenient to the buyer. Some insurance salesmen have learned, for instance, to call business men about mid-morning, blue collar individuals after supper, dentists before 9:30 A.M., and clergymen on Tuesday. Buyers should be addressed by name and made to feel important. Salesmen must refrain from interrupting, arguing, and monopolizing the conversation. Salesmen must make every word contribute to gaining their objectives as they enthusiastically convert product features into buyer benefits. Brevity is desirable. Short, crisp statements and questions of 15 to 20 words are recommended. Salesmen must persist up to a point after the buyer has pled "no time" or "not interested," but they must not push so hard as to "close the door" on a subsequent call. Salesmen need to experiment with various presentation plans and to keep notes and records of the calls they make.

Telephoning does not replace planning, thinking, working, or, for most salesmen, personal calls. It must not be used as a crutch on which to lean; it should increase, not decrease the number of personal calls made. It must not be asked to do what it cannot do; it clearly is not so effective as a personal visit.

The quality of telephone communication must be maintained at a high level. Salesmen are advised against drifting into over-familiarity, against gossiping, against calling just to pass the time of day. Buyers must not feel that a salesman is unwilling to call in person; nor must they feel that a telephone call was routine to the salesman, an item in a big, mechanical schedule, made because a certain buyer's name came up for a call on that day.

Above all, the salesmen dare not seem arrogant or inconsiderate. Certain businessmen, grossly overestimating their own importance and status, instruct their secretaries to get the other party on the wire and to call them to the telephone only when and if the other party is ready to talk. The person being called is supposed to get on the wire and wait until the man placing the call is notified by his secretary that he is on the line. Salesmen are clearly in no position to indulge in this type of maneuver. It is equally disrespectful for the salesman to hang up first. Not only is this discourteous, but also it ends the conversation before the buyer has had the opportunity to say all he wants to say.

Many salesmen have found a telephone company credit card quite useful. With one, a salesman can avoid making paid telephone calls; he does not need change; he does not have to call collect. A credit card helps a salesman avoid embarrassment when he wants to make a toll call over the buyer's telephone. Incidentally, many salesmen invite certain buyers to telephone them collect. Such an invitation is quite timely when a salesman has tried to telephone a distant buyer three or four times without success.

If a salesman wants or needs to see a buyer face-to-face, he should not let the buyer persuade him to make his selling presentation over the telephone. Should the buyer say, "Suppose you summarize your story over the telephone," the salesman must *not* panic and comply. A good tactic here is for the salesman to have something he and the buyer must examine together and for the telephone call to be an offer to show it to the buyer. Diagrams, maps, pictures, drawings, floor plans, models, and color assortments are examples.

RECORD KEEPING

The Need for Records

It is impossible for a salesman to plan and control his work or to direct himself most efficiently without records. Remember that his objectives have to do with calls on and sales to buyers. Only records can tell the salesman what he needs to know about each. The best methods the salesman can devise to obtain information on buying and selling and the mass of such data he accumulates are of limited value unless and until he organizes them into readily usable records.

The amount of time that is required in keeping records is justified by the improvement that results in the quality of the salesman's selling. Records enable the salesman to organize his work. The salesman leans heavily on them in managing himself. His daily accomplishments must be known if he is to make his quotas. As an example of the tactical use of records, the salesman can use them to shorten his calls, thus permitting more calls to be completed each week. For instance, on call-backs, records relieve him of spending time in finding out where he left off on the last visit. He can stress only those points that need stressing.

There is a "snowballing" aspect to keeping and using records. If he is to sell effectively, the salesman needs records. The more effective the salesman is, the more prospects and customers he acquires. The more buyers he deals with, the more pressing is the need for records.

All large companies consider records to be indispensable. For example, International Harvester says:

> A correctly operated prospect system will aid the salesman in organizing his time so that the "hit and miss" method of contacting prospects will be eliminated. He will be able to arrange his calls in routes to prevent excessive traveling from one part of a territory to another. In this way, too, he can use his time more advantageously. At the beginning of each 15-day period, he can plan the calls to be made and route himself accordingly. This route should be followed as closely as possible until all prospects have been seen.
>
> With a record of each previous call at his fingertips, the salesman is thoroughly acquainted with the prospect, his needs, and the status of the prospective call. Thus, he is familiar with all details concerning the prospective sale. When a prospect is called upon and not sold, the salesman should make a notation on the prospect record as to what occurred and list the date on which the next call should be made. This will keep him in direct contact with each prospect and enable him to make his calls at the proper time.

Keeping and Handling Records

No record is worth keeping unless it is both designed and maintained in such a way that its information can be and is used to advantage. Records that demand too much paper work can easily contain much useless detail. Records that are complete yet simple are the ones that are kept up-to-date and used.

If at all possible, the salesman should fill out immediately after each call any daily reports he keeps. His records will then contain fewer mistakes and fresher facts; they will also be more complete. Furthermore, the practice saves time and permits earlier mailings to the home office. In addition, the salesman is caught up with his work should some emergency arise. If orders, too, can be written up on the spot, time will not have to be spent at night or on weekends reprocessing them. In any event, a good habit is that of checking each day to see that the day's paper work is in good condition.

Orders and reports, particularly the former, should be mailed in to the company promptly. They should be checked for clarity and completeness prior to mailing.

What Records to Keep

It is not possible to prescribe in detail in a textbook all the records that salesmen will need. Instead, the attempt here is to point out most of the major areas in which most salesmen will need some form of records. It goes without saying that the salesman will keep whatever records his company requires, be the information for the use of the sales department or for other departments such as credit or advertising. In addition to those required, any other records that contribute to the salesman's success are worth keeping and using.

Prospects and Customers. These two sets of records are commented on together because they are so similar, each consisting of a card which contains a complete history of the salesman's attention to and experience with each individual buyer. Each card will contain the prospect information the salesman collected about the buyer, any other facts the salesman finds useful, an account of the salesman's work on and progress with the buyer, and plans for the next interview. Time spent in keeping these records is extremely well invested.

Daily Calls. This record tells where the salesman works and on whom he calls. It is a basic record because it shows the number of attempts the salesman makes to sell. It notes any prices quoted and any promises made by the salesman. It records the results of each call and, when sales are lost, it gives a brief reason. Any suitable facts can be transferred from the daily call record to the prospect and customer records.

Sales. There are many breakdowns for sales volume. The total dollar figure may be classified according to product line if the salesman handles more than one product, or to price line if he sells more than one. The breakdown may be by day, week, and month. It may be by size of order. It may be by type of buyer or by type of sale. These are only a few examples of the breakdown possibilities from which each salesman must select the ones to compile and maintain.

Expenses. If expenses are to be kept in a healthy ratio to sales volume, as they must, they need to be carefully controlled. This demands records. Considerable itemization is needed so that the total figure will be complete and so that the various expense items can be analyzed and compared with common or control figures. If the salesman's expense groupings are too detailed, they require too much of his time; if the groupings are too broad, control and comparison are difficult. Guesses and lump sum estimates are not adequate.

Time. Time records are for the purpose of clocking the salesman's hour-and-minute expenditures by days. The immediate result is that the salesman learns exactly how much time he is spending on each of his activities. The long-range result should be that he manages to spend more time in the presence of buyers.

Tickler File. A date tickler file is particularly valuable in reminding the salesman of two things each day of each month: whom to see and things to do. As to the former, the tickler file tells *whom* and *when*. By referring to his prospect and customer files, the salesman reviews *what* he needs to see them about and *how* he should plan to approach them. As to the things to do, the tickler identifies the day the quarterly report should be mailed to the home office, the day of the salesman's annual medical check-up, etc.

CHECKING ACCOMPLISHMENTS

Performance Standards

Plans and quotas, objectives and records are of little value unless the salesman checks the results of his selling efforts against what he had scheduled for himself to do. Students going to work as salesmen for well-managed companies know that their employers will measure the accomplishments of the newly hired salesmen. The basic question asked is, "What does the salesman have to show for his management of himself and his territory?" Only by answering this question frankly and accurately in terms of each day's performance against that day's plans can the salesman determine what kind of a job he is doing and how he can improve. If the salesman is to avoid fooling himself about how much he is working and how much he is playing, then he must measure and analyze his achievement.

To measure his accomplishments, the salesman must have standards against which to check. When he undertakes the task of measuring his productive effort, he automatically assumes that standards of activity and achievement can be set. Yet, the very nature of selling makes the establishment of absolute standards of achievement difficult. In selling, there is a human relations element that makes the job of the analyst

FORM 500-800-4-1-55
RECORD OF FIELD OBSERVATIONS
FIELDMAN

Route 1 _____
2 _____
3 _____
4 _____
5 _____

DATES WORKED

AREA WORKED

SUPERVISER'S CAR SPEEDOMETER READING:

Check (✔) as follows:
A — Outstanding
B — Good
C — Above Average
D — Average
E — Fair
F — Poor

SALESMAN'S ACTIVITIES	A	B	C	D	E	F		CUSTOMER CONTACTS	A	B	C	D	E	F
1. Are his files orderly?								1. Reception by Customers						
2. Does he plan itinerary intelligently?								2. Handling of Sales Presentations						
3. Does he plan daily calls intelligently?								3. Holding Customers Attention						
4. Does he make good use of plan sheets?								4. Knowledge of Products & Prices						
5. Does he plan sales presentations?								5. Use of Advertising Material						
6. Does he have sufficient samples?								6. Use of Promotional Material (brochures, etc.)						
7. Does he have sufficient sales material?								7. Understanding & Use of Sales Statistics						
8. Does he put in a good days work?								8. Intelligent Use of Retail Call Reports						
9. What is the condition of his car?								9. Efforts To Sell Items New to Account						
10. Condition of equipment and sales material								10. Efforts To Improve Distribution: Wholesale / Retail						
PERSONAL								11. Giving Promotional Ideas to Customers						
1. Appearance and Conduct								12. Asks for & Gets Orders during Calls						
2. Attitude								13. Handling of Co-op Advertising						
3. Punctuality								14. Working with ALL Hqtrs. Personnel						
4. Enthusiasm								15. Work with Retail Store Personnel						
5. Aggressiveness								16. Follow-Up: Prev. HQ Call Reports / Retail Call Reports / Contacts						
6. Judgment														
7. Organization								Comments:						
8. Imagination & Resourcefulness														
9. Health														
10. Initiative — Is he a self-starter?														

A. Indicate his Functioning on Present Work:
☐ Doing Outstanding Job
☐ Handling Job Capably
☐ Needs To Improve
☐ Unsatisfactory

B. Does he participate in RAK or WG Salesmen's Meetings?

C. His outstanding strong points are:
1. _____
2. _____

D. List chief weaknesses, in order of their importance, which you feel should be corrected.
1. _____
2. _____

E. What steps have been taken to correct weaknesses listed above and on previous reports?

NOTE: Use Reverse Side For Additional Remarks
White - to N. Y. Office
Green - to Regional Supervisor

Executive _____

An evaluation report

This form is used by sales supervisors to provide management with detailed reports on total effectiveness of sales personnel.

and evaluator less scientific than, let us say, that same job in the field of production. For an extreme example, how can a missionary salesman or other "goodwill" representative of a manufacturer tell how good a job he is doing? Despite this, the salesman is still under pressure to check his accomplishments. Otherwise, he may develop weaknesses.

Performance standards for salesmen are of two types, the first being *quantitative* or *statistical*. These are not difficult to construct; they are objective and concrete, and quite an assortment of them can be created. Standards for volume of sales, for number of calls, for new customers, and for expenses are examples. In operation, quantitative standards are based on a comparison of the salesman's current performance against his previous performance, or against some budget figure or quota. The standards can be used for both control and incentive purposes.

The second type of performance standard is *qualitative, nonstatistical,* and *subjective*. Examples of these inexact standards are those for goodwill, customer loyalty and esteem, planning ability, and industry. Outstanding or unsatisfactory performance in these areas shows up soon in matters that can be quantitatively measured, for example, sales.

Quantitative Checks

If the question is raised as to how many quantitative checks are necessary to measure a salesman's performance, an argument for having only one might be attempted. This one test would be *net profit* from his selling, and the reasoning would be that this single yardstick is adequate, as everything the salesman does in the line of selling is reflected in the net profit figure. But, as there is need for more detail, a double check might be recommended, consisting of *gross margin* and *expenses*. Or three checks might be suggested, the two just mentioned plus *sales volume*.

There is no sacred number of criteria by which the salesman's effectiveness and production should be tested. Some of the common, more revealing tests are:

TIME
Number of days worked.
Number of hours worked.
Number of hours selling to
  buyers.
Average length of call.

CALLS
Number of calls per day.
Number or demonstrations
  made.
Number of calls per sale.
Cost per call.

SALES
Sales per week or month.
Per cent increase in sales.
Average size of order.
Per cent of quota sold.
  How meaningful this figure is depends on the validity of the quota.
  If the quota is accurate, then the figure works out to be a valuable
  ratio of actual sales to potential sales.
Turnover in accounts.
  The main concern here is the number of new customers added and
  the number of old customers lost.

Degree of balance in sales.

Balanced selling keeps sales in proportion. Elements of balance include number of customers, size of customers, frequency of purchase by customer, composition of orders when checked against the salesman's complete line, average size of order, unit of sale, seasonal fluctuation, sales volume to cost of sales, and proportion of new business to old. The salesman needs to guard against letting sales drift out of satisfactory balance. Such a drift is both easy to develop and treacherous because many salesmen unknowingly tend to concentrate their selling in certain lines, in certain markets, at certain prices, during certain seasons, or to certain groups of buyers.

PROFIT

Expenses to sales.

Expenses to gross margin.

Dollar profit on sales.

Qualitative Checks

Qualitative evaluation of a salesman's performance also involves matters that influence net profit, but these matters are more elusive and vague than the quantitative gauges. Here are typical questions:

How much growth and development has the salesman shown in his ability to plan and to administer?

How much goodwill does he create, and how much is it worth?

How does he react to the demands of the creative phase of his job for imagination, vision, tact, or versatility? This is an area where there are no instruction sheets for him, no formulas, and no standard operating procedures.

How does he rate on *esprit de corps*?

How much allowance should be made for changing conditions in evaluating the job he does — changes in sales potential, in the business cycle, in competitors' activities, or in the policies of the salesman's own company?

These samples are matters of a nonstatistical, subjective nature. Because the salesman finds it impossible to do an objective job of evaluating his performance in such areas, he must ask an unbiased third person for an impartial rating.

HEALTH

Necessity for Good Health

If any businessman needs to be a level head on a healthy body, it is the salesman. As a matter of fact, few other lines of work are so demanding in this regard. For the salesman, health literally is wealth. And unlike car or clothes or even customers, health is not replaceable.

The salesman is under contant pressure and strain; great demands are made daily on his physical, emotional, and mental resources. Indefinite hours, tiring travel, irregular meals, the on-then-off character of the drain on his reserves, exasperating buyers, unfriendly weather, a sales manager who is insatiable, and unpredictable situations all add up to a strenuous life. The salesman's only sensible course of action is to follow the dictates of common sense and good judgment in health matters. These call for his building up large enough funds of nervous and physical energy to meet the demands of each day's work.

Unhealthy salesmen are apt to be unsuccessful, unattractive, and unprofitable salesmen; they can succeed, but they have handicapped themselves unnecessarily. Robust, vibrant health gives the salesman the drive he needs to overcome resistance. If his supply of energy is abundant, he can conquer laziness. Vitality that is not allowed to become depleted provides endurance, and an excellent physical condition resists illness and disease. Health helps determine appearance, and appearance helps determine the amount of success the salesman enjoys. If the salesman is to guard against being gruff or stale; if he is to look and feel poised, yet is eager to begin his day's work; if he is to avoid nonselling days caused by poor health; if he is to be active, energetic, and enthusiastic, then he must stay in good physical and mental health.

The Healthy Mind

Worry is a killer. It joins fear, pessimism, and tension to form a quartet of vicious foes dreaded particularly by young salesmen. The salesman's only hope in this regard is to work for and achieve tranquillity of mind. Sometimes this is a gradual and painful process.

The tranquil mind must be won by each individual in his own way. Thorough preparation for selling encourages this tranquility. Learning to live one day at a time helps. (Yesterday is gone, so don't worry about it, and tomorrow is a new day.) Being able to realize that the prospect "pulls on his pants just as the salesman does" is comforting. Keeping busy allows less time for moping. The art of relaxing mentally can be developed. A hobby or two may contribute toward tranquillity. Finally, religious faith has enabled many persons to convert troubled, tortured minds into peaceful minds.

The Healthy Body

A salesman needs to construct and to observe a set of "training regulations" just as much as does an athlete. If he is to match his healthy mind with a healthy body, he should concern himself with *diet, exercise,* and *rest.*

Proper diet is necessary to good health because of the obvious fact that we are what we eat. The three most common faults of salesmen in this respect are eating too much, eating the wrong foods, and eating on an erratic schedule.

Proper exercise is necessary for good health because no satisfactory substitute has been discovered that will keep the body fit and in good condition. It is an excellent protection against the common cold, flu, and even headaches. Furthermore, the grand feeling, the confidence that borders on cockiness, and the exuberant vitality that result from a good workout are worth many times their cost. The salesman must be careful to select what for him is the proper type of exercise, then take it in proper amount, and according to safe timing.

Proper rest is necessary to good health because of the individual's need for relaxation, recreation, and recovery. The amount and type of rest must complement and harmonize with the salesman's working activities. It may or may not be true that few persons work themselves to death, but there is a sense in which the salesman can do himself irreparable harm by overwork. Late hours and partying are neither a form of nor a substitute for rest.

The golden mean of centuries ago, moderation, is still the safest, soundest method of obtaining and maintaining health. In addition to its more common application, moderation should also govern diet, exercise, and rest.

HABITS

You are a walking assortment of habits. The way you dress, read your newspaper, listen to and watch your favorite radio and television shows, light your cigarettes, speak to people, eat — even what you do about studying is a result of forming habits. Habits are regular ways of doing things which establish themselves so firmly that they are routine. They become mechanical to such a degree that they require little or no thinking from you.

Habits can help or hurt; they can be a powerful ally or just as powerful an enemy. If mastered, they will take good care of you in many ways and in many situations. If they master you, you are at their mercy. The way to master them is to select your actions carefully and with conscious intent to make habits of them. Repeat the action until practice has made it yours. Permit no exceptions.

Habits and the Salesman

Every salesman soon begins to form selling habits — good and bad. Then, after this brief, early period, the odds are that he will continue throughout his selling career with the same techniques and methods he adopted at the beginning. He will have become a salesman of habits, doing many or most of the jobs that constitute selling in the same way time after time. This argues convincingly for the young salesman's appropriating the desirable and avoiding the undesirable in the realm of habit. If he starts correctly, he will not face the difficult duty of having to abandon an established but inefficient method by learning and mastering a new method. He continues right because of his right start.

The right habits must be employed by the salesman if an acceptable, profitable job is to be done. A few attempts to make weekly or monthly quotas without their aid will be enough to prove that truth. The more he relies on sound habits, the more time he has to spend face-to-face with buyers, in thinking about large problems that demand his best thought, or in other necessary activities. In a word, habits control both the amount and the expenditure pattern of the salesman's time, and, as a result, they determine the upper limit of his potential productivity.

The salesman's objective is to convert as many phases of his operations as he can into routine. This calls for making habits, first, of all standard practices and all regular tasks, and, second, of those tactics and procedures of selling which allow themselves to be translated into routines. Making habit a sort of "automatic pilot" increases the salesman's efficiency because such a step puts many reflexes and reactions on an involuntary, instantaneous basis and makes them as smooth and effortless as blinking your eyes. This reduces the number of topics or problems that require specific, tailored thinking, thus allowing the salesman to concentrate his attention and do a better job on those matters that do make that type of demand of him. A salesman seems weak and sells less effectively if he writes up his orders with obvious concentration and study on the act of writing, or if he hesitates during a demonstration, uncertain of what to do next. He looks equally weak if he has no habitually used and habitually satisfactory response to some situations that may develop quickly. Two examples are groping for an answer to a prospect's demand to be quoted a price within the first minute of the interview, or playing for time in an obvious manner while deciding what to do when the prospect is joined by a third party. Automatic responses are the solutions in such circumstances.

Bad Habits

Regardless of whether it be good or bad, a habit holds its victim in a tenacious grip. In addition, the bad habits seem more attractive — almost irresistible. So it is the salesman's concern to stay on the alert against acquiring habits that will reduce his success and his earnings.

Bad habits are sly. It is so easy and natural to gradually drift into them that the salesman often does not realize that that is what he is doing. It may well be some time before he perceives that his story is stale and uninspiring, that his delivery is lifeless, that his zest for his job has diminished, and that he himself has become uninterested and uninteresting. Or perhaps he has allowed matters to slide to such an extent that he is neglecting some phases of his job such as prospecting or devising more effective methods of demonstrating his products. Or it may be the appearance and growth of some mannerism that prospects dislike. Just because these practices become hard-and-fast habits by easy stages reduces not one bit the terribly difficult job of breaking them. Rationalization is so easy, isn't it?

A powerful will and a ruthless determination are needed to change bad habits. They can be abandoned only if replaced by good habits.

Examples of Good Habits

No all-inclusive list of good habits for salesmen can be offered here. It would be too long, and it would be too complete for any one salesman. Consequently, this section on good habits lists only some examples of habits that many successful salesman have found to be good:

> Make a habit of using habits constructively.
> Make planning a natural and permanent part of selling.
> Do what is planned, working according to schedule.
> Increase the ability to take advice and criticism and benefit therefrom.
> Become discouraged or disappointed infrequently, and then don't let it show.
> Maintain complete control of self when baited or abused by unpleasant buyers.
> Rule out of working hours all pointless and personal matters.
> Guard against becoming temperamental.
> Use the best selling hours of the day for nothing but selling.
> Work off a slump and boost morale by being busier than usual.
> Leave prejudices at home when calling on buyers.
> Follow the rules and requests of the sales manager.
> Ride every winning streak, for things may be tough tomorrow.
> Assume success and act on the assumption.
> Be alert and interested in prospects.
> Open interviews with courtesy, sincerity, and optimism.
> Have dental and medical checkups regularly.

SOME LONG-RANGE MATTERS

Training oneself to be an outstanding salesman is not the type of program that can be undertaken, completed, and then forgotten. It is a lifetime task. The first phase consists of formal education that helps prepare the future salesman for his duties. A second phase consists of approximately the first two years after college; this is the period when many, many things are learned the hard way. The third phase is the remainder of the individual's selling career. The book now calls attention to some matters that are of continuing concern.

Keeping Up to Date

If a person is to stay abreast of the times, he must know what is going on in two areas, his own specific line of work, and the world at large. It is hoped that by now the student realizes that he must continuously study, in the first area, what his product will do for the prospect and how to get it in the prospect's possession. In keeping posted in this area, the salesman will lean on and draw from the several departments and facilities of his own company, correspondence courses, competitors, business and trade papers, newspapers, books, observation with both eyes and ears, and, most important of all, experience.

As for the second area, the salesman cannot afford to be ignorant of current happenings and developments of a general nature. He must be all things to all buyers. This means that he must have at least some idea of what is going on in the worlds of economics, politics, society, education, science, religion, and athletics. Newspapers and magazines are the two most valuable sources in this area. Movies, radio, television, and association with informed persons are other sources.

Self-Discipline

Growth is impossible without discipline, hence, because there is a permanent need for growth in the salesman, his need for self-discipline will never disappear. Every salesman is a person of strength and weakness. Because of this, he must identify his strong and his weak characteristics, increase the strong, eliminate as far as possible the weak, and then adjust for any residual weakness which cannot be destroyed. This is a distasteful chore. It is essential, however, because one of the most accurate measures of a man is his ability to make himself do what he would rather not do.

A salesman should develop his memory as long as he sells because of the tremendous assistance he enjoys from a trained memory. He must force himself to exercise will power and self-control. His personality should improve indefinitely because he steadily improves it. He should encourage his power of imagination to grow by making himself dream up new ways of doing things. He must hold his morale at a high level. Unceasingly he must sharpen his power of observation through exercise so that it retains its keenness.

Second only to providing for complete self-discipline, which is a personal problem for each salesman, is the matter of being adamant in enforcing discipline. Pampering oneself by winking at a point of weakness instead of correcting it is sheer rationalization. Rather than condone or camouflage, the salesman must face facts squarely and take action. The salesman who kids himself usually kids *only* himself.

Personal Rating Chart

Cub salesmen sometimes find that they can benefit for even a rather long period of time from daily use of a personal rating chart. The purpose of the chart is to enable the salesman to check quickly on points of personal strength and weakness so that he can take steps to maximize the former and minimize the latter. By grading himself on specific matters, the salesman is better able to effect improvement.

Tailored construction of the chart is essential. It must fit the specific circumstances and requirements of the individual salesman. It must certainly include the most important matters and those in which the salesman is inclined to be remiss. It must be possible for quick and honest answers to be given at the close of the day's work.

While it is true that each chart must be built to fit the particular salesman, the component elements should follow a consistent pattern. The specific items can be no more than a one-word characteristic or quality, or they can be in the form of a question. The salesman can grade himself for the day with per cent figures, with letter grades, with numbers, with "yes or no" answers, or with any other system he finds appropriate. Examples of qualities are:

Appearance	Courtesy	Honesty	Obedience
Alertness	Enthusiasm	Loyalty	Tact

Examples of questions are:

Did I make today's decisions on the basis of facts?
Did I follow up today's leads promptly?
Did I spend some time hunting for new prospects?
Did I organize my hours and duties and then follow my plan?
Did I waste any time?
Did I waste any of the company's or my money?
Did I learn anything new today about my company, my product, my prospects, or myself?
How can I do more and better tomorrow?

After-Call Analysis

A salesman should be one of his own best teachers; a really good salesman is just that. Hence, regardless of whether or not a sale was made, the salesman should analyze his conduct of each interview in a critical, ruthless fashion. This can best be done if he faithfully keeps an account of each call, each account being one chapter in the case history of that particular buyer. As these case histories grow, the salesman will find them extremely valuable sources of information about buying motives, objections, the effect of different sales approaches, and other vital matters. The record should be made as soon as possible after the salesman leaves the buyer, while the details of the call are still remembered and a note can be made of each important aspect. The main concern of the salesman is what he did well, what he did badly, what changes of a general nature he should make, and what he should do the next time he calls on that buyer.

The young novice is not the only one who needs to ask himself why the interview turned out as it did. The more experienced salesman, too, can keep out of undesirable ruts and can avoid forming harmful habits only by giving careful scrutiny to his performances.

This section on lost sales is from the training material of the Addressograph-Multigraph Corporation and it lists some very good questions for a salesman to ask himself after every interview:

— Did I contact the right man?
— Was my approach effective?
— Was I confident during my approach?
— Did I talk too much or too fast?
— Did my prospect understand my story?
— Did I talk the prospect's language, or did I use technical and trade terms not understandable to him?
— Did I lack poise during my approach and thereby detract from the effectiveness of my reasoning?
— Was my explanation and presentation of proof effective?
— Did I qualify my prospect on each point as I submitted my proposition?
— Was any question raised regarding my recommendations that I could not or did not answer?
— How did I handle the objections raised? Were my answers reasonable, logical, and effective?
— Did I offend my prospect by discourtesy?
— Did I argue rather than sell?
— Did I make a bid for my order at the proper time?

The Experimental Attitude

The same questioning search that the salesman makes in his effort to increase the effectiveness of his calls must be translated into his complete operation. If there is a better way to tell his story, then might there not also be a better way to route himself? This determination to seek and find ways of doing things can best be described as an *experimental attitude*.

Thought and study highlight this experimental attitude. The well-managed, self-managed salesman ponders about his problems and speculates about their solutions. He encourages his mind to demonstrate its independence by daring to think new, constructive, creative thoughts. He studies what he does and the results he gets day by day and week by week. He makes tests and experiments a part of his self-management, learning what needs revising and using what has been found to be best. He recognizes that change will always be present, and he provides for ease in adapting to change by refusing to outgrow the habit of study. Finally, he obeys the most fundamental commandment in all selling, "Never think you are so good that improvement is impossible." Maintaining the "successful salesman" status requires continual effort.

STUDY ASSIGNMENTS

1. What rewards can be promised to systematic salesmen?
2. Are there times when a salesman should call on his sales manager for help in selling to or in working with some specific buyer? Why do salesmen do so little of this?
3. Can a salesman get helpful pointers about his performance from other than his own analysis of his record? Explain.
4. Why is it so important for salesmen to *have* and to *keep* their good health?
5. In what ways does selling use up a person's energies? What can be done about it?
6. "The salesman's workday is 24 hours long." How is this true?
7. How are time budgets and financial budgets alike? How different?
8. Would a salesman just starting out on his own be more apt to draft schedules that are too flexible or not flexible enough?
9. What can a salesman do to increase the number of calls he makes in a day?
10. Why should the salesman train himself to be a keen observer? How? What should he observe?

CASE STUDY 17A

Bill Woodson has been employed as a salesman for Allied Products Company. After receiving his factory training, Bill was sent out into a territory to work under Harold Greeley, senior salesman in the area. Mr. Greeley has been in the field of selling for seven years. During Bill's first week in the area, Mr. Greeley has allowed him to go out into the territory alone. The conversation below takes place in a restaurant when the two meet on Friday evening after Bill has been out all week alone.

Bill: Hi there, Mr. Greeley, it's good to see you. Here, have a seat and I'll get you a cup of coffee.

Greeley: Hello, Bill. No, keep your seat, I'll get it. Oh, Miss! Cup of coffee, please.

Bill: Boy, it sure is good to be back.

Greeley: How did you get along this week, Bill?

Bill: All right, I guess, Mr. Greeley. However, I didn't get as much accomplished as I thought I would. Everything was all so confused.

Greeley: Well, Bill, it'll take a few weeks until you get settled down to a good daily routine, and until that time, you will naturally have some backtracking and some wasted effort. As soon as you really learn to manage your time, Bill, your work will be a lot more productive. It's all a matter of learning to utilize your time, and you're also going to find that more sales are made if more and more time is spent with the buyers. No, I don't mean that every interview should be long and drawn out, but I mean that you should see as many as you can each day. You should spend as much time as possible in doing the actual work of selling.

Bill: When I was at the home office there seemed to be a lot of emphasis on these reports that we have to send in.

Greeley: Well, Bill, those things are all part of a salesman's job, and naturally they're important, especially from the home-office point of view. They have to stress that all reports be sent in on time. But once you learn to budget your time properly, these things will seem to you a natural and inherent part of the job which you can easily fit in with the plan that you want to make for yourself each day.

Bill: You mean that salesmen really make a schedule to go by? I thought that was just something that they told us at the home office to get us to work harder.

Greeley: No, Bill, it is good, sound advice. A salesman must plan his daily activities right down to the last mile he travels. This is going to mean that he's got to know his territory, the location of his prospective customers, and the most expeditious means of "working" them. This will save travel time and will also help to establish regularity. Set up a schedule, Bill, and stay with it; that's really the only way to manage your time properly. Time is about the most important thing that a salesman has. If he doesn't utilize it to his best advantage, then he's only defeating himself.

Bill: You know, I guess you've got something there, Mr. Greeley. I've never thought about it quite like that.

Greeley: It's important, Bill; it's as important as having good habits or, I might say, as not developing bad habits.

Bill: I don't quite see what you mean.

Greeley: Well, Bill, take it from an old hand. People judge you by your habits and your mannerisms, which, I suppose, are nothing more than habits. You'd be surprised how these habits can work for you or against you. Just as good working habits are a definite asset, poor working habits can very definitely cause you to lose time, money, customers, and even your job. It's not hard to adopt bad habits, but it is hard to break them. Bill, you're in a position where you're young, and you're just starting your career. Begin with good habits, and you won't have to worry about breaking bad ones later on.

Bill: That certainly sounds like good advice.

Greeley: I have an appointment, and I'm going to have to leave now. I'd like for you to be out on your own again for a couple of days next week, and then meet me back here next Wednesday afternoon at three o'clock. I think that you'll be able to get yourself a little better organized. Next Wednesday we'll talk over anything else you'd like to discuss. I can't teach you to sell, Bill, but I'll do all I can to help you to do a good job. So I'll see you here next Wednesday?

Bill: Sure, fine, Mr. Greeley, and thanks a lot. I've got a feeling that things are going to look a lot better by next Wednesday.

QUESTION:

Why do you think Mr. Greeley chose time, schedules, and habits to stress?

CASE STUDY 17B

The Midwest Manufacturing Company makes a line of appliances which includes such products as clothes washers and driers for the home. The line is marketed through distributors and retail dealers. Distribution is national, and the products are well-advertised. The size and quality of the sales force are in line with those of Midwest's leading competitors.

It has been the sales manager's practice to spend as much time as he can out in the field. During such trips, he has conferences with members of his sales force, and he accompanies individual salesmen on their calls to see and sell buyers in customers' firms. In every instance, the sales manager and the salesman discuss and plan strategy in advance for each call. It is the sales manager's conviction that the reactions to this type of call are decidedly favorable from buyers and salesmen alike. He realizes, of course, that these three-person interviews are more restricted than are two-person interviews.

The sales manager recently received word from one of the company's good customers that it was dissatisfied with the salesman managing its account. The buyer expressed a desire for a confidential conference with the sales manager. Such a meeting was scheduled and held. As he returned to his office from this interview, the sales manager did some concentrated thinking on a potential course of action. He debated whether he should begin calling on various buyers alone and without notifying in advance the salesman concerned.

There are certain situations which seem to the sales manager to justify such solo calls. The case at point, that of a dissatisfied customer, is one. Another is that of company dissatisfaction with a particular salesman whose performance continues to be inadequate. A somewhat similar situation is the account which month after month buys far less than its potential. Genuine emergencies seem to warrant solo calls. If a salesman is to be replaced, unaccompanied customer visits seem justified. And, when the sales manager is making a giant jump from one territory to a distant one, it is natural for him to call on customers in the territories in between.

The unaccompanied, unannounced calls the sales manager has in mind are not to be *selling* calls. He feels strongly that he should engage in no selling activities unless he is accompanying one of his salesmen. If he were to make a sale, there would be the problem of not taking credit away from the salesman. Too, each sale calls for follow-up and service — by and from the individual who made the sale. The sales manager's calls, then, would not be to sell, but to get acquainted and to cultivate goodwill. The sales manager also knows that he would learn what impressions his salesmen are making; he is realist enough to know that the calls would keep salesmen on their toes.

The sales manager sees some risks in the plan, but he believes he can avoid any serious damage. He is convinced that his tact and discretion will protect against the danger of buyers feeling that the sales manager is a detective checking up on the salesman. He does not believe buyers will seize upon his call as an opportunity to mislead him for their own advantage. He thinks his calls can be made without detracting from a salesman's standing and without harming the salesman's status as a manager of the account. He is positive that personnel problems exist in every sales force; he wants to identify just what these problems are before attempting to correct them. He does not see these calls as a breach of business etiquette. He does not think his leadership or his relations with his salesmen will suffer.

QUESTIONS:

1. What would the sales manager of the Midwest Manufacturing Company gain specifically from solo calls?
2. If you were one of his salesmen, how would you be affected by them?

Part

D

Industrial and Retail Selling

Part

D

Industrial and Retail Selling

CHAPTER 18

INDUSTRIAL SELLING

CHAPTER 19

SELLING IN RETAIL STORES

CHAPTER 18

INDUSTRIAL SELLING

THE INDUSTRIAL MARKET

Both products and services are sold to the industrial market. The product may be an entire *plant* — a factory, a mill, or a warehouse. The product may be *equipment*. *Heavy* equipment might involve a loom or a locomotive, a press or a lathe; *light* equipment includes typewriters, hand tools, and scales. Or, the product could be a *material*. Cotton, tobacco, and wheat are *raw* materials; flour, steel, and brick are *processed* materials; batteries, buttons, and packages are *fabricating* materials. Or, the product could be one of the *operating supplies* — fuel, stationery, soap. Operating supplies may be highly standardized and bought mainly on the basis of price. Banking, advertising, transportation, and insurance are examples of *services*.

Typically, industrial products are either (a) put into other products or (b) used in the buying firm's operation. They differ from consumer products more in their uses and in their buying procedures than in their physical features or appearances. Identical tires, batteries, and even automobiles are bought by purchasing agents in industry as well as by ultimate consumers.

Where the Buyers Are

Buyers of industrial products and services are usually found in one of three groups — business firms, institutions, or governmental units. Business firms include manufacturers, public utilities, processors, and sellers of services. Institutions include hotels, hospitals, churches, and schools. Governmental buying is found at the local, state, and federal levels.

Wholesalers and retailers make *two* types of purchases. One involves merchandise for resale. The other is industrial in nature and could be the purchase of a cash register or a delivery truck. When making this second type of purchase, wholesalers and retailers are industrial buyers.

Procurement Sequence

The first step toward an industrial purchase is the recognition of a need. A firm may realize its need to replace obsolete machinery or feel pressure to expand its factory. Recognition of a need may well be reflected in a requisition from the needing department to the purchasing agent's office. It is quite possible, however, that as many as one-half of all industrial purchases may be in answer to needs that were unsuspected until pointed out to industrial buyers *by salesmen.*

The next step is a tentative decision on the type of product to take care of the need. In a few cases, the buying firm will draft specifications for the product it has made a firm and final decision to buy. More often, though, the purchasing office will select one or several potential sources of supply and begin negotiations. The purchasing agent may keep lists of "approved" suppliers for various products. All sellers on such lists are considered suitable and satisfactory vendors. Interestingly, 75 per cent of the dollars spent by purchasing agents go for products requisitioned in a *general* way — with no particular vendor specified.

Once the source of supply has been selected and negotiations completed, the buyer issues a purchase order and thus makes the transaction official.

Next, the goods are received, inspected (for correctness, quantity, and quality), and checked into stores or inventory. When the seller's invoice has been checked and found in order, payment is authorized and made; the transaction is completed.

Channels

In the marketing of industrial products, there is considerable manufacturer-direct-to-user selling, with purchasing agents of business firms, institutions, and government buying direct from manufacturers. Sometimes the product involved must be tailored to the buyer's needs and is bought on the buyer's specifications, thus ruling out any middleman. Sometimes the buyer needs technical advice which can come only from the product's maker — or, sometimes a small seller needs technical advice from a larger firm that will be using the product. The large amounts of money involved in many transactions makes direct dealing feasible.

There is, of course, some indirect selling. This channel is widely used when the product involved is low in price, standardized, and widely used by buyers who are small and scattered. The middlemen may be *merchant* middlemen (industrial wholesalers, mill supply firms), or they may be *agent* middlemen (brokers, manufacturers' agents, selling agents). Industrial middlemen operate only at the wholesale level.

The industrial salesman, thus, may sell for a manufacturer, a merchant middleman, or an agent middleman.

Features

Certain features of the industrial market are of particular interest to salesmen. The typical unit of sale is *much* larger, both in dollars and in units, than that of the consumer market. Industrial demand is derived, fluctuating, and often postponable; it is much influenced by the business cycle. Unlike consumer markets, industrial markets ignore our population distribution; they may be concentrated geographically and may consist of relatively few buyers.

In sharp contrast to the ultimate consumer, the purchasing agent is an expert — a trained, professional buyer. He can indulge in no (or certainly very little) impulse buying because he is spending money which belongs to someone else. Profits are his guide and goal. Often the purchasing agent is not the only buying influence affecting purchasing decisions, and the identification of those other individuals can be a real challenge. Selling to a *group* can be quite different from selling to *one* individual.

Some prices in industrial procurement are negotiated by the buyer and vendor together. Some purchases go to the "lowest bidder." Often a comparison of prices can be most difficult. Try to compare, for example, the cost of locating a new factory in Pennsylvania with the cost of locating it in Georgia. Buying by specification and buying on the basis of performance help explain why brand names play a less prominent role in industrial buying than they play in consumer buying.

Much time may elapse between a salesman's first call on an industrial buyer and his first sale to that buyer. In some instances, the salesman must first sell the buyer on letting the salesman make a survey of the buyer's operations and circumstances. Then the salesman makes the survey, and this can be quite time consuming. Next, the salesman and his firm's engineers analyze the findings and draft a proposal. The salesman tries to identify all the buying influences to whom he should present his proposal. Some demonstration work may be necessary before the sale is closed.

Always and everywhere the salesman must convince the buyer that the product will be suitable, that supply will be dependable, that service will be outstanding, and that price will be acceptable.

THE JOB AND ITS REQUIREMENTS

The job of the industrial salesman differs in several respects from that of most other salesmen, particularly those who sell merchandise to middlemen for resale and those who sell to ultimate consumers. It is common for a manufacturer of *industrial* products to have fewer salesmen on his salesforce than does a manufacturer of *consumer* products. The performance of each is more significant to his firm than is that of each salesman who sells consumer goods. The industrial salesman makes fewer calls per month than does the consumer goods salesman, and each of his calls is longer because he usually must see *several* persons in each company. Because these individuals are often in different departments and on different management levels, great demands are made of the salesman's human and personal relations. The industrial salesman is responsible for fewer buyers or accounts than is the man selling consumer products. Few industrial salesmen are supported by anything like the advertising and sales promotion programs many other salesmen enjoy. One survey on how industrial salesmen spend their working hours reported these figures: 41% in face-to-face selling; 32% in traveling and waiting; 19% in handling reports and other paperwork, and in attending sales meetings; and 8% in making service calls.

The first and major duty of the industrial salesman is to bring in orders so that his firm's production can be kept going. He gets orders by being able to answer the universal questions of purchasing agents, "Mr. Salesman, just how will your product or service make money for my company? How will it reduce costs or increase sales so as to make our profits greater?" The salesman answers these by discovering needs, converting them into wants, and then converting wants into purchases. This requires a high quality of creative selling, particularly where, before he can sell a new product or the new use of an old product, the salesman must uncover a need or problem of which the buyer *is unaware*.

The salesman must be a competent, honest consultant to purchasing agents. He is required to have a great store of technical information about (a) his own products or services, and (b) the requirements of buyers. It is hardly possible for an industrial salesman to have too much knowledge about his type of product and its possible applications.

Job Requirements

Industrial selling can be done only by someone technically competent. This person may have taken a business administration course and then added whatever technical specialty he needed, or he may have studied engineering and added marketing. In either event, as is true for all salesmen, the individual must love to sell and must have faith in himself and his ability to see and grasp buyers' problems quickly. If possible, of course, he should know about those problems in advance.

The industrial salesman needs an intelligent and inquiring mind. He must always be curious as to how he, his product, and his company can help each buyer do a better job. And, this curiosity must be teamed with patience, persistence, and determination, because some salesmen find themselves making 75 per cent of their "first" sales only after five or more calls. Many purchasing agents are prejudiced in favor of the old and slow to accept the new.

A company wants its industrial salesman to set his sights high, to have work goals and personal goals that are high, and to make satisfactory progress toward their attainment. The sales manager is delighted by the salesman who wants and works for personal status in the company and who also seeks to build up his personal prestige in his community.

If purchasing agents are to have confidence in a salesman, he must inspire it by being confident and poised, by appearing keen and imaginative, by looking expectant and progressive, and by impressing buyers as being open to new ideas. Honesty and dependability are as essential here as in other areas of selling, perhaps even more so. The ability to organize is a great asset, as are initiative, enthusiasm, resourcefulness, and competitive spirit. Purchasing agents quickly sense whether or not a salesman is genuinely interested in them and their problems.

The Company

In industrial buying, the vendor-company can be and often is a most influential consideration in the source selection decisions of purchasing agents. It is not uncommon for the company to be *the* most important factor. And, because the salesman is the main, if not the only, contact purchasing agents have with supplier companies, purchasing agents are almost forced to judge, to a degree, a salesman's company by the impression the salesman makes.

As for information of a broad nature, the industrial salesman should know the background of his company and its position in its industry. He needs to be informed about company organization and structure, about how the firm operates, and, certainly, about all company policies and procedures affecting him and the buyers for whom he is responsible. Purchasing agents are understandably interested in a vendor's reputation, which depends on such matters as previous performance, research activities, and financial stability, and on its salesmen's reliability. In similar manner, purchasing agents are keenly curious about a vendor's capability to serve his customers and about the amount of help he gives them.

More specifically, the salesman cannot sell satisfactorily without knowing about his firm's size, experience, physical plant, equipment, and facilities, including warehousing and storage. Maintenance standards are of interest to buyers, sometimes of great enough interest that purchasing agents visiting a vendor's factory take particular note of plant house-keeping and maintenance standards. Where selling to industry makes use of teamwork and group effort, and this is not at all unusual, the salesman obviously needs to know and to know about various officials and other persons working for his company.

INDUSTRIAL PRODUCTS AND SERVICES

Perhaps one can begin to appreciate the magnitude of the salesman's job of acquiring and mastering information about what he sells by glancing at the type of questions purchasing agents are constantly asking themselves. Here are samples:

Should we be *making* this product instead of *buying* it, or should we *supply* the service instead of *buying* it?

Just what does this product or service add to the value of *our* end product or to the service *we* sell?

Is this added value proportionate to the cost of the product or service involved?

Does the product or service we are buying need all its present features?

Are we buying a *tailored* product or service when standard or simplified would do just as well?

Is there a different *type* of product or service which would be more satisfactory?

The big story then about products and services is that an industrial salesman simply *must* have a huge fund of facts about what he sells. He needs accurate, complete, and pertinent information about the uses and applications of his wares — about how they can be used to solve buyers' problems more profitably.

Specific items of product data include: materials, specifications, manufacturing processes, sizes, designs, features, dangers, limitations, performance under different operating conditions, and service or maintenance required. The area of price is a "must"; here the salesman must be able to quote prices, credit terms, and discounts (trade, quantity, cash). Often he must have complete knowledge of the contracts his company uses. The salesman must be especially effective in comparing his product with other products the purchasing agent's firm may buy or even make. Such a comparison would certainly include price, features, performance, vendor's reputation for quality, accompanying services, net cost, and value contributed. If the salesman's company follows a policy of product-specialization, there are some strong points he can make — and some handicaps or resistance he might otherwise not experience.

A salesman cannot know too much about his products because he never knows just what questions will be asked him by influential members of the purchasing agent's company.

INDUSTRIAL BUYERS

Industrial salesmen create customers in several ways. Sometimes the buyer directs an inquiry about some specific product to that product's manufacturer or its salesman. Sometimes the buyer's communication is nothing more than a description of a problem on which he would appreciate help. Sometimes happy customers refer salesmen to prospects who later become customers. Sometimes happy customers are excellent prospects for other products the salesman handles. All of these combined, however, do not produce enough customers. They must be supplemented by what is probably the greatest customer-producing activity of all, namely, the discovery *by a salesman* of a need, a problem, a use for which his product can be successfully recommended.

Buyer Information Needed

The need for buyer information is almost as all-inclusive as the need for product information. Broadly, the salesman is under pressure to know just as much as he possibly can about the business and the scope of the purchasing agent's company. He benefits from knowing what goals and objectives that company seeks to attain, and what plans and problems are involved in reaching them. Because what the industrial salesman sells must make a contribution to (sometimes even become a *part* of) what the purchasing agent's firm sells, he must acquaint himself with a prospect company's *marketing* as well as with its production.

Salesmen need to know the size of a prospect company, its financial rating, and the location of its plants and buying offices. Also of value is knowledge of purchasing policies, procedures, and personnel — how it buys, who does the buying, who influences the buying, when and where key persons can be seen, and what their backgrounds are. Prerequisite to a sale is learning what the buyer now does about the problem for which the salesman's product is a solution; this involves what the buyer thinks about the salesman's particular product and about competing products.

Sources of Buyer Information

What sources of buyer information are useful to industrial salesmen? A study of the buyer's end product, done perhaps by the research staff of the salesman's company, can reveal much, especially to sellers of raw materials and fabricating parts. If retailers handle that end product, their opinions and actions can be helpful. Sometimes literature or advertising concerning that end product can supply hints or tips that are beneficial. On occasion, firms allied with or otherwise close to the buying company are able to contribute to the industrial salesman's information about a buyer; among these may be the buyer's competitors and his customers. Non-competing salesmen are another source.

A particular problem is caused by the presence of a need in the buyer's company that is *unrecognized* by the buyer — or one existing in a department *not visited* by the salesman. This suggests that the salesman would benefit from a tour of the buyer's plant, factory, mill, garage, warehouse, mine, or shop. Chats with operators, maintenance men, and other personnel might reveal an impending change of product or plant, improvements needed, or perplexing problems. By examining and seeing, listening and questioning, salesmen often identify specific needs or requirements which can lead to sales.

Buying Influences

As the term implies, *buying influences* are those persons in the buying firm whose attitudes and activities carry some weight in the firm's buying. These buying influences are found at various levels and range from users and operators all the way up through top management. The participation of top management in buying decisions is most common (a) as the size of a contemplated purchase increases, and (b) as the size of the buying firm decreases. Foremen and supervisors are between users and top management, as are the operating managers in production, research, and engineering departments. The purchasing agent usually issues the purchase orders and has great authority in the purchase of some items but less in the case of others. In a real sense, the sales manager in the purchasing agent's company has much to say about what *quality* to buy — because price usually reflects quality, and cost to the buyer must be recovered when he sells his end product. Thus, the industrial salesman selling a fabricating part may quickly find himself "selling" the sales manager in some company on incorporating his product into what the sales manager sells.

Heavy equipment for use in factories provides an example of a purchase in which many buying influences function. Included might well be these:

Manager of manufacturing	Plant engineer
Production manager	Industrial engineer
General superintendent	Materials handling engineer
Department head	Master mechanic
Supervisor	Operator

An industrial salesman of plastics would want the approval of persons in design, research, purchasing, production, sales; he might also need the blessing of some members of top management.

What about a salesman selling a new packaging material? He needs to influence the product development, sales, advertising, production, purchasing, legal, and customer service departments.

One selling roofing, flooring, or plumbing faces the same complex pattern — he must "sell" architects, owners, builders, engineers, specification writers, designers, and draftsmen.

In each of his prospect companies, the industrial salesman needs to know the names and titles of the buying influences who can help or hurt his cause; this can be quite a challenge. The response to business paper advertising helps to identify some unsuspected prospects and even to identify some unknown buying influences. Sometimes, perhaps after a salesman has offered some very technical information to a purchasing agent or has asked a highly technical question, the purchasing agent refers the salesman to some of the firm's technical personnel who are buying influences. Often, when a salesman is in doubt, he can simply ask the purchasing agent, or even the receptionist, for the names of individuals who would be interested and involved in any purchase of his products. A complication, of course, stems from the fact that a job title — plant engineer, for example — does not mean the same from company to company. In fact, a man's name and title constitute minimal information. Actually, the salesman would like to know the interests and motives of each buying influence and how best to cultivate each.

Another difficulty is caused by the continuous changing which takes place among the buying influences within each company. Men are promoted and transferred; their titles and duties change; they join other firms; they retire and die. It is quite possible that fewer than 50 per cent of key buying influences stay put throughout one year.

In many companies and for certain products, the purchasing agent is not the most powerful buying influence; instead, that individual is a higher executive. In such circumstances, the purchasing agent would probably be most active early in the buying process — and then at the end when a purchase order is to be issued. If a salesman must "sell" three buying influences in a company, and if, in that same company, two-thirds of all buying influences seldom or never see salesmen (and these assumptions are realistic and true to life), then we understand why some salesmen feel they have done a very good job if they get in touch with one-third of the buying influences in the organizations they visit.

Sometimes a team, a buying group, or a committee is set up to make a large purchase. Getting in touch with each member is not easy, especially if all members are not in the same locality. Another group not easy to see consists of the operating and technical men. Typically, the industrial salesman does not know them because he does not see them.

WHAT PURCHASING AGENTS BUY

Most writing on the subject of industrial procurement pictures purchasing agents as buying quality, service, and price — in that order. Many salesmen sneer cynically at this idea, maintaining stoutly that purchasing agents would buy from the Devil — if his price was the lowest by even one-thirty-second of a cent. Who is right?

Quality

No one can quarrel with the claim that unless a product is correct and proper for the use to which the buyer puts it, it is *not* the product which should be bought. In this sense, quality is *suitability* — technical suitability. In this sense, quality can easily be too high as well as too low. Just as a superior tool can do a better job in the production process, so can a superior package, for example, increase a brand's dealer and consumer acceptance, even, in some cases, to the point of establishing dealer and consumer preference.

There is a quality of salesman and a quality of vendor-company, too, back of a product. For example, the purchasing agent wants to enjoy good personal relations with reputable salesmen, and he wants to deal with companies that are financially responsible.

Service

Purchasing agents must buy satisfactory service from vendors just as surely as they must buy satisfactory products. A hypothetical transation involving heavy equipment can give us an example. Pre-purchase service could start with a survey of the buyer's needs — a survey done by the salesman and his company. Survey findings are then studied and, after thorough analysis, they become the basis for a report and recommendations which actually constitute a proposal. Assume a purchase follows. Post-purchase service could start with installation of the equipment and then lead to the training of those employees who will be using or operating the equipment. Other post-sale activities of the vendor could include maintenance and repairs.

Another feature of service that purchasing agents buy is dependability of supply. Industrial buyers must be able to count on a vendor's delivering exactly what was ordered when it is scheduled to be delivered. Previous dealings with vendors carry much weight with purchasing agents, and one of the reasons for this is pressure on buyers to patronize only those suppliers whose delivery promises are reliable.

Buyers welcome services which help them sell their finished products. Service of this sort is highly appropriate where the seller's product is an identifiable part of the buyer's end product.

Price

Although it is true that purchasing agents buy quality and service, they buy them *at a price*. The buying firm is in business to sell some product or service at a profit. The price charged for that product or service influences the dollar volume of sales and the gross margin on those sales. Certainly, purchasing agents want to buy at *low* prices — at the *lowest* prices, under most circumstances. The qualification "under most circumstances" must be included because, in a real sense, a purchasing agent can be too expert or effective in prevailing upon sellers to cut their prices — lower and lower. And he knows this. If he beats down a supplier's price to a point where the supplier loses money on the sale, he almost forces that supplier (a) to skimp on quality of product in the hope of breaking even, or (b) to quit selling to him, forcing him to find a new source of supply.

An industrial salesman must be extremely effective in getting buyers to see that quoted prices are meaningless apart from other considerations, such as suitability of product-type, quality of product, service, and nature of buyer-vendor relations. In attempting this, many salesmen shift the buyer's attention from *price* and focus it on *long-run cost*, including such considerations as cost of storing, cost of handling, cost of rejections, and cost of using. These salesmen point out that the price-buying purchasing agent asks for poor materials, shoddy workmanship, and skimpy attention, whereas the best purchasing agent buys *value* — not price. Interestingly, very few "price buyers" like to think of themselves as buying price.

Other Considerations

In addition to quality, service, and price, purchasing agents have other interests in what is bought. One is the total cost to their companies of each alternative purchase. Vendor A's price may be $1.29 and vendor B's $1.28, yet the total cost may be less with the higher-priced product. Flexibility in buying is another feature attractive to purchasing agents. Delivery dates have been pictured as important — so are delivery methods. Most purchasing agents watch closely what competition is buying, and are as apt to do likewise as to do otherwise.

Employees who use, operate, or work with what is bought have preferences. They are for whatever makes their jobs less tiring and demanding. They want working conditions to be pleasant. They want the purchasing agent to buy convenience, quietness, cleanliness, and safety.

The sales manager and his staff want whatever makes the product or service more marketable — easier to sell — superior to competition's offerings. Engineers want the purchasing agent to buy high quality so the sales manager can sell high quality. The production manager dreams of *greater* production and *less costly* production. He fights a never-ending battle for reductions of time, labor, stores, space, machine down-time, and rejections of finished products. He wants more speed and less delay, more efficiency and less waste.

PURCHASING AGENTS ARE HUMAN, TOO

Sometimes we are inclined to think of the purchasing agent as a mechanically rational buyer whose behavior between 9 A.M. and 5 P.M. is under the complete control of cold logic. We picture his leaving at home everything in his nature that is emotional and impulsive — a puppet whose strings are in the hands of Reason.

Although the purchasing agent is hired to spend a firm's money wisely, and although he dare not buy between 9 A.M. and 5 P.M. as he, a consumer, may buy between 5 P.M. and 9 A.M., he *is* a human being while on his job. Add to this the fact that products, services, and prices are becoming more standardized and identical. Add, too, the fact that buying on specification practically eliminates competition among sellers on any *rational* basis. Our conclusion is unavoidable — where quality, service, and price are identical, the purchasing agent can hardly avoid basing his selection of vendor on some emotional consideration.

The industrial salesman is well advised, then, to recognize purchasing agents as being motivated to a degree by their emotions. *Fear*, for example, can be quite an influence on the actions of a purchasing agent. He knows that in any purchase he could make a mistake on quality, on service, or on price, and if he does, there will be two regrettable results: (1) his company will suffer because of the unfortunate purchase, and (2) his own pride will receive a blow because his company cannot avoid questioning his ability as a buyer. Or, fear can urge a purchasing agent to oppose change — fear of incurring the wrath of his boss or inviting the ill will of his associates. And, it is quite possible that the considerable store he places in doing as he has done can have such an emotional explanation as *pride*, or *emulation*, or the *corporate image* he has of the vendor from whom he buys.

The normal purchasing agent is human in still another way. He is anxiously ambitious for his firm and for himself. He wants his company to outsmart its competitors, to pioneer, to innovate. One way to achieve this goal would be to take a chance — and win. But, another nature whispers to the purchasing agent that he would be smart to play safe, to hold on to the old and known, to take no chances.

Another reflection of the "human-ness" of purchasing agents is their inclination to buy from salesmen with whom they enjoy pleasant and friendly personal relations. Industrial salesmen invite a buyer's esteem and liking by making the buyer feel important, by not taking him for granted, by offering him support and reassurance, by treating him as a *professional* man, by being attentive, and by expressing appreciation.

GETTING AND OPENING INDUSTRIAL SALES INTERVIEWS

As a general rule, any purchasing agent doing a creditable job is accessible to those salesmen who deserve to see him. It is not uncommon at all for a purchasing agent to "call in" two or three salesmen when he is searching for a source of supply for a purchase which he will soon be making. Incidentally, a comparison of vendors' literature bears an important influence on which salesmen get these invitations.

Many industrial selling calls are made on an appointment basis. Both letters and telephone calls are used to make appointments; the letters can be sent by the salesman's company or by the salesman himself. Sometimes a salesman can schedule his *next* call as he leaves a call. Sometimes appointments can be arranged at trade shows and expositions. Appointments are particularly appropriate if the salesman's story is long, if he calls on others (engineers, for instance) in the purchasing agent's company, or if the purchasing agent involved prefers to interview by appointment.   There is much "lunching" of industrial salesmen and purchasing agents, and many sales are made over the luncheon table.

Unless salesman and purchasing agent have known each other for a considerable length of time, the salesman is usually smart to open the interview by identifying himself *and* his company. He should do this call after call on the same purchasing agent, remembering that that individual may have seen scores of salesmen since last seeing him. From here, the industrial salesman opens the interview pretty much as any other salesman does. He may ask a question — a "why" type of question, for example, or make a request for advice. He may ask the purchasing agent to do something; he may show something to the purchasing agent. He may offer do do something in the purchasing agent's plant in the hope, perhaps, of looking around and asking questions in order to get needed information. When the salesman knows that the buyer is not ready to buy, he can open with information helpful to the buyer or with questioning which he intends to develop in a way that will benefit the agent and his company.

TWO-STEP SELLING

Frequently the first call an industrial salesman makes on a prospective customer is not opened by an attempt to sell a product. Instead, the salesman's intent and hope are to "sell" the buyer on giving permission to the salesman to make a survey of the buyer's circumstances. In other words, the salesman's first job is to sell the idea of a survey, and that is the first step in two-step selling. A life insurance salesman might offer to examine the policies held by a business man; a cash register salesman might offer to study how cash sales, credit sales, payments on accounts receivable, and pay-outs are now being handled in a retail operation. In selling the survey, the salesman obviously must sell himself, his company, his ability to make a sound survey, and the buyer's need for the survey findings. Usually the survey is offered "free" and is described as not obligating the prospective customer in any way. Occasionally the buyer does help defray the costs of the survey.

The purpose of the survey is to get current, correct, and complete information about the buyer's state of affairs. The salesman is particularly alert to spot any problem for which his products or services will be solutions. Just as a doctor diagnoses before prescribing, so the salesman collects facts and knowledge before recommending, Basically, the salesman wants to determine whether the buyer can make advantageous use of his product, and if so, exactly how.

While the survey is being made, the salesman may make use of personnel and facilities from his own company. This is particularly common if the survey is extensive and technical. In addition, he usually works with other than purchasing personnel in the buyer's organization because their participation in the survey may be mandatory. Working with this latter group gives the salesman an opportunity to "sell" to those employees, and they, at a later time, may be able to help "sell" for our salesman.

Once the survey has been completed, its findings are analyzed and then interpreted. If the buyer has no problem or need requiring action on his part, there is no second step in that particular instance. But, that is the rare case. Most of the time, survey findings constitute a foundation for a sales story for the salesman's product or service. And that story can be convincing in its recommendations because of the bases provided by a thorough survey. By knowing how things are *now*, the salesman can make an effective and persuasive comparison between present conditions and the better conditions which will prevail once the buyer has bought what the salesman suggested he buy.

Step two in two-step selling is selling the proposal to the buyer.

SELLING TO A GROUP

When an industrial salesman is telling his sales story to just one person, perhaps to a purchasing agent, he observes the principles expressed in the earlier chapter, "Telling the Story." Many industrial sales presentations, however, are made to groups, to two or more individuals who constitute a sort of buying committee. Most sales presentations to a group start with the salesman's making the presentation to one person, a presentation which has as its purpose getting the one person to approve and to schedule a meeting between the salesman and the group. In some ways, the group behaves as a unit; at the same time, each member is an individual buying influence. A five-man group might consist of the vice president for production, the works manager, the general superintendent, the general foreman, and the purchasing agent. Presentations to groups are made in various places. Perhaps most are made in a conference room in the buyer's quarters; but, sometimes the seller designs and equips a vehicle which can accommodate as many as eight buying influences and provide for product displays and demonstrations.

General Suggestions

Before the meeting with the buying group, the industrial salesman is quite busy. He would like to do a preapproach on each member of the group to determine the needs, preferences, prejudices, plans, and interests of each. He would like to discover what each member likes and dislikes about *his* product and about *competing* products. If there is one person who is clearly the "leader" of the group, and this is typical of most groups, our salesman may be smart to try to see that person before the group meets in the hopes of making an ally of him ahead of time.

The salesman then goes about constructing his presentation. He stresses advantages and proof as he drafts his story. And he backs these up with appropriate visual aids. Industrial salesmen have found these visual aids to be particularly effective: samples, models, sketches, slides, photographs, movies, testimonials, advertisements, and performance records. Thorough rehearsal of the story and of the use of visual aids is strongly recommended.

The final, finished plan can then be drawn. The salesman knows what he will need in a physical way, and he assembles these items. He lists the questions and the most probable objections, with answers for each. He sets up in 1-2-3 order the steps or phases of his performance. Finally, he clocks each step or phase and sets up a time schedule.

Once the presentation starts, the salesman must know what he is doing so completely from his rehearsals that he maintains almost continuous eye contact with his group, watching their facial expressions and their movements so that he can sense their reactions. If at all practicable, he will encourage members to interrupt with comments and questions, once again alert to "feel" how developments are going. Seldom, however, will the salesman ask for agreement as he does when selling to an individual. Nor will he stress any one advantage so much that he must skimp on other benefits; this procedure would usually cause the salesman grief because the various buying influences comprising the group have different interests and operate under different pressures. Benefits will be presented in a thorough, patient manner.

During the presentation the industrial salesman has a difficult job in respect to the "leader" of the group. He wants to get the leader on his side. At the same time, no other member of the group should be given cause to feel slighted or inferior. The salesman hopes to appear impartial even though he both refers and defers more to the leader than to any other one member. Perhaps it is well for the salesman to remember that the leader *can* be influenced — even won over — by the rest of the group.

When responding to member A's question, comment, or objection, the salesman must answer in a manner which includes members B, C, D, and E, too. This helps each member feel that he had a part in shaping the ultimate decision. The salesman tries to avoid arguments, at almost any cost. This includes arguments between and among members of the buying group as well as between himself and one of the group. Control of the session may be more easily maintained if a top official of the buyer company shares the stage with the salesman. In some situations the salesman will want to arrange for the members of the group to talk among themselves privately. If literature or other printed material is to be distributed, this is best done after the salesman has made his presentation, just before the question-and-answer period, if one has been scheduled.

Problems

When the buying group is made up of persons from different levels of authority (and this is not unusual), the salesman faces the problem of communicating to individuals who differ in background, training, education, personality, and goals. Each member has his own motivation pattern, and each pattern differs from the others. A complete story seems to be the best solution to this problem.

Then there is the problem of how to identify the "leader" of a group about which the salesman was able to learn little before the meeting. The leader may be the oldest person, or the one with the most impressive title, or the one who asks the best questions, or the one with the most definite, most specific program in mind, or the last man to join the group. On occasion, the salesman simply must try to sense who the leader is. Not always is the leader the most vocal, the most active, or the most prominent person.

Should the industrial salesman selling to a group bring in one or more persons to help make the presentation? Sometimes he has no choice — he must have help to do what he needs to do, or, in rare cases, the buying group may have asked the salesman to bring someone with him. A two-man selling team has certain merit. Salesman A can interrupt Salesman B, he can ask questions of B, he can take over every now and then to give B a break. One can take notes or just observe the group while the other is performing. Of course, the selling team ought not be so large that it appears to overwhelm the buying group.

Questions directed to the salesman before the question-and-answer period pose another problem. These premature questions should be discouraged, and any treatment of them should be brief.

Closing, too, can be awkward. Seldom can it be attempted at the end of the presentation as it is normally in selling to *one* person. Seldom is it practicable to ask a buying group for the order.

RECIPROCITY

Reciprocity is the practice followed by Company A of buying from Company B because Company B buys from Company A. The original idea could have first come to Company A — or to Company B. The more recessed business activity is, the more likely is it for *both* companies to toy with the idea.

It is possible, of course, for reciprocity to be a clear and simple matter. If Company B's and Company C's offerings to Company A are identical in all respects, *and* if Company B is a substantial customer of Company A whereas Company C buys nothing from Company A, then it would be difficult to criticize A for buying from B rather than from C. It is the complicated case, however, that causes difficulty and controversy. Even if B's price is slightly higher than C's, the price differential or premium may be less than the value of the A-B relationship to Company A.

Should Company A follow a policy of reciprocity in its buying and selling? That question is not one to be answered by either the sales manager or the purchasing agent; it is a question for top management. Reciprocity is a "pressure" type of selling argument; it is strictly competitive in that it does not increase the total market for the salesman's product. The policy is attractive to firms whose costs and prices are high, or whose products are inferior, or whose salesmen are weak; in a word, the policy of reciprocity appeals to the less efficient, the handicapped, the non-competitive seller.

Within their respective companies, purchasing agents as a group are understandably hostile to a policy of reciprocity. They see the policy as one which ties their hands, one which prevents an able and conscientious purchasing agent from doing the good procurement job he would otherwise do. The industrial salesman, too, is unhappy when he calls on a purchasing agent who tells him he would prefer to buy his product but cannot because of reciprocal arrangements. In such a situation, both salesman and purchasing agent will probably agree that no matter what advantages accrue to the buying company, these disadvantages cannot be denied: competition for the buyer's business is discouraged and probably falls off; the buyer's patronage is taken for granted by the present supplier as a "sure thing"; and the buyer is likely to get B- or C-grade treatment because the seller's customers that do not have the pressure of reciprocity deserve and get all the A-grade treatment.

WHAT BUYERS WANT FROM INDUSTRIAL SALESMEN

Buyers want and expect certain general things from industrial salesmen. Some of the more important aspects are covered in the following sections.

Thorough Product Knowledge

Purchasing agents obtain much of their product knowledge from salesmen. Quite naturally, the buyers come to depend on *all* salesmen to a degree and on *some* salesmen most heavily as sources of information about new products, improved products, and new applications or uses for present products. The purchasing agent's interest, of course, is in how he and his company can benefit. In this way, the industrial salesman functions as a product consultant and expert; he is a dependable supplier of accurate, helpful product information. Because he knows a product's limitations along with its merits, he can suggest with confidence. Because he has collected an assortment of case histories and experiences, he can assure the purchasing agent that the recommended product will do the job the buying firm wants done. He can promise *results*, and they are what a purchasing agent buys. If the salesman delivers enough product information, the purchasing agent will be able to explain and even defend his purchases should he be called upon to do so six or twelve months later.

Ideas from the Outside

Because of his traveling about and his many and diverse contacts, the industrial salesman can and should bring ideas to purchasing agents and report to them on conditions and developments. The salesman can describe what is going on within his own company, in companies which compete with the salesman's firm, and in retail stores if the end product of the purchasing agent's company is sold by retailers. He can even report on competitors of the purchasing agent's firm, provided he takes care to reveal nothing given to him in confidence.

Ideas from the outside may pertain to economic conditions, price behavior, the outlook within the industry of which the purchasing agent's company is a part, and even to business trends and developments in that company's market. It would not be out of line for an outstanding salesman to recommend new markets for the products made by the purchasing agent's firm — or even new products for it to consider making.

Help On Problems

Purchasing agents welcome help on their problems. These problems include those to which the purchasing agent is too close to see, as well as those problems of which he is painfully aware. Most welcome is the salesman who is interested in buyers' problems, who acquires an intelligent understanding of them, and who takes the initiative in hunting for better solutions. Such a salesman is always hunting for cost-cutting steps that purchasing agents can take. Such a salesman is always alert to see that his customers get all the service to which they are entitled. Typical here would be the salesman's following up a customer's order that involves a series of deliveries to see that exactly what was wanted is delivered according to schedule.

Industrial salesmen often work with the engineering personnel and the production personnel of the buyer company. For example, *all* Timken Roller Bearing Company salesmen are engineers. They render considerable engineering service to their customers. Because their suggestions and advice are technical in nature, these men must have integrity, honesty, and dependability.

The problem on which the salesman probably moves most quickly and with greatest concern is a problem the customer has in using his product.

Considerate Treatment

Because purchasing agents are human, they expect industrial salesmen to be thoughtful, proper, and understanding. Purchasing agents must budget their time with system and control; they do not have time to listen to idle chatter; they cannot treat themselves or salesmen to much general talk at the beginning or the end of sales interviews. Instead, purchasing agents want salesmen to use time to become informed — "educated," if you will — about the needs, personnel, procedures, and concerns of the buying company. Ideally, from the purchasing agent's point of view, no salesman would call unless he had some specific bit of helpful information, and then he should call, even when he knows that the purchasing agent is temporarily "out of the market."

Few purchasing agents have time for gossip. Let's hope that few indulge in it, at least on company time. By the same token, the salesman must keep confidential any information he acquires about the activities and plans of competing companies. Because of their extensive contacts and because they are asked questions about, for example, new products a company might be developing, salesmen often know about plans which are highly secret. Knowledge of this sort must not be revealed to competitors.

Most purchasing agents do not want to become obligated to salesmen by receiving substantial gifts, lavish entertainment, or expensive favors.

Most purchasing agents expect salesmen to get in touch with the purchasing office personnel first. Contacts with others (production, engineering) should be made through the purchasing agent. He should be kept posted on calls made on others in his company.

Willingness to Share Buyer's Business

In regard to the more essential, more significant products, many purchasing agents (perhaps most of them) do not want any one salesman to try to capture *all* of the company's business. Instead, each purchasing agent may well be inclined to buy such products from two or more suppliers as a matter of policy.

From a seller's point of view, interestingly, this idea, this course of action, may be most welcome. When Company X sells to Company Y *all* of its requirements of a vital product, a fire or a strike or even a shipping delay could tie up Company Y *for days*. Company X does not want to be the only one to feel the wrath of Company Y if Y's operations are forced to slow down or to quit temporarily.

Company X may not want all of a *small* customer's business; X may feel that the responsibility and the obligation are entirely too great. It would not be unrealistic for X to want 60 per cent of the small customer's business, hoping that Company V might have 25 per cent and Company W 15 per cent.

STUDY ASSIGNMENTS

1. Why does industrial selling appeal to more college students than does selling to retailers?
2. A manufacturer of industrial products, like other sellers, must always be anxious to add names to his prospect list. What features or characteristics probably are of interest to him in determining which buyers are his prospects?

3. If purchasing agents buy rationally, does an industrial salesman need to bother much about his personality and the personal impression he makes?

4. Is the preapproach in industrial selling similar to the preapproach in retail selling? Explain.

5. Can you argue successfully that an engineer who gets sales training is a better bet for future selling in the chemical field than is a marketing major who gets some engineering training?

6. If you should enter industrial selling upon finishing a program in business administration, you will undoubtedly find that many of your customers are 15 to 25 years older than you, and they may seem to think you too young to advise them. What can you do to avoid or remedy this?

7. Is there a proper place in industrial selling for trading-up? For suggestion-selling?

8. What do you consider to be the most serious problem confronted by industrial salesmen that seldom or never bothers other types of salesmen?

9. What values and dangers do you see in salesmen's practice of giving gifts to purchasing agents and other buying influences in industrial firms?

10. In industrial selling, what are some specific dangers of "overloading" customers?

CASE STUDY 18

Ted Broadwell is a sales engineer for International Chemical Corporation, a large chemical producer with plants throughout North America. His job is to sell and service accounts in the Carolinas which consume some 100 different chemicals produced by International. He has had the territory for five years.

John Phillips is the Director of Purchases for North Carolina Paper. While Phillips is an experienced buyer, Broadwell has noted on previous calls that he is increasingly hesitant to make buying decisions.

Broadwell has talked this over with his own boss, the International salesman who previously called on N. C. Paper. During these discussions, they recalled that Phillips joined N. C. about 15 years ago when it was a relatively small concern. Since then it has undergone a tremendous expansion and diversification. Phillips' job has evolved from the status of a routine buyer to Director of Purchases of a sprawling enterprise. Broadwell's superior has heard through the industry grapevine that Phillips is under constant fire from production management because of ever-increasing problems relating to purchasing and expediting of machinery and material requirements.

The purpose of this call is to sell Phillips on the idea of signing a contract for next year's requirements of 2,000 tons of caustic soda solution (sodium hydroxide). N. C. Paper currently divides purchases evenly among International and two other smaller suppliers. Price is not a prime problem because caustic soda is uniformly priced by all producers. Subtle forms of price-cutting such as delivery concessions are rather common, however.

After the usual hellos and small talk, Phillips turns the conversation to business.

Buyer: Ted, if you're here to talk about caustic soda, you couldn't have come at a worse time. I had my weekly meeting with production management, and they are really put out at our chemical suppliers — notably you. First, your last tank car of caustic arrived two days late, and we nearly had to shut down the plant waiting for it. Secondly, the engineers have been able to relate our process control troubles to caustic soda purity.

Salesman: Maybe I came at the *right* time, John. You know, my job is not only to sell chemicals, but to help you satisfy the production people. Tell me more.

Buyer: Well, I have the authority to buy from whichever company can give us the best product and service, but I have to keep the plant happy, too. Here's the picture. Our other two caustic suppliers have plants within 100 miles of here. Yours is 600 miles away. Delivery from either of them is two days; from you, five to seven days. When I'm in a hurry, I can no longer afford to order from you.

Salesman: What about the quality problem?

Buyer: You're in trouble again there. Those serious process control problems I told you about last time have definitely been traced to caustic soda purity. Both your competitors average 98%. Your purity, according to these figures I have here, is consistently 97.5%. On the basis of delivery and purity, I can't continue to give you one-third of our business.

Salesman: When I was at our plant last week, I made a point of seeing our Chemicals Technical Service people about your process control problem. I came across some facts that you'll be interested in. Two of our customers up north had similar problems a couple of years ago, and we were able to help them. Strangely enough, it was found that process fluctuations such as you're having were not related just to caustic soda purity but to *consistency* or purity. It was *consistency* which had the greatest effect. (Pause) What were the actual test results on your suppliers' products?

Buyer: (Glancing over his figures.) They varied from 97 to 99, averaging 98, but yours was only 97.5.

Salesman: But *constantly* 97.5%. The research explained in this report I've brought you proves that lack of consistency is the culprit rather than a one-half per cent difference in purity.

Buyer: (Leafing through the report handed to him by Broadwell.) Look, I'm not a chemical engineer. How can I be expected to understand these things I can't even read? Why don't you leave it with me. I'll take it to the Production Meeting next week. Ken Hamilton, the Production Manager, can read it over and check it. You leave it here, Ted, and drop back in a couple of weeks. By then we will have had a chance to read it.

Salesman: Why not send it in to him right now? If he mentioned the caustic problem only this morning, what better service can you give him than a report on it this afternoon? Any questions he might have, I can get today. Actually, it is a pretty open-and-shut proof that quality consistency and not percentage of purity is the prime requirement. It'll take him only 15 minutes to read.

Buyer: That guy gave me a rough time this morning. I'd like to show him he's barking up the wrong tree. Good idea. (To secretary) Miss Reed, please take this over to Hamilton and ask him to read it right now. Tell him I have the International representative in my office waiting, and I need his comments. (To Broadwell) How come your product is more consistent than our other suppliers' — they have newer plants.

Salesman: Good question. Our plant is about eight times the size of either of theirs. This lends itself to easier control and consistency. Since they have newer plants, their products have slightly greater purity, but this is not really what *you* are looking for.

Buyer: You realize that all this technical talk about consistency doesn't mean a thing to me unless you can get your orders here on time.

Salesman: We realize that our plant's being 600 miles away places us at a bit of a disadvantage relative to local suppliers. I've talked this over with the boss, and we've developed a purchase program which will lessen your work load and assure stock at all times.

Buyer: I'm not convinced, but I'm willing to listen.

Salesman: You use one tank car of caustic about every 9 to 12 days.

Buyer: Right.

Salesman: Our delivery time is usually 5 to 7 days.

Buyer: Except when there's a holiday or other disruption. That last order took 10 days.

Salesman: You mentioned last time I was here that when your storage tanks get below the half level, Production sends in a requisition. You then send out the order to whichever supplier you prefer for one tank car of solution.

Buyer: Right. And they take two days and you need seven. If anything unforeseen happens and your car is held up a couple of days, we're in the soup. If our other suppliers have a two-day holdup, it doesn't matter. If your proposal is for us to order earlier, forget about it. I can't see any reason why we should reorganize our methods to make up for your poor deliveries.

Salesman: You're right, John, that's *our* problem. Here's how we are solving it. We'll maintain on your rail siding one tank car of caustic at all times. When your storage tanks reach the half way mark, you send us an order as usual, but you are free to unload from the standby car as soon as you need it. Your work load is lessened in two ways: First, no more trouble contacting railroads, looking for shipments, expediting, and so forth. Second, you can send us a blanket order for the year's requirements, and your secretary can just call our office whenever the plant gives her the word, and we'll ship. The whole operation will work automatically and will be out of your hair. You'll be able to devote your time to those non-routine purchases that require your full personal attention.

Buyer: Are you trying to talk me into signing a contract? That's putting all my eggs into one basket. If you have a strike, fire, or something, I'm sunk.

Salesman: That's true, John, when you're dealing with a small supplier like these local ones. International has four plants in the country and one in Canada. If for some reason we had trouble at the plant that supplies you, there are four more to draw on. Since all prices are "delivered" it won't affect you in the least bit.

Buyer: What if the price changes when we're under contract with you?

Salesman: Under the terms of the agreement, if it goes down, you get the advantage right away. If it goes up, we give a 30-day protection at the old price. (Pause) I wonder how Ken Hamilton is making out with that report.

Buyer: (Picking up phone.) Miss Reed, connect me with Hamilton.

Hello, Ken, John here. What do you think of the International research report we sent over? . . . . Thanks a lot, Ken, I'll ask him to do that. See you later. (Hangs up.) (To Broadwell) You were right, Ted. Hamilton was really impressed with getting that information so quickly. Liked the report, too. What's more, it's convinced him. He'd like to meet the chemist that wrote it to talk over some technical stuff.

Salesman: (Sensing that Phillips is in a good mood) Sure thing, I'll arrange to get him down here as soon as we can. Well, John, our consistency will help your process fluctuations, and the purchase program will go a long way towards lessening your work load and will solve the delivery problem. Would you like to start immediately rather than waiting until the first of the year?

Buyer: (Takes contract from Broadwell, reads it over and signs.) January first will be fine, Ted. Let's work out the details after some coffee.

QUESTIONS:

1. Do you think Ted Broadwell had to be a chemical engineer as well as a sales engineer in order to make this sale?
2. How did the background information on the buyer help the salesman?
3. Where did Broadwell begin to close?

CHAPTER 19

SELLING IN RETAIL STORES

The phase of selling now to be considered takes place at one of the most decisive stages in all marketing. This is the stage where a consumer and a salesperson face each other across the counter in a retail store. The selling that takes place in that meeting is the heart of all retailing. All other activities that are undertaken by retailers and retail employees have a single justification — their contribution to the promotion of sales — profitable sales. It is in the retail store that a purchase for consumption purposes is or is not made, causing the spheres of production and marketing to be either balanced or uneven.

The *customer* is the person most immediately dependent on the salesperson. A consumer's ceaseless search for satisfactions will be more successful, or less, according to the help in buying he receives. Then the *retailer* is dependent, to a great degree, on the same salesperson. Merchants can, of course, sell to customers through salespeople who irritate instead of aid buyers; but, clearly, such a handicap should be avoided at almost any cost. It must be remembered that customers judge a store largely by its sales staff and that when a customer makes a purchase, he is really buying a package that involves product, salesperson, retailer, and manufacturer. Salespeople, therefore, have much to say about a retailer's future. Finally, *middlemen, manufacturers*, and *facilitating firms* – such as advertising media, transportation and storage facilities, advertising agencies, and buying offices – are much at the mercy of the sales force behind retail counters. All of their fine operations and promotion mean little unless the salesperson employed in a store succeeds in his selling.

The customer relations director of Neiman-Marcus in Dallas writes these views on retail store selling:

> To create the desire on the part of the customer for the fine quality, and in many cases, luxury items that we have at Neiman-Marcus requires the most expert salesmanship. Although we use all of the known devices to stimulate the buying desire of the public . . . we believe strongly that, in the final analysis, most sales are either made or lost at the point of sale. Retail selling is a highly technical vocation which is very remunerative

for those perceptive persons who know their products and master the selling techniques.

THE JOB OF RETAIL SELLING

Selling in retail stores breaks down into several standard steps. The customer is approached and greeted. The salesperson learns what the customer needs or wants. Suitable merchandise is selected from stock, and then it is shown, described, and explained to the customer. Buyer-benefits are stressed. After handling objections, the salesman closes the sale and attempts some suggestion selling if such seems desirable. A sincere desire to serve — to help the customer buy what he should have — is the most important factor. It separates the "salesclerks" from the "merchandise advisors." It is essential to retailing success, which has been correctly described as "selling products that won't come back to customers who will."

Duties

The duties of the salesperson in a store can be grouped into four classifications. First and foremost is the *duty to sell*. Satisfactory performance here rests on the salesman's knowing his merchandise, knowing his customers, and knowing how to sell those products to those buyers.

A second group of duties can be called *customer service duties.* Included here are merchandise instructions expected or needed by the buyer. When some products are to be serviced, the owner may prefer to use as his contact the salesperson who sold the item; in doing this, the owner hopes to get better treatment. Listening to customer complaints is a duty commonly assigned to the sales staff, and even where this is not done, customers may carry their complaints to the persons who made the sales. When customers want to exchange or to return goods, they may go first to the same salespersons. Directions within the store are often asked of the same employees.

A third classification is made up of *routine, nonselling duties.* Salespeople may be asked to work in the stock rooms, checking merchandise in and marking prices on it. They may be asked to get their departments open and ready for the day's business, and then to bed the departments down for the night. Adequate floor inventories must be maintained, usually by ordering replenishments from reserve stock. And these inventories must be kept clean and neat, in orderly arrangement. Salespeople will need to know how to wrap merchandise, make change, and write up charge sales. They may be asked to fill out want slips. Some are expected to build displays. Others must help take inventory, shop other stores, and serve as sponsors for new salespersons.

Finally, the sales staff has certain *duties to the store*. Typical would be the obligation not to be excessively absent or late. Then there is the duty to think and to plan in order to make a maximum contribution to the store's profitable operation. Closely allied is a determination to minimize mistakes, waste, and expense. Salespeople should keep ears and eyes open so that they will be in a position to make constructive suggestions to the store's management. A final obligation is to reflect to customers a loyalty to and a pride in the store.

The typical retail salesperson engages in a great amount of service selling and a limited amount of creative selling, much of which is of quite modest quality and complexity. Much of his working time is spent in nonselling activities. One study of what retail salespeople do with their employers' time, a project of the Domestic Commerce Division of the U. S. Chamber of Commerce, produced these figures:

Person-to-person selling..................	29%
Post-sale service to customers.............	13%
Information and help to customers........	8%
Stockkeeping...........................	17%
Idle time..............................	33%
Total.............................	100%

Here is a job specification from one of the country's best-known and best-respected department stores:

Division: Apparel

Job Title: Sales — Women's and Misses' Dresses

Duties: (A) *Sales* — Sell dresses through intelligent use of size, style, and fashion information; must explain washability, cleaning requirements, advantages through certain design features which tend to enhance the customer's figure; meet objections to certain competitive stores' claims and price advertisements; be familiar with sizing by manufacturer so as to provide merchandise which will fit well with a minimum of alteration. Try to be certain when selling merchandise that the item is one that will not be returned because of a hasty decision, that the item is "tried on" so that the customer will have an opportunity of seeing as well as feeling the fit and style advantages.

(B) *Stock* — Fill in sizes as required, help keep section stock in order by replacing in proper racks and in correct size sequence items which have been shown but not sold. Assist in maintaining section orderliness, straightening chairs, picking up hangers, etc.

Previous Experience Requirements: At least six months dress or similar selling experience.

Educational Requirements: High school minimum.
Working Hours: Regular store hours of 40 hours a week.
Overtime: None except for 48-hour weeks, 4 weeks a year.
Physical Demands: Standing, walking (to fitting rooms, stock rooms) with the usual seasonal rush pressures.
Promotional Lines: To head stock — sponsor
Machines and Equipment: Identification phones — cash registers
Method of Compensation: Straight commission with guaranteed minimum.

Distinctive Features

Although the fundamentals of selling are universal, the job of selling in retail stores differs from outside selling in several respects. In retail selling, buyers come to the salesman. The outside salesman may be said to stalk his buyers, but the store salesman has been said to lie in wait for his. As a result, the buyer is the guest, and the salesman is the host. These buyers are closer to buying — physically, financially, and emotionally — than are most of the buyers called on by outside salesmen. Buyer attention and buyer interest are usually present in strong enough degree to have caused the visit to the store. Furthermore, many buyers know the store, something about the merchandise in which they are interested, and even the salesperson himself. It must be admitted, however, that the buyers in stores are not, in an over-all way, so well-informed as the buyers many outside salesmen see — purchasing agents, for example.

The selling activity itself, as found in stores, is unlike outside selling in some ways. The store salesman handles *many* products, far more, indeed, than the typical outside salesman. The number of buyers to whom he talks is far greater also. He does his selling in an atmosphere of noise, hustle and bustle, time pressure, and interruptions. His influencing of buyers must be more subtle and less obvious than the influencing done by outside salesmen because his customers resent strongly anything that strikes them as being "salesmanship." Finally, the store salesman, unlike his outside counterpart, does not have the wide range of choice and decision with regard to when, where, how, and to whom he will sell.

SALES PERSONALITY

Retail employers and their customers unite in expecting store salespeople to exercise *good manners.* Practically all the research studies made in the field of customer-salesperson relations point up the universal and imperative demand for courtesy. As a matter of fact, more than a few customers want courtesy carried to the point of unmistakable deference. All customers want to be treated with tact; they want to be handled with consideration. Buyers are not attracted to aloof salesmen and saleswomen, nor, at the other extreme, do they like salespersons who are gushy and too familiar. A pleasant, friendly, smiling salesperson is the type that delights buyers. Incidentally, no one can succeed in being that type of salesperson all through the day, and day after day, without a generous amount of patience.

Customers in retail stores prefer salespeople who take a *genuine, understanding interest* in them. The buyer wants the salesman to become her ally immediately. She expects a sincere desire-to-help to be present in the way she is served by the salesman. The buyer insists that all claims and recommendations made to her be honest and sincere. If they are not, she will take her business elsewhere, and the retailer as well as the customer knows this. So, the retailer wants his salespeople to show real interest in their customers and to guide those customers to the best purchases possible. Otherwise, patronage is lost, and it can be lost for an immediate gain to the store that is pitifully small. For example, one can be quite generous and assume that a $10 purchase is involved. Few, if any, types of retailing have an average-sale figure that high. Then, being generous again, assume the store in question makes a net profit of 6 per cent on net sales. If a salesperson "pressured" a customer into making an unwise, unsuitable purchase, that customer could easily be driven away because of the transaction — a sale that increased the net profit of the store by 60 cents.

Finally, customers expect salespeople to have *competence* in their analyzing and recommending. This competence rests on the correct diagnosing of customer wants and then the proper prescribing for them. Indeed, selling cannot be sincere and sympathetic unless it is also able selling. By being qualified and competent, a salesperson avoids being classed with the lowest grade of so-called sales personnel, the order-takers, who do no more than make change and wrap merchandise. These order-takers should not be called salespeople — they are more correctly referred to as clerks or attendants. The store salesperson who has and shows a well-mannered, genuine, competent interest in customers invariably is self-reliant and thinks well of his job; otherwise, he would not be successful.

THE STORE

The most important information a salesman needs about his store relates to two areas, the first of which has to do with *policies*. One of the more significant policies concerns the *merchandise* the store stocks. The salesman needs to know what types of products are carried by his store, in what price ranges, and of what general quality.

A second basic policy involves the *services* the store makes available to its customers. For each service there is a small but essential fund of facts without which the salesman cannot function satisfactorily. For example, the store will or will not make credit sales; in either event, the salesman will need to be able to explain the policy and, in certain cases, to justify it. Delivery is another service that is or is not offered. Its frequency and its cost to customers, if any, are necessary information to the sales staff. A third service is that of adjustments, and here the salesman must know what the store does about refunds, exchanges, returns, and complaints. A fourth service, quite important in stores selling appliances, can be termed "product" service. As an example, a store selling washers and television sets must have policies about installation, repairs, service calls, and guarantees.

A store's *promotion* policy is a third vital area about which the salesman must know. Retailers, like other sellers, combine the three basic marketing forces of personal selling, advertising, and sales promotion into what they believe to be the most profitable combination. Some conception of the relationships among these three factors must be had by selling employees. In regard to more immediate concerns, the salesman should always keep informed about what items are being promoted currently and with what forms of promotion. He will delight his employer if he reads his store's advertisements and looks at his store's windows.

The second area of necessary information for a salesman is *procedures* or *store system*, sometimes referred to as the mechanics of selling. Knowledge of merchandise location within the store is a basic element here. Another essential element is knowing how to make a charge sale, a task which calls for credit clearing and the writing of a sales ticket. For cash sales, the salesman must be handy in operating the cash register and in making change. Finally, some salespeople in stores must be able to wrap a neat, safe package.

THE MERCHANDISE

Customers expect the sales staff of a retail store to know the merchandise the store carries. Nothing seems more natural than to look to the salesperson for answers to product-questions that arise in the customers' minds. Most buyers are willing — even eager — to become better informed about merchandise. Many buyers go even further than that when making certain purchases, asking a saleswoman for her views, her preferences, or her convictions. In such instances, the buyer is assuming that the saleswoman is an authority on merchandise and, of course, the saleswoman must live up to that description.

What does the salesman or saleswoman in a store need to know about the merchandise he or she sells? Specific product facts include the identity of the manufacturer, raw materials and composition, construction, finish and style, and, of course, price, size, color, and model. Then the salesperson should know what the product is used for, how it should be used or operated, its performance and its limitations, the care it requires, and the services, if any, available with it. Particularly desirable is the ability to compare any given product with its closest competitors and to highlight its various merits and points of superiority. While the general rule is that the amount of product information needed increases as price rises, retailers hope that each selling employee will know one or more influential facts about as many products as possible.

Where is product information to be found? There are several productive sources of merchandise information available to most store salespeople, one of which is the product itself. Many of the facts to be found on the label, the tag, or the package can help those who sell the item just as they help those who buy it. Products in some classifications, such as food, clothing, and beverages, can actually be tried under natural conditions, while products in all classifications can be inspected, examined, and studied personally. The vendors who sell to the retailer are another source of product information. Here are found the salesmen of manufacturers and wholesalers who call on and sell to the store. Here, too, are found the literature and visual aids and, in a few situations, plant tours made available by some manufacturers. Advertising is a third source of product information. It includes the manufacturer's advertisements, those of competing manufacturers, those of competing retailers, and, last but not least, those of the salesman's store. The individuals with whom the salesperson deals are another source — one group, the prospects, being able to tell why they *do not* use the product; the other group, the users, telling why they *do.* A final major source is the store itself. Its training program, its merchandise manuals, its product specifications, the results it obtained from testing bureaus, and the buying and selling personnel can all place valuable product information in the hands of the store's selling staff.

THE CUSTOMERS

The sales forces in retail stores do not have much of a prospecting job to do; their stores do the job for them. Advertising is one of the forces used by stores to attract buyers. The store's windows issue another invitation; they entice sidewalk traffic into becoming aisle traffic. Inside some stores are customer services or facilities such as telephones, post offices, and lounges; these bring individuals into the store, and some of those individuals become shoppers and customers. A few stores that can be termed *prestige* stores are found in most large markets; they are so widely and favorably known that they pull buyers in because of their reputations. Finally, some stores are adroit at obtaining considerable amounts of publicity — good publicity that recommends, even if subtly, the store as a place to shop.

Because the salesman in a store does not know who his next customer will be, obviously he cannot execute a personalized preapproach. The salesman can only assume that this next customer is in a buying mood and is curious about and interested in merchandise because of some need or desire. The majority of shoppers do not enter stores unless these conditions exist. Instead of a preapproach, the salesman is forced to rely on observation and experience. It is particularly helpful for the salesman to note the treatment *he* gets in the various stores when he is buying and to analyze his reactions to it.

MOTIVATION

Little needs to be added to the treatment of buying motives found in Chapter 8. Customers in stores buy ideas and satisfactions instead of merchandise the same as do customers in any buying situation. They don't want products — they want what products will do for them. Because store contacts are of such short duration, the salesman must identify customers' buying motives quickly. *Products* are bought which will deliver a feeling of importance, beauty, health, pride, comfort, convenience, romance, safety, durability, longevity, gain, or economy. *Stores* are patronized because of prices, quality, variety, assortments, location, friendship, prestige, fashion, or service.

COMPETITION

As far as competition is concerned, salespersons in stores need most of all to know what competing stores are offering. Some retailers help supply this necessary information. Salespersons themselves should read the advertisements of competing stores and, if practicable, visit those stores every now and then.

OPENING THE INTERVIEW

The Greeting

Because its sales force is charged with very little or no responsibility for attracting prospective buyers to a store, "getting" interviews is not a factor in retail selling. As has been mentioned, the store's promotional activities bring buyers to the salespeople.   This permits us to start this section with a consideration of the greeting.

Before examining certain greetings, it is well to realize that the salesperson's manner and manners are more significant than the particular words he or she decides to use.   Customers demand much.   They are in the store because of an invitation that, if not direct and specific, was clearly and intentionally implied.   Customers know that they are guests, and they want salespeople to act the role of hosts in the proper manner. Each customer wants to feel that the salesman is pleased by his visit to the store and by the opportunity to serve him.   So, customers want salespeople to be alert to give quick service when they are ready to buy.   If salespersons are gossiping or visiting with each other, or if they are concentrating on stock or housekeeping duties, this essential promptness is lacking.   The salesman's manner should always be friendly and polite. His brisk and confident actions should recommend him to the customer as an expert advisor on merchandise whose major interest at the moment is his customer's welfare.

When the salesman or saleswoman approaches, the customer is usually doing one of two things — looking for a salesperson or looking at merchandise.   In the first case, these openers are acceptable:

> May I help you?
> Are you being served?
> How do you do?
> Good morning (or afternoon).

Very good and very safe are the simple "Good morning" and "Good afternoon."   If the customer is a man, the word "sir" may well be attached; the use of "madam" is *not* recommended for feminine shoppers.   After voicing a sincere, cheerful "Good morning," the salesman can pause, thus passing the conversational ball to the customer.   She must do more than just return the greeting, and whatever she does will undoubtedly reveal a possible sales approach to the salesperson.

Among the *un*acceptable openers are these:

> Something?
> Something for you?
> What'll you have?
> Do you want something?

When the customer is looking at merchandise, the salesperson has two other options.   One, the silent approach, can be executed very nicely. Here the salesman steps up, physically and mentally alert, expectant, and obviously at the customer's service.   Practically always the customer will make a comment or ask a question that starts the interview.   The other option is the merchandise type of opener.   These are examples:

What Consumers Liked
When Shopping In Retail Stores

Salesperson was very much interested during the transaction

Gave helpful merchandise information

Displayed merchandise in an effective way

Answered questions or objections satisfactorily

Acknowledged customer in a courteous or friendly way

Thanked or invited purchase customer back

Suggested or showed something else

Gave reasonably prompt attention

Did not make non-purchase customer feel uncomfortable for not buying

Had the merchandise customer first asked to see

Salesperson handled purchase details quickly

Research Bureau for Retail Training, University of Pittsburgh

Pretty, aren't they?
That is one of our new spring colors.
Those just came in last week from Ireland.
That makes an appreciated gift.

When the salesman knows the customer, he can call the customer by name, and that is helpful. In addition, the salesman can ask a casual question or make some informal remark. An example would be, "Good morning, Mrs. Johnson, how was your trip?"

Determining the Customer's Wants

One handicap in store selling is the impossibility of the salesman's learning, in advance, what each of his customers needs or wants. The preapproach work that many outside salesmen can do simply cannot be done for store customers. Yet, if a sale is to be made, and if the customer (but not the merchandise) is to return, it is clear that the salesman must learn accurately what customers want. Unless the salesman translates merchandise into customer interests, and unless he helps each customer buy wisely, he will not be an outstanding salesman.

How can the wants of customers be determined? *Observation* helps. If the salesman observes the customer's attraction to and interest in merchandise, if he studies the apparent needs of customers, and if he watches closely the customer's reactions to various products, he will find some indications and guidance. *Listening* helps. Customers' comments may be vague or even inaccurate. They may be so rationalized that they camouflage the customer's deep desire or what she feels to be her urgent need. Even so, what the customer says must be analyzed and used. The sooner the salesman gets merchandise in the customer's hands and the sooner he gets the customer thinking about specific merchandise, the earlier there will be reactions to observe and comments to hear. *Headlining* helps. When the customer is examining a particular product, the salesman can mention quickly the three or four most outstanding benefits the product supplies and then watch and listen for reactions. Finally, *questioning* helps. Restrained, tactful questions can be used to point up the customer's problems. Questions about material, style, interests, uses, and purposes are quite in order. Questions about size are risky because they can make the salesman look ignorant. Questions about price are somewhat risky; answers may commit the customer to a price level the store does not have in stock, and, in addition, the answer may handicap any attempt at trading up. The smaller the retailer's stock, the fewer questions the salesman dares ask.

Typing Customers

Although several textbooks on retail selling recommend the "typing" of customers, it appears that the practice is just as dangerous in store selling as it is in outside selling. One quite basic factor is how customers feel about being "typed." They resent it. Customers do not want to be analyzed, classified, and then treated as specimens. They do not care to think of a salesperson as serving "types" of customers — to them he should be helping an *individual* solve some buying problem. Instead of routine selling tactics, customers want personalized interest and treatment.

Even if customers did not loathe the practice, it could still be attacked on the grounds of impracticality. If a "timid" customer is also impatient, should the saleswoman assure the buyer repeatedly of her friendship — or should she not talk too much? If a talkative customer is curious and inquisitive about some merchandise, should the salesman give the buyer all the information he has — or be a good listener? If a customer has little to say and is obviously pressed for time, should she be given the "silent" customer treatment — or the "hurried" customer treatment? In store selling, as in outside selling, each customer is an individual of many moods, different on each contact, and often reacting differently to the same situation.

It seems far sounder to see the salesman as dealing with (a) customers who know what they want, (b) customers who want something but don't know precisely what, and (c) casual visitors, usually called "lookers," who don't want anything particularly or strongly.

Handling Customers Who "Want"

In handling customers who know what they want, the salesman should work toward a short sales interview. He should quickly put some merchandise before the customer; he should avoid telling a lengthy sales story; and he should make his answers to questions specific and brief. If the customer has her heart set on some product she definitely should not have, about all the salesman can do is to recommend a more sensible product and urge the customer to compare the two items before buying.

The customers who want something but don't know just what need much help from salespeople. They need help in pinpointing their problems and in selecting merchandise which will solve those problems. The soundest general suggestion to the salesman in these circumstances is for him to start showing some merchandise immediately. Meanwhile, the salesman must attempt to analyze the customer's appearance and manner. Possibly the most baffling matter is that of trying to guess what price lines are most appropriate. Every salesperson knows that some customers spend less, while others spend much more than their appearance and impression would suggest. The course followed by some salesmen is to show two or three items in a middle price line with, perhaps, a single higher-priced item. From the moment she sees merchandise, the customer can hardly avoid revealing information about prices, uses, colors, and preferences. Another fairly safe rule is for the salesman to stick closely to whatever merchandise is in greatest demand at the moment. Questions by the salesman should be held to a minimum. Above all, a salesman must be careful not to show too much merchandise, for such a practice often serves only to confuse customers.

Handling "Lookers"

In many stores, well over half of the customers consider themselves to be "just looking," and, as "lookers," they pose a difficult problem. It appears that the sales personnel of a store are entitled to base their behavior on four assumptions. First, lookers are not intending nor planning to buy now. Second, their immediate wish is to be left alone to look at merchandise. Third, the looker in all probability wants to buy something and can finance the purchase; otherwise, he would not be looking. Finally, it is the salesperson's duty to discover what the looker needs.

Several courses of action are possible in handling a looker. One of the most logical is to leave the customer alone, hoping that examination of the merchandise will sell it. Many a customer raises his buying defenses at least a bit if a salesman immediately attaches himself to and stays right with the looker. Another course of action is to offer to escort the looker on a guided tour of merchandise inspection. This offer is particularly appropriate where products need to be demonstrated and the salesman is not busy. A third possibility is for the salesman to brief the looker on the general location of merchandise, to invite the looker to feel completely at home, and to assure the looker of prompt and interested service just as soon as such is desired. A fourth technique is to refer the looker to some specific merchandise, somewhat along the lines of the sales conversation openers mentioned previously. Such references to merchandise should be casual and somewhat offhand. For example, a saleswoman might say, "Take all the time you want. You'll undoubtedly want to see our new collection of scarfs, right over there." Other merchandise which can be brought to the looker's attention includes any "specials" being offered, products featured in the day's advertisements, items that are being pushed, and merchandise on display in the store's windows or interior.

Regardless of which method is used, it is the salesman's duty to work to get the goodwill of every looker. In those cases which develop favorably, the salesman should make a serious attempt to make a sale. Whether his goal is goodwill or a sale, the salesman should watch closely so that he can be ready to serve the looker just as soon as he is ready to be approached again.

Selecting the Merchandise

Having greeted the customer and made a start at determining what he wants, the salesperson then must select what merchandise to show and recommend. If the customer made a specific request to see a certain product, that, of course, is the one the salesman will show first. If the customer was somewhat vague, then the salesman must bring out what he or she believes the customer will like. Here the salesman is well advised not to lead off with either the highest- or the lowest-priced items. The safest as well as the most ethical guide in selecting merchandise to show is that of customer satisfaction. If a customer later regrets a purchase, if he feels that he made an unfortunate purchase, his natural reaction is to blame the store more than he blames himself. His resentment usually results in buying less at that store and in unfavorable word-of-mouth publicity for it.

Trading Up

In selecting the merchandise to show, the salesman must decide whether to attempt *trading up*. A salesman succeeds in trading up when he sells the customer a better-quality item than the customer was planning to buy — he sells a $10 item instead of a $7.50 one. Another version of trading up is selling a larger size of the product. Still another possibility is for the salesman to sell more items than the customer was intending to buy — six pairs of socks instead of three.

When the customer trades up and buys the better quality of a suit, for example, then he gets greater economy, or greater satisfaction of some other kind. This result leads to repeat buying at the store which served him so well. In this regard, the sales staff should appreciate the benefits, to the customer and to the store, of selling the better merchandise. Salespeople should practice until they can show their superior lines of merchandise smoothly and recommend them naturally.

Sears, Roebuck and Co. tells this to its salespeople about trading up:

> A salesperson isn't "good" unless he trades up. Trading up means selling better or top-quality merchandise. To do this . . . you must know your merchandise completely and be able to point out to the customer the benefits of buying better merchandise.
>
> Suppose, for example, an economy electric blanket is advertised. When a customer comes to buy, show the advertised merchandise and tell her its advantages. Also show the 4-Star Harmony House blanket and point out its superior value. Don't talk down the advertised blanket . . . just make the better-quality one sound more desirable . . . as it actually is!
>
> You know, of course, that 4-Star items are tops at Sears . . . proved in lab tests and actual shopping checks. From there on, however, 4-Star items depend on you! Learn as much as possible about 4-Star items so you'll be able to tell customers about the benefits of better merchandise. Trading up is the type of selling that is interesting and challenging!

Substitution

The issue of substitution is far more common in store selling than in outside selling. In some cases, the store will not have in stock the item or brand requested; in others the salesperson may attempt to redirect the customer's interest to some other product or some other brand, even though the item requested is in stock. In all cases there will be bad after-effects if either the salesman or the customer successfully insists on the sale and purchase of a product the customer should not buy. The more merchandise information the salesman has, the greater his chance of success.

If the store does not have the requested product in stock, the customer should be told this without any hesitation or apology. If the store *does* have something in that line which will give satisfaction, the item should be placed in the customer's hands quickly for inspection. The requested product should not be criticized, nor should the item shown be referred to as a substitute. The salesman can question the customer tactfully while showing the substitute item.

If the store has the requested item, then there must be sound justification for any attempt at switching. The soundest reason of all would be present when a customer plans to buy a product utterly inappropriate. In these circumstances, it is the salesman's duty to try to steer the customer away from what would be an unfortunate, unsatisfactory purchase and to recommend in its place a more suitable one. Such attempts to switch can even involve *type* of product, especially in the case of gift purchases. Often the salesman is wise in showing the more appropriate product along with what the customer asked to see, because many customers will see immediately and without aid that their original preference was not sound. For every attempted switch, the salesman must have a tactful, respectable, and acceptable reason. Switches attempted just because the store has a higher margin of profit on the substitute item often backfire.

TELLING THE STORY

Store salesmen tell a somewhat different story from that told by outside salesmen. One difference is in story length, the story told in the store being the shorter. For this reason, the salesman is wise to make his strongest and most persuasive points at the very start. Otherwise, he may not have the opportunity to make them. Another difference involves the salesman's familiarity with his story. Because he tells it so many times, the store salesman is apt to consider his story old. To him it *is* old, but it is new to each new customer. Still another difference is that the store salesman cannot plan his stories in advance to the degree that the outside salesman can. Standard or canned stories are impossible for store salespeople, although key words and phrases can, of course, be used effectively. The outside salesman can determine in advance just what he is going to say and how he will say it; but the store salesman must feel his way along, deciding and acting on the spur of the moment in selecting the treatment of each customer.

Most of the important principles of storytelling found in Chapter 12 are equally basic in store selling. The salesman's job is to identify or to create a human want and then to recommend a product to fill it. He must let the customer buy and avoid making him feel that he, the customer, is being sold. Customers do not buy until convinced that the purchase will be of personal benefit or advantage. It is the salesman's duty to make each customer feel important. Both overselling and underselling are to be avoided. The customer is entitled to the salesperson's complete attention, and, in turn, the salesman can hold or recapture the customer's attention by directing it to the product or by asking the customer to do something to or with the item. Agreements on small matters should be reached frequently. Value should be established before price is discussed. If the price of some product is asked, it should be quoted at once; immediately the customer should be told about product advantages and buyer benefits that justify the price. As the sales talk progresses, the sales story should become more specific and more emphatic.

Handling Several Customers at Once

During rush hours, there will be several customers wanting the service of the same salesperson. This situation creates a problem involving promptness and sequence of attention. The most essential principle for the salesman to be guided by is that customer #1 has top priority. This customer must not be given cause for feeling neglected, discriminated against, or rushed. A second essential principle is that customers must be served in turn. Of course, some customers will release the salesman for a few minutes, thereby easing his problem. In some situations, only the senior customer can initiate this clearance; in others, the salesman may feel entitled to suggest the move. The least the salesperson can do when additional customers approach is to smile a recognition and to promise prompt attention with such a phrase as, "I'll be right with you," or "Just one minute, please." At times the salesperson can excuse himself from a looker, permit him to shop or look, take care of the customer who is ready to buy quickly, and then return to the looker. Sometimes it is possible for the salesman to give something to customer #2 for examination while serving customer #1. A final possibility, practicable only for certain types of goods, is to serve two or even three customers at the same time. Examples of such types of goods are shoes, clothing, and greeting cards. Here the salesman's task is to keep the several customers at different stages in the buying process. The salesman starts off with customer #1 and places items in his hands for inspection or trial. While this inspection is being made, the salesman moves over to customer #2 and starts *him* off, then on to customer #3, or back to customer #1.

Handling Groups of Customers

Often the salesman in the store is approached not by a single customer but, instead, by a group of two or more customers shopping together. Typically, the group would be composed of a customer and a friend or two, or of a customer with one or more members of the family. A husband-and-wife shopping unit is not uncommon. The salesman must remember, as he moves to serve a group, that the person buying must think highly of the judgment and taste of his companions, else he would not have come shopping with them. So, the salesman is well cautioned not to ignore or neglect comments, questions, or opinions of any member of the group. The recommended course is for the salesman to say little and to stay neutral until he has attempted to sense which member of the group is the dominant one and what interests are involved. If the "leader" can be identified, then the major sales efforts and the strongest selling points should be aimed at that person. Members of the group should be given the opportunity to talk between or among themselves if they desire. If two persons who are shopping together cannot agree on merchandise, the best course for the salesman is to recommend the item he sincerely believes to be the wisest and most appropriate purchase under the circumstances.

DEMONSTRATING WITH SHOWMANSHIP

If one were making a list of unforgivable sins of store selling, he would certainly have to include the failure to show merchandise to the customer. Here, as in outside selling, the salesperson should show his products when explaining how the buyer can use them. Because the item the customer buys is practically always in the store at the time of purchase, there is hardly ever an excuse for *not* demonstrating. And, the desirability of identifying the product with the customer has already been noted.

How much merchandise should be shown? This decision must be left up to the salesman's best judgment. If he does not show enough, the customer may feel limited, slighted, and not well enough informed to buy. If shown too much, the customer only becomes confused. Definitely, the customer wants to see and ought to be shown all the items he feels he *should* examine. The customer wants to see what he deems to be a minimum assortment for making an intelligent, sound purchase. In every case, the customer should feel that the salesman has shown, or will gladly show literally every bit of the store's merchandise that is suitable for the customer's wants. The demonstration phase of the sale rarely lasts very long. There is usually time to repeat a demonstration, even in greater detail, if necessary.

Rules for demonstrating (Chapter 13) are equally valid in store selling. Customer participation is eminently desirable and can be obtained by the salesman's asking the customer to do something or by giving the customer something to watch. Whenever practicable, the product should be handled or operated by the customer just as it will be used after purchase. The customer can try on coats and shoes or he can write with a pen. A few passes made over the chin with an electric razor may be the convincing point in obtaining an affirmative purchasing decision in that line. All the while, the salesman can be describing the buyer benefits the customer is experiencing. Salesmen can also demonstrate the care that certain products should be given.

Store salespeople should be good demonstrators and, likewise, their demonstrations should be effective. Merchandise should be displayed in its best light and in an impressive, yet believable, way. The demonstrations should be designed to prove the advantages promised by the salesman; they should be more than just spectacles or shows. Throughout the sales story, the salesman should remember that the manner in which he handles his merchandise is quite revealing. His respect and care should be always in evidence. Nothing he does must be allowed to destroy or damage the customer's respect for the goods.

HANDLING OBJECTIONS

Most buying resistance met by store salespeople stems from the customer's uncertainty about the three buying decisions relating to *product*, *price*, and *time*. Not many objections are based on *need*, although need must always be established, and, for obvious reasons, even fewer are based on the *source* decision. So, the salesperson can expect to be dealing with many customers who are not completely certain that the product under consideration is the best buy. Then, there will be many customers who will tell themselves that the price of the item is really more than they can afford to pay. Finally, many times customers will start to leave, commenting that they must think the purchase over before buying or that they want to look around a bit more before making a final selection.

The general rule here, as in outside selling, calls for the avoidance of objections by explaining them away before the customer raises them. When the salesman selects the most appropriate and acceptable merchandise to recommend, he reduces the amount of product objection he must handle. When he points out all the outstanding satisfactions to be had from the product, he narrows the base of price objections. Difficulty with the time decision will become less frequent and less troublesome as the salesman does a more thorough job of getting solid agreements with regard to the matters of product and price.

It is sometimes obvious that a customer feels sincerely that he must "think it over" or "talk it over" before buying. In these circumstances, there are several steps the salesman may take. He may start by agreeing with the customer that deliberation or clearance is desirable before making the purchase. This might be followed by reminding the customer of the store's liberal policy on the return of merchandise. The salesman may offer to show even more merchandise to the customer before the customer leaves. If this offer is not accepted, the salesman can give the customer a summary of the most important benefits involved, these to be thought about or relayed to the absent person who must be consulted. These benefits can be given orally or in written form, which is much better if feasible. The salesman may try to schedule a meeting with the customer *and* that absent third party, at which he could sell to both. The salesman may indicate that he would be delighted to put the item aside for the customer. As the customer leaves, the salesman may give the customer literature or his card in an effort to get the customer to return — to him.

The concealed or camouflaged objection is the same tough problem in store selling that it is in outside selling. For example, the customer may try to prevent or postpone a product demonstration by saying, "No, let's not bother with that today." Or, after a sales presentation and demonstration, the customer may say nothing more than, "I'm afraid that isn't exactly what I had in mind." About all the salesperson can do in this situation is to observe the customer closely in an effort to sense, from the customer's action, comments, or facial expressions, what buying decision is causing the trouble. Meanwhile, the salesperson can once more present the most persuasive, the most desirable customer advantages of the product; sometimes this causes the buying difficulty to disappear. In some cases, the salesperson must ask the customer, "What have I failed to make clear?" Once the objection has been identified, it should be handled quickly and openly, fairly and completely.

CLOSING

There are closing clues in store selling just as there are in outside selling. Sometimes they indicate that the customer has decided to make a purchase; at all times they justify a trial close from the salesman. Closing clues can be found in customers' *words* and *actions*. Words could be in question form, asking about price, or size, or terms. Words could be a statement as, for example, "It *would* save me time each week." Actions indicating interest or even decision can be nothing more than changes in facial expression; or, they can be the reading of the product's tag or label, the checking of product size, or the moving to one side so as to see the product from a different angle.

As the salesman senses the approach of the end of the sales interview, there are certain suggestions or precautions he should remember. The salesman's manner should become more positive and masterful. The customer must feel the salesman's confidence in the product, his conviction as to its value, and his control over the situation. The customer must realize that the salesman has made a decision about which the salesman has no doubts or questions. No new merchandise should be brought out at this stage. Instead, items should be removed that did not strike the customer's fancy and, hence, are getting little or no consideration. Choice should be simplified; if the customer is going to buy one item, never should an assortment numbering more than three be left before her. The salesman should concentrate on those two or three items of particular interest to the customer, reviewing the outstanding merits of each. The salesman must not seem to be in a hurry, nor should it seem that he is attempting to hurry the customer into buying. The salesman will ask for customer agreements more often during this stage, and he will avoid talking too much or too long. He will be ready and eager to suggest a decision to an undecided customer or to make the final choice.

AFTER A SALE OR "NO SALE"

Immediately after making a sale, the salesman should record it, demonstrating his skill with arithmetic and the necessary mechanics. As the salesman wraps the purchase, he can at the same time assure the customer that he made an intelligent decision. A warm "thank you" should always be voiced to let the customer know that the purchase was appreciated, and a sincere personal invitation to return should be issued. If appropriate, the customer's name should be learned and associated with his appearance for possible future use. Also, if appropriate, the salesman can tell the customer *his* name or give the customer his business card.

Regardless of whether or not the interview ends in a purchase, the salesman must make the best selling attempt he knows how to make. When the customer postpones a purchase, the salesman will continue to be just as courteous and friendly as he was before the decision. He will not disclose in any manner the irritation, disappointment, hurt, or resentment he may feel. Instead, he will indulge in some excellent public relations as he builds goodwill for his store and himself by the way he treats a customer who did not buy. He lets the customer know that visits to the store are and will continue to be appreciated. His manner should encourage customers to return.

The enlightened salesman realizes that the customer has two undeniable rights — to postpone a purchase decision, and to shop further before buying. Any attempt to curtail these rights can be damaging to a store. If, therefore, a customer insists on asserting one or more of these rights, there's nothing to do except cooperate. The salesperson *can* summarize the advantages of his merchandise and ask the customer to investigate competing products on those points. It is clearly the salesman's responsibility to see that the customer knows thoroughly and completely before leaving what his store can supply in the product lines being considered. He should assume that the customer will return and will then buy; he might even try to make a definite appointment for the return visit. In some cases, the salesman can give a memo, a sketch, some literature, or his card to the customer in an effort to increase the chances of his return.

Some stores instruct each of their salespersons to bring another of the store's salesmen into the situation when he feels he will not be able to make a sale. This practice is sometimes referred to as "turnover," and sometimes as the "wring out" system. The salesman called in is often described and addressed as the "manager" whether he is or not. It is the hope of the store that the customer will be impressed by the personal attention of a second salesman, particularly if he answers to the title of "manager." This practice can be defended if the second salesman is better informed than the first. It cannot be defended if its sole purpose is to "pressure" the customer. If this salesperson is too obvious or aggressive, the customer will probably become suspicious and object even more strongly.

SUGGESTION SELLING

No treatment of closing sales in retail stores is complete if it omits the topic of suggestion selling. Suggestion selling is getting the customer to buy merchandise he had not planned to buy. It is the sale of items over and above those the customer requested and bought. It is additional sales volume, and that, of course, explains the store's as well as the salesperson's interest in it.

It can be said correctly that customers want suggestions from the sales staffs of retail stores. One explanation of this attitude is that suggestions can remind customers of products they need. Another explanation is that the consumer will run out of a product less often if he replenishes his stock more often. Suggestions can also help a consumer identify actual needs of which he was not aware. When made in a tactful way, suggestions are received by customers as favors and, hence, are appreciated. Suggested purchases can save both time and money and can increase the customer's personal satisfaction.

When should suggestion selling be attempted? It is usually best for the salesman to care for the customer's requests first and to have this purchase agreed on before suggesting other products. Then, before going through the mechanics of completing this sale physically — writing up the sales ticket, wrapping the merchandise, or making change — the salesman can make suggestions. Once in a while the salesman can make use of the ensemble technique before the first purchase is made in the customer's mind. Here, for example, the salesman might bring out a tie to show with a shirt the customer is examining. The tie often helps to sell the shirt; the purchase of the shirt recommends the purchase of the tie.

Because suggestion selling can be executed in such a way as to irritate or even drive customers away, certain rules or principles which have proved sound should be observed. The salesman's ideal suggestion should prove to be a better solution to a customer problem. If the suggested merchandise is something that will benefit the customer, the salesman is well on his way to customer acceptance of the suggestion. Furthermore, the suggestion should be realistic and suitable. This rules out products that would not be appropriate for the customer's needs. Then too, if the customer is in a tremendous hurry the salesman would be wise to avoid suggestion selling. If the salesman uses a tone of helpful concern and interest, he helps give his suggestion the appearance of a service to the customer.

Another rule is that suggestion selling must be moderate in intensity, in the amount of the recommended purchase, and in the number of items mentioned. A salesman can easily be too aggressive in his commendable ambition to increase the amount of the sale. If he sells too hard, the result will be customer resentment. If he tries to make too large an additional sale, his attempt smacks of overloading the customer. If he suggests too long a list of products, he certainly irritates and may even infuriate the customer.

Still another guide is that suggestions must be definite. The salesman does not make the mistake of using any of these:

> Now what else?
> Will that be all?
> Anything in socks today?

What merchandise is best suited to suggestion selling? A major group is composed of related items. Suits call for shirts, shoes, socks, ties, and hats; gasoline calls for oil; shaving cream calls for blades; frankfurters call for rolls and mustard. Then, moving away from related or complementary products, there are the "specials" of the day. There are new products with news value and old products for which new uses have been

found. There are the items currently featured in store displays and advertisements.   Merchandise that is timely because of its relationship to
"days," such as Mother's Day or Valentine's Day, is a natural choice for
suggestion selling. In somewhat the same manner, seasonal products can
be effectively suggested as the season arrives; antifreeze, straw hats, and
Christmas gifts are examples. Finally, merchandise immediately at hand
can often be suggested successfully because its examination and purchase
take so little time.

WORKING WITH CUSTOMERS

Retail stores constantly feel the necessity for continued patronage.
Similarly each salesperson has a strong desire to have *his* or *her* regular,
steady customers. Stated simply, customers return to and buy repeatedly
from those stores which satisfy and please them. Basically, customers
want good values, accurate and adequate information about products,
speedy service, and polite treatment. The customer especially wants to
feel that each purchase and each return visit is appreciated. He expects
the store and particularly its selling personnel to express appreciation
for the opportunity to serve him and for his repeated votes of confidence
in them. Sound selling plus sincere appreciation build a loyal clientele
whose esteem and goodwill are invaluable assets to a store.

No thorough attempt at working with customers can be made without
reviewing the reasons why customers quit buying at certain stores and
from individual salesmen and saleswomen. The indifference of salespeople
always ranks high on lists of causes of customer loss. Selling tactics that
smack of pressure or of too much aggressiveness can drive customers
away. If too many attempts at substitution are made or if the attempts are
too crude and obvious, customers are going to take their patronage elsewhere. Customer complaints include the charge that some salespeople
are haughty instead of friendly, while others are discourteous instead of
well-mannered. Also included is the accusation that some salespeople
are not well enough informed about their merchandise to supply the
product information required by customers. A more disturbing charge is
that some salespersons actually misrepresent their goods. When a salesman or a saleswoman promises something to a customer, such as a
delivery date and hour, but fails to comply, the effects are not good.
Finally, the mistakes of salespeople discourage and sometimes terminate
return visits and purchases.

There are certain steps salespersons in some stores can take in their
determination to work more successfully with their customers. One of
the simplest, yet most rewarding, is learning the names of as many cus-

Eleven Commandments
of good business . . .

A Customer
is the most important person in any business.

A Customer
is not dependent on us — we are dependent on her.

A Customer
is not an interruption of our work — she is the purpose of it.

A Customer
does us a favor when she calls — we are not doing her a favor by serving her.

A Customer
is a part of our business — not an outsider.

A Customer
is not a cold statistic — she is a flesh and blood human being with feelings and emotions like our own.

A Customer
is not someone to argue with but to help.

A Customer
is a person who brings us her needs and it is our job to fill those needs.

A Customer
is deserving of the most courteous and attentive treatment we can give her.

A Customer
is the person who makes it possible for us to earn our salary.

A Customer
is the life-blood of our business.

Saks Fifth Avenue

tomers as possible and addressing those individuals by their names. Another habit well acquired is that of remembering the preferences (and prejudices) of regular customers. In the higher-priced merchandise lines, some salesmen find it practicable and worthwhile to keep an individual record on some of their best customers. Such a record might include the customer's name, the date of his last visit, the items last bought, and any other significant facts about the customer. These customer records can be reviewed quickly each morning, permitting the salesman to give more tailored and personalized treatment to any of the recorded customers who drop in that day. The records also serve the salesman as a mailing list or as a telephone call list. Where installment credit is available, a salesman can keep posted on his customers' balances and recommend "add on" purchases at the appropriate times. Salespeople should convert as many salesperson-customer relations from a stranger-to-stranger type into an acquaintance-to-acquaintance type, and as many of these as possible into a friend-to-friend relationship.

RETURNED GOODS

A retail problem of obvious interest to retail salespersons is that of merchandise bought by customers but subsequently returned to the store. Returned goods are a significant element in a retailer's expenses. Returns must be handled, and this involves cost. An item being returned may show evidence of use, abuse, or deterioration; repair, renovation, or even markdown may be necessary. Then, for the time the merchandise was out of the store, it was neither "sold" nor available for sale; unless the retailer is to lose sales, his inventory must be large enough to allow for this out-of-stock time. In addition, some returns reflect an increase in customer ill-will. Finally, the volume of returns may suggest that buying and or selling are less efficient and more expensive than they should be.

Retail salesmen are often responsible for a significant proportion of returned goods. Sometimes a salesman makes a mistake unknowingly. Sometimes there is a misunderstanding between customer and salesman involving just what is being bought or its price. An ignorant, poorly trained salesman can expect returns; the same holds for the careless, indifferent salesman who does not bother to tailor merchandise recommendations to individual shoppers. The high-pressure salesman may as well brace for returns; so may the weak salesman who urges shoppers to take goods home on approval instead of *selling* goods to those buyers. Equally guilty is the casual salesman who allows customers to do a poor job of buying; customer disappointment over merchandise performance, be this a matter of operation, fit, color, or size, often leads to the return of

WHY SALES ARE LOST

Very often sales are lost through carelessness or indifference on the salesperson's part. Here are some reasons why:

1. Disinterest — Don't conduct a conversation with a fellow employee or another customer while waiting on someone. Give the customer your complete attention. Dead-pan expressions, daydreaming, or "take it or leave it" attitudes leave unsold merchandise.

2. Mistakes — If you show the wrong item or make a mistake in change, acknowledge it and make the customer feel you are genuinely sorry.

3. Appearing too anxious — Show customers you want to serve their interests. Over-insistence and high-pressure tactics are objectionable to customers.

4. Talking down other brands — Talk up the brand you want to sell. Do not make unfair remarks about a competitive brand.

5. Arguing — Never argue with a customer. If it appears that an argument might develop, shift the conversation to another topic. There's little profit in winning an argument and losing the customer. If a customer makes an absurd statement, don't laugh or argue. You may anger the customer, and an angry customer is a lost customer.

6. Being too long-winded — A flood of words doesn't make many sales. Some people take time to make up their minds, and silence at the right time allows the customer to think and decide. Being a good listener often makes more sales than being a fast talker.

7. Lack of courtesy — Discourteous salespeople rarely last long on a job; they lose too many customers.

8. Showing favoritism — Never wait on your friends or favorite customers before taking care of customers who were there first.

9. Being too hurried — Take time to find out what a customer wants and then take time to show the merchandise properly.

10. Embarrassing the customer — Never laugh at a person who speaks with a foreign accent or correct a person who mispronounces words or product names.

11. Misrepresenting merchandise — Never guarantee any cures or make any claims for products that cannot be backed up by facts.

12. Lack of product information — Salespeople who are not well informed cannot expect to build a steady clientele for their store.

13. Wasting customers' time — When a customer is in a hurry, finish the sale as quickly as possible.

14. Getting too personal — Assume a professional attitude. Be sincere and friendly, but keep a touch of dignity and formality in all customer contacts. Never let familiarity creep into the conversation, for it is usually resented.

E. R. Squibb & Sons

the item. Occasionally goods are returned because an unacceptable substitution was made on a customer's order.

Of course, some causes of goods being returned do not relate closely to the personal selling done by retail salespersons. For example, the reason could be a mistake in order filling, damage en route, or delay in delivery. Or, the item might be inherently faulty. Or, the customer may buy — then find the same item available in another store at a lower price. Or, as a final example, there are a few customers who simply cannot abstain from taking advantage of a store's policy that the customer is always right and that his money will be cheerfully refunded if he is not satisfied.

Retail salespeople have an interest in the returned goods problem — a considerable interest if they work in department, clothing, or furniture stores. Their earnings are usually affected directly because they are determined by their sales volume. There are more than a few cases where a salesperson made a big sale, spent the commission, and then found his commission account charged because the merchandise was returned. In addition, returns can take up a salesperson's selling time. Some stores ask their sales staffs to handle returns; some customers prefer to take merchandise back to the same individual from whom they bought it. Then too, there is often a make-up or replacement sale which must be made. For any salesman, a high returned-goods figure is hardly a cause for pride or joy.

If his store has a liberal policy about returns, the retail salesperson does have cause to be happy because such a policy works in the direction of greater sales. New customers are more easily attracted, and present customers are more easily held. It is a fact, incidentally, that a store's largest credit customers do the most returning. If his store's policy is generous, the salesman should not fail to emphasize this fact. But, at the same time, this fact does not relieve the salesman of the responsibility of helping customers make purchases that will not come back.

SELF-MANAGEMENT

Self-management is not nearly the complicated, challenging, and difficult matter for salespeople in stores that it is for outside salesmen. Typically, the store tells a salesperson how many hours a week he will work and when he will be on duty. In regard to planning their work, there is little that the salesman and saleswoman must decide — the store does that for them. Apart from store records, there are some personal records of performance a salesperson can keep, but such records are not so helpful to them as those kept by outside salesmen. Neither the salesman's health nor his habits is a major problem.

What, then, can or should a store salesperson do about managing himself? It would seem that he should concern himself mainly with *attitudes* and *activities*. As to attitudes, the starting step is to recognize that training and modification must go on indefinitely because improvement is always possible. The salesman must realize that his present as well as his future depends in large measure on how well he gets along with three groups — customers, associates, and the store's executives. Further, he must remember that few of the customers who quit buying at a store do so because of the store's merchandise, its prices, or its customer services; most quit because they find the salespeople ignorant or incompetent, uninteresting or uninterested. The salesman's attitude must reflect his understanding of the dependence of customers on salespeople and of the customer's need for help and advice. His attitude should reflect his awareness of the fact that customers are guests — his guests as well as the store's guests, and *invited* guests at that.

As for activities, they are whatever is needed to achieve self-improvement. They include such obvious practices as the analysis of selling attempts in order to identify elements of strength and elements of weakness. In particular, the well-managed salesman searches for the causes of lost sales and lost customers. Another activity involves the collection of all information needed; information about merchandise, about customers, and about how to sell the former to the latter. Still another activity is that of the improvement of his memory; otherwise, that information about merchandise, customers, and selling techniques will be of limited use because of its limited life. Then there is the matter of developing and even trying to perfect a pleasing personality. Finally, there is the never-ending practice of trying, week after week and month after month, to be of greater help to the salesman's real boss — his customers.

STUDY ASSIGNMENTS

1. Do you believe *trading-up* more risky than *suggestion-selling?* Why?
2. What does a retail salesperson need to know about his merchandise?
3. Why shouldn't retail salespeople open sales interviews with questions about size or price?
4. When a customer in a retail store asks for a product the store usually has but is temporarily out of, what should the salesperson do?
5. Why is it so important for salespeople to know and observe store policies and procedures?
6. Practically all salesmen must take some form of competition into account. What types of competition are of greatest concern to retail salespeople?

7. How can a retail salesperson try to develop the goodwill of customers after the sales transaction has been completed?

8. Make a list of the bad habits that retail salespeople should avoid at all costs.

9. In what ways does a group of loyal customers benefit an individual salesperson?

10. Why should returned goods be of concern to retail salespeople?

CASE STUDY 19A

A man has just entered a men's medium-priced clothing shop. The salesman judges him to be in his late twenties. He is tastefully dressed in a business suit. As the scene opens the salesman approaches him and says cheerfully:

Salesman: Good afternoon. May I help you, sir?

Prospect: I'm interested in a pair of shoes.

Salesman: Fine. Would you step back this way to our shoe department? (Prospect follows salesman to rear of shop.) Won't you have a seat? (Prospect sits down.)

Prospect: I'd like to see something in brown. Dark brown.

Salesman: Let's just slip off your shoe, and I'll get your size. We always like to get a new measurement for our customers so there'll be no question of fit. (Places customer's foot on measuring device.) Let's see . . . I make it about 9-D. Is that what you've been wearing?

Prospect: I don't remember, something like that.

Salesman: I think I've got something right here that you'll like. (Salesman goes over to shelf and pulls out one box.) This has been one of our most popular sellers this season. It's the finest Cordovan shoe that we have in the shop. You'll find this shoe right for dress or for sports occasions. A Cordovan wing-tip is never out of place, unless, of course, it's a full-dress formal dance or dinner party.

Prospect: How much is this shoe?

Salesman: This shoe runs you $22.95. And it's built to last for many years. See here . . . inside, it's got a full leather lining.

Prospect: That's more than I wanted to put in a pair of shoes.

Salesman: All right. Let's try another pair I have here. (Salesman gets two boxes down from shelf.) Let's slip this one on and see how it feels.

Prospect: Feels all right, but that solid, plain toe doesn't show me too much . . .

Salesman: You know, I've found that to be the case with a lot of people. They either like this shoe extremely well or they don't like it at all. (Puts that shoe back in box and opens second box.) Now here's my choice of the shoe that's going to be the most popular shoe of the season. It's the new Florsheim Lotop, really a smart shoe.

Prospect: Um . . . humn . . . That's not bad, let's slip it on.

Salesman: (Fitting shoe on and tying it.) How does it feel?

Prospect: Feels pretty good.

Salesman: Let's slip on the other one and let you walk around in it a bit. (Slips on other shoe.) Now try that.

Prospect: They sure feel light.

Salesman: That's the new style. They're cut low and don't have a heavy bulky sole for you to drag around.

Prospect: Um . . . humn . . . But do you suppose these light shoes will hold up as well as a heavier pair . . .

Salesman: Yes sir, you see these shoes are made of genuine pebble-grain calfskin. No shoe on the market today uses a finer leather than this.

Prospect: How much are these shoes?

Salesman: Those shoes are only $17.95; that's five dollars cheaper than the first pair you tried on. Would you like to wear them?

Prospect: I think I'll take them . . . No, I don't want to wear them . . . You can put them in a box for me, can't you?

Salesman: Surely, we'll be glad to. (He takes shoes, puts them in box and hands them to clerk with instructions to wrap.) While she's getting those ready for you, sir, could I suggest for you a pair of these brown and tan argyles. They're just the right shade to accent the tone of your new shoes.

Prospect: Say, they are right nice; let me have a pair of those, size 11.

Salesman: Fine, I'll have them put right in with your shoes. Let's see — that comes to $18.90, and .57 tax — $19.47 all told.

Prospect: Here you are.

Salesman: (Handing him change and package.) Here you are, sir, $19.47 out of $20 — $19.47, $19.50, and .50 is $20.00. Thank you very much, and come back again.

QUESTIONS:

1. What did the salesman do well?
2. What did the salesman do that could be improved?
3. What techniques are illustrated in the sale?

CASE STUDY 19B

A lady enters the home furnishings department of a large department store. She is well-dressed and poised, and she is looking about as if she were searching for a particular item. A salesman approaches her.

Salesman: (Smiling cheerfully) Good morning, may I show you something in particular?

Prospect: Yes, I'd like to see what you have in boudoir chairs.

Salesman: Fine. If you'll walk this way, I've just received several new styles that I think you'll like. I think they're really beautiful chairs. (Shows her three chairs grouped together.) Notice this new, nubby, bouclé fabric. Isn't it nice?

Prospect: Oh, that really is beautiful; I don't think I've ever seen it used on boudoir chairs.

Salesman: No, I imagine not. All three of these chairs were just purchased at the Chicago furniture market, and surprisingly enough, a great many of the manufacturers were showing their entire boudoir lines covered in this nubby bouclé. Of course, I think the other two chairs that are covered in that antique velvet are really softer and warmer looking than the nubby.

Prospect: Yes, that's true. If I got one, I'd be more interested in the velvet because Mother just couldn't understand having a modern fabric like that bouclé in the bedroom. I'm on one of those "hurry-up" decoration tours. Mother is coming to stay with us for two weeks, and I simply can't put her in that old bedroom the way it looks now. So I bought draperies and a new spread this morning, and it just occurred to me that a pretty boudoir chair would do wonders for the room.

Salesman: I'm sure she would like one like this. This one is called "The Debbie." (Slides chair forward.) It's one of our proudest offerings.

Prospect: It's so pretty.

Salesman: This chair was built by Eastern Galleries, Inc. We handle their boudoir line exclusively; we've found over the years that for beauty, quality, style, and price, they offer the best line of boudoir chairs obtainable. And another thing, we're proud to say that we stand back of an Eastern Galleries chair. These chairs are superbly constructed.

Prospect: Well, I surely don't want anything that's going to fall apart the first time you sit in it.

Salesman: Well, you can take this chair and know that you won't have to worry about that.

Prospect: What's this chair filled with?

Salesman: Eastern Galleries uses kapok exclusively in all its boudoir chairs. Kapok is far superior to cotton in that it is softer, more resilient, and will not mat or pack down. Would you like to sit on it?

Prospect: Why, yes . . . (She sits on it.) Hmm . . . Not as comfortable as a platform rocker.

Salesman: No, they're not. Most boudoir chairs are designed to enhance the beauty of your bedroom, and actually they're not quite so comfortable as some of your living room pieces.

Prospect: Yes, I suppose that's right. Now what colors do you have here in "The Debbie"?

Salesman: Here, let me get you our swatches for this chair. You can always tell more if you can actually see the colors. (Gets book of swatches.) Now let's see, "The Debbie" is listed 2320, so that gives us these four colors here . . . on hand. We have Emerald Green, Coffee Brown, Sage, and Rose. Which color do you prefer?

Prospect: Let me see, I've got a sample of my drapery material here in my bag. Yes, here it is . . . Humm . . . This brown seems to go with it pretty well, doesn't it?

Salesman: That looks nice. I like that drapery material with just a trace of green in it. It'll look real nice with this Coffee Brown.

Prospect: How much is this chair?

Salesman: "The Debbie" sells for $39.75 each or $77.50 for the pair. They're unconditionally guaranteed by both our department and by Eastern Galleries. You're receiving the finest quality available anywhere today. Why not take a pair of these chairs? Your Mother would love them in her bedroom, and you'll get years of satisfaction from them.

Prospect: My husband would kill me! Hou much did you say a pair costs?

Salesman: You may have the pair for only $77.50, and you'll have a pair of beautiful chairs you'll be proud to show your friends. We'd be glad to deliver them to you today.

Prospect: Well . . . I'll take them . . . the two in Coffee Brown . . . I just love them.

Salesman: They're going to be lovely in your bedroom with the drapes that you've chosen. Now, if you'll step over here, I'll write down your name and address so we can send them right out.

QUESTIONS:

1. What did the salesman do well?
2. What did the salesman do that could be improved?
3. What techniques are illustrated in the sale?
4. Why did the prospect buy the chairs?
5. Of what phase of the sale should the salesman be proudest?

Index

INDEX